EARLY CHRISTIANITY IN CONTEXT

Editor
John M.G. Barclay

Editorial Board
Loveday Alexander, Trocels Engberg-Pedersen,
Bart Ehrman, Joel Marcus, John Riches

Published under
JOURNAL FOR THE STUDY OF THE NEW TESTAMENT
SUPPLEMENT SERIES
293

Editor
Mark Goodacre

*To Barbara Groff,
my fellow-traveller
in search of Paul
and the truth
of the Gospel!*
L.L. Welborn

For

Paul Malcolm Puckett

Paul, the Fool of Christ

A Study of 1 Corinthians 1–4 in the Comic-Philosophic Tradition

L. L. Welborn

T & T CLARK INTERNATIONAL
A Continuum imprint
LONDON • NEW YORK

Published by T&T Clark International

The Tower Building,	15 East 26th Street,
11 York Road,	Suite 1703,
London SE1 7NX	New York, NY 10010

www.tandtclark.com

British Library Cataloguing-in-Publication Data
A catalogue record for this book is available from the British Library

Library of Congress Cataloging-in-Publication Data
Welborn, L. L., 1953-
    Paul, the fool of Christ : a study of 1 Corinthians 1-4 in the cosmic-philosophic tradition / Laurence L. Welborn.
        p. cm.   (Early Christianity in context) (Journal for the study of the New Testament. Supplement series ; 293)
    Includes bibliographical references and index.
    ISBN 0-567-03041-5
    1. Bible. N.T. Corinthians, 1st, I-IV–Language, style. I. Title. II. Series. III. Series: Journal for the study of the New Testament. Supplement series ; 293

BS2675.52.W45 2005
227′.206–dc22

2005041867

ISBN 0567030415 (hardback)
ISBN 0567030423 (paperback)

Typeset by Tradespools, Frome, Somerset
Printed on acid-free paper in Great Britain by
MPG Books Ltd. Bodmin Cornwall

CONTENTS

The Roman Prefect rebuking the martyr Saint Laurence:

impune tantas, furcifer, strophas cavillo mimico te
nexuisse existimas, dum, scurra, saltas fabulam?

Do you suppose, you scoundrel, that you can get away
with contriving such a display of the mime-jester's art
and your dancing clown's act?

(Prudentius *Peristeph.* 2. 317–18)

PREFACE

This book owes its origin to the one to whom it is gratefully dedicated – my friend and fellow student of Greco-Roman history, Paul Malcolm Puckett. In the spring of 2001, I sent three chapters of a manuscript entitled 'The Fool's Speech and the Apostle Paul' to Mac for comment. Among the questions that he raised in response was one which seemed easy to answer: Where and when did Paul appropriate the role of the 'fool' which he plays in 2 Cor. 11.1–12.10 with such devastating effect? I set about to write an introduction to my monograph on the 'fool's speech' in which I hoped to show that Paul's acceptance of the role of the 'fool' and, arising out of this, his evaluation of the message of the cross as 'folly' occurred in 1 Cor. 1–4 against the background of popular culture. The result is the book that you now hold in your hands. However, Mac Puckett's contribution to the present volume goes far beyond the question that instigated its composition. Taking responsibility for the detour in his friend's research, Mac faithfully read each chapter and generously offered suggestions and advice. For example, he insisted that I deepen my understanding of the psychology of 'gallows humor', and that I expand my treatment of Paul's self-parody in 1 Cor. 2.6–16. As the years roll on, I am increasingly conscious of the rare gift of such a friendship.

Conversations with Dieter Georgi on the occasion of the 'Symposium on the Interpretation of Scripture as a Force for Social Change' at the Evangelische Akademie Arnoldshain in the fall of 2001 encouraged me to pursue the popular theater as the most plausible social context for understanding Paul's language about the 'folly' of the message of the cross and his description of himself as a 'fool on account of Christ.' The footnotes of this book reveal how often Professor Georgi's insights anticipate the results of my research.

A conversation with Holt Parker of the Department of Classics of the University of Cincinnati in the spring of 2002 illuminated the process by which the term μωρός became the common generic name for a mimic fool. I am grateful for his insights.

The subtitle of the book reveals the abiding influence of my teacher Hans Dieter Betz upon my research interests. I continue to find inspiration in his *Paulus und die sokratische Tradition*.

I am especially grateful to the colleagues who read the entire manuscript and who offered valuable criticism and advice. At the top of the list is Dale Martin who provided page upon page of trenchant commentary. His incisive critique improved the argument of the book at crucial points. The book would be stronger had it been possible to follow his advice in full. My Australian friends, Mark Harding and Jim Harrison, likewise provided detailed comments on the entire manuscript, saving me from numerous errors and enriching the footnotes. Indeed, Mark Harding cheerfully endured the gestation of much of chapter 6 in many pleasant conversations during his sabbatical in Ohio in 2003. My teacher Gerd Lüdemann offered learned and timely advice on several key issues.

I am grateful to the librarians of United Theological Seminary and Wittenberg University, Brillie Scott and Suzanne Smailes, for tireless efforts to locate materials. Many thanks are due as well to John Barclay for accepting this work for publication in his distinguished series, and to Rebecca Mulhearn of T & T Clark for encouraging me through the process of editing.

The members of my immediate family – my wife Diane, my sons Locke and Mark, and my mother Ann – have shared in the genesis of this book with patience and genuine interest. Because of them, I take as my own the words of the poet of the most sublime comedy: *'Ciò ch' io vedeva mi sembiava un riso dell'universo; per che mia ebbrezza intrava per l'udire e per lo viso.'*

Dayton   L.L.W.
December, 2004

ABBREVIATIONS

AB	Anchor Bible
ABD	*Anchor Bible Dictionary.* Edited by D. N. Freedman. 6 vols. New York, 1992
AGJU	Arbeiten zur Geschichte des antiken Judentums und des Urchristentums
AJA	*American Journal of Archaeology*
AnBib	Analecta biblica
ANF	Ante-Nicene Fathers
ANRW	*Aufstieg und Niedergang der römischen Welt: Geschichte und Kultur Roms im Spiegel der neueren Forschung.* Edited by H. Temporini and W. Haase. Berlin, 1972-
AusBR	*Australian Biblical Review*
BA	*Biblical Archaeologist*
BAGD	Walter Bauer, W. F. Arndt, F. W. Gingrich, and F. W. Danker, *A Greek-English Lexicon of the New Testament and Other Early Christian Literature.* Chicago, 2000
BBB	Bonner biblische Beiträge
BDF	Friedrich Blass, A. Debrunner and R. W. Funk, *A Greek Grammar of the New Testament and Other Early Christian Literature.* Chicago, 1961
BETL	Bibliotheca ephemeridum theologicarum lovaniensium
BHTh	Beiträge zur historischen Theologie
Bib	*Biblica*
BibInt	*Biblical Interpretation*
BJRL	*Bulletin of the John Rylands University Library of Manchester*
BNTC	Black's New Testament Commentaries
BR	*Biblical Research*
BSac	*Bibliotheca Sacra*
BWANT	Beiträge zur Wissenschaft vom Alten und Neuen Testament
BZ	*Biblische Zeitschrift*
BZNW	Beihefte zur Zeitschrift für die neutestamentliche Wissenschaft
CAH	Cambridge Ancient History

CBQ	*Catholic Biblical Quarterly*
CIL	*Corpus inscriptionum latinarum*
CJ	*Classical Journal*
CP	*Classical Philology*
CPSP	*Cambridge Philological Society Proceedings*
CQ	*Classical Quarterly*
CNT	Commentaire du Nouveau Testament
CW	*Classical World*
EA	*Epigraphica Anatolica*
EBib	Etudes bibliques
EDNT	*Exegetical Dictionary of the New Testament.* Edited by H. Balz and G. Schneider. Grand Rapids, 1990–93
EKKNT	Evangelisch-katholischer Kommentar zum Neuen Testament
FGH	Die Fragmente der griechischen Historiker
FRLANT	Forschungen zur Religion und Literatur des Alten und Neuen Testaments
GCS	Griechische christliche Schriftsteller
GRBS	*Greek, Roman, and Byzantine Studies*
HDR	Harvard Dissertations in Religion
HNT	Handbuch zum Neuen Testament
HNTC	Harper's New Testament Commentaries
HR	*History of Religions*
HSCP	*Harvard Studies in Classical Philology*
HTR	*Harvard Theological Review*
ICC	International Critical Commentary
IG	*Inscriptiones Graecae*
ILS	*Inscriptiones Latinae Selecta.* Edited by H. Dessau. Leipzig, 1892–1916
Int	*Interpretation*
JAC	*Jahrbuch für Antike und Christentum*
JBL	*Journal of Biblical Literature*
JHS	*Journal of Hellenic Studies*
JR	*Journal of Religion*
JRH	*Journal of Religious History*
JRS	*Journal of Roman Studies*
JSHRZ	Jüdische Schriften aus hellenistisch-römischer Zeit
JSNT	*Journal for the Study of the New Testament*
JSNTSup	Journal for the Study of the New Testament: Supplement Series
JTS	*Journal of Theological Studies*
KEK	Kritisch-exegetischer Kommentar über das Neue Testament (Meyer)
KJV	King James Version

LCL	Loeb Classical Library
LSJ	H. G. Liddell, R. Scott, and H. S. Jones, *A Greek-English Lexicon*. 9th ed. with revised supplement. Oxford, 1996
LXX	Septuaginta
MRF	*Mimorum Romanorum Fragmenta*. Edited by M. Bonaria. Geneva, 1955
NEB	*New English Bible*
NHC	*Nag Hammadi Codices*
NHS	Nag Hammadi Studies
NKZ	*Neue kirchliche Zeitschrift*
NovT	*Novum Testamentum*
NovTSup	*Novum Testamentum*, Supplements
NRSV	New Revised Standard Version
NTAbh	Neutestamentliche Abhandlungen
NTD	Das Neue Testament Deutsch
NTOA	Novum Testamentum et Orbis Antiquus
NTS	*New Testament Studies*
OCD	*Oxford Classical Dictionary*
OGIS	*Orientis graeci inscriptiones selectae*
PG	*Patrologiae cursus completus … Series graeca*. Edited by J.-P. Migne. 166 vols. Paris, 1857–83
PGM	*Papyri graecae magicae*. Edited by K. Preisendanz
PL	*Patrologia cursus completus … Series prima [latina]*. Edited by J.-P. Migne. 221 vols. Paris, 1844–65
RE	*Real-Encyclopädie der classischen Altertumswissenschaft*. Edited by August Friedrich von Pauly and Georg Wissowa. Stuttgart, 1894-
RESuppl	Supplement to Pauly-Wissowa
RAC	*Reallexikon für Antike und Christentum*. Edited by T. Klauser, et al. Stuttgart, 1950-
RB	*Revue biblique*
RGG	*Religion in Geschichte und Gegenwart*
RhM	*Rheinisches Museum für Philologie*
SBB	Stuttgarter biblische Beiträge
SBL	Society of Biblical Literature
SBLDS	Society of Biblical Literature Dissertation Series
SBLSBS	Society of Biblical Literature Sources for Biblical Study
SBLSS	Society of Biblical Literature Semeia Studies
SBS	Stuttgarter Bibelstudien
SC	Sources chrétiennes
SCHNT	Studia ad corpus hellenisticum Novi Testamenti
SEÅ	*Svensk exegetisk årsbok*
SEG	*Supplementum epigraphicum Graecum*

Paul, the Fool of Christ

SHAW	Sitzungsberichte der Heidelberger Akademie der Wissenschaften
SHAW PH	Sitzungsberichte der Heidelberger Akademie der Wissenschaften. Philosophisch-historische Klasse
SIG	*Sylloge Inscriptionum Graecarum*. Edited by W. Dittenberger. Berlin, 1915–24
SNTSMS	Society for New Testament Studies Monograph Series
SNTU	Studien zum Neuen Testament und seiner Umwelt
SO	*Symbolae Osloenses*
SP	Sacra pagina
SUNT	Studien zur Umwelt des Neuen Testaments
SVF	*Stoicorum veterum fragmenta*. H. von Arnim. 4 vols. Leipzig, 1903–24
TAPA	*Transactions of the American Philological Association*
TDNT	*Theological Dictionary of the New Testament*. Edited by G. Kittel and G. Friedrich. 10 vols. Grand Rapids, 1964–76
Thes. Ling. Lat.	Thesaurus Lingua Latina
TLZ	*Theologische Literaturzeitung*
TRE	*Theologische Realenzyklopädie*
TU	Texte und Untersuchungen
TynBul	*Tyndale Bulletin*
TZ	*Theologische Zeitschrift*
WBC	Word Biblical Commentary
WMANT	Wissenschaftliche Monographien zum Alten und Neuen Testament
WUNT	Wissenschaftliche Untersuchungen zum Neuen Testament
YCS	Yale Classical Studies
ZDPV	*Zeitschrift des deutschen Palästina-Vereins*
ZNW	*Zeitschrift für die neutestamentliche Wissenschaft*
ZPE	*Zeitschrift für Papyrologie und Epigraphik*
ZThK	*Zeitschrift für Theologie und Kirche*

LIST OF ILLUSTRATIONS

INTRODUCTION

It is possible that this book will elicit the same response that Paul reported of his preaching: 'scandal!' and 'foolishness!' (1 Cor. 1.23). In part, this is because the book calls into question an understanding of Paul which goes back to the second century. Alluding to 1 Cor. 1–2, Justin Martyr describes the offense caused by the message about the crucified Christ as 'madness' (μανία) rather than 'folly' (μωρία).[1] This interpretation locates Paul's statement about the 'folly' of 'the word of the cross' (1 Cor. 1.18) in the long debate over the use and abuse of reason, as its first and most influential proposition.[2] The tradition has followed Justin with remarkably few exceptions. In his acclaimed study of 'Crucifixion in the Ancient World and the Folly of the Message of the Cross,' Martin Hengel cites Justin in the opening paragraph, and substitutes 'madness' for 'folly' in his paraphrase of Paul's thought.[3]

Our research into Paul's language has led in a different direction. For most Greek speakers in the time of Paul, the term μωρία meant 'stupidity' rather than 'absurdity.'[4] A social stigma attached to the Greek term μωρία that is not generally associated with the English word 'folly.' The term μωρία designated the attitude and behavior of a particular social type: the lower class moron. The 'foolishness' of this social type consisted in a weakness or deficiency of intellect, often coupled with a physical grotesqueness. Because the concept of the laughable in the Greco-Roman

---

1. Justin *Apol.* I, 13.4. As is often the case with Justin's allusions to scripture, the reference to 1 Cor. 1–2 in *Apol.* I, 13.4 has the quality of a reminiscence, rather than a citation. Some scholars question Justin's use of Paul; but see the allusion to 1 Cor. 10.4 in *Dial.* 13.1 and to 1 Cor. 11.19 in *Dial.* 35.3.

2. S. Stowers, 'Paul on the Use and Abuse of Reason' in *Greeks, Romans, and Christians: Essays in Honor of Abraham J. Malherbe*, ed. D. Balch, E. Ferguson, and W. Meeks (Minneapolis: Fortress Press, 1990) 253–86, esp. 255–62; F. Voss, *Das Wort vom Kreuz und die menschliche Vernunft: Eine Untersuchung zur Soteriologie des 1. Korintherbriefes*, FRLANT 199 (Göttingen: Vandenhoeck & Ruprecht, 2002).

3. M. Hengel, *Crucifixion in the Ancient World and the Folly of the Message of the Cross* (Philadelphia: Fortress Press, 1977) 1, 2, 7, 89.

4. See chs. 2 and 3 below.

world was grounded in contemplation of the base and defective,[5] those who possessed these characteristics were deemed to be 'foolish.' Paul means to say that the message about the crucified Christ was regarded by the cultured elite of his day as a coarse and vulgar joke. That this is the right understanding of Paul's characterization of 'the word of the cross' as μωρία, is demonstrated by the way in which Paul continues in 1 Cor. 1.26–28: those who are 'called' by 'the word of the cross' are, for the most part, persons without education, wealth, or birth; they are 'the foolish,... the weak,... the low-born,... the despised, the nobodies.' All of this makes better sense, when one understands that the cross, which was the special object of Paul's proclamation, was the 'slaves' punishment' (*servile supplicium*).[6]

This understanding of Paul's theology would be scandalous enough. But this is not the reason, one suspects, why our study may elicit the response of 'foolishness!' Rather, danger arises from a corollary of the main thesis: namely, that in his discourse about the 'folly' of the 'word of the cross,' Paul has recourse to the language of jest and mime. In this maneuver, Paul acts in accordance with a social constraint upon discussion of the cross in antiquity,[7] obeying what one might call the 'law of the euphemism.' The cross was an ominous lacuna at the center of public discourse.[8] When the cross was mentioned at all, it was generally as the subject of jest.[9] One usually encounters 'gallows humor,' whenever an account of crucifixion attains any length. In keeping with the law of the euphemism, the most vivid references to crucifixion in ancient literature are found in farce and mime.[10] Gallows humor was only an extreme expression of 'aesthetic disdain' towards the poor, weak and defective, in general.[11] The brutal, historical fact is that no one wanted to see the poor, the 'human trash,'

---

5.   Aristotle *Ars Poet.* 1449a30; Cicero *De Orat.* 2.236; Quintilian *Inst. Orat.* 6.3.8; cf. M. Grant, *The Ancient Rhetorical Theories of the Laughable* (Madison: University of Wisconsin Press, 1924) 19.

6.   W. L. Westermann, 'Sklaverei,' *RESuppl.* VI, 980–81; Hengel, *Crucifixion in the Ancient World*, 51–63.

7.   Cicero *Pro Rabirio* 5.16.

8.   On the concept of the lacuna in discourse, see G. Agamben, *Remnants of Auschwitz: The Witness and the Archive* (New York: Zone Books, 2002).

9.   J. Meggitt, 'Laughing and Dreaming at the Foot of the Cross: Context and Reception of a Religious Symbol', *Journal for the Critical Study of Religion, Ethics, and Society* 1.1 (1996) 9–14.

10.   See, esp., the comedies of Plautus, with the commentary and analysis of E. Segal, *Roman Laughter: The Comedy of Plautus* (Cambridge, MA: Harvard University Press, 1952) 137–69, and the *Laureolus* mime in *Mimorum Romanorum Fragmenta*, ed. M. Bonaria (Geneva: Instituto di Filologia Classica, 1955) 112.

11.   On 'aesthetic disdain' for the poor, see P. Veyne, *A History of Private Life I: From Pagan Rome to Byzantium* (Cambridge, MA: Harvard University Press, 1992) 61–62, 134–37.

who were becoming more numerous on the streets of the cities in the early Empire, as a result of changes in the economy.[12] Realistic portraits of the beggardly poor are rare in Greco-Roman literature.[13] The few authors who describe the beggars whom they happen to meet invariably use language which likens these poor creatures to fools in the mime.[14] The mimic elements in these portraits measure the aesthetic distance between the authors (even the most sympathetic) and a subject which no one wanted to hear mentioned.

It is the thesis of this book that Paul was governed by a social constraint in his discourse about the cross and in his account of the sufferings of the apostles of Christ. Like his contemporaries Horace and Seneca, Paul employs the language and imagery of the mime, when he speaks about these socially shameful subjects. The theatrical metaphor becomes explicit in 1 Cor. 4.9–10: 'For I think that God has put us apostles on show last of all, as people condemned to death, because we have become a theater-act (θεάτρον) to the world, both to angels and to human beings. We are fools (μωροί) on account of Christ...' But it will be argued that allusions to the mime are present throughout 1 Cor. 1–4, from the *narratio* of the letter (1.11–17), where Paul portrays the quarrelsome Corinthians as the partisans of star-performers in the theater, to a well-developed allusion to the 'Guardian' mime, at the conclusion of the rhetorical unit (4.14–21). Awareness of the comic tradition to which Paul makes reference gives access to a number of texts that have long puzzled interpreters (e.g., 2.6–16).

Does Paul make use of the mime? It is this suggestion that is likely to make our study controversial. For it is widely held that, as a Christian and a Jew, Paul would have had nothing to do with such a vulgar form of art. Did not the church fathers, such as Tatian and Tertullian, fiercely denounce the mime for its obscenity?[15] Were not the mime artists excommunicated?[16] Hence, New Testament scholars routinely dismiss the notion that Paul derived the role of the fool and the genre of the 'fool's speech' (2 Cor. 11.1–12.10) from the Greek and Roman mime.[17] The goal

---

12. See, e.g., Seneca *De Clem.* 2.7; cf. G. E. M. de Ste. Croix, *The Class Struggle in the Ancient Greek World* (Ithaca: Cornell University Press, 1981) 189–91, 195; G. Alföldy, *The Social History of Rome* (Baltimore: Johns Hopkins University Press, 1991) 135.

13. F. Millar, 'The World of the *Golden Ass*', *JRS* 71 (1981) 63, 65, 75. On the highly realistic portrait of the beggar Lazarus in Luke 16.19–21, see ch. 7 below.

14. Philo *In Flacc.* 6.36–38: Seneca *Epist. Mor.* 12.3; Apuleius *Met.* 1.6–7.

15. Tatian *Oratio ad Graecos* 22; Tertullian *Apologeticus* 15; *De Spectaculis* 23; Cyprian *De Spectaculis* 6.

16. A. Nicoll, *Masks, Mimes and Miracles: Studies in the Popular Theatre* (New York: Harcourt, Brace, 1931) 135–50.

17. E.g., U. Heckel, *Kraft in Schwachheit. Untersuchungen zu 2. Kor. 10–13*, WUNT 56 (Tübingen: Mohr-Siebeck, 1993) 20: '...bei seiner Narrenrede hat er [Paulus] das Bild des

of this introduction must be to forestall the immediate reaction of indignation, and to win a provisional hearing for what may be regarded as an implausible notion.

We may begin with a clarification and a definition. It is important to emphasize that the ancient mime was not mute, like the modern form bearing this name.[18] Although a variety of performances might be covered by the term, the 'mime' may be defined as a reproduction in character and language of a typical scene of everyday life in the form of a short monologue or dialogue.[19] The essential elements in this definition are character and realism. The interest of mime was in the depiction of character, rather than plot. So much is indicated by the surviving titles of mimes, e.g., 'The Soothsayer,' 'The Courtesan,' 'The Fisherman.'[20] The realism of the mime is manifest in the fact that mime, unlike traditional comedy, was presented without masks.[21] Moreover, the subject matter of the mime was realistic, with themes drawn, for the most part, from everyday life, such as, 'a man drunk and going on a revel to his lover,'[22] or 'a slave who deceives his master.'[23] It is not difficult to see what made the mime so attractive to the ancient audience: the mime portrayed the rich variety of everyday life with such frankness and realism that spectators of all classes recognized themselves and their contemporaries.

Toren aus der jüdischen Weisheitstradition vor Augen, nicht der Komödiantenrolle der Mimus, den er – wenn er ihn überhaupt aus eigener Anschaung kannte – wegen seiner oft obszönen Szenen vermütlich abgelehnt haben dürfte.' Similarly, M. Hengel, 'Der vorchristliche Paulus' in *Paulus und das antike Judentum*, ed. M. Hengel and U. Heckel, WUNT 58 (Tübingen: Mohr-Siebeck, 1994) 184. These judgments are based upon Josephus' description of the theater and amphitheater as 'alien to Jewish custom' in *Ant.* 15.8.1. But from the Herodian period onwards, there were theaters and amphitheaters in Caesarea, Jericho, and Jerusalem, as well as a stadium in Tiberias; see E. Schürer, *The History of the Jewish People in the Age of Jesus Christ*, Vol. II, ed. G. Vermes (Edinburgh: T. & T. Clark, 1979) 54–55.

18.   On the mime in general, see H. Reich, *Der Mimus. Ein litterar-entwickelungsgeschichtlicher Versuch* (Berlin: Weidmann, 1903); E. Wüst, 'Mimos,' *RE* 15.2 (1932) 1727–64.

19.   Compare the definition quoted by the grammarian Diomedes, for which Theophrastus may originally have been responsible: 'The mime is an imitation of life encompassing both things accepted and things forbidden,' μῖμός ἐστιν μίμησις βίου τά τε συγκεχωρημένα καὶ ἀσυγχώρητα περιέχων (*Ars grammatica* 3, *Grammatici latini*, ed. H. Keil [Leipzig: Teubner, 1857–80] 1.490).

20.   The titles of mimes by Decimus Laberius; see *Mimorum Romanorum Fragmenta* I, 9–103; for discussion, see W. Beare, *The Roman Stage* (London: Methuen, 1977) 144–47.

21.   Wüst, 'Mimos', 1747.

22.   Athenaios (*Deip* 14.621c) gives this as the subject of a mime troupe.

23.   O. Crusius, *Untersuchungen zu den Mimiamben des Herondas* (Leipzig: Teubner, 1892) 53, 69.

One might defend the idea that Paul made use of the mime by observing that not all mimes were crude, vulgar, and subliterary. On the contrary, there is evidence that, at this very period, the mime was regarded as sophisticated entertainment, appealing to the highest social levels.[24] The Roman knight, Decimus Laberius, composed mimes that were praised for the elegance of their versification and the novelty of their language.[25] Seneca praises the 'sagacious verses' of the mime-writer Publilius Syrus for their philosophical content.[26] Pliny considered the mimes of one Vergilius Romanus to be equal to the best of Plautus and Terence,[27] and praises his friend Arrius Antoninus for his talent at composing mimes in Greek.[28] The emperor Augustus was famously devoted to the mime: he employed mime actors at his private banquets and spent lavishly on public shows.[29] According to Horace, the audience for a farcical contest between two professional jesters (*scurrae*) included the millionaire Maecenas and the poets, Virgil and Varius.[30] If the mime appealed to the same audience as elegaic poetry and philosophy, one might reasonably allow that Paul exploited elements of the mime in his correspondence with the sophisticated Corinthians, who were so rich in speech and knowledge (1 Cor. 1.5).

But let us concede the point about the vulgarity of the mime in general.[31] Judging from the extant fragments of mime and references in literature, it is clear that mime was a low form of comedy.[32] Mime focused on humble characters, with the emphasis upon parody of low-class trades and professions.[33] The humor was coarse and the action exaggerated; there was much slapstick and noisy violence.[34] An aspect of the vulgarity of the mime

24. See the important essay by J. C. McKeown, 'Augustan Elegy and Mime', *CPSP* 25 (1979) 71–84.

25. Gellius *NA* 16.7.

26. Seneca *Epist. Mor.* 8.8. A vast collection of maxims is attributed to Syrus, many doubtless genuine; see O, Friedrich, *Publilii Syri Mimi Sententiae* (Leipzig: Teubner, 1880).

27. Pliny *Ep.* 6.21.

28. Pliny *Ep.* 4.3: 'What sensitivity, what grace! How delightful they are, so full of love, and how humorous and tasteful!'

29. Ovid *Trist.* 2.497–516; Suetonius *Aug.* 43, 74.

30. Horace *Sat.* 1.5.

31. See esp. E. Rawson, 'The Vulgarity of the Roman Mime' in *Tria lustra. Liverpool Classical Monthly* 150 (1993) 255–60.

32. See the discussion in Reich, *Der Mimus*, 50–53; Wüst, 'Mimos,' 1736, 1747; Beare, *The Roman Stage*, 150–53; R. Beacham, *The Roman Theatre and its Audience* (Cambridge, MA: Harvard University Press, 1992) 130–31.

33. Crusius, *Untersuchungen zu den Mimiamben des Herondas*, 22; Rawson, 'The Vulgarity of the Mime,' 259.

34. Catullus 42.8–9; Juvenal 8.185–92; Martial 2.72.3–4; 5.61.11; *POxy* 413 ('Charition').

was its indecency.[35] Adultery was a favorite theme.[36] Mime actresses sometimes appeared naked on the stage.[37]

In assessing the vulgarity of the mime, with respect to Paul's moral scruples, two considerations are crucial. First, it is necessary to bear in mind that the values and attitudes of the Greco-Roman audience were different from those of scholars in the twenty-first century, who have been brought up in the Judeo-Christian tradition.[38] Modern visitors to an ancient Roman city would be shocked by two aspects of the experience in particular: the routine nature of violence and the explicitness of sex.[39] Violence had entertainment value in the Greco-Roman world, and a considerable number of holidays were devoted to games of death.[40] Suetonius reminds us that a Roman city was a place where a dog might pick up a human hand in the street.[41] Moreover, Roman cities were 'full of erotic images, from Priapus' grotesque erection in the gardens of villas to paintings of copulation on the walls inside.[42] Out in the streets, prostitutes plied for hire practically naked.'[43] This was the world inhabited by Paul and the Corinthian Christians, however distasteful it may be to modern scholars. It would have been impossible for Paul to shut his eyes to everything, even if he disapproved of what he saw. Nor is it clear how Paul would have reacted, given his own penchant for violent and sexually explicit humor. One wonders whether the author of the 'sarcastic and bloody joke'[44] at the expense of the Judaizers in Gal. 5.12 would have laughed or blushed at what he saw on the streets of Roman Corinth.

---

35. On mimic obscenity, see Cicero *De Orat.* 2.59.242; Horace *Sat.* 1.2.57; Ovid *Trist.* 2.497, 515; Valerius Maximus 2.10.8; Plutarch *Quaes. Conviv.* 7.8, 712E; Quintilian *Inst. Orat.* 6.1.47; 6.3.8; Juvenal 6.44; 8.187–98, 197; Martial 3.86; Macrobius *Sat.* 2.1.9.

36. See esp. R. W. Reynolds, 'The Adultery Mime,' *CQ* 40 (1946) 77–84.

37. Valerius Maximus 2.10.8; Seneca *Ep.* 97.8; Martial 1; 35.8.

38. On modern attitudes as opposed to Roman *mores*, see the remarks of T. P. Wiseman, *Catullus and his World. A Reappraisal* (Cambridge: Cambridge University Press, 1985) 1–4.

39. Rightly, K. Hopkins, *Death and Renewal* (Cambridge: Cambridge University Press, 1983); Wiseman, *Catullus and his World*, 4–14.

40. M. Wistrand, *Entertainment and Violence in Ancient Rome. The Attitudes of Writers of the First Century A.D.* (Gotheborg: Universitatis Gothoburgensis, 1993); R. Auguet, *Cruelty and Civilization: The Roman Games* (London: Routledge, 1994).

41. Suetonius *Vesp.* 5.4.

42. Wiseman, *Catullus and his World*, 14. For evidence, see M. Grant and A. Mulas, *Eros in Pompeii: The Erotic Art Collection of the Museum of Naples* (New York: Stewart, Tabori & Chang, 1975) 84–166.

43. Wiseman, *Catullus and his World*, 14, citing Propertius 2.22.8; Ovid *Trist.* 2.309–12; Tacitus *Ann.* 15.37.3; for Corinth, see Strabo.

44. The comment of H. D. Betz, *Galatians. A Commentary on Paul's Letter to the Churches in Galatia*, Hermeneia (Philadelphia: Fortress Press, 1979) 270, on Gal. 5.12, ὄφελον καὶ ἀποκόψονται οἱ ἀναστατοῦντες ὑμᾶς ('I wish that those who are troubling you [about

Secondly, and more importantly, the vulgarity of the mime is a reflection of the audience at which the mime was directed.[45] Although rich and sophisticated persons might enjoy the mime, the surviving fragments leave little doubt that the mime was primarily aimed at the humbler part of the audience – freedmen, slaves, and the poor. The Campanian freedman Trimalchio (in Petronius' *Satyricon*) greatly admires the moral sentiment of Publilius' verses, and has a song from a mime sung at his banquet.[46] A real first-century freedman from Rome had two lines of Laberius engraved on his tombstone.[47] One may suppose that the mime was even more appealing to slaves and the poor, even if they had to watch from the back rows of the theater. Indeed, the mime offers one of the few means of access to the thought world of the poorer classes in the Roman Empire, since 'it was on the theatre that the culture of the poor was largely dependant.'[48] As a context for reading Paul's correspondence with a community whose members derived mainly from the lower classes (1 Cor. 1.26–28), the mime may prove to be more appropriate than the literature of Roman Stoicism or the Jewish Wisdom Tradition.

Paul and his readers in Corinth would have had many opportunities for contact with the mime. Apuleius attests what we should otherwise have surmised: that the mime was performed in the theater of Corinth.[49] The theater of Corinth was rehabilitated at the end of the reign of Augustus, and was fully operational in the time of Paul.[50] The structure held upwards of 15,000 spectators.[51] It is difficult to overestimate the importance of the theater in the daily life of a city like Corinth.[52] In the theater, all the classes crowded together: elites and the underclass, rustics and city folk, veterans

circumcision] would cut their own off!'): 'As an after-thought Paul adds a sarcastic and indeed "bloody" joke,' observing (n. 164) that 'Translations sometimes tend to avoid the obscene language Paul is using.' See also Phil. 3.2, βλέπετε τὴν κατατομήν.

45.   Rawson, 'The Vulgarity of the Mime', 255.

46.   Petronius *Satyr.* 55.6; 35.6; cf. the comments of Rawson, 'The Vulgarity of the Mime', 258.

47.   F. Leo, 'Inschriftliches Citat aus Laberius' in *Hermes* 48 (1913) 147; Rawson, 'The Vulgarity of the Mime', 258.

48.   Rawson, 'The Vulgarity of the Mime,' 260, citing Ovid's account of theatrical songs at a picnic of the plebs in *Fast.* 3.535.

49.   Apuleius *Met.* 10.29.

50.   R. Stillwell, *Corinth II: The Theatre* (Princeton: The American School of Classical Studies at Athens, 1952) 135–41. The reign of Augustus inaugurated a period of theater construction throughout the Empire; by the end of the first century A.D., even the smallest cities had acquired a theater. A section of Vitruvius' great work on architecture (*De arch.* 5.5.7), written at the beginning of this period, provides details on theater construction, in anticipation of the erection of theaters at Rome and elsewhere. See Beacham, *The Roman Theatre*, 166–69.

51.   D. Engels, *Roman Corinth* (Chicago: University of Chicago Press, 1990) 47.

52.   Engels, *Roman Corinth*, 47–48.

and matrons – a true microcosm of society.[53] The entertainment which Greco-Roman audiences increasingly chose to attend was the mime,[54] which, by the middle of the first century A.D., was so popular that it 'practically monopolized the stage'.[55] It would be a mistake to assume that diaspora Jews would have refused to attend the theater.[56] The attendance of Jews at the theater of Aphrodisias is well attested.[57] An inscription in the theater of Miletus indicates that Jews even had assigned seats.[58] Among the crowds who thronged into the theater in search of entertainment were doubtless many of Paul's converts. Indeed, one of the Corinthian Christians may have been a patron of the theater. Erastus, the Corinthian *aedile*, who laid the limestone pavement adjacent to the theater of Corinth,[59] may well be 'the city treasurer' (ὁ οἰκονόμος τῆς πόλεως) from whom Paul sends greetings in Rom. 16.23.[60] Like aediles in other Roman cities, Erastus of Corinth would have been responsible for supervising the theater and amphitheater.[61]

It is even more likely that Paul observed the mime in the streets and marketplaces of the city, where plays were regularly enacted on hastily erected stages.[62] Small companies of players traveled from town to town giving their shows wherever an audience could gather.[63] Cicero refers to

53.   Horace (*Ars poet.* 212–13) describes the spectators as 'an unlettered throng just freed from toil, rustics mixed up with city folk, vulgar with the serious-minded.' See R. Beacham, *Spectacle Entertainments of Early Imperial Rome* (New Haven: Yale University Press, 1999) 139–40.

54.   Beare, *The Roman Stage*, 139–48; Beacham, *The Roman Theatre*, 129–39.

55.   W. Beare, 'Mimus', *OCD* (1970) 688.

56.   Rightly, D. Georgi, 'Jüdischer Synkretismus,' (unpublished essay).

57.   R. Smith and K. Erim, *Aphrodisias Papers 2: The Theatre* (Ann Arbor: University of michigan Press, 1991).

58.   Photographic plate of inscription in A. Deissmann, *Light from the Ancient East* (Grand Rapids, MI: Baker Book House, 1978) 451, Fig. 84, with discussion 452–53.

59.   Text in J. H. Kent, *Corinth – Inscriptions, 1926–1950* (Princeton: Princeton University Press, 1966) no. 232.

60.   In favor of the identification of the two Erasti, see O. Broneer, 'Corinth, Center of St. Paul's Missionary Work in Greece,' *BA* 14 (1951) 94; Kent, *Corinth – Inscriptions, 1926–1950*, 27, 99–100 (Princeton: American School of Classical Studies, 1966); J. Wiseman, 'Corinth and Rome I: 228 B.C. – A. D. 267,' *ANRW* 2.7.1 (1981) 499 n. 226; Engels, *Roman Corinth*, 108.

61.   Engels, *Roman Corinth*, 18.

62.   Beare, *The Roman Stage*, 151; Beacham, *The Roman Theatre*, 132.

63.   Evidence for the movement of mimes and mime companies throughout the Roman world is provided by epitaphs, such as that of Protogenes, a slave of Greek origin, found near the town of Amiternum (*CIL* I.[2] 1861), or that of the young mime actress Eucharis, slave, and later freedwoman of Licinia, found at Rome (*CIL* VI.[2] 10096). See also the farewell poem addressed by Antipater of Sidon to the mime actress Antiodemis on the occasion of her departure for Rome (*Anth. Pal.* 9.587). See the discussion in Reich, *Der Mimus*, 167–68, 558, 561; Beare, *The Roman Stage*, 151–52; E. Rawson, 'Theatrical Life in Republican Rome and Italy,' *Proceedings of the British School at Rome* 53 (1985) 111.

extempore performances by mime troupes of farcical themes like 'The Beggar Turns Millionaire.'[64] The staging requirements of such troupes were minimal. A rough platform served to raise the actors above the heads of the crowd. For scenery, a portable curtain hung from columns or posts was sufficient.[65] The actors were concealed behind the curtain intil their turn came; then, parting the curtain in the middle, they stepped into view.[66] While the mimes performed, a colleague might be collecting coins from the spectators, as one sees in a wall painting from Rome.[67] It is impossible that Paul would not have encountered the mimes in the marketplaces of Roman cities, where they performed during the day, and where they slept at night upon mats and pallets in booths that they shared with conjurers, dancers, and the like.[68]

Mimes were frequently presented as entertainment at banquets in private houses.[69] As wealth accumulated in the late Republic and early Empire, it became the fashion for well-to-do Romans to include mime actors on their household staffs.[70] Augustus himself employed mime actors as entertainment at his private banquets.[71] The 'Room of the Masks' in the house of Augustus on the Palatine hill depicts a brightly colored wooden structure thought to be a temporary comic stage.[72] The tastes of the emperor were widely imitated. The parvenu Trimalchio in Petronius' *Satyricon* confesses over dinner that although he employs a troupe of comic actors, he in fact prefers them to perform Atellan farces.[73] Pliny the Younger acknowledges that although he prefers to amuse himself and his guests with the more refined art of poets, musicians, and comedians, many others favor at dinner the antics and coarse humor of clowns and buffoons from the mime.[74]

It is also likely that Paul encountered the mime in literary form during the course of his education. The mimes of Sophron, for example, were

---

64. Cicero *Phil.* 2.65.

65. Seneca *Dial.* 9.11.8; Juvenal 8.185; Apuleius *Met.* 10.29; cf. Beare, *The Roman Stage*, 270–72; Beacham, *The Roman Theatre*, 132, 172.

66. See the scholiast to Juvenal 8.185; see also Cicero *Prov. Cons.* 14. See the discussion of staging in Beare, *The Roman Stage*, 149.

67. Reich, *Der Mimus*, 540.

68. Martial 6.39.

69. Beare, *The Roman Stage*, 149.

70. Polybius 31.25.4; Sallust *Jug.* 85.39; cf. Beacham, *The Roman Theatre*, 129.

71. Suetonius *Aug.* 74.

72. Beacham, *The Roman Theatre*, 71–72.

73. Petronius *Satyr.* 53. For discussion of Atellan farce and its relationship to the mime, see Nicoll, *Masks, Mimes and Miracles*, 65–79; Beare, *The Roman Stage*, 137–48. Atellan farces might be performed in Greek in the first century A.D.; Suetonius *Nero* 39.2–3.

74. Pliny *Ep.* 1.3b; 9.17, 36.

widely read and greatly admired.[75] Books of his mimes were introduced to Athens by none other than Plato,[76] who read them avidly and alludes to them.[77] According to Diogenes Laertius, it was from Sophron that Plato learned the art of character drawing employed in his dialogues.[78] A copy of Sophron's mimes was reportedly found under Plato's pillow on his deathbed.[79] Theocritus adapted one of Sophron's mimes in his second idyll, 'The Spell.'[80] An influential commentary on the mimes of Sophron was composed by Apollodorus of Athens in the second century B.C.[81] According to Statius,[82] the mimes of Sophron were read by students in the schools in the first century A.D. Did Paul read Sophron in the school at Tarsus?

The mime significantly influenced the style and content of other genres: comedy and satire, naturally, but also elegy, philosophical dialogue, and the novel.[83] From these sources, as well, Paul may have derived his knowledge of the mime and the role of the fool. Herodas unquestionably took the subject matter of his subtle, iambic poems from the tradition of the mime.[84] The comedies of Plautus contain much jesting and buffoonery of a kind that can scarcely have been found in the literary originals of Greek New Comedy, but that was characteristic of the mime.[85] The satires of Horace and Juvenal contain much mime-inspired material.[86] The

75.   A. Körte, 'Sophron', *RE* 3 (1930) 1100–1103; S. Eitrem, 'Sophron', *SO* 12 (1933) 10–13.

76.   Diogenes Laertius 3.18.

77.   Plato *Rep.* 451C, 606C. On Plato's admiration of Sophron, see also Douris of Samos in *FGH* 76 F 72. For Sophron's influence on Plato, see Reich, *Der Mimus*, 380–88.

78.   Diogenes Laertius 3.18.

79.   Quintilian *Inst. Orat.* 1.10.17; Diogenes Laertius 3.18.

80.   Scholion on Theocritus *Id.* 2; U. von Wilamowitz-Moellendorf, *Die Textgeschichte der griechischen Bukoliker* (Berlin: Weidmann, 1906) 270; see also P. E. Legrand, 'Théocrite', *Revue des études anciennes* 36 (1934) 28.

81.   K. Vretska, 'Sophron', *Der Kleine Pauly. Lexicon der Antike* 5 (1975) 281. Note also the numerous quotations of Sophron in Ps.-Demetrius *De eloc.* and Athenaios *Deip.*

82.   Statius *Silv.* 5.3.158.

83.   R. E. Fantham, 'Mime: The Missing Link in Roman Literary History', *CW* 82.3 (1989) 153–63.

84.   Crusius, *Untersuchungen zu den Mimiamben des Herondas*, 22; I. C. Cunningham, *Herodas. Mimes*, LCL (Cambridge, MA: Harvard University Press, 1993) 203–206.

85.   A. M. Little, 'Plautus and Popular Drama', *HSCP* 49 (1938) 205–28. Cf. Beare, *The Roman Stage*, 151: 'Plautus' very name, "Flatfoot", may perhaps suggest that he had himself acted as a *planipes* or barefooted mime.'

86.   On mime-inspired material in Horace, Propertius, and Ovid, see McKeown, 'Augustan Elegy and Mime'; K. Freudenburg, *The Walking Muse: Horace on the Theory of Satire* (Princeton: Princeton University Press, 1993) esp. 21–33; M. Hubbard, *Propertius* (London: Duckworth, 1974) 52–53; N. Horsfall, 'Epic and Burlesque in Ovid *Met.* VIII 260ff.', *CJ* 74 (1979) 19–32. For mime in Juvenal, see G. Highet, *Juvenal the Satirist. A Study* (Oxford: Clarendon, 1954) 274.

reminiscences of mime in Seneca's Menippean satire, the *Apocolocyntosis*, are so numerous and forceful as to suggest that the work was originally written for performance as a mime in four scenes.[87] Many of the features of the character Trimalchio in the *Satyricon* – his vulgarity and pretentiousness, but also his vitality – doubtless are owing to Petronius' familiarity with the fools of the mime stage.[88] Mime routines are constant points of reference in Apuleius' cunning novel, the *Golden Ass*.[89]

Beyond these opportunities for contact with the mime, it is possible that Paul's relationship to the theater was more direct and occupational. Readers of the revised article on σκηνοποιός in *A Greek-English Lexicon of the New Testament* by Frederick Danker will make the surprising discovery that the traditional understanding of the term used to describe Paul's occupation in Acts 18.3 as 'tentmaker' is wholly without lexical support outside the Bible and literature that the Bible has influenced, and furthermore is undermined by a variety of practical considerations.[90] Instead, Danker proposes the meaning 'maker of stage properties',[91] appealing to Pollux, who explains that the word is a synonym for μηχανοποιός, which is either a 'stagehand' who moves stage properties or a 'manufacturer of stage properties.'[92] Danker concludes: 'In the absence of any use of the term σκηνοποιός, beyond the passages in Pollux and the Hermetic Writings, and the lack of specific qualifiers in the text of Acts 18.3, one is left with the strong probability that Luke's publics in urban areas, where theatrical productions were in abundance, would think of σκηνοποιός in reference to matters theatrical.'[93] If the report of Paul's occupation in Acts 18.3 is historically reliable, then Paul was a 'prop

87. For mime elements in the *Apocolocyntosis*, see O. Weinreich, *Senecas* Apocolocyntosis. *Die Satire auf Tod/Himmel-und Höllenfahrt des Kaisers Claudius* (Berlin: Weidmann, 1923) 6–8; P. T. Eden, *Seneca. Apocolocyntosis* (Cambridge: Cambridge University Press, 1984) 13–17, 64, 95. For the suggestion that 'Seneca has reworked in the narrative form of Menippean satire his own original libretto, written for intimate staging at Nero's *Saturnalia* as a mime in four scenes', see Fantham, 'Mime: The Missing Link', 160–62.

88. G. Sandy, '*Scaenica Petroniana*', *TAPA* 104 (1973) 329–46. For a thorough analysis of theatrical elements in the *Satyricon*, see C. Panayotakis, *Theatrum Arbitri: Theatrical Elements in the* Satyrica *of Petronius*, Mnemosyne Suppl. 146 (Leiden: Brill, 1995).

89. J. J. Winkler, *Auctor & Actor. A Narratological Reading of Apuleius's* Golden Ass (Berkeley: University of California Press, 1991).

90. W. Bauer, *A Greek-English Lexicon of the New Testament and other Early Christian Literature*, 3rd ed., rev. and ed. by F. W. Danker (Chicago: University of Chicago Press, 2000) 928–29.

91. Bauer, *Greek-English Lexicon*, *s.v.* σκηνοποιός 1.

92. Pollux *Onom.* 7.189. See also Dio Cassius 67.2.

93. Bauer, *Greek-English Lexicon*, 929. Danker continues: 'In addition, Acts 20.34; 1 Cor. 4.12; 1 Thess. 2.9; 2 Thess. 3.8 indicate that Paul's work was of a technical nature and was carried out in metropolitan areas, where there would be a large demand for such kind of work.'

maker'. This would go far to explain the number, specificity, and richness of Pauline metaphors drawn from the world of the theater and amphitheater (e.g., 2 Cor. 11.1–12.10; Phil. 3.12–4.3, etc.).[94] In assessing the subtlety and ingenuity of the theatrical metaphor that runs through 1 Cor. 1–4, one should not forget Strabo's comment on 'the facile speed (εὐχέρεια) which is common among Tarsians, making them improvise endlessly on a given theme'.[95]

Two final words of explanation are necessary: first, on the intellectual tradition in which Paul is located; and then, on the textual basis of this study. In these areas, too, our study is vulnerable to the verdict of 'foolishness!' As the subtitle of the book indicates, it is our conviction that Paul's exposition of the folly of the message about the cross is best understood in the context of an intellectual tradition which, for want of a better term, we have designated the 'comic-philosophic tradition'. The intent of this phrase is to suggest that a common cultural perspective connects Socrates, satire, and the mime. The existence of such a connection is mostly asserted here, though the affinities that we establish within the literature may lend support to the claim. Nor has the history of this tradition yet been written, although many of the materials were gathered and discussed by Reich at the beginning of the last century.[96] Yet, a growing number of researchers into Greco-Roman culture have begun to trace a trajectory that reaches from Epicharmus to Lucian, and that includes, as one of its high points, Menippus of Gadara.[97] What these authors have in common is what John Winkler has called 'the grotesque perspective'.[98] In this tradition, the world is viewed from the perspective of the poor, the dishonored, the deformed, the outsiders. The hero of this

---

94. H. Windisch, *Der zweite Korintherbrief*, KEK 6 (Göttingen: Vandenhoeck & Ruprecht, 1924) 316, 349; L. L. Welborn, 'The Runaway Paul: A Character in the Fool's Speech', *HTR* 92 (1999) 115–63; D. J. Williams, *Paul's Metaphors – Their Context and Character* (Peabody, MA: Hendrickson, 1999); E. Krentz, 'Paul, Games, and the Military' in *Paul in the Greco-Roman World. A Handbook*, ed. P. Sampley (Harrisburg, PA: Trinity Press International, 2003) 344–83; S. Payne, 'Imagery of Paul the Stagehand' (unpublished paper).

95. Strabo 14.5.14. Compare Cicero *De Orat.* 3.194 on the ability of Antipater of Sidon to extemporise verses in a variety of meters, and the extempore verses of Achias the poet of Antioch, *Arch.* 18. A. Hardie (*Statius and the Silvae* [Liverpool: S. Cairns, 1983] 97–100) demonstrates that the origin of those who are celebrated for improvisation on a theme is the cities of the Eastern Mediterranean – Sidon, Antioch, and Tarsus.

96. Reich, *Der Mimus* (1903).

97. Winkler, *Auctor and Actor* (1985); R. Bracht Branham, *Unruly Eloquence: Lucian and the Comedy of Traditions* (Cambridge, MA: Harvard University Press, 1989); J. Relihan, *Ancient Menippean Satire* (Baltimore: Johns Hopkins University Press, 1993); Freudenburg, *The Walking Muse* (1993); Panayotakis, *Theatrum Arbitri* (1995).

98. Winkler, *Auctor and Actor*, 286–91. On the concept, see already M. Bakhtin, *Rabelais and His World* (Cambridge, MA: MIT Press, 1968) esp. 18–30.

tradition is the 'wise fool', who, in grotesque disguise, is allowed to utter critical truths about authority. Popular examples of this figure are Aesop of folk-tale and the fool in the mime; for intellectuals, Socrates was the model of the wise man who cloaked his wisdom in foolishness. As we hope to show, Paul participates fully in this tradition in his discourse about the folly of the word of the cross. The major components of Paul's argument in 1 Cor. 1–4 (the divine reversal of wisdom and foolishness, the necessity of becoming a fool, etc.) find their closest analogies in the tradition that valorizes Socrates, Aesop, and the mimic fool. The Paul who emerges from this study has more in common with Menippus than Gamaliel.

Finally, the textual basis of our study is the first four chapters of 1 Corinthians. The reader may rightly question this restriction, and may ask about the implications of our findings for the rest of 1 Corinthians. We might defend our choice of textual basis by observing that chapters 1–4 are manifestly a rhetorical unit, the beginning and end clearly marked by hortatory periods in 1.10 and 4.16.[99] But I will not conceal from the reader the fact that I do not regard canonical 1 Corinthians as a unified text. Almost one hundred years ago, Johannes Weiss, whose commentary on 1 Corinthians remains unsurpassed, expressed doubts about the integrity of canonical 1 Corinthians, noting breaks in the train of thought, discrepancies in reports of events, sudden changes of tone, and differences in outlook and judgment.[100] In my view, the questions raised by Weiss have not been answered by recent attempts to defend the integrity of 1 Corinthians on the basis of rhetorical analysis.[101] Hence, I follow Weiss in the hypothesis that 1 Cor. 1.1–6.11 was originally an independent letter, the last of three substantial fragments preserved in canonical 1 Corinthians.[102] With a number of scholars,[103] I also regard canonical 2

99. C. J. Bjerkelund, *Parakalo: Form, Funktion und Sinn der Parakalo-Sätze in den paulinischen Briefen* (Oslo: Universitetsforlaget, 1967) 141–42, 145–46.

100. J. Weiss, *Der erste Korintherbrief*, KEK 7 (Göttingen: Vandenhoeck & Ruprecht, 1910) xxxix–xliii.

101. E.g., M. M. Mitchell, *Paul and the Rhetoric of Reconciliation: An Exegetical Investigation of the Language and Composition of 1 Corinthians*, HUNT 28 (Tübingen: Mohr-Siebeck, 1991). For critique of the hypothesis that all of 1 Corinthians qualifies as deliberative rhetoric, see R. Dean Anderson, *Ancient Rhetorical Theory and Paul*, CBET 18 (Kampen: Kok Pharos, 1996).

102. In the original sequence of composition: Letter A: On Association with Idolators and the Immoral (6.12–20; 10–11); Letter B: Response to the Corinthians' Questions (7–9, 12–16); Letter C: Counsel of Concord (1.1–6.11).

103. E.g., G. Bornkamm, *Die Vorgeschichte des sogenannten Zweiten Korintherbrief*, SHAW.PH 1961, 2. Abhandlung (Heidelberg: Winter, 1961); D. Georgi, *The Opponents of Paul in Second Corinthians* (Philadelphia: Fortress Press, 1986); H. D. Betz, *2 Corinthians 8 and 9. A Commentary on Two Administrative Letters of the Apostle Paul*, Hermeneia (Philadelphia: Fortress Press, 1985).

Corinthians as a collection of letters, the earliest of which is preserved in 2 Cor. 10–13.[104] The implication of this literary hypothesis for our study is as follows: having appropriated the role of the fool in 1 Cor. 1–4, Paul goes on to deliver a 'fool's speech' in 2 Cor. 11.1–12.10,[105] as the conflict with the Corinthians sharpened, and as Paul embraced more completely the identity of the fool of Christ.

104.   For the hypothesis that 2 Cor. 10–13 is the earliest of the letter-fragments preserved in canonical 2 Corinthians, see A. von Hausrath, *Der Vier-Kapitel-Brief des Paulus an die Korinther* (Heidelberg: Bassermann, 1870); J. H. Kennedy, *The Second and Third Epistles of St. Paul to the Corinthians* (London: Methuen, 1900); L. L. Welborn, 'The Identification of 2 Corinthians 10–13 with the Letter of Tears', *NovT* 37 (1995) 138–53.

105.   For the interpretation of 2 Cor. 11.1–12.10 as a 'fool's speech' based upon the performances of fools in the mime and mime-inspired literature, see Windisch, *Der zweite Korintherbrief*, 316; Welborn, 'The Runaway Paul'.

Chapter 1

TRADITIONAL INTERPRETATIONS

Paul's description of the gospel as 'foolishness' (μωρία), although it is found in only one epistle,[1] has played a crucial role in the history of Christian thought.[2] Theologians as diverse as Tertullian and Chrysostom in the early church,[3] and Erasmus and Kierkegaard in the modern period,[4] have seen in Paul's characterization of the Christian message as 'folly' the formulation of an essential truth of their own religious philosophies. The meaning of Paul's declaration, 'the message about the cross is foolishness' (1 Cor. 1.18), is usually taken to be self-evident,[5] so that it functions as a cipher for whatever ideal is central to a given theological system. So, for dialectical theologians, the μωρία τοῦ κηρύγματος is the paradox by which God determines the existence of

---

1. 1 Corinthians, esp. 1.18–25, 27; 2.14; 3.18–19; 4.10.
2. The history of the reception of Paul's idea has not been written; see, however, the study of W. Nigg, *Der christliche Narr*. (Zürich: Artemis, 1956), which traces the 'fool of Christ' through selected literature from Simeon of Edessa to Dostoyevsky's *Idiot*.
3. Tertullian, *Adversus Marcionem* 5.5–7; *De Carne Christi* 4–5 in *Tertulliani Opera* I. ed. E. Dekkers (Turnholti: Typographi Brepols, 1954); John Chrysostom, *Homiliae in Epistulam I ad Corinthios*, ed. Migne, *PG* 61.9–382.
4. D. Erasmus, *Moriae Encomium* in *Opera Omnia*, ed. C. Miller (Amsterdam: North-Holland Publishing Company, 1979); English translation by B. Radice, *Erasmus. Praise of Folly* (London: Penguin Books, 1993); see esp. the final section in which Erasmus praises the Christian folly of Paul in a touching and earnest manner. S. Kierkegaard, 'Of the Difference Between a Genius and an Apostle' in *The Present Age*, trans. A. Dru (New York: Harper & Row, 1962) 89–108.
5. In most commentaries on 1 Cor., the terms μωρία, μωραίνω, μωρός generate little discussion, so e.g., H. Lietzmann, *An die Korinther I/II*, HNT 9 (Tübingen: Mohr-Siebeck, 1949) 9; C.K. Barrett, *A Commentary on the First Epistle to the Corinthians*, HNTC (New York: Harper & Row, 1968) 52; H. Conzelmann, *1 Corinthians*, Hermeneia (Philadelphia: Fortress, 1975) 41, 45, 47; A. Lindemann, *Der erste Korintherbrief*, HNT 9/I (Tübingen: Mohr-Siebeck, 2000) 44, 45, 47; so also in monographs devoted to 1 Cor. 1–2, e.g. U. Wilckens, *Weisheit und Torheit: Eine exegetisch-religionsgeschichtliche Untersuchung zu I. Kor. 1 und 2*, BHT 26 (Tübingen: Mohr-Siebeck, 1959) 24; and even in the lexica, e.g., G. Bertram, 'μωρός', *TDNT* 4 (1967) 845: 'The word of the cross is foolishness to those who are lost (1 Cor. 1.18), to Gentiles or Greeks (1.23), to the natural man in general (2.14). Paul is obviously right in this.'

human beings in the world,[6] while for theologians of the death of God, it provides the occasion for human beings to reestablish an authentic relation to time and history.[7] That Paul's formulation should have proven so influential is testimony to the power of his thought and rhetoric. But the assumption of self-evidence and the familiarity of the theme have erected an invisible barrier to exploration of one of Paul's most astonishing formulations. Until such an investigation is undertaken, a chapter in the history of Christian theology remains unread, and it is one of the most interesting.

When the attempt is made to determine what Paul meant by 'foolishness', it is generally explained that 'foolishness' (μωρία) is defined negatively, as the opposite of 'wisdom' (σοφία).[8] This seems a reasonable assumption given the dialectical manner in which Paul introduces the discussion in 1 Cor. 1.17: with calculated abruptness,[9] the gospel (εὐαγγελίζεσθαι) is defined negatively as the rejection of 'eloquent wisdom' (σοφία λόγου).[10] Paul then proceeds to explain this contrast,[11] beginning with the thesis statement: 'For the message about the cross is foolishness...' (1.18a). The meaning of 'foolishness,' then, logically depends upon the content of 'wisdom,' and varies, naturally, as 'wisdom' is understood differently by the interpreters.[12] So, when 'wisdom' is understood as 'cleverness in speaking'[13] or

6.   Conzelmann, *1 Corinthians*, 38, 41, 43, 45, 46, 88, referring to Karl Barth, *The Resurrection of the Dead* (New York: Revell, 1933) 15–21; similarly, E. Käsemann, 'The Saving Significance of the Death of Jesus in Paul' in idem, *Perspectives on Paul* (Philadelphia: Fortress, 1971) 40–41.

7.   Harvey Cox, *The Feast of Fools*, (Cambridge, MA: Harvard University Press, 1969) 27, 43, responding to T. J. J. Altizer, *Toward a New Christianity* (New York: Harcourt, Brace, 1967) 11, 13.

8.   Wilckens, *Weisheit und Torheit*, 24: 'Μωρία ist ein allgemeines Urteil, gemessen an dem was σοφία λόγου ist.' Similarly, Lindemann, *Der erste Korintherbrief*, 44.

9.   For the stylistic device of abruptness and contrast in order to introduce a theme, compare Rom. 1.16; Phil. 1.20; see the insightful comments of J. Weiss, *Der erste Korintherbrief*, 23.

10.   On the translation of σοφία λόγου in 1 Cor. 1.17, see W. Bauer, *A Greek-English Lexicon of the New Testament and Other Early Christian Literature* (Chicago: University of Chicago Press, 2000) 934; S. Pogoloff, *Logos and Sophia: The Rhetorical Situation of 1 Corinthians*, SBLDS 134 (Atlanta: Scholars Press, 1992) 108–13; and the discussion below.

11.   The conjunction γάρ marks vs. 18 and the paragraph it introduces (1.18–25) as the explanation of vs. 17b; thus Weiss, *Der erste Korintherbrief*, 24; cf. Conzelmann, *1 Corinthians*, 41 n. 9.

12.   On the diverse understandings of σοφία in 1 Cor. 1.17 among modern interpreters, see D. Litfin, *St. Paul's Theology of Proclamation: 1 Corinthians 1–4 and Greco-Roman Rhetoric*, SNTSMS 79 (Cambridge: Cambridge University Press, 1994) 2–4.

13.   In the sense of rhetoric, e.g., J. Calvin, *Commentarius in epistolam priorem ad Corinthios*, CR 77 (Brunsvigae, 1892) 320; C. F. G. Heinrici, *Das erste Sendschreiben des Apostel Paulus an die Korinther* (Berlin: Hertz, 1880) 91; E. B. Allo, *Saint Paul. Première Épître aux Corinthiens* (Paris: Gabalda, 1934) 21; H. D. Betz, 'The Problem of Rhetoric and

'eloquence',[14] 'foolishness' is defined as simple, straight-forward proclamation of what was ordinarily an unfit subject for declamation.[15] And when 'wisdom' is understood as philosophy,[16] or gnostic theology,[17] then 'foolishness' is taken to be the stark, historical account of the crucifixion of Jesus Christ.[18]

There is truth in this common sense approach to the meaning of foolishness in 1 Cor. 1–4. Paul clearly contrasts 'the foolishness of preaching' (ἡ μωρία τοῦ κηρύγματος) with the 'wisdom' (σοφία) of 'the world' (ὁ κόσμος, 1.21);[19] he denies that he came to the Corinthians 'with the superiority of eloquence or wisdom' (καθ᾽ ὑπεροχὴν λόγου ἢ σοφίας

Theology according to the Apostle Paul' in *L'Apôtre Paul: Personalité, Style et Conception du Ministére*, ed. A. Vanhoye, BETL 73 (Leuven: Leuven University Press, 1986) 34–36; T. Lim, 'Not in Persuasive Words of Wisdom, but in the Demonstration of the Spirit and Power,' *NovT* 29 (1987) 146–48; Pogoloff, *Logos and Sophia*, 108–113; Litfin, *St. Paul's Theology of Proclamation*, 2–8, 17–18, 187–209, 244–45.

14. In the sense of sophistry, J. Munck, 'The Church without Factions: Studies in 1 Corinthians 1–4' in *Paul and the Salvation of Mankind* (Richmond: John Knox Press, 1959) 148–67; L. Hartman, 'Some Remarks on 1 Cor. 2.1–5,' *SEÅ* 39 (1974) 115–16; B. W. Winter, *Philo and Paul among the Sophists*, SNTSMS 96 (Cambridge: Cambridge University Press, 1997) 145–61.

15. So, e.g., Pogoloff, *Logos and Sophia*, 119–21; Litfin, *St. Paul's Theology of Proclamation*, 197; Winter, *Philo and Paul among the Sophists*, 161.

16. Weiss, *Der erste Korintherbrief*, xxxiii, 23; G. Stählin, *Skandalon. Untersuchungen zur Geschichte eines biblischen Begriffs* (Gütersloh: Mohn, 1930) 201–203; R. Asting, *Die Verkündigung des Wortes im Urchristentum, dargestellt an den Begriffen 'Wort Gottes', 'Evangelium' und 'Zeugnis'* (Stuttgart: Kohlhammer, 1939) 145; R. M. Grant, 'The Wisdom of the Corinthians' in *The Joy of Study. Papers on New Testament and Related Subjects Presented to Honor Frederick Clifton Grant*, ed. S. E. Johnson (New York: Macmillan, 1951) 51–55; F. W. Grosheide, *Commentary on the First Epistle to the Corinthians* (Grand Rapids, MI: Eerdmans, 1953) 41; H. Schlier, 'Kerygma und Sophia. Zur neutestamentlichen Grundlegung des Dogmas' in *Die Zeit der Kirche. Exegetische Autsätze und Vorträge* (Freiburg: Herder, 1956) 206–32; E. Best, 'The Power and the Wisdom of God: 1 Corinthians 1.18–25' in *Paolo a una Chiesa Divisa (1 Cor. 1–4)*, ed. L. de Lorenzi (Rome: Abbazi di S. Paolo, 1980) 21, 30.

17. W. Schmithals, *Die Gnosis in Korinth. Eine Untersuchung zu den Korintherbriefen*, FRLANT 48 (Göttingen: Vandenhoeck & Ruprecht, 1965) 131–53; Wilckens, *Weisheit und Torheit*, 24–27; idem, 'σοφία' *TDNT* 7 (1972) 522; idem, 'Zu 1 Kor 2, 1–16' in *Theologia Crucis – Signum Crucis*, ed. C. Andersen and G. Klein (Tübingen: Siebeck-Mohr, 1979) 503; R. Baumann, *Mitte und Norm des Christlichen. Eine Auslegung von 1 Korinther 1,1–3,4*, (Münster: Aschendorff, 1968) 67, 78–79; G. Sellin, 'Das "Geheimnis" der Weisheit und das Rätsel der "Christuspartei" (zu 1 Kor 1–4)', *ZNW* 73 (1982) 80; M. Wolter, 'Verborgene Weisheit und Heil für die Heiden', *ZThK* 84 (1987) 303.

18. So, e.g., Schlier, 'Kerygma und Sophia,' 222–23; Wilckens, *Weisheit und Torheit*, 214–24; Schmithals, *Die Gnosis in Korinth*, 131–33; E. Schwarz, 'Wo's Weisheit ist, ein Tor zu sein,' *Wort und Dienst* 20 (1989) 225, 229–30.

19. Weiss, *Der erste Korintherbrief*, 29 perceptively senses the correspondence between the phrases διὰ τῆς σοφίας and διὰ τῆς μωρίας τοῦ κηρύγματος in vs. 21; cf. Baumann, *Mitte und Norm des Christlichen*, 97–98.

2.1);[20] he acknowledges that his speech and his proclamation were 'not in persuasiveness of wisdom' (οὐκ ἐν πειθοῖ σοφίας 2.4).[21] In these instances[22] and others (1.20,22–23,25,27; 2.14; 3.19) it is clear that 'foolishness' is constructed as the antithesis of worldly 'wisdom'.

But what Paul means by 'foolishness' is not exhausted when foolishness is construed as the opposite of wisdom. For Paul's exposition of 'the word of the cross' (1.18–2.5), which he describes as 'foolishness', abounds in rhetorical devices: antithetical parallelism, anaphora, rhetorical question, paronomasia, graduation, and irony;[23] its method of argumentation is the enthymeme, developed by means of the rhetorical strategies of redefinition and self-deprecation.[24] So that, it is impossible to reduce the meaning of 'foolishness' to the anti-rhetorical.[25] Similarly, Paul insists that he speaks

20.   Bauer, *Greek-English Lexicon*, 1034; cf. Hartman, 'Some Remarks on 1 Cor. 2.1–5', 118; Pogoloff, *Logos and Sophia*, 131–36; Winter, *Philo and Paul among the Sophists*, 156–57.

21.   On the textual difficulties that riddle the phrase ἐν πειθοῖ[ς] σοφίας [λόγοις], see B. M. Metzger, *A Textual Commentary on the Greek New Testament* (London & New York: United Bible Societies, 1971) 546. The text adopted here follows the suggestion of Weiss, *Der erste Korintherbrief*, 49 that the original wording was ἐν πειθοῖ σοφίας, a reading that seems to lie behind some of the Old Latin versions, and that balances nicely with the following phrase, ἐν ἀποδείξει πνεύματος. Cf. G. Zuntz, *The Text of the Epistles: A Disquisition upon the Corpus Paulinum* (London: Oxford University Press, 1953) 23–25; J. Héring, *The First Epistle of St. Paul to the Corinthians* (London: Epworth, 1962) 15; G. D. Fee, *The First Epistle to the Corinthians* (Grand Rapids, MI: Eerdmans, 1987) 88; Pogoloff, *Logos and Sophia*, 137.

22.   A number of interpreters rightly observe that 2.1–5 is a restatement and amplification of 1.17–18, e.g., C. F. G. Heinrici, *Der erste Brief an die Korinther*, KEK 5 (Göttingen: Vandenhoeck & Ruprecht, 1896) 65–66; Weiss, *Der erste Korintherbrief*, 23; Pogoloff, *Logos and Sophia*, 129; Litfin, *St. Paul's Theology of Proclamation*, 190; J. S. Vos, 'Die Argumentation des Paulus in 1 Kor 1,10–3,4' in *The Corinthian Correspondence*, BETL 125, ed. R. Bieringer (Leuven: Leuven University Press, 1996) 103–04.

23.   J. Weiss, 'Beiträge zur paulinischen Rhetorik' in *Theologische Studien, Bernhard Weiss zu seinem 70. Geburtstag dargebracht* (Göttingen: Vandenhoeck & Ruprecht, 1897) 165–247; idem, *Der erste Korintherbrief*, 25, 27, 29, 35–36; Conzelmann, *1 Corinthians*, 39, 49; R. F. Collins, *First Corinthians*, SP 7 (Collegeville, MN: Michael Glazier, 1999) 75–76, 91, 99, 117.

24.   R. A. Humphries, 'Paul's Rhetoric of Argumentation in 1 Corinthians 1–4', GTU Ph.D. Dissertation (Berkeley, CA, 1979); K. Plank, *Paul and the Irony of Affliction*, SBLSS (Atlanta: Scholars Press, 1987) 34–42; Vos, 'Die Argumentation des Paulus', 104–105; Collins, *First Corinthians*, 116–17.

25.   Contra Hartman, 'Some Remarks on 1 Cor. 2.1–5', 120; Litfin, *St. Paul's Theology of Proclamation*, 197–201; Winter, *Philo and Paul among the Sophists*, 161, 201–202. Interpreters have variously attempted to resolve the contradiction between Paul's professed disavowal of rhetoric and his evident use of the art in 1 Cor. 1–4: F. Siegert (*Argumentation bei Paulus*, WUNT 34 [Tübingen: Mohr-Siebeck, 1985] 248–51) argues that Paul's attitude is an instance of the phenomenon of 'rhetoric against rhetoric', which has a long tradition in classical Greek thought; Lim ('Not in Persuasive Words of Wisdom,' 146–49) proposes that Paul rejected a sophistic rhetoric in favor of a plain style; Betz ('The Problem of Rhetoric and Theology', 138–46) suggests that Paul and the Corinthians participated in the debate between rhetoric and philosophy which goes back to Isocrates; Pogoloff (*Logos and Sophia*. 120–21) explains

'wisdom' (σοφία) among those who are mature enough to receive it (2.6; cf. 3.1–4),[26] and proceeds to characterize this 'wisdom' in language derived from the mystery religions (2.7–16).[27] Consequently, it is not possible to subsume Paul's 'foolishness' under the category of the anti-philosophical.[28]

Indeed, it is not 'wisdom' (σοφία) that is the counterpoint to 'foolishness' (μωρία) in the thesis statement in 1.18, but the 'power of God' (δύναμις θεοῦ).[29] This insight has not escaped interpreters.[30] But its significance is usually sought in the limitation of the concept of 'wisdom' that is implied,[31] or in the boundless scope and effect of the kerygma that is assumed.[32] What is

that Paul rejects not rhetoric, but the cultural values underlying it, appealing to E. A. Judge, 'The Reaction against Classical Education in the New Testament', *Journal of Christian Education* 77 (1983) 7–14.

26. On the meaning of τέλειος, see P. J. du Plessis, ΤΕΛΕΙΟΣ: *The Idea of Perfection in the New Testament* (Kampen: Kok, 1959); G. Delling, 'τέλειος', *TDNT* 8.69–72.

27. R. Reitzenstein, *Hellenistic Mystery-Religions* (Pittsburgh: Pickwick, 1978) 431–36; Wilckens, *Weisheit und Torheit*, 52–89; H. Jonas, *Gnosis und spätantiker Geist* (Göttingen Vandenhoeck & Ruprecht, 1966) 57–65; Conzelmann, *1 Corinthians*, 60; H. Koester, 'Gnostic Writings as Witnesses for the Development of the Sayings Tradition' in *The Rediscovery of Gnosticism*, Vol. 1, ed. B. Layton (Leiden: Brill, 1980) 248–49.

28. Contra J. Moffat, *The First Epistle of Paul to the Corinthians* (London: Hodder & Stoughton, 1938) 15, citing Milton's line: 'Down, reason, then; at least vain reasonings down!'; Asting, *Die Verkündigung des Wortes*, 145: 'Paulus will also sagen, dass die Eigenart seiner Evangeliumsverkündigung nicht in einer Mitteilung einer Einsicht in das Wesen der Vernunft besteht, die als Beherrscherin dieser Welt gedacht wurde.' Similarly, W. Lütgert, *Freiheitspredigt und Schwarmgeister in Korinth*, BFCT 1213 (Gütersloh: Bertelsmann, 1908); W. G. Kümmel, Supplemental notes (165–214) to Hans Lietzmann, *An die Korinther I/II.*, HNT 9 (Tubingen: Mohr-Siebeck, 1949); Best, 'The Power and Wisdom of God,' 14; Lindemann, *Der erste Korintherbrief*, 44; 'μωρία... gemeint ist ein Urteil, das den Inhalt der Predigt als unlogisch und unvernunftwidrig bezeichnet.'

29. On the concept of δύναμις, see W. Grundmann, 'δύναμαι', *TDNT* 2. 284–371; K. Prümm, 'Dynamis in griechisch-hellenistischer Religion und Philosophie als Vergleichsbild zu göttlicher Dynamis im Offenbarungsraum', *ZThK* 83 (1961) 393–430.

30. Weiss, *Der erste Korintherbrief*, 26: 'An unsrer Stelle sollte man als Gegensatz zu μωρία σοφία erwarten, δύναμις θεοῦ wirkt also überraschend'; similarly, Wilckens, *Weisheit und Torheit*, 24; Baumann, *Mitte und Norm des Christlichen*, 86; Conzelmann, *1 Corinthians*, 41; Lindemann, *Der erste Korintherbrief*, 44; Collins, *First Corinthians*, 102: 'One might have expected *sophia*, wisdom, in contrast to *moria*, the 'foolishness' of the first antithesis. Instead, Paul has *dynamis*.'

31. Wilckens (*Weisheit und Torheit*, 24) argues that Paul avoids the term σοφία in 1.18 in view of the negative definition of the gospel in vs. 17 as οὐκ ἐν σοφίᾳ λόγου. Cf. Schmithals, *Gnosis in Korinth*, 132–33; Baumann, *Mitte und Norm des Christlichen*, 86. See also Conzelmann, *1 Corinthians*, 41 n. 15: 'The choice of δύναμις θεοῦ instead of σοφία points to the fact that faith is not a habitus which – on a higher plane – again makes possible the independent operation of a wisdom of our "own".'

32. So, already, Heinrici, *Der erste Brief an die Korinther*, 67–68: 'Der Gegensatz ist starker als wenn es σοφία θεοῦ hiesse; δύναμις θεοῦ hat nämlich das Gegentheil von μωρία zur nothwendigen Voraussetzung, weil die Kraft Gottes Erleuchtung, Busse, Heiligung, Liebe, Friede, Hoffnung zu Wege bringt. Der Apostel wählt diesen Gegensatz, weil der

seldom recognized is the consequence for the concept of 'foolishness' entailed in the contrast with the 'power of God': namely, the origin and significance of 'foolishness' in Paul's discourse is not to be found in antithesis to 'wisdom'.[33]

Nor is it, finally, in the form or manner of Paul's proclamation that interpreters have sought the meaning of 'foolishness', but rather in the content:[34] that is, 'the message about the cross' (ὁ λόγος τοῦ σταυροῦ, 1.18). It belongs to the fundamental assumptions of Christian interpreters throughout history that the proclamation of the crucified Christ was 'foolishness' to the people of the ancient world, and remains 'folly' to all those who encounter this message from a human standpoint.[35] When Paul described the message of the crucified Christ as 'foolishness,' he was

Erkenntnissgrund des Evangeliums nicht auf dem Gebiete des Intellectuellen, sondern auf dem Gebiete des effectus historiae liegt.' Cf. Weiss, *Der erste Korintherbrief*, 26; Wilckens, *Weisheit und Torheit*, 24: 'Dagegen für das Urteil δύναμις θεοῦ gibt es offenbar keinen Massstab, eben weil es sich um die Macht *Gottes* handelt.' Similarly, Conzelmann, *1 Corinthians*, 41–42.

33. There is partial insight in Stählin, *Skandalon*, 203; H. O. Gibb, '*Torheit*' und '*Rätsel*' im Neuen Testament. Der antinomische Strukturcharakter der neutestamentlichen Botschaft (Stuttgart: Kohlhammer, 1941) 8; 'In 1, 18 steht μωρία in kontradiktorischem Gegensatz zu δύναμις, in 1, 23 steht es in konträrem Gegensatz zu σκάνδαλον. Diese Beziehungen sind charakteristisch: μωρία ist also das Gegenteil einer Kraft, das heisst etwas Lähmendes, mit dem man nichts anfangen kann; seine Wirkung kommt somit der eines "Falles" gleich.'

34. Heinrici, *Der erste Brief an die Korinther*, 72–73, on the expression διὰ τῆς μωρίας τοῦ κηρύγματος in 1.21: 'd.i. mittelst der den Inhalt der Predigt (des Evang.) ausmachenden Torheit. Das ist die Lehre vom Kreuze, v. 18, die im Gegensatz gegen jene vom κόσμος fruchtlos zum Erkenntnissmittel benutzte Weisheit eine thörichte Lehre ist.' J. B. Lightfoot, *Notes on the Epistles of St. Paul* (London: Macmillan, 1904) 161: 'It refers to the subject, not to the manner of preaching.' Moffat, *The First Epistle of Paul to the Corinthians*, 14: 'It is the content rather than the form of the utterance that engages his attention ... *the story of the cross*.' Baumann, *Mitte und Norm des Christlichen*, 82, 98: 'Diese charakterisierung seiner Verkündigung als "Wort vom Kreuz" mag bereits andeuten, dass das Evangelium von seinem Inhalt her alles andere als "Weisheit" ist. Denn mit dem verachtetsten Namen der damaligen Welt ist es benannt: Es ist "Predigt vom Galgen"'; and 'wie die These in v. 18 bereits zum Ausdruck brachte, dass "Torheit" wesentlich den *Inhalt* des Kerygmas bezeichnet, den gekreuzigten Christus, das Wort vom Kreuz.' Conzelmann, *1 Corinthians*, 41: 'ὁ λόγος τοῦ σταυροῦ, "the word of the cross," is, as is shown by 2.1 f., an exhaustive statement of the content of the gospel.' H. Conzelmann, *An Outline of the Theology of the New Testament* (London: SCM Press, 1969) 241: 'The folly lies exclusively in the content of the preaching.' Wilckens, 'Zu 1 Kor 2, 1–16,' 503: 'Mit dieser μωρία τοῦ κηρύγματος ist der Inhalt der Verkündigung gemeint.'

35. E.g., Justin, *Dial. Cum Tryph*, 69; Tertullian, *De Carne Christi*, 4–5; *Advers. Judaeos*, 10; Origen, *Philocalia*, 18; Calvin, *Commentarius in epistolam priorem ad Corinthios*, 320, 322; J. A. Bengel, *Gnomon of the New Testament*, Vol. 2. (Edinburgh: T & T Clark, 1877) 205, 207; Käsemann, 'The Saving Significance of the Death of Jesus in Paul', 40: 'The cross always remains scandal and foolishness for Jew and Gentile, inasmuch as it exposes man's illusion

reflecting the harsh experience of his missionary preaching and the response that the gospel elicited, particularly from Greeks and Romans.[36]

Now it is one of the results of historical-philological research that the term 'folly' is nowhere connected with the cross in pre-Christian literature, Greek or Latin.[37] The cross is described as 'terrible' (*maxuma mala*),[38] 'infamous' (*infamis*),[39] 'barren' (*infelix*),[40] 'criminal' (πανουργικός),[41] an 'evil instrument.'[42] Crucifixion is called 'cruel and disgusting' (*crudelissimus taeterrimusque*),[43] 'shameful' (αἴσχιστος),[44] 'the supreme penalty' (*summum supplicium*),[45] 'the most wretched of deaths' (θανάτων τὸν οἴκτιστον).[46] But nowhere is the cross associated with any of the terms that make up the rich vocabulary of 'foolishness' in Greek and Latin.[47]

that he can transcend himself and effect his own salvation . . . In light of the cross God shows all this, and ourselves as well, to be foolish, vain and godless'; similarly, Conzelmann, *1 Corinthians*, 46–47.

36. G. Bertram, 'μωρός' 845–46; M. Hengel, *Crucifixion* 89.

37. This is the (unintended?) outcome of the meticulous investigation of Hengel, *Crucifixion*, which draws upon the rich materials of the *Thesaurus Linguae Latinae* and the *Thesaurus Graecae Linguae*, supplemented by the concordances to various writers; see the introduction and the bibliography for other resources. It is indicative of the state of the evidence that the word 'folly' does not appear in the book outside of summary statements in the first chapter and the conclusion. Pliny (*Epistulae* 10.96.4) describes the adherents of the new sect of the Christians as *amentiae*. But the primary meaning of *amentia* is 'madness'. B. Radice (*Pliny Letters*, Vol. 2, LCL [Cambridge, MA: Harvard University Press, 1976] 287) rightly translates the term 'fanatical'. *Amentia* means 'folly' only in a transferred sense in poetical texts, such as those of Horace. Similarly, Justin (*Apol.* I, 13.4) describes the offense caused by the message of the crucified as μανία, but this is 'madness' rather than 'folly'. Christian writers, such as Theophilus of Antioch (*Ad Autolycum* 2.1) and Origen (*Contra Celsum* 1.9), who place the term 'foolishness' (μωρία) in the mouth of pagan interlocutors as a judgment upon the Christian message, are demonstrably under the influence of Paul's formulation in 1 Cor. 1.18–31.

38. Esp. in Plautus *Captivi* 469; *Casina* 611; *Menaechmi* 66, 849; *Poenulus* 347; *Persa* 352, *Rudens* 518; *Trinummus* 598; see other texts cited by Hengel, *Crucifixion*, 7 n. 13.

39. *Anthologia Latina* 415.23–24: *Noxius infami districtus stipite membra, sperat et a fixa posse redire cruce.* ('The criminal, outstretched on the infamous stake, hopes for escape from his place on the cross').

40. Seneca *Epist. mor.* 101.14: cf. Hengel, *Crucifixion*, 7 n. 12.

41. *PGM* 5.73, ed. K. Preisendanz, *Papyri Graecae Magicae. Die griechische Zauberpapyri I* (Stuttgart: Teubner, 1973) 184.

42. Lucian *Iudicium vocalium* 12; cf. Hengel, *Crucifixion*, 8.

43. Cicero *In Verr.* 2.5.165; cf. Seneca *Epist. mor.* 14.5; Apuleius *Met.* 1.15.4; *Scriptores Historiae Augustae* 8.5; Hengel, *Crucifixion*, 22–32.

44. Achilles Tatius 2.37.3; cf. Origen *c. Cels.* 6.10.

45. Cicero *In Verr.* 2.5.168, 169; cf. Hengel, *Crucifixion*, 33–38.

46. Josephus *War* 7.202–203.

47. Greek is rich in the vocabulary of 'foolishness'; usage varies according to genre and author. The basic terms for 'folly' are μωρία, ἄνοια, ἀμαθία, ἀφροσύνη, ἀβουλία, ἀσυνεσία. The 'foolish person' is called μωρός, ἀνόητος, ἀμαθής, ἄβουλος, ἀσύνετος, ἄνους, ἄφρων, but also terms

The fact that pagan writers do not describe the cross as 'folly' is hardly surprising. In a well known passage, Cicero asserts that 'the very word "cross" should be far removed not only from the person of a Roman citizen but from his thoughts, his eyes and his ears. ... The mere mention of such a thing is shameful to a Roman citizen and a free man.'[48] The cross was evidently not a subject of levity among the upper classes of the Roman Empire.[49] But it is only when this fact is acknowledged that one can begin to appreciate the audacity of Paul's formulation, 'the message about the cross is foolishness'.

The signs of novelty are apparent in Paul's articulation of the thesis. The expression, ὁ λόγος τοῦ σταυροῦ,[50] by which Paul summarizes the gospel,[51] is

which denote the humorous response which such a figure evokes, such as γελοῖος, γελωτοποιός, and καταγέλαστος; with lower-class fools, the emphasis falls upon the wretchedness of their condition, and so they are termed τλήμων and ταλαίπωρος. Foolish talk is λῆρος and φλυαρία. See the various articles in H. G. Liddell and R. Scott, *A Greek-English Lexicon*, rev. H. S. Jones (Oxford: Clarendon Press, 1968). The most general Latin term for 'folly' is *stultitia*, then *fatuitas, insipientia, dementia, ineptia*. The 'foolish person' is generally called *stultus*, sometimes *fatuus, ineptus, demens, insipiens*. See the entries in P. G. W. Glare, *Oxford Latin Dictionary* (Oxford: Clarendon Pres. 1982).

48.   Cicero *Pro Rabirio* 5.16: '... *et nomen ipsum crucis absit non modo a corpore civium Romanorum sed etiam a cogitatione, oculis, auribus... mentio ipsa denique indigna cive Romano atque homine libero est.*' The passage is often quoted in exposition of 1 Cor. 1.18, e.g., Heinrici, *Der erste Brief an die Korinther*, 75; G. Bertram, 'μωρός', 845 n. 112; Baumann, *Mitte und Norm des Christlichen*, 85; Hengel, *Crucifixion*, 41–42. H.-W. Kuhn ('Jesus als Gekreuzigter in der frühchristlichen Verkündigung bis zur Mitte des 2. Jahrhunderts', *ZThK* 72 [1975] 7–8) correctly insists that the aesthetic judgment of a man of Cicero's social class should not be taken as representative of the attitude of antiquity.

49.   Note the explanation of Cicero's learned contemporary, Varro *De Lingua Latina*: 'To say "pleasure" is gentle on the ears, but to say "cross" is harsh. The harshness of the latter word matches the pain brought on by the cross' (*lene est auribus cum dicimus 'voluptas', asperum cum dicimus 'crux' ... ipsius verbi asperitas cum doloris quem crux efficit asperitate concordet*) in *M. Terenti Varronis de Lingua Latina quae supersunt*, ed. G. Goetz and F. Schoell (Leipzig: Teubner, 1910) 239, quoted by Hengel, *Crucifixion*, 10. On the use of the term 'cross' in the gallows-humor of the lower classes, see below.

50.   The text chosen by Nestle-Aland, *Novum Testamentum Graece*, 27th ed. (Stuttgart: Deutsche Bibelgesellschaft, 1993) 442 is ὁ λόγος γὰρ ὁ τοῦ σταυροῦ. But the postpositive use of the genitive with the article is rare in the New Testament. Blass-Debrunner, *A Greek Grammar of the New Testament and Other Early Christian Literature* (Chicago: University of Chicago Press, 1961), 271 assumes a kind of anaphora (following vs. 17). The reading chosen here, which omits the article after γάρ, is supported by P46, B, and several other manuscripts. Cf. Zuntz, *The Text of the Epistles*, 67.

51.   Wilckens, *Weisheit und Torheit*, 24: 'ὁ λόγος τοῦ σταυροῦ ist eine abgekürzte Redewendung. Gemeint ist, wie 1, 23 und 2, 2 zeigen, die Verkündigung Christi als des Gekreuzigten.'

unique, not only in the *corpus Paulinum*,[52] but in the New Testament.[53] Thus it is not a *terminus technicus* of the Pauline kerygma, but an ad hoc formulation,[54] growing out of the terse, antithetical phrases at the end of 1.17 (οὐκ ἐν σοφίᾳ λόγου, ἵνα μὴ κενωθῇ ὁ σταυρὸς τοῦ Χριστοῦ).[55] The synecdoche, which replaces the content of the gospel metaphorically with a *signum crudelitatis*, is intentionally harsh.[56] The reader, who does not yet know how Paul will expound his thought in the following paragraphs (esp. 1.23 and 2.2), must have experienced this reduction of the content of the gospel to a single, shameful event as stunning.[57] And then, when the message about this cruel and disgusting death is immediately declared to be 'foolishness' (μωρία), the effect must have been shocking. The paradox is stupefying.

If Paul were the first to describe 'the word of the cross' as 'foolishness', then the question of the meaning of 'foolishness' in Paul's discourse takes on fresh urgency. For the term cannot previously have possessed the profound, theological significance that Paul confers upon it in the course of his exposition.[58] Close examination of Paul's argument reveals that the apostle uses the word 'foolishness' (μωρία) in three senses in 1 Cor. 1–4, corresponding to three moments in his encounter with the concept: appropriation, evaluation, and affirmation.[59] If we would understand the meaning of Paul's surprising assertion, 'the message about the cross is foolishness', we must rehearse the drama of his struggle with this concept,

52. Heinrici, *Der erste Brief*, 66 rightly observes that Paul speaks of the cross (σταυρός) relatively seldom in his epistles (1 Cor. 1.17,18; Gal. 5.11, 6.12, 14; Phil. 2.8, 3.18; see also the verb form in 1 Cor. 1.13,23; 2.2,8; 2 Cor. 13.4; Gal. 3.1, 5.24, 6.14), but always with emphasis. Cf. Kuhn, 'Jesus als Gekreuzigter', 27–41.

53. Collins, *First Corinthians*, 101.

54. Lindemann, *Der erste Korintherbrief*, 43.

55. Heinrici, *Der erste Brief an die Korinther*, 66; Wilckens, *Weisheit und Torheit*, 21; Lindemann, *Der erste Korintherbrief*, 43.

56. Heinrici, *Der erste Brief an die Korinther*, 66.

57. Weiss, *Der erste Korintherbrief*, 26–27.

58. Contra Bertram, 'μωρός', 845: 'The transvaluation of values in the Gospel is the basis of the use of the word group by Paul … the transvaluation of values in the sense of the New Testament revelation was accomplished by Jesus Himself, not by Paul.'

59. So, already, Weiss, *Der erste Korintherbrief*, 25, commenting on 1 Cor. 1.18 ff.: 'Der lebhaft erregte Apostel spielt im folgenden mit dem Ausdruck μωρία in verschiedene Weise: einerseits spricht er dieser Urteilsweise ihr eigenes Urteil, in dem er sagt vs. 18a, dass nur Verlorenen das Wort vom Kreuz als μωρία erscheinen könne, andererseits greift er dies beschimpfend gemeinte Wort als eines Ruhmestitel auf: gewiss, Torheit, da eben die Weisheit nicht zu brauchen war (vs. 20 f.); und schliesslich mündet er darin aus, dass diese "Torheit," die immer noch weiser ist als menschliche Weisheit (vs. 25) die wahre "Weisheit" ist, weil sie eben die σωτηρία wirklich bietet (vs. 18b, 21b, 24, 30).' Bertram, 'μωρός', 845–47, also finds that the apostle uses the term 'folly' in three senses in 1 Cor. 1–4.

from the application of the term as a judgment upon his preaching, to his acceptance of the word as the truth of his life in fellowship with the suffering of Christ.

Chapter 2

THE PROVENANCE OF THE CONCEPT

We begin our search, accordingly, at the point where Paul appropriates the term 'foolishness' (μωρία) as a description of his proclamation, since this is the earliest moment in the process of meaning that is ascertainable in the text. Determination of the original import of the word is crucial, since whatever significance the term acquires in the course of Paul's exposition is, in some sense, a reflex of the meaning it possessed at the point of appropriation. So, whence has Paul derived the concept of 'foolishness' (μωρία) that he applies to his preaching of the message about the cross?

It is clear, from the outset, that the source of the term is not to be found in the Old Testament.[1] To be sure, Paul repeatedly cites the Scriptures to justify and explicate his assertions about wisdom and foolishness.[2] But the term 'foolishness' (μωρία) does not appear in any of the passages which Paul quotes.[3] Indeed, 'μωρός ("fool") and its cognates are not common in

---

1. W. Caspari, 'Über den biblischen Begriff der Torheit', *NKZ* 39 (1928) 690; Gibb, '*Torheit*,' 8.

2. There are six explicit citations of Scripture in 1 Cor. 1–4: Isa. 29.14 in 1.19; Jer. 9.22–23 in 1.31; Isa. 64.3 (52.15) in 2.9; Isa. 40.13 in 2.16; Job 5.12–13 in 3.19; and Ps. 93.11 in 3.20. On Paul's use of Scripture in this section of 1 Cor., see D. A. Koch, *Die Schrift als Zeuge des Evangeliums. Untersuchungen zur Verwendung und zum Verständnis der Schrift bei Paulus*, BHTh 69 (Tübingen: Mohr-Siebeck, 1986) 31, 36–37, 42, 71–72; G. R. O'Day, 'Jeremiah 9.22–23 and 1 Corinthians 1.26–31: A Study in Intertextuality', *JBL* 109 (1990) 259–67; C. Stanley, *Paul and the Language of Scripture. Citation Technique in the Pauline Epistles*, SNTSMS 74 (Cambridge: Cambridge University Press, 1992) 185–94; R. Hays, *First Corinthians*, Interpretation (Louisville, KY: John Knox, 1997) 28–29, 34–35, 44–45, 59–60; Collins, *First Corinthians*, 94–96.

3. The closest that Paul comes to the vocabulary of foolishness in the texts that he cites is the term πανουργία 'craftiness,' in 3.19 (Job 5.13) and the term 'futile,' μάταιος, in 3.20 (Ps. 93.11). Πανουργία is the antithesis to σοφία in Plato *Menex.* 247a: πᾶσα τε ἐπιστήμη χωριζομένη δικαιοσύνη καὶ τῆς ἄλλης ἀρετῆς πανουργία οὐ σοφία, φαίνεται. Μάταιος can mean 'foolish' in reference to persons; see Liddell-Scott-Jones, *Greek-English Lexicon*, 1084 s.v. Cf. Plato *Soph.* 231b: περὶ τὴν ματαίαν δοξοσοφίαν. In neither case does Paul's quotation agree with the majority tradition of the LXX: he substitutes πανουργίᾳ for φρονήσει in the citation of Job in 3.19, and replaces ἀνθρώπων with σοφῶν in the citation of Ps. 93.11 in 3.20. Whether Paul has modified the texts that he quotes in the interest of his argument, or follows a minority

the Greek Old Testament'.[4] Where μωρός is used to translate נָבָל (Deut. 32.6, Isa. 32.5–6)[5] or כְּסִיל (Ps. 94.8),[6] the reference is to a lack of the true knowledge of God,[7] that expresses itself as impiety and iniquity.[8] 'The folly condemned here is thus apostasy from God, or practical atheism',[9] a meaning that has no relationship to the senses in which Paul uses the term in 1 Cor. 1–4.[10] Only in the Wisdom of Jesus ben Sira, where the adjective is common, is μωρός used in a general sense to designate the opposite of practical wisdom in social and moral matters.[11] But Paul's willingness to accept the term as a description of his proclamation distinguishes his attitude fundamentally from that of ben Sira.[12] Indeed, at points it seems that Paul's use of the word is an attack upon the conventional notion of 'foolishness' found in wisdom literature.[13] The reversal of wisdom and foolishness described in Isaiah 19.11 and the Syriac Apocalypse of Baruch 70.2–5 is reminiscent of Paul's statements in 1 Corinthians, especially 1.20, 27; 3.18–19.[14] But the resemblance is purely formal, the content is dissimilar: in the former, the reversal of normal relations is a sign of divine judgment, an eschatological catastrophe resulting in confusion; in the latter, it is a paradoxical sign of present salvation in a new social order established by God.[15] In sum, the several meanings of 'foolishness' in the Old Testament, all defined in a religious context,[16] from which the sense of

tradition within the textual history of the LXX, see Weiss, *Der erste Korintherbrief*, 87–88; B. Schaller, 'Zum Textcharakter der Hiobzitate im paulinischen Schriftum'. *ZNW* 71 (1980) 21–26; Stanley, *Paul and the Language of Scripture*, 189–94; Collins, *First Corinthians*, 165.

4.   Bertram, 'μωρός', 833; similarly, Caspari, 'Über den biblischen Begriff der Torheit', 683. In most of the wisdom literature of the Greek OT (Ps., Prov., Eccl., Wis., Sol.), ἄφρων is used exclusively or almost exclusively for the 'fool'.

5.   In the LXX of Deut. 32.6, the people are addressed as λαὸς μωρός καὶ οὐχὶ σοφός. See also Jer. 5.21: λαὸς μωρός καὶ ἀκάρδιος. For נָבָל = μωρός, see also Sir. 4.27; 21.22a; 50.26. Cf. Caspari, 'Über den biblischen Begriff der Torheit' 684; Bertram, 'μωρός', 833–34.

6.   Caspari, 'Über den biblischen Begriff der Torheit', 676; Bertram, 'μωρός', 834–35.

7.   Caspari, 'Über den biblischen Begriff der Torheit', 676, 683–84, 690; Gibb, '*Torheit*', 7–8; Bertram, 'μωρός', 833–34.

8.   Cf. Ps. 14.1; Isa. 32.5–6; Bertram, 'μωρός', 834.

9.   Bertram, 'μωρός', 834.

10.   Caspari, 'Über den biblischen Begriff der Torheit', 690; Gibb, '*Torheit*', 8.

11.   E.g., Sir. 18.18; 19.11,12; 20.13,16,20; 21.14 ff.; 22.9 ff.; 27.13; 33.5. See Caspari, 'Über den biblischen Begriff der Torheit', 684; Bertram, 'μωρός', 833–36.

12.   Caspari, 'Über den biblischen Begriff der Torheit', 690–91.

13.   Ibid., 691. n. 1.

14.   Isa. 19.11: καὶ μωροὶ ἔσονται οι ἄρχοντες Τάνεως ἡ βουλῆ αὐτῶν μωρανθήσεται. Syr. Apoc. of Bar. 70.5: 'The wise are silent and fools will speak'. For comparison with 1 Cor. 1.20, 26–31, see Weiss, *Der erste Korintherbrief*, 27; E. von Dobschütz, 'Religionsgeschichtliche Parallelen zum Neuen Testament', *ZNW* 21 (1922) 69–72; Bertram, 'μωρός', 835.

15.   Gibb, '*Torheit*', 13.

16.   Caspari, 'Über den biblischen Begriff der Torheit', 676–78; Bertram, 'μωρός', 836.

'ungodly' is never entirely absent,[17] have contributed nothing to the content of the concept that Paul appropriates as a description of his gospel in 1 Cor. 1–4.

It is equally apparent that the use of μωρός in the tradition of Jesus' sayings has exercised no influence upon Paul's concept of foolishness. Neither the use of the verb μωραίνω in the difficult saying about salt in Matt. 5.13 // Lk. 14.34, with the probable meaning of 'become insipid',[18] nor the condemnation of the use of μωρέ as an abusive epithet in Matt. 5.22,[19] nor the evaluation of the actions of the builders and the virgins in the parables (Matt. 7.24–27; 25.1–13) as 'foolish' in the sense of 'imprudent',[20] nor, finally, the polemical description of the scribes and Pharisees as 'fools and blind' (μωροὶ καὶ τυφλοί) in the sense of 'ungodly' in Matt. 23.17,[21] motivate Paul's paradoxical application of the term μωρία to his preaching. Jesus' use of μωρός falls within the parameters of the concept in the Old Testament,[22] even if his condemnation of the use of μωρέ as reprehensible and culpable puts an end to that development, by departing from tradition on a critical tangent.[23] We may conclude that Paul's discussion of the 'foolishness' of his preaching is not informed by the use of the term μωρός in the tradition of Jesus' sayings.[24]

Finally, we must guard against the systematic tendency to interpret Paul's statements about the folly of the message of the cross in 1 Cor.

17. Not even in texts such as Sir. 16.22–23, where folly implies a practical denial of God as judge, nor in Sir. 22.12, where the 'fool' is coordinate with the 'ungodly man'.

18. On the difficulty of this saying, see L. Köhler, 'Salz, das dumm wird', *ZDPV* 59 (1936) 133–34; Bertram, 'μωρός', 837–39; O Cullmann, 'Das Gleichnis vom Salz' in idem, *Vorträge und Aufsätze*, ed. K. Fröhlich (Tübingen: Mohr-Siebeck, 1966) 192–201; H. D. Betz, *Sermon on the Mount*, Hermeneia (Minneapolis: Fortress, 1995) 158–60. For the meaning 'become insipid', see Dioscurides Medicus, *De Mat. Med.* 4.19, who speaks of insipid roots (ῥίζαι γευσαμένῳ μωραί).

19. The interpretation of μωρέ in this passage is attended by philological difficulties; see A. Fridrichsen, 'Exegetisches zum Neuen Testament', *SO* 13 (1934) 38–40; Bertram, 'μωρός', 839–42; Betz, *Sermon on the Mount*, 220–22.

20. Bertram, 'μωρός', 842–44; Betz, *Sermon on the Mount*, 557–67.

21. Caspari, 'Über den biblischen Begriff der Torheit', 687.

22. Ibid., 687–88.

23. Ibid., 690.

24. Gibb ('*Torheit*', 11–12) suggests that when Paul composed 1 Cor. 1.18–31 he had in mind the saying of Jesus in Matt. 11.25 and Lk. 10.21 contrasting the 'wise' (σοφοί) and 'understanding' (συνετοί), from whom things are hidden, with the 'babes' (νήπιοι) to whom they are revealed; similarly, T. Zahn, *Das Evangelium des Matthäus* (Leipzig: Hinrichs, 1903) 439 n. 46; E. Klostermann, *Das Matthäusevangelium*, HNT 4 (Tübingen: Mohr-Siebeck, 1971) 102. The suggestion is difficult to evaluate, owing to the difference in vocabulary. But in Jesus' contrast of the σοφοί and the νήπιοι there is missing that ironic and self-conscious moment that is characteristic of Paul's concept of Christians as μωροὶ διὰ Χριστόν (1 Cor. 4.10). Jesus' νήπιοι are such by nature and God's good pleasure as Paul's readers must become by choice, after having disabused themselves of the opinion that they are 'wise' (1 Cor. 3.18).

1.18–31 as a concise, provisional formulation of the doctrine of the blinding and hardening of the world through sin, which is more fully expounded in Rom 1.18–32.[25] The theodicy recounted in the latter passage is regularly taken as the presupposition for the judgment of 'foolishness' that the world passes upon the gospel in the former: it is the result of a divinely willed darkening of human understanding (Rom. 1.21).[26] But there is no mention of the blinding of the world by God in 1 Cor. 1.18–31. When Paul asks rhetorically, 'Has not God made foolish the wisdom of the world?' in 1 Cor. 1.20, he uses the verb μωραίνειν in a declarative sense, as he elsewhere frequently uses the verbs ἁγιάζειν, δικαιοῦν, and καθαίρειν;[27] that is, God has demonstrated that what the world regards as wisdom is actually foolishness.[28] But the idea of a divinely willed incapacitation of human understanding on account of sin is remote from Paul's thought in 1 Corinthians, and even seems to be excluded by the logic of his argument.[29] Indeed, there is a little noticed contradiction between Paul's statements about human knowledge of God in 1 Cor. 1.21 and Rom. 1.18–32. In the former passage, Paul explains that the world (that is, humankind) failed to attain knowledge of God through wisdom (οὐκ ἔγνω ὁ κόσμος διὰ τῆς σοφίας τὸν θεόν), whereas in the latter text, Paul insists that human beings possessed knowledge of God (γνόντες τὸν θεόν) from what was revealed in creation, but suppressed the truth by their wickedness.[30] The contradiction may be formal and may find its resolution at a deeper, conceptual level.[31] But in any case, it is

---

25. Heinrici, *Der erste Brief an die Korinther*, 71, commenting on ἐμώρανεν ὁ θεός in 1.20: 'Es ist in diesem Ausspruch in knappster Form und in sorgfältig abgewogenem Ausdrucke eine Gesammtanschauung zusamengedängt von der religiösen Weltentwickelung, welche Rom. 1.18–3.20; 9–11 ihre volle Darlegung findet.' Similarly, Lietzmann, *An die Korinther*, 9; Conzelmann, *1 Corinthians*, 40, 44, commenting on 1.21 ff: 'For what follows we have constantly to keep in view the analgous exposition in Rom. 1.18 ff., which can provide a commentary on the briefer hints of 1 Corinthians.'

26. Bertram, 'μωρός', 846; more recently, P. Lampe, 'Theological Wisdom and the "Word About the Cross": The Rhetorical Scheme in 1 Corinthians 1–4', *Interpretation* 44 (1990) 123.

27. Rightly, Weiss, *Der erste Korintherbrief*, 27.

28. Heinrici, *Der erste Brief an die Korinther*, 70, commenting on ἐμώρανεν in 1.20: '*thöricht gemacht*, d.i. nicht: er hat sie zur Erkenntnissunfähigkeit gemacht, was auf den Begriff der Verstockung hinausliefe, sondern: er hat sie thatsächlich als Thorheit ausgewiesen, als "*insaniens sapientia*." '

29. Weiss, *Der erste Korintherbrief*, 27.

30. Weiss, *Der erste Korintherbrief*, 29. See now K. Gaca, 'Paul's Uncommon Declaration in Rom. 1.18–32 and Its Problematic Legacy for Pagan and Christian Relations', *HTR* 92.2 (1999) 165–98, who demonstrates that Paul's argument in Rom 1.18–32 is a radical departure from the conventional Hellenistic Jewish and early Christian polemic against polytheism.

31. Weiss, *Der erste Korintherbrief*, 29, finds no essential, theological difference between Paul's thought in 1 Cor. 1.18 ff. and Rom. 1.18 ff., asserting that οὐκ ἔγνω in 1 Cor. 1.21 corresponds to οὐκ ὡς θεὸν ἐδόξασαν in Rom. 1.21.

methodologically illegitimate to presuppose the results of Paul's mature reflection in the interpretation of statements in one of his earlier epistles.[32] The meaning of Paul's description of the gospel as 'foolishness' must be sought in the immediate context of 1 Cor. 1–4, or, at most, within the scope of the Corinthian correspondence.[33]

There is no need for a wider search for the source of the concept that Paul applies to his preaching in 1 Cor. 1–4, for the apostle states very clearly in which provenance the judgment of 'foolishness' is formulated: those for whom the message about the cross is 'foolishness' are initially described (1.18) in apocalyptic terms[34] as 'the ones who are perishing' (οἱ ἀπολλύμενοι),[35] without an attempt to identify this group in a narrower social sense.[36] But as Paul proceeds to explain[37] his assertion (1.23), he characterizes those for whom his proclamation is 'foolishness' (μωρία) as

---

32. On methodology in the interpretation of the Pauline epistles, see W. Wrede, 'Über Aufgabe und Methode der sogenannten neutestamentlichen Theologie' (1897) in *Das Problem der Theologie des Neuen Testaments*, ed. G. Strecker (Darmstadt: Wissenschaftliche Buchgesellschaft, 1975); idem, *Paulus* (Tübingen: Mohr-Siebeck, 1907).

33. Collins, *First Corinthians*, 100, 188–89, rightly refers to the 'fool's speech' in 2 Cor. 11.1–12.10 in seeking to interpret Paul's statements in 1 Cor. 1–4.

34. On the eschatological perspective that comes to expression in the division of humankind into 'the lost' (ἀπολλύμενοι) and 'the saved' (σῳζόμενοι), cf. 1 Thess. 1.10; 2 Cor. 2.15; Rom. 5.9–10, and the discussion in Weiss, *Der erste Korintherbrief*, 25–26. See esp. Wilckens, *Weisheit und Torheit*, 22, on the concepts ἀπολλύμενοι and σῳζόμενοι: 'Es handelt sich um geprägte Termini der frühchristlichen Predigt mit streng eschatologischem Sinn: Gemeint sind die durch das jüngste Gericht geschiedenen Gruppen, deren Urteilsspruch für sie entweder Zorn, Fluch, Verwerfung, ewiges Feuer, Tod, Verderben usw. – oder Segen, Rettung, Erlangung der Erbes, Reichtum usw. bedeutet.' On ἀπόλλυσθαι in this eschatological sense, see A. Oepke, 'ἀπόλλυμι', *TDNT* 1 (1964) 394–97. The division into 'lost' and 'saved' at the last judgment is a central aspect of Jewish eschatology; see P. Volz, *Die Eschatologie der jüdischen Gemeinde im neutestamentlichen Zeitalter* (Tübingen: Mohr-Siebeck, 1934) 272–419, esp. 321 on ἀπώλεια.

35. On the implications of the present tense of the participle, see Heinrici, *Der erste Brief an die Korinther*, 67; Weiss, *Der erste Korintherbrief*, 25–26; Wilckens, *Weisheit und Torheit*, 23. On the ambiguity of the dative case of the participle, see Wilckens, *Weisheit und Torheit*, 21–22, who argues that it implies both a subjective view and an objective relationship; see further Conzelmann, *1 Corinthians*, 42 n. 18; Collins, *First Corinthians*, 101: 'The phrase is to be read subjectively and construed to mean that the word of the cross is considered as folly by some who perish as a result', appealing to Blass-Debrunner-Funk, *A Greek Grammar of the New Testament* § 190 (1).

36. H. Weder, *Das Kreuz Jesu bei Paulus*, FRLANT 125 (Göttingen: Vandenhoeck & Ruprecht, 1981) 142–43; Lindemann, *Der erste Korintherbrief*, 44.

37. On the explanative force of ἐπειδή in 1.22 and the structure of the sentence embraced by 1.22–24, see Heinrici, *Der erste Brief an die Korinther*, 73–74; Wilckens, *Weisheit und Torheit*, 29; Lindemann, *Der erste Korintherbrief*, 46.

'Gentiles' (ἔθνη),[38] in contrast to 'Jews' (Ἰουδαῖοι) for whom the message of 'Christ crucified' is an 'offense' (σκάνδαλον).[39] Thus it would appear that the locus of the judgment 'foolishness' is that portion of the human race which is distinguished from the Jews by religion and nationality.[40] But a more precise definition of this group emerges from Paul's account of the attitude and motivation underlying the judgment of 'foolishness': 'Greeks desire wisdom' (Ἕλληνες σοφίαν ζητοῦσιν), Paul explains (1.22).[41] The term Ἕλληνες in Paul,[42] as in ancient literature generally,[43] designates those who are distinguished from the βάρβαροι by the possession of Greek language and culture.[44] Their distinctive characteristic, as Paul states clearly, is the pursuit of 'wisdom' (σοφία).[45] Those who embraced Hellenism,[46] whether of Greek nationality or not, participated in a learned culture through philosophy, rhetoric, and art as represented in the gymnasium, the assembly, and the theater.[47] Thus the concept of 'foolishness' that Paul applies to his preaching is not derived from the Gentile

38. On the meaning of ἔθνη in 1 Cor. 1.23, see K. L. Schmidt, 'ἔθνος in the NT', *TDNT* 2 (1964) 369–72; Bauer, *Greek-English Lexicon*, 276–77; Lindemann, *Der erste Korintherbrief*, 47.

39. On σκάνδαλον in 1 Cor. 1.23, see Stählin, *Skandalon*, 201–210.

40. Schmidt, 'ἔθνος in the NT', 370.

41. On the meaning of ζητεῖν here, see Conzelmann, *1 Corinthians*, 46 n. 75.

42. See the excellent article of H. Windisch, '"Ἕλλην', *TDNT* 2 (1964) 504–16, esp. 512–16 on Paul's use of the term. In Rom. 1.14 Paul differentiates Gentiles into two subgroups, Greeks and barbarians.

43. U. Wilcken, 'Hellenen und Barbaren', *Neue Jahrbücher des Klassischen Altertums* 17 (1906) 457–71; J. Jüthner, *Hellenen und Barbaren* (Leipzig: Dieterich, 1923) *passim*; Windisch, '"Ἕλλην', 504–508.

44. W. Jaeger, *Paideia: The Ideals of Greek Culture*, Vol. 1 (New York: Oxford University Press, 1939); Jüthner, *Hellenen und Barbaren*, 4–7, 34; Windisch, '"Ἕλλην', 504–505. On the use of the term Ἕλληνος to designate those who share in Greek language and culture, see esp. Isocrates 4.50: καὶ τὸ "Ελλήνων ὄνομα πεποίηκε μηκέτι τοῦ γένους ἀλλὰ τῆς διανοίας δοκεῖν εἶναι, καὶ μᾶλλον Ἕλληνας καλεῖσθαι τοὺς τῆς παιδεύσεως τῆς ἡμετέρας ἢ τοὺς τῆς κοινῆς φύσεως μετέχοντας ('the name "Hellenes" suggests no longer a race but an intelligence, and the title "Hellenes" is applied rather to those who share our culture than to those who share a common blood').

45. The desire for 'wisdom' (σοφία) among the Greeks was proverbial. See Herodotus 4.77.1: ' Ἕλληνας πάντας ἀσχόλους εἶναι ἐς πᾶσαν πλὴν Λακεδαιμόνιων ('All Greeks were zealous for every kind of learning, save only the Lacedaimonians'). See also Aelian *VH* 12.25, and Aelius Aristides *Or.* 1.330, where the Athenians are said to be ἡγεμόνες... σοφίας ἀπάσης. Cf. Heinrici, *Der erste Brief an die Korinther*, 11, 75; Lindemann, *Der erste Korintherbrief*, 46.

46. For barbarians who embraced Hellenism, see Strabo 14.2.28: οἱ βάρβαροι οἱ εἰσαγόμενοι εἰς τὸν ἑλληνισμόν. Josephus *c. Ap.* 1.180, speaks of a Hellenized Jew, Ἑλληνικὸς ἦν οὐ τῇ διαλέκτῳ μόνον, ἀλλὰ καὶ τῇ ψυχῇ. See also Plutarch *Alex. Fort. Virt.* 1.6. Cf. R. Laqueur, *Hellenismus, Schriften der hessischen Hochschulen* (Giessen: Universität Giessen, 1925) *passim*.

47. W. Jaeger, *Paideia, passim*; Windisch, '"Ἕλλην', 504–505.

inhabitants of the Roman Empire in general, but, more specifically, from those whose identity as Hellenes centered on the possession of wisdom.[48]

It is in the Greek world that we must seek the meaning of 'foolishness' as it applies to Paul's discourse. This insight puts us on a different path from the majority of interpreters, who tend to deny that the term 'foolishness' retains a pre-Christian meaning in Paul.[49] But it does not yet serve to focus our investigation, for the term 'foolishness' (μωρία) takes on various meanings as it occurs in different contexts in Greek literature.[50] In Greek tragedy, μωρία is a kind of 'madness', a rash and impulsive action that seems to be impelled by a power that confuses human understanding and hides the right path.[51] In a political context, μωρία denotes a naïveté that is unable to calculate the consequences of actions,[52] and that is consequently

48. See the conclusion of Windisch, '"Ελλην', 515: 'in 1 Cor. 1.22, 25 the "Ελληνες are concrete Greeks with their culture centered on wisdom, not Gentiles'.

49. E.g., Gibb, '*Torheit*', 8; Bertram, 'μωρός', 845; Conzelmann, *1 Corinthians*, 43: 'The judgment of "foolishness" is strictly related to revelation'; P. Fiedler, 'μωρία', *Exegetical Dictionary of the New Testament*, Vol. 2. (Grand Rapids: Eerdmans, 1981) 449: 'The secular meaning which was adopted by wisdom literature, can no longer be discerned in Paul'; Lampe, 'Theological Wisdom and the "Word About the Cross"', 120–21.

50. Bertram, 'μωρός', 832.

51. Gibb, '*Torheit*', 6; Bertram, 'μωρός', 833. Thus the chorus that watches Antigone violate the law and risk punishment exclaims, 'There is no one foolish (μωρός) enough to desire death' (Sophocles *Ant*. 220). And Antigone, who seems ironically aware of folly as fate, challenges Creon: 'If you think my actions foolish, that amounts to a charge of folly by a fool!' (σοὶ δ' εἰ δοκῶ νῦν μῶρα δρῶσα τυγχάνειν, σχέδον τι μώρῳ μωρίαν ὀφλισκάνω, Sophocles *Ant*. 469–70). See also Sophocles *El*. 1326: 'You utter fools, you senseless people' (ὦ πλεῖστα μῶροι καὶ φρενῶν τητώμενοι), do you take no heed any longer for your lives, or have no inborn sense, that you fail to see that you are not merely close to but are in the midst of the greatest dangers.' Cf. also Euripides *Medea* 614. The sense of 'folly' as 'madness' is also found in Demosthenes'' third Philippic (*Or*. 9.54): 'But you have reached such a height of folly or of madness (ἀλλ' εἰς τοῦτ ἀφῖχθε μωρίας ἢ παρανοίας) or – I know not what to call it, for this fear too has often haunted me, that some demon is driving you to your doom'; and Epictetus *Diss*. 1.6.36: μωρία τοῦτο καὶ μανία. Elsewhere in tragic drama, μωρία retains the more basic sense of a weakness or defect in understanding. Thus Oedipus confronts Creon: 'Come, tell me, I beg you, was it because you saw in me some cowardice or folly (δειλία ἢ μωρία) that you decided to act thus?' (Sophocles *Oed. Tyr*. 535–36.) See also Sophocles *Ajax* 594: 'I think you are a fool (μωρά μοι δοκεῖς φρονεῖν), if you mean now to try to educate my character'; Sophocles *El*. 889–90: 'Listen, I beg you, so that you can learn it from me, and then pronounce me sensible or foolish (τὸ λοιπὸν ἢ φρονοῦσαν ἢ μώραν λέγης).'

52. Thucydides 5.41.3. For this political sense in tragedy, see e.g., Sophocles *Oed. Tyr*. 540–42, where Oedipus suggests that Creon operates out of a naïve political understanding: 'Is not your attempt foolish (ἆρ' οὐχὶ μῶρόν ἐστι τοὐγχείρημά σου), without wealth and without friends to try to steal a kingdom, a thing that is captured with massed supporters and with money?'

expressed as imprudent counsel.[53] In the teaching of the philosophers and moralists, μωρία is a lack of reason[54] or self-understanding, the absurdity of an unexamined life.[55] For the rhetorician, it is 'sheer folly' not to adapt one's style of speaking to the audience and the circumstances of the case.[56] The wise counselor warns against the 'silly talk', μωρολογία, of the 'chatterer'.[57]

Some of these uses may have relevance to Paul's concept of 'foolishness'.[58] But before we begin to analyze these uses and assess their significance, it is essential to recognize that there is one meaning which is so common in the Greco-Roman world that it would have been uppermost in the minds of Paul's readers and, apart from clear indications to the contrary, must be assumed to be the meaning that Paul intended. For most Greek readers in the time of Paul, and especially for those who viewed the world from the perspective gained through their participation in learned culture, the term μωρία designated the attitude and behavior of a particular social type: the lower class buffoon.[59] The 'foolishness' of this social type

53. E.g., Sophocles *Oed. Tyr.* 433: 'No, I did not know that your words would be foolish (οὐ γάρ τί σ' ἤδη μῶρα φωνήσοντ'), else I would hardly have summoned you to my house.' See also Aristophanes *Eccl.* 474: 'There is a legend of the older time, that all our foolish plans and vain conceits (ὅσ' ἂν ἀνόητ' ἢ μῶρα βουλευσώμεθα) are overruled to work the public good.'

54. Plato *Leg.* 818d: 'To suppose then, that all these studies [arithmetic, geometry, astronomy] are not "necessary" for a man who means to understand almost any single one of the fairest sciences is a most foolish assumption (πολλὴ καὶ μωρία τοῦ διανοήματος)'; Ps.-Plato *Epin.* 983e: 'Hence to say that all we behold in the heavens is due to some other source and not produced in the fashion we describe by soul and body, is pure folly and unreason (μωρία καὶ ἀλογία).' See also Epictetus *Diss.* 2.1.33; 2.2.16.

55. Diogenes *Ep.* 36.4; Epictetus *Diss.* 3.24.86. Grant, 'The Wisdom of the Corinthians', 52, adduces Sextus Empiricus *Adv. Math.* 7.432 for the skeptics' view that 'all men are fools'; but the term used here is φαῦλοι, not μωροί.

56. Quintilian *Inst. Orat.* 12.10.69 (*stultissimus*), cited by Litfin, *St. Paul's Theology of Proclamation*, 197 n. 55.

57. Plutarch *De Garr.* 4 (*Mor.* 504B), cited and discussed in connection with 1 Cor. 1–4 by Pogoloff, *Logos and Sophia*, 153–54.

58. Particularly those in Epictetus. Heinrici, *Der erste Brief an die Korinther*, 67 suggests that Epictetus uses μωρία in a sense similar to Paul in *Diss.* 1.6.36; 1.22.18; 1.23.8; 2.1.33; 2.20.25., see also 4.8.38–39.

59. This sense predominates in popular literature (e.g., Homeric Apocrypha, *Margites* fr. 4; *Vit. Aesop.* 18–19; *POxy* 413), and is not infrequent in poetic and philosophical texts: the μωρός is one who suffers from a weakness or deficiency of intellect; the context often makes clear that the person is of lower class origin. E.g., Sophocles *Oed. Tyr.* 388–433: Oedipus describes Tiresias as a 'crafty beggar' (388); Tiresias denies being Oedipus' slave or Creon's partisan (410–411); there follows this exchange: Oedipus – 'No, I did not know that your words would be foolish (μῶρα); else I would hardly have summoned you to my house'; Tiresias replies – 'That is what I am; foolish (μῶροι), as you think, but the parents who gave you birth found me wise.' Sophocles *El.* 870–90: Chrysothemis enters in haste, in a manner that recalls

consisted in a weakness or deficiency of intellect,[60] often coupled with a physical grotesqueness.[61] Because the concept of the laughable in the Greco-Roman world was grounded in contemplation of the ugly and defective,[62] those who possessed these characteristics were deemed to be 'foolish'. As a source of amusement, these lower class types were widely represented on the stage in the vulgar and realistic comedy known as the 'mime' (μῖμος).[63] Through its use in this context, μωρός became 'the common generic name for a mimic fool'.[64]

the figure of the 'running slave': his face is red, his body warm (887–88); he prefaces his news – 'Listen, I beg you, so that you can learn it from me, and then pronounce me sensible or foolish (μῶρα)!' See also Epictetus *Diss.* 1.23.8; 3.24.86.

60.   Bertram, 'μωρός', 832.

61.   G.M.A. Richter, 'Grotesques and the Mime', *AJA* 17 (1913) 148–56; P. Veyne, *A History of Private Life I*, 134–36.

62.   Aristotle *Ars. Poet.* 1449a30: 'the laughable is a species of the base or ugly'; Cicero *De Orat.* 2.236; Quintilian *Inst. Orat.* 6.3.8: 'Laughter has its basis in some kind or other of deformity or ugliness'; cf. Grant, *Ancient Rhetorical Theories*, 19; R. Garland, *The Eye of the Beholder: Deformity and Disability in the Graeco-Roman World* (Ithaca: Cornell University Press, 1995) 73–86.

63.   The mime was a reproduction in character and language of a typical scene of everyday life in the form of a short monologue or dialogue. On mime in general, see C. J. Grysar, *Der römische Mimus, Sitzungsberichte der königliche Akademie der Wissenschaften zu Wien*, Phil-hist. Klasse 12 (1854) 237–337. H. Reich, *Der Mimus*; E. Wüst, 'Mimos'; H. Wiemken, *Der griechische Mimus: Dokumente zur Geschichte das antiken Volkstheaters* (Bremen: Schüne-mann, 1972).

64.   Nicoll, *Masks, Mimes and Miracles*, 28. For evidence of the generic use of the term, see the lexicographers, e.g. Nonius Marcellus, who defines the term *sannio* (another name for the fool) by reference to the Greek μωρός: 'The *sanniones* derive their title from their grimaces. They are foolish in speech, in manners, and in action. The Greeks call them *moroi*' (*sanniones dicuntur a sannis qui sunt in dictis fatui et in moribus et in schemis quos moroi vocant Graeci*); ed. W. M. Lindsay, *Nonii Marcelli De Compendiosa Libros* (Leipzig: Tuebner, 1903). The Alexandrian lexicographer Hesychius defines the word σάνναρος as the name of a μωρός in the play *Tarantinos* by Rhinthon: σάνναρος· μωρός παρὰ Ῥίνθωνι Ταραντίνῳ, ed. M. Schmidt (Jena,1858–68); cf. Dieterich, *Pulcinella*, 236. Similarly, Eustathius glosses the word σάννας in a comedy of Cratinus, explaining that the term does not indicate the mildly foolish, but the regular μωρός, or fool: *Commentarii ad Homeri Iliadem et Odysseam*, ed. G. Stallbaum (Leipzig: Teubner, 1825–30) p. 1761, lines 21–22: ὁ παρὰ τῷ κωμικῷ κρατίνῳ σάννας· αὐτὸς μέντοι οὐ τὸν εὐήθη ἁπλῶς δηλοῖ, ἀλλὰ τὸν μωρός. The author of the account of the martyrdom of a certain Genesius (300 A.D.) explains that this actor was a μωρός, or fool, the theatrical type whom the Romans call *stupidus; Acta Sanctorum*, ed. T. Ruinart (Paris, 1689) 282–83, cited and discussed in Reich, *Der Mimus*, 84; Nicoll, *Masks, Mimes and Miracles*, 87.

Chapter 3

THE GENERIC MEANING

We meet one of these lower class types in the first tale of Apuleius' brilliant novel, *The Golden Ass*.[1] On his way to the baths in Hypata, the principal city of Thessaly, a merchant chances to see a companion of former days, a certain Socrates, sitting upon the ground, covered with a torn and coarse mantel, so thin and pale and miserable that he scarcely recognizes him. The merchant wonders what crime or misfortune has reduced his friend to such a state that he appears to be like a 'common beggar' who stands in the streets asking a hand-out of passersby. As he approaches his old friend, the poor wretch, blushing for shame, attempts to cover his face with his ragged mantle, and in the process exposes the parts of his body below the navel all naked. From beneath the mantle, Socrates cries out: 'Let fortune finish the job she has started!'[2]

One might have encountered such a fool on the streets of any city in the Roman Empire, including Corinth, the home of Lucius, the hero of *The Golden Ass*.[3] Yet, realistic descriptions of lower class life, such as Apuleius provides, are rare in Greek and Latin literature.[4] The lives of

---

1.   The *Metamorphoses* or *Golden Ass* is a Latin work of the second century A.D., but as Apuleius explicitly tells the reader (*Met.* 1.1), the story is derived from an older Greek original. On the sources of *The Golden Ass* and its relationship, in particular, to the Greek short story entitled *Lucius or the Ass* preserved in the works of Lucian, see H. van Thiel, *Der Eselsroman* 2 Vols. (München: Beck, 1971–72); H. J. Mason, 'Fabula Graecanica; Apuleius and his Greek Sources' in B. L. Hijmans and R. Th. Van der Paardt, *Aspects of Apuleius' Golden Ass* (Groningen: Bouma's, 1978) ch. 1.

2.   Apuleius *Met.* 1.6-7; see the discussion of this episode in Winkler, *Auctor and Actor*, 126.

3.   For Lucius as a Corinthian and Apuleius' knowledge of Corinth and Cenchreae, see P. Veyne, 'Apulée à Cenchrées,' *Revue Philologique* 39 (1965) 241; H. J. Mason, 'Lucius at Corinth,' *Phoenix* 25 (1971) 160.

4.   On the rarity of social realism in Classical literature, see Millar, 'The World of the Golden Ass', 63, 65, 75. Two further examples of this lower class type appear in the literature of the High Empire. Philo (*In Flacc.* 6.36-38) relates an incident involving a poor street-creature named Carabas, 'whose madness was not of the fierce and savage kind, ... but of the easy-going, gentler style.' This poor fool 'spent day and night in the streets naked, shunning neither heat nor cold, made game of by the children and lads who were idling about.' In a politically tense situation, he was driven by rioters into the gymnasium, and mocked, 'as in

Figure 1: Bronze statuette caricaturing a hunchbacked beggar.
Alexandrian work of the second to the first century B.C. Berlin Museum.

the poor were not generally deemed to be worthy of serious literary effort.[5] It was as a source of amusement that lower class types found representation in literature[6] and art (Fig. 1),[7] and especially in the

theatrical mimes' (ὡς ἐν θεατρικοῖς μίμοις). Seneca (*Epist. Mor.* 12.3) describes a decrepit creature upon whom he one day happened to cast his eyes as he was leaving his house. In a brutal reversal of fortune, this old dotard, once Seneca's favorite slave, has become the very image of the mimic fool, with whose little terracotta statues the youthful Seneca once gave delight as presents at the Saturnalia. He is poor and old and broken down; his teeth are dropping out; he is like one who is ready to be carried out for burial. Seneca pronounces him 'perfectly silly' (*perfecte delirat*).

5.   On 'aesthetic disdain' for the poor, see P. Veyne, *A History of Private Life I*, 61–62, 134–37.

6.   For literary portraits of the low class 'fool', see Thersites in Homer *Il.* 2.212-65; Margites in Homeric Apocrypha *Margites* fr. 4; Aesop in *Vit. Aesop.*

7.   Bronze statuette caricaturing a hunchbacked beggar; Alexandrian work of the first century B.C., pictured in G. Becatti, *The Art of Ancient Greece and Rome* (Englewood Cliffs, NJ: Prentice, 1975) 272, Fig. 258. For further examples of Hellenistic genre sculpture, see H. P. Laubscher, *Fischer und Landleute. Studien zur hellenistischen Genreplastik* (Mainz: von Zabern, 1982).

mime.[8] Even the description of the foolish Socrates in the *Golden Ass*, despite its sympathetic realism, is imbued with the upper class values of the author of the novel,[9] as evidenced by mimic elements in the portrayal:[10] the *centunculus* in which Socrates is dressed,[11] a rag garment stitched together from odd scraps, is the motley costume of the fool in the mime;[12] the scene in which he pulls the mantle over his head, exposing his private parts, was repeatedly enacted on the stage, a predictable cause of mirth.[13]

The mime was by definition 'an imitation of life',[14] and took as its subject matter the coarse reality of everyday existence among the urban lower classes.[15] As a representation of an extreme social type, the mimic fool provoked laughter at both ends of the class structure. To the rich, the intellectual weakness and physical deformity of the fool were welcome reminders of what it was like to be a fully human part of society – educated, unmaimed, independent.[16] Hence the numerous caricatures of grotesque persons in Greek and Roman art (Fig. 2).[17] On the other hand, the transgressive behavior of the fool, his mockery of the words and deeds of the serious actors, gave delight to members of the lower class, as

8. On the social types represented in mime, see Grysar, *Der römische Mimus*, 250; Reich, *Der Mimus*, 1.214; R. C. Beacham, *The Roman Theatre and Its Audience* (Cambridge, MA: Harvard University Press) 130–31.

9. Millar, 'The World of the *Golden Ass*', 64–65.

10. Rightly pointed out by Winkler, *Auctor and Actor*, 126.

11. Apuleius *Met.* 1.6: *Et cum dicto sutili centunculo faciem suam iamdudum punicantem prae pudore obtexit.*

12. Seneca *Epist. Mor.* 11.1.8; Apuleius *Apol.* 13; cf. A. Dieterich, *Pulcinella. Pompejanische Wandbilder und römische Satyrspiele* (Leipzig: Teubner, 1897) 143–45; Nicoll, *Masks, Mimes and Miracles*, 91.

13. See *POxy* 413 ('Adulteress') p. 41, lines 153–57; for iconographic evidence, see Nicoll, *Masks, Mimes and Miracles*, 30, 88–89. For exposure as a gesture of the comic type, see Theophrastus *Char.* 4.4-5.

14. See the definition of the grammarian Diomedes: μῖμός ἐστιν μίμησις βίου τά τε συγκεχωρημένα καὶ ἀσυγχώρητα περιέχων ('mime is an imitation of life encompassing both things accepted and things forbidden'), in *Grammatici Latini*, Vol. 1, ed. H. Keil (Hildesheim, 1961) 490–91.

15. Note Euanthius' observation on the mime: *mimos dictos esse a diurna imitatione vilium rerum et levium personarum*, in *Excerpta de comoedia*, ed. P. Wessner (Leipzig: Teubner, 1902) 1.21; cf. Wüst, 'Mimos,' 1728–30; J. Carpocino, *Daily Life in Ancient Rome* (New Haven: Yale University Press, 1977) 230.

16. Quintilian *Inst. Orat.* 6.3.8: 'Laughter is never far removed from derision … Laughter has its basis in some kind or other of deformity or ugliness … Laughter, … an emotion frequently awakened by buffoons, actors, or fools': cf. Veyne, *A History of Private Life*, 136.

17. On this bronze statuette from the Metropolitan Museum of Art, see Richter, 'Grotesques and the Mime', 148–56. See also Garland, *The Eye of the Beholder*, 108–110.

Figure 2. **Bronze statuette of a mimic fool. Probably Greek.**
Metropolitan Museum of Art, New York.

instances of resistance to privilege and authority, otherwise dangerous to express.[18]

The fool (μωρός, *stupidus*)[19] was the secondary actor in the mime (μῖμος δεύτερος, *actor secundarum partium*);[20] that is, he aped the performance of

18. See the discussion in Z. Yavetz, *Plebs and Princeps* (Oxford: Oxford University Press, 1988) 18–20; Winkler, *Auctor and Actor*, 289–91.

19. On the identity of the μωρός and the *stupidus*, see Grysar, *Der römische Mimus*, 266–67. The *stupidus* is mentioned in literature, e.g., Juvenal 8.196-97, and on inscriptions, e.g., *CIL* VI. 1063, 1064; see the discussion in Wiemken, *Der griechische Mimus*, 179–81. Cf. W. Kroll, 'Stupidus', *RE* 4 (1931) 422–23.

20. The 'second part' is frequently mentioned, e.g., *I.L.S.* 5198; Horace *Sat.* 1.9.46; *Epist.* 1.18.14; Suetonius *Calig.* 57.4; most clearly, Festus, in *Glossaria Latina* ed. W. M. Lindsay,

Figure 3.   Terracotta head of a mimic fool. Glyptothek, Munich.

the archmime,[21] comically misinterpreting and reacting to him.[22] Like other mimes, the fool appeared barefoot,[23] and maskless,[24] his grimaces and gesticulations an essential part of the performance.[25] The fool typically had a shaven head (Fig. 3),[26] and might be endowed with a prominent

(Paris, Societe Belles Lettres 1930) Vol. 4, p. 438.23: *s.v. sulva res est: quod C. Volumnius secundarum partium fuerit, qui fere omnibus mimis parasitus inducatur.* See also the account of the martyrdom of Gelasinus, ὅστις ἦν μῖμος δεύτερος, cited in Reich, *Der Mimus*, 82 n.3, 93. Cf. Dieterich, *Pulcinella*, 145–48; Wüst, 'Mimos', 1747–48.

21.   See esp. Horace's description of a parasite in *Epist.* 1.18.10-14: 'The man, over-prone to servility, a jester of the basest sort, so trembles at the rich man's nod, so echoes his speech and picks up his words as they drop, that you might suppose... a mime player was acting the second part *(partis mimum tractare secundas)*.' See the discussion of the role of the secondary actor in the mime in Nicoll, *Masks, Mimes and Miracles*, 87; Wiemken, *Der griechische Mimus*, 67–68; Beacham, *The Roman Theatre*, 132.

22.   See the discussion of the antics of the fool in the Oxyrhynchus mime, *POxy* 413, in Nicoll, *Masks, Mimes and Miracles*, 115–18; Wiemken, *Der griechische Mimus*, 60–80; and below.

23.   Seneca *Epist.* 8.8; Quintilian *Inst. Orat.* 5.11.24; Juvenal 8.191; Aulus Gellius *Noct. Att.* 1.11.12; Macrobius *Sat.* 2.1.9. Diomedes *Ars grammatica* 3 (ed. Keil, I. 490) explains that the common Latin term for the mimes, *planipes*, means 'with bare feet'. Cf. Wüst, 'Mimos', 1747; Nicoll, *Masks, Mimes and Miracles*, 83–84; Beare, *The Roman Stage*, 153.

24.   Quintilian *Inst. Orat.* 6.3.29; Athenaios *Deip.* 10.452; see the discussion in Reich, *Der Mimus*, 527–29, 598; Wüst, 'Mimos', 1747; Beare, *The Roman Stage*, 150.

25.   See the epitaph of one Vitalis, a virtuoso solo performer of the imperial period, who boasts of his skill in moulding his features and describes the effect upon the audience, in *Minor Latin Poets*, ed. J. W. Duff, LCL (Cambridge, MA: Harvard University Press, 1934) 637–39. Quintilian (*Inst. Orat.* 6.3.29) warns the orator against using 'those distorted grimaces and gestures which we are accustomed to laugh at in the mimes.' See also Cicero *De Orat* 2.61.251; Diodorus Siculus 37.12.2; Nonius Marcellus 61.2.

26.   Juvenal 5.170-72; Arnobius *Adv. nat.* 7.33, *stupidi capitibus rasis*; Pliny *Nat. Hist.* 7.54; see the other texts cited and discussed by Dieterich, *Pulcinella*, 149–51; Reich, *Der Mimus*, 23, 66, 470, 578, 831; for iconographic evidence, see, e.g., Fig. 3, and the other examples in Nicoll, *Masks, Mimes and Miracles*, 47–49. See also H. Yilmaz and S. Sahin, 'Ein Kahlkopf aus Patara', *EA* 21 (1993) 78–91.

Figure 4.   Mime actors. Terracotta lamp of the third century B.C. National Museum, Athens.

phallus.[27] Although he might wear a variety of costumes, those most often associated with the fool were the χιτών, a short frock, and the *centunculus*, a colorful patchwork tunic.[28] The fool sometimes carried a stick with which his misbehavior was punished;[29] we read much of the blows that rained down upon the fool's humped back or bald head.[30]

Vivid portraits of mimic fools survive in terracotta statuettes of the Hellenistic age and the early Empire.[31] A terracotta lamp found in

27.   See the scholiast to Juvenal 6.66: *penem, ut habent in mimo*; Arnobius *Adv. nat.* 7.33, on what pagans enjoy most in the mimes: 'they love the morons with their shaved heads, the resonant sound of the heads being boxed, the applause, the shameful jokes and gestures, the huge red phalluses.' Cf. Reich, *Der Mimus*, 258; Wüst, 'Mimos', 1747–48; Beare, *The Roman Stage*, 153.

28.   Apuleius *Apol.* 13; Seneca *Epist. mor.* 11.1.8; Varro *Ling.* 5.132; Nonius Marcellus 14, p. 869 (Lindsay); Arnobius *Adv. nat.* 6.25; Festus 342, 20 (Lindsay); cf. A. Dieterich, *Pulcinella. Pompejanische Wandbilder und römische Satyrspiele* (Leipzig: Teubner, 1897) 143–45; Reich, *Der Mimus*, 448–49, 578–79; Wüst, 'Mimos', 1747; Nicoll, *Masks, Mimes and Miracles*, 90–91; Beare, *The Roman Stage*, 153.

29.   Wüst, 'Mimos', 1748.

30.   Martial 2.72.3; 5.61.11; Tertullian *De Spectac.* 23; Procopius *Hist. arc.* 9.14; Gregory Nazianzus in Migne, *PG* 37.1517; John Chrysostom in Migne, *PG* 59.28; Synesius Φαλακρᾶς ἐγκώμιον 77; cf. Wüst, 'Mimos,' 1748; Nicoll, *Masks, Mimes and Miracles*, 88.

31.   F. Winter, *Die Typen der figürlichen Terrakotten* II (Berlin: Spemann, 1903) 411, 432–34, 437; M. Bieber, *Die Denkmäler zum Theaterwesen im Altertum* (Berlin: Vereinigung Wissenschaftlicher Verleger, 1920) 175–78, Tab. 108; Nicoll, *Masks, Mimes and Miracles*, 45, 47–49.

Figure 5. Pair of mimic fools. Terracotta statuette. Pelizaeus Museum, Hildesheim.

Athens[32] depicts three maskless performers standing in a group (Fig. 4).[33] That they are mime actors is proven by the inscription on the side: μιμολόγοι ὑπόθεσις Ἕκυρα, that is, 'mime actors: the theme (or subject of the play), The Mother-in-Law'.[34] Of the three mimes represented, the one in the middle, facing front, is clearly the fool. He wears a short *chiton* and lays his right hand over his protruding belly. He has a bald head, large ears, a broad nose, small eyes, and a wry mouth. He stands, rather dejectedly, between the other characters, as though he had just received a heavy lecture from them. To the left is a young man with long hair, clad in a *himation* draped in the usual fashion. The scroll in his hand identifies him as an ambitious young scholar, perhaps of rhetoric or philosophy. To the right stands a second *himation*-clad figure, beardless but older than his companion, with a bald head and thick lips. He holds his hands before his

32. This terracotta lamp is dated to the end of the third century B.C. by C. Watzinger 'Mimologen', *Mittheilungen des deutschen archäologischen Instituts, Athenische Abteilung* 26 [1909] 1–8, but it may be more recent; see Reich, *Der Mimus*, 553–55.

33. For detailed description of the figures and the scene represented, see Bieber, *Die Denkmäler zum Theaterwesen*, 176–77; Nicoll, *Masks, Mimes and Miracles*, 46–47; Wiemken, *Der griechische Mimus*, 39–40.

34. The title, Ἕκυρα, is familiar through its use by Apollodorus of Carystus (ca. 258 B.C.) and Terence; cf. M. Bieber, *The History of the Greek and Roman Theater* (Princeton: Princeton University Press, 1961) 107; A. Lesky, *Geschichte der griechischen Literatur*, 2nd ed. (Bern-München, 1963) 800.

body and throws his head back. Both men are on the verge of withdrawing from the central character but turn back to look at him, creating the impression of lively interaction. Another statuette (Fig. 5), probably from Alexandria,[35] shows two mimic fools with shaved heads, broad noses, and full lips, dressed in short *chitons*, engaged in animated dialogue. One fool places his arm around the shoulders of the other, who leans toward him, listening, endeavoring to imitate with his right hand the gesture of his companion.[36]

One gains some impression of the antics of the fool from an Oxyrhynchus papyrus of the first century A.D.[37] The piece is a farce, with a plot based, however remotely, on Euripides' *Iphigenia in Tauris*.[38] The characters are marked by symbols,[39] but references in the text enable us to identify them. The chief part is that of A, named in the dialogue as Charition, a young Greek woman who has fallen into the hands of some barbarians. The king of the land intends to sacrifice her to Selene, in whose temple she has taken refuge. The second actor, marked B in the manuscript, is a fool.[40] That he is to be so identified is indicated not only by his behavior,[41] but also from the way in which he is addressed: 'O fool!' (μωρέ),[42] and 'poor fool' (ταλαίπωρε).[43] It is upon the low humor of this buffoon that the amusement of the play chiefly depends. His methods of raising laughter are obvious: he plays off the heroine and others, making retort to their words and mocking their actions. He is, alternately,

---

35. Cf. Nicoll, *Masks, Mimes and Miracles*, 47–48; A. Swiderek, 'Le Mime Grec en Egypte', *Eos* 47 (1954) 63–74.

36. Bieber, *Die Denkmäler zum Theaterwesen*, 177 no. 188, Tab. 108, 5; Nicoll, *Masks, Mimes and Miracles*, 47–48, Fig. 31.

37. *POxy* 413 ('Charition'). Originally published in B. P. Grenfell and A.S. Hunt, *The Oxyrhynchus Papyri* (London: Egypt Exploration Fund, 1903) no. 413 (3.41); text and English translation in *Select Papyri* III, ed. D. L. Page, LCL (Cambridge, MA: Harvard University Press, 1988) 336–49. For analysis and commentary, see S. Sudhaus, 'Der Mimus von Oxyrhynchos', *Hermes* 41 (1906) 273–74; M. Winter, *De mimis Oxyrhynchiis* (Ph.D. diss. Leipzig Universität, 1906); E. Rostrup, 'Oxyrhynchus Papyrus 413' in *Oversigt over het Kgl. Danske Videnskabernes Selskabs Forhandlinger* (Copenhagen, 1915) 63–91; Wiemken, *Der griechische Mimus*, 48–80.

38. Winter, *De mimis Oxyrhynchiis*, 26; Page, *Select Papyri III*, 336–39.

39. On the decipherment of the symbols, see Winter, *De mimis Oxyrhynchiis*, 32–35.

40. Nicoll, *Masks, Mimes and Miracles*, 116; Wiemken, *Der griechische Mimus*, 67–68; Wüst, '*Mimos*', 1753.

41. See the detailed analysis of the behavior of the character marked B in Wiemken, *Der griechische Mimus*, 60–68.

42. *POxy* 413, line 52; the text is cited according to the complete version found in Wiemken, *Der griechische Mimus*, 52. At line 191, the fool retorts to his mistress Charition with the address μωρέ.

43. *POxy* 413, line 207.

Figure 6.   Scene from a mime. From the pulpitum of the theater at Sabratha.

boastful, cowardly, cunning, sacrilegious, and obscene.[44] Repeatedly associated with the fool is the word πορδή, evidently a stage direction that plays an integral part in the action; it implies a noise of a vulgar sort, for at one point it clearly signifies flatulence.[45] However obscene the humor of the fool may be, his importance to the mime is obvious. Without the fool as a foil, the play is mere melodrama, lacking in originality, with little dramatic effect.[46]

A fool appears in a second mime from Oxyrhynchus entitled Μοιχεύτρια, or 'Adulteress.'[47] What we learn about him from the text defines his role as that of the μωρός, or fool:[48] he appears only in the company of the

44.   Wiemken, *Der griechische Mimus*, 67–68: 'Die oft recht derben Knotenspässe, die er dem Bühnengeschehen beisteuert, charakterisieren seine Rolle hinreichend als die der lustigen Person. Wenn auch zumeist am Rande des Geschehens, ist er Verkörperung all dessen, was der Mimus an eigenen Mitteln dem Stück beisteuern konnte: der ursprünglich-mimischen Wandlungsfähigkeit, der feig-verschlagenen Stupidität, der hemmungslosen Zoten – und Possenreisserei.'

45.   For discussion of the meaning and function of this stage direction, see Winter, *De mimis Oxyrhynchiis*, 43, 45; Wiemken, *Der griechische Mimus*, 60.

46.   The fool is the only character who is continuously on the stage throughout the course of the action. It is the fool who effects the heroine's rescue by making her captors drunk. Cf. Wiemken, *Der griechische Mimus*, 68.

47.   *POxy* 413. Originally published in Grenfell and Hunt, *The Oxyrhynchus Papyri III*, 41. An additional small fragment of the papyrus was published in G. von Manteuffel, *De opusculis Graecis Aegypti e papyris ostracis lapidibusque collectis* (Warsaw: Société des sciences et des letters de Varsovie, 1930) 132. The mime was entitled Μοιχεύτρια by Crusius, *Herondae Mimiambi*, 110. See the discussion in Sudhaus, 'Der Mimus von Oxyrhynchos', 247–77; Rostrup, 'Oxyrhynchus Papyrus 413', 88–91; H. Lyngby, 'De dramatiska problememi Oxyrhynchus-mimen Μοιχεύτρια', *Eranos* 26 (1928) 23–55; Wiemken, *Der griechische Mimus*, 81–106. Greek text and English translation in Page, *Select Papyri III*, 350–61.

48.   Wiemken, *Der griechische Mimus*, 102.

archimima,[49] and is, thus, the 'secondary actor' in the mime; the name by which he is addressed, Μαλακός, means 'debauchee';[50] he instigates a burlesque scene with a phallus;[51] his stupidity is responsible for the unraveling of the plot;[52] in the final scene, he sings a parody of a dirge;[53] he is punished for his misbehavior with a sound thrashing.[54] A marble relief from the theater at Sabratha depicts a scene from the adultery mime in which the bald-headed fool is about to receive his punishment (Fig. 6).[55] A fool speaks at the beginning of a fragmentary papyrus of the second century A.D., now in the British Museum.[56] In response to the question of the *archimima*, 'Where is justice to be found?', the fool, designated B in the manuscript, answers with an impertinent joke, 'Among those who spit at each other!'[57] A papyrus fragment, now in Warsaw,[58] contains a piece of dialogue between a person marked B in the text and a partner. It seems certain that the character B plays the role of the fool in this mime, as well:[59] he is described as 'witless' or 'silly' (ἀνούτατος);[60] like the fool in the

49. Except for the final scene – following the distribution of parts by Crusius, *Herondae Mimiambi*, 102.

50. Mentioned by name at lines 145, 158, 170, 176; line numbers cited according to the complete text in Wiemken, *Der griechische Mimus*, 82–89. On the meaning of the word μαλακός, see Bauer, *Greek-English Lexicon of the New Testament*, 613, esp. Plautus *Miles gloriosus* 668, *cinaedus malacus* = catamite; see also *PHib* 54.10 and *PBerol* 13927.2.4, where the word has the meaning 'lascivious dancer.'

51. 'Adulteress', lines 153–57; for this interpretation of the scene, see Sudhaus, 'De Mimus von Oxyrhynchos', 255–58; Wiemken, *Der griechische Mimus*, 97.

52. 'Adulteress', lines 171–72; see the interpretation of Wiemken, *Der griechische Mimus*, 99, 102.

53. 'Adulteress', lines 184–85; see the discussion in Lyngby, 'Der dramatiska problememi', 58; Wiemken, *Der griechische Mimus*, 101.

54. 'Adulteress', line 186; cf. Wiemken, *Der griechische Mimus*, 101–102.

55. Picture and interpretation in Bieber, *The History of the Greek and Roman Theater*, 237–38, Fig. 786.

56. *PLond* 1984. Originally published by A. Körte, 'Bruchstück eines Mimus,' *Archiv für Papyrusforschung* 6 (1913) 1–5; text and English translation in Page, *Select Papyri* III, 362–67; see the discussion in S. Srebrny, 'De mimi Graeci fragmento Londinensi', *Eos* 30 (1927) 401–12; G. von Manteuffel, 'Zwei Bemerkungen zu den griechischen Mimen aus Ägypten', *Hermes* 65 (1930) 126–27; Wiemken, *Der griechische Mimus*, 111–26.

57. For this interpretation of the fragmentary text of line 2, see Manteuffel, 'Zwei Bemerkungen zu griechischen Mimen aus Ägypten', 126; Page, *Select Papyri III*, 362–63.

58. *PVarsoviensis* 2. Published by G. von Manteuffel, *Papyri Varsovienses* (Warsaw: Univ. Varsovie facult. Litt., 1935) 5, Tab. I, 2. See the discussion in G. Von Manteuffel, 'Über einige Papyri der Warschauer Sammlung', *Münchener Beiträge zur Papyrus-Forschung* 19 (1934) 437–38; Wiemken, *Der griechische Mimus*, 135–38.

59. Manteuffel, *Papyri Varsovienses*, 5; Wiemken, *Der griechische Mimus*, 138.

60. *PVars* 2, line 2; cf. Wiemken, *Der griechische Mimus*, 138.

Oxyrhynchus mime, he is associated with a vulgar noise;[61] what he says meets with the strict disapproval of his partner in the dialogue.[62] These papyri and other remains of the mime,[63] however fragmentary, make clear what a large part the fool played in the popular entertainment of the Greco-Roman world.

Numerous references to the fool in literature delineate a lively portrait of this theatrical type. In the chapters on ridicule in *De Oratore*,[64] Cicero often refers to the mimes and speaks of their general deformity, their baldness, and their ridiculous grimaces. He warns the orator against that kind of ridicule, and in the process gives a portrait of the fool. Cicero asks, 'What can be so ridiculous as a fool (*sannio*)? We laugh at his grimaces, his mimicry of other people's characteristics, his voice, in short, his whole person. I call him witty, not, however, in the way I should wish an orator to be witty, but only the mime. That is why this method, which makes people laugh, does not belong to us. I mean the peevishness, super-stitiousness, suspiciousness, boastfulness, foolishness (*stultus*). Such characters are in themselves ridiculous: we jeer at such roles on the stage; we do not act them.'[65]

Diodorus describes a certain Latin mime named Sannio, 'a buffoon (γελωτοποιός) with a wonderful gift for raising laughter': 'for he not only aroused laughter by his words, but even when silent, the slightest movement of his body would bring smiles to all who watched him'.[66] In a withering satire on the Roman ruling class, Juvenal likens the behavior of the patricians to the 'buffooneries' of the 'bare-footed mimes', whom the spectators laugh to see 'cuffing each other'.[67] In this connection Juvenal mentions a particularly well known 'fool' (*stupidus*) named Corinthus,[68]

---

61.   Manteuffel (*Papyri Varsovienses*, 5) interprets the term βροντή in line 1 as a paraphrase for the ἐρεγμὸς τῆς πορδῆς of *POxy* 413, line 19.

62.   *PVars* 2, lines 2, 7; cf. Wiemken, *Der griechische Mimus*, 138.

63.   An ostracon of the second or first century B.C. portrays a drunken fool on his way to a revel with his lover; text in Crusius, *Herondae Mimiambi*, 137; text and translation in Page, *Select Papyri III*, 332–33. That the drunkard is a fool is indicated by the description ὁ τλήμων (line 1) and by the drunkard's confession, με παραφρονεῖν (line 10). Athenaios (*Deip.* 14.621c) gives as the subject of a mime troupe, 'a man drunk and going on a revel to his lover.' A fool was probably prominent in Decimus Laberius' mime *The Man with a Bad Memory* ('Cacomnemon') with its fragment, 'This is that dolt who came to me from Africa two months ago' (*hic est ille gurdus, quem ego me abhinc menses duos ex Africa*), quoted in Aulus Gellius *NA* 16.7.1; see the notes and commentary in M. Bonaria, *Mimorum Romanorum Fragmenta I* (Genova: Instituto di Filologia Classica, 1955) no. 25, pp. 21–22.

64.   Cicero *De Orat.* 2.61-72.

65.   Cicero *De Orat.* 2.61.251-52; see the discussion of this text in Grysar, *Der römische Mimus*, 267.

66.   Diodorus Siculus 37.12.1-2.

67.   Juvenal 8.190-92.

68.   Juvenal 8.196-97.

who played the role of a deceived husband in an adultery mime.[69] Martial repeatedly mentions a fool named Panniculus, who gets his ears boxed by another mime actor in punishment for his behavior.[70] A fool figures in a tale from Apuleius' *Golden Ass*,[71] which is recognized to derive from a mime.[72] This foolish slave is described as a miscreant and an unabashed liar;[73] when his mischief is discovered, he becomes deathly pale, breaks out in a cold sweat, trembles in every part of his body, stumbles about uncertainly, scratching now this, now that part of his head, and begins 'to stammer forth some foolish trifles'.[74] A learned fool called σχολαστικός is the principal character in the jokebook *Philogelos*,[75] some of whose material goes back as far as the first century.[76] The essence of these jokes consists in an ironic conflict between acuity and fatuousness: thinking himself to be wise, the 'professor' becomes a fool.[77]

69. Reich, *Der Mimus*, 89–90; Wiemken, *Der griechische* Mimus, 147.

70. Martial 2.72.1-4; 5.61.11-12; cf. 1.4.5.; 9.28; see the discussion in Dieterich, *Pulcinella*, 145–46; Grysar, *Der römische Mimus*, 266.

71. Apuleius *Met.* 10.2-12.

72. Reich, *Der Mimus*, 589–91; S. Sudhaus, 'Der Mimus von Oxyrhynchos', 262–64; Wiemken, *Der griechische Mimus*, 139–46.

73. Apuleius *Met.* 10.4, 7.

74. Apuleius *Met.* 10.10.

75. E.g., *Philogelos* 3, 9, 17, 22, 29, 43, 45, 54, 56, 73. On the figure of the σχολαστικός, see B. Baldwin, 'The Philogelos: An Ancient Joke Book,' *Roman and Byzantine Papers* (Amsterdam: Gieben, 1989) 629.

76. The extant recension is from the fourth century, but some of the material is much older, e.g., *Philogelos* 193 = Cicero *De Orat.* 2.276; 148 = Plutarch *Mor.* 177A; 263 = Plutarch *Mor.* 235E; 264 = Plutarch *Mor.* 178F; 78 = Velleius Paterculus 1.13.4; A. Thierfelder, ed., *Philogelos der Lachfreund, von Hierokles und Philagrios* (Munich: Heimeran, 1968); B. Baldwin, trans., *The Philogelos or Laughter-Lover* (Amsterdam: Gieben, 1983); A. Rapp, 'A Greek "Joe Miller" ', *CJ* 46 (1951) 286–90, 318. For other collections of jokes, see B. Baldwin, 'The Philogelos', 628. On the solitary evidence of the *Suda*, Reich (*Der Mimus*, 589–96) identifies Philistion, a Greek writer of the Augustan era, as the source of the mime-inspired material in the *Philogelos*; on the problems with this identification, see the review of Reich by A. Körte in *Neue Jahrbücher für das klassische Altertum* 11 (1903) 537–49.

77. E.g., *Philogelos* 75: 'Once the professor was sick, and when he became hungry but the dinner wasn't being announced, he distrusted his attendants and told them to bring the sundial into his bedroom so he could see for himself'; 78: 'A professor bought some very old paintings in Corinth and on boarding a ship he said to the captain, "If you lose these, I will make you replace them with new ones!" '; 43: 'The professor heard some people say "Your beard is coming in" – so he went to the city gates to wait for it. Another professor asked him what he was doing there and when he heard the reason said, "No wonder people think we are fools! How do you know it's not coming in by another gate?" '; 52: 'A professor fell into a well, but no one heard his cries for help. So he said to himself, "I'm a fool, I shall climb out and go and punish them to make them come here with a ladder to rescue me" '; 56: 'A barber accompanies a professor and a bald-head on a journey. When they stop for the night, they agree to keep watch in turns. During his watch, the barber shaves the head of the sleeping

The fool was a familiar figure in the cities of the Roman Empire, where the mime was so popular that it 'practically monopolized the stage.'[78] The ubiquity of the figure in popular consciousness made it possible to denigrate a rival or ridicule an inferior by comparison with a mimic fool.[79] Seeking to diminish Clodius' influence upon the masses, Cicero refers to his opponent as 'that arch-buffoon.'[80] Horace attempts to dissuade a young friend from becoming the client of a wealthy man by portraying his future conduct as that of a fool in the mime: he warns the youthful Lollius that he will become 'a jester of the basest sort, who so trembles at the rich man's nod, so echoes his speech and picks up his words as they drop, that you might suppose ... a mime-player was acting the second part.'[81] Martial slurs a contemporary by alleging that one of his sons is the natural offspring of a well known fool in the mime: his bald, pointed head and his long, ass-like ears reveal his mother's escapade on a truckle bed with a certain moron named Cyrta.[82] Juvenal ridicules an acquaintance who is eager to become the client of a parsimonious patron: in his capacity to endure insults and indignities, he is like the fool in the mime who offers his head to be shaved and slapped, and receives blows as his proper payment.[83]

Politicians might be denigrated by comparison with a fool, particularly if something about their appearance, speech or demeanor furnished a basis

professor. When he awakes and finds himself without hair, the professor exclaims: "Oh, that fool of a barber; he has awakened the bald-head instead of me!"' See the insightful discussion of this material by Winkler, *Auctor and Actor*, 160–65.

78. W. Beare, 'Mimus,' *OCD* (1970) 688; idem, 'Mime. Greek,' *OCD* (2003) 982; E. Fantham, 'Mime. Roman,' *OCD* (2003) 982–83. similarly, Bieber, *History of the Greek and Roman Theater*, 237.

79. On the use of humorous invective to denigrate political rivals, see A. Corbeill, *Controlling Laughter: Political Humor in the Late Roman Republic* (Princeton: Princeton University Press, 1996).

80. Cicero *Pro Sest.* 116–17: *ipse ille maxime ludius, non solum spectator sed actor et acroama, qui omnia sororis embolia novit,...* See the analysis of this passage and of the theatrical references in the *pro Caelio*, which seek to reduce the dignity of Clodius' sister, Clodia, by describing her as a mime writer, in Wiseman, *Catullus and his World*, 26–30, 35–38. See also Cicero *De Haurus. Resp.* 42, where Clodius is placed in the company of the *scurrae*.

81. Horace *Epist.* 1.18.10-14; text and translation in *Horace. Satires, Epistles, and Ars poetica*, ed. H. Fairclough, LCL (Cambridge, MA: Harvard University Press, 1991) 368–69. See the discussion of this passage in D. Armstrong, *Horace* (New Haven: Yale University Press, 1989) 131–33; W. R. Johnson, *Horace and the Dialectic of Freedom: Readings in Epistles 1* (Ithaca: Cornell University Press, 1993) 88–90, 96–100.

82. Martial 6.39.1-5, 15-17: *Pater ex Marulla, Cinna, factus es septem non liberorum: namque nec tuus quisquam nec est amici filiusve vicini, sed in grabatis tegetibusque concepti materna produnt capitibus suis furta ... hunc vero acuto capite et auribus longis, quae sic movetur ut solent asellorum, quis morionis filium negat Cyrtae?*

83. Juvenal 5.170-73. Cf. Grysar, *Der römische Mimus*, 266.

for the comparison.[84] As is well known, the emperor Claudius, who ruled when Paul wrote to Corinth, suffered from a cerebral palsy which left him with certain physical impairments: his head and hands shook; he dragged his right leg; he had a cracked and hardly intelligible voice; when he was angry, it was even more unpleasant: he stammered and snarled and slobbered.[85] When he was young, his grandfather Augustus kept him out of the public eye.[86] But when he unexpectedly came to power, he was widely ridiculed as a fool.[87] Two anecdotes in the historian Suetonius illustrate how widespread was this ridicule. A Greek litigator, in hot debate with Claudius as a judge, let slip the remark, 'You are both an old man and a fool (μωρός)!'[88] After Claudius' death, Nero 'vented on him every kind of cruelty; for it was a favorite joke of his to say that Claudius had ceased "to play the fool" among mortals, lengthening the first syllable of the word *morari*, "to linger, remain", so that it became *mōrari* = μωραίνειν, "to play the fool"'.[89]

Seneca composed a splenetic parody of the deification of Claudius, with a title, *Apocolocyntosis*, that translates loosely 'The Apotheosis of a Pumpkinhead'.[90] To make sure that readers recognize the role in which Claudius is cast, Seneca describes the subject of his satire as a 'born fool' in the prologue,[91] and later twice refers to the divinized emperor as a 'fool,'

84. Suetonius (*Iulius* 51) reports that, as the soldiers of Julius Caesar returned from their triumph in Gaul, they mocked their hero, in accordance with military custom, with a song that compared him to a bald-headed mime (*moechus calvus*); cf. Reich, *Der König mit der Dornenkrone*, 29. For the ridicule of the bald Tiberius as a μωρὸς φαλακρός, see Dio Cassius 58.19. Suetonius (*Domit.* 10, 18) also reports that Domitian, who in later life was bald, with a protruding belly, and spindling legs, was mocked as a bald-headed buffoon.

85. See Suetonius *Claud.* 30, and the other texts assembled and discussed in B. Levick, *Claudius* (New Haven: Yale University Press, 1990) 13–15, 200 n. 7–12.

86. Suetonius *Claud.* 2.2; 4.2-3; Dio Cassius 55.27.3. Cf. Garland, *The Eye of the Beholder*, 40–42.

87. Suetonius *Claud.* 3.2; 15.4; 38.3.

88. Suetonius *Claud.* 15.4.

89. Suetonius *Nero* 33.1.

90. On the title, authorship, and date of the satire, see P.T. Eden, *Seneca. Apocolocyntosis* 1–17. The title and attribution to Seneca are found in a passage of Dio Cassius 60.35.2: συνέθηκε . . . καὶ ὁ Σενέκας σύγγραμμα ἀποκολοκύντωσιν αὐτὸ ὥσπερ τινὰ ἀποθανάτισιν ὀνομάσας. For the association of the 'gourd' (κολοκύντη, Latin *cucurbita*) with folly and empty-headedness, see Petronius *Satyr.* 39.12 and Apuleius *Met.* 1.15.2; cf. Tacitus' comment on Claudius in *An.* 12.3. There is no reason to doubt the authorship of Seneca; on the place of the *Apocolocyntosis* in Seneca's life and work, see M. Griffin, *Seneca, a Philosopher in Politics* (Oxford: Oxford University Press, 1976) 129–31, 216–17, 219–20. For the suggestion that the *Apocolocyntosis* was produced for the Saturnalia beginning on 17 December 54 A.D., see H. Furneaux, *The Annals of Tacitus* (Oxford: Oxford University Press, 1907) Vol. 2, 23–24 n. 11, 45 n. 10, 171 n. 1.

91. Seneca *Apoc.* 1.1: *qui verum proverbium fecerat, aut regem aut fatuum nasci oportere*; this is the Latin counterpart of the Greek proverb cited by Porphyrion on Horace *Sat.* 2.3.188,

cleverly substituting μωρός for θεός in phrases familiar from Greek drama and traditional Greek prayers.[92] It seems probable that it was from the personality of the emperor Claudius that the figure of the fool received new life in the literature of the first century A.D. According to Suetonius, 'Claudius did not even keep quiet about his own stupidity, but in certain brief speeches he declared that he had purposely feigned it under Gaius (Caligula), because otherwise he could not have escaped alive and attained his present situation. But he convinced no one, and within a short time a book was published, the title of which was "The Elevation of Fools" (μωρῶν ἐπανάστασις), and its thesis, that no one feigned folly.'[93]

μωρῷ καὶ βασιλεῖ νόμος ἄγραφος ('for a fool and a king the law is unwritten'); see the commentary in Eden, *Seneca. Apocolocyntosis*, 64. See also *Apoc.* 7.1, *tu desine fatuari*, where Claudius is too foolish to be let into heaven; see the commentary on *fatuari* in Eden, *Seneca. Apocolocyntosis*, 92.

92.   At *Apoc.* 7.3 the author comments on Hercules' tirade: *nihilo minus mentis suae non est et timet* μωροῦ πληγήν. The phrase μωροῦ πληγή, 'a blow from a fool', is a parody of θεοῦ πληγή, 'a blow of a god', as found in Greek tragedy, for example, Sophocles *Aj.* 278–79, δέδοικα μὴ 'κ θεοῦ πληγή τις ἥκει, 'I am afraid some blow is going to come from a god'; Sophocles *fr.* 961, θεοῦ δὲ πληγήν οὐκ ὑπερπηδᾷ βροτός, 'a mortal cannot escape a god's blow'. Μωροῦ is substituted for θεοῦ again at *Apoc.* 8.3 in the phrase μωροῦ εὐιλάτου τυχεῖν, a parody of a traditional Greek prayer, for example, as found in an inscription from Corcyra: μή γένοιτο εὐιλάτου τυχεῖν Δάματρος, 'May an encounter with a gracious Demeter not occur'; see C. Wachsmuth, 'Senecas *Apocolocyntosis*', *Rh.M.* 18 (1863) 370–76; Eden, *Seneca. Apocolocyntosis*, 95, 105.

93.   Suetonius *Claud.* 38.3. Tacitus exploits the conventions of the mime to portray Claudius as a fool in books 11 and 12 of the *Annals*, according to S. K. Dickison, 'Claudius: Saturnalicius Princeps', *Latomus* 36 (1977) 634–47. For evidence that Claudius was remembered as a fool long afterwards, see *Historia Augusta, Tyr.* 30.33.

Chapter 4

CONFIRMATION AND CLARIFICATION

When we return to 1 Corinthians 1–4 with this understanding of 'foolishness,' we discover that many of Paul's statements become more intelligible. We begin at the end of the section,[1] because Paul has constructed his argument in such a way that he comes to speak last of the criticism that has given rise to the discussion.[2] Thus Paul declares in 1 Cor. 4.10, 'We are fools on account of Christ' (ἡμεῖς μωροὶ διὰ Χριστόν). The sense in which Paul intends the term μωρός is now clear from contemporary usage. Paul does not mean, merely, that he and his fellow apostles are regarded as simple and unsophisticated because of a lack of rhetorical or philosophical training.[3] Rather, Paul acknowledges that, on account of his apostolic calling (4.9), he is viewed as an example of a lower

1. For purposes of this investigation, we define the rhetorical unit as consisting of 1 Cor. 1–4. It may be that these chapters, with the paraenesis in 5.1–6.11, originally constituted an independent letter. Weiss (*Der erste Korintherbrief*, xxxix–xliii) doubted the integrity of the canonical epistle, basing his conclusions upon breaks in the train of thought, discrepancies in reports of events, sudden changes of tone, and differences in outlook and judgment. Weiss' arguments were strengthened by the observations of W. Schenk, 'Der 1. Korintherbrief als Briefsammlung', *ZNW* 60 (1969) 219–43; C. Senft, *La première épitre de Saint Paul aux Corinthians*, CNT 7 (Neuchatel: Neuchatel-Delachaux, 1979) 17–25; M. Bünker, *Brief-formular und rhetorische Disposition im 1. Korintherbrief* (Göttingen: Vandenhoeck & Ruprecht, 1983) 51–59. But even if 1 Cor. 1.1–6.11 is not an independent letter, chs. 1–4 are manifestly a rhetorical unit, the beginning and end clearly marked by hortatory periods in 1.10 and 4.16; see C. J. Bjerkelund, *Parakalo*, 141–42, 145–46; N. A. Dahl, 'Paul and the Church at Corinth according to 1 Corinthians 1.10–4.21' in *Christian History and Interpretation: Studies Presented to John Knox*, ed. W. R. Farmer and C. F. D. Moule (Cambridge: Cambridge University Press, 1967) 313–35.

2. On the logic of Pauline argumentation, that is, his tendency to delay mention of the cause of a dispute until he has defined key terms in his own sense, see Conzelmann, *1 Corinthians*, 249; and, in general, F. Siegert, *Argumentation bei Paulus*, 195–99.

3. Contra Hartman, 'Some Remarks on 1 Cor. 2.1–5', 120; Pogoloff, *Logos and Sophia*, 119–21, 153–54; Litfin, *St. Paul's Theology of Proclamation*, 197–201; Winter, *Philo and Paul among the Sophists*, 161, 165, 201–202; Lindemann, *Der erste Korintherbrief*, 44.

class type,[4] one whose weaknesses and deficiencies (ἡμεῖς ἀσθενεῖς, 4.10) make him seem to be 'foolish'. That is, Paul knows that the wealthy and powerful in Corinth (4.8) regard him with disdain (ἡμεῖς ἄτιμοι, 4.10), much as Seneca once smiled with condescension upon his decrepit slave.[5] What is worse, Paul knows that the type to which he seems to belong makes him vulnerable to mistreatment (κολαφιζόμεθα, 4.11), like the poor street creature Carabas, whom the mob abused in Philo's Alexandria.[6]

But evidence also suggests that Paul's acknowledgement of his resemblance to a lower class type includes an awareness of the comical associations which this figure evoked, and that his identification with this social type involves a conscious appropriation of the corresponding theatrical role. This is hardly surprising, given what we have learned about the social function of the mimic fool. Indeed, each of the examples of this lower class type which we have encountered in the literature of the High Empire included mimic elements in the portrayal.[7] Evidence that Paul has done the same in his self-presentation in 1 Cor. 1–4 appears, first of all, in his word-choice.

1 Cor. 4.9–13

We begin with Paul's explicit, but little noticed,[8] reference to the 'theater' in the preceding verse. In 4.9 Paul explains, θέατρον ἐγενήθημεν τῷ κόσμῳ. The phrase is usually translated, 'we have become a spectacle to the world'.[9] But the generalizing translation conceals Paul's meaning. Θέατρον

4. So, already, G. Theissen, *The Social Setting of Pauline Christianity. Essays on Corith* (Philadelphia: Fortress Press, 1982) 72–73, commenting on 1 Cor. 4.10: 'Paul contrasts his circumstances with those of the Corinthians in terms bearing indisputable sociological implications ... Paul puts himself at the bottom of the scale of social prestige'; similarly, P. Marshall, *Enmity in Corinth: Social Conventions in Paul's Relations with the Corinthians*, WUNT 23 (Tübingen: Mohr-Siebeck, 1987) 210–211: 'The contrast in 4.10 is primarily a social one and the terms belong to the "rhetoric of status". ... Paul's description of himself as a socially and economically disadvantaged person becomes clear in 4.11–13'; followed by R. Pickett, *The Cross in Corinth: The Social Significance of the Death of Jesus*, JSNTSS 143 (Sheffield: Sheffield Academic Press, 1997) 42–43.
5. Seneca *Epist. Mor.* 12.3, with the comments of Veyne, *A History of Private Life I*, 136.
6. Philo *In Flaccum* 6.36–38; cf. Reich, *Der König mit der Dornenkrone*, 24–27.
7. Specifically, Seneca's reference to the little terracotta figurines (*sigillaria*) in *Epist. Mor.* 12.3; Apuleius' description of the *centunculus* in which Socrates is dressed, the motley costume of the fool in the mime, in *Met.* 1.6–7; Philo's explicit reference to the 'theatrical mimes' (θεατρικοὶ μῖμοι) in his account of the mocking of Carabas in *In Flacc.* 6.36–38.
8. An exception is M. Kokolakis, *The Dramatic Simile of Life* (Athens, 1960) 35.
9. Thus the NRSV, as well as the KJV; also in the commentaries, e.g., Conzelmann, *1 Corinthians*, 85; Collins, *First Corinthians*, 188.

4. *Confirmation and Clarification* 51

is, literally, 'a place for seeing', especially dramatic performances.[10] It was a place used increasingly for public assemblies in the early Empire,[11] corresponding to the growing significance of the theater in public life.[12] Then, θέατρον means 'what one sees at a theater, a play'.[13] It is in the latter sense that Paul uses the term here,[14] and not in the general sense of 'spectacle'.[15] Dio Chrysostom distinguishes between the plays one sees 'in the theater' (ἐν τῷ θεάτρῳ) and the races one sees 'in the stadium' (ἐν τῷ σταδίῳ), while deploring the infatuation of the public with both.[16] In the theater are to be seen the scurrilities of 'mimes and buffoons'

10. Herodotus 6.67.3; *IG* 2.1176; Philo *Abr.* 103; *In Flacc.* 95; *Leg. Gai.* 368; Dio Chrysostom *Or.* 32.4, 32, 41; cf. Liddell-Scott-Jones, *Greek-English Lexicon*, 787 *s.v.* θέατρον; Bauer, *A Greek-English Lexicon*, 446 *s.v.* θέατρον.

11. *SIG* 976.4; Diodorus Siculus 16.84.3; Philo *In Flacc.* 41, 74, 84; Chariton 8.7.1; *POxy.* 2190, lines 4,46; Polyaenus 8.21; *IBM* 3.481.395; Josephus *B. J.* 7.47; *Ant.* 17.161; *OGIS* 480,9; Acts 19.29,31; cf. Bauer, *A Greek-English Lexicon*, 446 *s.v.* θέατρον, 1.

12. E. Tengström, 'Theater und Politik im Kaiserlichen Rom', *Eranos* 75 (1977) 43–56; J. Blänsdorf, *Theater und Gesellschaft im Imperium Romanum* (Tübingen: Franke, 1990); D. Potter, 'Performance, Power, and Justice in the High Empire' in *Roman Theatre and Society*, ed. W. J. Slater (Ann Arbor: University of Michigan, 1996) 144.

13. Ps.-Plato *Axiochus* 371c: θέατρα ποιητῶν; Philo *Leg. Gai.* 79: 'then, as in a play (ὥσπερ ἐν θεάτρῳ), he assumed different costumes at different times'; Philo *In Flacc.* 19: 'acting as in a play (ὥσπερ ἐν θεάτρῳ) the part of genuine friends'; cf. Bauer, *A Greek-English Lexicon*, 446 *s.v.* θέατρον 2. On the distinctions in meaning between the terms θέα, θέαμα, and θέατρον, see B. Bergmann, *The Art of Ancient Spectacle* (New Haven: Yale University Press, 1999) 10–11.

14. So, already, Heinrici, *Der erste Brief*, 155, on the phrase ὅτι θέατρον ἐγενήθημεν: 'Es heisst: *da wir ein Schauspiel geworden sind.* Θέατρον kann heissen Schaubühne, die Zuschauer, die Schauspieler, das Schauspiel. Hier das letztere'; citing, in support, Aeschines *Dial. Socr.* 3.20; Achilles Tatius 1.55; Polybius 3.91.10.

15. Commentators, e.g. Conzelmann, *1 Corinthians*, 88 n. 36, are drawn toward the general meaning 'spectacle' by the figurative use of *spectaculum* in Latin texts that seem to furnish nice parallels to the figurative use of θέατρον by Paul, e.g. Sallust *Jug.* 14.23: 'While I, poor wretch, hurled from my father's throne into this sea of troubles, present a spectacle of human vicissitude (*rerum humanarum spectaculum praebeo*)'; Pliny *Panegyr.* 33.3, praising the public entertainments provided by the emperor Trajan: 'No spectator found himself turned spectacle' (*nemo ex spectatore spectaculum factus*). But commentators overlook the figurative use of θέατρον in the specific sense of a 'play' in Polybius 3.91.10; Philo *In Flacc.* 19; *Leg. Gai.* 79, cited above n. 13, 14. See also the counsel which Dio Cassius placed in the mouth of Maecenas in a speech that he imagined this adviser making to Octavian: 'For you will live as it were in a theater of the whole world (καθάπερ γὰρ ἐν ἑνί τινι τῆς ὅλης οἰκουμένης θεάτρῳ ζήσῃ), and it will not be possible for you to escape detection if you make even the most trivial mistake' (Dio Cassius 52.34.2). The same metaphor is used by Cicero *Quin. Fr.* 1.1.42.

16. Dio Chrysostom *Or.* 32.4, 32; see esp. 32.41, ὅταν δὲ εἰς τὸ θέατρον εἰσέλθωσιν ἢ τὸ στάδιον; 32.74–75, where Dio concludes discussion of disorders in the theater, and turns to consider behavior in the stadium: καὶ ταῦτα μὲν δὴ τὰ περὶ τὸ θέατρον. Ἀλλ' ὅταν εἰς τὸ στάδιον ἔλθητε, κτλ.

(μίμοι καὶ γελωτοποιοί).[17] Paul acknowledges that he and his fellow-apostles have become a vulgar comedy in the eyes of the world.

Paul describes the audience before which the apostolic 'theater' is enacted as consisting of 'both angels and human beings' (καὶ ἄγγελοι καὶ ἄνθρωποι). This way of analyzing the beings that make up the cosmos, unusual in the letters of Paul,[18] is illumined by reference to a basic aspect of the theater in the Roman world. Theatrical performances were believed to be observed by the gods, as well as human beings.[19] A special chair was placed in the orchestra or the main seating area, 'from which the god...could watch the performance, through the medium of the symbol which represented him'.[20] The chair was carried in procession from a temple to the theater, having been prepared in a ritual in which it was draped, and emblems of the gods were placed on its cushions.[21] The practice is described in detail by historians and others,[22] and is attested by a bilingual inscription from the theater at Ephesus,[23] a building with which Paul was familiar.[24] Even 'temporary theaters were constructed near

17. Dio Chrysostom *Or.* 32.4: δήμου γάρ ἐστιν ἀκοὴ τὸ θέατρον· εἰς τοῦτο δὲ καλὸν μὲν ἢ τίμιον οὐδὲν ὑμῖν ἢ σπανίως ποτὲ εἰσέρχεται· κρουμάτων δὲ ἀεὶ μεστόν ἐστι καὶ θορύβου καὶ βωμολοχίας καὶ σκωμμάτων οὐδὲν ἐοικότων χρυσῷ. Διὰ τοῦτο οὖν ὀρθῶς ἔφην ἀπορεῖν ὑμᾶς σπουδῆς. οὔτε γὰρ αὐτοὶ σπουδαῖοί ἐστε οὔτε οἱ ὑμέτεροι συνήθεις καὶ πολλάκις εἰς ὑμᾶς εἰσιόντες, μῖμοί τ' ὀρχησταί τε χοροιτυπίησιν ἄριστοι...; 32.86: τοὐναντίον δὲ ὡς φαύλους τοὺς ἀνθρώπους διαβεβλῆσθαι, μίμους καὶ γελωτοποιοὺς μᾶλλον οὐκ ἄνδρας ἐρρωμένους.

18. Elsewhere Paul analyzes the spiritual beings that make up the cosmos differently, e.g. Phil. 2.10, ἐπουράνια καὶ ἐπίγεια καὶ καταχθόνια, in keeping with the ancient conception of the three-story universe; Col. 1.10, 16 (if authentically Pauline), εἴτε τὰ ἐπὶ τῆς γῆς εἴτε τὰ ἐν τοῖς οὐρανοῖς. See the observations of Weiss, *Der erste Korintherbrief*, 109–10. Also infrequent in Paul is the καὶ...καὶ construction; cf. 1 Cor. 1.22; Rom. 14.9.

19. J. A. Hanson, *Roman Theater-Temples* (Princeton: Princeton University Press, 1959); M. Hülsemann, *Theater, Kult und bürgerlicher Widerstand im antiken Rom* (Frankfurt: Peter Lang, 1987). On the religious belief and fervor that animated theater audiences in the Roman world, see Polybius 6.56; Cicero *Har. Resp.* 2.22–24; Tertullian *De Spect.* 10; see the discussion in Beacham, *Spectacle Entertainments*, 32.

20. Hanson, *Roman Theater-Temples*, 85.

21. Hanson, *Roman Theater-Temples*, 82–85; Beacham, *Spectacle Entertainments*, 27. In addition, an altar was located in the orchestra, and the stage was sprinkled with saffron and incense; Lucretius *De Re. Nat.* 2.416–17; Ovid *Ars Amat.* 1.103–106; Propertius 4.1.15–16, and the discussion in Hanson, *Roman Theater-Temples*, 87–89.

22. Dionysius of Halicarnassus *Ant. Rom.* 2.71; Lucretius *De Re. Nat.* 4.78–80; Dio Cassius 44.6.3; 53.30.6; 58.4.4; 72.31.2; 73.17.4; 75.4.1.; Tertulian *De Spect.* 10.1–2.

23. *OGIS* 480, cited and discussed in A. Deissmann, *Light from the Ancient East* (Grand Rapids: Baker Book House, 1980) 112–13. The inscription records the gift of a silver image of Diana and other statues by C. Vibius Salutaris, who directed 'that they be set up at every assembly in the theater upon the pedestals' (ἵνα τίθηνται κατ' ἐκκλησίαν ἐν τῷ θεάτρῳ ἐπὶ τῶν βάσεων).

24. Acts 19.23–42; P. Lampe, 'Acta 19 im Spiegel der ephesinischen Inschriften', *BZ* 36 (1992) 59–76; perhaps also 1 Cor. 15.32; cf. Lindemann, *Der erste Korintherbrief*, 107.

temples to enable the gods to observe the performances'.[25] In keeping with his Christian (and ultimately Jewish) conception of the numinous world, Paul replaces the θεοί with ἄγγελοι.[26] As in the theater, the comedy of the apostolic calling plays out before an audience supernal and mundane.[27]

At the beginning of the sentence in which Paul employs the explicitly theatrical metaphor, he waxes ironical:[28] 'For I suppose God has exhibited us apostles as last of all, like people condemned to death' (δοκῶ γάρ, ὁ θεὸς ἡμᾶς τοὺς ἀποστόλους ἐσχάτους ἀπέδειξεν ὡς ἐπιθανατίους).[29] The vocabulary of the sentence, unusual in Paul,[30] contributes powerfully to the theatrical image which he seeks to evoke.[31] The verb ἀποδεικνύναι is used here, not in the sense of 'make' or 'proclaim',[32] but rather with the meaning 'display',

25. Beacham, *Spectacle Entertainments*, 27; on the relation between theater sites and temples, see Hanson, *Roman Theater-Temples*, 13 ff.

26. So, already, Weiss, *Der erste Korintherbrief*, 108: 'An Stelle der θεοί treten bei Paulus die ἄγγελοι', with reference to a striking parallel in the Stoic definition of the κόσμος in Stobaeus *Ecl.* I, p. 184, 8: κόσμον δ' εἶναί φησίν ὁ Χρύσιππος σύστημα ἐξ οὐρανοῦ καὶ γῆς καὶ τῶν ἐν τούτοις φύσεων· ἢ τὸ ἐκ θεῶν καὶ ἀνθρώπων σύστημα. See also Posidonius *apud* Diogenes Laertius 7.138; Ps.-Aristotle *De Mundo* 2; Epictetus *Diss.* 1.9.4. Paul shares this world-view with the Stoics; but the immediate context of Paul's thought is supplied by his reference to the θέατρον.

27. Lietzmann (*An die Korinther I*, 20) calls attention to a parallel passage in Seneca *Prov.* 2.9, where the struggle of the wise man against destiny is described as a 'spectacle' admired by God: *Ecce spectaculum dignum ad quod respiciat intentus operi suo deus, ecce par deo dignum, vir fortis cum fortuna mala compositus, utique si et provocavit. Non video, inquam, quid habeat in terris Iuppiter pulchrius, si eo convertere animum velit, quam ut spectet Catonem iam partibus non semel fractis stantem nihilo minus inter ruinas publicas rectum*; similarly, Seneca *Ep.* 64.4–6; Epictetus *Diss.* 2.19.25. But there are differences in outlook and tone between Paul's metaphor and the Stoic analogy; see Weiss, *Der erste Korintherbrief*, 110: 'Aber die Stimmung ist hier gerade entgegengesetzt. Bei Paulus keine Spur von diesem Stolz, kein Wort eigentlich auch davon, dass er mit seinem Geschicke ringt; ein klägliches, erbarmungswürdiges Schauspiel gibt er der Welt zu schauen'; see also the observations of H. Braun, 'Exegetische Randglossen' zum Ersten Korintherbrief' in idem, *Gesammelte Studien zum Neuen Testament und seiner Umwelt* (Tübingen: Mohr, 1962) 181–91.

28. See the astute and subtle observations on the expression δοκῶ γάρ by Heinrici, *Der erste Brief*, 154: 'In δοκῶ liegt eine fühlbare Spitze des Ausdrucks'; Weiss, *Der erste Korintherbrief*, 109: 'Aber Paulus meint das nicht mehr ganz ernst, wie δοκῶ γάρ gezeigt hat'; similarly, Lindemann, *Der erste Korintherbrief*, 105–106.

29. The asyndetic construction of the sentence (see Blass-Debrunner, *Greek Grammar*, 461.2) adds to the rhetorical and emotional effect. The best mss. (P46 א* A B C D* F G, *et. al.*) omit ὅτι after δοκῶ γάρ.

30. The verb ἀποδείκνυμι is not otherwise found in Paul's authentic letters; ἐπιθανάτιος is *hapax legomenon* in the New Testament; ἔσχατος is used in a different sense than in 1 Cor. 15.8, cf. Collins, *First Corinthians*, 188; Lindemann, *Der erste Korintherbrief*, 106: 'Dass die Apostel "letzte" sind, sagt Paulus sonst durchaus nicht.'

31. So, already, Collins, *First Corinthians*, 188; Lindemann, *Der erste Korintherbrief*, 106–107.

32. As in 2 Thess. 2.4; Lk. 10.1; thus, rightly, Heinrici, *Der erste Brief*, 155; Weiss, *Der erste Korintherbrief*, 109.

'put on show'.[33] It is the equivalent of the Latin *edere*,[34] used to describe the exhibition of actors and gladiators.[35] Paul thus portrays God as the 'producer' (*editor*) of a cosmic spectacle which culminates in the performance of the apostles, much as Julius Caesar and his successors enhanced their power and dignity by giving games (theatrical and circus) and staging gladiatorial combats.[36] Following his decisive victory over the remnant of the Pompeian forces in 46 B.C., Caesar staged *ludi* which surpassed all that had gone before them in splendor and expense, gladiatorial displays in the Forum, and combats in the Circus Maximus, culminating in a contest between mime writers in the theater.[37] Augustus 'surpassed all his predecessors in the frequency, variety, and magnificence of his public shows... Sometimes plays were shown in all the various city districts, and on many stages, with the actors speaking in all languages.'[38] The elite in Roman provincial cities, such as Athens, Corinth and Ephesus, gave shows in the theater and amphitheater to gain office and enhance their reputations.[39]

When Paul says that the apostles are exhibited 'last', he uses the term ἔσχατοι in an ironic double sense.[40] On the one hand, Paul describes the apostles' social status: the apostles are the lowest, the meanest, the basest of people.[41] Mime actors, together with gladiators and prostitutes,

---

33.   In this sense, see esp. Plato *Phd.* 72c: 'You must realize that in the end everything would show Endymion to be foolish' (οἶσθ ὅτι τελευτῶντα πάντ <ἂν> λῆρον τὸν Ἐνδυμίωνα ἀποδείξειεν), with the comment of D. Wyttenbach, *Platonis Opera, Platonis Phaedon*, (Lugduni-Batavorum: H. W. Hazenberg, 1830) *ad loc*: λῆρόν τι ἀποδεικνύναι, *aliquid nugas ostendere, aliquid ita superare, ut nugae et nihil esse videatur*. See also Plato *Symp.* 179c: ὥστε ἀποδεῖξαι αὐτοὺς ἀλλοτρίους ὄντας τῷ υἱεῖ. Cf. Heinrici, *Der erste Brief*, 155; Weiss, *Der erste Korintherbrief*, 109.

34.   Rightly, J. B. Lightfoot, *Notes on the Epistles of St. Paul*, 43; Heinrici, *Der erste Brief*, 155.

35.   See esp. Livy 28.21 and Suetonius *Aug.* 43, 45; see also Tacitus, *et al.* in Glare, *Oxford Latin Dictionary*, *s.v.* edo.

36.   See the first chapter on 'murderous games' in K. Hopkins, *Death and Renewal*, 1–30. H. N. Parker, 'The Observed of All Observers: Spectacle, Applause, and Cultural Poetics in the Roman Theater Audience' in *The Art of Ancient Spectacle*, ed. B. Bergmann and C. Kondoleon (New Haven: Yale University Press, 1999) 163–79, esp. 168.

37.   Suetonius *Iul.* 391; Dio Cassius 43.22.2–23; Macrobius *Sat.* 2.7.1–9; cf. N. Purcell, 'Does Caesar Mime?' in Bergmann and Kondoleon, eds. *The Art of Ancient Spectacle*, 181–93; Beacham, *Spectacle Entertainments*, 76–81.

38.   Suetonius *Aug.* 43.1; cf. K. Galinsky, *Augustan Culture* (Princeton: Princeton University Press, 1996) 322–31; Beacham, *Spectacle Entertainments*, 128–30.

39.   J.-C. Golvin, *L'amphithéâtre romain* (Paris: Du Cerf, 1988) 237–46; K. Welch, 'Negotiating Roman Spectacle Architecture in the Greek World: Athens and Corinth' in Bergmann and Kondoleon, eds. *The Art of Ancient Spectacle*, 125–45.

40.   Cf. Conzelmann, *1 Corinthians*, 88; Lindemann, *Der erste Korintherbrief*, 106.

41.   Diodorus Siculus 8.18.3, the ἔσχατοι are those living in the most miserable conditions; Dio Cassius 42.5, 'Thus Pompey, who previously had been considered the most powerful of the Romans,... was now butchered like one of the lowest (ἔσχατος) of the Egyptians';

belonged to a group of persons who were considered degraded, that is, they had lost the status of respectable citizens, in the court of public opinion and even in the provisions of law.[42] On the other hand, Paul refers to the position of the actors in the spectacle: the performance of the apostles is the last of all. In the lavish theatrical entertainments given by the Roman elite, the mimes and buffoons were the last upon the stage.[43] Because the mime occupied the position of the concluding play, it was called an *exodium* ('after-piece').[44] By their witty speeches and jests, the buffoons relieved the tears and sadness caused by tragic drama.[45]

What does Paul mean when he describes the apostles 'as people condemned to death' (ὡς ἐπιθανατίους)?[46] Tertullian rendered ὡς ἐπιθανατίους with *veluti bestiarios* ('like one who fights with wild beasts

Alciphron 3.43, ὡς ἔσχατον ἀνδράποδον. See the vivid description of such a social type in Apuleius *Met.* 4.31: 'the most miserable creature living, the most poor, the most crooked, and the most vile, that there may be none found in all the world of like wretchedness' (*hominis extremi, quem et dignitas et patrimonii simul et incolumitatis ipsius fortuna damnavit, tamque infirmi ut per totus orbem non inveniat miseriae suae comparem*). Cf. Heinrici, *Der erste Brief,* 154: 'als homines infimae sortis'; similarly, Weiss, *Der erste Korintherbrief,* 109; J. T. Fitzgerald, *Cracks in an Earthen Vessel: An Examination of the Catalogues of Hardships in the Corinthian Correspondence* (Atlanta: Scholars Press, 1988) 136–37. Bauer, *Greek-English Lexicon,* 398 *s.v.* ἔσχατος 3.

42. See Cicero's grouping of actors, gladiators and criminals in *Cat.* 2.9; Cornelius Nepos *Vit.* pref. 5 on the *infamia* of appearing on the stage; Paulus *Sent.* 5.26, on the husband's right to kill his wife's lover if the lover is a slave, condemned criminal, gladiator, or actor. See in general, H. Leppin, *Histrionen: Untersuchungen zur sozialen Stellung von Bühnenkünstlern im Westen des Römischen Reiches zur Zeit der Republik und des Principats* (Bonn: Habelt 1992) 71–83; T. Wiedemann, *Emperors and Gladiators* (London: Routledge, 1992) 26, 28–30; M. Ducos, 'La condition des acteurs à Rome. Données juridiques et sociales' in *Theater und Gesellschaft im Imperium Romanum,* ed. J. Blänsdorf (Tübingen: Francke, 1990) 19–33.

43. Beacham, *Spectacle Entertainments,* 2–11, 80–81; A. I. Kessissoglu, 'Mimus Vitae,' *Mnemosyne* 41 (1988) 385: 'the mime constituted the formal close of theatrical performances'.

44. Cicero *Ad Fam.* 9.16.7, compares the post-script of his letter to Paetus to a mime, noting that the mime had taken the position of after-piece once occupied by the Atellan farce. O. Hirschfeld ('Augustus und sein Mimus vitae', *Wiener Studien* 5 [1883] 116–19) interprets Augustus' dying words about the *mimus vitae* as a description of the final act of his life as an *exodium*. On the mime as *exodium,* see Nicoll, *Masks, Mimes and Miracles,* 99; Bieber, *History of the Greek and Roman Theater,* 160.

45. See the scholiast to Juvenal 3.175: 'The *exodiarius* came on the stage in ancient times at the end of the play. He uttered witty speeches in order to relieve a little the tears and the sadness resultant upon tragic action by the merriness of his performance'; ed., J. E. B. Mayor, *Juvenal* (Cambridge: Macmillan, 1853) 62.

46. For the meaning 'condemned to death,' see Dionysius of Halicarnassus *Ant. Rom.* 8.18.2 (referring to the Tarpeian Rock): ὅθεν αὐτοῖς ἔθος βάλλειν τοὺς ἐπιθανατίους ('from which they used to hurl those condemned to death'); see also the LXX, Bel et Draco 31; cf. G. Hotze, *Paradoxien bei Paulus. Untersuchungen zu einer elementaren Denkform in seiner Theologie* (Göttingen: Vandenboeck & Ruprecht, 1997) 149–53.

in the public spectacles'),[47] and was followed in this interpretation by a number of commentators.[48] But this restriction of the reference of the term to gladiators is unwarranted.[49] Actors, as well as gladiators, were subject to corporal punishment.[50] As *infames*, they were assimilated to the category of slaves by the law, and suffered the loss of the citizen's right of the inviolability of body.[51] Actors, even if freeborn, might be beaten by the magistrates at will, or might be put to death.[52] Even Augustus, whose interest in the mime is well attested,[53] and who took steps to curb the magistrates' power of punishing actors anywhere and everywhere,[54] exercised the severest discipline upon actors who transgressed social norms: he had an actor named Stephanio whipped with rods through the three theaters of Rome, and publicly scourged a pantomimic actor named Hylas in the atrium of his own house.[55]

Indeed, it is possible that Paul has in mind the action of a particular play, when he describes the apostles 'as people condemned to death' – namely, a mime in which the buffoons were crucified. The most popular mime of Paul's day was the *Laureolus* of a certain Catullus.[56] References by historians and poets make it possible to reconstruct the plot:[57] Laureolus is a slave who runs away from his master and becomes the leader of a band of

47.   Tertullian *De pudic.* 14.7.

48.   Beza, Calvin, Grotius, among others; cited in Heinrici, *Der erste Brief*, 155; more recently, Collins, *First Corinthians*, 188; Lindemann, *Der erste Korintherbrief*, 106–107.

49.   So, already, Heinrici, *Der erste Brief*, 155: '. . . eine willkürliche Beschränkung'.

50.   Ducos, 'La condition des acteurs à Rome', 19–33; Parker, 'The Observed of All Observers', 165–66.

51.   A. H. J. Greenidge, *Infamia: Its Place in Roman Public and Private Law* (Oxford: Oxford University Press, 1894); Leppin, *Histrionen*, 71–83. The matter is well explained by C. Edwards, 'Beware of Imitations: Theater and the Subversion of Imperial Identity' in *Reflections of Nero: Culture, History and Representaiton*, ed. J. Elsner and J. Masters (Chapel Hill, NC: University of North Carolina Press, 1994) 84: 'the rationale . . . may be found in Roman ideas of the dignity required of the citizen's body. For the bodies of actors, like those of gladiators and prostitutes, were seen as lacking dignity. They were paraded on stage for financial gain. They served the pleasures of others. And just as actors (along with gladiators and prostitutes) resembled slaves in their lack of control over their own bodies, so they were assimilated to slaves by the law.'

52.   For examples, see Plautus *Cist.* 785; Cicero *Planc.* 30–31; Tacitus *Ann.* 1.77; Suetonius *Aug.* 45.3–4; *Calig.* 27.4; *Domit.* 10.4; Paulus *Sent.* 5.26. See T. Frank, 'The Status of Actors at Rome', *CP* 26 (1931) 11–20.

53.   Ovid *Trist.* 2.509–17; Suetonius *Aug.* 43, 74; cf. A. I. Kessissoglu, 'Mimus Vitae', 385–88.

54.   Suetonius *Aug.* 45.3.

55.   Suetonius *Aug.* 45.4.

56.   On the popularity of the *Laureolus* mime and the identity of the author, see Nicoll, *Masks, Mimes and Miracles*, 110–11; Wisemann, *Catullus and His World*, 183–98; Beacham, *The Roman Theatre*, 136.

57.   Josephus *Ant.* 19.94; Martial *De spect.* 7; Juvenal 8.187–88; Suetonius *Calig.* 57.

robbers; in the final scene, he is crucified.[58] The crucifixion was enacted with a considerable degree of stage realism. Josephus reports that 'a great quantity of artificial blood flowed down from the one crucified'.[59] Suetonius records a performance on the day of Caligula's assassination, at the close of which a number of mimic fools (*plures secundarum*) 'so vied with one another in giving evidence of their proficiency at dying that the stage swam in blood'.[60]

Paul follows the assertion, 'We are fools on account of Christ', with an account of his experience as an apostle, which is remarkably harsh in tone and content: 'We are weak, ... we are held in disrepute; ... we are hungry and thirsty, we are naked, we are beaten, we are homeless, and we toil, laboring with our own hands; [we are] reviled, ... persecuted, ... slandered ...; we have become like the refuse of the world, the scum of all things' (4.10–13). The severity of the language has puzzled interpreters,[61] and has sometimes been explained by reference to Paul's emotional state,[62] or his rhetorical purposes.[63] Some interpreters soften the impression produced by these verses, by suggesting that they constitute a brief catalogue of hardships, such as the philosophers employed to depict the adversities faced by the lover of virtue, and that the vocabulary is, therefore, conventional.[64] But the account as a whole, and each of its details, is an accurate portrait of the social experience of the mimes,[65] and

---

58. Cf. Reich, *Der Mimus*, 564–66.

59. Josephus *Ant.* 19.94: αἷμα τεχνητὸν πολὺ τὸ περὶ τὸν σταυρωθέντα ἐκκεχυμένον.

60. Suetonius *Calig.* 57.

61. Heinrici, *Der erste Brief*, 156–57; Lindemann, *Der erste Korintherbrief*, 108: 'Der ironische Sarkasmus der Aussagen in v. 10 ist überraschend.'

62. Weiss (*Der erste Korintherbrief*, 112) speaks of the 'Bitterkeit' resulting from Paul's extremely adverse experiences; a similarly autobiographical interpretation in Barrett, *The First Epistle*, 111–13.

63. Some interpreters characterize the language as ironic hyperbole, e.g., K. Plank, *Paul and the Irony of Affliction*, 33–69; others regard the passage as a 'paradoxical encomium,' e.g. M. M. Mitchell, *Paul and the Rhetoric of Reconciliation*, 220–21; adopting both explanations, B. Witherington, *Conflict and Community in Corinth: A Socio-Rhetorical Commentary on 1 and 2 Corinthians* (Grand Rapids, MI: Eerdmans, 1995) 142–44.

64. Conzelmann, *1 Corinthians*, 89–90; R. Hodgson, 'Paul the Apostle and the First Century Tribulation Lists,' *ZNW* 74 (1983) 59–80, esp. 65; Fitzgerald, *Cracks in an Earthen Vessel*, 132–48; M. Ebner, *Leidenslisten und Apostelbrief. Untersuchungen zu Form, Motivik und Funktion der Peristasenkataloge bei Paulus* (Würzburg: Echter, 1991) 20–92. Even if Paul employs the literary form of the *peristasis* catalogue in this passage, the resulting account cannot have diverged too widely from his actual experience, a point well made by Lindemann, *Der erste Korintherbrief*, 108.

65. Much of the account also applies, naturally, to other members of the lower class; thus, rightly, Theissen, *The Social Setting of Pauline Christianity*, 72–73, 97–98; Pickett, *The Cross in Corinth*, 42–43. But the immediate reference of the terms is controlled by the theatrical metaphor introduced in vs. 9.

gives substance to the theatrical metaphor announced in the preceding
verse. The mime actors' social status was miserably low.[66] They were held
in contempt, certainly by 'polite' society.[67] They were widely regarded as
parasites.[68] Commentators frequently lumped them together with other
low-life denizens – whores, pimps, and thieves.[69] The mimes were
repeatedly banished from the cities of the Empire.[70] 'The mimes' life was
a precarious one,... most were slaves, and those who were not eked out a
dubious living, greatly dependent on the largess and indulgence of patrons,
the taste of the public, and the availability of suitable opportunities for
performances.'[71] The poet Martial pictures the mimes haunting the
marketplaces, where they performed during the day, and where they slept
at night upon mats and pallets in booths that they shared with conjurers,
dancers, and the like.[72]

'We are weak', Paul concedes (4.10). The term ἀσθενής describes the
social condition of the poor in general, both in perception and in reality.[73]
But the term applies specifically to the mimic fool, whose caricature of the
weakness of a lower class type engendered derisive laughter.[74] The fool is
portrayed as weak in every respect – physically, intellectually, and
morally.[75] Thus, the fool in the adultery mime from Oxyrhynchus is too

66. Quintilian *Inst. Orat.* 6.3.8: *scurrae mimi insipientes*; see in general, Wüst, 'Mimos,'
1748; Ducos, 'La condition des acteurs à Rome', 19–33; Leppin, *Histrionen*, 71–83. This does
not mean that individual actors did not occasionally move in high society, like the *mima*
Cytheris; see Cicero *Ad Fam.* 9.26.2; *Ad Att.* 10.16.5; *Phil.* 2.24.58.

67. Cicero *De Orat.* 2.239, 242; *Ad Fam.* 12.18; Horace *Sat.* 1.2.55, 57; Aulus Gellius *Att.
Noct.* 16.7.4; 19.13.3; cf. E. Rawson, 'The Vulgarity of the Roman Mime', 255–60.

68. On the parasitism of mime actors, see esp. Cicero *Phil.* 2.27.67; Horace *Epist.* 1.18.10–
14; Martial 9.28; Suetonius *Domit.* 15; cf. Wüst, 'Mimos', 1748.

69. See *inter alia*, Horace *Sat.* 1.2.55, 57; Valerius Maximus 2.10.8; Martial 3.86;
Quintilian *Inst. Orat.* 6.3.8; 6.47; Juvenal 8.187–90; cf. Wüst, 'Mimos', 1748; Beacham, *The
Roman Theatre*, 131.

70. Suetonius *Aug.* 45.4; *Tib.* 37.2; Tacitus *Ann.* 1.77; cf. D. Potter, 'Performance, Power
and Justice', 129–60.

71. Beacham, *The Roman Theatre*, 131.

72. Martial 6.39.

73. See esp. Plato *Resp.* 364a, who contrasts men who are rich and powerful with 'those
who are in any way weak or poor' (οἳ ἄν πῃ ἀσθενεῖς τε καὶ πένητες ὦσιν) ; Prov. 22.22 (LXX):
'Do not rob the poor (πένης) because he is poor (πτωχός), and do not dishonor the weak
(ἀσθενῆ) at the gates'; Philo *De Som.* 155, who speaks of 'poor men' and 'weak men' (ἀσθενεῖς).
See the other texts cited and discussed by C. Forbes, ' "Strength" and "Weakness" as
Terminology of Status in St. Paul: The Historical and Literary Roots of a Metaphor, with
Special Reference to 1 and 2 Corinthians' (B. A. Thesis, Macquarie University, 1978); see also
Theissen, *The Social Setting*, 72; Pickett, *The Cross in Corinth*, 43.

74. Quintilian *Inst. Orat.* 6.3.8; see the discussion of the derision of the weak, deformed,
and disabled in the Greco-Roman world, with reference to the representation of these types in
comedy and mime, by Garland, *The Eye of the Beholder*, 73–86, 110, and *passim*.

75. Reich, *Der Mimus*, 23, 448, 470, 578–79; Nicoll, *Masks, Mimes and Miracles*, 87–88.

Figure 7.   Terracotta statuette of a mimic fool from Myrina, third century B.C. Louvre, Paris.

weak to fend off the blows of his master;[76] his name, Μαλακός, means 'soft' or 'effeminate'.[77] The dolt in Laberius' *Cacomnemon* suffers from a faulty memory.[78] The fool in the *Chariton* mime cowers before a group of women as they return from the hunt; he exclaims at the size of their bows, and cries out to his mistress for help.[79] The fool's baldness is a sign of his weakness, for the fool is bald not by nature, but from anxiety.[80] Synesius explains that

76.   *POxy* 413 ('Adulteress') lines 184 ff.; cf. Wiemken, *Der griechische Mimus*, 100–101, 102.

77.   Addressed by name at lines 145, 158, 170, 176, *POxy* 413 ('Adulteress'). On the meaning of the term, see Bauer, *Greek-English Lexicon*, 613 *s.v.* μαλακός 2, esp. of catamites, of men and boys who are sodomized; Plautus *Miles* 668: *cinaedus malacus*. See also the *cinaedus* who is a solo mime-performer in Petronius *Satyr.* 23. For actors as essentially effeminate, see Pliny *Panegyr.* 46.5; 54.1; Quintilian *Inst. Orat.* 1.10.31; Tacitus *Ann.* 15.1; Juvenal 3.95–97; Athenaeus *Deip.* 14.621d; Tertullian *De spect.* 10; Arnobius *Adv.nat.* 7.33, on what spectators see when they witness the performance of the fools: 'they see men weakening themselves to the effeminacy of women.' Cf. Parker, 'The Observed of All Observers', 166.

78.   Bonaria, *Mimorum Romanorum Fragmenta I*, no. 25, pp. 21–22; cf. Beare, *The Roman Stage*, 146.

79.   *POxy* 413 ('Chariton') lines 188–208; note, esp. the self-pitying conclusion at line 209: 'Nothing but trouble for me!' (πάντα μοι κακά); see the discussion in Wiemken, *Der griechische Mimus*, 177.

80.   Reich, *Der Mimus*, 23, 470, 578; Nicoll, *Masks, Mimes and Miracles*, 47, 87.

the fool laboriously makes himself bald 'by going to the barbers' shops several times each day'.[81] The actors who played the part of the fool in farce and mime were often persons with abnormally ugly bodies, chosen, evidently, on account of their weaknesses and defects.[82] Among the extant terracottas (e.g., Fig. 7)[83] are a number which share the same bodily deformity: the baldness, the extreme thinness and gauntness, the moodiness and anxiety of expression.[84] Because the weakness of the fool was a standard feature of the type, it is emphasized in literary parodies that are influenced by the mime. In his satire of Claudius as a fool,[85] Seneca caricatures the native weakness of the emperor, finding in each of his defects an opportunity for humor: he continually 'wags his head' and 'drags his right foot';[86] his sounds are 'confused' and 'unintelligible'; he is feverish, and his hands shake uncontrollably.[87] Seneca summarizes the life of the weakling: 'For forty-six years he struggled against the breath of life';[88] when Claudius died, 'he ceased to have even the appearance of existence'.[89] Like a fool of this type, Paul is characterized by weakness.[90]

Paul continues, 'We are in disrepute' (4.10). The term ἄτιμος refers, first of all, to social status.[91] The poor and weak in Greco-Roman society were regarded as persons without honor,[92] and consequently were treated with

---

81. Cited in Nicoll, *Masks, Mimes and Miracles*, 47; see also John Chrysostom *Poenit.* 4.3 (PG 59, col. 760), describing how the fool 'cuts his hair off with a razor'. Nonius (*De compendiosa doctrina*, ed. W. M. Lindsay [Leipzig: Teubner, 1902] 1.10) explains another respect in which the fool's baldness signifies weakness in his definition of the word *calvitur*: '*Calvitur* means "he is deceived"; it is derived from the *calvis mimicis* (baldheaded mimes) because they are deceived by all.'

82. Bieber, *History of the Greek and Roman Theater*, 248; similarly, Garland, *The Eye of the Beholder*, 110.

83. Terracotta statue of a mimic fool from Myrina, third century B.C., now in the Louvre (no. 324); Nicoll, *Masks, Mimes and Miracles*, 43.

84. Richter, 'Grotesques and the Mime', 148–56, esp. 154; Bieber, *History of the Greek and Roman Theater*, 247–48; Garland, *The Eye of the Beholder*, 110.

85. For the influence of mime upon the *Apocolocyntosis*, see O. Weinreich, *Senecas Apocolocyntosis*, 6–8; Eden, *Seneca. Apocolocyntosis*, 13–17, 64, 95; E. Fantham, 'Mime', 160–62.

86. Seneca *Apoc.* 5.2.

87. Seneca *Apoc.* 6.1–2; see also Suetonius *Claud.* 4.6, 21.6, 30; Dio Cassius 60.2.1–2; cf. Eden, *Seneca. Apocolocyntosis*, 66, 83, 92.

88. Seneca *Apoc.* 3.1.

89. Seneca *Apoc.* 4.2.

90. Cf. 2 Cor. 11.29a ('Who is weak, and I am not weak?') in the 'fool's speech'.

91. Rightly, Theissen, *The Social Setting*, 72–73; Pickett, *The Cross in Corinth*, 42–43.

92. Forbes, '"Strength" and "Weakness"', 83; Marshall, *Enmity in Corinth*, 210; Fitzgerald, *Cracks in an Earthen Vessel*, 140. Cicero's letters and speeches are full of scorn for the lower classes: e.g., they are 'the dregs (*faex*) of the city'. *Pro Flacc.* 17–18; 'dirt' (*sordes*), *Ad Att.* 1.16.11; 'the bilge-water of the city' (*sentina urbis*), *Ad Att.* 1.19.4. Dionysius

disrespect.[93] Paul acknowledges that he and his apostolic colleagues are reckoned to belong to this socially inferior group. But in the context of the theatrical metaphor introduced in vs. 9, the term 'dishonored' describes the status of actors, particularly actors in the mime.[94] Roman law and public opinion defined actors as *infames* (literally, 'of ill repute').[95] The reason for this classification is clear: 'public performers such as actors and gladiators sold their bodies for the delectation of others'.[96] Thus, to make an exhibition of oneself, as the actor did, to invite the gaze of others, was to degrade oneself.[97] Cornelius Nepos records the automatic *infamia* of appearing on stage as one of the cultural differences between Romans and other peoples: 'Even to come forth on the stage to make oneself a spectacle to the people was not a shame to any of these nations; but all these acts among us are classed as disreputable (*infamia*), low-class (*humilia*), and beyond the bounds of honor (*honestate*).'[98] This attitude toward actors spread to the upper classes in the provinces under the High Empire. Dio Chrysostom admonishes the Alexandrians: 'Nothing beautiful or honorable (τίμιον οὐδέν) enters into your theater; but it is always full of buffoonery and scurrility.'[99] Mime actors were especially disreputable, owing to the obscenity that was characteristic of the genre.[100] References abound to the performers' shocking behavior, and the disgrace of associating with them.[101] Persons of rigid morals were ashamed to

of Halicarnassus (*Ant. Rom.* 8.71.3) speaks of the lower classes as 'the indigent and unwashed.' Cf. Yavetz, 'Plebs sordida', *Athenaeum* 43 (1965) 295–311; G. Highet, *Juvenal the Satirist*, 8: 'Greek and Latin literature has many references to the shame of poverty.'

93.   Note the close association of poverty with dishonor in, e.g., Plato *Resp.* 364a, 'and to dishonor (ἀτιμάζειν) and disregard those who are in any way weak or poor'; see also Prov. 22.22 (LXX), which warns, 'do not dishonor (μὴ ἀτιμάσῃς) the weak of the gates'. For examples of the treatment of the poor with contempt, see e.g., Juvenal 3. 153; Pliny *Ep.* 9.6; Petronius *Satyr.* 57; Dio Chrysostom *Or.* 7.115; Lucian *Saturn.* 20, 22; cf. R. MacMullen, *Roman Social Relations 50 B.C. to A.D. 284* (New Haven: Yale University Press, 1974) 111–12, 138–41.

94.   Frank, 'The Status of Actors in Rome', 11–20.

95.   See, in general, Greenidge, *Infamia*; F. Dupont, *Acteur-Roi ou le théâter dans la Rome antique* (Paris: Du Cerf, 1985) 95–98. On the nature of *infamia* and the wide vocabulary associated with it, see B. Levick, 'The Senatus Consultum from Larinum,' *JRS* 73 (1983) 108–110.

96.   T. Wiedemann, *Emperors and Gladiators* (London: Routledge, 1992) 26.

97.   Parker, 'The Observed of All Observers', 165.

98.   Cornelius Nepos *Vitae* pref. 5.

99.   Dio Chrysostom *Or.* 32.4.

100.   On the obscenity of the mime, see in general Reich, *Der Mimus*, 50–53; Nicoll, *Masks, Mimes and Miracles*, 92–93, 107, 123–24; Wüst, 'Mimos', 1747; Beacham, *The Roman Theatre*, 130–31.

101.   See *inter alia*, Cicero *De Orat.* 2.59.242; Horace *Sat.* 1.2.55, 57; Valerius Maximus 2.6.7; 2.10.8; Ovid *Trist.* 2.497, 515; Quintilian *Inst. Orat.* 6.1.47; Juvenal 6.44; 8.187–89, 197; Martial 3.86.4; Macrobius *Sat.* 2.1.9.

watch.[102] The elder Cato famously left the theater during a performance at the Floralia, 'in order that his presence might not hinder the customary spectacle'.[103] Among the actors in the mime, the fool was the most shameful, because his routine regularly involved the phallus.[104] We recall that Paul's only other use of the term ἄτιμος is in reference to the body's private parts (1 Cor. 12.23).[105]

'We are hungry and thirsty' (πεινῶμεν καὶ διψῶμεν), Paul avers (4.11). The expression refers concretely to the physical experience of the poor,[106] the gnawing pain that makes poverty urgent. Judging from the literary evidence, hunger seems to have been endemic among the lower classes of the Roman Empire,[107] exacerbated by periodic famines and frequent interruptions of the grain supply.[108] A sympathetic commentator, such as Lucian, describes the poor hovering just above the starvation line.[109] Even

102. E.g., Dio Chrysostom *Or.* 32; Pliny *Ep.* 1.36; 9.17,36; Cyprian *De Spect.* 6: 'But now to pass from this to the shameless corruption of the stage. I am ashamed to tell what things are said; I am even ashamed to denounce the things that are done – the tricks of arguments, the cheatings of adulterers, the immodesties of women, the scurrilous jests, the base parasites, the very toga-clad family men themselves, sometimes foolish, sometimes obscene, stupid in all things, shameless in all things'; Tiberius Donatus *Ad Verg. Aen.* 5.64; Arnobius *Adv. nat.* 7.33.

103. Valerius Maximus 2.10.8: [Catone] *ludos Florales, quos Messius aedilis faciebat, spectante populus ut mimae nudarentur postulare erubuit. quod cum ex Favonio amicissimo sibi una sedente cognosset, discessit e theatro, ne praesentia sua spectaculi: consuetudinem impediret.* The story is also told by Lactantius *Divin. Inst.* 1.20.10, and is cited by Seneca *Ep.* 97.7, and Martial *Praef.* 1; cf. Bonaria, *Mimorum Romanorum Fragmenta*, 28.

104. *POxy* 413 ('Adulteress') lines 153–57; the scholiast to Juvenal 6.66; Wüst, 'Mimos', 1747–48. See esp. Arnobius *Adv. nat.* 7.33: '... the performers which your law has decided to be dishonored and to be considered infamous,... the morons with their shaved heads, ... their shameful jokes and gestures, their huge red phalluses.'

105. Conzelmann, *1 Corinthians*, 214 n. 32.

106. Interpreting the phrase in a sociological sense, Theissen, *The Social Setting*, 72–73; Fitzgerald, *Cracks in an Earthen Vessel*, 134; J. Meggitt, *Paul, Poverty and Survival* (Edinburgh: T. & T. Clark, 1998) 76, 96.

107. See, for example, Plautus *Stichus* 155–70: *Menaechmi* 77–109. Note Cicero's description of the lower class as 'wretched and hungry' (*misera ac ieiuna*) in *Ad Att.* 1.16.11. Martial 10.5 portrays the poor craving morsels of bread fit only for dogs. See esp. the complaint of the poor over hunger in Lucian *Saturnalia*; and the account of the hunger of rural peasants in Galen *De bonis malisque sucis*, ed. G. Helmreich, *Corpus Medicorum Graecorum* V.4.2. (Leipzig: Teubner, 1923) 389–91. Cf. G. E. M. de Ste. Croix, *The Class Struggle*, 13–16; Meggitt, *Paul, Poverty and Survival*, 59–60.

108. On famines and the response of the plebs, see Appian *B. C.* 5.18; Dio Cassius 55.26.1–3; Tacitus *Ann.* 2.87; Suetonius *Tib.* 48; cf. de Ste. Croix, *The Class Struggle*, 13–16, 195–96, 219–21. On other interruptions in the grain supply, see P. Garnsey and R. Saller, *The Roman Empire: Economy, Society, and Culture* (London: Duckworth, 1987) 100.

109. See the repeated complaint of the poor that they are 'starving' in Lucian *Saturn.* 19, 'while others are dying of hunger' (τοὺς δὲ λιμῷ διαφθείρεσθαι); 31, 'in the grip of famine' (λιμῷ ἐχόμενοι); 38, 'they were thirsty and well acquainted with starvation' (ὡς ἐδίψησαν καὶ ὡς λιμῷ συνῆσαν).

Figure 8. Terracotta statuette of a mimic fool. British Museum, London.

artisans often went hungry, despite having worked day and night.[110] As a hand-worker,[111] Paul would have frequently suffered hunger,[112] and not merely, as has been suggested,[113] on the occasion of journeys and imprisonments. Here, again, the terms that Paul uses have an indisputable sociological significance.[114] But the reference to hunger and thirst acquires a special resonance in the context of the theatrical image which Paul employs.[115] Hunger and thirst were among the most conspicuous features of the fool in the mime.[116] As the secondary actor in the mime, the fool

110. Lucian *Gallus* 1; *Cataplus* 20; *Saturn.* 20.

111. 1 Thess. 2.9, κόπος καὶ μόχθος. 1 Cor. 4.12, κοπιῶμεν ἐργαζόμενοι ταῖς ἰδίαις χερσίν. 2 Cor. 11.27, κόπῳ καὶ μόχθῳ. Acts 18.3, σκηνοποιός. Cf. R. Hock, *The Social Context of Paul's Ministry: Tentmaking and Apostleship* (Philadelphia: Fortress, 1980) 21.

112. Phil. 4.12; 2 Cor. 11.27, ἐν λιμῷ καὶ δίψει. Rightly, Meggitt, *Paul, Poverty and Survival*, 76.

113. Lindemann, *Der erste Korintherbrief*, 108: 'Paulus hungert gewiss nicht ständig und wahrscheinlich selten im strengen Sinne des Wortes; aber Hunger gehört offenbar zu den möglichen Begleiterscheinungen der apostolischen Existenz, z. B. auf Reisen oder während einer Gefangenschaft.'

114. Theissen, *The Social Setting*, 72.

115. It goes without saying that mime actors suffered from physical hunger, like other members of the lower class. Most mime actors seem to have been paid only for the days on which they gave performances; this is the best explanation of the term *diurnus* applied to mime actors in *CIL* III. 7343, where *diurnus* is best interpreted: *in perpetuum diurnam mercedem accipiens*; cf. Wüst, 'Mimos', 1749.

116. See already the allusion to hungry, buffoonish characters from Megarean mime in Aristophanes *Vesp.* 56–60, with the explanation of the scholiast, cited in Nicoll, *Masks, Mimes and Miracles*, 27. Note also the obsession with food and drink of the buffoons in the adultery mime from Oxyrhynchus, *POxy* 413 ('Adulteress') lines 169–73. See also Juvenal 5. 156–174; Lucian *Saturn.* 4, 9, with allusions to the hunger of the poor portrayed as mimic fools.

often, if not always, played the part of a parasite.[117] That is, he was portrayed as a perpetually hungry client or beggar at the table of some rich man (Fig. 8).[118] The humor of the role resulted from the fool's frustration at being passed over in the distribution of food and drink,[119] or in the abuse he was willing to endure to fill his empty stomach,[120] or in the disastrous results of his greedy over-consumption.[121] Of the many examples of the fool as a hungry parasite, one must suffice. In his fifth satire, Juvenal seeks to warn an acquaintance of the insults with which he will have to pay for

117.   See esp. Festus, in *Glossaria Latina* ed. Lindsay, Vol. 4, p. 438.23: *quod C. Volumnius secundarum partium fuerit, qui fere omnibus mimis parasitus inducatur*; Wüst, 'Mimos', 1748. See also Horace *Epist.* 1.18.10–14; Arnobius *Adv. nat.* 7.33; cf. Beacham, *The Roman Theatre*, 132. Note the παρασιτός who is one of the buffoons in the adultery mime from Oxyrhynchus, *POxy* 413, mentioned by name at lines 164, 165, 167, 173, 178, 180, and the discussion of this character by Wiemken, *Der griechische Mimus*, 103. See already the *parasitus ridiculus* in the comedies of Plautus and the discussion of this figure by P. B. Corbett, *The Scurra* (Edinburgh: Scottish Academic Press, 1986) 11–26. Note, esp., the speech of Gelasimus, whose name implies that he is a 'laughter man,' at the beginning of Plautus *Stichus* 155–56: 'I suspect that Hunger herself was my Mother, for ever since I was born I have never had my fill'; the following lines (157–70) enlarge upon the theme in true parasitic style. See also the speech of the parasite jester Ergasilus at the beginning of Act 1 of Plautus' *Captivi*, and the speech of Peniculus in *Menaechmi* 77–109. One of the most popular themes of farce and mime was the 'hungry Hercules,' a mythological burlesque in which the hero was portrayed as a clownish parasite; Athenaeus (*Deip.* 4. 164b-d) quotes some lines from a play, which he attributes to Alexis, depicting Hercules in this role: Linos. 'The fellow has a morbid hunger.' Hercules. 'Say what you like of me. I *am* hungry, let me tell you!' (πεινῶ γάρ, εὖ τοῦτ' ἴσθι). The theme remained popular under the Roman Empire; Tertullian (*Apologeticus* 15) lists among the themes of the mime 'three hungry Herculeses treated ridiculously'. A Phlyax vase found at Ruvo depicts Hercules stuffing his hungry face with food from the table of an angry Zeus; picture in Bieber, *Denkmäler zum Theaterwesen*, Fig. LXXVII.

118.   Fig. 8, a mimic fool as parasite, clutching bread and cup; terracotta statuette in the British Museum; picture in Nicoll, *Masks, Mimes and Miracles*, 49. For literary portraits, see Horace *Epist.* 1.18.10–14; Juvenal 5.1–11, 156–73; Lucian *Saturn.* 22, 32, 38, with repeated allusion (13, 24, 34, 35) to bald-headed buffoons (φαλακροί) and mimic jests (σκώμματα), which establish an association between the poor parasites who are the object of concern in this dialogue and the fools in the mime. See also H. G. Nesselrath, *Lukians Parasitendialog. Untersuchungen und Kommentar* (Berlin: de Gruyter, 1985) 15–53, 65–70, 92–111.

119.   Juvenal 5.156–70; Lucian *Saturn.* 22, 32; see also Plautus *Stichus* 183–84, 217; *Captivi* 71, 77; *Persa* 58.

120.   Plautus *Captivi* 88–90; Juvenal 5.170–73; Cyprian *De Spect.* 8.

121.   A commentator on Horace has preserved an anecdote about a parasitic fool who injured himself while attempting to imitate an orator when drunk: Porphyry on Horace *Ep.* 1.19.15: ' "Timagenes burst Iarbuthas." He has included the stock case of the Stupid Mimic. This Iarbuthas was a moor who mimicked Timagenes holding forth after a dinner party and in his cups. Because he was not used to the imitation he was attempting, he ruptured himself'; cited by Purcell, 'Does Caesar Mime?', 190 n.3. The fool in the 'Charition' mime evidently drinks some of the wine meant for the barbarians, and joins in their drunken dance, *POxy* 413, lines 58–95. See also the injunction against forcing a parasite to drink more than he is able in Lucian *Saturn.* 18.

his dinner, if he carries out his plan to become the client of a wealthy patron.[122] At the end of the satire, the would-be parasite is explicitly compared with a fool in the mime:

> For what comedy, what mime, is so amusing as a disappointed belly? The rich man's one object, let me tell you, is to compel you to pour out your wrath in tears, and to keep gnashing your squeaking molars. You think yourself a free man, and a guest of a grandee; he thinks—and he is not far wrong—that you have been captured by the savoury odours of his kitchen. For who could tolerate such a patron for a second time, however destitute he might be? It is the hope of a good dinner that beguiles you: 'Surely he will give us,' you say, 'what is left of a hare, or some scraps of a boar's haunch; the remains of a fattened fowl will come our way by and by.' And so you sit in dumb silence, your bread clutched, untasted, and ready for action. In treating you thus, the great man shows his wisdom. If you can endure such things, you deserve them; some day you will be offering your head to be shaved and slapped![123]

Like a fool of this kind, a parasite, Paul describes himself as 'hungry and thirsty'.

'We are naked', Paul complains (4.11). The verb γυμνιτεύειν, found only here in the New Testament,[124] means, literally, 'to be naked', but also describes one who is poorly clothed.[125] Seneca explains: 'One who has seen a man wretchedly clad and in rags says that the man he saw was "naked" (*nudum*).'[126] So this term, like the others employed in the paragraph, has a primary, sociological significance.[127] To be poorly clothed was a sign of destitution.[128] Micyllus the shoemaker laments that he is 'barefooted and

---

122. See the commentary on this satire, with notes on its sources, analogues, and allusions, esp. to the mime, in Highet, *Juvenal the Satirist*, 83–88, 262–63.

123. Juvenal 5.157–72; trans. G. G. Ramsay, *Juvenal*, LCL (Cambridge, MA: Harvard University Press, 1979) 81, 83. The identification of the would-be parasite with the mimic fool is especially clear in the expression *vertice raso* in 5.171, for this is the mark of the *stupidus* in the mimes, the *morio* of private dinner parties; cf. Pliny *Ep.* 9.17; Lucian *Conviv.* 18; Tertullian *De Spectac.* 23.

124. But see γυμνότης in 2 Cor. 11.27; Rom. 8.35. The verb γυμνιτεύω is late Greek; see the alternate spelling γυμνητεύω in Dio Cassius 47.34.2; Plutarch *Aem.* 263; cf. Heinrici, *Der erste Brief*, 157; Weiss, *Der erste Korintherbrief*, 111.

125. As in Dio Chrysostom *Or.* 25.3; cf. Bauer, *Greek-English Lexicon*, 208 *s.v.*

126. Seneca *De Ben.* 5.13.3.

127. Rightly, Theissen, *The Social Setting*, 72–73; Fitzgerald, *Cracks in an Earthen Vessel*, 134; Meggitt, *Paul, Poverty and Survival*, 76, 96.

128. For the association of poverty and nakedness, see, e.g., Epictetus *Diss.* 3.22.45: 'And how is it possible for a man who has nothing, who is naked (γυμνόν), without home or hearth, in squalor, … to live serenely?' Rev. 3.17: σὺ εἶ ὁ ταλαίπωρος καὶ ἐλεεινὸς καὶ πτωχὸς καὶ τυφλὸς καὶ γυμνός. Martial 10.5 pictures the poor beggar 'flapping his rags to drive off noxious birds'.

half-naked' (ἀνυπόδητος τε καὶ ἡμίγυμνος).[129] Because ragged clothing was the most visible manifestation of poverty, it was often a source of ridicule. Juvenal observes:

> The poor man gives food and occasion for jest if his cloak be torn and dirty; if his toga be a little soiled; if one of his shoes gapes where the leather is split, or if some fresh stitches of coarse thread reveal where not one, but many a rent has been patched? Of all the woes of luckless poverty none is harder to endure than this, that it exposes men to ridicule.[130]

In keeping with this cultural logic, the fool, who portrayed the poor man on the stage, was dressed in wretched garments; indeed, it was by means of his ragged costume that the fool was identified by the audience.[131] In literature, the fool is closely associated with the *centunculus*, a rag tunic stitched together from (literally, a 'hundred') odd scraps.[132] Patching is a sign of poverty, the attempt of the poor to get as much as possible out of the clothes they have.[133] The variety of colors in the patchwork create a comical, harlequin effect.[134] In a number of the terracotta statuettes, the fool wears a *chitōn*, or short frock.[135] The shortness of the garment is another sign of poverty.[136] The *chitōn* also gave occasion for vulgar comedy, when its shortness led to the exposure of the fool's private parts. The *archimima* in the adultery mime from Oxyrhynchus repeatedly calls attention to the middle of the fool's frock, and to what it leaves exposed.[137] Indeed, several of the surviving statuettes depict the mimic fool as entirely

---

129. Lucian *Cataplus* 20. For the poor clad in rags, see Lucian *De Merc. Cond.* 39; Apuleius *Met.* 9.12. The poor in Lucian's *Saturnalia* complain that they are unshod and have but a single cloak, *Saturn.* 11, 19, 31. See also Firmicus *Math.* 4.14.3: 'The mendicant poor, covered with rags and sunk in the calamity of their wretchedness'. For the correlation between the clothes worn by slaves and the low esteem in which they were held, see esp. Achilles Tatius *Leucippe* 5.17; Martial 14.127, 129, 158; and the discussion in K. Bradley, *Slavery and Society at Rome* (Cambridge: Cambridge University Press, 1994) 96–98.

130. Juvenal 3.147–153; trans. Ramsay, *Juvenal*, 43; on the protagonist of this satire and Juvenal's own view and experience of poverty, see Highet, *Juvenal the Satirist*, 7–8, 37–38, 72–73.

131. Dieterich, *Pulcinella*, 143–48; Nicoll, *Masks, Mimes and Miracles*, 90–91.

132. Apuleius *Apol.* 13: *quid enim, si choragium thymelicum posiderem? num ex eo argumentarere uti me consuesse tragoedi syrmate, histrionis crocota, mimi centunculo?*; Seneca *Epist. mor.* 11.1.8; cf. Grysar, *Der römische Mimus*, 270; Wüst, 'Mimos', 1747.

133. Mark 2.21; Juvenal 3.151; rightly, Meggitt, *Paul, Poverty and Survival*, 61.

134. Dieterich, *Pulcinella*, 145; Nicoll, *Masks, Mimes and Miracles*, 91.

135. Nicoll, *Masks, Mimes and Miracles*, 47 fig. 31, 48 fig. 34; Bieber, *History of the Greek and Roman Theater*, 107 fig. 415.

136. Artemidorus *Oneirocritica* 2.3: to dream of a short garment presages poverty.

137. *POxy* 413 ('Adulteress') lines 155–57, esp. 156: ποῦ σοῦ τὸ ἥμισυ τοῦ χιτωνίου; τὸ ἥμισυ; see the interpretation of this episode in Wiemken, *Der griechische Mimus*, 97, 102.

naked (e.g. Fig. 9),[138] a crude illustration of the fool's poverty and shamelessness.[139] Paul evokes this image of destitution when he laments that he and his fellow apostles are 'naked'.

'We are beaten', Paul reveals (4.11). With this statement, the evocation of the image of the fool becomes clearer and sharper (if that were possible) than in the preceding phrases. Not that beatings were not part of the experience of the poor in general in the Roman world,[140] where the law did little to constrain the *hybris* of the rich and powerful.[141] Thus, a poor man might be thrashed for making an impertinent joke,[142] or cudgeled if the barking of his dog disturbed the sleep of his neighbor.[143] Juvenal's account of a nocturnal assault by a drunken young bully, full of insults and blows, has the bitter ring of something lived through; the poet concludes: 'Such is the liberty of the poor man: having been pounded and cuffed into a jelly, he begs and prays to be allowed to return home with a few teeth in his head!'[144] Slaves were beaten even more cruelly,[145] flogged through the streets,[146] and

138. Terracotta statuette of a mimic fool in the British Museum, pictured in Nicoll, *Masks, Mimes and Miracles*, 49 fig. 35; see also 88 fig. 80, 81. For naked fools on the stage, see also Cyprian *De Spect.* 8.

139. On nudity as a sign of destitution, see Fitzgerald, *Cracks in an Earthen Vessel*, 134; Meggitt, *Paul, Poverty and Survival*, 61 n. 111.

140. See the section on 'cruelty' in Wiseman, *Catullus and his World*, 5–10; see also M. Harding, ' "Killed All Day Long": The Powerful and Their Victims in the New Testament Era,' unpublished paper delivered at the Annual Meeting of the Society of Biblical Literature, 2001.

141. The emperor could beat or torture whomever he wished, since there was no one who could invoke the law against him, e.g. Suetonius *Calig.* 27–33; *Nero* 26. But the law also extended indulgence to provincial governors, e.g., Cicero *Verr.* 5.163–64; *Ad Fam.* 10.32.3, and even private citizens, if they were powerful enough, e.g., Sallust *Hist.* 1.44 M; Valerius Maximus 9.2.1; Cicero *Phil.* 11.5–7; Seneca *De Ira* 3.18.1; Plutarch *Cic.* 49.2. The explanation lies in the fact that Roman cities lacked a police force; citizens had to resort to self-help for protection; wealthy men went about with armed escorts; for late-Republican examples, see A. Lintott, *Violence in Republican Rome* (Oxford: Clarendon Press, 1968) 22–34, 83–85; that the same situation existed under the Empire is attested by Juvenal 3.282–85.

142. Gellius *Noct. Att.* 10.3.5.

143. Juvenal 6.413–18.

144. Juvenal 3.288–301, the quotation 3.299–301. The verbal abuse that precedes the beating illustrates the fact that the blows are offered as an insult; cf. Plato *Grg.* 527 A-D; 486 C; Demosthenes *Or.* 21.72. Cynic philosophers also suffered such ignominious blows, e.g., Ps.-Diogenes *Ep.* 20; Diogenes Laertius 6.89, cited in Fitzgerald, *Cracks in an Earthen Vessel*, 143 n. 89.

145. For the beating of slaves with the fist or hand, see, e.g., 1 Peter 2.20; Longinus *De Subl.* 44.4; Philo *Ebr.* 198; Seneca *Apoc.* 15.

146. E.g., Plautus *Most.* 56; see Wiseman, *Catullus and his World*, 6–7, emphasizing the publicity of such floggings as an exemplary warning to unruly slaves.

Figure 9.   Terracotta statuette of a mimic fool. British Museum, London.

whipped in the atrium of the house,[147] or handed over to the professional torturers (*carnifices*), who scourged and crucified the slave for a standard fee of 4 *sesterces* per person.[148] As members of the lower class, mime actors were frequently and publicly beaten.[149] With his reference to the beatings he experiences as an apostle, Paul identifies himself with slaves and actors, and with the poor in general.

147.   Suetonius *Aug.* 45.4; for beatings in other public places see Livy 2.36.1; Dionysius of Halicarnassus 7.69.1; Valerius Maximus 1.7.4.

148.   On the dreadful *carnifices* and the agony they inflicted on slaves and criminals, see, e.g., Plautus *Miles*. 359–60; Martial 2.17.2; cf. Wiseman, *Catullus and his World*, 5–8. On the standard fee for flogging and execution, see *L'année épigraphique* (1971) 88.2.10, an inscription from Puteoli, trans. in J . F. Gardner and T. Wiedemann, *The Roman Household: A Sourcebook* (London: Routledge, 1991) no. 22; and the discussion in O. F. Robinson, 'Slaves and the Criminal Law,' *Zeitschrift der Savigny-Stiftung für Rechtsgeschichte* 98 (1981) 223–27; Bradley, *Slavery and Society at Rome*, 166–67.

149.   For examples of actors beaten or killed, see Plautus *Cist.* 785; Cicero *Planc.* 30–31; Tacitus *Ann.* 1.77; Suetonius *Aug.* 45.3–4; *Calig.* 27.4; *Domit.* 10.4; Paulus *Sent.* 5.26; cf. the comments of Parker, 'The Observed of All Observers', 165–66.

But the precise verb that Paul chooses to describe his mistreatment has a history of usage which connects it with comedy and mime, and specifically evokes the punishment employed to censure the misbehavior of the mimic fool. The verb κολαφίζειν,[150] a non-Attic word derived from κόλαφις,[151] means 'to strike with the fist or knuckles'.[152] Κόλαφος ('Knucklehead') already appears as the proper name of a fool in *The Rustic* of Epicharmus,[153] author of the earliest literary mimes.[154] A fool (*sannio*) in Terence's comedy *The Brothers* uses this term to protest his mistreatment: 'my head is lumpy from his blows' (*colaphis tuber est totum caput*).[155] The connections to comedy and mime are greatly expanded, when one recognizes that κολαφίζειν is the vernacular equivalent of κονδυλίζειν;[156] for the latter term is used frequently,[157] even proverbially,[158] to describe the 'knuckle-sandwich' given to the fool. In describing the theater, Gregory of Nazianzus speaks of the mimic fool as 'accustomed to knuckles' (κονδύλοις εἰθισμένοι).[159] Moreover, since Hesychius equates κολαφιζόμενος with ῥαπιζόμενος,[160] the numerous passages which describe the mimic fool as one who gets 'slapped' become relevant to Paul's statement here.[161] Thus,

---

150. See the articles by K. L. Schmidt, 'κολαφίζω', *TDNT* 3 (1965) 818–21; idem, ' Ἰησοῦς Χριστὸς κολαφιζόμενος und die "colaphisation" der Juden' in *Aux sources de la tradition chrétienne*, Mélanges M. Goguel (Neuchâtel: Delachaux & Niestle, 1950) 218–27. As Fitzgerald (*Cracks in an Earthen Vessel*, 143 n. 89) observes, neither of the articles by Schmidt is particularly illuminating in regard to 1 Cor. 4.11, so that a fresh discussion is needed.

151. Bauer, *Greek-English Lexicon*, 555 *s.v.* κολαφίζω.

152. Heinrici, *Der erste Brief*, 157: 'κολαφιζόμεθα, ganz eigentlich: wir werden mit Fäusten geschlagen'; Fitzgerald *Cracks in an Earthen Vessel*, 143 n. 89: 'Basic to the meaning of the verb is the idea of striking with the fist or knuckles (κόλαφος = κόνδυλος).'

153. Epicharmus Ἀγρωστῖνος fr. 1: ὡς ταχὺς Κόλαφος περιπατεῖ δίνος, in G. Kaibel, *Comicorum Graecorum Fragmenta I* (Berlin: Weidmann, 1958) 91; cf. Liddell-Scott-Jones, *Greek-English Lexicon*, 971 *s.v.* κόλαφος.

154. See the careful study of the life and writings of Epicharmus by A. W. Pickard-Cambridge, *Dithyramb, Tragedy and Comedy* (Oxford: Clarendon Press, 1927) 353–413; see also Nicoll, *Masks, Mimes and Miracles*, 38–41.

155. Terence *Adelphi* 245; the preceding line completes the picture: 'Is your man utterly shameless? He's loosened every tooth in my head.' See also Plautus *Capt.* 88–90: *nisi qui colaphos perpeti potest parasitus frangique aulas in caput.*

156. Hesychius *Gloss.* κόλαφος = κόνδυλος; Liddell-Scott-Jones, *Greek-English Lexicon*, 971 *s.v.* κόλαφος; Fitzgerald, *Cracks in an Earthen Vessel*, 143 n. 89.

157. E.g., Aristophanes *Vesp.* 254, 1503; Liddell-Scott-Jones, *Greek-English Lexicon*, 977 *s.v.* κόνδυλος.

158. Aristophanes *Pax* 123, κολλύραν καὶ κόνδυλον ὄψο ἐπ᾽ αὐτῇ, 'pudding and knuckle-sauce to it,' i.e. a good thrashing; Liddell-Scott-Jones, *Greek-English Lexicon* 977 *s.v.* κόνδυλος.

159. Gregory of Nazianzus *Carm.* 2.2 in Migne, *PG* 37, col. 1582.

160. Bauer, *Greek-English Lexicon*, 551 *s.v.* κολαφίζω.

161. On slapping as an insult and humiliation, whether the person being struck is a slave, a condemned criminal, or a fool, see the texts assembled in Fitzgerald, *Cracks in an Earthen Vessel*, 144 n. 89; Betz, *Sermon on the Mount*, 290.

John Chrysostom refers to the mimic fool as one who is 'slapped at public expense' (δημοσίᾳ ῥαπίζεται).[162]

Descriptions of the fool being beaten or slapped, and references to such scenes in literature, are so numerous as almost to defy citation.[163] Martial refers repeatedly to the blows (*alapae*) given a fool named Panniculus; his ears are boxed with a loud smack, and his sorry face is slapped.[164] Juvenal evokes the image of buffoons 'cuffing each other' on the stage, and speaks of the laughter which such antics incited.[165] Elsewhere, Juvenal alludes to the professional clown who shaves his head and allows himself to be beaten (*pulsandum*) for public amusement.[166] The fool in the adultery mime from Oxyrhynchus is beaten when his mischief is discovered.[167] Arnobius describes what most delights spectators at the mime: 'the shaved heads of the fools, the resonant sound of the heads being boxed, the noise of applause'.[168] Indeed, it seems that part of the equipment of the fool upon the stage was a stick with which his beating was administered.[169] A terracotta statuette from the British Museum (Fig. 10) shows a mimic fool holding in his right hand a short, crooked stick.[170]

It is not difficult to comprehend why the beating of the fool provided amusement: the explanation lies in the complex social function of this theatrical type. For the rich in the audience, the blows that rained down upon the fool's bald head were a sign of his helplessness and humiliation, and thus welcome reminders of the power of the rich to inflict punishment, and their invulnerability to such mistreatment.[171] On the other hand, the formal appearance of punishment enabled poor spectators to respond with

---

162.   John Chrysostom *Poenit.* 4.3. in Migne, *PG* 59, col. 760.

163.   In addition to the texts discussed below, see Novius Frag. 3 in Ribbeck, *Comicorum Romanorum Fragmenta*, 254; Tertullian *De Spectac.* 23; Macrobius *Sat.* 2.7.4; Cyprian *De Spect.* 8; Synesius Φαλακρᾶς ἐγκώμιον 77; Procopius *Hist. arc.* 9.14; cf. Wüst, 'Mimos', 1748; Nicoll, *Masks, Mimes, and Miracles*, 88.

164.   Martial 2.72.1–4; 5.61.11–12; cf. 1.4.5; see the discussion in Dieterich, *Pulcinella*, 145–46; Grysar, *Der römische Mimus*, 266. A Latin gloss, cited by Reich, *Der Mimus*, 448, explains the term *alopus* used to describe the mimic fool as follows: 'one who receives blows as his proper payment' (*qui propter mercedem alapas patitur*).

165.   Juvenal 8.189–92.

166.   Juvenal 5.171–72, with the comments of Highet, *Juvenal the Satirist*, 87, 263 n.7.

167.   *POxy* 413 ('Adulteress') line 186, with the comments of Wiemken, *Der griechische Mimus*, 99, 102. A worse beating, including torture, is inflicted upon the fool in the mime-inspired tale in Apuleius *Met.* 10.10.

168.   Arnobius *Adv. nat.* 7.33.

169.   Wüst, 'Mimos,' 1748: 'Wahrscheinlich führte nur der *secundarum* den Stock, mit dem die häufigen Prügelszenen durchgeführt werden (ῥαπίζεσθαι).'

170.   Terracotta statuette from the British Museum collection, pictured in Nicoll, *Masks, Mimes and Miracles*, 48.

171.   See the insightful remarks of Highet, *Juvenal the Satirist*, 87.

Figure 10.   Terracotta statuette of a mimic fool. British Museum, London.

free delight to the outrageous behavior of the fool.[172] In any case, the beating of the fool is emphasized in literary parodies inspired by the mime, precisely because it is a standard feature of the type. Thus, in Seneca's *Apocolocyntosis*, the foolish Claudius is 'flogged, caned, and beaten (*colaphis vapulantem*)' by Caligula, who suddenly turns up at the end of the satire to claim Claudius as his slave.[173] The appearance here, in a work so deeply influenced by the mime,[174] of the very term (*colaphis*) used by Paul to describe his mistreatment is as clear an indication as we are likely to obtain of the provenance of the language and images employed by Paul in this paragraph.

'We are homeless', Paul laments (4.11). Homelessness was the condition of many of the poor in the Roman Empire.[175] According to Gregory of

172. See the critical insights of Winkler, *Auctor and Actor*, 290.

173. Seneca *Apoc.* 15. For other indications that Caligula treated Claudius as a professional buffoon during his lifetime, see Suetonius *Calig.* 23.3; *Claud.* 9.1; *Nero* 6.2; cf. Eden, *Seneca, Apocolocyntosis*, 149.

174. On the relation of the *Apocolocyntosis* to mime, see the suggestion of E. Fantham, 'Mime', 160: 'Indeed, the reminiscences [of mime] are so many and the dramatic potential of Seneca's scenario so irresistible that I would like to suggest that Seneca has reworked in the narrative form of Menippean satire his own original libretto, written for intimate staging at Nero's *Saturnalia* as a mime in four scenes'.

175. The numbers of homeless are difficult to estimate. MacMullen (*Roman Social Relations*, 92–93) laments the failure of archaeology and epigraphy to provide data. We are left to draw inferences from literature. See the references to the masses of the poor in Seneca *Ad. Helv.* 12.1; Strabo 14.2.5, and to beggary in Appian *B.C.* 2.120; Juvenal 5.8.

Nyssa, homeless beggars were to be seen everywhere: 'The open air is their dwelling, their lodgings are the porticoes and street corners and the less frequented parts of the marketplace.'[176] This account is from the later Empire, as are other graphic testimonies.[177] But such statements are not to be dismissed as evidence of decline.[178] The problem of homelessness was there in the first century, as well, for those who had eyes to see it.[179] Martial pictures a poor man wandering (*erret*) through the city, seeking shelter beneath bridges and beside slopes, driven (*exul*) from doorways, shivering through a wet and cold December.[180] Some of the homeless sought shelter in tombs, cellars, and vaults,[181] while others constructed lean-tos against the walls of permanent buildings, between the columns of porticoes, or beneath aqueducts.[182] As the apostle of Christ, Paul acknowledges that he shares the plight of these homeless poor.[183]

But the verb that Paul chooses to describe his condition, ἀστατεῖν, is a frequentative verb that expresses incessant movement: it means, literally, 'to be unsettled', 'to be without a permanent residence'.[184] It depicts the life of the 'vagabond',[185] who is constantly moving from place to place.[186] Thus, the term is more consonant with the theatrical metaphor than one might have assumed. For the mime's life was a vagabond life, constantly roving from town to town, in search of audiences and suitable venues for performance.[187] Indeed, one of the terms by which mime actors were

---

176. Gregory of Nyssa *De pauper. amand.* 1, in Migne, *PG* 46, col. 457, cited in MacMullen, *Roman Social Relations*, 87.

177. Firmicus Maternus *Math.* 4.14.3; Augustine *Sermo* 345.1.

178. MacMullen, *Roman Social Relations*, 87.

179. E.g. Luke 16.20.

180. Martial 10.5.

181. A. Scobie, 'Slums, Sanitation and Mortality in the Roman World,' *Klio* 68 (1986) 403.

182. Dio Chrysostom *Or.* 40.8–9; Ulpian *Digest* 43.8.2.

183. Fitzgerald, *Cracks in an Earthen Vessel*, 134–35; Meggitt, *Paul, Poverty and Survival*, 96.

184. Bauer, *Greek-English Lexicon*, 145 *s.v.* ἀστατέω; Fitzgerald, *Cracks in an Earthen Vessel*, 134.

185. F. Field, *Notes on the Translation of the New Testament* (Oxford: Oxford University Press, 1899) 170.

186. Weiss, *Der erste Korintherbrief*, 111: 'Dies Wort bezeichnet die ruhelose, unstäte "Heimatlosigkeit" des Wanderers, der nicht hat, wo er sein Haupt niederlegen könnte (Theophylactus: ἐλαυνόμεθα, φεύγομεν), den es von Ort zu Ort treibt'; similarly, Fitzgerald, *Cracks in an Earthen Vessel*, 134.

187. See in general Reich, *Der Mimus*, 167–68, 558, 561; Beare, *The Roman Stage*, 141–43, 142: 'We can picture these small companies of strolling players, men, women, and children, traveling from town to town like gypsies, setting up their simple stage and curtain in some market-place and giving their show'; Beacham, *The Roman Theatre*, 131–32. Cicero (*Phil.* 2.65) refers to extempore performances by traveling mime troupes. Martial (6.39) pictures the mimes sleeping on truckle beds and mats in the market-place.

known is *circulatores*,[188] because they circulated from place to place,[189] either as solo-performers,[190] or as members of strolling companies.[191] The wandering life of the mime is attested by several well known epitaphs, such as that of Protogenes, a slave of Greek origin, who amused Italian crowds with his 'merry trifles',[192] and that of the young mime actress Eucharis, slave, and later freed woman of Licinia, found at Rome.[193] The distances that might be traveled by mime actors in the course of what was, too often, a short life, and the relationships that might be destroyed as a result, are illustrated by the touching farewell poem addressed by Antipater of Sidon to the mime actress Antiodemis on the occasion of her departure for Rome.[194]

Moreover, in the context of the theatrical metaphor that Paul has been developing throughout the paragraph, the verb ἀστατεῖν is evocative of one of the principal roles in which the fool was cast in farce and mime, namely,

---

188.   On the mimes as *circulatores*, see the texts assembled and discussed by Corbett, *The Scurra*, 55–57. See esp. Petronius *Satyr*. 68.6–7, describing a clever slave who has been trained as a mimic: 'I had him taught by sending him to the *circulatores*.'

189.   Corbett, *The Scurra*, 55 on the meaning of the term, drawing upon references in the *Thes. Ling. Lat., s.v.*

190.   See the epitaph of one Vitalis in *Anthol. Lat.* 487a, who boasts of his skill in molding his features and voice to suit his part. For another example of a solo-performer, see the κίναιδος in Petronius *Satyr*. 23. On solo-performers in general, see Wüst, 'Mimos', 1745, 1751; Beare, *The Roman Stage*, 142.

191.   For evidence of mime troupes, see esp. *CIL* XIV. 2408, an inscription from Bovillae in honor of the *archimimus* Eutyches, which lists sixty members of his company, and the other evidence adduced by Grysar, *Der römische Mimus*, 269; Nicoll, *Masks, Mimes and Miracles*, 85–87.

192.   *CIL* I. 1861: *Protogenes Clouli suauei heicei situst mimus, plourima que fecit populo soueis gaudia nuges.* The inscription was found near the town of Amiternum; it seems to be the earliest Latin record of a mimus. See E. Rawson, 'Theatrical Life in Republican Rome and Italy', 111.

193.   *CIL* VI. 10096. See the observations of Beare, *The Roman Stage*, 142: 'Eucharis was a mime actress who had just been reaching renown when she was cut down by death at the age of fourteen. The epitaph tells of the grief of the girl's father at the early death of this little maiden, beloved by her parents and her mistress, and so skilled in her profession that it seemed that the Muses themselves had taught her. She had recently danced at games given by the "nobles," and she is described as the first actress to have appeared [in Rome] on the "Greek stage".' See also the perceptive discussion of this inscription in Wiseman, *Catullus and his World*, 30, with text and translation.

194.   *Anthol. Pal.* 9.587: 'Antiodemus, the nursling of Aphrodite, who from her babyhood slept on purple cloth, the glance of whose melting eyes is softer than sleep, the halcyon of Lysis, the delightful toy of Methe (Intoxication), whose arms flow like water, who alone among women has no bones at all (for she was all cream-cheese), has crossed to Italy, that by her softening charm she may make Rome cease from war and lay down the sword'; trans. by W. R. Paton, *The Greek Anthology*, Vol. 3, LCL (Cambridge, MA: Harvard University Press, 1993).

the 'vagabond' or 'runaway'.[195] In this role, the fool is portrayed as a ne'er-
do-well, most often a slave, who is forced, whether by circumstances or his
own misdeeds, to 'hit the road'.[196] Such a runaway fool is the subject of a
play by Novius entitled 'Maccus the Exile' (*Maccus Exul*).[197] Only a few
lines of the play survive, but they afford a glimpse of the fool in flight. In
one of the fragments, Maccus bids farewell to his door: 'Lintel, whereon I
have often banged my unlucky head, and threshold, where I have many a
time broken all my toes.'[198] Other preserved lines picture the fool passing
through Etruria 'at a full trot' (*tolutim*), 'flogged' and 'beaten', wearing a
'tattered garment'.[199] Juvenal refers to a mime by Catullus which seems to
have been entitled 'The Runaway Buffoon' (*Fugitivus Scurra*): 'Such a one
plays a mime-part, like the runaway buffoon of the witty Catullus.'[200] A
scholiast informs us that 'this is a mime in which a fugitive slave (*servus
fugitivus*) distracts his master'.[201] Seneca mentions a mime depicting the

195. On this type of fool, see Corbett, *The Scurra*, 68; E. Fantham, 'Mime', 158–59; E.
Rawson, 'The Vulgarity of the Roman Mime' 259; L. L. Welborn, 'The Runaway Paul', 152–
59.
196. Clownish, thievish slaves who attempt to flee are already established as stock
characters of Dorian mime: such actors are depicted on Corinthian vases; see G. Löschke,
'Korinthische Vasen mit der Rückführung des Hephaistos', *Mittheilungen des kaiserlichen
deutschen archäologischen Instituts, Athenische Abteilung* 19 (1894) 521; G. Thiele, 'Die
Anfänge der griechischen Komödie,' *Neue Jahrbücher für das klassische Altertum* 5 (1902)
413–16; and they are alluded to by Aristophanes *Vesp.* 56–60 and Athenaios *Deip.* 14.621d-
22b. For discussion of the evidence, see Reich, *Der Mimus*, 497–98; Pickard-Cambridge,
Dithyramb, Tragedy and Comedy, 229; Nicoll, *Masks, Mimes and Miracles*, 21, 25–27.
Odysseus seems to have become a type of the runaway fool in farce and mime: Odysseus is
pictured on a Phlyax vase as a thief in flight, Fig. 41 in Nicoll, *Masks, Mimes and Miracles*, 54;
see also Epicharmus' play entitled Ὀδυσσεὺς Ἀυτόμολος ('Odysseus the Deserter'); for the title
and fragments, see Kaibel, *Comicorum Graecorum Fragmenta*, 108–110. In the *Curculio* (288–
95), Plautus provides a comic sketch of a runaway slave turned philosopher. In a mime which
he wrote and performed before Julius Caesar, the Roman knight Decimus Laberius acted the
part of a Syrian slave, 'whom he represented as flogged by whips and beating a hasty retreat',
according to Macrobius *Sat.* 2.7.4. The scholiast to Juvenal 8.185–88 (p. 147 Wessner) tells us
that the bandit Laureolus, crucified on stage in the mime of that name by Catullus, was a
runaway slave; cited in the appendix to Wiseman, *Catullus and his World*, 258.
197. Fragments in O. Ribbeck, *Scaenicae Romanorum Poesis Fragmenta II, Comicorum
Romanorum Fragmenta* (Hildesheim: Olms, 1962), 254. Maccus was one of the stock
characters of Atellan farce; his name, Greek in origin (μακκοᾶν), means 'to be stupid';
Aristophanes *Eq.* 396 uses μακκοᾷ in the sense 'be stupid'; see also Dieterich, *Pulcinella*, 85–86,
235–36; Nicoll, *Masks, Mimes and Miracles*, 72.
198. Frag. 2 in Ribbeck, *Comicorum Romanorum Fragmenta*, 254.
199. Frag. 1, 3, 4 in Ribbeck, *Comicorum Romanorum Fragmenta*, 254.
200. Juvenal 13.110–11 (describing a bold-faced cheat): *mimum agit ille urbani qualem
fugitivus scurra Catulli*.
201. Scholiast on Juvenal 13.109–11 (p. 250 Wessner): *Talis est enim mimus, ubi servus
fugitivus dominum suum trahit*.

'runaway slaves' of a rich man.[202] Allusions to the figure of the runaway fool abound in the literature of the early Empire,[203] demonstrating how well established was this theatrical type in popular consciousness. Paul evokes the image of this stock character with his reference to his vagabond existence. Like such a fool, Paul is 'driven from pillar to post, and forced to flee'.[204]

'We toil', Paul insists, 'working with our own hands' (4.12).[205] Arduous, physical labor marked the experience of the majority of the poor in the Roman Empire.[206] Even a skilled artisan, such as Lucian's shoemaker Micyllus, had to work hard from sun-up to sun-down to earn his daily bread.[207] Unskilled workers and slaves, like the mill-workers sympathetically described by Apuleius, faced a bitter struggle for survival.[208] The verb that Paul uses here, κοπιᾶν, elsewhere describes the work of fishermen and

202. Seneca *Ep.* 114.6, describing Maecenas as muffled up in scarves like the runaway slaves of mime: *non aliter quam in mimo fugitivi divitis solent.*

203. E.g., Cicero's allusion (*Pro Cael.* 27.65) to the typical mime-plot, with the pursuit and last-minute escape of a foolish character (*fugit aliquis e manibus*); Horace *Sat.* 2.7, a satire on the question, 'Who is the greater fool (*stultior*), the master or the slave?' contains an allusion to the runaway in lines 111–15, esp. 113: *teque ipsum vitas fugitivus et erro*; see also the derision of the *scurra* Sarmentus as a runaway in Horace *Sat.* 1.5.67–69, with the comments of Corbett, *The Scurra*, 68; Seneca *Apoc.* 15: Caligula claims Claudius as a runaway slave and drags him off to spend eternity in the slavish office of secretary for petitions; Petronius *Satyr.* 103, a scene that is adapted from the mime: the heads of Encolpius and Giton are shaved and branded with the usual mark of runaway slaves; see the commentary on the theatrical elements in this episode by C. Panayotakis, *Theatrum Arbitri*, 148–49; Propertius 2.29, where the poet is seized as a runaway and dragged before his mistress for punishment; Suetonius' account of the flight of Nero in *Nero* 46.3–48.4 abounds in features that belong to the portrait of the fool as a vagabond; see comments of S. Bartsch, *Actors in the Audience: Theatricality and Doublespeak from Nero to Julian* (Cambridge, MA: Harvard University Press, 1994) 56–62; Lucian uses the figure of the runaway slave to attack Cynic philosophers in his comic dialogue *Fugitivi*, esp. 27, 30, 33, with the comments of R. Branham, *Unruly Eloquence*, 86–89.

204. Reflecting the paraphrase of ἀστατοῦμεν by Theophylactus: ἐλαυνόμεθα, φεύγομεν, cited in Heinrici, *Der erste Brief*, 157.

205. Cf. Paul's other references to his labor in 1 Thess. 2.9; 1 Cor. 9.6; 2 Cor. 11.27.

206. See, in general, M. Maxey, *Occupations of the Lower Classes in Roman Society* (Chicago: University of Chicago Press, 1938); S. Treggiari, 'Urban Labour in Rome: *Merecenarii* and *Tabernarii*' in *Non-Slave Labour in the Graeco-Roman World*, ed. P. Garnsey (Cambridge: Cambridge Philological Society, 1980) 48–64; Veyne, *A History of Private Life I*, 117–37.

207. Lucian *Gallus* 1; similarly, *Cataplus* 15, 20. The smith Philinus in Lucian's *Dial. Meretr.* 6.293 leaves no savings behind after his death, so that his widow is forced to sell their daughter into prostitution. See also Lucian's description of the trades of cobblers, builders, fullers, and carders as 'laborious and barely able to supply them with just enough' in *Fugitivi* 12–13. Dio Chrysostom *Or.* 7.103, 125 connects poverty and manual labor. The poverty of the artisan is emphasized by Hock, *The Social Context of Paul's Ministry*, 34–37.

208. Apuleius *Met.* 9.12 describes the slaves toiling in a flour mill, dressed in rags, their half-naked bodies scarred from beatings, their foreheads branded, their heads half-shaved,

farmers.[209] The adjective by which Paul qualifies his labor, ἰδίαι, is emphatic as well as possessive: 'working with our *own* hands'.[210] With his reference to his manual labor, Paul associates himself with the hard-working crowd of urban plebs and rural peasants, some slave, and some free.[211]

The lives of the working poor were the subject matter of the mime.[212] So much is clear from the surviving titles of plays, many of which are called after low-class trades and occupations.[213] Sophron's mimes were divided into 'mimes of men' (ἀνδρεῖοι) and 'mimes of women' (γυναικεῖοι), with titles such as 'The Tunnyfisher' (Θυννοθήρας) and 'The Seamstresses' ('Ακέστριαι).[214] The mimes of Herodas portray low-life professions from the Hellenistic city: a 'Brothel-keeper' (Πορνοβοσκός) prosecutes a sea-captain for assaulting one of his girls; a 'Schoolmaster' (Διδάσκαλος) thrashes a boy for his pranks.[215] A number of Laberius' mimes have titles which indicate central characters belonging to lower class professions, e.g., 'The Fuller' (*Fullo*), 'The Soothsayer' (*Augur*), 'The Fisherman' (*Piscator*), 'The Courtesan' (*Hetaera*), 'The Salt-Miner' (*Salinator*), 'The Rope-Dealer' (*Restio*).[216] A guest at Trimalchio's banquet in Petronius' *Satyricon* boasts of a clever slave who has been trained as a mime and who gives imitations of a mule-driver, a cobbler, a cook, and a baker; as his master proudly exclaims, 'He is a Jack of All Trades!'[217] In his description of mimic characters, Choricius lists: 'household slaves, inn-keepers, sausage-sellers, cooks, the hosts and their guests, notaries.'[218]

A mimic fool in the role of a common laborer is depicted by a terracotta statuette from Tarsus (Fig. 11) dated to the first half of the first century

---

their feet chained, their complexions sallow, all of them covered in a fine ash of flour. On the large numbers of unskilled workers in Greco-Roman cities and the dangerous conditions of their life and work, see Maxey, *Occupations of the Lower Classes*, 44;

209. Luke 5.5; 2 Tim. 2.6; Bauer, *Greek-English Lexicon*, 558 *s.v.* κοπιάω 2.

210. Bauer, *Greek-English Lexicon*, 446 *s.v.* ἴδιος 2; Weiss, *Der erste Korintherbrief*, 112: 'das ἰδίαις ist hier nicht bloss als Possessivum zu verstehen, sondern emphatisch – wir müssen *selber* arbeiten'.

211. Fitzgerald, *Cracks in an Earthen Vessel*, 135; Meggitt, *Paul, Poverty and Survival*, 75–76.

212. See, in general, Grysar, *Der römische Mimus*, 250; Reich, *Der Mimus*, 214; Rawson, 'The Vulgarity of the Mime', 259.

213. E. Wölfflin, 'Atellanen und Mimentitel', *Rheinisches Museum* 43 (1888) 308–309.

214. G. Kaibel, *Comicorum Graecorum Fragmenta* I/1 152–81.

215. O. Crusius, *Untersuchungen zu den Mimiamben des Herondas* 22; Cunningham, *Herodas. Mimes*, 203–206.

216. Titles and fragments in *Mimorum Romanorum Fragmenta I*, ed. M. Bonaria, 9–103.

217. Petronius *Satyr.* 68.6–7; see the comments of Panayotakis, *Theatrum Arbitri*, 100–102.

218. Choricius *Apol. Mim.* 110: οἰκέτας, καπήλους, ἀλλαντοπώλας, ὀψοποιούς, ἑστιάτοπα, συμβόλαια γράφοντας.

Figure 11. **Terracotta statuette of a mimic fool from Tarsus, first century A.D. Metropolitan Museum of Art, New York.**

A.D.[219] 'The lean body speaks of privation and physical misery. The face with its lined and sunken cheeks, its thick-lipped open mouth and heavy nose and its pervasive air of stupidity, corruption, and sordid cunning, might at first glance be taken for nothing more than a realistic representation of some low fellow at home among the rabble which frequented the Tarsus water front. The loin-cloth, garb of the common laborer, and the attitude which suggests that of a rower, would well accord with this interpretation. But there are three features which demand a different classification: they are the large phallus, the startling asymmetry of the eyes, designed as a conventional comic effect, and the pointed cap, identified with the clown or buffoon as early as the days of the Old Comedy. Thus our terracotta, by its facial peculiarities and by its costume, is identified with those public performers who wore no masks, ... one and all mimes.'[220] One of the principal terms for the fool in the mime, ταλαίπωρος, emphasizes his endurance of toil and labor.[221] It is with such a character that Paul identifies himself, when he describes his labor with his own hands.

In consequence of the way Paul and his colleagues are perceived, they are 'reviled..., harassed, ... slandered' (λοιδορούμενοι..., διωκόμενοι...,

219.   H. Goldman, 'Two Terracotta Figurines from Tarsus', *AJA* 47 (1943) 22–34.

220.   Ibid., 22–24.

221.   *POxy* 413 ('Charition') line 207, the fool is addressed as ταλαίπωρε. See also *POxy* 413 ('Adulteress') line 184: οὐαί σοι, ταλαίπωρε.

δυσφημούμενοι) (1 Cor. 4.12–13). Each of these terms individually has a history of usage related to the theater,[222] and together describe a slap-stick scene from the mime. The theater was infamous as a place of 'abuse' (λοιδορία),[223] and one who visited the theater could expect to hear persons 'reviled and reviling'.[224] Dio Chrysostom describes the Athenians as 'frequenting the theatre for the express purpose of hearing themselves abused (συνιόντες εἰς τὸ θέατρον ὡς λοιδορηθησόμενοι), and having established a contest with a prize for the most proficient in that sort of thing'.[225] In the theater, the fool was the special object of abuse. Plutarch explains that 'fools make terms of abuse (λοιδόρημα) out of "pauper" (πτωχός), "bald" (φαλακρός) and "short" (μικρός)'.[226] Plutarch affords a glimpse of a typical mime scene: bald-headed buffoons exchanging insults. Indeed, 'theatrical' behavior, even when exhibited outside the play-house, seems to have consisted largely in an exchange of verbal abuse (λοιδορία).[227] Philo recounts how the Alexandrian mob, 'a multitude well practiced in idle talk, who devote their leisure to slandering and evil speaking', was permitted by the Roman governor of Egypt to vilify the Jewish king Agrippa, 'through revilings' (διὰ τῶν λοιδοριῶν): 'Thus started on their course they spent their days in the gymnasium jeering (χλευάζοντες) at the king and bringing out a succession of gibes (σκώμματα) against him. In fact they took the authors of mimes and farces for their instructors and thereby showed their natural ability in things of shame.'[228]

222. Fitzgerald (*Cracks in an Earthen Vessel*, 142) already calls attention to the theatrical context, though the terms may also be used to describe others who are perceived as lacking in honor, e.g. 'the poor,' Plutarch *Mor*. 607A.

223. Dio Chrysostom *Or*. 32.5, castigating the people of Alexandria for their preoccupation with the theater, and the buffoonery and scurrility of the mimes: 'That indeed is the nature of what you regularly see, and you are devoted to interests from which it is impossible to gain intelligence or prudence or a proper disposition or reverence toward the gods, but only stupid contention, unbridled ambition, vain grief, senseless joy, and raillery (λοιδορία) and extravagance.'

224. E.g., Dio Chrysostom *Or*. 32.89, where Dio describes the behavior of the spectators in the theater, 'using abominable language and often reviling (λοιδοροῦντες)'. See also Tatian *Or*. 25.5.

225. Dio Chrysostom *Or*. 33.9.

226. Plutarch *Mor*. 607A.

227. E.g., Demosthenes 10.75: in the assembly, the Athenians 'turn the subject into ridicule and raillery' (τὸ πρᾶγμ' εἰς γέλωτα καὶ λοιδορίαν ἐμβαλόντες); Posidonius 87 frag. 108, ed. Jacoby: ἐξεθεάτριζον ὀνειδίζοντες. According to Diodorus Siculus (34/35.2.46), Eunus, the leader of a slave revolt in Sicily, taunted the Romans by 'staging a production of mimes, in which the slaves acted out (ἐξεθεάτριζον) scenes of revolt from their individual masters, heaping abuse (ὀνειδίζοντες) on their arrogance and the insubordinate insolence that led to their destruction.' See also Hebrews 10.33, ὀνειδισμοῖς τε καὶ θλίψεσιν θεατριζόμενοι.

228. Philo *In Flacc*. 33–34.

The middle term in the series by which Paul describes his mistreatment, διωκόμενοι, is conventionally translated 'persecuted'.[229] But in the context of the other expressions, and the images they evoke, διωκόμενοι should probably be rendered 'harassed' or 'driven away'.[230] Altercations that begin with verbal abuse predictably degenerate into physical violence.[231] The sequence is especially prominent in stories that form the subject-matter of comedy and mime.[232] Such is the case in the twice-told tale of the Athenian messenger Chlidon.[233] Ordered to ride at full speed to the Attic border, Chlidon hastened home, brought out his horse, and asked for the bridle. His wife, however, had lent it to a neighbor, and was embarrassed to admit that she could not give it to him. So she spent a long time in the storeroom, rummaging through the contents as if looking for it. When she had enough of making a 'fool' of her husband, she at last admitted lending it to a neighbor the evening before. 'Words of abuse (λοιδορίαι) were followed by insults (δυσφημίαι).'[234] Finally, Chlidon was so overcome by anger that he beat her (τέλος δὲ μέχρι πληγῶν προαχθεὶς ὑπὸ ὀργῆς).[235] In this little comic episode, we find all the elements of Paul's account of his mistreatment, including the term 'slander' (δυσφημία), also connected with 'reviling' (λοιδορία) in one of Menander's comedies.[236] Taken together, the terms used by Paul describe the boisterous conclusion of a mime, a scene familiar from allusions in literature: a fool is derided; there are blows, and an attempt to flee, with further insults hurled at the fool's retreating back.[237]

As the climax of the account, Paul echoes the judgment of the world upon the clownish apostles: 'We have become like the refuse (περικαθάρματα) of the world, the scum (περίψημα) of all things, to this very day' (1 Cor.

---

229. Thus the KJV and the NRSV and in most commentaries, e.g., Conzelmann, *1 Corinthians*, 85; Collins, *First Corinthians*, 190.

230. Bauer, *Greek-English Lexicon*, 254 *s.v.* διώκω 2,3; Liddell-Scott-Jones, *Greek-English Lexicon*, 440 *s.v.* διώκω. This is not to deny that Paul elsewhere uses the term in the sense of 'persecuted,' e.g. 2 Cor. 4.9; Gal. 5.11.

231. Polybius (5.15.4) recounts how the guests at Philip's victory banquet, emboldened by drink and passion, went looking for their enemy, Aratus, after the banquet had broken up, and meeting him as he was on his way home, 'first of all abused him (ἐλοιδόρουν), and then began to pelt him with stones'.

232. Petronius *Satyr.* 74; Arnobius *Adv. nat.* 7.33; Nicoll, *Masks, Mimes and Miracles*, 88–89.

233. Plutarch *Pel.* 8.5; *Mor.* 587F.

234. Plutarch *Pel.* 8.5; cf. *Mor.* 587F: καὶ κακῶς αὐτὴν λέγοντος τρέπεται πρὸς δυσφημίας.

235. Plutarch *Mor.* 588A.

236. Menander 715, 716 (Kock): 'He who rails at his father with reviling words (ὁ λοιδορῶν τὸν πατέρα δυσφήμῳ λόγῳ) rehearses blasphemy against divinity.'

237. E.g., Cicero *Pro Cael.* 27.65; Arnobius *Adv. nat.* 7.33 (derision, slapping, running, bruising and maiming, shouting out noisily); Cyprian *De Spect.* 8–9.

4.13). These two, practically synonymous terms[238] were 'the worst terms of abuse in the Greek language'.[239] Etymologically, both terms describe 'that which is removed as a result of cleansing, dirt, off-scouring'.[240] How these terms came to have such an opprobrious sense is a long, sad story with its roots in Greek religion.[241] The terms κάθαρμα and περίψημα were applied to those unfortunate men in ancient times who were put to death 'for the purification of the city'.[242] Those who were chosen to suffer this fate were, for the most part, condemned criminals, paupers, and the deformed, that is, persons for whom life was assumed to be a burden.[243] In the course of time, the terms κάθαρμα and περίψημα were transferred to all those whom society held in contempt.[244] By the time of Paul, the use of these terms as vulgar epithets, in the sense of 'refuse' or 'scum', was firmly established,[245] as abundant parallels demonstrate.[246]

In popular usage, the terms κάθαρμα and περίψημα express the judgment of the rich upon the poor,[247] and others, such as parasites and vagabonds,[248] who lived at the margins of society. Thus, according to Demosthenes, the arrogant Meidias claimed to be the only rich man, and

238.   Conzelmann, *1 Corinthians*, 90 n. 49; Lindemann, *Der erste Korintherbrief*, 110; Collins, *First Corinthians*, 191.

239.   M. P. Nilsson, *A History of Greek Religion* (New York: Norton & Co., 1968) 87.

240.   Bauer, *Greek-English Lexicon*, 801 *s.v.* περικάθαρμα; 808 *s.v.* περίψημα.

241.   See esp. H. Usener, *Kleine Schriften IV* (Leipzig: Teubner, 1912) 257–58.

242.   E. Rohde, *Psyche* (New York: Harcourt, Brace, 1925) 296. At the festival of the Thargelia, or on occasions of general affliction, such as famine or plague, in Ionian cities, and even in Athens, ritual victims were carried around the town and country in order to absorb all the impurity, and then, like a rag with which one wipes a dirty pot, they were 'thrown away', that is, they were destroyed entirely, burned up or cast into the sea, so that the impurity might be altogether removed along with them.

243.   G. Stählin, 'περίψημα', *TDNT* 6 (1968) 86.

244.   Nilsson, *History of Greek Religion*, 87; Stählin, 'περίψημα', 87.

245.   It is unlikely that the cultic sense of the terms as 'expiatory sacrifice' was intended by Paul; thus, rightly, Heinrici, *Der erste Brief*, 158–59; Weiss, *Der erste Korintherbrief*, 114: 'Aus den so reichlich zur Verfügung stehenden Parallelstellen bekommt man nun doch den Eindruck, dass die kultische Bedeutung des Worts so gut wie garnicht mehr empfunden wird; es scheint lediglich zu einem verächtlichen Schimpfwort geworden zu sein: Armseliger, Elender, Nichtswürdiger'; similarly, Conzelmann, *1 Corinthians*, 90 n. 49.

246.   See the collection of Greek and Latin texts in J. J. Wettstein, *Novum Testamentum Graecum* (1751; repr. Graz, Oesterreich: Akademische Druck-und Verlagsanstalt, 1962) 2. 114–15; see also H. D. Betz, *Lukian von Samosata und das Neue Testament*, TU 76 (Berlin: Akademie-Verlag, 1961) 67 n. 7. See esp. *Vit. Aesop.* 14.

247.   Rightly, Weiss, *Der erste Korintherbrief*, 114: 'Und zwar bezieht es sich meist auf die niedrige, verächtliche, soziale, finanzielle oder Bildungsstufe solcher Menschen'; citing Josephus *B. J.* 4.241; Demosthenes *Or.* 21.198; Lucian *Hermot.* 81; Philo *Virt.* 174; Pollux 3.66; 5.163.

248.   On parasites as 'scum,' see Lucian *Pisc.* 34; *De Merc. Cond.* 24; on vagabonds, Philo *Vit. Mos.* 1.30; Lucian *Paras.* 42.

treated all others as if they were 'beggars' (πτωχοί), 'scum of the earth' (καθάρματα), and 'mere nobodies' (οὐδέν).[249] Philo describes the man who has begun to enjoy some prosperity, and boasts himself greater than humbler men, 'and miscalls them offscourings (καθάρματα) and nuisances and cumberers of the earth and suchlike names'.[250] Elsewhere, Philo elaborates the portrait of the type: 'He considers himself superior to all in riches, ... while everyone else he regards as poor, disesteemed, dishonored, foolish, unjust, ignorant, scum (καθάρματα), nothings.'[251]

Through constant association with the poor and destitute, these terms acquired a fundamentally opprobrious sense, and came to be used as general terms of abuse.[252] This is particularly true of the simplex form κάθαρμα ... 'vile wretch'.[253] For example, in Lucian's satirical account of a debate between philosophers, Timocles lashes out at Damis, who has bested him in argument: 'Are you mocking me, you ghoul, you miscreant (μιαρέ), you abomination, you gallows-bird (μαστιγία), you scum of the earth (κάθαρμα)?'[254] Here, as in 1 Cor. 4.13, the term κάθαρμα climaxes a series of vulgar epithets.[255]

In a number of passages in which these epithets are found, the verb λοιδορεῖν ('to revile') also appears,[256] as in 1 Cor. 4.12. And again, predictably, verbal abuse devolves into physical violence – hitting, spitting, etc. – in these passages,[257] as it does in 1 Cor. 4.12 (διωκόμενοι). More significant are the numerous instances in which the epithet 'scum' is found in connection with derisive laughter.[258] Lucian sketches the denouement of the contest between the philosophers, mentioned above, which culminates in the abusive term κάθαρμα: 'One is going away laughing (γελῶν), and the other is following him up with abuse (λοιδορούμενος), because he can't

249. Demosthenes *Or.* 21.185, 198; cf. Fitzgerald, *Cracks in an Earthen Vessel*, 142 n.86.

250. Philo *Vit. Mos.* 1.30.

251. Philo *Virt.* 174.

252. Epictetus *Diss.* 3.22.78: Priam's fifty sons are περικαθάρματα. Diogenes Laertius 6.32: One day Diogenes shouted out for men, and when people collected, hit out at them with his stick, saying, 'It was men I called for, not scoundrels (καθάρματα).' See also Lucian *Pisc.* 34; *POxy* 2190, line 10.

253. Dio Chrysostom *Or.* 7.30; Lucian *Symp.* 40; *Demonax* 30; *De Merc. Cond.* 24; *Charon* 10; Philostratus *Vit. Soph.* 1.12; Julian *Or.* 6.197c; cf. Weiss, *Der erste Korintherbrief*, 114.

254. Lucian *Jup. Trag.* 52.

255. Other examples of κάθαρμα as the climax of a series of epithets: Demosthenes *Or.* 21.185; Philo *Virt.* 174; Dio Chrysostom *Or.* 32.50.

256. E.g., Dio Chrysostom *Or.* 7.30; Lucian *Paras.* 42; *Symp.* 40; *Jup. Trag.* 53.

257. Petronius *Satyr.* 74; Lucian *Pisc.* 34; *Symp.* 16; Diogenes Laertius 6.32; Julian *Or.* 6.197c; Pollux 3.66.

258. Dio Chrysostom *Or.* 7.29–30; Lucian *Pisc.* 34; *Hermot.* 81; *Symp.* 16, 40; *Demonax* 30; *Catapl.* 16; Julian *Or.* 6.197c.

stand the mockery; it looks as if he would hit him on the head with the brickbat.'[259] This passage and others reveal the nexus of Paul's vocabulary in 1 Cor. 4.12–13: reviling, blows, and vulgar epithets characterize the treatment of low, farcical types in literature as in life, in accordance with the Greco-Roman concept of the laughable.[260]

In view of all the connections which word-study has brought to light, it is no longer surprising to discover that several of the texts in which the epithets appear are influenced by the mime. This is demonstrably the case in the *Cena Trimalchionis* of Petronius,[261] where Fortunata's jealousy of her husband's affection towards a slave leads her to revile him as 'scum' (*pergamentum ...* κάθαρμα) and 'a dog' (*canis*), which in turn gives rise to a physical assault, followed by the cruelest slander.[262] Several passages in Lucian which contain the epithet κάθαρμα are set in the context of *symposia*. The drinking-party was a primary context for the hurling of verbal excrement,[263] and naturally so, since drunkenness inflames prejudices and reduces inhibitions. We know from a report by Cicero that a burlesque symposium of philosophers and poets was a typical mime theme.[264] In Lucian's *Symposium*, a group of philosophers debate the proposal that they should have their wives in common, so as to be devoid of jealousy. When the idea is rejected with laughter as inappropriate, the proponent lashes out: ' "What, do you dare open your mouth, you scum of the earth (κάθαρμα)?" said Ion, and Dionysodorus began to give him back his abuse (ἀντελοιδορεῖτο) in due form.'[265] In the *Piscator*, Lucian portrays a group of quack-philosophers at a banquet; they are servile, thievish, and quarrelsome; they let themselves in for ridicule by their parasitic behavior, stuffing themselves shamelessly. Lucian summarizes the reaction of his fellow-symposiasts, as if he were reporting the response of spectators at the mime: 'All those present who are not of the profession laugh at them, naturally, and spit philosophy to scorn for breeding such scum (καθάρματα).'[266]

---

259. Lucian *Jup. Trag.* 53.
260. Garland, *The Eye of the Beholder*, 73–86.
261. Petronius *Satyr.* 74. cf. Panayotakis, *Theatrum Arbitri*, 107.
262. Petronius *Satyr.* 74. See the comments of Panayotakis, *Theatrum Arbitri*, 107: 'Note the dramatic and exaggerated manner in which everything is performed: Fortunata's hands tremble, she shouts, covers her face, quivers all over her body, cries and groans. Fortunata is over-acting. It is interesting to discover from her husband's tirade against her that Fortunata was a flute-girl, an occupation which shows that in her past she was connected with the stage.'
263. See the section on 'symposiastic jokes in poor taste' in Garland, *The Eye of the Beholder*, 83–86.
264. Cicero (*Pro Gall.* frag. 2) reports having witnessed a mime presenting a symposium of poets and philosophers that anachronistically included at a single gathering Euripides, Socrates, Menander, and Epicurus.
265. Lucian *Symp.* 40.
266. Lucian *Pisc.* 34.

As might be expected, the surviving fragments of the mime are full of vulgar epithets, with the fool as the special object of abuse. In the adultery mime from Oxyrhynchus, the slaves and parasites are repeatedly called 'miscreant' (μιαρέ) and 'gallows-bird' (μαστιγία),[267] vulgar synonyms of κάθαρμα. The fool in the Warsaw papyrus is described as 'cursed' (κατάρατε).[268] The fact that κάθαρμα is not found in the surviving fragments of the mime can only be an accident. For the term appears in Dio's address to the Alexandrians, in which he castigates his hearers for their infatuation with the theater. Picking up the abusive language of the actors, Dio applies the epithets to members of the audience in a climax of vulgarity, calling them 'poor wretches' (ταλαίπωροί), 'slaves' (ἀνδραπόδοι), 'luckless creatures' (κακοδαίμονες), and 'low-born scum' (κάθαρμα ἀγεννής).[269] Indeed, the Latin name for the fool of private dinner parties, *scurra*, is best defined by the Greek σκῶρ and σκωρία in the sense of 'refuse', 'scum', 'off-scouring', as the glossaries indicate.[270] Like these stupid fools, Paul and his apostolic fellows are 'pure trash'.

When one looks back over this remarkable paragraph, it is clear what care Paul has taken with its composition.[271] Each term, motif, and aspect of character contributes something to the theatrical metaphor. But content is not the only level at which the theatrical metaphor operates. Theatrical conventions also determine aspects of the style and structure of the passage.[272]

The striking, rhetorical contrast that Paul establishes between the wealthy, sophisticated Corinthians and the poor, moronic apostles is an instance of the theatrical metaphor at the structural level.[273] The contrast is

---

267. *POxy* 413 ('Adulteress') lines 5, 110, 137, 154, 155.

268. *PVars* 2, line 4.

269. Dio Chrysostom *Or.* 32.49–50.

270. See the explanation of Corbett, *The Scurra*, 2: 'The spelling *scur* suggests a connection with σκῶρ and σκωρία in the sense of "refuse", "trash", "ordure". The Latin derivative *scoria* (*scuria*) is glossed as *sordes metallorum* and *quod de ferro cadit* (*CGLV*. 243, 21 and 22) and cf. *stercus ferri* "dross", "slag", while the cognate *scorio* is glossed as *stultus fatuus* (ibid. 610, 44) and *scories* as *stulti stolidi fatui* (ibid. 614, 54), both obvious echoes of Plautus *Bacch.* 1088–89: *stulti, stolidi, fatui, fungi, bardi, blenni, buccones, solus ego omnis longe antideo stultitia et moribus indoctis* – "I outstrip in stupidity and ignorant behavior all these stupid dullard fools, these slow-witted blockhead babblers". It would seem then from these examples that *scurra* has a meaning similar to *nugator* "trifler", "jester" and to *nugae* itself, which has a similar basic meaning of "trash", "scouring", etc., but in its normal figurative sense ... *ineptiae* (cf. *nugas agere*) and even *inepti homines* (cf. Cicero *Ad Att.* 6.3.5, *amicos habet meras nugas* – "he has friends who are pure trash").'

271. On the composition and structure of 1 Cor. 4.8–13, see J. Weiss, 'Beiträge zur Paulinischen Rhetorik', 209–10; Fitzgerald, *Cracks in an Earthen Vessel*, 129–32.

272. For the three levels (content, structure, style) of a theatrical 'reading' of a text, see Panayotakis, *Theatrum Arbitri*, ix.

273. On the rhetorical figure of *synkrisis* and the structure of the paragraph 1 Cor. 4.8–13, see Fitzgerald, *Cracks in an Earthen Vessel*, 129–32.

most explicit in 1 Cor. 4.10 ('We are fools, but you are wise. We are weak, but you are strong. You are held in honor, but we in disrepute.'), but in fact runs throughout the paragraph (4.8–13).[274] Thus the Corinthians are described as satiated, rich, royal (4.8),[275] while the apostles are hungry, naked, homeless, etc. (4.11–13). The humor of the mime depended upon the dramatization of these contrasts, paradoxically embodied in the relationship between the archmime and the mimic fool. The archmime was portrayed as wealthy (the master or mistress of a household),[276] physically sound (sometimes beautiful, like the lady Charition),[277] intelligent,[278] and noble; the fool, by contrast, was a slave or parasite, physically grotesque (often deformed), stupid and sordid. The mime elicited laughter by exploiting this contrast. For example, when the heroine of the *Charition* mime rejects with horror the fool's sacrilegious plan to steal some of the temple offerings, the fool agrees: 'You mustn't touch them – I will!'[279] The contrast between the behavior of the upper class noble and that of the lower class buffoon was repeatedly staged in the mime and was the principal cause of mirth.[280] In this highly stylized paragraph of the letter, Paul employs every rhetorical artifice to point precisely this contrast: ironic antitheses (4.10), an absence of copulas (4.10) and connectives (4.12b-13a), strong oxymora (4.12b-13a), and two uses of chiasmus (4.10–13).[281]

At the level of style, the theatrical metaphor manifests itself, first of all, in the use of hyperbole. The Corinthians are not merely rich, they have

274.   Rightly, Fitzgerald, *Cracks in an Earthen Vessel*, 132.

275.   For satiety (κόρος) as a characteristic of the rich, in contrast to the hungry, abject poor, see esp. Philo *In Flacc.* 77; Dio Chrysostom *Or.* 7.17; Lucian *De Merc. Cond.* 8. For the connection of satiety with wealth and kingship, see Luke 6.24–25; Dio Chrysostom *Or.* 1.67; 30.19. See the other texts cited in connection with 1 Cor. 4.8 in Marshall, *Enmity in Corinth*, 183–84, 188–89; Fitzgerald, *Cracks in an Earthen Vessel*, 133–35.

276.   In both of the Oxyrhynchus mimes, 'Charition' and 'Adulteress,' the *archimima* is a wealthy noblewoman; in the former, the lady Charition is modeled on Euripides' Iphigenia; see the comments of Wiemken, *Der griechische Mimus*, 67, 102. Similarly, the heroine of the mime-inspired tale in Apuleius *Met.* 10. 2–12; cf. Wiemken, *Der griechische Mimus*, 140–45.

277.   The lady Charition is reminiscent of the beautiful heroine of the first-century romance *Chaereas and Callirhoe*; cf. Nicoll, *Masks, Mimes and Miracles*, 115–16.

278.   See the description of the heroine of the 'Adulteress' by Page, *Select Papyri III*, 353: 'This *archimima* has indeed an excellent part to play, varied and vivid , – first furious and vindictive, then repentant and sentimental; first exultant, then subtly cunning and sinister.'

279.   *POxy* 413, lines 44–49, 219–24. The contrast between the character and behavior of the archmime and the fool runs through the entire play, e.g. lines 190–91, in response to the heroine's pious exclamation, 'Great are the gods!' the fool retorts, 'What gods, you fool?' and makes a vulgar noise.

280.   Winkler, *Auctor and Actor*, 290; Beacham, *The Roman Theatre*, 132.

281.   Weiss, 'Beiträge zur Paulinischen Rhetorik', 209–10; Fitzgerald, *Cracks in an Earthen Vessel*, 129–32.

'become kings' (4.8);[282] the apostles are not simply poor,[283] they are 'the scum of the earth' (4.13). This is the graphic, exaggerated style of the mime. For example, the fool in the *Charition* mime refers to the barbarian huntresses as 'daughters of little swine'; he calls the ship's captain a 'catastrophe', and suggests that he be thrown overboard 'to kiss the ship's arse'.[284] Similarly, the fool in the 'Adulteress' calls his master 'miserable, hapless, troublesome, unlovable', in the mock dirge that he sings over his body.[285] To the mimic style also belongs the series of exclamations with which Paul introduces the paragraph in 4.8 ('Already you are satiated! Already you have become rich!' etc).[286] Critics of the mime mention its noisy exclamations. Arnobius describes mime actors 'vociferating uselessly, … shouting out noisily…, bursting into exclamation.'[287] Examples of exclamations are found on virtually every page of surviving mime text.[288]

Finally, Paul's account of the response of the apostles to mistreatment in 4.12b-13a ('When reviled, we bless; when harassed, we put up with it; when slandered, we speak kindly') poignantly evokes the compliant, servile demeanor of the fool in his accustomed role as a parasite. In Terence's *Eunuchus*, Gnatho explains to a man whom he has just met in the street and who, like himself, has been reduced to beggary, what it takes to be a successful parasite: it is not enough to be a 'funny-man' (*ridiculus*); one must also be a flatterer.[289] Gnatho describes his relation to his patrons: 'Whatever they say I approve. If someone says No, I say No; he says Yes, I

282. The hyperbolic trope seems to be overlooked by commentators who explain ἐβασιλεύσατε by reference to the Stoic paradox of the wise man as the true king; cf., for example, E. L. Hicks, 'St. Paul and Hellenism,' *Studia Biblica et Ecclesiastica* 4 (1896) 1–14; H. Braun, 'Exegetische Randglossen zum I. Korintherbrief,' *Gesammelte Studien zum Neuen Testament und seiner Umwelt* (Tübingen: Mohr, 1962) 182–86; Fitzgerald, *Cracks in an Earthen Vessel*, 135–36.

283. It is interesting that Paul does not use the general terms πενία, πένης, πεῖνα, nor even πτωχός, in this paragraph, but the graphic and vivid terms analyzed above, with all of their connections to the mime.

284. *POxy* 413 ('Charition') lines 38, 102–103.

285. *POxy* 413 ('Adulteress') lines 184–85.

286. Fitzgerald, *Cracks in an Earthen Vessel*, 129.

287. Arnobius *Adv. nat.* 7.33; cf. Tatian *Or.* 25.5; Cyprian *De Spect.* 8–9.

288. For example, Page, *Select Papyri III*, 339–49, 350–61, punctuates the *Charition* mime with 36 exclamations, the 'Adulteress,' with 22 exclamations. Working with more complete texts, Wiemken, *Der griechische Mimus*, 50–59, 82–89, punctuates *Charition* with 51 exclamations and the 'Adulteress' with 31. It should be borne in mind that these texts are very fragmentary.

289. Terence *Eun.* 232–45; cf. Corbett, *The Scurra*, 19. For the existence of this character in the mimus, see Seneca *Nat. Quaest.* 4A Praef.12.

say Yes. In a word, I have trained myself to agree to everything.'[290] Similarly, Horace warns a youthful acquaintance against becoming a client by portraying his future as that of a fool in the mime: he will be like 'a man over-prone to servility, a jester of the basest sort, who so trembles at the rich man's nod, so echoes his voice and picks up his words as they fall, that you might think ... a mime-player was acting the second part'.[291] One who accepted such a role in life must not only learn to answer agreeably, but must also be prepared to endure abuse. Juvenal tells a would-be client that he will have to put up with being slapped and whipped, alluding to the treatment of the fool in the mime.[292] Paul makes it clear that he and his fellow apostles are prepared to endure such mistreatment, not to receive a hand-out, but as emissaries of the crucified Christ.[293] Despite the difference in motivation, the style of Paul's account of his response to mistreatment operates entirely within the logic of the theatrical metaphor which dominates the paragraph.

1 Cor. 4.14–21

Nor is the theatrical metaphor exhausted at the end of the paragraph. Allusions to the mime echo in the following section (4.14–21), where Paul portrays himself as an anxious father, the Corinthians as unruly children, and other apostles and ministers of the gospel as guardians (παιδαγωγοί).[294] Indeed, a proper understanding of Paul's ironic purpose in this paragraph depends upon recognition of the mime-scene to which he is making reference. Cicero gives the title of the play as 'The Guardian' (*Tutor*), and describes it as 'an ancient and exceedingly ridiculous mime'.[295] The plot, in some form, goes back to Sophron,[296] and was still popular in Paul's day, as one can see from the allusions which enliven the pages of Paul's younger contemporary Persius.[297] A father, distressed at his son's lack of progress, confronts the pedagogue and insists upon discipline; as the punishment is about to be administered, the truant escapes with the help of a clever and

---

290. Terence *Eun.* 250–53; see the comments of Corbett, *The Scurra*, 19–21.
291. Horace *Epist.* 1.18.10–14; cf. Nicoll, *Masks, Mimes and Miracles*, 87; Johnson, *Horace and the Dialectic of Freedom*, 88–90, 96–100.
292. Juvenal 5.170–73; cf. Highet, *Juvenal the Satirist*, 262–63.
293. On this point, see M. Ebner, *Leidenslisten und Apostelbrief. Untersuchungen zu Form, Motivik und Funktion der Peristasenkataloge bei Paulus* (Würzburg: Echter, 1991) 77–89.
294. For general background, see N. H. Young, '*Paidagogos*: The Social Setting of a Pauline Metaphor', *NovT* 29 (1987) 150–76.
295. Cicero *De Orat.* 2.259; cf. R. Fantham, 'Mime: The Missing Link in Roman Literary History,' *Classical World* 82.3 (1989) 156.
296. O. Crusius, *Untersuchungen zu den Mimiamben des Herondas*, 53.
297. Persius *Sat.* 3.44–51. See also Petronius *Satyr.* 46.

sympathetic slave.[298] Scenes from this mime are depicted on a wall-painting at Herculaneum and a well known relief panel now in the Naples Museum. In the former, a slave throws the boy over his shoulders, so that the tutor can inflict a beating upon the boy's naked backside.[299] In the latter, an enraged father emerges from the door of his house, bearing a staff with which he intends to beat his son, who comes home drunk, swinging in his hand the festive fillet worn at banquets. The pedagogue attempts to restrain the father, holding his right arm, while another slave supports the young master, urging him to make his escape (Fig. 12).[300]

The most original adaptation of the theme is found in the third mime-poem of Herodas entitled Διδάσκαλος ('Schoolmaster').[301] In this short, clever piece, a mother brings her delinquent son to the schoolmaster for punishment. She narrates the failure of his father's attempt to teach the boy to spell and to recite speeches.[302] She complains that the boy spends all his time in gambling, and that his dissolute ways have pillaged the house.[303] The lament persuades the schoolmaster that a beating is required, and he proceeds to inflict it, with the help of the under-teachers.[304] When the mother urges that the lash be laid on more heavily, however, the boy succeeds in making his escape, evidently with the help of one of the slaves.[305] Discomfited, the mother resolves angrily to go home and tell the old man what has happened, and to come back with fetters, so that the boy's feet may be tied together.[306]

It is to this well known mime that Paul makes reference in this crucial paragraph of the letter,[307] the allusion clearer and more exact than in the

---

298. For this reconstruction of the plot, found in New Comedy as well as mime, see Crusius, *Untersuchungen zu den Mimiamben des Herondas*, 53–79; M. Bieber, *Die Denkmäler zum Theaterwesen im Altertum*, 157.

299. Described by Crusius, *Untersuchungen zu den Mimiamben des Herondas*, 69.

300. M. Bieber, *Die Denkmäler zum Theaterwesen im Altertum*, 157, Plate 89; idem, *The History of the Greek and Roman Theater*, 92, Fig. 324. See also Beacham, *The Roman Theatre*, 175. The panel has not been reliably dated; the scene seems to represent a situation from New Comedy, but the stage facade behind the actors suggests Roman theater buildings.

301. Text and translation in Cunningham, *Herodas. Mimes*, 242–53; see the commentary by Crusius, *Untersuchungen zu den Mimiamben des Herondas*, 53–79.

302. Herodas *Mime* 3.22–36.

303. Ibid., lines 5–8, 19–21.

304. Ibid., lines 58–88; for the interpretation of those who help to administer the beating as ὑποδιδάσκαλοι, see Crusius, *Untersuchungen zu den Mimiamben des Herondas*, 69.

305. Herodas *Mime* 3.88–92.

306. Ibid., lines 93–97.

307. On the function and significance of this paragraph of the letter, see R. Funk, 'The Apostolic Parousia: Form and Significance' in *Christian History and Interpretation: Studies Presented to John Knox*, ed. W. R. Farmer, C. F. D. Moule (Cambridge: Cambridge University Press, 1967) 249–69; W. Schenk, 'Der 1. Korintherbrief als Briefsammlung', *ZNW* 60 (1969) 219–43.

Figure 12.   Marble relief of a comic scene. Museo Nazionale, Naples.

pages of his contemporaries, Persius and Petronius.[308] Paul apportions the
roles and assigns the parts with the confidence of a regisseur. Paul himself
is the father 'through the gospel' (1 Cor. 4.15). Like the father in the
'Guardian' mime, Paul is solicitous for the welfare of his children,[309] but is
not above assuming a minatory posture to bring about improvement
(4.19–21). The Corinthians are clearly cast as the children (τέκνα); they are
'beloved' (4.14) but immature,[310] as evidenced by their need for guardians.
Like the boy in the mime, the Corinthians are inattentive to their studies,[311]
and full of youthful arrogance (4.18–19).[312] The other apostles and

308.   Persius *Sat*. 3.44–51; Petronius *Satyr*. 46; see the comments of M. Rosenblüth,
Beiträge zur Quellenkunde von Petrons Satiren (Berlin: Weidmann, 1909) 54.
309.   Compare Paul's language of earnest concern (οὐκ ἐντρέπων...ἀλλ᾽ νουθετῶν
...παρακαλῶ, κτλ.) in 4.14–21 with Herodas' portrait of the anxious parents of a truant,
'weeping' and 'weary', in *Mime* 3.10, 14, 32, and with Persius' account of his father 'sweating'
as he listened, with his invited friends, to his son's attempt to recite the speech of the dying
Cato in *Sat*. 3.45–47. See also the comic *pater ardens* Demea in the *Adelphi* of Terence.
310.   Compare Paul's description of the Corinthians as 'infants' (νήπιοι) who are not ready
for solid food in 3.1–2.
311.   The description of Timothy as a 'faithful child' in 4.17 implies the inconstancy of
Paul's Corinthian children. Because of their inattentiveness, the Corinthians need to be
reminded of Paul's ways (4.17). Compare the portrait of the inattentive boy in Herodas *Mime*
3.19–26: 'He does not even know how to recognize the letter A, if one does not shout the same
thing at him five times. Two days ago when his father was teaching him to spell "Maron," this
fine fellow made 'Maron' into "Simon".'
312.   Compare Paul's account of the arrogant behavior of the Corinthians in 4.18–19 with
Herodas' account of the boy's disrespectful treatment of his parents in *Mime* 3.5–6, 36–49: he
has 'pillaged' his parents house and 'fleeces' his grandmother; if his parents try to speak more
forcibly to him, he runs away from home.

ministers of the gospel are the 'guardians' (παιδαγωγοί). That Paul is not altogether pleased with their performance is suggested by his hyperbolic reference to their number ('ten thousand'),[313] and by the need for parental intervention. While the pedagogues remain anonymous, the role of 'schoolmaster' is explicitly assigned to Timothy, who is 'trustworthy', and who will 'remind' the Corinthians of Paul's ways in Christ, as he 'teaches' them everywhere in every church (4.17). The warning to the Corinthians is implicit in the plot of mime: if the Corinthians will not accept instruction from Timothy, Paul will come with his 'stick' (ῥάβδος), like the father in the 'Guardian,' and administer the needed discipline (4.21). This explicit mention of the stick that belonged to the standard equipment of the mime[314] is a final, decisive indication of the scenario to which Paul has been making reference throughout the paragraph.

Interpreters who are not aware of the background of Paul's thought in this passage have largely mistaken Paul's purposes, seeing in the assumption of a paternal role (4.15), the call for imitation (4.16), and the threat of punishment (4.18–21) evidence of Paul's desire to set himself up as the sole authority over the community and to reinforce his privileged position.[315] However, as we have discovered, the father in the 'Guardian' mime is a figure of considerable irony. He is tricked and his purposes are frustrated by the delinquency of his son and the connivance of a slave.[316] Indeed, the mother in Herodas' 'Schoolmaster' pronounces herself 'foolish' (ἄνους) for trying to teach her son booklearning instead of to feed asses.[317] She describes the father in a manner that clearly recalls the fool in the mime: 'an old man with tired, drooping ears'.[318] The stick that the father

313. Cf. Plutarch *Mor.* 589F; N. H. Young, '*Paidagogos,* 167; Lindemann, *Der erste Korintherbrief*, 113–14.

314. Wüst, 'Mimos,' 1748, with references to literature. For artistic representations, see H. Goldman, 'Two Terracotta Figurines from Tarsus', 31, Fig. 12; Nicoll, *Masks, Mimes and Miracles*, 48 Fig. 34, 63 Fig. 59, 73 Fig. 73, 75 Fig. 76, 79 Fig. 77; Bieber, *The History of Greek and Roman Theater*, 92 Fig. 324.

315. G. Shaw, *The Cost of Authority. Manipulation and Freedom in the New Testament* (Philadelphia: Fortress, 1982) 68–69; E. Castelli, *Imitating Paul: A Discourse of Power* (Louisville, KY: Westminster/John Knox, 1991) 98–111.

316. For example, Persius (*Sat.* 3.44–47) recounts how, as a boy, he used to smear his eyes with oil to avoid reciting speeches before his father and the schoolmaster. The humor of the 'Guardian' mime as described by Cicero (*De Orat.* 2.259, 274) seems to have depended upon salacious *double entendres*, misunderstandings and cross purposes, with the father as the principal butt of the jokes.

317. Herodas *Mime* 3.26–29; see the comments of Crusius, *Untersuchungen zu den Mimiamben des Herondas*, 60–61.

318. Herodas *Mime* 3.31–32. For drooping, ass-like ears of the mimic fool, see Martial 6.39.15–17; Dieterich, *Pulcinella*, 151; Bieber, *Die Denkmäler zum Theaterwesen*, 176–77; for terracotta examples, see Winter, *Die Typen der figürlichen Terrakotten II*, 411 nr. 8, 436 nr. 4, 438 nr. 6.

brings with him upon the stage remains unused, because the boy escapes.[319] To be sure, Paul's allusion to the 'Guardian' mime is a warning to the Corinthians. But the warning is imbued with an ironic consciousness of the possibility of his own discomfiture.

In the context of the theatrical metaphor that Paul has developed throughout these paragraphs, the appeal for mimesis in 4.16 takes on a profound and ironic significance. Paul's admonition, 'become my imitators' (μιμηταί μου γίνεσθε), is not merely an attempt to reinforce his authority by presenting himself as the model for the community.[320] Rather, Paul understands himself to be a secondary actor, the fool of Christ (4.10), who mimics the performance of the archmime. His appeal to the Corinthians to become his imitators is an invitation to become the colleagues of a clown.[321] The mimic fool often appeared with a fellow.[322] Juvenal mentions 'the colleague of the clown Corinthus' (*stupidi collega Corinthi*).[323] A terracotta statuette, pictured above (Fig. 5), shows two mimic fools, one endeavoring to imitate the gestures of the other.[324]

1 Cor. 2.1–5

Moving backwards through the discourse,[325] we come to Paul's account of his preaching on the occasion of his appearance in Corinth in 2.1–5: 'When I came to you, brothers and sisters, I did not come proclaiming the mystery of God in lofty words or wisdom ... I came to you in weakness and in fear and in much trembling. My speech and my proclamation were not with

319.   Even in Herodas' 'Schoolmaster,' there are indications that the beating of the boy is a mock-beating staged in order to trick the mother, *Mime* 3.58–90. At line 92, Cunningham rightly infers the boy's escape from his laughter; see Cunningham, *Herodas. Mimes*, 253 n: 'Rejoicing at his release and his mother's discomfiture.' Cf. Crusius, *Untersuchungen zu den Mimiamben des Herondas*, 76–77.

320.   B. Sanders, 'Imitating Paul: 1 Cor. 4.16', *HTR* 74 (1981) 353–63; E. Castelli, *Imitating Paul*, 108–111.

321.   For μιμητής as 'one who impersonates characters, an actor', see Liddell-Scott-Jones, *Greek-English Lexicon*, 1134 s.v. μιμητής II. This meaning is usually disregarded by commentators, who emphasize uses of the term in a religious or philosophical context, e.g. Lindemann, *Der erste Korintherbrief*, 114–15, referring to Xenophon *Mem.* 1.2.3; 1.6.3; Musonius 17.

322.   E.g., Panniculus and Latinus, in Martial 2.72.1–4; 5.61.11–12.

323.   Juvenal 8.197.

324.   Bieber, *Die Denkmäler zum Theaterwesen*, 177 no. 188, Tab. 108,5; Nicoll, *Masks, Mimes and Miracles*, 47–48, Fig. 31.

325.   We pass over Paul's explicit references to fools and foolishness in 3.18–19 and 2.14. These passages will be treated in ch. 6 below, in connection with Paul's evaluation of the role of the fool.

plausible words of wisdom, etc.'. This passage, like the others we have examined, has puzzled interpreters, who have sometimes viewed it as a digression in the argument,[326] or an autobiographical account.[327] We may rule out the possibility that Paul's weakness was the result of a failure of nerve.[328] Nor is there any mention of persecution as the cause of anxiety.[329] So, what is the point of Paul's self-portrait in this passage?

It is clear that Paul intends to contrast his proclamation with that of certain missionary rivals who have made use of the art of rhetoric.[330] Hence Paul's choice of a number of terms that belong to the technical vocabulary of Hellenistic rhetoricians (ὑπεροχή, πειθώ, ἀπόδειξις, πίστις, δύναμις).[331] Yet, the hyperbolic language by which Paul describes his demeanor in verse 3 ('weakness, fear, much trembling') is not sufficiently explained on the hypothesis that this passage embodies Paul's renunciation of rhetoric.[332] To be sure, professional orators sometimes affected inexperience and inability in order to win the good will of their audiences.[333] In a show of mock humility, Dio Chrysostom warns the audience in his native Prusa not to expect a 'highminded' discourse, but an 'amateurish and commonplace' speech appropriate to the situation.[334] Dio seeks to win support for his project by deprecating his rhetorical ability. But he hardly describes himself as 'weak' or 'fearful', or as one who 'trembled much'.[335] What is the

326. W. Wuellner, 'Haggadic Homily Genre in 1 Corinthians 1–3', *JBL* 89 (1970) 201.

327. Weiss, *Der erste Korintherbrief*, 44, 47; Barrett, *The First Epistle to the Corinthians*, 64.

328. Weiss (*Der erste Korintherbrief*, 47–48) explains Paul's weakness, fear and trembling in Corinth as the result of the failure of his attempt to communicate the gospel to the philosophers in Athens (Acts 17.16–34); similarly, G. Lüdemann, *Paul: The Founder of Christianity* (Amherst, NY: Prometheus Books, 2002) 126–30. Cf. Litfin, *St. Paul's Theology of Proclamation*, 209. Psychological explanations are rightly rejected by Heinrici, *Der erste Brief*, 87.

329. Heinrici, *Der erste Brief*, 87.

330. For the interpretation of this passage as Paul's renunciation of rhetoric, see E. A. Judge, 'Paul's Boasting in Relation to Contemporary Professional Practice', *Aus BR* 16 (1968) 38; T. H. Lim, 'Not in Persuasive Words of Wisdom', 147–48; L. Hartman, 'Some Remarks on 1 Cor. 2.1–5', 117.

331. As demonstrated by Pogoloff, *Logos and Sophia*, 131–43; Winter, *Philo and Paul among the Sophists*, 153–61.

332. Litfin (*St. Paul's Theology of Proclamation*, 302 n.1) recognizes that the rhetorical sources do not provide a basis for explaining the three terms used by Paul in 2.3, ἀσθενεία, φόβος and τρόμος.

333. Quintilian *Inst. Orat.* 4.1.8–10. Cf. Judge, 'Paul's Boasting in Relation to Contemporary Professional Practice', 37; Pogoloff, *Logos and Sophia*, 136.

334. Dio Chrysostom *Or.* 47.8; see also *Or.* 42.3. Cf. Pogoloff, *Logos and Sophia*, 136; Winter, *Philo and Paul among the Sophists*, 152–53.

335. Winter (*Philo and Paul among the Sophists*, 158) attempts to diminish the difference between Dio's rhetorical apology in *Or.* 47.8 and Paul's self-description in 1 Cor. 2.3 by construing 'weakness' as the opposite of rhetorical 'strength', appealing to Philo *Det.* 35. But for the terms 'fear' (φόβος) and 'trembling' (τρόμος), Winter offers no parallels from the

basis for these elements in Paul's self-portrait?[336]

In keeping with the theatrical metaphor, Paul portrays himself as a well known figure in the mime: the befuddled orator.[337] The figure was popularized by Sophron, whose mimes were widely read and greatly admired.[338] One of Sophron's fools, Boulias the orator, is repeatedly mentioned in literature as an example of incoherent speech. The author of the late Hellenistic or early Roman treatise *On Style* (Περὶ ἑρμηνείας), traditionally, but wrongly, ascribed to Demetrius of Phalerum,[339] adduces as an example of rambling, ambiguous speech, 'Boulias who, when orating in Sophron's mime, delivers an utterly incoherent speech' (ὥσπερ ὁ παρὰ Σώφρον ῥητορεύων Βουλίας οὐδὲν γὰρ ἀκόλουθον αὐτῷ λέγει).[340] The incoherence of Boulias' oratory became proverbial, as demonstrated by the adage quoted by Mnaseas: 'he pleads like Boulias'.[341] It is regrettable that the mime has not survived, since it may have been known to Paul.[342] According to Statius, the mimes of Sophron were still being read in the

rhetorical sources. The fact that the expression φόβος καὶ τρόμος occurs frequently in the Septuagint (Ex. 15.16; Deut. 2.25; 11.25; Jdt. 2.28; 4 Macc. 4.10; Ps. 54.6; Isa. 19.16), and is found elsewhere in Paul (2 Cor. 7.15; Phil. 2.12) does not explain Paul's use of the terms here to describe the manner of his proclamation.

336.   Dieter Georgi (*Theocracy in Paul's Praxis and Theology* [Minneapolis: Fortress, 1991] 55 n. 65) calls attention to the 'vulgarity' of the description of Paul's appearance in Corinth in 2.1–5, 'which must have struck Hellenistic eyes and ears as a virtual caricature'.

337.   This point is anticipated by Georgi, *Theocracy in Paul's Praxis and Theology*, 54–55. On the ridicule of orators on the mimic stage, see Reich, *Der Mimus*, 458–75. The persona of the bad orator remained a common feature even in the later mime; Choricius *Apol. Mim.* 26, 109.

338.   Books of Sophron's mimes were introduced to Athens by none other than Plato (Diogenes Laertius 3.18), who read them avidly and alludes to them, *Rep.* 451c, 606c. On Plato's admiration of Sophron, see also Douris of Samos in *FGH* F 72. For Sophron's influence on Plato, see Reich, *Der Mimus*, 380–88. According to Diogenes Laertius (3.18), it was from Sophron that Plato learned the art of character drawing employed in his dialogues. A copy of Sophron's mimes was reportedly found under Plato's pillow on his deathbed (Quintilian *Inst. Orat.* 1.10.17). Theocritus 'adapted' one of Sophron's mimes in his second idyll, 'The Spell'; U. von Willamowitz-Moellendorff, *Die Textgeschichte der griechischen Bukoliker*, 270; see also P. Legrand, 'Théocrite', *Revue des études anciennes* 36 (1934) 28. An influential commentary on the mimes of Sophron was composed by Apollodorus of Athens in the second century B.C.; Vretska, 'Sophron', 281. On Sophron's influence in general, see Körte, 'Sophron', 1100–1103; Eitrem, 'Sophron', 10–13.

339.   See the discussion of authorship and date in G. M. A. Grube, *A Greek Critic: Demetrius on Style* (Toronto: University of Toronto Press, 1961) 39–56, and the appendices.

340.   Text and translation in W. Rhys Roberts, *Demetrius On Style*, LCL (Cambridge, MA: Harvard University Press, 1973) 398–99.

341.   Mnaseas in Zenobius 3.26: Βουλίας δικάζει ἐπὶ τῶν τὰς κρίσεις ἀναβαλλομένων ἀεὶ καὶ ὑπερτιθεμένων, quoted in Crusius, *Untersuchungen zu den Mimiamben des Herondas*, 51.

342.   Note the numerous quotations of Sophron in Ps.-Demetrius *De eloc.* and Athenaios *Deip.* On Sophron's influence in the Hellenistic and early Roman period, see Cunningham, *Herodas. Mimes.*

schools in the first century A.D.[343] Judging from the comments of Ps.-
Demetrius and Mnaseas, it would appear that Sophron's 'Boulias' was a
parody of a court scene, such as was popular in comedy and mime.[344] The
speech of Boulias was evidently a masterpiece of confusion, its arguments
inconclusive, its expressions hyperbolic, utterly wanting in sequence, but
abounding in unexpected mirth.[345]

In literature influenced by the mime, we repeatedly meet with the
befuddled orator, usually a simple man who has been thrust before the
assembly or dragged into court, and finds himself weak in the head and
trembly. The parodist, Hegemon of Thasos,[346] derisively nicknamed 'Lentil
Porridge', casts himself in this role in a passage quoted by Athenaios from
Polemon:[347]

> When I came to Thasos, they pelted me with lumps of filth tossed high,
> and one standing beside me said, 'Foulest man in all the world, who
> persuaded you to mount our fair platform with such feet as yours?' To
> them all I then answered one little word: ''Twas the lucre that persuaded
> me, in my old age and unwillingly, to come up here, and my poverty,
> which drives many Thasians aboard a merchantman, ... to them even I
> did yield, for I crave food sorely.'[348]

Poor 'Lentil Porridge' then stands dumbfounded, ruminating on his
shameful situation, and the insults his poor wife has had to endure from
other women, who have chided her for the meagerness of her loaves and
the smallness of her cakes.[349] In a mock-epic conclusion to the episode,
Pallas Athena intervenes to help the tongue-tied poet: touching 'Lentil
Porridge' with her golden wand and giving him heart, she sends her poor
champion forth to paradoxical victory in the contest.[350]

The most brilliant portrait of a foolish orator is found in the second
mime-poem of Herodas, in which an effeminate brothel-keeper prosecutes

343. Statius *Silv.* 5.3.158.
344. Crusius, *Untersuchungen zu den Mimiamben des Herondas*, 51.
345. Cf. the comments of Crusius, *Untersuchungen zu den Mimiamben des Herondas*, 51–52; Roberts, *Demetrius. On Style*, 398–99.
346. On Hegemon of Thasos, see Aristotle *Poet.* 2.1448a12; Athenaios *Deip.* 1.56; some describe him as a poet of Old Comedy, a contemporary of Alcibiades; but Athenaios *Deip.* 15.699 suggests a later date for him. See, in general, W. G. Waddell, 'Hegemon,' *OCD* (1978) 492; W. Kraus, 'Hegemon,' *Der Kleine Pauly. Lexicon der Antike* 2 (1979) 967.
347. The Greek text with *testimonia, varietas lectionis* and *Homeri loci similes* is found in *Corpusculum Poesis Epicae Graecae Ludibundae 1. Parodorum Epicorum Graecorum et Archestrati Reliquiae*, ed. P. Brandt (Leipzig: Teubner, 1888) 42–44, with commentary, 45–49.
348. Athenaios *Deip.* 15.698d-e. The translation slightly modifies C. Gulick, *Athenaeus. The Deipnosophists*, Vol. 7, LCL (Cambridge, MA: Harvard University Press, 1993) 243, 245.
349. Athenaios *Deip.* 15.698e-f.
350. Athenaios *Deip* 15.698f-699a, with allusions to Homer *Od.* 3.222; 19.33–34; *Il.* 1.92.

a sea-captain for assaulting one of his girls.[351] In Greek courts, plaintiffs and defendants had to represent themselves, so that the mime consists of the brothel-keeper's speech to the jury. To make sure that we recognize the role in which the complainant is cast, Herodas has given him the name of Battaros, which means 'stammerer'.[352] The speech is a magnificent epitome of the characteristics of bad oratory.[353] Battaros speaks constantly in platitudes and commonplaces.[354] The humorous master-stroke comes midway through the speech, when Battaros apologizes to the gentlemen of the jury for wearing them out with a long speech delivered in a proverbial style, and then proceeds to quote the old adage about the mouse trapped in the pitch.[355] Other traits of bad oratory are represented, as well, including shrill hyperbole,[356] dry rhetorical formulae,[357] and obscure allusions to history and myth.[358] There are revolting vulgarities typical of Battaros' profession, but inappropriate to the forensic context.[359] Throughout, the speech is characterized by incoherence, like that of Sophron's Boulias.[360] Battaros 'attempts to follow the usual pattern of a legal speech, but is

351. Text and translation in Cunningham, *Herodas. Mimes*, 230–41; commentary, with a number of important suggestions for alternate readings, in Crusius, *Untersuchungen zu den Mimiamben des Herondas*, 28–52.

352. The onomatopoeic word βατταρίζω means 'stammer'; see Hipponax fr. 108; Plato *Tht.* 175d; Cicero *Ad Att.* 6.5.1; Lucian *Iup. trag.* 27; Liddell-Scott-Jones, *Greek-English Lexicon*, 311 s.v. For the connotations of similar names in literature, e.g., βάττος, βάτταλος see Crusius, *Untersuchungen zu den Mimiamben des Herondas*, 50–51.

353. At the same time, Herodas also engages in devastating parody of several contemporary Hellenistic rhetoricians, such as Theodectes of Phaselis, as demonstrated by Crusius, *Untersuchungen zu den Mimiamben des Herondas*, 40.

354. For Battaros as a παροιμιαζόμενος ('one who is fond of quoting proverbs'), and for analysis of the many proverbial expressions in the speech, see the detailed and insightful commentary of Crusius, *Untersuchungen zu den Mimiamben des Herondas*, 28, 30–31, 33, 37, 40–41, 49.

355. Herodas *Mime* 2.60–63, with the comments of Crusius, *Untersuchungen zu den Mimiamben des Herondas*, 40–41.

356. E.g., Herodas *Mime* 2.25–27, where the brothel-keeper warns the members of the jury that the 'security' and 'freedom' of their city will be lost, if a customer is able to take one of his girls by force, a parody of the warning against oligarchical plots (δῆμον κατάλυσις) in ancient rhetoric; cf. Crusius, *Untersuchungen zu den Mimiamben des Herondas*, 29.

357. E.g. Herodas *Mime* 2.60–61; cf. Aeschines *De falsa leg.* 22.

358. Herodas *Mime* 2.48, referring to Chaerondes, a lawgiver, and 2.95–98, alluding to Merops, legendary king of Kos, Herakles, Asklepios, and Leto; cf. Crusius, *Untersuchungen zu den Mimiamben des Herondas*, 34–37, 48–49.

359. E.g. Herodas *Mime* 2.18–20, where Battaros compares his profession with that of the ship-captain: 'For neither does he [give] the wheat [to grind] for nothing, nor again do I give them to screw'; 2.42–45, where Battaros compares the waterclock, which had a hole and plug in its base, to an anus about to 'speak' and 'soil the bed'.

360. The principal instances of incoherence are at Herodas *Mime* 2.60–65 and 2.74–78; see the discussion in Crusius, *Untersuchungen zu den Mimiamben des Herondas*, 34, 46, 51–52.

regularly diverted from his theme and repeats himself endlessly.'[361] With an eye to Paul's use of the topos of the befuddled orator, it is especially interesting that Battaros depicts himself as poor and humble, weak, fearful, and trembling. Battaros 'wears a rough coat and shuffles along in rotten shoes'.[362] Knowing who he is and from what kind of clay he is mixed, he 'trembles before even the humblest of common people'.[363]

The figure of the foolish orator was so popular that actors specialized in the representation of this type. The epitaph of a player of Tiberius' household boasts of his ability 'to mimic barristers'.[364] The popularity of the befuddled orator has left an abundant record in terracotta: a gallery of low-class types with bald heads and stupid, coarse features, mouths open, hands lifted in gestures (e.g. Fig. 13).[365]

Because the figure of the foolish orator was so firmly established in popular consciousness, one might ridicule a politician, even the most powerful, by portraying him as an example of this comic type. Thus, Cicero is ridiculed as a comic Bambalio ('stutterer') in a piece of invective which Dio Cassius attributes to Q. Fufius Calenus: 'Why, you always come to the court trembling, as if you were going to fight as a gladiator, and after uttering a few words in a meek and half-dead voice, you take your leave, without having remembered a word of the speech you thought out at home before you came, and without having found anything to say on the spur of the moment.'[366] In his satire on the deification of the emperor Claudius, Seneca casts Claudius in this role. Exhorted by Hercules to 'stop playing the fool' and tell the truth about himself,[367] Claudius makes a speech to justify his claim to be a god. The speech is obviously intended as a parody of Claudius' own pronouncements, with their rambling style and familiar tone.[368] Claudius begins by appealing to Hercules as the one god

---

361. Cunningham, *Herodas. Mimes*, 209.

362. Herodas *Mimes* 2.22–23.

363. Herodas *Mimes* 2.28–30.

364. *CIL* VI.4886: *Caesaris lusor mutus et argutus imitator Ti Caesaris Augusti qui primus invenit causidicos imitari.* See the discussion of this epitaph by Purcell, 'Does Caesar Mime?' 181–83. See also the anecdote of the fool who injured himself while attempting when drunk to imitate an orator after dinner, in Porphyry's commentary on Horace *Ep.* 1.19.15.

365. See, for example, F. Winter, Die *Typen der figurlichen Terrakotten* II, 429, nr. 6; 430, nr. 5–8; 437, nr.6; Bieber, *History of the Greek and Roman Theater*, 100, Fig. 372, 374, 376, 377.

366. Dio Cassius 46.7.

367. Seneca *Apoc.* 7.1: *tu desine fatuari.* Elaborating the portrait of Claudius as a fool, Hercules threatens: 'Tell me the truth, and quickly, or I'll shake your absurdities (*alogias*) out of you!' On *alogias* as a plebian Grecism, see Eden, *Seneca. Apocolocyntosis*, 93.

368. C. F. Russo, *L. Annaei Senecae Divi Claudii* ΑΠΟΚΟΛΟΣΥΝΤΩΣΙΣ (Firenze: Nuova Italia, 1981) 77–79.

Figure 13.   Terracotta statuette from Myrina. German Archaeological Institute, Athens.

who he hoped would stand up for him, if he should ever need a voucher.[369]
He then proceeds to recall the tribulations which he endured as president
of the court which met 'for whole days at a time' in front of Hercules'
temple, 'miseries' which he ventures to compare with Hercules' labors.[370]
At this point, the text breaks off; a considerable lacuna intervenes.[371] The
loss is unfortunate, given the historical proximity to Paul. But enough
survives to permit us to form a rough concept of the speech: Claudius is
plaintive, boastful, officious, and silly.[372] Seneca completes the portrait by
emphasizing Claudius' weakness: his head and hands shake uncontrollably; his speech is a 'confused mumbling' which others find 'unintelligible'.[373]

A final example of the befuddled orator is found in Lucian's *Juppiter
Tragoedus*.[374] Like other works of Lucian, this dialogue is inspired by the
satires of Menippus of Gadara (third century B.C.).[375] What has caused the

369.   Seneca *Apoc.* 7.4; cf. Petronius *Satyr.* 92.11.

370.   Seneca *Apoc.* 7.5. For the 'miseries' suffered by Claudius as the 'plaints' of the
litigants, see Eden, *Seneca. Apocolocyntosis*, 97. Cf. Tacitus *Dial.* 1.1.; Suetonius *Claud.* 14;
Dio Cassius 60.4.3.

371.   On the extent of the lacuna, see Eden, *Seneca. Apocolocyntosis*, 99: 'At least one
complete *folium* of a codex, either the archetype or an ancestor of it, must have been lost.'

372.   See the discussion in O. Weinreich, *Senecas* Apocolocyntosis, 6–8, 80–94; Eden,
Seneca. Apocolocyntosis, 13–17, 64, 95, 99.

373.   Seneca *Apoc.* 5.2; 6.1–2.

374.   Text and translation in *Lucian*, Vol. 2, ed. A. H. Harmon, LCL (Cambridge, MA:
Harvard University Press, 1968) 90–169.

375.   R. Helm, *Lucian und Menipp* (Leipzig: Teubner, 1906) 115–64. J. Bompaire, *Lucian
écrivain: Imitation et création* (Paris: Boccard, 1958) 587–656; B. P. McCarthy, 'Lucian und

father of the gods to 'rant'[376] is a debate about providence between the philosophers, in which an Epicurean has asserted that the gods do not exist.[377] Zeus is thus obliged to convoke an assembly of the gods to determine how to meet the danger.[378] In the prologue, Lucian makes skillful use of the techniques of parody to represent Zeus as a foolish orator.[379] In striking contrast to his stone portraits, which convey the image of mature strength and assurance,[380] Zeus is depicted as distraught over the speech that he must give: care consumes his heart and soul, pallor preys upon his face, he paces about fretfully, giving vent to his anxiety in 'deep, deep sighs'.[381] When the time finally comes for Zeus to address the assembly, the thunderer is mute: he who was once so confident and loud-spoken in assembly, frightening the gods with his threats to pull up earth and sea from their foundations, is himself struck dumb.[382] Zeus confesses: 'I am confused in the head and trembly (ὑπότρομος) and my tongue seems to be tied.'[383] Worst of all, Zeus has forgotten the introduction to the speech which he has prepared, and gladly accepts the advice of Hermes that he make use of one of Demosthenes' speeches, with a little modification: 'Good! That is a short cut to speechmaking and a timely help to anyone who doesn't know what to say.'[384] The joke that is thus played on Zeus is especially good, in that the proem of Demosthenes' first Olynthiac, which is imitated here, introduces a deliberative discourse (λόγος συμβουλευτικός),[385] whereas Zeus has no counsel to offer his fellow-

---

Menippus', *YCS* 4 (1934) 3–58. On the relationship of the *Juppiter Tragoedus* to Lucian's other works, esp. the *Jup. Conf.* and the *Deor. conc.*, see V. Gazza, 'I tre scritti affini di Luciano: Ζεὺς ἐλεγχόμενος, Ζεὺς τραγῳδός, θεῶν ἐκκλησία', *Aevum* 27 (1953) 1–17.

376.   On the difficulty of an adequate translation of τραγῳδός, see J. Coenen, *Lukian Zeus tragodos: Überlieferungsgeschichte, Text und Kommentar*. Beiträge zur klassischen Philologie 88 (Meisenheim am Glan: Hain, 1977) 39.

377.   Lucian *Jup. trag.* 4; see M. Caster, *Lucien et la pensée religieuse de son temps* (Paris: Les Belles Lettres, 1938) 201, 205.

378.   Lucian *Jup. trag.* 6. On Lucian's use of the *concilium deorum* motif and its antecedents, see Helm, *Lucian und Menipp*, 158–65.

379.   On the parody technique of Lucian, see Bompaire, *Lucien écrivain*, 625–30. Zeus was already a subject of burlesque in Phlyax comedy and the mime; see Nicoll, *Masks, Mimes and Miracles*, 54–58.

380.   F. Beare, 'Zeus in the Hellenistic Age' in *The Seed of Wisdom*, ed. W. McCullough (Toronto: University of Toronto Press, 1964) 92–113.

381.   Lucian *Jup. trag.* 1. On anxiousness as a mark of the fool, see the comments of Reich, *Der Mimus*, 374: 'Vor allem zeichnet er sich als echter μωρός durch eine übertriebene Ängstlichkeit aus.'

382.   Lucian *Jup. trag.* 14.

383.   Lucian *Jup. trag.* 14; cf. Coenen, *Lukian Zeus tragodos*, 38–39.

384.   Lucian *Jup. trag.* 14.

385.   Bompaire, *Lucien écrivain*, 393; Helm, *Lucian und Menipp*, 159–60; cf. E. Drerup, *Demosthenes im Urteile des Altertums* (Würzburg: Becker, 1923) 144–47.

deities, and has called them together to ask their advice![386] The speech concludes with an anxious summary in which Zeus again reveals his lack of confidence.[387]

Paul evokes the well-known figure of the befuddled orator in the account of his appearance and proclamation at Corinth in 1 Cor. 2.1–5, a description 'which must have struck Hellenistic eyes and ears as a virtual caricature'.[388] Thus Paul repeatedly emphasizes his lack of rhetorical ability: his coming was 'not with the superiority of eloquence or wisdom' (2.1); his speech and proclamation were 'not in persuasiveness of wisdom' (2.4). The repetition is meant to convey Paul's heightened emotional state.[389] Between the repeated disavowal of rhetorical ability, at the center of the paragraph, lies Paul's account of his 'weakness', 'fear', and 'much trembling' (2.3). Precisely those elements of Paul's self-portrait which interpreters are at a loss to explain[390] characterize the foolish orator in the mime and in mime-inspired literature. Like Seneca's Claudius, Paul is weak and impotent. Like Lucian's Zeus, Paul is frightened and confused. Like Herodas' 'stammerer' Battaros, Paul trembles before his audience.

The figure of the befuddled orator was used in self-parody long before Paul, as the case of Hegemon of Thasos demonstrates. Socrates stands in this tradition, as well, as he is depicted in Plato's *Gorgias*.[391] Callicles tries to get Socrates to see how 'ridiculous' (καταγέλαστος) he appears to the men of Athens because of his mode of discourse.[392] Callicles prophesies ominously that Socrates would 'reel to and fro and gape openmouthed, without a word to say', if he were ever to be arrested and brought into court.[393] In Callicles' opinion, Socrates is a fool, who 'may be boxed on the ears with impunity'.[394] Berated by Callicles for incessantly talking about

---

386.   Coenen, *Lukian Zeus tragodos*, 67–68.

387.   Lucian *Jup. trag.* 18.

388.   Georgi, *Theocracy in Paul's Praxis and Theology*, 55 n. 65.

389.   On repetition as a conveyor of heightened emotion, see J. D. Denniston, *Greek Prose Style* (Oxford: Clarendon Press, 1952) 78–98. Pogoloff (*Logos and Sophia*, 129–30) explains the repetition in 2.1 and 2.4 as an instance of the rhetorical figure of *expolitio* (refining or embellishing). But as an aspect of Paul's portrayal of himself as a bad orator, the repetition is probably meant to convey emotional distress.

390.   Litfin, *St. Paul's Theology of Proclamation*, 209, 302; Winter, *Philo and Paul among the Sophists*, 158.

391.   On the Socratic self-parodies and the influence of the mime, see Reich, *Der Mimus*, 354–60.

392.   Plato *Grg.* 485D; E. R. Dodds, *Plato. Gorgias* (Oxford: Oxford University Press, 1959) 277, 324, 368; P. Friedländer, *Plato. The Dialogues, First Period* (Princeton: Princeton University Press, 1965) 143.

393.   Plato *Grg.* 486B.

394.   Plato *Grg.* 486C; Dodds, *Plato. Gorgias*, 278, 352, 358. See esp. the observation of A. W. Nightingale, *Genres in Dialogue: Plato and the Construct of Philosophy* (Cambridge: Cambridge University Press, 1995) 90: 'Callicles thus portrays Socrates as a comic character

'food and drink and cobblers and fullers and cooks and doctors',[395] Socrates resorts to self-parody, seeming to revel in the foolishness and vulgarity of his language, and the discomfort it causes his aristocratic companions.[396] Callicles finds Socrates' mode of discourse 'shameful',[397] But the point of Socrates' self-parody, as it is of Paul's, is to call into question what is vulgar and what is noble, what is ridiculous and what is serious.[398] Paul follows a Socratic precedent in making himself and his manner of speaking the object of parody. Indeed, Paul's formulation of his decision 'not to know anything (οὐ τι εἰδέναι) except Jesus Christ, and him crucified' in 2.2 probably owes something to Socrates' famous disavowal of knowledge, 'what I do not know, I do not think that I know' (ἃ μὴ ὃιδα οὐδὲ οἴομαι εἰδέναι),[399] and to Socrates' repeated claim that he knows nothing except how much he desires knowledge.[400]

1 Cor. 1.18–25

We return, then,[401] to the thesis statement and to the intense, theological reflection which it introduces: 'The message about the cross is foolishness.... We proclaim Christ crucified,...foolishness to Gentiles' (1.18, 23). It now seems likely that Paul's astonishing and paradoxical equation of the cross and foolishness was mediated by the mime. The most popular mime of Paul's day was the *Laureolus* of Catullus, mentioned above.[402]

---

very much in keeping with the comic persona delineated in the *Philebus* – the ignorant fool who is powerless to retaliate when harmed. In the eyes of the non-philosophical person, we infer, a philosopher like Socrates appears both foolish and comic.'

395. Plato *Grg.* 490C, 491A.

396. Plato *Grg.* 494 B-E: Socrates speaks of birds that defecate while they eat, of compulsive itchers, and of the shocking κίναιδος.

397. Plato *Grg.* 494E.

398. Nightingale, *Genres in Dialogue*, 91; Georgi, *Theocracy*, 54–55.

399. Plato *Apol.* 21D. See W. Kalinka, 'Das Nichtwissen des Sokrates', *Wiener Studien* 50 (1932) 36–46; E. L. Burge, 'The Irony of Socrates', *Antichthon* 3 (1969) 5–17; W. C. K. Guthrie, *Socrates* (Cambridge: Cambridge University Press, 1971) 85–89, 122–25. Socrates' statement should not be taken as an absolute disavowal of knowledge. It should be understood in the context of the contrast between Socrates and men such as Gorgias of Leontini and Hippias of Elis (*Apol.* 19E-20C), who claim to possess expert knowledge and who teach for a fee. Whereas each of these men thinks that he knows something which he does not know, Socrates is conscious of his ignorance.

400. E.g., Plato *Symp.* 177D. See S. Lowenstam, 'Paradoxes in Plato's *Symposium*', *Ramus* 14 (1985) 85–104, esp. 88.

401. Passing over, for the moment, Paul's reference to τὰ μωρὰ τοῦ κοσμοῦ in 1.27; this passage will be discussed below in chs. 6 and 7.

402. *Mimorum Romanorum Fragmenta*, ed. M. Bonaria, 112. On the popularity of the *Laureolus* mime, see Nicoll, *Masks, Mimes and Miracles*, 110–11; Beachman, *The Roman Theater*, 136. T. P. Wiseman (*Catullus*, 183–98) argues for the identity of Catullus the mime

References by historians, poets, and commentators make it possible to reconstruct the plot.[403] Laureolus is a slave who runs away from his master and becomes the leader of a band of robbers. Some record of his crimes must have been presented; there was a scene in which he was captured, and a final scene in which he was crucified.[404] The crucifixion was enacted with a considerable degree of stage realism. Josephus reports that 'a great quantity of artificial blood flowed down from the one crucified'.[405] Suetonius records a performance on the day of Caligula's assassination, in which the chief actor fell and vomited blood.[406] Suetonius notes that the performance was immediately followed by a humorous afterpiece in which 'several mimic fools (*plures secundarum*) so vied with one another in giving evidence of their proficiency at dying that the stage swam in blood'.[407] According to Martial, a condemned criminal was forced to take the part of Laureolus at a performance during the reign of Titus, and actually died on the cross.[408] Paul may have this mime in mind when he describes the message of the crucified Christ as 'foolishness'. Martial compares the fate of Laureolus with the suffering of Prometheus, the other 'crucified god' of antiquity.[409]

The 'humor' of the *Laureolus* mime is a complex instance of the 'gallows joke' popular in antiquity, particularly among the lower classes.[410] There is

writer with the late-Republican love poet of that name. Wiseman discusses other mimes which are attributed to Catullus: *Phasma, Pharmakeutria, Priapus*, and *Phormio*. A commentator on Lucan describes a book by Catullus evidently entitled 'An Essay on Mimes' (περὶ μιμολογιῶν); Schol. Bernensis on Lucan 1.544, cited as Appendix no. 101 in Wiseman, *ibid.* p. 259.

403.   Josephus *Ant.* 19.94; Suetonius *Calig.* 57; Martial *De Spect.* 7; Juvenal 8.187–88; Tertullian *Adv. Val.* 14; see also the scholiast on Juvenal 8. 185–87, cited as Appendix 98 in Wiseman, *Catullus*, 258.

404.   For the reconstruction of the plot, see Reich, *Der Mimus* 564–66; Nicoll, *Masks, Mimes and Miracles*, 110–11.

405.   Josephus *Ant.* 19.94: ἅιμα τεχνητὸν πολὺ τὸ περὶ τὸν σταυρωθέντα ἐκκεχυμένον. Cf. H. Reich, *Der König mit der Dornenkrone* (Leipzig: Teubner, 1905) 14.

406.   Suetonius *Calig.* 57.4.

407.   Suetonius *Calig.* 57.4. On the *plures secundarum*, see the note in J. C. Rolfe, *Suetonius*, Vol. 1, LCL (Cambridge, MA: Harvard University Press, 1979) 492.

408.   Martial *De Spect.* 7. Cf. Reich, *Der König mit der Dornenkrone*, 14–15.

409.   Martial *De Spect.* 7. Martial compares the fate of Laureolus with that of Prometheus on the Scythian crag. On Prometheus as a 'crucified god' in antiquity, see Hengel, *Crucifixion*, 11–14, citing Lucian *Prometheus* 1–2, who describes how Prometheus is nailed to two rocks above a ravine in the sight of all, in such a way as to produce the effect of 'a most serviceable cross' (ἐπικαιρότατος...ὁ σταυρός): 'nailed up... in full sight of everyone as he hangs there... We must not crucify him low and close to the ground, ...crucify him above the ravine with his hands stretched out... crucified in your stead (προσηλῶσθαι,...καὶ οὗτος ἅπασι περιφανὴς εἴη κρεμάμενος,...οὔτε γὰρ ταπεινὸν καὶ πρόσγειον χρή..., ...ὑπὲρ τῆς φάραγγος ἀνεσταυρώσθω ἐκπετασθεὶς τὼ χεῖρε...ἀντὶ σοῦ ἀνασκολοπισθῆναι αὐτίκα).

410.   On the popularity of the 'gallows joke' in antiquity, see already J. Meggitt, 'Laughing and Dreaming at the Foot of the Cross', 9–14.

evidence of the use of *crux* and related terms (*cruciarius*, *furcifer*, μαστιγίας, *patibulatus*) as a vulgar taunt in comedy, mime and farce, with the meaning 'gallows-bird'.[411] The abusive expression *i in malam maximam crucem* thus meant something like 'be hanged!'[412] Jokes about crucifixion are frequently found on the lips of slaves in Plautus' comedies. For example, in Plautus' *Mostellaria* the slave Tranio, realizing that his demise is imminent, asks: 'Anybody here want to make some easy money? Anybody ready to be crucified in my place today? .... I'm offering a talent to anyone prepared to jump on a cross..., after that he can come and claim the money, cash on the nail.'[413] The function of this gallows humor was clearly to alleviate the terrifying and unavoidable in the everyday lives of those who found themselves at the bottom of ancient society, the slaves and the free poor.[414] For the rich in the audience, such gallows humor served to trivialize the evil instrument by which the upper class maintained its dominance. In sum, the gallows joke was the most extreme example of the paradoxical humor of the mime in general.

In a number of instances, the slave who is taunted with the vulgar epithet 'gallows-bird' is also said to be a 'fool'. Thus, Plautus' Menaechmus confesses 'I'm a fool' (*ego stultus sum*) in a passage which culminates with the sarcastic question, 'Why don't you go be hanged?' (*Quin tu is in malam crucem*).[415] In Petronius' *Satyricon*, the young slave Giton is described as a fool at the Saturnalia, just before he is pronounced a piece of 'gallows meat' (*crucis offla*).[416] Finally, the fool in the mime-inspired tale from the tenth book of Apuleius' *Golden Ass* is explicitly described as a *cruciarius*.[417] These instances make it clear that the 'fool' and the 'gallows-bird' would have been associated in the minds of Paul's readers. Associations created by the mime evidently mediated Paul's provocative description of 'the message of the cross' as 'foolishness'.

---

411.   For *crux* in this sense, see Plautus *Aul.* 522; *Bacch.* 584; *Cas.* 416; *Persa* 795; Terence *Eun.* 383; Petronius *Satyr.* 58.2; 126.9. For *cruciarius*, Apuleius *Met.* 10.7.5. For μαστιγίας, *POxy* 413 ('Adulteress') lines 5, 110, 137, 154, 155; Lucian *Jup. Trag.* 52. For *patibulatus*, Plautus *Mostel.* 53; Apuleius *Met.* 4.10.4. Cf. Hengel, *Crucifixion*, 9–10.

412.   Plautus *Asin.* 940; *Bacch.* 902; *Cas.* 93, 641, 977; *Cur.* 611, 693; *Menaech.* 915, 1017; *Mostel.* 1133; *Poen.* 271, 495, 511, 789, 1309. Cf. Hengel, *Crucifixion*, 10.

413.   Plautus *Mostel.* 359–64; cited in Meggitt, 'Laughing and Dreaming at the Foot of the Cross', 10.

414.   Rightly, Meggitt, 'Laughing and Dreaming at the Foot of the Cross', 10, 13.

415.   Plautus, *Menaech.* 904, 915. See also Plautus *Cur.* 611; *Bacch.* 584, where fools in the accustomed role of parasite are addressed in this way.

416.   Petronius *Satyr.* 58.1–3; see also 126.1–10, where a slave who is 'condemned for crucifixion' (*in crucem mittam*) is associated with 'an actor disgraced by exhibiting himself on the stage'. See the commentary by Panayotakis, *Theatrum Arbitri*, 164–66.

417.   Apuleius *Met.* 10.7.5.

Chapter 5

APPROPRIATION OF THE ROLE

We may now tell the story of Paul's appropriation of the role of the fool in his correspondence with Corinth. When Paul came to Corinth, he preached a gospel of Jesus the Christ crucified (1 Cor. 1.17,18; 2.2). He made converts, mainly among the lower classes (1 Cor. 1.26–28).[1] But it seems that at Corinth the Pauline mission also succeeded, for the first time, in winning adherents from the better educated and cultured circles.[2] After Paul left Corinth, another Christian missionary arrived, a Jew named Apollos, a native of Alexandria.[3] According to the author of the book of Acts, Apollos was 'an eloquent man,... skilled in the exposition of Scriptures' (Acts 18.24).[4] He made a strong impression upon the Corinthians, especially upon the elite who valued proficiency in philosophy and rhetoric.[5] Factions formed within the church, with members declaring support for one teacher or another (1 Cor. 1.10–12; 3.4).[6] In the resulting debates, members of the Apollos party said that, in comparison with their eloquent teacher, Paul appeared to be a 'fool'. Perhaps they also

---

1. Cf. Georgi, *Theocracy*, 54; Meggitt, *Paul, Poverty and Survival*, 75–76, 96.

2. Betz, 'The Problem of Rhetoric and Theology according to the Apostle Paul', 24; C. S. de Vos, *Church and Community Conflicts: The Relationship of the Thessalonian, Corinthian, and Philippian Churches with Their Wider Civic Communities* (Atlanta: Scholars Press, 1999) 197–203.

3. The reconstruction offered here follows the account of Apollos' role in Corinth by Weiss, *Der erste Korintherbrief*, xxxi–xxxiv. For a similar reconstruction of the situation, see, more recently, J. F. M. Smit, 'What is Apollos? What is Paul? In Search for the Coherence of First Corinthians 1.10–4.21', *NovT* 44 (2002) 231–51, esp. 246–47.

4. See the analysis of this tradition by G. Lüdemann, *Early Christianity according to the Traditions in Acts* (Minneapolis: Fortress Press, 1989) 207–209.

5. Similarly, Litfin, *St. Paul's Theology of Proclamation*, 162; Winter, *Philo and Paul among the Sophists*, 175–76; de Vos, *Church and Community Conflicts*, 219–20.

6. On the dynamics at work in the formation of factions in the Corinthian church, see L. L. Welborn, *Politics and Rhetoric in the Corinthians Epistles* (Macon, GA: Mercer University Press, 1997) 1–42; H. A. Stansbury, 'Corinthian Honor, Corinthian Conflict: A Social History of Early Roman Corinth and its Pauline Community' (Ph.D. dissertation, University of California at Irvine, 1990) 20, 275–76, 424.

contrasted the 'wisdom' of Apollos' interpretation of Scripture with the simplicity of Paul's preaching of the cross.

Several aspects of Paul's argument in 1 Cor. 1–4 suggest that the terms 'fool' and 'folly', as they appear in the Corinthian correspondence, did not originate with Paul himself, but were put forward by certain members of the Christian community in Corinth to describe the impression made upon them by Paul and his gospel. First, there is the antithetical manner in which Paul formulates his commission as an apostle in 1.17: 'For Christ did not send me to baptize but to proclaim the gospel, not with eloquent wisdom, so that the cross of Christ might not be emptied of its power.' The abrupt introduction of the subject of Paul's preaching (ἀλλὰ εὐαγγελίζεσθαι),[7] and the negative definition of its style and content (οὐκ ἐν σοφίᾳ λόγου),[8] suggest that the Corinthians have found something wanting in Paul's proclamation, and indicate in what respect they have found it deficient.[9] That Paul himself did not present the gospel as 'wisdom' is demonstrated by what he says about the divine inversion of wisdom and foolishness in 1.21, and by the account of his appearance and proclamation in Corinth in 2.1–5.[10] Indeed, the term σοφία is hardly found in the Pauline corpus outside of this context.[11] It is clear that the term σοφία has been forced upon Paul by others.[12] Paul appropriates the concept only in order to show in what sense the gospel is really 'wisdom'.[13] To be sure, abruptness and contrast is a stylistic device,[14] used by Paul with great effect, here and

7. On the abruptness with which the subject of Paul's preaching is introduced in 1.17 and its implications, see esp. Weiss, *Der erste Korintherbrief*, 23; Pogoloff, *Logos and Sophia*, 108; Litfin, *St. Paul's Theology of Proclamation*, 187: 'As of 1.17, however, we note only a certain as yet unexplainable abruptness in the introduction of the subject along with the unexpected qualifying phrase οὐκ ἐν σοφίᾳ λόγου.'

8. The phrase οὐκ ἐν σοφίᾳ λόγου qualifies εὐαγγελίζεσθαι, rather than ἀπέστειλεν; thus, rightly, Heinrici, *Der erste Brief*, 65; Lindemann, *Der erste Korintherbrief*, 43. There is considerable debate among interpreters whether σοφία λόγου refers more to the style or content of preaching, whether, that is, Paul rejects rhetorical skill or philosophical argument; on this point, see esp. Weiss, *Der erste Korintherbrief*, 22–23; Barrett, *The First Epistle*, 49; Pogoloff, *Logos and Sophia*, 108–13; Litfin, *St. Paul's Theology of Proclamation*, 188–92; Winter, *Philo and Paul among the Sophists*, 186–87; Smit, 'What is Apollos? What is Paul?' 244–46.

9. So, already, Heinrici, *Der erste Brief*, 64–65; Weiss, *Der erste Korintherbrief*, 22–23; Litfin, *St. Paul's Theology of Proclamation*, 187; J. S. Vos, 'Die Argumentation des Paulus in 1 Kor 1,10–3,4', 96–97.

10. Heinrici, *Der erste Brief*, 64.

11. The term σοφία is found 15 times in 1 Cor. 1.17–2.13, elsewhere only in 2 Cor. 1.12 and Rom. 11.33; σοφός appears 9 times in 1 Cor. 1.19–3.20, otherwise only 4 times in Romans. On this point, see already Heinrici, *Der erste Brief*, 64; Lindemann, *Der erste Korintherbrief*, 43.

12. Heinrici, *Der erste Brief*, 64; Vos, 'Die Argumentation des Paulus,' 96–97.

13. Heinrici, *Der erste Brief*, 64.

14. Identified and analyzed by Weiss, *Der erste Korintherbrief*, 23. Collins (*First Corinthians*, 75–76, 85) designates this as the rhetorical figure of *contradictio*.

elsewhere,[15] in order to introduce a theme.[16] But the figure corresponds to a situation, which it exposes in a forceful manner: by means of the abrupt negation, 'not with eloquent wisdom', Paul unmistakably distinguishes his charisma as a missionary from that of another, for whom σοφία λόγου is characteristic.[17] The best explanation of the antithesis between σοφία λόγου and ὁ λόγος τοῦ σταυροῦ, which is introduced in this verse and which structures the discussion that follows, is that it reflects a contrast which some in Corinth have drawn between the eloquent wisdom of Apollos' preaching and the foolishness of Paul's gospel.[18]

A second feature of the rhetoric of the passage which suggests that the term 'foolishness' has been applied as a judgment upon Paul's preaching is the concessive manner in which he introduces the subject of his appearance and proclamation in Corinth in 2.1,3, and also in 3.1. The emphatic particle κἀγώ in 2.1, repeated for rhetorical effect in 2.3, and resumed in 3.1, is adverbial in usage,[19] and has an assentient force:[20] '*Indeed, I did* come to you, brothers and sisters, without eloquence or wisdom (as you say)…, *Indeed, I did* come to you in weakness and in fear and in much trembling…, *Indeed, I* was *not* able to speak to you, brothers and sisters, as spiritual people,…(and this was because…).' [21] By means of the emphatic κἀγώ and the apostrophe, ἀδελφοί, Paul indicates that he is responding to a negative evaluation of his preaching by some at Corinth.[22]

15.   Phil. 1.20–21; Rom. 1.16.

16.   See esp. the insightful comments of Weiss, *Der erste Korintherbrief*, 23: 'Paulus bringt plötzlich und unvermittelt durch οὐκ ἐν σοφίᾳ λόγου ein Stichwort, von dem noch garnicht die Rede war und gewinnt damit das Thema des folgenden Abschnitts. Diese Art, "unhörbar", aber doch ziemlich ruckweise das Thema des Folgenden einzuführen, ist auch sonst ein stilistisches Mittel des Paulus, vgl. Röm 1.16; Phil. 1.20 und 21. Schon der kleine, bei lautem Lesen deutlich spürbare Einschnitt vor οὐκ und die dadurch gegebene lebhafte Betonung des οὐκ weckt die Aufmerksamkeit – es muss wohl zwischen εὐαγγελίζεσθαι und σοφία λόγου ein merkwürdiges Verhältnis bestehen!'

17.   Weiss, *Der erste Korintherbrief*, 22.

18.   Smit, 'What is Apollos? What is Paul?' 236, 246–48.

19.   On adverbial καί, see H. W. Smyth, *Greek Grammar* (Cambridge, MA: Harvard University Press, 1956) 2881–84; Blass and Debrunner, *A Greek Grammar of the New Testament and Other Early Christian Literature*, 438–39, 442.

20.   On καί assentient, see J. D. Denniston, *The Greek Particles* (Oxford: Clarendon Press, 1987) 396.

21.   Similarly, H. A. W. Meyer, *Der erste Brief an die Korinther*, KEK 1 (Göttingen: Vandenhoeck & Ruprecht, 1839) *ad loc.*, cited in Heinrici, *Der erste Brief*, 115, with the observation: 'Die Fassung: "auch ich" (Meyer) führt zur Eintragung eines unausgesprochenen Vergleichs zwischen dem Apostel und anderen Lehrern.'

22.   So, already, Smit, 'What is Apollos? What is Paul?' 248: 'In 2.1–5 as well as in 3.1–4, …Paul is clearly on the defensive. In 2.1–5 he stresses the qualities which he lacked during that visit… In 3.1–4 he explicitly draws attention to the manner in which he could not address them at the time… Paul evidently offers resistance to a negative valuation of his founding visit of which he suspects a number of Corinthian believers.'

Paul agrees with the evaluation, adding an explanation of his theological motivation (2.3–5), and finally shifting responsibility from himself to the Corinthians (3.1–3).[23]

A third characteristic of Paul's rhetoric which suggests that the epithet 'fool' has been applied to him by others is the apologetic orientation of the entire exposition in 1.17–4.21.[24] Paul is clearly on the defensive when he speaks of the 'foolishness' of his preaching.[25] The defensive tone is sharpest in those passages where Paul addresses himself in the first person singular (ἐγώ) to the Corinthians in the second person plural (ὑμεῖς), that is, in 2.1–5, 3.1–4, and 4.1–5.[26] In the latter passage (4.3), Paul explicitly rejects any judgment that the Corinthians may pass upon him.[27] The reason for the apologetic stance in these passages may be inferred from the way in which Paul continues the discussion in 3.5–15 and 4.6–7: 'What then is Apollos? What is Paul?... I have applied all of this to Apollos and myself.'[28] Evidently some in Corinth have made invidious comparisons between Paul and Apollos.[29]

Several aspects of Paul's defense of himself and his gospel in 1 Cor. 1–4 suggest that the adherents of Apollos are those who harbor deprecatory opinions about him. First, there is the way in which Paul returns to the subject of the factions in ch. 3. Although four party slogans are subjected to parody in 1.12, only two are repeated in 3.4 – 'I belong to Paul,' ... 'I belong to Apollos'. From this we may conclude that the preceding apology (1.18–3.4) has been written with a view to the Apollos party, and that the other factions have been left out of consideration.[30] It is evidently the adherents of Apollos who have pointed out a deficiency of σοφία λόγου (1.17) or πειθὼ σοφίας (2.4) in Paul's proclamation.

Second, in an important summary of his purposes in the letter, Paul states explicitly (4.6): 'I have applied (μετεσχημάτισα) these things to myself and Apollos for your benefit, brothers and sisters,[31] ... so that none of you

---

23. Smit, 'What is Apollos? What is Paul?' 248–49.

24. Heinrici, *Der erste Brief*, 64: 'In dieser Darlegung ist alles apologetisch orientiert'; similarly, Weiss, *Der erste Korintherbrief*, xxxi, 22. Winter (*Philo and Paul among the Sophists*, 147) also speaks of Paul's *apologia*. Smit, 'What is Apollos? What is Paul?' 250: '... in 1 Cor. 1.10–4.21 Paul deploys a well-considered strategy following the classical status theory. This definitely is an apology.'

25. Heinrici, *Der erste Brief*, 64; Smit, 'What is Apollos? What is Paul?' 241–42.

26. Smit, 'What is Apollos? What is Paul?' 236–38.

27. On the significance of the verb ἀνακρίνειν that Paul uses three times in 4.1–5, see Weiss, *Der erste Korintherbrief*, 96–97.

28. Similarly, Smit, 'What is Apollos? What is Paul?' 242.

29. Heinrici, *Der erste Brief*, 12, 64.

30. So, already, Weiss, *Der erste Korintherbrief*, xxxiii.

31. I pass over here the debated phrase τὸ μὴ ὑπὲρ ἃ γέγραπται, since it is not crucial to our investigation. See Welborn, *Politics and Rhetoric in the Corinthian Epistles*, 43–75.

106 *Paul, the Fool of Christ*

may be puffed up in favor of one (ὑπὲρ τοῦ ἑνός) against the other (κατὰ τοῦ ἑτέρου).' The best way to understand the term μετεσχημάτισα here is in the sense of the 'application of a figure'.[32] The figures of speech to which Paul makes reference are the illustrations from agriculture and building in ch. 3.[33] The point of these illustrations is to demonstrate the collegiality of those who labor toward a 'common purpose' as defined by God (3.5–9). The lessons are necessary because of the tendency of some in Corinth to become 'inflated' in favor of Apollos and against Paul.[34]

Finally, it is possible that Paul alludes to the adherents of Apollos in the opening lines of his defense of the 'foolishness' of the gospel.[35] In 1.18 Paul designates those for whom the word of the cross is foolishness as οἱ ἀπολλύμενοι ('the ones who are perishing'). Paul elucidates his point by means of a quotation from Scripture: 'I will destroy (ἀπολῶ) the wisdom of the wise, and the cleverness of the clever I will thwart' (1.19). Both verses seem to contain a paronomasia: οἱ ἀπολλύμενοι is a pun on the 'Apollonists,' and ἀπολῶ a play on the name of their revered teacher. Three observations support this conclusion. First, the repetition of the verb ἀπόλλυμι serves to make the term conspicuous.[36] Second, there is a well-established connection between the name Apollo and the verb ἀπόλλυμι in the literature of antiquity.[37] And third, there is Paul's demonstrated tendency to employ paronomasia elsewhere, as in the epistle to Philemon, where Paul plays repeatedly with the name Onesimus.[38] By means of a word-play in 1.18–19, Paul makes it clear that the adherents of

32. M. D. Hooker, '"Beyond the things which are written"? An Examination of I Corinthians 4,6', *NTS* 10 (1963) 127–32; J. S. Vos, 'Der ΜΕΤΑΣΧΗΜΑΤΙΣΜΟΣ in 1 Kor 4,6,' *ZNW* 86 (1995) 154–72.

33. D. P. Ker, 'Paul and Apollos – Colleagues or Rivals?' *JSNT* 77 (2000) 91–92.

34. Weiss (*Der erste Korintherbrief*, 104) rightly holds that 'the one' and 'the other' in 4.6 refer to Apollos and Paul.

35. For what follows, see Smit, 'What is Apollos? What is Paul?' 243–44.

36. It is not the verb ἀπόλλυμι as such, but the repetition of the verb which signals a word-play; thus, Smit, 'What is Apollos? What is Paul?' 243: 'By itself the qualification οἱ ἀπολλύμενοι in verse 18 is not unique and occurs elsewhere in the Pauline corpus, as for instance in 2 Cor. 4.3. In 2 Cor. 2.15 we even find the same antithesis between οἱ ἀπολλύμενοι and οἱ σῳζόμενοι as we have here. What sets 1 Cor. 1.18–19 apart is that οἱ ἀπολλύμενοι is elucidated by means of the quotation from Scripture beginning with ἀπολῶ, a form which is almost identical to the name of Apollos as mentioned by Paul in 1.12.'

37. See the references in D. E. Aune, *Revelation*, WBC 52B (Nashville: Thomas Nelson, 1998) 535; cf. Smit, 'What is Apollos? What is Paul?' 244.

38. Phlm. 10–11, where the adjectives ἄχρηστος ('useless') and εὔχρηστος ('useful') play upon the meaning of the name Ὀνήσιμος ('the useful one'); see also vs. 20, ναὶ ἀδελφέ, ἐγώ σου ὀναίμην ἐν κυρίῳ. See the comments of J. B. Lightfoot, *St. Paul's Epistles to the Colossians and to Philemon* (repr. of 1879 edition; Grand Rapids, MI: Zondervan, 1976) 340, 344–45; J. Knox, *Philemon Among the Letters of Paul* (New York: Harper, 1959) 12–13.

Apollos are the main target of the defense of his gospel against the charge of 'foolishness'.

What we learn about Apollos from the Acts of the Apostles (18.24–28) suggests that this teacher would have found an enthusiastic reception among those at Corinth who participated in learned culture.[39] The author of Acts describes Apollos as 'a Jew, a native of Alexandria... an eloquent man, skilled in the exposition of Scriptures' (Acts 18.24).[40] As a native of Alexandria,[41] Apollos would have benefited from the rich intellectual culture of this teeming cosmopolis,[42] to which Jews made significant contributions in the early Roman period.[43] The expression ἀνὴρ λόγιος describes a person with rhetorical training, one who had mastered the art of oratory,[44] but also designates a 'learned man' generally,[45] one who had studied philosophy and literature.[46] The additional characterization of Apollos as δυνατὸς ἐν γραφαῖς probably refers to his ability to expound the deeper, allegorical meaning of religious texts through the application of a

39. Indeed, according to codex D of Acts 18.27, Apollos came to Corinth at the invitation of certain Corinthians who were visiting in Ephesus and were impressed by his speech (ἐν δὲ Ἐφέσῳ ἐπιδημοῦντες τινες Κορίνθιοι καὶ ἀκούσαντες αὐτοῦ παρεκάλουν διελθεῖν σὺν αὐτοῖς εἰς τὴν πατρίδα αὐτῶν).

40. There is no reason to doubt the historicity of the information contained in Acts 18.24; problems begin only with the next verse; see the analysis in Weiss, *Der erste Korintherbrief*, xxxi n.1; G. Lüdemann, *Early Christianity according to the Traditions in Acts* (Minneapolis: Fortress Press, 1989) 207–209.

41. On the disputed issue of whether Luke's expression Ἀλεξανδρεὺς τῷ γένει implies that Apollos was a citizen of the Greek polis, see Winter, *Philo and Paul among the Sophists*, 175 n. 142. On the social and political status of Jews in Alexandria, see A. Kasher, *The Jews in Hellenistic and Roman Egypt: The Struggle for Equal Rights* (Tübingen: Mohr-Siebeck, 1985) 197–207.

42. C. Haas, *Alexandria in Late Antiquity: Topography and Social Conflict* (Baltimore: Johns Hopkins University Press, 1997).

43. J. Modrzejewski, *The Jews of Egypt: From Ramses II to Emperor Hadrian* (Princeton: Princeton University Press, 1995).

44. Philo *Post.* 53 describes one engaged in σοφιστικαὶ τεχναί as a λόγιος ἀνήρ. See the definition of ἀνὴρ λόγιος in Phrynichus 198 (ὡς οἱ πολλοὶ λέγουσιν ἐπὶ τοῦ δεινοῦ εἰπεῖν καὶ ὑψηλοῦ), supported by Lobeck's citations. Cf. Field, *Notes on the Translation of the New Testament*, 129; Heinrici, *Der erste Brief*, 12 n.; Winter, *Philo and Paul among the Sophists*, 176.

45. Plutarch *Cicero* 49.5, where Augustus calls Cicero a λόγιος ἀνήρ. See E. Orth, *Logios* (Leipzig: Norske, 1926) esp. 46. Cf. Liftin, *St. Paul's Theology of Proclamation*, 123, 240; Ker, 'Paul and Apollos', 77–78.

46. Weiss, *Der erste Korintherbrief*, xxxi, n. 1. Compare, for example, the curriculum of Tiberius, who studied rhetoric, philosophy, and literature, and whose writings 'reveal a preference for the learned and elaborate; that is, for the Alexandrian', according to B. Levick, *Tiberius the Politician* (London: Routledge, 1999) 15–17, esp. 16.

philosophical framework.[47] Perhaps we should picture Apollos to ourselves as a man like Philo, with similar education and abilities, though not of so lofty a social class.[48] He was the kind of man who could have composed a writing like the so-called Epistle to the Hebrews, as Luther suggests.[49] Such a 'man of culture'[50] might well have engendered among his admirers comparisons derogatory to the apostle Paul.

Paul's rhetorical strategy makes it difficult to assess whether Apollos may have had some role in instigating a derogatory estimate of Paul. Paul's over-arching purpose in 1 Cor. 1–4 is to quell the outbreak of faction and to restore the Christian community to concord.[51] Accordingly, Paul presents himself and Apollos as examples of harmonious relation: they are 'one' (3.8); they are 'co-workers' (3.9). Yet precisely at the point where Paul emphasizes unity and collegiality, there are signs of tension and subtle distinctions.[52] In the agricultural metaphor in 3.5–9, it is Paul who has 'planted' and Apollos who has 'watered' (3.6). Although both activities are necessary for growth, the one who plants has priority, and might be thought to have a greater claim upon the produce.[53] The distinction is clearer in the building metaphor that follows in 3.10–15, where Paul describes himself as a 'skilled master builder' (σοφὸς ἀρχιτέκτων) who has laid the foundation of the community, while Apollos is, figuratively, one of the anonymous workers who have added something to the structure.[54] Indeed, the anonymity of Apollos in this figure ('someone else is building on it', 3.10) may be the clearest indication of Paul's feeling of rivalry.[55] A distinction between functions that are essential and those that are

47.   Weiss, *Der erste Korintherbrief*, xxxi, n. 1. Cf. R. A. Horsley, 'Wisdom of Word and Words of Wisdom at Corinth', *CBQ* 39 (1977) 224–39, esp. 232.

48.   Weiss, *Der erste Korintherbrief*, xxxi, n. 1.; Winter, *Philo and Paul among the Sophists*, 176.

49.   Luther *WA* 10, Ia. 134; *WA* 45.389; followed by H. Appel, *Der Hebräerbrief: Ein Schreiben des Apollos an Judenchristen der korinthischen Gemeinde* (Leipzig: Deichert, 1918); T. W. Manson, 'The Problem of the Epistle to the Hebrews', *BJRL* 32 (1949) 1–17, esp. 13–17. See the evaluation of Luther's suggestion in H. Attridge, *The Epistle to the Hebrews*, Hermeneia (Philadelphia: Fortress Press, 1989) 4.

50.   The rendering of ἀνὴρ λόγιος suggested by J. H. Moulton and G. Milligan, *The Vocabulary of the Greek Testament* (London: Hodder & Stoughton, 1930; repr. Grand Rapids, MI: Eerdmans, 1980) 378.

51.   L. L. Welborn, 'A Conciliatory Principle in 1 Cor. 4.6', *NovT* 29 (1987) 320–46, esp. 333–40; idem, *Politics and Rhetoric in the Corinthian Epistles*, 56–65; M. M. Mitchell, *Paul and the Rhetoric of Reconciliation*.

52.   Ker, 'Paul and Apollos', esp. 85–90.

53.   Collins, *First Corinthians*, 146: 'The image highlights the complementarity of Apollos' role to Paul's ministry and suggests the truly seminal nature of Paul's ministry.' Similarly, Ker, 'Paul and Apollos', 86.

54.   Collins, *First Corinthians*, 148–50; Ker, 'Paul and Apollos', 88–89.

55.   Rightly, Ker, 'Paul and Apollos', 89.

supplementary is implicit in these metaphors, and serves to diminish the contribution of Apollos to the Corinthian community. We must also assume that Apollos is reckoned among the 'pedagogues' mentioned in 4.15.[56] The inclusion of Apollos in the latter group is a gesture of contempt,[57] since the pedagogues in the 'Guardian' mime, to which Paul alludes here,[58] are guilty of connivance in the delinquency of the schoolboy.[59] In the logic of the metaphor, Apollos has aided the unruly elements in the church at Corinth. The distinctions implicit in Paul's metaphors suggest that Apollos has played a more than passive role in inspiring criticism of Paul.[60] Indeed, the possibility cannot be excluded that it was Apollos himself who originally applied the term 'fool' (μωρός) to Paul.[61] We are not permitted to forget that Alexandria, of which Apollos was a native, was the home of the mime, and that it was from this city that mimic plots and characters flowed to other places.[62]

We have seen that for the denigration of a public figure as a 'fool' to be successful, there must be some basis for the comparison.[63] In the case of Paul, several aspects of his person, way of life, and self-presentation may have given his opponents opportunities to portray him as a 'fool'. The most obvious of these was Paul's manner of speaking, to which reference is repeatedly made in 1 Cor. 1–4 (esp. 1.17, 21; 2.1, 3, 4; 3.1). As we have seen, Paul acknowledges that his manner of speaking made him appear to be foolish, by alluding in his self-portrait in 2.1–5 to the figure of the

---

56. Weiss, *Der erste Korintherbrief*, xxxii; Ker, 'Paul and Apollos', 85.

57. So, already, Weiss, *Der erste Korintherbrief*, xxxii.

58. See ch. 4 above, on 1 Cor. 4.14–21.

59. Herodas *Mime* 3.58–90; cf. Crusius, *Untersuchungen zu den Mimiamben des Herondas*, 76–77.

60. P. Richardson, 'The Thunderbolt in Q and the Wise Man in Corinth', in *From Jesus to Paul: Studies in Honor of Francis Beare Wright*, eds. P. Richardson and J. C. Hurd (Waterloo: Laurier, 1984) 100: 'Apollos hovers over the difficulties in Corinth to a very much larger extent than many recent commentators allow.'

61. If this were the case, then Apollos would be following the conventional practice among rivals in the late Roman Republic and early Empire, when humorous invective was routinely used to denigrate political rivals; see Corbeill, *Controlling Laughter*, 4: '*Ad hominem* attacks characterize the bulk of political humor during this period.'

62. Cicero *Pro Rab. Post.* 12.35: 'We have heard of old of Alexandria; now we know it. There we find all the race of jugglers; there we find all their tricks; it is from its inhabitants that writers of mimes draw all their plots.' For further evidence, see Swiderek, 'Le Mime Grec en Egypte', 63–74.

63. See ch. 3 above, particularly the denigration of Claudius as a fool (μωρός) in Suetonius *Claudius* 3.2; 15.4; 38.3; *Nero* 33.1; Seneca *Apoc.* 1.1; 7.1; 7.3; 8.3; with the comments of Eden, *Seneca. Apocolocyntosis*, 64, 92, 95, 105; Garland, *The Eye of the Beholder*, 40–42; S. K. Dickison, 'Claudius: Saturnalicius Princeps,' *Latomus* 36 (1977) 634–47. For the principal topics of humorous invective, see Corbeill, *Controlling Laughter*, esp. 14–56.

'befuddled orator'.[64] In 2 Cor. 10.10, Paul's detractors are quoted: 'His letters are weighty and strong,... but his speech is contemptible (ὁ λόγος ἐξουθενημένος).'[65] A few verses later, Paul concedes the point: 'I am untrained (ἰδιώτης) in public speaking' (2 Cor. 11.6).[66]

Next, there was something about Paul's demeanor that gave the impression of 'weakness'. Paul repeatedly acknowledges his weakness in 1 Cor. 1–4: 'Indeed, I came to you in weakness and in fear and in much trembling' (2.3); 'We are weak, but you are strong' (4.10). In 2 Cor. 10.10, again, Paul quotes anonymous critics who say, 'his bodily presence is weak'.[67] As we have seen, 'weakness' is a standard feature of portraits of the fool in the mime and in mime-inspired satire.[68] Because the Greek word for 'weakness,' ἀσθενής, implies illness, a physical ailment,[69] Paul's opponents may have been ridiculing his 'thorn in the flesh' (2 Cor. 12.7). There has been much speculation about the nature of Paul's condition: epilepsy, weakened eyesight, a speech impediment, have all been proposed.[70] Perhaps Paul suffered, like his contemporary Claudius, from the effects of infantile paralysis.[71] In any case, Paul's opponents exploited his weakness to make him look like a fool.[72] However cruel this humor may seem to us, it is in keeping with the Greek and Roman concept of the

64. See above, ch. 4 on 1 Cor. 2.1–5. Compare, especially, the portrayal of Claudius as a 'befuddled orator' in Seneca *Apoc.* 7.1–5; in this case, too, the portrayal is a parody of Claudius' own manner of speaking; see C. F. Russo, *L. Annaei Senecae Divi Claudii* ΑΠΟΚΟΛΟΣΥΝΤΩΣΙΣ, 77–79.

65. On the meaning of the description of Paul's λόγος as ἐξουθενημένος in 2 Cor. 10.10, see Furnish, *II Corinthians*, 486; Martin, *2 Corinthians*, 313; Winter, *Philo and Paul among the Sophists*, 211–13.

66. See the discussion of the meaning of the expression ἰδιώτης τῷ λόγῳ in Winter, *Philo and Paul among the Sophists*, 213–15, referring to Philodemus 2.134; Philo *Agr.* 143, 159–60; Isocrates *Antidosis* 201, 204; Epictetus *Diss.* 3.7.1; 16.13; Alcidamas 1.4.15; Aristides *Or.* 51.29, in order to argue that ἰδιώτης τῷ λόγῳ designates one who is not a professional orator (a sophist), but rather an 'amateur'. See also Epictetus *Diss.* 3.9.14: οὐδὲν ἦν ὁ Ἐπίκτητος, ἐσκολοίκιζεν, ἐβαρβάριζεν.

67. On the phrase ἡ παρουσία τοῦ σώματος ἀσθενής in 2 Cor. 10.10, see the discussion in Betz, *Der Apostel Paulus und die sokratische Tradition*, 53–54; Furnish, *II Corinthians*, 468; Winter, *Philo and Paul among the Sophists*, 211–13.

68. See above, ch. 4 on 1 Cor. 4.10. In addition to the texts cited above, see the weak, anxiety-ridden fisherman, ironically named 'Asphalion,' in the mime-inspired poem of Theocritus *Id.* 21, with the comments of Reich, *Der Mimus*, 374: 'dieser alte Fischer ... gehört zur Gattung der mimischen stupidi, der μωροί, ... Vor allem zeichnet er sich, als echter μωρός, durch eine übertriebene Ängstlichkeit aus'.

69. Bauer, *A Greek-English Lexicon*, 142–43.

70. Furnish, *II Corinthians*, 547–50.

71. Levick, *Claudius*, 13–15, 200 n. 7–12; Garland, *The Eye of the Beholder*, 40–42.

72. Weakness, often construed as effeminacy, was one of the principal topics of humorous invective between rivals; see Corbeill, *Controlling Laughter*, 128–73.

laughable, in which 'usually only the defects of the weak are represented as truly ridiculous'.[73]

Third, Paul's occupation as a handworker (1 Cor. 4.12) placed him among the urban proletariat whose lives were caricatured in the mime.[74] Numerous references in the Corinthian correspondence make it plain that Paul's decision to work with his hands was a source of shame for the wealthy members of the church in Corinth.[75] Indeed, it is possible that Paul's occupation was related to the theater. According to Acts 18.3, Paul was a σκηνοποιός by trade, an occupation which he shared with his missionary colleagues, Aquila and Priscilla.[76] The traditional rendering of this term is 'tentmaker'.[77] Recently, it has been argued that σκηνοποιός should be defined more precisely as 'leather-worker'.[78] But neither of these interpretations is well supported by linguistic evidence.[79] The only non-metaphorical use of the term σκηνοποιός outside the Bible (and literature it has influenced) suggests that σκηνοποιός should be understood as a 'maker of stage properties'.[80] According to Pollux, the word was used in comedy as a synonym for μηχανοποιός,[81] which is either a 'stagehand' who moves stage properties,[82] or a 'manufacturer of stage

73. Grant, *The Ancient Rhetorical Theories of the Laughable*, 19: 'That laughter has its origin in the contemplation of the ugly or defective is a fundamental and frequently recurring definition in Greek and Roman theories of the laughable, and it is equally significant that usually only the defects of the weak are represented as truly ridiculous.'

74. See, in general, Grysar *Der römische Mimus*, 250; Reich, *Der Mimus*, 214; Rawson, 'The Vulgarity of the Mime', 259; Beacham, *The Roman Theatre*, 131, 137.

75. 1 Cor. 9.1–27; 2 Cor. 11.7–15; see the discussion in G. Theissen, 'Legitimation und Lebensunterhalt: Ein Beitrag zu Soziologie urchristlicher Missionare', *NTS* 21 (1975) 192–221; Hock, *The Social Context of Paul's Ministry*, esp. 50–65.

76. For evaluation of this tradition in Acts, see Weiss, *Das Urchristentum*, 135; Lüdemann, *Early Christianity according to the traditions in Acts*, 198, 202: 'The further information in Acts that like Aquila and Priscilla he [Paul] was a *skenopoios* cannot be demonstrated from the letters. However, because of the historical reliability of the other information in vv. 2–3 we should not doubt this report.'

77. Thus the KJV, RSV, REB, NRSV; advocated by P. Lampe, 'Paulus als Zeltmacher,' *BZ* 31 (1987) 256–61; C. J. Hemer, *The Book of Acts in the Setting of Hellenistic History*, WUNT 49 (Tübingen: Mohr-Siebeck, 1989) 119, 233.

78. E. Haenchen, *The Acts of the Apostles* (Philadelphia: Westminster Press, 1971) 534 n. 3; Hock, *The Social Context of Paul's Ministry*, 21.

79. See the detailed analysis of the linguistic evidence and other considerations which militate against the interpretations 'tentmaker' and 'leatherworker' by F. Danker in the 3rd ed. of Bauer, *Greek-English Lexicon*, 928–29, *s.v.* σκηνοποιός.

80. Bauer, *Greek-English Lexicon*, 928, *s.v.* σκηνοποιός 1; see also Liddell-Scott-Jones, *Greek-English Lexicon*, 1608, *s.v.* σκηνοποιός II.

81. Pollux *Onom.* 7.189. See also Dio Cassius 67.2 for σκηνοποιέω as 'building a theater'.

82. Aristophanes *Pax* 174.

properties'.[83] One must reckon with 'the strong probability that Luke's readers in urban areas, where theatrical productions were in abundance, would think of σκηνοποιός in reference to matters theatrical',[84] that is, as a 'prop maker'.

Finally, we cannot exclude the possibility that Paul's physical appearance bore some resemblance to a mimic fool. The only physical description of Paul to come down to us from the early church, in the *Acts of Paul and Thecla*, portrays 'a man small of stature, with a bald head and crooked legs, in good condition, with eyebrows meeting and nose somewhat hooked, full of friendliness'.[85] Whatever the historical accuracy of this description may be, it is clear that Paul is depicted in accordance with a particular type, the 'bald-headed buffoon' (μωρὸς φαλακρός) of the mime.[86]

Perhaps it came as a surprise to Paul's Corinthian detractors that he accepted their labeling of him as a fool, though not without considerable hesitation,[87] and only after he had redefined the key terms in his own sense.[88] But as it turns out, the adoption of the role of the fool was a strategy practiced by a number of intellectuals in Greek and Roman antiquity. The attraction of the role lay in the freedom it permitted for the utterance of a dangerous truth.[89] Numerous anecdotes relate how, especially in the early Empire, the mimes became voices for what no one else dared to say.[90]

83. Bauer, *Greek-English Lexicon*, 928, *s.v.* σκηνοποιός I: 'Associated terms include σκηνογράφος Diogenes Laertius 2.125 and σκηνογραφία Aristotle *Poet.* 1449a and Polybius 12.28a.1, in reference to painting of stage scenery.'

84. Danker in Bauer, *Greek-English Lexicon*, 929.

85. Text in *Acta Apostolorum Apocrypha*, ed. R. A. Lipsius and M. Bonnet (Darmstadt: Wissenschaftliche Buchgesellschaft, 1959) 1.237.6–9: εἶδεν δὲ τὸν Παῦλον ἐρχόμενον ἄνδρα μικρὸν τῷ μεγέθει, ψιλὸν τῇ κεφαλῇ, ἀγκύλον ταῖς κνήμαις, εὐεκτικόν, σύνοφρυν, μικρῶς ἐπίρρινον, χάριτος πλήρη. Translation in E. Hennecke and W. Schneemelcher, *New Testament Apocrypha* (trans. R. McL. Wilson; Philadelphia: Westminster Press, 1964) 2.354.

86. Rightly, Betz, *Der Apostel Paulus und die sokratische Tradition*, 54–55. For alternative views of this literary portrait of Paul, see R. M. Grant, 'The Description of Paul in the *Acts of Paul and Thecla*', *VC* 36 (1982) 1–4; A. Malherbe, 'A Physical Description of Paul', *HTR* 74 (1986) 170–75. On mockery of a deviant physical appearance as a strategy of denigration, see Corbeill, *Controlling Laughter*, 14–56.

87. The point is rightly made by Caspari, 'Über den biblischen Begriff der Torheit', 692: 'Zu allem bleibt aber beachtlich, wie lange der 1. Kor. zögert, bis er nur überhaupt eine persönliche Wortform unseres Begriffs 3, 18 verwendet.' See below, ch. 6 'Evaluation of the Role'.

88. Thus, rightly, Weiss, *Der erste Korintherbrief*, 25; Conzelmann, *1 Corinthians*, 249. See ch. 6 below for detailed analysis of Paul's redefinition of the key terms μωρία and σοφία.

89. Winkler, *Auctor and Actor*, 290–91.

90. E.g., Suetonius (*Calig.* 27.4) relates how Caligula 'burned a writer of Atellan farces alive in the middle of the arena of the amphitheatre, because of a humorous line of double

The exercise of the fool's license is well illustrated by the encounter between the Roman knight Decimus Laberius and Julius Caesar in 46 B.C.[91] Although a member of the upper class, Laberius wrote professionally for the stage, and won fame by means of his clever and pungent mimes.[92] Politicians, like the demagogue Clodius,[93] were the object of his 'wit-bolts',[94] and Caesar himself felt their sting.[95] In revenge, Caesar compelled Laberius (then age sixty) to perform in a competitive presentation of one of his own mimes.[96] Laberius took the role of the fool,[97] and uttered two pointed *dicta* which the audience rightly interpreted as an attack upon Caesar.[98] Dressed as a

meaning'. See also Suetonius *Domit.* 10; Anthenaeus *Deip.* 14.621A; *Historia Augusta, Duo Maxim.* 9.3–5; *Historia Augusta, M. Antonin.* 29; other anecdotes are collected by Reich, *Der Mimus*, 182–92; Nicoll, *Masks, Mimes and Miracles*, 124–26.

91. The account of the episode is preserved in Macrobius *Sat.* 2.7.2; 2.7.6–7, and was evidently part of the lost eighth book of Gellius *Noctes Atticae*. On the sources, see E. Turk, *Macrobius. Die Quellen seiner Saturnalien* (Diss. Freiburg, 1961). References to the incident are found in Cicero *Ad Fam.* 12.18 and Suetonius *Caes.* 39.

92. Of the mimes of Laberius we have forty-two titles and about one hundred and forty lines, in Bonaria, *Mimorum Romanorum Fragmenta I*, 9–103. Laberius is praised by Gellius (*NA* 16.7) for the elegance of his verses and the freedom with which he coined new words. Horace (*Sat.* 1.10.6) shows a grudging respect for Laberius' mimes, which he nevertheless considered obscene. See, in general, Reich, *Der Mimus*, 563–67; Nicoll, *Masks, Mimes and Miracles*, 111–12; Beare, *The Roman Stage*, 154–58; Beacham, *The Roman Theatre*, 133–34. On the social status of Laberius, see L. R. Taylor, 'Republican and Augustan Writers Enrolled in the Equestrian Centuries', *TAPA* 99 (1968) 469–72. For the fame of Laberius, see Cicero *Ad Fam.* 7.11.2; 12.18.

93. For Laberius' refusal of Clodius' request for a mime and his taunt at him, see Macrobius *Sat.* 2.6.6, and the discussion in R. Till, 'Laberius und Caesar', *Historia* 24 (1975) 261–62.

94. Fronto (61.155) characterizes Laberius' sayings as 'wit-bolts' or 'wit-flashes' (*dictabolaria*); cf. Nicoll, *Masks, Mimes and Miracles*, 111.

95. For Laberius' jibes at Caesar for nominating six aediles and favoring polygamy, see his mime *Necyomantia*, frag. 78 in Bonaria, *Mimorum Romanorum Fragmenta I*, 52–54.

96. Macrobius *Sat.* 2.7.2; 2.7.6–7. See the analysis of this incident by Till, 'Laberius und Caesar', 260–86; E. J. Jory, 'Publilius Syrus and the Element of Competition in the Theatre of the Republic' in *Vir Bonus Discendi Peritus. Studies in Celebration of Otto Skutsch's Eightieth Birthday*, ed. N. Horsfall (London: University of London Institute of Classical Studies, 1988) 73–81, esp. 77–81.

97. Till, 'Laberius und Caesar,' 278: 'Laberius spielte die Rolle eines syrischen Sklaven, bezog die in dieser Rolle üblichen Prügel'; n. 78: 'Daraus könnte man schliessen, dass Laberius *actor secundarum partium* war.'

98. Macrobius *Sat.* 2.7.5: 'And at those last words the audience as one man turned and looked at Caesar, thus indicating that this scathing gibe was an attack on his despotism'; trans. P. V. Davies, *Macrobius. The Saturnalia* (New York: Columbia University Press, 1969) 181.

slave,[99] and flogged by whips (the fool's usual punishment), Laberius cried out, 'Thus, citizens of Rome, do we lose our liberties!' and 'Many must he fear whom many fear.'[100]

In an exceptionally ferocious satire (*Sat.* 2.7),[101] the Augustan poet Horace dissects the hypocrisy of his own social class by portraying himself as a fool. The scene is set at Rome during the Saturnalia, when slaves enjoyed a season of license.[102] Davus, the slave of Horace, is thus permitted to speak his mind freely to his master.[103] The satire revolves around Davus' audacious question, 'What if you, the master, are found to be a greater fool (*stultior*) than I, your slave?'[104] In the diatribe that follows, Davus portrays his master in a variety of roles played by the fool in the mime: the adulterer, the parasite, and finally, the runaway.[105] Although Horace is represented as the auditor of the sermon, and feigns an outburst of anger, it would be more correct to regard the slave Davus, the preacher of wisdom, as Horace's alter ego.[106] In the slave's lecture, the face of Horace's own opinion begins to show through the mask of mirth, as silver seeps through a mirror. It is Horace's own voice that we hear in the servant's speech indicting the members of the ruling class for their addictions, inconstancies, and complacencies.

In the role of a fool, Paul is able to challenge the reliance upon wealth and knowledge by the leaders of the church at Corinth (1 Cor. 1.5; 4.8),[107]

---

99.   Laberius' dress was a sarcastic reference to the origins of his rival in the competition, Publilius Syrus, a manumitted slave; Macrobius *Sat.* 2.7.4; Till, 'Laberius und Caesar,' 278. On Publilius Syrus, see O. Skutsch, 'Publilius Syrus', *RE* 23 (1959) 1920–23.

100.   Macrobius *Sat.* 2.7.4. On the sayings, see F. Giancotti, *Mimo e Gnome* (Firenze: G. D'anna, 1967) 183, 186; Till, 'Laberius und Caesar', 278–79. See the comment of Th. Mommsen, *The History of Rome*, trans. W. Dickson (London, 1880) 4.581: 'One sees from this that Laberius understood how to exercise the fool's privilege and Caesar how to permit the fool's freedom.'

101.   On the character of this satire and the sustained violence of its self-criticism, see Johnson, *Horace and the Dialectic of Freedom*, 3–5.

102.   Horace *Sat.* 2.7.4–5; see also 2.3.5.

103.   Horace *Sat.* 2.7.1–5, with the summary of Fairclough, *Horace. Satires, Epistles and Ars Poetica*, 221.

104.   Horace *Sat.* 2.7.42–43. Davus asserts that the terms 'weak' (*imbecillus*), 'lazy' (*iners*) and 'parasitic' (*popino*) apply to Horace in greater measure than himself (*Sat.* 2.7.39–40), employing terms that were routinely associated with the fool in the mime.

105.   In fact, the rogues' gallery is more complete: Horace is portrayed as an adulterer (*Sat.* 2.7.46–67), a leading slave (*Sat.* 2.7.68–82), a braggart warrior (*Sat.* 2.7.83–87), a learned impostor (*Sat.* 2.7.95–101), a parasite (*Sat.* 2.7.102–111), and a runaway (*Sat.* 2.7.111–115) – all parts played by the fool in the mime. For a similar interpretation of Horace Sat. 2.7, see Freudenburg, *The Walking Muse*, 225–26.

106.   Rightly, Fairclough, *Horace*, 223; Johnson, *Horace and the Dialectic of Freedom*, 3.

107.   On Paul's critique of the Corinthians' wealth in 'speech' (λόγος) and 'knowledge' (γνῶσις), see esp. Heinrici, *Der erste Brief*, 11–12, 45–46, 152–53; Weiss, *Der erste*

and the sense of superiority which these things engendered (3.21; 4.6).[108] At the beginning of the epistle (1.5), Paul's criticism is implicit in his thanksgiving for the intellectual attainments of the Corinthians; his irony is half revealed in hyperbole,[109] in qualifications,[110] and in the passive voice of the verb used in describing the Corinthians' 'enrichment'.[111] But as the letter unfolds, and Paul acknowledges the 'foolishness' of his preaching (1.18–2.16), he speaks with greater freedom of the spiritual immaturity of the Corinthians. Paul's critique of the superficiality of the Corinthians in 3.1–3 is cutting and direct: 'To be sure, brothers, I was not able to speak to you as spiritual people, but rather as people of the flesh, as infants in Christ. I gave you milk to drink, not solid food, for you were not able (to digest it), nor are you able even now, for you are still of the flesh.'[112] Yet it is only after Paul brings himself to use a personal form of the concept in 3.18 (μωρός),[113] and finally appropriates the role of the fool, that he is able to exercise the fool's license to the fullest degree. Thus in 4.7, Paul asks with savage irony: 'For who sees anything different in you? What do you have that you did not receive? And if you received it, why do you boast as if it were not a gift?'[114] And in 4.8, Paul addresses the Corinthians with a series of exclamations possessed of a bitter and mounting sarcasm:

Korintherbrief, 7, 108–109; H. D. Betz, 'The Problem of Rhetoric and Theology according to the Apostle Paul', 26–39. Rhetorical skill and sophistical knowledge are the attainments which are most valued by those who participate in Hellenistic culture.

108.   The verb φυσιοῦσθαι ('to be puffed up, to have an exaggerated self-conception'), which occurs so frequently in the Corinthian correspondence (1 Cor. 4.6,18–19; 5.2; 8.1; 13.4; see also 2 Cor. 12.20), is especially important as an indication of Paul's understanding of the source of the conflict in Corinth; see Heinrici, *Der erste Brief*, 12: Weiss, *Der erste Korintherbrief*, 104; Collins, *First Corinthians*, 180–81. In ancient literature, the verb φυσιόω (φυσάω) designates a symptom of the *hybris* that gives rise to factions; see Fitzgerald, *Cracks in an Earthen Vessel*, 133, 144; Welborn, *Politics and Rhetoric in the Corinthian Epistles*, 5–6, 39, 55–56.

109.   The hyperbole is embodied in the repetition of πᾶς/πᾶσα in the phrases ἐν παντὶ ἐπλουτίσθε . . . , ἐν παντὶ λόγῳ καὶ πάσῃ γνώσει (1.5); see Weiss, *Der erste Korintherbrief*, 7.

110.   On the critical intention expressed by the qualifying phase ἐν αὐτῷ in 1.5, see Lindemann, *Der erste Korintherbrief*, 30: 'mit dem betont nachgestellten ἐν αὐτῷ wird auf das ἐν Χριστῷ Ἰησοῦ von V. 4 zurückgegriffen: Nicht aus sich selbst heraus sind die korinthischen Christen "reich", sondern sie sind es geworden "in Christus".'

111.   On Paul's use of the passive voice of the verb (ἐπλουτίσθητε) in 1.5, see Collins, *First Corinthians*, 62: 'Paul's critical perspective on the gifts is foreshadowed in the phrase "enriched in him" (*eploutisthēte en autō*). The use of the divine passive of *ploutizō*, hapax in 1 Corinthians, is a reminder that the Corinthians are merely the recipients of these gifts.'

112.   On the directness of Paul's discussion of the spiritual defects of the Corinthians in 3.1–4, see Heinrici, *Der erste Brief*, 114–17; Weiss, *Der erste Korintherbrief*, 72–73; Fitzgerald, *Cracks in an Earthen Vessel*, 121; Collins, *First Corinthians*, 139–41.

113.   W. Caspari, 'Über den biblischen Begriff der Torheit', 692.

114.   On the irony in 4.7, see Weiss, *Der erste Korintherbrief*, 105–106; Fitzgerald, *Cracks in an Earthen Vessel*, 121.

'Already you have all you want! Already you have become rich! Quite
apart from us you reign like kings! Indeed, I wish that you had become
kings, so that we might share the reign with you!'[115] Paul is fully aware of
the punishment he will have to endure for his free speaking: he alludes,
metaphorically, to verbal abuse and physical mistreatment (4.11–13). And
yet, in the role of the fool, Paul is able to rebuke the educational privilege
and social authority of the Corinthian elite.

By his appropriation of the role of the fool, Paul joins a submerged
tradition in Greco-Roman culture that views dominant society from the
perspective of the poor and weak, the deformed and grotesque.[116] At the
center of this tradition stands the figure of the 'wise fool', who speaks a
critical truth, in jesting-earnest, against the tyranny of conventional
wisdom. The most popular example of this figure is Aesop of folk-tale.[117]
For intellectuals in the early Empire, however, it was Socrates who was the
model of the σοφός who cloaked his wisdom in foolishness.[118] The image of
Socrates that was current in the time of Paul had many elements in
common with the mimic fool.[119] When we have mentioned Aesop and
Socrates, we have touched upon the tradition in which Paul undertakes his
re-evaluation of the concepts of 'wisdom' and 'folly'.

115. The irony of this passage is appreciated by P. Schmiedel, *Die Briefe an die
Thessalonicher und an die Korinther*, HNT (Freiburg: Mohr, 1893) 114; Weiss, *Der erste
Korintherbrief*, 106–108; Fitzgerald, *Cracks in an Earthen Vessel*, 137.

116. The history of this tradition has not been written, though Reich (*Der Mimus*)
gathered many of the materials. Winkler (*Auctor and Actor*, 279–91) traces the connections
between Epicharmus, the *Life of Aesop*, Socrates, Phlyax farce, Herodas, and the mime. See
also Garland, *The Eye of the Beholder*.

117. B. E. Perry, *Aesopica* (New York: Arno Press, 1980); L. W. Daly, *Aesop without
Morals* (New York: Thomas Yoseloff, 1961); Winkler, *Auctor and Actor*, 279–86.

118. Reich, *Der Mimus*, 354–60; O. Gigon, *Sokrates, sein Bild in Dichtung und Geschichte*
(Bern: Francke, 1947) 19–22, 58–62, 112, 209; A.-H. Chroust, *Socrates, Man and Myth*
(London, 1957) 69–100; K. Döring, *Exemplum Socratis. Studien zur Socratesnachwirkung in
der kynisch-stoischen Popularphilosophie der frühen Kaiserzeit und im frühen Christentum*,
Hermes 42 (Wiesbaden: Franz Steiner, 1979) 2–12.

119. Reich, *Der Mimus*, 354–60; Betz, *Der Apostel Paulus und die sokratische Tradition*,
48–49, 80–81; P. Zanker, *The Mask of Socrates: The Image of the Intellectural in Antiquity*
(Berkleley: University of California Press, 1995) 34.

Chapter 6

EVALUATION OF THE ROLE

Before Paul is able to accept the role that has been thrust upon him, he subjects the concept of 'foolishness' (μωρία) to a theological analysis, in order to indicate in what paradoxical sense 'foolishness' might be the characteristic of authentic existence, in a world where the rulers had crucified the Messiah. The analysis embraces three moments – acknowledgement, assertion, affirmation – in each of which the term 'foolishness' acquires a somewhat different meaning.[1] First, Paul acknowledges that, from the point of view of the rich and powerful, the message about the crucified Christ appears to be 'foolishness' (1 Cor. 1.18a,23; 2.14).[2] Second, Paul asserts that God has secretly inverted the concepts of 'wisdom' and 'foolishness', so that what is regarded as 'foolishness' by the elite is actually 'wisdom' (1.18b,19–20,24–25,30; 2.6–8).[3] And third, Paul affirms that 'the word of the cross' nevertheless remains 'foolishness' in this present age, so that those who are 'called' by this word must become 'fools' (1.21,26–28; 3.18–19).[4] Paul then spells out the consequences of these paradoxical insights for the Corinthians, for his missionary rivals, and for himself and his colleagues (3.1–4.21).

In order to comprehend Paul's analysis, it is essential to grasp the motivation, structure, and tone of the argument in 1 Cor. 1–4. The explanation of the first of these is already implied in the reconstruction of events that preceded the composition of the letter.[5] We recall that the term 'fool' (μωρός) was not introduced into the discussion by Paul, but was employed by certain members of the church at Corinth in a derogatory comparison of Paul with the eloquent and learned Apollos. The insult was a severe one and could not go unanswered: for to allow oneself to be called a μωρός was to accept relegation to a social category whose ignominy was so great as to render one faceless and voiceless in Greco-Roman society,

---

1. Weiss, *Der erste Korintherbrief*, 25; Bertram, 'μωρός', 845–47.
2. Weiss, *Der erste Korintherbrief*, 25; Wilckens, *Weisheit und Torheit*, 36.
3. Weiss, *Der erste Korintherbrief*, 25; Wilckens, *Weisheit und Torheit*, 36.
4. Weiss, *Der erste Korintherbrief*, 25; Wilckens, *Weisheit und Torheit*, 37.
5. See ch. 5 above.

except as the object of ridicule in the mime.[6] On the other hand, Paul could not simply refuse the denomination, and insist, on the contrary, that he was a σοφός, like Apollos; for this would result in the reification of the values and criteria of the rich and educated in Corinth who had judged him in this fashion.[7] How difficult it was to respond to such an insult in a straightforward manner is illustrated by Claudius' feeble attempt to counter his contemporaries' jokes by explaining that he had merely 'feigned folly'.[8] The only way that remained open to Paul was that taken by mime writers and satirists: he could exploit intellectual paradox to call into question the Corinthians' assumptions about wisdom and foolishness.

The structure of Paul's argument also provides insight into his purposes. Through its formulation, 1.18 is clearly marked as the thesis statement of the argument:[9]

Ὁ λόγος γὰρ ὁ τοῦ σταυροῦ
τοῖς μὲν ἀπολλυμένοις μωρία ἐστίν,
τοῖς δὲ σῳζομένοις ἡμῖν δύναμις θεοῦ ἐστιν.

For the word of the cross
is foolishness to those who are perishing;
but is the power of God to us who are being saved.

By means of antithesis and *parallelismus membrorum*,[10] Paul draws a sharp contrast between two responses to the same subject.[11] The contrast is heightened by the use of the particles (μέν . . . δέ), seldom found in Paul,[12] and by the repetition of the copula (ἐστίν) in both parts of the sentence.[13] Paul's argument thus begins with an account of the diametrically opposed responses of two groups to 'the word of the cross'. The summation of the argument is also clearly indicated in 3.18–19, both in terms of style and content:

Μηδεὶς ἑαυτὸν ἐξαπατάτω·
εἴ τις δοκεῖ σοφὸς εἶναι ἐν ὑμῖν ἐν τῷ αἰῶνι τούτῳ,
μωρὸς γενέσθω,
ἵνα γένηται σοφός.

6. See the insightful observations of Veyne, *A History of Private Life I*, 61–62, 134–37; Winkler, *Auctor and Actor*, 279–91.
7. Similarly, Wilckens, *Weisheit und Torheit*, 38.
8. Suetonius *Claud.* 15.4; 38.3.
9. So, already, Weiss, *Der erste Korintherbrief*, 24–25; Wilckens, *Weisheit und Torheit*, 21.
10. On the parallelism: τοῖς ἀπολλυμένοις corresponds to τοῖς σῳζομένοις, just as μωρία corresponds to δύναμις θεοῦ. See the comments of Weiss, *Der erste Korintherbrief*, 25; Wilckens, *Weisheit und Torheit*, 21; Collins, *First Corinthians*, 102.
11. The single subject, ὁ λόγος τοῦ σταυροῦ, holds both parts of the sentence together; cf. Wilckens, *Weisheit und Torheit*, 21.
12. Blass-Debrunner, *A Greek Grammar* §447; Weiss, *Der erste Korintherbrief*, 25.
13. Wilckens, *Weisheit und Torheit*, 21.

ἡ γὰρ σοφία τοῦ κόσμου τούτου
μωρία παρὰ τῷ θεῷ ἐστιν.

Let no one deceive himself:
if someone among you thinks himself to be wise in this age,
let him become a fool,
so that he may be wise.
For the wisdom of this world
is foolishness with God.

The expression μηδεὶς ἑαυτὸν ἐξαπατάτω characterizes the sentence that follows as the conclusion of the argument, the resolution that must be enacted.[14] The sentences which are thus introduced are a highly artful composition, marked, like the thesis statement in 1.18, by formal parallelism and conceptual contrast.[15] The dialectical formulation is a concentrated summary of the content of the argument from 1.18 on, focused upon the antithetical concepts of σοφός and μωρός.[16] But now the terms μωρός and σοφός have acquired a wholly paradoxical sense.[17] Thus, the argument moves from the abstract to the personal, from the doxastic to the paradoxical. The strategy by which the argument is developed is that of redefinition.[18] Having been labeled a 'fool' (μωρός), Paul first abstracts the concept, then redefines the term 'folly' (μωρία), repeatedly insisting that God has inverted the values of 'wisdom' and 'foolishness', before he finally accepts a personal form of the concept (μωρός) as the truth of his life, now understood in a deeper, paradoxical sense.

Even more crucial for an understanding of Paul's argument is an appreciation of the tone of the exposition. Because this aspect of Paul's discourse has seldom been appreciated,[19] there is puzzlement over particular expressions,[20] and misconstrual of entire sections of the

---

14.   Wilckens, *Weisheit und Torheit*, 8: 'Durch die Wendung μηδεὶς ἑαυτὸν ἐξαπατάτω ist der folgende Satz als hervorgehobene, besonders zu beachtende "Regel" gekennzeichnet.' Cf. Epictetus *Diss.* 2.22.15: καθόλου γὰρ – μὴ ἐξαπατᾶσθε πᾶν ζῷον οὐδενὶ οὕτως ᾠκείωται ὡς τῷ ἰδίῳ συμφέροντι. See also the quotation of Epicurus in Epictetus *Diss.* 2.20.7: μὴ ἐξαπατᾶσθε.

15.   Wilckens, *Weisheit und Torheit*, 9; Collins, *First Corinthians*, 162–63.

16.   Wilckens, *Weisheit und Torheit*, 9; Collins, *First Corinthians*, 87.

17.   Wilckens, *Weisheit und Torheit*, 9.

18.   Humphries, 'Paul's Rhetoric of Argumentation in 1 Corinthians 1–4'; Collins, *First Corinthians*, 116–17.

19.   The exception in the modern history of interpretation is Weiss, who is especially sensitive to the nuances of tone, e.g., *Der erste Korintherbrief*, 25, 27, 29–30, 35, 44, 106.

20.   See, for example, the debate over the meaning of the prepositional phrase ἐν τῇ σοφίᾳ τοῦ θεοῦ in 1.21: the preposition is taken in a temporal sense by Lietzmann, *An die Korinther*, 9; but is construed in a local manner by Schlier, 'Kerygma und Sophia,' 484–85 and Wilckens, *Weisheit und Torheit*, 33–34; for a causal interpretation, see Schottroff, *Der Glaubende und die feindliche Welt*, 196–206. The dispute results from the failure to recognize the word-play.

argument.[21] Numerous features of the text make it clear that Paul wrote 1 Cor. 1–4 in a state of controlled excitement, whose dominant tone is that of irony.[22] Thus the rhetoric exhibits a tendency toward hyperbole and antithesis; the thought takes the form of paradox; throughout there is a search for humorous effect. For example, irony is already apparent in Paul's exaggerated praise of the Corinthians' enrichment 'in everything, in all speech and in all knowledge' (1.5).[23] Paul's account of the behavior of the factions in 1.12 takes the form of parody.[24] A three-fold anaphora (ποῦ) in 1.20 introduces a series of mocking questions which escalate in power and scope.[25] In 1.21, Paul plays provocatively with the meaning of σοφία, exploiting two opposed senses of the term in the tradition.[26] The paradox embodied in expressions such as 'the foolishness of preaching' (1.21) and 'the foolishness of God' (1.25) is so extreme that it approaches blasphemy.[27] Even Paul's account of the drama of salvation in 2.6ff. is deeply ironical in character: as in the theater, the actors in the drama – in this case, 'the rulers of this age' – remain ignorant of the significance of actions which are revealed to the reader 'through the Spirit' (2.6–10).[28]

21.   The most significant of these is the interpretation of Paul's argument in 1 Cor. 1–2, esp. in 2.6–16, as a response to incipient Gnosticism by Schmithals, *Die Gnosis in Korinth*; Wilckens, *Weisheit und Torheit*, esp. 52–89; Lührmann, *Das Offenbarungsverständnis bei Paulus*, 113–17. It has even been suggested (M. Widmann, '1 Kor. 2, 6–16: Ein Einspruch gegen Paulus', *ZNW* 70 [1979] 44–53) that 1 Cor. 2.6–16 is an interpolation by the hand of a Corinthian gnostic!
22.   Repeatedly emphasized by Weiss, *Der erste Korintherbrief*, 25, 27, 29–30, 106; more recently, Plank, *Paul and the Irony of Affliction* esp. 33–70.
23.   Weiss, *Der erste Korintherbrief*, 7: 'ἐν παντὶ λόγῳ καὶ πάσῃ γνώσει – eine hyperbolische Schilderung des Reichtums, mit dem sie überschüttet sind'; similarly, Welborn, *Politics and Rhetoric*, 38.
24.   1 Cor. 1.12, 'What I mean is that each of you says "I belong to Paul", or "I belong to Apollos", or "I belong to Cephas", or "I belong to Christ".' See Welborn, *Politics and Rhetoric*, 60–61; Mitchell, *Paul and the Rhetoric of Reconciliation*, 83, 86.
25.   1 Cor. 1.20. 'Where is the wise man? Where is the scribe? Where is the debater of this age?' See Weiss, *Der erste Korintherbrief*, 27.
26.   Weiss, *Der erste Korintherbrief*, 29: 'Pointiert ist das Nebeneinander ἐν τῇ σοφίᾳ τοῦ θεοῦ...διὰ τῆς σοφίας. Dies Wortspiel erklärt sich begriffsgeschichtlich aus dem Sprachgebrauch der Weisheitsbücher, wo σοφία bald die göttliche Eigenschaft oder Betätigung (oder auch ein Mittelwesen oder eine Weltkraft), bald ein Besitz, eine Befähigung, ein Bestreben der Menschen ist.'
27.   Rightly, Weiss, *Der erste Korintherbrief*, 29–30, on the phrase διὰ τῆς μωρίας τοῦ κηρύγματος in 1.21: 'Hier tritt die Paradoxie des paulinischen Gedankens packend hervor. Fast klingt es lästerlich, dass Gott, um die Menschen zu retten, Torheit angewandt habe.' See also Weder, *Das Kreuz Jesu bei Paulus*, 150.
28.   Cf. J. Schniewind, 'Die Archonten dieses Äons, 1 Kor. 2,6–8', *Nachgelassene Reden und Aufsätze*, ed. E. Kähler (Berlin: Töpelmann, 1952) 104–109; Schottroff, *Der Glaubende und die feindliche Welt* (Tübingen: Mohr-Siebeck, 1970) 201–27; A. W. Carr, 'The Rulers of this Age – 1 Corinthians ii.6–8,' *NTS* 23 (1976/77) 20–35.

When Paul turns to address the Corinthians directly (in 3.1–4), it is in a derisive manner, the way one chides children.[29] The irony of the apostrophe in 4.8 is so intense that it breaks over into sarcasm: 'Already you are satiated! Already you are enriched! Quite apart from us you reign as kings!' The determinative particle ἤδη, which introduces the first two exclamations in this verse, has a taunting, sneering quality that is impossible to translate exactly into English; it designates a false certainty that is grounded upon superficial perception: 'evidently', 'surely!' 'manifestly'.[30] When Paul turns his irony upon himself (as in 2.1–5 and 4.9–13), he seems most fully a 'dissembler', in keeping with the original meaning of the term εἴρων:[31] by simulated ignorance and self-deprecating humor, Paul entraps the Corinthians in his argument and exposes the inadequacy of their values and perceptions.

A final consideration is necessary before undertaking a detailed examination of Paul's argument. It is essential to bear in mind that Paul carries out his re-evaluation of the concepts of 'wisdom' and 'foolishness' in the context of a specific intellectual tradition, which some have named 'the grotesque perspective'.[32] In this tradition, the world is viewed from the perspective of the poor, the uneducated, and the dishonored. The tradition was largely submerged in Greco-Roman culture, the unwritten repertoire of an unlettered populace. Yet, through all periods of antiquity, the grotesque perspective found expression. Among the witnesses may be named Epicharmus, Sophron, Herodas, the authors of phlyax plays and Atellan farces, and the writers of mimes.[33] The hero of this tradition is the 'wise fool' – a figure of shocking ugliness, often deformed, invariably a member of the lower class, a slave, vulgar and obscene in his behavior, in open disregard of convention.[34] Because the fool is a grotesque outsider, deformed, and without honor, he is able to give voice to irreverent thoughts about the rulers, thoughts that are forbidden to normal members of society.[35] It is our contention that Paul has drawn upon this tradition in

29. Emphasizing the irony in 3.1–4, G. Fee, *The First Epistle to the Corinthians*, 102–103.

30. So, already, Weiss, *Der erste Korintherbrief*, 106.

31. Aristophanes *Nubes* 449, etc.; Aristotle *Eth. Nic.* 1124 b30; Theophrastus *Char.* 1.1; O. Ribbeck, 'Über den Begriff des εἴρων', *Rheinisches Museum* 31 (1876) 381–400.

32. G. M. A. Richter, 'Grotesques and the Mime', 149–56; G. Nagy, *The Best of the Achaeans* (Baltimore: Johns Hopkins University, 1979) 229–30, 280–90; Winkler, *Auctor and Actor*, 286–91; R. Garland, *The Eye of the Beholder*.

33. The history of this tradition has not been written, though many of the materials are gathered and discussed by Crusius, *Herondae Mimiambi*; Nicoll, *Masks, Mimes and Miracles*, 38–128; Winkler (*Actor and Actor*, 287) recognizes that a common perspective connects these writers.

34. Reich, *Der Mimus*, 587–93; Nicoll, *Masks, Mimes and Miracles*, esp. 47–50, 87–90; Winkler, *Auctor and Actor*, 286–91.

35. Reich, *Der Mimus*, 182–92; Nicoll, *Masks, Mimes and Miracles*, 124–26; Winkler, *Auctor and Actor*, 287, 290–91.

his critique of the conventional concepts of 'wisdom' and 'foolishness': in the guise of a 'fool,' who is weak, dishonored and beaten, Paul is able to speak a critical truth to those in authority.

Paul is not the only intellectual in this period to adopt 'the grotesque perspective' as a vehicle for critical truth. Much of the Socratic tradition, especially that promulgated by the Cynics, portrays the philosopher as a common βάναυσος, with a laughable exterior, the inventor of a game of provocative questions aimed at conventional wisdom.[36] According to the story-tellers who contributed to the *Life of Aesop*, Aesop is an ugly, deformed slave, who is beaten and tormented, but who triumphs over mistreatment with astonishing cleverness, and solves problems that have perplexed the philosophers with an earthy wisdom.[37] It is important to emphasize Paul's participation in this tradition as a corrective of the persistent tendency to generalize and spiritualize Paul's account of the folly of the message of the cross. In the history of Christian theology, 'folly' is usually taken to be the response of all those who regard the gospel from a human standpoint.[38] Paul's injunction to 'become a fool' (μωρὸς γενέσθω) is often interpreted as an exhortation to suprarationality, evidence of Paul's intoxication with the Spirit.[39] When Paul's analysis of the foolishness of the gospel is interpreted in this way, without reference to the intellectual tradition in which he stands, the political and social thrust of his thought is completely dissipated.

It remains only to suggest why foolishness was necessary. The brutal, historical fact is that no one wanted to see the μωρός. The poor man on the street, hungry and half-naked, was virtually invisible in Greco-Roman society. Whenever the gaze of an historian or a moralist falls incidentally upon one of these husks of men, attention is quickly averted. One may speculate about the social and psychological causes of this aversion, whether it is an expression of 'aesthetic disdain',[40] or the reflex of an instinct for self-preservation[41] among the upper classes. But the rarity of

---

36. Gigon, *Sokrates*, 112; Helm, *Lucian und Menipp*, 211; Betz, *Der Apostel Paulus und die sokratische Tradition*, 48–49; Döring, *Exemplum Socratis*, 2–12 and *passim*.

37. Daly, *Aesop without Morals*, esp. 19–23; Winkler, *Auctor and Actor*, 279–86.

38. E.g., Justin *Dial. cum Trypho*, 69; Tertullian *De Carne Christi*, 4–5; *Advers. Judaeos*, 10; Origen *Phiocalia* 18; Calvin, *Commentarius in epistolam priorem ad Corinthios*, 320, 322; Bengel, *Gnomon of the New Testament* 2.205, 207; Käsemann, 'The Saving Significance of the Death of Jesus in Paul,' 40; Conzelmann, *1 Corinthians*, 46–47; Hengel, *Crucifixion*, 89; Wolter, 'Verborgene Weisheit und Heil für die Heiden', 304; R. Penna, 'The Wisdom of the Cross and Its Foolishness as Foundation of the Church' in *Wisdom and Folly of the Cross*, vol. 2 of *Paul the Apostle: A Theological and Exegetical Study* (Collegeville, MN: Liturgical Press, 1996) 54–55.

39. Nigg, *Der christliche Narr*, 15–26.

40. Veyne, *A History of Private Life I*, 134–37.

41. For the rare recognition that the rich created others' poverty and attendant miseries, see Josephus *Ant.* 18.274; Dio Chrysostom *Or.* 77.10.5; Julian *Ep.* 89; see the comments of MacMullen, *Roman Social Relations*, 116–17.

realistic portraits of these social outcasts in Greco-Roman literature is a fact that must be acknowledged.[42] Evidently the sight of those whom fate had demolished, human trash, was unbearable to the majority of authors of ancient literature. The conclusion which the evidence suggests is that the μωρός might be publicly represented only under the guise of humor, as the object of ridicule.

The social constraint upon the representation of the μωρός serves to explain the mimic elements that invariably appear in the rare portraits of the type in the literature of the early Empire. Thus, when the philosopher Seneca describes a half-dead slave whom he meets outside his gate, he predictably uses language which likens the poor creature to a fool in the mime.[43] One day, as Seneca was leaving his house, he happened to cast his eyes on a slave lying by his door and found him so pathetic that he turned to his majordomo and asked, 'Where did this decrepit creature come from?' Whereupon the slave, hearing what Seneca had said, spoke up: 'Don't you recognize me sir? I am Felicio, to whom you used to bring little figurines as presents.'[44] In a brutal reversal of fortune, this old dotard, once Seneca's favorite slave, has become the very image of the mimic fool, with whose little terracotta statues the youthful Seneca once gave delight as presents at the Saturnalia.[45] He is poor and old and broken-down; his teeth are dropping out; he is like one who is ready to be carried out for burial.[46] Seneca pronounces him 'perfectly silly'.[47]

Seneca's perspective on a μωρός is that of a member of the upper class, however sympathetic to the plight of the slave he may be.[48] But even those who had adopted 'the grotesque perspective' were obliged to obey the social constraint and to represent the poor man as a deformed and comical character, a 'fool'.[49] The slave is allowed to speak in defiance of authority,

---

42. F. Millar, 'The World of the *Golden Ass*', 63, 65, 75; de Ste. Croix, *The Class Struggle in the Ancient Greek World*, 441–42.

43. Seneca *Epist. Mor.* 12.3; text and translation in R. Gummere, *Seneca IV: Ad Lucilium Epistulae Morales*, LCL (Cambridge, MA: Harvard University Press, 1979) 66–67.

44. Seneca *Epist. Mor.* 12.3: *Ego sum Felicio, cum solebas sigillaria adferre.*

45. On the *sigillaria* as terracotta statues of mimic fools, cf. Macrobius *Sat.* 1.11.49: *sigilla ... pro se atque suis piaculum.*

46. On the jesting allusions to the toothlessness of second childhood and the preparation of a corpse for a funeral, see the notes in Gummere, *Seneca IV*, 66.

47. Seneca *Epist. Mor.* 12.3: *perfecte delirat.*

48. Elsewhere, Seneca argues against cruelty by masters to slaves, e.g. *Ep.* 47.2–5, 11–13; *De Bene.* 3. But it is symptomatic how quickly Seneca averts his gaze from the decrepit slave and turns his attention to himself in *Epist. Mor.* 12.3, composing a meditation on the ravages of time upon his own person.

49. See esp. *POxy* 413 ('Charition') line 52, 207; *PVars* 2, line 2; *Vit. Aesop.* 18.

but only as the object of ridicule,[50] and then he is punished with slapsticks on the spot.[51] Yet there is this difference with the witnesses to the submerged tradition: here the poor man is the center of value and insight.[52] The μωρός may be ugly and he may be beaten, but he is the hero of his own genre.

1. *Acknowledgement*

Paul begins his theological analysis by acknowledging that 'the message about the cross is foolishness' to a certain class of people (1.18).[53] This group is initially described in evaluative terms, employing first apocalyptic, and then anthropological categories: they are 'those who are perishing' (οἱ ἀπολλύμενοι),[54] and 'natural' or 'unspiritual' (ψυχικός) persons (2.14).[55]

---

50. E.g., *POxy* 413 ('Charition') esp. lines 38–57; *PVars* 2, lines 2, 7; see the comments of Wiemken, *Der griechische Mimus*, 67–68, 138; see also *Vit. Aesop.* 36.

51. E.g., *POxy* 413 ('Adulteress') line 186; Apuleius *Met.* 10.10.

52. E.g., *PLond* 1984, line 2, with the comments of G. von Manteuffel, 'Zwei Bemerkungen zu griechischen Mimen aus Ägypten', 126. Aesop is especially portrayed as a source of wisdom in the running battle of wits between master and slave that makes up the central section of the *Vit. Aesop.* (20–91); see the comments of Winkler, *Auctor and Actor*, 282–83.

53. On Paul's division of humankind into two groups, cf. 2 Cor. 2.15. See the comments of Heinrici, *Der erste Brief*, 67; Lietzmann, *An die Korinther I*, 9; Collins, *First Corinthians*, 92–93.

54. On the apocalyptic perspective reflected in the division of humanity into 'the lost' (ἀπολλύμενοι) and 'the saved' (σῳζόμενοι), see Weiss, *Der erste Korintherbrief*, 25–26; Wilckens, *Weisheit und Torheit*, 22–23; Lindemann, *Der erste Korintherbrief*, 44; Collins, *First Corinthians*, 92–93. While not denying the overriding eschatological sense of the terms 'lost' and 'saved' in 1.18, it is nevertheless important to note that Epictetus makes similar use of ἀπόλλυσθαι and σῴζεσθαι in *Diss.* 2.9. 1–12 to distinguish between the loss and the preservation of human dignity; see esp. *Diss.* 2.9.9: τί οὖν θαυμαστόν, εἰ καὶ ἄνθρωπος ὡσαύτως μὲν σῴζεται, ὡσαύτως δ᾿ ἀπόλλυται;

55. The term ψυχικός has proven extraordinarily difficult to interpret. Some suggest that the term reflects early Gnosticism, so Wilckens, *Weisheit und Torheit*, 60, 88–89; more recently, W. Schrage, *Der erste Brief an die Korinther*, vol. 1, EKKNT 7/1 (Neukirchen-Vluyn: Neukirchener Verlag, 1991) 240. Others look for the background of the term in Hellenistic Judaism, specifically in Philonic exegesis; thus, B. Pearson, *The Pneumatikos-Psychikos Terminology in 1 Corinthians: A Study in the Theology of the Corinthian Opponents of Paul and Its Relation to Gnosticism*, SBLDS 12 (Missoula, MT: Scholars Press, 1973) 17–21; R. Horsley, 'Pneumatikos vs. Psychikos: Distinctions of Spiritual Status Among the Corinthians,' *HTR* 69 (1976) 274–84; G. Sterling, 'Wisdom Among the Perfect: Creation Traditions in Alexandrian Judaism and Corinthian Christianity,' *NovT* 37 (1995) 360–72. For our purposes it suffices to notice that the category is anthropological and that Paul's use of the term is ironical, whatever the origin of the term may be; thus, rightly, R. Jewett, *Paul's Anthropological Terms: A Study of Their Use in Conflict Settings*, AGJU 10 (Leiden: Brill, 1971) 353–54; Collins, *First Corinthians*, 136.

But in the course of his exposition, Paul uses a variety of descriptive expressions, ethnic and cultural, that make it possible to identify those who pass the judgment of 'foolishness' upon the gospel: they are 'Greeks' ("Ελληνες) devoted to the search for wisdom (1.22);[56] they are 'Gentiles' (ἔθνη) for the most part, rather than 'Jews' (1.23).[57] These designations make it clear that those for whom the message of the 'crucified Christ' is 'foolishness' are persons who have embraced Hellenism, and who participate in a learned culture through philosophy, rhetoric, and art.[58] Elsewhere, Paul uses sociological and political categories to refer to the members of this group. As the opposites of those who are 'called' by the word of the cross (1.26–28), these persons are 'wise' (σοφοί), 'powerful' (δυνατοί), and 'well-born' (εὐγενεῖς). The adjectives which Paul uses here are those employed throughout antiquity to describe the members of the upper class, those who are distinguished by education, wealth, and birth.[59] Specifically, Paul is describing the 'honorable men' (*honestiores*), the local elites gathered in the *ordines decurionum*,[60] although the group that Paul envisions may also include some freedmen who by wealth had acquired power and influence.[61] At the acme of this social group, Paul mentions 'the rulers of this age' (οἱ ἄρχοντες τοῦ αἰῶνος τούτου) as the parties responsible for the crucifixion of Jesus through ignorance of God's hidden purposes (2.6–8).[62] Specifically, 'the rulers' are the holders of high offices in the

---

56. On the meaning of "Ελληνες, see esp. Wilcken, 'Hellenen und Barbaren', 457–71; Jüthner, *Hellenen und Barbaren passim*; Windisch, ' "Ελλην', 504–16. See above, ch. 2, n. 43–45.

57. Schmidt, 'ἔθνος in the NT', 369–72. See above, ch. 2, n. 38, 40.

58. Jüthner, *Hellenen und Barbaren*, 4–7, 34; W. Jaeger, *Paideia*; Windisch, ' "Ελλην', 512–16. For texts supporting this conclusion, see above, ch. 2, n. 44–48.

59. See esp. Aristotle *Ars Rhet.* 2.12.2; *Pol.* 6.1.9; Philo *De Virt.* 187–277; Plutarch *Mor.* 58E; Josephus *B. J.* 1.17.2; 2.14.1; 2.14.4; 7.8.1; Dio Chrysostom *Or.* 15.29; 31.74; with the analysis of J. Bohatec, 'Inhalt und Reihenfolge der "Schlagwörte der Erlösungsreligion," 1 Kor. 1.26–31,' *TZ* 4 (1948) 252–71; Theissen, *The Social Setting of Pauline Christianity*, 70–73; D. Sänger, 'Die δυνατοί in 1 Kor. 1, 26', *ZNW* 76 (1985) 285–91; L. L. Welborn, 'On the Discord in Corinth: 1 Corinthians 1–4 and Ancient Politics', *JBL* 106 (1987) 96–97; A. D. Clarke, *Secular and Christian Leadership in Corinth: A Socio-Historical and Exegetical Study of 1 Corinthians 1–6*, AGJU 18 (Leiden: Brill, 1993) 41–45.

60. On the distinction between the *honestiores* and the *humiliores*, see esp. P. Garnsey, *Social Status and Legal Privilege in the Roman Empire* (Oxford: Oxford University Press, 1970). On the decurion class that administered the cities, see G. Alföldy, *The Social History of Rome*, 106–15. On education, wealth and birth as the defining characteristics of the upper classes, see MacMullen, *Roman Social Relations*, 88–120.

61. On the means of advancement for freedmen, see A. M. Duff, *Freedmen in the Early Roman Empire* (Cambridge: Cambridge University Press, 1958) 63–66; Alföldy, *The Social History of Rome*, 106–107.

62. The question of the identity of 'the rulers of this age' mentioned in 2.6 and 2.8 has long been in dispute. Some interpreters identify 'the rulers' with spiritual, demonic powers: M. Dibelius, *Die Geisterwelt im Glauben des Paulus* (Göttingen: Vandenhoeck & Ruprecht, 1909)

administration of the Empire and in the command of the army, offices that were reserved for senators and knights (*equites*).[63] Therefore, the group that pronounces the judgment of 'foolishness' upon the gospel is identified with the upper strata of the Roman Empire, that small percentage of the population upon whom wealth, education and birth had conferred enormous privileges.[64] To such persons, the message about the crucified Messiah appeared to be 'foolishness'.

Among those for whom 'the word of the cross' is 'foolishness' Paul reckons certain members of the Christian community in Corinth.[65] This is the ineluctable conclusion to which analysis of Paul's rhetoric in 1.26 and 4.8, 10 leads the attentive reader, however surprising the conclusion may

24; Lietzmann, *An die Korinther*, 12; Conzelmann, *1 Corinthians*, 61; this interpretation is favored by those who seek to explain Paul's terminology against the background of Gnosticism: thus, Schmithals, *Gnosticism in Corinth*, 137; Wilckens, *Weisheit und Torheit*, 61; Schrage, *Der erste Brief*, 1.250, 253–54. Other interpreters identify 'the rulers' as earthly, political authorities: so, Heinrici, *Der erste Brief*, 95; Schniewind, 'Die Archonten dieses Äons, 1. Kor. 2, 6–8', 104–109; G. Miller, 'ἀρχόντων τοῦ αἰῶνος τούτου – A New Look at 1 Corinthians 2.6–8,' *JBL* 91 (1972) 522–28; A. W. Carr, 'The Rulers of this Age – 1 Cor. ii. 6–8,' *NTS* 23 (1976) 20–35; G. D. Fee, *The First Epistle to the Corinthians*, 104; Clarke, *Secular and Christian Leadership in Corinth*, 116–18; Lindemann, *Der erste Korintherbrief*, 63. Decisive for the resolution of the debate would seem to be the fact that the plural form of ἄρχων is never used in the New Testament to designate demonic powers; see esp. Rom. 13.3, where οἱ ἄρχοντες are earthly, political authorities; see also Luke 23.13, 35; 24.20, where οἱ ἄρχοντες are human authorities responsible for the crucifixion of Jesus. Of equal importance is Schniewind's inference from the broader context of Paul's argument in 1 Cor. 1–4, with specific reference to the language of 1.26–28: 'Dem Gedankenzug von 1. Kor. 1, 20–2, 16 entspricht nicht die Deutung der Archonten auf Geister, sondern die Deutung auf die Vornehmen, Führenden, Gebildeten unter den Menschen' ('Die Archonten dieses Äons', 105).

63.   For the reference of οἱ ἄρχοντες to the political authorities responsible for the death of Jesus, specifically the emperor Tiberius, the governor Pilate (an *eques*), and their clients in Galilee and Judea, Herod and Caiaphas, see already F. Godet, *Commentary on St. Paul's First Epistle to the Corinthians*, Vol. 1 (Edinburgh: T. & T. Clark, 1889) 135; J. B. Lightfoot, *Notes on the Epistles of St. Paul*, 177; Heinrici, *Der erste Brief*, 95 (adducing Theodoret in support). On the restriction of high offices to the members of the *ordo senatorius*, the *ordo equester*, and the *ordo decurionum* of the various cities, see Alföldy, *The Social History of Rome*, 106.

64.   This conclusion is already found in Heinrici, *Der erste Brief*, 95: 'τῶν ἀρχόντων τοῦ αἰῶνος τούτου. Dies sind die Herrschenden überhaupt (vgl. Act 13.27), die Gewaltträger (*proceres*) der Zeit unter Juden und Heiden. Vgl. vs. 8. Man darf sowohl an die einflussreichen Gelehrten und Philosophen denken (Theodoret, vgl. Neander: "die geistigen Machthaber der antiken Welt"), als auch an Würdenträger und Besitzende, die durch die Verwerfung Christi seinen Tod mit verschulden.'

65.   *Contra* Conzelmann, *1 Corinthians*, 42, who, emphasizing the pronoun ἡμῖν in 1.18, reckons all Christians among 'the saved' for whom 'the word of the cross' is 'the power of God': 'Paul embraces all Christians regardless of their groupings: theologically speaking, they are saved and there is no more to be said.' Similarly, Lietzmann, *An die Korinther I*, 9; Allo, *Première Épitre aux Corinthians*, 21; Barrett, *First Epistle*, 30, 59, 69.

be.[66] For Paul's use of litotes (οὐ πολλοί for ὀλίγοι) in 1.26 reveals that a few, if only a few, of the Corinthian Christians possessed the characteristics which distinguished members of the upper class – education, wealth, and birth.[67] To this group may be reckoned with certainty only Gaius,[68] 'the host of the whole church', and Erastus,[69] 'the treasurer of the city' of Corinth (Rom. 16.23), although other individuals may have been included.[70] While the number of such persons may have

66. One can trace the emergence of a new consensus on the social composition of the Christian community in Corinth in the works of E. A. Judge, *The Social Pattern of the Christian Groups in the First Century* (London: Tyndale Press, 1960) 59–60; Theissen, *The Social Setting of Pauline Christianity*, 55, 70–72; D. Sänger, 'Die δυνατοί in 1 Kor. 1, 26', 290–91; Clarke, *Secular and Christian Leadership in Corinth*, 42; D. Gill, 'In Search of the Social Élite in the Corinthian Church,' *Tyndale Bulletin* 44 (1993) 324; D. Martin, *The Corinthian Body* (New Haven: Yale University Press, 1995) 61.

67. On the litotes in 1.26 and its implications, see Heinrici, *Der erste Brief*, 78; Judge, *The Social Pattern of the Christian Groups*, 59; Theissen, *The Social Setting of Pauline Christianity*, 70, 72; Martin, *The Corinthian Body*, 61; Lindemann, *Der erste Korintherbrief*, 49.

68. On Gaius, see 1 Cor. 1.14, where Gaius is mentioned as one of the few whom Paul himself had baptized, and Rom. 16.23, where Paul sends greetings from 'Gaius, who is host to me and to the whole church'. One may reasonably infer that, as 'host of the whole church', Gaius possessed the largest house and was the Christian of highest social standing in Corinth. If, as the author of Acts reports, the Corinthian congregation was large, a λαὸς πολύς (18.10), then Gaius' residence must have been substantial indeed. The linking of the names of Gaius and Erastus in the greetings of the Epistle to the Romans suggests that the two men must be of similar social standing; indeed, the fact that Gaius is mentioned first may imply that he is socially superior to Erastus, 'the treasurer of the city'. For this view of Gaius, see esp. Theissen, *The Social Setting of Pauline Christianity*, 55, 89 and De Vos, *Church and Community Conflicts*, 201–202; similarly, Stansbury, 'Corinthian Honor, Corinthian Conflict: A Social History of Early Roman Corinth and its Pauline Community'. (Ph.D. diss., University of California at Irvine, 1990), 460–62; Clarke, *Secular and Christian Leadership in Corinth*, 46.

69. The Erastus from whom Paul sends greetings in Rom. 16.23, described as ὁ οἰκονόμος τῆς πόλεως, is likely to be identified with an Erastus who laid the limestone pavement adjacent to the theater at Corinth, in return for his election as aedile. Text in J. H. Kent, *Corinth – Inscriptions* 1926–1950 (Princeton: Princeton University Press, 1966) no. 232: *Erastus pro aedilit[at]e s.p. stravit*. In favor of the identification of the two Erasti, see Broneer, 'Corinth, Center of St. Paul's Missionary Work in Greece', 94; Kent, *Corinth – Inscriptions*, 27, 99–100; J. Wiseman, 'Corinth and Rome I: 228 B.C. – A.D. 267', 499 n. 226; Engels, *Roman Corinth*, 108; cautiously, Clarke, *Secular and Christian Leadership in Corinth*, 55–56; de Vos, *Church and Community Conflicts*, 199–201. On the social status of Erastus, see already the conclusion of Kent, *Corinth – Inscriptions*, 27: 'Erastus was probably a Corinthian freedman who had acquired considerable wealth in commercial activities' (an inference from the absence of a patronymic or tribal abbreviation on the inscription).

70. Other named individuals who may have belonged to the upper class include: Crispus, the former ἀρχισυνάγωγος (Acts 18.8; 1 Cor. 1.14), Chloe, whose 'people' (probably slaves) visited Paul in Ephesus (1 Cor. 1.11), and Stephanas, a householder who also visited Paul in Ephesus bringing material support (1 Cor. 1.16; 16.15–18). For evaluation of the social status of these individuals, see E. A. Judge, 'The Early Christians as a Scholastic Community', *JRH*

been small, their influence was great, because they functioned as patrons of the Christian community.[71] How large these representatives of the upper class loomed in Paul's mind is reflected in the fact that, at one point, Paul addresses his Corinthian readers as if they were identical with this small group of elite (4.8,10),[72] although earlier he had stated clearly that the majority of the Corinthian Christians were persons of low social status (1.26–28).[73] For this small group of upper-class Christians, 'learned eloquence' (σοφία λόγου) would have held a special attraction, because the attainment and exercise of public office depended upon mastery of the art of rhetoric.[74] Such persons would have admired the eloquent and learned

1 (1960) 128–30; Theissen, *The Social Setting of Pauline Christianity*, 73–75, 83–96; H. J. Klauck, *Hausgemeinde und Hauskirche im frühen Christentum* (Stuttgart: Katholisches Bibelwerk, 1981) 33; Welborn, *Politics and Rhetoric*, 23–24, 26–27; de Vos, *Church and Community Conflicts*, 197–99.

71. So, already, Judge, 'The Early Christians as a Scholastic Community,' 8; Theissen, *The Social Setting of Pauline Christianity*, 72–73; J. K. Chow, *Patronage and Power: A Study of Social Networks in Corinth*, JSNTSS 75 (Sheffield: Sheffield Academic Press, 1992) esp. 88–93; Welborn, *Politics and Rhetoric*, 24, 27; de Vos, *Church and Community Conflicts*, 204, 216–17. There are numerous indications of patronage within the Corinthian church. Note the provision of food for the common meal (1 Cor. 11.17–34); see the insightful analysis of Theissen, *The Social Setting of Pauline Christianity*, 153–63. The term ξένος, used to describe Gaius in Rom. 16.23, normally rendered 'host', is also a polite term for 'patron', e.g. in *IG* 10.2.1.255, where the cognate term ξενισμός describes a certain Xenainetos acting as a patron of the cult of Isis and Sarapis; cited by de Vos, *Church and Community Conflicts*, 204 n. 100. Paul's description of the wealthy in the Corinthian congregation as 'kings' in 1 Cor. 4.8 recalls the client's practice of referring to his rich patron as *rex*: see Horace *Ep.* 1.7.37–38; Juvenal 5.14, 130, 137, 161; 7.45; 10.161; cited by D. Martin, *Slavery as Salvation: The Metaphor of Slavery in Pauline Christianity* (New Haven: Yale University Press, 1990) 210 n. 13. On Paul's ambivalence toward the patronage of the wealthy few, see ch. 7 below.

72. 1 Cor. 4.8, 10: 'Already you are satiated (κεκορεσμένοι)! Already you have become rich (ἐπλουτήσατε)! Quite apart from us you reign as kings (ἐβασιλεύσατε)! Indeed, I wish that you did reign as kings, so that we might be kings with you! ... We are fools for the sake of Christ, but you are wise (φρόνιμοι) in Christ. We are weak, but you are strong (ἰσχυροί). You are held in honor (ἔνδοξοι), but we are dishonored.' The terms 'satiety' (κόρος), 'wealth' (πλοῦτος) and 'kingship' (βασιλευειν) are constantly found in connection with one another as epithets of the ruling class, e.g., Herodotus 3.80.3; 4.146; Dio Chrysostom *Or.* 1.67; 30.19; Theognis 153–54; Aeschylus *Agam.* 382; Sophocles *OT* 872–74; Pindar *Isthm.* 3.2; *Ol.* 1.56; Maximus of Tyre *Or.* 34.7a; Diogenes Laertius 1.59; see Fitzgerald, *Cracks in an Earthen Vessel*, 133–35. On the terms 'wise' (φρόνιμοι), 'strong' (ἰσχυποί) and 'held in honor' (ἔνδοξοι) as epithets for the rich, see, e.g., Plato *Soph.* 223b; Xenophon *Mem.* 1.2.56; Isocrates 1.37; cf. Theissen, *The Social Setting of Pauline Christianity*, 70–73; Welborn, *Politics and Rhetoric*, 23.

73. The point is well made by Theissen, *The Social Setting of Pauline Christianity*, 72–73.

74. See, e.g., Petronius *Satyr.* 48; Plutarch *Mor.* 801D-802E; Dio Chrysostom *Or.* 18.1–3; cf. Theissen, *The Social Setting of Pauline Christianity*, 97; Winter, *Philo and Paul among the Sophists*, 170–78; Clarke, *Secular and Christian Leadership in Corinth*, 36–39; de Vos, *Church and Community Conflicts*, 217.

Apollos, as argued above,[75] and may have been the prime movers in the formation of factions.[76] To such elite Christians, Paul would have been an embarrassment, owing to the weakness of his person, the defects of his oratory, his banausic occupation, and the content of his gospel.[77] It is these upper-class Christians, in the immediate instance, who are responsible for the formulation of the judgment of 'foolishness' upon 'the message about the cross.'

A comprehensive survey of references to crucifixion in Greek and Roman writers demonstrates the accuracy of Paul's observation regarding the effect of any public discourse involving 'the cross' upon members of the upper class.[78] And this, in turn, provokes reflection upon the social causes and psychological mechanisms of the response that Paul describes with such unstinting candor. Cicero is representative of his social class, when he insists, in the speech quoted above,[79] that 'the very word "cross" should be far removed not only from the person of a Roman citizen but from his thoughts, his eyes and his ears. . . . The mere mention of such a thing is shameful to a Roman citizen and a free man'.[80] The surviving literature

75.   Ch. 5 above; see already Winter, *Philo and Paul among the Sophists*, 170, 174–75, 177; Litfin, *St. Paul's Theology of Proclamation*, 162, 232–33; Smit, 'What is Apollos? What is Paul?' 246–47; Ker, 'Paul and Apollos – Colleagues or Rivals?' 91–92.

76.   Welborn, *Politics and Rhetoric*, 23–27.

77.   Marshall, *Enmity in Corinth*, 339–41; Chow, *Patronage and Power*, 102–105; D. Gill, 'In Search of the Social Élite in the Corinthian Church', 331; Litfin, *St. Paul's Theology of Proclamation*, 162–63, 232–33; Winter, *Philo and Paul among the Sophists*, 170–78; de Vos, *Church and Community Conflicts*, 219–20. See above ch. 5.

78.   Research and interpretation builds upon the study of crucifixion by Martin Hengel, originally published as '*Mors turpissima crucis*: Die Kreuzigung in der antiken Welt und die "Torheit" des "Wortes vom Kreuz"' in *Rechtfertigung. Festschrift für Ernst Kasemann zum 70. Geburtstag*, ed. J. Friedrich, W. Pöhlmann and P. Stuhlmacher (Tübingen: Mohr-Siebeck, 1976), revised and considerably enlarged for the English translation, *Crucifixion in the Ancient World and the Folly of the Message of the Cross* (Philadelphia: Fortress Press, 1977). Hengel endeavored to include all available material in his study (x–xii). But he devoted insufficient attention to the material from 'popular' culture (mime, farce, satire, novels) owing to his conviction that accounts of crucifixion in these sources served only the purposes of 'entertainment and sensationalism' (p. 88).

79.   See ch. 1. The context of the passage quoted is significant: Cicero's speech in defense of the senator C. Rabirius against the charge of having murdered a tribune of the people. The prosecutor had threatened Rabirius with hanging upon the *arbor infelix*, the archaic form of the death penalty in cases of high treason. The crucial sentences form the rhetorical climax of Cicero's account of the dangers with which Rabirius had been threatened by the prosecutor: disgrace by a public court, the imposition of a fine, banishment, and the death penalty. Cicero's point is that crucifixion is qualitatively different from the other punishments with which Rabirius had been threatened, in that it is unworthy of a Roman citizen and a free man (*Pro Rabirio* 5.9–17).

80.   Cicero *Pro Rabirio* 5.16. See the discussion in Kuhn, 'Jesus als Gekreuzigter in der frühchristlicher Verkündigung bis zur Mitte des 2. Jahrhunderts', 7–8; Hengel, *Crucifixion in the Ancient World*, 41–43.

illustrates how consistently members of the upper class adhered to this principle. There are no references to the cross (*crux*) in learned Roman writers such as Lucretius, Virgil, Statius, or Aulus Gellius;[81] and there is little or no mention of crucifixion (ἀνασκολοπίζειν or ἀνασταυροῦν) in Greek writers like Plutarch, Dio Chrysostom, Aelius Aristides, or Maximus of Tyre.[82] What is truly remarkable is the absence of the words *crux* or *patibulum* from the works of Caesar,[83] despite the fact that he is known to have used crucifixion as a punishment;[84] the same is true of the younger Pliny, who as governor of Bithynia must have condemned many criminals to the cross.[85] Inevitably, there are references to crucifixion in Greek and Roman historians who recount wars and rebellions;[86] but even in such cases, there is reticence, and a tendency to portray crucifixion as a barbarian mode of execution, an atrocity.[87] The only detailed descriptions of crucifixion in antiquity are those found in the Christian gospels.[88] It is clear that the rarity of references to crucifixion in ancient literature is not an historical accident, but a reflection of the aesthetic and moral values of

81.   According to Hengel, *Crucifixion in the Ancient World*, 38.

82.   Plutarch *Mor.* 554 AB cites the general principle, 'every criminal condemned to death bears his cross on his back' (καὶ τῷ μὲν σώματι τῶν κολαζομένων ἕκαστος κακούργων ἐκφέρει τὸν αὑτοῦ σταυρόν); cf. *Mor.* 554 D; 499 D. Dio Chrysostom *Or.* 17.15 mentions only the famous case of Polycrates of Samos. Cf. Hengel, *Crucifixion in the Ancient World*, 77.

83.   See Hengel, *Crucifixion in the Ancient World*, 38.

84.   *De Bello Hispaniensi* 20.5, where it is reported that Caesar had three slaves crucified who had been sent out as spies.

85.   Hengel, *Crucifixion in the Ancient World*, 38.

86.   E.g. Livy 30.43.13, the crucifixion of Roman deserters as traitors; cf. Valerius Maximus 2.7.12; Appian *Bell. Civ.* 1.120, the crucifixion of six thousand slaves who had joined the revolt of Spartacus; Strabo 3.4.18, the crucifixion of the Cantabrians of northern Spain; Dio Cassius 49.12.4, the crucifixion of slaves who had enlisted to fight under Sextus Pompeius. Of course, there are numerous references to crucifixion in Josephus' account of the Jewish revolt against Rome, esp. *B. J.* 5.449–51. But the Romans regarded the Jewish rebels not as enemies, but as common bandits and slaves; see Hengel, *Crucifixion in the Ancient World*, 47–48 and the literature cited there. Hence the greater willingness to discuss crucifixion. On crucifixion as the 'slaves' punishment' (*servile supplicium*), see the discussion below.

87.   For references to crucifixion among the Persians, see Herodotus 1.128.2; 3.125.3; 3.132.2; 3.159.1; 4.43.2; 6.30.1; 7.194.1–2; Thucydides 1.110.1; among the Assyrians, see Diodorus Siculus 2.1.10; the Scythians, Diodorus Siculus 2.44.2; the Celts, Diodorus Siculus 5.32.6; the Germani, Tacitus *Ann.* 1.61.4; 4.72.3; Dio Cassius 54.20.4; the Britanni, Tacitus *Ann.* 14.33.2; the Carthaginians, Polybius 1.11.5; 1.24.6; 1.79.4–5; 1.86.4; Diodorus Siculus 25.5.2; 26.23.1; Livy 22.13.9; 28.37.2; 38.48.13; used by Mithridates, the arch-enemy of Rome, Appian *Mith.* 97; Valerius Maximus 9.2, ext. 3; used by two cruel kings of Thrace, Diodorus Siculus 33.15.1; 34/35.12.1. See already the conclusion of Hengel, *Crucifixion in the Ancient World*, 23: 'Both Greek and Roman historians were fond of stressing *barbarian* crucifixions, and playing down their own use of this form of execution.'

88.   So, already, Hengel, *Crucifixion in the Ancient World*, 25.

upper-class writers.[89] The cultured elite of the Roman world wanted nothing to do with crucifixion, and as a rule kept silent about it.

What makes the silence of the upper class with respect to crucifixion more significant is the fact that the practice was so widespread in the Roman world. In speaking of the ubiquity of the cross, we do not have in mind the occasional use of crucifixion as the 'supreme penalty' (*summum supplicium*) in notorious cases of high treason,[90] nor the more frequent use of crucifixion as a means of suppressing rebellious subjects in the provinces,[91] but rather the daily employment of the cross as a punishment for slaves in cities throughout the Roman Empire.[92] Just outside the Esquiline Gate at Rome, on the road to Tibur, was a horrific place where crosses were routinely set up for the punishment of slaves.[93] There a torture and execution service was operated by a group of funeral contractors who were open to business from private citizens and public authorities alike.[94] There slaves were flogged and crucified at a charge to their masters of 4 *sesterces* per person.[95] Passing references in the satirists disclose aspects of the grisly scene: Varro mentions rotting corpses;[96] Horace speaks of

89. Hengel, *Crucifixion in the Ancient World*, 38: 'the relative scarcity of references to crucifixions in antiquity, and their fortuitousness, are less a historical problem than an aesthetic one, connected with the sociology of literature'.

90. See esp. the famous case of Verres, who as governor of Sicily inflicted the *crudelissimum taeterrimumque supplicium* upon a Roman citizen, P. Gavius, for serving as a spy of Spartacus in the slave revolt, Cicero *In Verr.* 2.5.158–165. Paulus *Sententiae* 5.19.2; 5.21.4; 5.23.2; 5.25.1 gives a list of other crimes which are punished by crucifixion. See Garnsey, *Social Status and Legal Privilege in the Roman Empire*, 122–31; cf. Hengel, *Crucifixion in the Ancient World*, 33–45.

91. Josephus gives numerous examples of the use of crucifixion to suppress rebellious subjects in Judaea, e.g., *B. J.* 2.75; 2.241; 2.253; 2.306, 308; 3.321; 5.289; 5.449–51; *Ant.* 17.295; 20.129. We do not possess similar sources for other provinces, but must assume that crucifixion was used there to punish unruly provincials. Cf. Hengel, *Crucifixion in the Ancient World*, 46–47.

92. See in general, J. Vogt, *Ancient Slavery and the Ideal of Man* (Cambridge, MA: Harvard University Press, 1975) 49–50, 60, 86–90; Hengel, *Crucifixion in the Ancient World*, 51–63; Robinson, 'Slaves and the Criminal Law', 223–27; K. Hopkins, *Conquerors and Slaves: Sociological Studies in Roman History* (Cambridge: Cambridge University Press, 1978) 118–23; K. Bradley, *Slaves and Masters in the Roman Empire: A Study in Social Control* (New York and Oxford: Oxford University Press, 1987) 113–37.

93. Plautus *Miles Gloriosus* 359–60 (punishment of slaves *extra portam*); Tacitus *Ann.* 2.32.2; 15.60.1 (*locus servilibus poenis sepositus*). Archaeology reveals that the place was part cemetary, part garbage dump; R. Lanciani, *Ancient Rome in the Light of Recent Discoveries* (London: Macmillan, 1888) 64–67. Official notices tried to limit the dumping of dung and carrion: *CIL* VI.31577, 31615; cf. Wiseman, *Catullus and his World*, 7–8.

94. Robinson, 'Slaves and the Criminal Law', 223–27; Wiseman, *Catullus and his World*, 7–8; Bradley, *Slavery and Society at Rome*, 166.

95. For the 4 sesterces, see *L'année épigraphique* (1971) 88.2.10.

96. Varro *Ling. Lat.* 5.25; see also Festus *Gloss. Lat.* 240–41.

whitened bones;[97] Juvenal describes the way in which the Esquiline vulture
disposed of the bodies: 'The vulture hurries from dead cattle and dogs and
crosses to bring some of the carrion to her offspring.'[98] An inscription from
Puteoli confirms that such places of execution, with crosses and other
instruments of torture, were found throughout Italy,[99] and probably
outside the gates of every large city in the Roman Empire.[100]

   At these places of execution, it is impossible not to recognize the real
reason for the silence of the upper class with respect to crucifixion:
crucifixion was the 'slaves' punishment' (*servile supplicium*).[101] One can still
hear the tone of shock and revulsion in the voices of Roman writers of a
certain class, when they speak of the exceptional circumstances under
which the 'slaves' punishment' came to be inflicted upon Roman citizens
and free men.[102] The overwhelming majority of references to crucifixion in
Greek and Roman literature are found in connection with the punishment
of slaves.[103] Examination of these passages indicates what a large space the
spectre of the cross occupied in the consciousness of the servile class.[104] The
slave Sceledrus in Plautus' *Miles Gloriosus* confesses: 'I know the cross will
be my tomb. That's where my ancestors rest – father, grandfather, great-
grandfather, and great-great-grandfather.'[105] How vulnerable slaves were
to this cruel punishment is abundantly illustrated by texts from the early
Empire. Horace criticizes a master who crucified his slave for finishing off
a half-eaten plate of fish which he had been told to remove from the

   97.   Horace *Sat.* 1.8.8–13.
   98.   Juvenal 14.77–78; also cited in this connection by Hengel, *Crucifixion in the Ancient
World*, 54.
   99.   Text in *L'année épigraphique* (1971) 88 and 89; inscription translated in J. F. Gardner
and T. Wiedemann, *The Roman Household*, no. 22.
   100.   For a similar conclusion, see Hengel, *Crucifixion in the Ancient World*, 54; Bradley,
Slavery and Society at Rome, 166.
   101.   See Westermann, 'Sklaverei', and ch. 8 in Hengel, *Crucifixion in the Ancient World*,
51–63.
   102.   E.g., Livy 29.18.14, in connection with executions during the Second Punic War;
Valerius Maximus 2.7.12, on the crucifixion of Roman deserters by Scipio Africanus: 'I will
not pursue this matter further, both because it concerns Scipio and because Roman blood
should not be insulted by paying the slaves' penalty (*servile supplicium*), however deservedly';
Tacitus *Hist.* 4.11.3, the treacherous freedman Asiaticus 'paid for his hateful power by a
slave's punishment (*servili supplicio*)'. For additional texts, see Hengel, *Crucifixion in the
Ancient World*, 51 n. 1.
   103.   Hengel, *Crucifixion in the Ancient World*, 51: 'In most Roman writers crucifixion
appears as the typical punishment for slaves.'
   104.   For thoughts in this direction, see already J. Meggitt, 'Laughing and Dreaming at the
Foot of the Cross', 10–12.
   105.   Plautus *Miles* 372–73; trans. P. Nixon, *Plautus III*, LCL (Cambridge, MA: Harvard
University Press, 1970) 163.

table.[106] In his novel, Petronius tells how one of Trimalchio's slaves was crucified for having cursed the soul of Caligula; the notice of his death is read out by a clerk from a long list of things which had happened that day on Trimalchio's estate, such as the harvesting of wheat, and the breaking in of oxen.[107] Juvenal describes a Roman matron blithely sending a slave to the cross, merely because she is of a humor to do so; when her husband asks what offense the slave has committed worthy of death, the lady replies that she has no reason, but, after all, a slave is not really a man.[108] The sources so far cited come from the Latin West, but the situation was not different in the Greek-speaking East: here, too, crucifixion was the 'slaves' punishment'.[109] The novelist Chariton, who was probably writing in the middle of the first century A.D.,[110] gives a grim depiction of the crucifixion of sixteen slaves who were working on a chain gang in Caria. Shut up in a dark hut, under miserable conditions, the slaves broke their chains in the night and tried to escape, but failed because the dogs' barking gave them away. Chariton relates the outcome: 'Without even seeing them or hearing their defense, the master at once ordered the crucifixion of the sixteen men. They were brought out of the hut chained together at foot and neck, each carrying his cross.'[111]

Because crucifixion was almost always inflicted upon slaves,[112] the occasions for the excessive use of crucifixion tended to coincide with

---

106. Horace *Sat*. 1.3.80–83. See also the conversation with his slave, which Horace reports in *Ep*. 1.16.46–48: 'If a slave were to say to me, "I never stole or ran away," my reply would be, "You have your reward; you are not flogged." "I never killed anyone." "You'll not hang on the cross to feed crows"'.

107. Petronius *Satyr*. 53. Cf. Hengel, *Crucifixion in the Ancient World*, 59.

108. Juvenal 6.219–23: ' "Crucify that slave!" says the wife. "But what crime worthy of death has he committed?" asks the husband; "Where are the witnesses? Who informed against him? Give him a hearing a least; no delay can be too long when a man's life is at stake!" "What a fool you are! Do you call a slave a man? He has done no wrong, you say? Be it so; this is my will and my command: let my will be the voucher for the deed." '

109. On crucifixion in the Greek-speaking world, see Hengel, *Crucifixion in the Ancient World*, 69–83, esp. 82 and the conclusion on p. 83: 'in the Greek-speaking East crucifixion was no less well-known, feared and abhorred than in the Latin West – particularly among the lower classes'. H.-W. Kuhn ('Die Kreuzesstrafe während der frühen Kaiserzeit. Ihre Wirklichkeit und Wertung in der Umwelt des Urchristentums' in *ANRW* 2.25.1 [1982] 719–21) asserts that crucifixion was the 'slaves' punishment' only in Rome and Italy. But see the depiction of the crucifixion of a group of slaves in Asia Minor in the first-century novel by Chariton (4.2).

110. On the authorship and date of the novel *Chaereas and Callirhoe*, see B. P. Reardon, *Collected Ancient Greek Novels* (Berkeley: University of California Press, 1989) 17.

111. Chariton 4.2; trans. in Reardon, *Collected Ancient Greek Novels*, 67.

112. Hengel, *Crucifixion in the Ancient World*, 51, 56, and more broadly, 34: 'because of its harshness, crucifixion was almost always inflicted only on the lower class (*humiliores*); the upper class (*honestiores*) could reckon with more "humane" punishment. Here we have a real case of "class justice".' In a number of instances, the crucifixion of robbers is also the

outbreaks of slave rebellions,[113] and incidents of violence by slaves against their masters.[114] The size of the slave population in Italy and throughout the Empire made frequent and rigorous application of the *servile supplicium* a necessity.[115] Tacitus makes explicit the rationale of the ruling class in a speech attributed to Caius Cassius, delivered in the senate during the reign of Nero: 'only by fear can you keep such scum under control'.[116]

The most vivid references to crucifixion in ancient literature are found in the comedies of Plautus,[117] where the lives of slaves are portrayed with unparalleled sympathy. It is here that one encounters a phenomenon that is essential to an understanding of Paul's dictum on the 'folly' of 'the word of the cross': references to crucifixion in Plautus' comedies almost always take the form of jokes![118] For example, the deceitful slave Chrysalus in the *Bacchides* pauses to consider what will happen when his master, whom he has sent on a wild goose chase, returns and discovers his scheme: 'I suppose he'll change my name for me, and transform me from Chrysalus to Crucisalus on the spot';[119] that is, instead of a 'gold-bearer' he will be a 'cross-bearer', and will have to carry his cross to the place of execution.

crucifixion of slaves, since, as Hengel observes (p. 50), 'robbers often drew their recruits from runaway slaves'. The crucifixion of rebellious subjects also falls under the rubric of the *servile supplicium*, since the Romans regarded subject peoples, such as the British and the Jews, not as enemies of equal status, but as their slaves; for this view of the British, see the speech of Paulinus before the battle against the British leader Boudicca in Dio Cassius 62.11.3–4; for a similar view of the Jews, see the sources cited in M. Hengel, *Juden, Griechen und Barbaren* (Stuttgart: Katholisches Bibelwerk, 1976) 78–79.

113. On crucifixion as a punishment following the great slave rebellions, see Cicero *In Verr*. 2.5.3; Livy 22.33.2; 33.36.3; Appian *Bell. Civ*. 1.120; Valerius Maximus 6.3.5; Orosius *Historiae* 5.9.4. Cf. E. M. Staerman, *Die Blütezeit der Sklavenwirtschaft in der römischen Republik* (Wiesbaden: Steiner, 1969) 238–42, 257–60; Hengel, *Crucifixion in the Ancient World*, 54–56.

114. For the accounts of the crucifixion of slaves who had murdered their masters, see Appian *Bell. Civ*. 3.98; Valerius Maximus 8.4.2–3; Tacitus *Ann*. 14.44; cf. Hengel, *Crucifixion in the Ancient World*, 59.

115. On the size of the slave population of the Roman Empire, see K. Hopkins, *Conquerors and Slaves*, 99–102. On the size of the slave population and the frequency of crucifixion, see Hengel, *Crucifixion in the Ancient World*, 56.

116. Tacitus *Ann*. 14.44.3; cf. Wiseman, *Catullus and his World*, 6. The quotation is in connection with the murder of the prefect P. Secundus by one of his slaves and its grim aftermath, the execution, presumably by crucifixion, of all 400 household slaves. For analysis of this episode and what it reveals about the vulnerability of slaves to torture and crucifixion, see M. Harding, '"Killed All the Day Long": The Powerful and their Victims in the New Testament Era', 3–4 (paper presented at the annual meeting of the Society of Biblical Literature, Denver, 2001).

117. G. E. Duckworth, *The Nature of Roman Comedy* (Princeton: Princeton University Press, 1952) 288–92; cf. Hengel, *Crucifixion in the Ancient World*, 52.

118. See the insightful analysis of Segal, *Roman Laughter*, 137–69.

119. Plautus *Bacch*. 362; cf. Segal, *Roman Laughter*, 149–50.

The pages of Plautus are full of such 'gallows humor'.[120] Even more frequent are the passages in which slaves use the word *crux* in vulgar taunts, calling one another 'cross-meat' and 'cross-bird',[121] or bidding one another to 'go be hanged!'[122]

Gallows humor was also a significant feature of the mime, judging from the extant remains and allusions in literature. Here, too, the vulgar taunts of μαστιγίας and *crucis offla* are hurled at the fool.[123] And here foolish slaves are frequently threatened with hanging on the cross. In the opening scene of the adultery mime from Oxyrhynchus, the *archimima* orders that two of her slaves be 'fastened to the trees'.[124] When the fool's complicity in the plot to murder his master is uncovered, at the conclusion of the same mime, the master loudly calls for the 'stake' to be brought.[125] In the denouement of a mime-inspired tale in the tenth book of Apuleius' *Metamorphoses*, the foolish slave who has assisted his mistress in an attempt to murder her stepson is hanged on the cross.[126] In the final scene of the *Laureolus* mime, the runaway slave turned robber-chieftain is crucified.[127] Contemporary accounts of the performance of this mime stress the realism of the stage

120. E.g., *Miles* 539–40, 610–14; *Persa* 855–56; *Stichus* 625–26; *Asinaria* 314, 545–61; *Epidicus* 610–14; esp. the grim humor in the speech of the slave Tranio in *Mostellaria* 359–64: realizing that his demise looks imminent, he asks, 'Anybody here want to make some easy money? Anybody ready to be crucified in my place today? ... I'm offering a talent to anyone prepared to jump on a cross ..., after that he can come and claim the money, cash on the nail.' There is also considerable humor in the speech of the slave Sceledrus, cited above: since in Roman law a slave was *nullo patre*, the four generations of ancestors whom Sceledrus places in the 'tomb' of the cross would have sounded ridiculous to a Roman audience (*Miles* 372–73); cf. M. Hammond, *Plautus. Miles Gloriosus* (Cambridge, MA: Harvard University Press, 1997) 111.

121. E.g., *Aul.* 522; *Bacch.* 584; *Cas.* 416; *Persa* 795; etc. Note the concentration of epithets such as *furcifer* ('gallows-bird'), *mastigia* ('whip-worthy'), and *verbero* ('flog-worthy') in the *Captivi* 551, 563, 577, 600, 659. On the frequency of such 'torture titles' in Plautus, see Segal, *Roman Laughter*, 138.

122. For the abusive expression *i in malam maximam crucem* ('be hanged!'), see *Asin.* 940; *Bacch.* 902; *Cas.* 93, 641, 977; *Cur.* 611, 693; *Menaech.* 915, 1017; *Mostel.* 1133; *Poen.* 271, 495, 511, 789, 1309.

123. For μαστιγίας ('flog-worthy'), see *POxy* 413 ('Adulteress') lines 5, 110, 137, 154, 155. for *crucis offla* ('gallows-meat'), see the mime-inspired scene in Petronius *Satyr.* 58.1–3. For *cruciarius*, see the mime-inspired tale in Apuleius *Met.* 10.7.5.

124. *POxy* 413 ('Adulteress') lines 123–24: ὑμῖν λέγω, ἀπαγαγόντες αὐτοὺς κατὰ ἀμφότερα τὰ ἀκρωτήρια καὶ τὰ παρακείμενα δένδρα προσδήσατε. Cf. Wiemken, *Der griechische Mimus*, 94–95.

125. *POxy* 413 ('Adulteress') line 186: ξύλα ἐπὶ τοῦτον. Cf. Wiemken, *Der griechische Mimus*, 101.

126. Apuleius Met. 10.12: *servus vero patibulo suffigitur*. On the comedic elements in this scene, see Winkler, *Auctor and Actor*, 77–78.

127. *Mimorum Romanorum Fragmenta*, ed. M. Bonaria, 112; cf. Reich, *Der Mimus* 546–66; Nicoll, *Masks, Mimes and Miracles*, 110–11.

crucifixion.[128] Suetonius records that the gallows humor was prolonged by 'several mimic fools' who aped the death of Laureolus on the cross.[129]

Accounts of crucifixion in novels and romances have undeniably comic elements. The humor is most conspicuous in the Milesian tale of the 'Widow of Ephesus,' inserted in Petronius' *Satyricon*.[130] In this salacious story, an Ephesian matron, overcome by grief at the death of her husband, follows the dead man into the tomb, and weeps over the body night and day. Near to the place where the lady was mourning, a soldier happened to be supervising a crucifixion, watching over the crosses to prevent anyone from taking the bodies down. Discovering the lady in the vault, the soldier first consoled her, then induced her to eat, and finally seduced her. While the soldier was taking his pleasure with the woman, the parents of one of the crucified came and removed their son from the cross. Foreseeing the punishment that awaited him, the soldier decided to take his own life. But the clever widow had a solution: she ordered her husband's body to be taken out of the coffin and nailed up to the empty cross, saying, 'I would rather make a dead stiff useful, than send a live stiff to his death.'[131] The characters and plot of this ribald tale obviously owe a great deal to the mime.[132] The sailors to whom the tale is told in the *Satyricon* respond as an audience would in the theater – that is, with laughter.[133] But accounts of crucifixion in other novels, not so directly influenced by the mime, also contain comedic elements. To mention only one example: the reader is meant to laugh at the sight of Habrocomes, the hero of Xenophon's *Ephesian Tale*, floating down the Nile, tied to a cross.[134]

It is hardly surprising to discover gallows humor in genres that are meant to amuse, such as comedy, mime, and romance, still less unexpected to encounter the occasional 'gallows joke' in a jokebook like the

---

128.   See esp. Josephus *Ant.* 19.94, which mentions 'a great quantity of artificial blood that flowed down from the one crucified'. Cf. Martial *De Spect.* 7; Juvenal 8.187–88.

129.   Suetonius *Calig.* 57.4.

130.   Petronius *Satyr.* 111–12. The story of the 'Widow of Ephesus,' first found in the fabulist Phaedrus (15 B.C. – A.D. 50), was enormously popular in antiquity, and even in the middle ages. See G. Huber, *Das Motiv der 'Witwe von Ephesus' in lateinischen Texten der Antike und des Mittelalters* (Tübingen: Mohr-Siebeck, 1990).

131.   Petronius *Satyr.* 112.

132.   For a comparison of the Ephesian widow with the adulteress of *POxy* 413, see M. Rosenblüth, *Beiträge zur Quellenkunde von Petrons Satiren* (Berlin: Weidmann, 1909) 46. Mimic characteristics in the widow's tale are noted by D. Gagliardi, *Il Comico in Petronio* (Palermo: Palumbo, 1980) 111. For theatrical elements in the story, see N. W. Slater, *Reading Petronius* (Baltimore: Johns Hopkins University Press, 1990) 108–11.

133.   Petronius *Satyr.* 113: *Risu excepere fabulam nautae.*

134.   Xenophon of Ephesus *Ephesiaca* 4.2; Reardon, *Collected Ancient Greek Novels*, 155–56. For similarly comic elements in novelistic accounts of crucifixion, see Iamblichus *Babyloniaca* 2, 21.

Philogelos.[135] If these were the only instances of humor in connection with the cross in ancient literature, then one might dismiss the phenomenon as insignificant, the macabre 'entertainment' of jaded audiences.[136] But, in fact, the paradoxical combination of crucifixion with comedy appears in a number of other genres, particularly when the attention of the author lingers for a moment upon the one crucified, so that the account assumes the dimensions of a λόγος, as Paul would have it. The satirists, for example, are earnest moral critics of the ease with which masters sent their slaves to the cross; yet humor accompanies even the harshest critique. To return to the passages cited above, Horace's disapproving account of a master who would have his slave crucified because he surreptitiously tasted some fish soup[137] is offered as an example of 'the faults that cleave to fools (*stulti*)',[138] and the cavalier master is compared to the crazy jurisconsult Labeo.[139] Petronius the moralist seeks to emphasize the heartless attitude taken toward slaves, when he depicts an *actuarius* in the employ of Trimalchio mentioning the crucifixion of a slave *en passant*, among other trivialities.[140] Yet the scene in which the crucifixion is reported abounds in mimic laughter: Trimalchio gets drunk and invites his wife to perform a lascivious mimic dance,[141] while he proceeds to imitate the gestures of the actor Syrus,[142]

---

135. E.g., *Philogelos* 121: 'On seeing a runner who had been crucified, an Abderite remarked, "By the gods, now he does fly – literally!".' Cited by Meggitt, 'Laughing and Dreaming at the Foot of the Cross,' 10.

136. This is the way in which Hengel interprets the accounts of crucifixion in the romances (*Crucifixion in the Ancient World*, 88): 'In the romances, ... crucifixion made for exciting entertainment and sensationalism. Here the suffering was not really taken seriously. The accounts of the crucifixion of the hero served to give the reader a thrill.' Hengel mentions the *Laureolus* mime, but diminishes its significance by describing it as 'popular entertainment' (p. 35). The novels are similarly dismissed as 'recreational literature' (p. 81).

137. The scenario is not purely hypothetical: Cato the Elder had his cooks flogged for preparing a dinner which failed to please him, according to Plutarch *Cato Maior* 25.

138. Horace *Sat*. 1.3.76–77.

139. Horace Sat. 1.3.82–83. Horace's reference to Labeo causes one to wonder whether this prominent Roman jurist was the object of ridicule in the mime, as an instance of the type of the 'learned impostor' (*alazon doctus*); cf. O. Ribbeck, *Alazon. Ein Beitrag zur antiken Ethologie* (Leipzig: Teubner, 1882) 10–18.

140. G. Highet, 'Petronius the Moralist' in *The Classical Papers of Gilbert Highet*, ed. R. J. Ball (New York: Columbia University Press, 1983) 193–95.

141. Petronius *Satyr*. 52. On Trimalchio's drunkenness as an allusion to a recurrent motif in the mime, see K. Preston, 'Some Sources of Comic Effect in Petronius', *Classical Philology* 10 (1915) 264. For the drunken fool as a familiar type in the mime, see Athenaios *Deip*. 14.621c and the fragment of a mime preserved on an ostracon of the second or first century B.C. in Page, *Select Papyri III*, 332–33. On the κόρδαξ as an indecent mimic dance, see Sandy, 'Scaenica Petroniana', 337 n. 16.

142. For a discussion of the identity of this Syrus and his possible identification with the mimograph and actor Publilius Syrus, see Giancotti, *Mimo e Gnome*, 231–34.

to the choral accompaniment of the whole household.[143] In the midst of these theatrical follies, the notice of the slave's death is suddenly read out: 'The slave Mithridates was crucified for having damned the soul of our Gaius (=Caligula).'[144] The momentary boredom induced by the reading of the 'court-circular' is suddenly relieved by the entrance of acrobats.[145] Thus, the report of the crucifixion of a slave is sandwiched between a mimic dance and a gymnastic spectacle.[146] The point of the dialogue between a Roman matron and her husband in Juvenal's sixth satire (' "Crucify that slave!" says the wife,' etc.) is to denounce the viciousness of rich women who would crucify their slaves on a whim.[147] But for all Juvenal's moral indignation, there is humor when he approaches the subject of the cross: the callous wife pronounces her husband a 'numskull' (*demens*) for suggesting that the crucifixion be delayed until the slave can be given a hearing.[148]

The unexpected conjunction of crucifixion and comedy appears in political writings, as well. Philo gives a grim account of the pogrom against the Jews of Alexandria during the reign of Caligula.[149] In the torture and crucifixion of the Jews, the Greek persecutors 'assumed the roles of actors in the mimes' and 'mimicked' the suffering of those whom they tormented.[150] Indeed, Philo reports that the Roman prefect Flaccus staged the torture and crucifixion of Jews in the middle of the theater as a 'play' (θέα) in two acts:[151] 'The first part of the show, lasting from dawn until the third or fourth hour, consisted of Jews being scourged, hung up, bound to the wheel, brutally mauled, and haled for their death march through the middle of the orchestra.'[152] In the final act, the Jews were crucified,

---

143. On the chorus which the slaves sing in accompaniment to Trimalchio's mimic gestures, see A. De Lorenzi, '*Madeia Perimadeia* in Petronio e un mimo perduto di P. Siro', *Rivista Indo-Greca-Italica di Filologia* 13 (1929) 10–11; P. Perrochat, *Pétrone. Le Festin de Trimalcion* (Paris: Presses Universitaires de France, 1952) 84.

144. Petronius *Satyr*. 53.3.

145. Petronius *Satyr*. 53.11. For the performances of acrobatic entertainers at dinners, cf. Martial 5.12.3–4.

146. Panayotakis, *Theatrum Arbitri*, 83–84.

147. Juvenal 6.219–23. For this satire as a denunciation of the vice and folly of Roman society ladies, see Highet, *Juvenal the Satirist*, 91–92.

148. Juvenal 6.222. The theme of the vicious woman was popular in the mime: see, e.g., Herodas *Mime* 5 and 6; Publilius Syrus in O. Ribbeck, *Scaenicae Romanorum Poesis Fragmenta II, Comicorum Romanorum Fragmenta* (Hildesheim: Olms, 1962) 369–70.

149. See esp. the fine introduction, translation and commentary of H. Box, *Philonis Alexandrini in Flaccum* (London: Oxford University Press, 1939).

150. Philo *In Flacc*. 72: καὶ οἱ μὲν ταῦτα δρῶτες ὥσπερ ἐν τοῖς θεατρικοῖς μίμοις καθυπεκρίνοντο τοὺς πάσχοντας. Cf. the translation of Box, *Philonis Alexandrini in Flaccum*, 27: 'the perpetrators mimicked the sufferers as in the mimes of the theater.'

151. Philo *In Flacc*. 84–85: ζῶντας δ' ἀνασκολοπίζεσθαι προσέταττεν, . . . καὶ ἡ θέα διενενέμητο.

152. Philo *In Flacc*. 85; trans. by F. H. Colson, *Philo IX*, LCL (Cambridge, MA: Harvard University Press, 1985) 349.

surrounded by 'dancers and mimes and flute players and all the other favorites of theatrical contests'.[153] It is worthy of note that, in this case, the humor connected with crucifixion is not merely a feature of Philo's narrative, but is a product of the actors in the real-life drama, as though it were impossible to participate in such a cruel deracination of fellow human beings without the protection provided by mimic laughter.

One should not suppose that it was only in Alexandria, where the populace was infatuated with the mime,[154] that mockery and derision accompanied crucifixion. On the contrary, jesting and ridicule seem to have been concomitant features of crucifixion everywhere, judging from the accounts of historians. This element appears clearly in Josephus' account of the crucifixion of Jews who attempted to escape from the besieged city of Jerusalem:

> They were first scourged and subjected to torture of every description, before being killed, and then crucified opposite the walls. Titus felt pity for them, five hundred or sometimes more being captured daily, but their number was too great for him to risk either letting them go or putting them under guard. But his main reason for not stopping the crucifixions was the hope that the spectacle might induce them to surrender, for fear that continued resistance would involve them in a similar fate. So the soldiers, out of rage and hatred, nailed those they caught in different postures, *by way of jest* (πρὸς χλεύην), and so great was their number that space could not be found for the crosses nor crosses for the bodies.[155]

Ridicule is also found in Tacitus' well-known account of the crucifixion of Christians by Nero in Rome: 'And derision (*ludibria*) accompanied their end: they were covered with wild beasts' skins and torn to death by dogs; or they were fastened on crosses, and, when daylight failed were burned to serve as lamps by night.'[156] Even more remarkable are those instances in which the crucified laugh and jest in the face of death, or mock and deride their tormentors. Seneca refers to persons who, 'when stretched upon crosses', nevertheless 'are slanderous and witty in heaping insult on others', and even 'spit upon spectators from their own cross!'[157] Silius Italicus tells

---

153.   Philo *In Flacc.* 85; trans. by Box, *Philonis Alexandrini in Flaccum*, 31.

154.   On the popularity of the mime in Alexandria, see Cicero *Pro Rab. Post.* 12.35; Dio Chrysostom *Or.* 32.86, 99.

155.   Josephus *B.J.* 5.449–51; the translation slightly modifies H. Thackeray, *Josephus III: The Jewish War, Books IV–VII*, LCL (Cambridge, MA: Harvard University Press, 1979) 340–41.

156.   Tacitus *Ann.* 15.44; text and trans. J. Jackson, *Tacitus V, The Annals, Books XIII–XVI*, LCL (Cambridge, MA: Harvard University Press, 1981) 284–85.

157.   Seneca *De vita beata* 19.3; text and trans. J. Basore, *Seneca. Moral Essays II*, LCL (Cambridge, MA: Harvard University Press, 1994) 148–49.

of a Spanish slave who demanded to be crucified along with his master, and taunted the torturers for flagging in their task.[158] Josephus mentions a Jew of Jotapata who was tortured and crucified by Roman soldiers, and laughed at his tormentors as he died.[159]

Of course, the most infamous case of mockery and jest in connection with crucifixion is that of Jesus of Nazareth.[160] The earliest account of the incident is that found in the Gospel of Mark:[161] after Jesus had been flogged and remanded for crucifixion,

> The soldiers led him into the courtyard of the palace (that is, the governor's headquarters); and they called together the whole cohort. And they clothed him in a purple cloak; and after twisting some thorns into a crown, they put it on him. And they began saluting him, 'Hail, King of the Jews!' They struck his head with a reed, spat upon him, and knelt down in homage to him. After mocking him, they stripped him of the purple cloak and put his own clothes on him. Then they led him out to crucify him.

Given the constancy of the connection of humor with crucifixion in antiquity, there is good reason to regard the buffoonery of the soldiers in the gospels as a plausible action. Indeed, more attention should be given to the suggestion, made almost a century ago,[162] that the mockery of Jesus is based upon a theatrical mime, which would have been familiar to both the soldiers and the populace.[163]

---

158. Silius Italicus *Punica* 179–81.

159. Josephus *B.J.* 3.321; cf. *B.J.* 2.153; 7.418.

160. See, in general, R. E. Brown, *The Death of the Messiah: From Gethsemane to the Grave: A Commentary on the Passion Narratives in the Four Gospels*, Vol. 1 (New York: Doubleday, 1994) 862–77, with the bibliography, 674–75.

161. Mark 15.16–20, 29; Matt. 27.27–31, 38–39; cf. John 19.2–3; Luke 23.11, 36–37, 39; Gospel of Peter 3.7–9.

162. Reich, *Der König mit der Dornenkrone*; K. Kastner, 'Christi Dornenkrönung und Vespottung durch die römische Soldateska', BZ 6 (1908) 378–92.

163. Reich argues that the soldiers who mocked Jesus were enacting a mime in which kingship was caricatured. In favor of this suggestion is Philo's account of the mockery of the poor simpleton Carabas in *In Flaccum* 36–40: the Greek mob put on Carabas' head a sheet of papyrus spread out like a diadem; they threw around his body a rug as a royal robe, and gave him a papyrus reed as a scepter. 'And when, as in theatrical mimes, he had received the insignia of kingship and had been arrayed in the character of a king, young men bearing staffs on their shoulders took their stance on either side in place of spearmen, mimic lancers. Then the others approached, some as if to greet him, others as though to plead their causes, others as though to petition him about public matters. Then from the surrounding multitude rang forth an outlandish shout of "Marin" – the name by which it is said that kings are called in Syria' (*In Flacc.* 38–39). Although no mime is extant in which a king is mocked in this way, *POxy* 413 ('Charition') contains a burlesque of a drunken king.

Figure 14.   Graffito from the Palatine Hill, Rome.

A well-known graffito from the Palatine Hill in Rome, dated ca. A.D. 225, depicts a crucified figure with the head of an ass.[164] Facing the crucified is a smaller, beardless man clad in a tunic, his left hand raised in supplication. A crudely lettered inscription reads: ᾿Αλεξαμενὸς σέβετε [= σέβεται] θεόν, that is, 'Alexamenos worships god' (Fig. 14). The drawing was discovered in one of the rooms of a building which served as a training school for imperial guards.[165] There can be no doubt that the caricature was meant as a parody of the faith of a Christian convert by one of his pagan comrades.[166] The ass's head has been interpreted as a derogatory reference to the Jewish origins of the Christian religion.[167] But the ass-man was a theme featured in mimes, as illustrated by a first-century A.D. bronze relief depicting a scene in which a man with an ass's head is beaten

164.   The graffito was discovered in 1856; for discussion of the archaeological context, publication, and early efforts at interpretation, see Reich, *Der König mit der Dornenkrone*, 3–4.

165.   In one of the rooms of the Domus Gelotiana; cf. Reich, *Der König mit der Dornenkrone*, 3; Brown, *The Death of the Messiah*, Vol. 1, 875.

166.   Thus the consensus of scholars, e.g., Reich, *Der König mit der Dornenkrone*, 6; E. Dinkler, *Signum Crucis. Aufsätze zum Neuen Testament und zur Christlichen Archäologie* (Tübingen: Mohr-Siebeck, 1967) 150–53; Hengel, *Crucifixion in the Ancient World*, 19. This conclusion is strengthened by another inscription found in a neighboring building of the same complex: ᾿Αλεξαμενὸς *fidelis*. Reich's reconstruction of the relationship between the two inscriptions is quite plausible: a pagan guard in the imperial palace first sought to denounce a Christian comrade by writing on the wall, 'Alexamenos is a Christian'; when this did not produce the desired result, he sketched a caricature of Alexamenos as the devotee of an ass-headed god. For pagan mockery of the crucified Christ during the period of the expansion and persecution of the faith, see Tertullian *Apol.* 16.6–8; *Ad. Nat.* 1.12; *Adv. Val.* 1.14.

167.   This interpretation is an inference from the fact that one of the themes of ancient anti-Judaism was the accusation that the Jews worshipped an ass in the temple. See Hengel, *Crucifixion in the Ancient World*, 19, and the literature he cites: I. Opelt, 'Esel,' *RAC VI*, 592ff.; J.–G. Préaux, 'Deus Christianorum Onocoetes' in *Hommages L. Hermann* (Bruxelles:

in a mimic dance.[168] Thus the Palatine graffito is a final example of the paradoxical connection between humor and the cross that we have traced through the literature: here the central mystery of the Christian faith is parodied as a scene from the mime, in which the crucified god of the Christians is mocked as a grotesque, much-slapped ass.

It is now time to confront the issue of the social motivation of gallows humor, for the light that may be cast upon Paul's statement about the 'folly' of 'the word of the cross'. The explanation suggested by ancient theorists of the laughable is that gallows humor is an extreme expression of 'aesthetic disdain' towards the weak and defective.[169] Quintilian summarizes a tradition that goes back to Plato, when he states: 'Laughter is never far removed from derision . . . . Laughter has its basis in some kind or other of deformity or ugliness.'[170] To be sure, the philosophers made a distinction between liberal and illiberal jests, insisting that humor should not cause pain, and questioning the ethics of laughter directed at the unfortunate.[171] But practice was always less scrupulous than theory, especially among the Romans. Politicians, orators, and satirists routinely ridiculed the deformities and disabilities of their opponents.[172] In the very passage of the *De Oratore* in which Cicero seeks to restrain the ridicule of ugliness and physical blemishes, he cites examples of jests illustrating the

Latomus, 1960) 639–54. But this interpretation deserves to be critically evaluated. The crucified figure portrayed in the Palatine graffito is not an ass, but a man, clad in a short tunic, with the head of an ass.

168.   Figure with discussion in Reich, *Der König mit der Dornenkrone*, 9–15; idem, 'Der Mann mit dem Eselskopf, ein Mimodrama, von klassischen Altertum verfolgt bis auf Shakespeares Sommernachtstraum', *Jahrbuch der deutschen Shakespeare-Gesellschaft* 40 (1904) 18–19; cf. Nicoll, *Masks, Mimes and Miracles*, 75. Winkler (*Actor and Actor*, 286–91) sees the theme of the ass-man in the mime behind the plot and humor of Apuleius' *Golden Ass*.

169.   For ancient theories on the source of the laughable, see E. Arndt, *De ridiculi doctrina rhetorica* (Kirchain: M. Schmersow, 1904); Grant, *The Ancient Rhetorical Theories of the Laughable*. The term 'aesthetic disdain' is taken from Veyne, *A History of Private Life* I, 134–32.

170.   Quintilian *Inst. Orat.* 6.3.8, citing Cicero *De Orat.* 2.236; Aristotle *Ars Poet.* 1449a30: 'the laughable is a species of the base or ugly.' In the *Philebus* (48–50), Plato explains that the ridiculous is a name applied to the vice of self-ignorance, especially as it occurs in the weak.

171.   The condemnation of laughter directed at the unfortuate is already found in Chilon, one of the so-called 'Seven Wise Men': 'Do not laugh at the unfortunate' (τῷ δυστυχοῦντι μὴ ἐπιγέλα) in H. Diels, *Die Fragmenta der Vorsokratiker* (Berlin: Weidmann, 1906–10) p. 521, 24. See also a fragment of Democritus: 'Do not laugh at the misfortunes of men, but pity them' (ἄξιον ἀνθρώπους ὄντας ἐπ᾽ ἀνθρώπων συμφοραῖς μὴ γελᾶν ἀλλ᾽ ὀλοφύρεσθαι) in Diels, *Fragmenta der Vorsokratiker*, p. 405, 15. Both Plato and Aristotle agree in limiting the ridiculous to slighter defects which are not painful or injurious to others: Plato *Leges* 9, 934–36; Aristotle *Ars. Poet.* 1449a30; cf. Cicero *De Orat.* 2.238. For the distinction between liberal and illiberal jests, see Aristotle *Eth. Nic.* bk. 4, 1128ab; Cicero *De Off.* 1.104.

172.   Corbeill, *Controlling Laughter*, esp. 30–42; more broadly, Garland, *The Eye of the Beholder*, 73–86.

different *genera ridiculi* which contain ridicule of bodily defects – smallness, blindness, lameness, baldness, etc.[173] Cicero cannot conceal his approval of this humor.[174] Indeed, Cicero illustrates the principle that 'caricatures are leveled against ugliness or some physical defect' by reference to his own practice, telling how he once ridiculed his opponent Helvius Mancia by comparing his appearance with a picture of a deformed Gaul with twisted body, hanging cheeks and extended tongue.[175] Because the weak and the defective were considered laughable, slaves and the poor were assigned the principal roles in comedy.[176] By an extension of this logic, slave-beating was a standard feature of comedy,[177] and whiplash marks seem to have been the sign by which slaves were identified on the comic stage.[178] Of course, the special object of ridicule in the mime was a grotesque, deformed figure, upon whose humped back or bald head blows rained down for the amusement of the audience.[179] The crucified slave, flogged and tortured, and nailed up by way of jest, represents the extreme limit of the human.[180] Along the continuum of aesthetic disdain, gallows humor is the ultimate expression of what Greeks and Romans regarded as laughable in general.

The existence of such a continuum of aesthetic disdain, uniting the weak and the deformed with the victims of crucifixion, is illustrated by a verse which Seneca quotes from Maecenas:

Fashion me with a palsied hand,
Weak of foot, and a cripple;
Build upon me a crook-backed hump;
Shake my teeth till they rattle;
All is well, if my life remains.
Save, oh, save it, I pray you,
Though I sit on the piercing cross![181]

173. Cicero *De Orat.* 2.245, 246, 249, 250; cf. Grant, *Ancient Rhetorical Theories of the Laughable*, 79–80.

174. E.g., the jest of Glaucia on the limping gait of Calvinus in *De Orat.* 2.249.

175. Cicero *De Orat.* 2.266.

176. Grant, *Ancient Rhetorical Theories of the Laughable*, 39–47.

177. See, already, Aristophanes *Pax* 743–44; *Vesp.* 1292–96; and numerous instances in Plautus, for which see Segal, *Roman Laughter*, 138–43.

178. See esp. Plautus *Amphitruo* 443–46, with the observations of Segal, *Roman Laughter*, 139.

179. On the psychology of audience response to the abuse of the fool in the mime, see the remarks of Grant, *Ancient Rhetorical Theories of the Laughable*, 48–51; Winkler, *Auctor and Actor*, 290–91.

180. The extreme, limit status of the crucified is reflected in Columella's statement in *De re rustica* 1.7.2: 'the ancients regarded the extreme of the law as the extreme of the cross' (*summum ius antiqui summam putabant crucem*).

181. Seneca *Ep.* 101.11.

As Seneca observes, Maecenas has arranged the list of sufferings in the form of a climax: weakness, deformity, and the ultimate pain of crucifixion.[182] Seneca despises Maecenas' desire to live under such pitiable conditions: he asks repeatedly, 'What is more foolish?' (*Quid stultius*),[183] and confesses that he 'laughs heartily' (*cum multo risu*) at such a 'contemptible' and 'effeminate' creature.[184]

In accordance with this conception of the laughable, the upper class responded to gallows humor with amusement. The crucifixion of a slave or a poor man, one who was socially inferior or physically defective, was a welcome reminder of what it was like to be a fully human part of society – wealthy, unmaimed, independent –, and thus invulnerable to such cruel punishment. For such persons, the representation of crucifixion in an artistic medium, such as the mime, must have been especially pleasurable, because of the economy in the expenditure of affect.[185] But one must also allow that some members of the lower class took pleasure in gallows humor, since crucifixion was a regular feature of the mime, and the mime appealed to persons of all classes. Here, too, a milder form of aesthetic disdain must have operated, especially among that minority of the poor who imagined that their interests coincided with those of their rulers. Plautus' good and fearful slave Messenio in the *Menaechmi* delights in contemplating the pains that his disobedient fellows will suffer for their misdeeds: 'Their masters will reward them, let the worthless slaves be told, the lowly, lazy louts get whips and chains, and millstones, great fatigue, starvation, freezing cold, the price for all their misbehaviors – pains. I therefore fully fear this fate and very gladly remain determined to be good, so I won't end up badly.'[186] Messenio is hardly typical of a Plautine slave, who is usually scheming and impudent.[187] But he may be representative of a minority in the audience who joined in laughter at their unfortunate fellows, seeking to warm their bones on the suffering of others.[188] It goes without saying that he is also the mouthpiece of the masters whose interests he seeks to safeguard.

182. Seneca *Ep.* 101.10, 13.
183. Seneca *Ep.* 101.4, 7.
184. Seneca *Ep.* 101.9, 12–13.
185. In accordance with Freud's insights into the mechanism of humor, as arising from 'an economy in the expenditure of affect'; see *Jokes and Their Relation to the Unconscious*, trans. J. Strachey (New York: Norton, 1963) 229, where Freud deals with *Galgenhumor* ('gallows humor').
186. Plautus *Menaechmi* 973–77, trans. Segal, *Roman Laughter*, 142.
187. Segal, *Roman Laughter*, 142–43.
188. Cf. Cicero *In Verr.* 5.65: the populace 'longed to feast their eyes and satisfy their souls with the spectacle of torture and crucifixion'.

But psychology teaches that motivation is seldom simple or singular. Indeed, certain figures evoke an emotional ambivalence.[189] One should not be surprised if the crucified were one of these figures. Tacitus' comment about the cruelty necessary to preserve order among the slave population ('only by fear can you keep such scum under control') reveals a second motivation of gallows humor: fear.[190] What if public execution, with all its attendant horrors, should prove insufficient? Gallows humor relieved this anxiety by trivializing the evil instrument by which the upper class maintained its dominance. Among the lower classes, fear must have been the primary emotion aroused and released by gallows humor, particularly in the case of slaves, who lived constantly in the shadow of the cross.[191] In comedy, mime, and romance, this anxiety finds expression in the motif of escape from crucifixion. Students of Plautus have often noted that the crucifixions and other tortures, with which roguish slaves are constantly threatened, are never carried out.[192] Plautine slaves consistently elude the cross, giving thanks to 'holy trickery'.[193] The pleasure which the audience derived from this momentary absolution was no doubt sweetened by awareness of what would have happened under ordinary circumstances.[194]

189. On the emotional 'ambivalence', see S. Freud, 'Instincts and Their Vicissitudes' in *General Psychological Theory*, ed. P. Rieff (New York: Collier, 1963) 91–92; idem, *Introductory Lectures on Psychoanalysis*, ed. J. Strachey (New York: Norton, 1966) 427–28.

190. Tacitus *Ann.* 14.44.5.

191. See Cicero's account of what occurred at the emancipation (*manumissio*) of slaves in *Pro Rabirio* 16: the touch of the praetor's staff liberated slaves 'from the fear of all these torments,' including '... flogging, the executioner's hook, and finally the terror of the cross (*cruces denique terrore*)'.

192. This aspect of Plautine comedy has greatly puzzled modern interpreters, e.g., Legrand, *The New Greek Comedy* 110, 240, 455; Duckworth, *The Nature of Roman Comedy* 253, 288, 290. P. Spranger ('Historische Untersuchungen zu den Sklavenfiguren des Plautus und Terenz,' *Akademie Mainz. Geistes und Sozialwissenschaftlichen Klasse* 8 [1960] 58 repr. *Historiche Untersuchungen zu den Sklavenfiguren des Plautus und Terenz* (Wiesbaden: Steiner, 1961) suggests that the immunity of Plautine slaves from punishment reflects good relations between masters and slaves in the Greek sources from which Plautus drew his comedies. Segal (*Roman Laughter*, 141–69) argues that the slaves' escape from punishment represents a 'saturnalian overthrow' of the ordinary practices of Roman society.

193. The best example is Libanus' triumphant speech in the *Asinaria* (545–51): 'We give our great and grateful thanks to holy trickery, for by our shrewdness, wiles, deceits, and clever machinations, our shoulders bold, displaying courage in the face of rods, we've just defied hot-iron tortures, crucifixion, chains, strappadoes, fetters, dungeons, locking, stocking, manacles, and harsh persuasive whippers well acquainted with our backs!' For other examples and commentary, see Segal, *Roman Laughter*, 143–46.

194. The awareness of the spectators is mirrored in the plays, where the slaves themselves are fully conscious of the fact that the circumstances which permit them to escape are exceptional: e.g., Plautus *Asin.* 561–74; *Bacch.* 358–62; *Persa* 264–71; see also Terence *Phormio* 248–51, where the slave Geta reveals his awareness of tortures to come. See the analysis of Segal, *Roman Laughter*, 146–52.

It is the same in the mime, where the master calls for the stake,[195] but the foolish slave escapes from his clutches, the clappers sound, and curtain![196] Indeed, it is even possible that the robber-chieftain Laureolus escaped from the cross at the end of the mime by that name: Suetonius relates that at a performance on the day of Caligula's assassination, the chief actor fell 'as he was making his escape' (*proripiens se*) and vomited blood.[197] Likewise in the romances, the heroes and heroines are constantly in danger of suffering this fearful punishment, but are rescued at the last moment.[198]

Our conclusion with respect to Paul's statement about the 'folly' of 'the word of the cross' may take the form of an argument *a minori ad maius*: if the crucifixion of a slave or a poor man provoked humor, for the reasons given above, then how much more a message about the crucifixion of the anointed one of God! That one who had suffered the death of a slave, and had experienced the extreme limit of human misery, should be proclaimed as God's agent in the last days (1 Cor. 1.7–8), the one who had been awaited so long (2.7) – this was surely the purest folly. That a piece of human trash, one of those whom life had demolished, should be called the 'Lord of glory' (2.8) – was the most laughable scenario imaginable.[199] In Paul's gospel of the cross of Christ, we have, so to speak, the finale of a mime, not a proper play. Thus Paul acknowledges that his message about the 'crucified Christ' is foolishness to many of his contemporaries, especially those upon whom wealth and power had conferred the privilege of participating in learned culture. Indeed, Paul sharpens the humorous effect of his message by choosing a perfect participle,[200] ἐσταυρωμένος (1.23; 2.2), rather than an aorist,[201] to describe the Christ whom he proclaims: over against the Corinthian elite, Paul insists, provocatively, that the

---

195. E.g., *POxy* 413 ('Adulteress') line 186.

196. The typical conclusion of a mime, according to Cicero *Pro Cael*. 27.65: *Mimi ergo est iam exitus, non fabulae; in quo cum clausula non invenitur, fugit aliquis e manibus, deinde scabilla concrepant, aulaeum tollitur.*

197. Suetonius *Calig*. 57.4. Further evidence that Laureolus escaped death on the cross is found in Josephus' reference to 'stage blood' (αἷμα τεχνητόν) in *Ant*. 19.94, and in Juvenal's satirical account of impecunious nobles selling their stage-deaths by appearing in the Laureolus mime (8.187–88). Martial's description of a more gruesome production in which the unfortunate actor did not survive the ordeal (*De Spect*. 7) would seem to be the exception. Cf. J. G. Griffith, 'Juvenal and Stage-Struck Patricians', *Mnemosyne* 15 (1962) 259–60.

198. Chariton *Chaereas and Callirhoe* 4.2.6–8, 4.3.3–5, Xenophon *Ephesiaca* 2.6, 4.2.1–3, 4.6.2; Iamblichus *Babyloniaca* 2,21. This aspect of crucifixion in the Greek romances is already noted by Hengel, *Crucifixion in the Ancient World*, 81–82.

199. Cf. Weder, *Das Kreuz Jesu bei Paulus*, 167–68.

200. Blass-Debrunner, *A Greek Grammar of the New Testament*, § 342.1: the perfect is used 'to denote a continuing effect on a subject or object'.

201. For examples of the use of the aorist participle to speak of the past event of Jesus' crucifixion, see Gospel of Peter 13.56: τίνα ζητεῖτε; μὴ τὸν σταυρωθέντα ἐκεῖνον; Justin Martyr

continuing and present significance of Christ, even after his resurrection, consists in nothing other than the fact that he *is* the crucified.[202]

Not only does Paul acknowledge that the message about the 'crucified Christ' appears to be 'foolishness', he admits that those who are 'called' by this message are regarded as 'foolish' (μωρά) by the wise and the strong (1.27).[203] Paul employs the most astonishing hyperbole to dramatize the disdain in which the mostly impoverished Christians at Corinth (1.26) are held by the elite: they are 'weak' (ἀσθενῆ), 'low-born' (ἀγενῆ), 'despised' (ἐξουθενημένα), 'mere nothings' (τὰ μὴ ὄντα).[204] As has been shown, the terms that Paul uses here are descriptive of the social status of the majority of the Corinthian Christians.[205] But several features of Paul's rhetoric suggest that the expressions also embody derisive judgments upon those who have been 'called' by 'the word of the cross'. First, there is the genitive 'of the world' (τοῦ κόσμου), by which the terms are repeatedly qualified.[206] While it is possible that the genitive is used in a purely partitive sense ('the portion of humanity that is foolish, weak, and low-born'),[207] it seems more likely that Paul also intended the meaning which the majority of older interpreters discovered in this genitive: namely, 'those whom the world regards as foolish, etc'.[208] Second, Paul's use of the neuter plural (τὰ μωρά κτλ.) to designate persons in 1.27–28, not only emphasizes the abstract qualities of those who have been chosen by

---

Apol. I. 13.3: Ἰησοῦν Χριστόν, τὸν σταυρωθέντα; *Apol.* I. 13.4: …ἀνθρώπῳ σταυρωθέντι διδόναι; Irenaeus *Adv. Haer.* 2.32.4, frag. 9 (= Eusebius *Hist. Eccl.* 5.7.5.): ἐν τῷ ὀνόματι Ἰησοῦ Χριστοῦ τοῦ σταυρωθέντος ἐπὶ Ποντίου Πιλάτου; Lucian *De Mort. Peregr.* 11: ἀνασκολοπισθέντα.

202.   The theological significance of Paul's choice of the perfect participle, ἐσταυρωμένος, to describe more precisely the Christ whom he proclaims, has long been recognized: Deissmann, *Paulus*, 153–54; J. Schneider, 'σταυρός', *TDNT* 7 (1971) 582; E. Ellis, 'Christ Crucified' in *Prophecy and Hermeneutic in Early Christianity* (Grand Rapids, MI: Eerdmans, 1980) 73–74; H.-W. Kuhn, 'Kreuz,' *TRE* 19 (1990) 720; most recently, and with strong arguments, T. Heckel, 'Der Gekreuzigte bei Paulus und im Markusevangelium', *BZ* 46 (2002) 196–200.

203.   On τὰ μωρὰ τοῦ κόσμου (1.27) as 'those whom the world regards as foolish', see esp. Heinrici, *Der erste Brief*, 79.

204.   1 Cor. 1.27–28; on the background and significance of these terms, see Theissen, *The Social Setting of Pauline Christianity*, 71; Collins, *First Corinthians*, 111.

205.   J. Bohatec, 'Inhalt und Reihenfolge der "Schlagworte der Erlösungsreligion" in I Kor 1, 26–31', 252–71; Theissen, *The Social Setting of Pauline Christianity*, 71–73; Martin, *The Corinthian Body*, 61.

206.   1.27 τὰ μωρὰ τοῦ κόσμου, … τὰ ἀσθενῆ τοῦ κόσμου; 1.28 τὰ ἀγενῆ τοῦ κόσμου.

207.   So Meyer, *Der erste Brief, ad loc*: 'die thörichten Bestandtheile der Welt'; Weiss, *Der erste Korintherbrief*, 36: 'diejenigen aus der Menschheit, welche töricht sind'.

208.   Heinrici, *Der erste Brief*, 79: 'Doch scheint die von den Meisten (Theodoret, Luther, Grotius, Estius, *et. al.*) bevorzugte Erklärung: *nach dem Urtheile der Welt* mehr für sich zu haben, da die Analogie des Ausdrucks von V. 25 dafür spricht, und es sich hier um relative Grössen handelt (vgl. τὰ μὴ ὄντα V. 28). Dass dem Urtheile der Welt die Lage der Berufenen entsprochen habe, ist dadurch selbstverständlich nicht ausgeschlossen.'

God,[209] it also denigrates this class of subjects by objectification: in comparison with the educated and powerful who are fully human participants in society, those who have been 'called' by 'the word of the cross' are 'foolish things, etc.'.[210] Third, Paul adds to the objective terms which describe the majority of the Corinthians as coming from the lower classes of society (μωρά, ἀσθενῆ, ἀγενῆ) the fact that they are 'despised' (ἐξουθενημένα), employing the participle of a verb that consistently suggests disdain and derision elsewhere in Paul.[211] Finally, there is Paul's choice of the highly unusual expression τὰ μὴ ὄντα as the climactic description of the insignificance of those who have responded to the message of the 'crucified Christ'.[212] The expression has philosophical and even theological connotations,[213] in addition to its sociological reference,[214] so that it does not suffice to translate: 'the nobodies'; rather, Paul means to say that, in the view of the cultured elite, those who have been 'called' by 'the word of the cross' simply do not exist at all.[215]

Later, in 4.8–13, a paragraph we have analyzed in detail,[216] Paul acknowledges that he and his fellow apostles are regarded as 'fools on account of Christ' (4.10). The vocabulary that Paul uses in reference to himself and his colleagues is first of all descriptive of their social status, and makes it clear that the apostles belong to a socially inferior group.[217] The first three terms in this collocation – 'fools', 'weak', and 'dishonored' – overlap, for the most part, with the epithets applied to the Corinthian Christians in 1.27–28. But in 4.11–13, Paul moves beyond whatever

---

209. Heinrici, *Der erste Brief*, 79; Weiss, *Der erste Korintherbrief*, 36; Collins, *First Corinthians*, 110–11.

210. The contrast is particularly sharp if the noun 'strong' ἰσχυρά in 1.27 was originally masculine, like 'wise' (σοφούς) in the same verse: see the reconstruction of the text of this verse proposed by Weiss, *Der erste Korintherbrief*, 36: ἀλλὰ τὰ μωρὰ τοῦ κόσμου ἐξελέξατο ὁ θεὸς, ἵνα καταισχύνῃ τοὺς σοφούς, καὶ τὰ ἀσθενῆ τοῦ κόσμου ἐξελέξατο ὁ θεὸς, ἵνα καταισχύνῃ τοὺς ἰσχυρούς.

211. 1 Thess. 5.20; 1 Cor. 6.4; 16.11; Gal. 4.14; 2 Cor. 10.10; Rom. 14.3, 10. For this point, see Weiss, *Der erste Korintherbrief*, 36; Collins, *First Corinthians*, 111.

212. On this expression, see esp. Theissen, *The Social Setting of Pauline Christianity*, 71–72.

213. So, already, Weiss, *Der erste Korintherbrief*, 37; but esp. Theissen, *The Social Setting of Pauline Christianity*, 71, citing Plato *Phaedr.* 234E; *Tht.* 176C; Epictetus *Diss.* 3.9.14; 4.8.25.

214. Theissen, *The Social Setting of Pauline Christianity*, 71, calling special attention to Philo *De Virt.* 173–74; followed by Collins, *First Corinthians*, 111: 'Paul's jargon is roughly equivalent to the contemporary contrast between the "haves" and the "have-nots".'; Lindemann, *Der erste Korintherbrief*, 50: 'τὰ μὴ ὄντα bezeichnet das "Nicht-Seiende" und enthält insofern die schärfste Form sozialer Diskriminierung.'

215. So, rightly, Heinrici, *Der erste Brief*, 80: '*das wie nicht existierend Angesehene*, d.i. was so völlig nichtsgeltend war, als ob es gar nicht vorhanden wäre'; Weiss, *Der erste Korintherbrief*, 37: 'das nicht Existierende.'

216. See Ch. 4 above.

217. Theissen, *The Social Setting of Pauline Christianity*, 72–73.

ambiguities reside in euphemisms such as 'foolish' and 'weak', and speaks a more literal language, using terms that the elite did not want to hear mentioned: 'hungry and thirsty, naked, beaten, homeless, laboring, reviled, harassed, slandered, scum, trash'. As we have shown, each of these terms has a history of usage related to the mime, and together reinforce the theatrical metaphor explicitly articulated at the beginning of the paragraph (4.9). Thus the terms are not merely descriptive of Paul's abject social condition, but embody the disdain in which Paul is held by the rich at Corinth. In the logic of his argument, Paul acknowledges that, as the apostle of the 'crucified Christ', he is regarded as a low-class buffoon.

With Paul's acknowledgment that he and his apostolic colleagues are regarded as 'fools' by the elite, Paul places himself in a tradition of cultural criticism that is informed by a 'self-denying intelligence'.[218] The speaker in this tradition is permitted to utter a critical truth about those in authority, but only after he has assumed the role of a grotesque outsider.[219] Aesop and Socrates belong to this group of 'wise fools', who speak a critical truth in jesting-earnest against the tyranny of conventional wisdom.[220] Because the fool in the mime is grotesque, deformed, and without honor, he is able to utter irreverent thoughts about the rulers that are forbidden to ordinary citizens.[221] Thus Paul's acknowledgement of 'foolishness' is an essential first step in his critique of the values of the rich and powerful in Corinth. As we shall discover, the assumption of the guise of a 'fool' is a standard maneuver in that intellectual tradition which takes up a dialectical relation to authority.

One already encounters such a moment in the Homeric tradition, when Odysseus, the wisest of all the Greeks, assumes the guise of a fool, upon his return to Ithaca, in order to destroy the suitors. Odysseus is described as 'an old outcast, a beggar man, leaning most painfully upon a stick, his poor cloak, all in tatters, looped about him'.[222] In this burlesque role, Odysseus became a popular character of farce and mime.[223] Epicharmus' play entitled 'Odysseus the Runaway' ('Οδυσσεὺς Αὐτόμολος)[224] dealt with the story of Odysseus' spying expedition to Troy.[225] Odysseus plays the

218. The term is taken from Winkler, *Auctor and Actor*, 279, 286–87, for whom it is the essential characteristic of 'the grotesque perspective' in Greco-Roman literature.
219. On the early history of the figure of the 'grotesque outsider' in Greek literature, see Nagy, *The Best of the Achaeans*, 280–90.
220. Daly, *Aesop without Morals*, 19–23; Döring, *Exemplum Socratis* (Weisbaden: Franz Steiner, 1979), 2–12.
221. Nicoll, *Masks, Mimes and Miracles*, 47–50, 87–90, 124–26.
222. Homer *Od*. 17.202–203; trans. by R. Fitzgerald, *Homer. The Odyssey* (New York: Farrar, Straus and Giroux, 2000) 316.
223. Nicoll, *Masks, Mimes and Miracles*, 39–41, 54.
224. For the title and fragments, see Kaibel, *Comicorum Fragmenta*, 108–10.
225. A mission that, according to *Od*. 4.240–64, Odysseus carried out with great success.

deserter, deciding that it is safer not to enter Troy, but only to pretend to have gone there.[226] In one of the extant fragments, Odysseus rehearses to himself the extravagant story he will tell his comrades when he returns from his supposed spying expedition.[227] A foolish Odysseus also appears as a comic hero in Phlyax farce. A Phlyax vase in the British Museum (Fig. 15) depicts Odysseus as a thief in flight, half-naked, draped in a mantle, wearing on his head a *pilos*, or peaked hat, the habitual headgear of the mimic fool.[228]

As is well known,[229] Socrates is depicted in the writings of his followers as a teacher who affected naïveté and ignorance in order to bring his contemporaries to self-knowledge.[230] With humor which verged upon insolence, employing common, even vulgar terms,[231] Socrates sought to disabuse the Athenians and to lead them to a true conception of the good.[232] Those who were insensitive to Socrates' irony viewed the philosopher as 'ridiculous' (καταγέλαστος), as a foolish, comic figure.[233]

226. For this interpretation of the plot of Epicharmus play, see Pickard-Cambridge, *Dithyramb, Tragedy and Comedy*, 380–81.

227. Frag. 99 in Kaibel, *Comicorum Fragmenta*, 110.

228. Nicoll, *Masks, Mimes and Miracles*, 54, Fig. 41. On the *pilos* as the hat of the mimic fool, see Dieterich, *Pulcinella*, 153–81. For another example of Odysseus wearing the peaked hat, see Bieber, *Denkmäler zum Theaterwesen*, 131 no. 77, Tab. 67.3.

229. The figure of Socrates is already discussed in relation to Paul's assumption of the role of the 'fool' by Betz, *Der Apostel Paulus und die sokratische Tradition*, 34–35, 48–49, 60–63, 80–82. The criticism of Betz as too narrowly focused on the Socratic tradition, which, since the publication of E. A. Judge, 'St. Paul and Socrates,' *Interchange* 13 (1973) 106–16, has become general, e.g. J. T. Fitzgerald, 'Paul, the Ancient Epistolary Theorists, and 2 Corinthians 10–13' in *Greeks, Romans, and Christians*, ed. D. Balch, E. Ferguson and W. A. Meeks (Minneapolis: Augsburg Press, 1990) 197–98; Witherington, *Conflict and Community in Corinth*, 436–37, does not take sufficient account of the diffusion of the image of Socrates, which not only permeated the philosophical schools, but also impacted popular consciousness; see Döring, *Exemplum Socratis*, passim; Zanker, *The Mask of Socrates*, 32–39, 57–74, 173–79.

230. On Socrates' avowal of ignorance and his educational intent, see in general E. Zeller, *Die Philosophie der Griechen*, 2.1: *Sokrates und die Sokratiker* (Leipzig: Teubner, 1922; repr. 1963) 124–26; Gigon, *Sokrates, sein Bild in Dichtung und Geschichte*, 58–62; P. Friedländer, *Plato. An Introduction* (Princeton: Princeton University Press, 1969) 137–53; Guthrie, *Socrates*, 122–29; G. Vlastos, *Socrates, Ironist and Moral Philosopher* (Ithaca: Cornell University Press, 1991.) ch. 1.

231. E.g., Plato *Euthyd.* 218D-293A; *Grg.* 490C, 491A, 494 B-E.

232. W. Jaeger, 'Socrates als Erzieher' in *Paideia. Die Formung des griechischen Menschen*, Vol. 2 (Berlin: Walter de Gruyter, 1954) 74–77; G. Vlastos, 'The Socratic Elenchus', *Oxford Studies in Ancient Philosophy* 1 (1983) 71–91; M. Stokes, 'Socrates' Mission' in *Socratic Questions. New Essays on the Philosophy of Socrates and Its Significance*, ed. B. S. Grower (London: Routledge, 1992) 26–31.

233. See the texts assembled and discussed by Reich, *Der Mimus*, 354–60; see also Gigon, *Sokrates*, 58–61; V. de Magalhäes-Vilhena, *Le problème de Socrate* (Paris: Presses Universitaires de France, 1952) 90, 231–33.

Figure 15.   Phlyax vase. British Museum, London.

Socrates did not seek to correct this impression.[234] On the contrary, he spoke of his own wisdom as 'a sorry thing, and questionable, like a dream'.[235] His characteristic utterance took the form of a disavowal of knowledge: 'I know that I do not know.'[236] Instead, Socrates described himself as vulgar and foolish in memorable self-parodies.[237]

Plato makes no attempt to conceal the fact that Socrates was regarded by the public, and even by other intellectuals, as a 'fool'. The faithful Crito confides in Socrates his embarrassment at hearing dialectic described as 'nonsense' (λῆρος) and the master himself as a 'fool' (ἄτοπος) by a sophist who has witnessed one of Socrates' conversations.[238] Callicles tries to get Socrates to see how 'laughable' (καταγέλαστος) he appears to the men of Athens for shunning the city center and the market place, and spending his life sunk in a corner, whispering with three or four boys.[239] Callicles embellishes his comic portrait with the ominous prophecy that Socrates would 'reel to and fro and gape openmouthed, without a word to say', if he were ever to be arrested and

234. As acknowledged by Plato *Apol.* 21A-24A.

235. Plato *Symp.* 175 E.

236. Plato *Apol.* 21D. See the discussion in W. Kalinka, 'Das Nichtwissen des Sokrates', 36–46; E. L. Burge, 'The Irony of Socrates', 5–17; Guthrie, *Socrates*, 85–89, 122–25.

237. E.g., Xenophon *Symp.* 4.20, 5.1–9; *Mem.* 3.11. Cf. Reich, *Der Mimus*, 358–59; Friedländer, *Plato*, 138–50.

238. Plato *Euthyd.* 304E-305A. Cf. Reich, *Der Mimus*, 356; Friedländer, *Plato*, 145–46.

239. Plato *Grg.* 485D. Cf. Dodds, *Plato. Gorgias*, 277, 324, 368; P. Friedländer, *Plato*, 143.

brought into court.[240] In Callicles' opinion, Socrates is a harmless fool, who 'may be boxed on the ears with impunity'.[241] 'Callicles thus portrays Socrates as a comic persona – the ignorant fool who is powerless to retaliate when harmed. In the eyes of the non-philosophical person, we infer, a philosopher like Socrates appears both foolish and comic.'[242]

Contributing to the perception of Socrates as a fool was his physical appearance. The historical Socrates must have been extraordinarily ugly, judging from all that the ancient sources report.[243] While the focus on Socrates' unfortunate appearance may derive from the offensive nature of his intellectual activities,[244] even his friends had to concede that he resembled nothing so much as a satyr and a flatfish.[245] His chief features, and those that are repeatedly mentioned, were a broad and flat face with bulging eyes, a large mouth with thick, fleshy lips, a bald head, and a squat body with protruding belly.[246] So Socrates is depicted on a bronze relief from Pompeii, with unmistakably ugly and deviant features, small of stature and with a bulging belly, just as he is described in the literary sources (Fig. 16).[247] These traits were all considered, by the standards of ancient aesthetics, not only ugly, but tokens of a base nature, and therefore comical.[248]

240. Plato *Grg.* 486B.

241. Plato *Grg.* 486C; cf. Dodds, *Plato. Gorgias*, 278, 352, 358.

242. Nightingale, *Genres in Dialogue*, 90. This perception of Socrates as a comic character is dramatized in the *Gorgias* when Polus, the most tractable of Socrates' opponents, actually laughs in Socrates' face at the suggestion that the tyrant is the most unhappy of men (473E). At the end of the argument, Polus declares that Socrates' conclusions seem 'absurd' (ἄτοπα), even if they are consistent with his premise (480E). The laughter of Polus is echoed by Callicles, who pronounces him right to have laughed at Socrates (482D). Cf. C. Kauffman, 'Enactment as Argument in the *Gorgias*', *Philosophy and Rhetoric* 12 (1979) 114–29.

243. References to Socrates' physical appearance in Xenophon and Plato are collected by E. Edelstein, *Xenophontisches und platonisches Bild des Sokrates* (Berlin: Ebering, 1935) 7–9, 22; see the discussions in Guthrie, *Socrates*, 66–70; Zanker, *The Mask of Socrates*, 34–39.

244. The Aristophanic portrait of Socrates in the *Clouds* (101 ff., 348 ff., 414) is widely recognized to be a caricature based upon a conventional topos; see A. Weiher, 'Philosophen und Philosophenspott in der attischen Komödie' (Diss. Munich, 1913) 5–12; Gigon, *Sokrates, sein Bild in Dichtung und Geschichte*, 19; T. Gelzer, 'Aristophanes und sein Sokrates', *Museum Helveticum* 13 (1956) 65–93, esp. 76, 91–92; Zanker, *The Mask of Socrates*, 32–35.

245. Plato *Symp.* 215B; *Meno* 80A.

246. Xenophon *Symp.* 2.18, 5.5–7; Plato *Symp.* 215F. Cf. Edelstein, *Xenophontisches und platonisches Bild des Sokrates*, 7–8, 22; I. Scheibler, 'Zum ältesten Bildnis des Sokrates', *Münchner Jahrbuch der bildenden Kunst* 40 (1989) 25–33.

247. The scene depicts Socrates' initiation into the mysteries of love by Diotima. The relief, which is about fifteen centimeters in height, was made as a furniture appliqué; dated to the first century B.C., now in Naples, Museo Nazionale. Picture in Zanker, *The Mask of Socrates*, 37, Fig. 23.

248. Cicero *Tusc. Disp.* 4.81; cf. Grant, *Ancient Rhetorical Theories of the Laughable*, 19; Zanker, *The Mask of Socrates*, 34.

Figure 16.   **Bronze relief of Socrates and Diotima. Pompeii, first century B.C. Museo Nazionale, Naples.**

Whatever may be the historical accuracy of these portraits, the image of Socrates that was transmitted to subsequent generations, and became current in the popular philosophy of the early Empire, was that of the σοφός who cloaked his wisdom in foolishness.[249] Thus, in the pseudo-Platonic *Hippias Major*, the famous orator and ambassador admonishes Socrates to abandon his 'petty arguments' and devote himself to the useful art of public speaking, unless he wishes to be accounted a 'complete fool' (λίαν ἀνόητος) because he occupies himself with 'frivolity and nonsense' (λήρους καὶ φλυαρίας).[250] Enemies and detractors construed Socrates' foolishness as malicious irony. Timon of Phlius lampooned Socrates as a 'sneerer' (μυκτήρ), and a 'dissembler' (εἰρωνευτής),[251] no genuine philosopher, but a mimic 'character-painter' (ἠθολογός).[252] Zeno of Sidon coined the disparaging term *scurra Atticus* ('Attic jester') in reference to Socrates.[253] Quintilian explains that 'Socrates was called an ironist because he assumed the role of an ignorant man lost in wonder at the wisdom of

249. See Reich, *Der Mimus*, 354–58; Gigon, *Sokrates, sein Bild in Dichtung und Geschichte*, 19–22, 59–60, 112; Chroust, *Socrates, Man and Myth*, 69–100; Döring, *Exemplum Socratis*, 2–12.

250. Plato *Hipp. Maj.* 304B; cf. Reich, *Der Mimus*, 356 n. 4.

251. Diogenes Laertius 2.19; cf. Reich, *Der Mimus*, 354 n. 1.

252. Sextus Empiricus *Adv. Math.* 1.10; cf. Reich, *Der Mimus*, 355 n. 1.

253. Cicero *De Nat. Deor.* 1.91; see also Minucius Felix *Octavius* 38.5: *proinde Socrates scurra atticus viderit*. Cf. Reich, *Der Mimus*, 354 n. 2; Döring, *Exemplum Socratis*, 5.

others'.[254] Maximus of Tyre adumbrates the features of the image of Socrates that were firmly established in popular consciousness as clichés attached to the philosopher's name: 'Poor man Socrates, ugly Socrates, ignoble Socrates, low-born Socrates, dishonored Socrates ... the snub-nosed, the pot-bellied, the object of ridicule, etc'.[255] Diogenes Laertius, who speaks of the 'mockery' (χλευασμός) of Socrates,[256] summarizes the response which the philosopher evoked: 'for the most part he was despised and laughed at'.[257]

Even closer to Paul's letter in outlook and tone is the *Life of Aesop*, a genuine folk-book, the repository of an inherited tradition.[258] A Berlin papyrus-fragment demonstrates that the *Life of Aesop* had achieved written form by the second century A.D., at the latest.[259] But before this, there must have existed an oral repertoire of Aesop stories going back for centuries.[260] The material in the *Life* is of diverse origin.[261] But the character of Aesop is a fixed feature. The work as a whole is pervaded by an anti-Hellenic bias: the claims of the educated elite to have a monopoly on wisdom are subjected to vulgar and witty criticism.[262]

According to the stories in the inherited tradition, Aesop is an ugly, deformed slave who is beaten and tormented, but who triumphs over mistreatment with astonishing cleverness, and solves problems that have perplexed the philosophers with a wisdom that is earthy, practical, and

254. Quintilian *Inst. Orat.* 9.2.46.

255. Maximus of Tyre *Or.* 39.5: Σωκράτης πένης, Σωκράτης αἰσχρός, Σωκράτης ἄδοξος, Σωκράτης δυσγενής, Σωκράτης ἄτιμος...ο σιμός, ο προγάστωρ, ο κωμῳδούμενος, κτλ.

256. Diogenes Laertius 2.38.

257. Diogenes Laertius 2.21. Cf. Reich, *Der Mimus*, 359.

258. Text in Perry, *Aesopica*, 35–130; trans. by Daly, *Aesop without Morals*.

259. On the history of the text and its tradition, see B. E. Perry, *Studies in the Text History of the Life and Fables of Aesop*, American Philological Association, Philological Monographs no. 7 (Haverford, PA, 1936) 24–26; H. Zeitz, 'Der Aesoproman und seine Geschichte: eine Untersuchung im Anschluss an die neugefundenen Papyri', *Aegyptus* 16 (1936) 225–56. Cf. Daly, *Aesop without Morals*, 22: 'Internal evidence makes it likely that the *Life* was written by a Greek-speaking Egyptian, in Egypt, probably in the first century after Christ.'

260. Two episodes in the Aesop saga were already known to Greek writers of the fifth century B.C.: his servitude to Xanthus on Samos and his death at Delphi; see Herodotus 2.134–35; Aristophanes *Vesp.* 1446–48.

261. The substance of sections 101–23 was drawn from the old Eastern tale of Achiqar, the wise vizier at the court of Sennacherib. An Aramaic version of the Achiqar romance is extant in the fifth-century papyrus; see E. Meyer, *Der Papyrusfund von Elephantine* (Leipzig: Teubner, 1912) 102–28. Two fragments of a Demotic version, dated to the first century A.D., were published by K.-Th. Zaurich, 'Demotische Fragmente zum Ahikar-Roman', *Folia Rara W. Voigt LXV. d. n. celebranti ... dedicata*, ed. H. Franke (Wiesbaden: Franz Steiner, 1976) 180–85.

262. *Vit. Aesop.* 36: κατάρατε, εἰς τὸ κοινὸν τῆς Ἑλλάδος βλασφημῶν λέγεις. Cf. Daly, *Aesop without Morals*, 20–22; Winkler, *Auctor and Actor*, 282.

aporetic. Despite Aesop's demonstrated ingenuity, he is consistently regarded by those who see him as a 'fool'.[263] This perception is not only occasioned by Aesop's servile origin, but is also, and primarily, the result of his physical deformity. The opening lines of the *Life* consist of a list of pejorative adjectives describing Aesop's appearance: 'revolting to look at, putrid and worthless, potbellied, misshapen of head, snub-nosed, swarthy, stunted, bandy-legged, short-armed, squint-eyed, liver-lipped – a portentous monstrosity'.[264] The ugliness of Aesop is remarked throughout the *Life*, and is an essential feature of his character: he is 'a goose egg',[265] 'a turnip with teeth',[266] 'a completely misshapen pot'.[267] Indeed, the ugliness of Aesop may even be built into his name, if the etymology that has been suggested is correct: αἰσ-ωπος = 'base face'.[268]

Especially in that portion of the *Life* in which Aesop is still a slave, the impression of his foolishness predominates.[269] The account of the journey to the slave-market in Asia dramatizes the play of misperceptions.[270] Ordered to help with the baggage, Aesop chooses the heaviest load of all, a basket full of bread. The slaves say to themselves: 'We've never seen a worse fool than this fellow' (οὐδένα μωρότερον τούτου τοῦ ἀνθρωπαρίου εἴδομεν). But as the journey progresses, and the slaves stop to eat, Aesop's burden grows progressively lighter. When the basket is emptied, Aesop tosses it on his shoulder and runs ahead of everyone else. One of the slaves observes: 'You underestimated the little fellow's wit.' Another retorts, 'Bah, the fellow ought to be crucified!'

A number of the episodes in which Aesop's foolishness is emphasized reveal connections to the mime.[271] Indeed, in one case, the story may even be said to be self-consciously theatrical: the scene in which Aesop is presented to his new mistress, the wife of the philosopher Xanthus.[272] Concluding that Xanthus has purchased a physically repulsive slave in order to insult her, the philosopher's wife demands the return of her dowry, and prepares to leave the house. Aesop agrees that the woman should go and be damned. Pronouncing Aesop a 'piece of trash' (κάθαρμα)

263. E.g., *Vit. Aesop.* 18, 21, 22, 25, 30, 31, 87.

264. *Vit. Aesop.* 1 (ms. G): κακοπινὴς τὸ ἰδέσθαι, εἰς ὑπηρεσίαν σαπρός, προγάστωρ, προκέφαλος, σιμός, σόρδος, μέλας, κολοβός, βλαισός, γαλιάγκων, στρεβλός, μυστάκων, προσημαῖνονα ἁμάρτημα.

265. *Vit. Aesop.* 14.

266. *Vit. Aesop.* 22.

267. *Vit. Aesop.* 21.

268. Nagy, *The Best of the Acheans*, 229, 280.

269. *Vit. Aesop.* 1–90.

270. *Vit. Aesop.* 18–19 (ms. G).

271. E.g., *Vit. Aesop.* 22, 29, 32, 75–76 (ms. W), 131; cf. Winkler, *Auctor and Actor*, 280–82.

272. *Vit. Aesop.* 29–32.

and a 'contemptible fool' (ταπεινός),[273] Xanthus commands the slave to use his keen wit to conciliate his wife. Aesop says, 'I'll play the role you choose' (ὑποκρινοῦμαι ὡς θέλεις).[274] Striking the pose of the leading slave (θεράπων ἡγέμων), a stock character of comedy and mime,[275] Aesop proceeds to supply in fantasy the liaison with a handsome slave which the lascivious wife has been seeking,[276] evoking the plot of the popular adultery mime.[277] It is hardly surprising to discover allusions to the mime in the *Life of Aesop*, since, as has been observed,[278] the appearance of Aesop has much in common with the statuettes of mimic fools from the late Hellenistic era and the early Empire (Fig. 17).[279]

Nowhere in the *Life* does Aesop seek to dispel the impression of his foolishness. On the contrary, Aesop insists that his knowledge is minimal and wholly uncertain. When the slave Aesop is put up for sale in the market, and a potential buyer asks what he knows how to do, Aesop answers, 'Nothing at all' (ἐγὼ ὅλως οὐδέν).[280] When the governor of Samos asks Aesop where he is going, Aesop says, 'I don't know' (οὐκ οἶδα). Recognizing Aesop as a slave, and suspecting he is a runaway, the governor puts Aesop in jail. Aesop then says, 'See, I really didn't know where I was going'.[281] Nor does Aesop attempt to divert attention from his dopey appearance. On the contrary, Aesop makes his ugliness a provocation to thought and a challenge to convention: 'As the slave dealer saw what a piece of human garbage Aesop appeared to be, ... he started to leave. But Aesop caught him by the tail of his cloak and said, "Listen .... Don't you have any undisciplined fellows in your slave market who are always asking for food?" Slave dealer: "Yes." Aesop: "Buy me and make me their trainer. They'll be afraid of my ugly face and will stop acting so unruly".[282]

---

273. *Vit. Aesop.* 31 (ms. G).

274. *Vit. Aesop.* 31.

275. On this character type in comedy, farce and mime, see Pollux *Onom.* 4.150; Plautus *Pseudolus* 38–81, 383, 458–61, 1218–19; see the discussion in Ribbeck, *Alazon*, 18–24; C. Robert, *Die Masken der neueren attischen Komödie* (Halle: Niemeyer, 1911) 76, 108–109; Bieber, *The History of the Greek and Roman Theatre*, 159–60; Nicoll, *Masks, Mimes and Miracles*, 28–30.

276. *Vit. Aesop.* 32.

277. *POxy* 413 ('Adulteress') 37–45, 51–58, 64–65; cf. R. W. Reynolds, 'The Adultery Mime', 77–84.

278. Winkler, *Auctor and Actor*, 288.

279. Fig. 17 is a terracotta of a mimic fool in the British Museum, in Nicoll, *Masks, Mimes and Miracles*, 45, Fig. 29;. Cf. Richter, 'Grotesques and the Mime', 149–56.

280. *Vit. Aesop.* 25 (ms. G).

281. *Vit. Aesop.* 65 (ms. G).

282. *Vit. Aesop.* 14–15. For other instances of Aesop's ugliness as a provocation to thought, see *Vit. Aesop.* 26, 30, and esp. 87–88.

Figure 17. Terracotta statuette of a mimic fool. British Museum, London.

What is being suggested here is that Paul chose to place himself in the tradition of Aesop and Socrates, taking upon himself the guise of a fool, in order to offer resistance to elite privilege and authority. Like Socrates,[283] Paul acknowledges that his discourse is regarded as 'foolishness' by those who seek wisdom (1 Cor. 1.18, 23). Indeed, Paul echoes the language of Socrates' famous disavowal of knowledge,[284] in the account of his decision 'not to know anything' (οὐ τι εἰδέναι) except Christ crucified (2.2), as we have argued above.[285] Paul's proximity to the Aesopic tradition is even greater. Here one finds the very term μωρός applied to Aesop[286] that was used at Corinth to insult Paul (4.10). Like Aesop, Paul is 'hungry' and 'beaten' (4.11), and must endure hard labor (4.12). A cluster of stories in the Aesop saga are essentially 'food jokes', dealing with lost food, stolen food, trampled food, etc., and betraying the constant concern of slaves and

---

283. See esp. *Grg.* 490C-491A, where Socrates is berated by Callicles for incessantly talking about frivolties, such as 'food and drink and cobblers and fullers and cooks and doctors', and Socrates acknowledges that he is always 'saying the same things about the same things'. Cf. Xenophon *Mem.* 4.4.6 for a similar complaint and acknowledgement, in conversation with Hippias.

284. Plato *Apol.* 21D: ἃ μὴ οἶδα οὐδὲ οἴομαι εἰδέναι. See further Plato *Apol.* 21B: 'I know very well that I am not the least bit wise'; 23A-B, for Socrates' acknowledgement of his own ignorance.

285. See ch. 4 above, on 1 Cor. 2.1–5.

286. *Vit. Aesop.* 18.

the poor with finding something to eat.[287] Another group of episodes features the attempt by Aesop's master to find an excuse to give Aesop a beating.[288] Frequent reference is made to Aesop's 'mattock,' the emblem of his arduous physical labor.[289] In view of all these parallels, it is not surprising to hear the term περικάθαρμα ('scum') hurled at Aesop[290] that was used to revile the apostle Paul (4.13). While these parallels are not so exact or extended as to demonstrate the direct influence of the *Life of Aesop* upon Paul, they serve to indicate that Paul has located his analysis of the foolishness of the gospel in a comic-philosophic tradition that would have been recognized by ancient readers.

What, then, is the significance of Paul's acknowledgement of the foolishness of his preaching and his person, in the context of the tradition of cultural criticism associated with Aesop and Socrates? What assumptions and implications are embraced in this self-effacing gesture, that would have been understood by Paul's audience in first-century Corinth? First, it is clear that acknowledgement of foolishness in this tradition is the assumption of a guise. Odysseus, the quick-witted and well-spoken, is disguised as an old fool by Athena in order to deceive the suitors: to all who meet him upon his return, Odysseus appears to be an old beggar, dressed in wretched sacking, dirty and contemptible.[291] Because Odysseus is taken for a fool, he is reviled and abused, kicked in the shins and struck with a stool.[292] Alcibiades explains to his companions in the *Symposium* that Socrates 'loves to appear utterly uninformed and ignorant', and that his foolishness is 'his outward appearance' (τὸ σχῆμα αὐτοῦ), a cloak that he 'puts around himself on the outside'.[293] Aesop repeatedly warns those whom he meets that his appearance is deceptive, and urges them to examine the soul that lies beneath.[294] Paul's acknowledgment of foolishness should not be mistaken for willingness to participate in the mindless antics of the rabble; rather, by hiding himself behind a grotesque façade, Paul seeks to call into question the conventional assumptions about wisdom and foolishness.

---

287.   In the first story in the *Life*, Aesop is accused of having eaten stolen figs, *Vit. Aesop.* 2–3; in *Vit. Aesop.* 18, his fellow slaves suspect Aesop of scheming to eat more than his share of bread from the basket; see also the low-class food jokes in *Vit. Aesop.* 37, 39, 42, 44.

288.   *Vit. Aesop.* 42, 50, 56, 58, 61; see also *Vit. Aesop.* 2, where Aesop's fellow-slaves conspire to have him beaten; 9, where Aesop protests against the beating of a fellow slave by the overseer with his 'stick' (ῥάβδος).

289.   *Vit. Aesop.* 4, 9, 13.

290.   *Vit. Aesop.* 14; see also the simplex form κάθαρμα in 30, 31, 69.

291.   *Od.* 13.500–507; 17.281.

292.   *Od.* 17.298–99, 604–605.

293.   Plato *Symp.* 216D.

294.   *Vit. Aesop.* 18, 26, 87.

Second, it is clear that the term 'foolishness', as it first appears in Paul's argument, embodies the subjective judgment of a certain class of persons upon Paul's gospel,[295] and should not be construed as a description of the objective effect of the gospel.[296] This conclusion, which had already been reached on the basis of Paul's grammar (sc. the force of the datives, τοῖς ἀπολλυμένοις in 1.18 and ἔθνεσιν in 1.23),[297] is strengthened by the indication that Paul participates in a comic-philosophic tradition that exploits incongruity and paradox. Alcibiades explains to his companions that one who is not initiated into Socrates' philosophy is likely to misjudge him: 'Anyone who isn't used to his style and isn't very quick on the uptake would naturally take his arguments for the most utter nonsense.'[298] The unphilosophical man of affairs, such as Callicles, judges Socrates to be a fool.[299] The majority of Aesop's fellow slaves mistake him for a fool, and mistreat him accordingly. The slaves suffer the consequences of their misjudgment: the beatings and the burdens they seek to inflict upon Aesop rebound upon themselves.[300] Aesop's master, the philosopher Xanthus, consistently misjudges him, despite Aesop's admonition: 'Don't look at my appearance, but examine my wits.'[301] As the embodiment of the proud wisdom of the Greeks, Xanthus cannot get beyond the impression that the repulsive little slave is a fool, however often he is outwitted.[302] Thus, when Paul acknowledges that the gospel is 'foolishness', he uses the term in accordance with the value system of the elite. Like the author of the *Life of Aesop*, Paul acknowledges the existence of a realm of elite 'wisdom' and acknowledges that his 'message about the cross' stands outside that realm.

Third, and most importantly, an acknowledgement of foolishness in this tradition is a provocation to thought and a challenge to convention. The provocation is intended to force a decision: how one responds to the appearance of 'foolishness' determines whether one is saved or lost. When Antinous lets fly a stool at Odysseus, whom he regards as a stinking

295. So, already, Weiss, *Der erste Korintherbrief*, 25, commenting on 1.18 ff: 'Der lebhaft erregte Apostel spielt im folgenden mit dem Ausdruck μωρία in verschiedene Weise: einerseits spricht er dieser Urteilsweise ihr eigenes Urteil, in dem er sagt v. 18a, dass nur Verlorenen das Wort vom Kreuz als μωρία erscheinen könne, etc.'
296. Contra Wilckens, *Weisheit und Torheit*, 21–23; Conzelmann, *1 Corinthians*, 42.
297. Collins, *First Corinthians*, 101: 'The phrase is to be read subjectively and construed to mean that the word of the cross is considered as folly by some who perish as a result,' appealing to Blass-Debrunner-Funk, *A Greek Grammar of the New Testament*, } 190 (1).
298. Plato *Symp.* 221E-222A. Cf. Xenophon *Mem.* 1.2.32–37.
299. Plato *Grg.* 485D-486C.
300. *Vit. Aesop.* 2–4, 18–19.
301. *Vit. Aesop.* 26.
302. *Vit. Aesop.* 20–91, a running battle of wits between master and slave in which the deformed little man consistently outthinks the vain philosopher.

beggar, 'Odysseus only shook his head, containing thoughts of bloody work'.[303] The audience of the great poem knows that Antinous, like the other suitors who have misjudged Odysseus, will soon be destroyed. Callicles, who utters an ominous prophecy about Socrates, makes himself complicit in the greatest moral crime in Athenian history.[304] The ugliness and foolishness of Aesop is a specific challenge to Hellenic culture.[305] Contrast the fates of the Samians and the Delphians in respect to the provocation of Aesop's ugliness. Because the citizens of Samos look beyond Aesop's deformity and perceive his native wit, they are saved from the armed might of the Lydian king.[306] The proud Delphians, by contrast, despise the grotesque little man and refuse to listen to him; they drag him outside the city to the edge of a cliff, where he throws himself off, as if he were a wretched φαρμακός.[307] The *Life of Aesop* concludes with the dire warning that Aesop's death will be avenged upon the Delphians by famine and sword.[308]

When Paul, having placed himself in this tradition, acknowledges that his gospel is foolishness and that he is a fool, he implies a verdict upon those who have judged him and his gospel in this fashion. Because the elite are unable to see beyond the appearance of foolishness and weakness which attends the gospel and its messenger, to grasp the underlying wisdom and power, they are 'doomed to perish' (1.18, 2.6). Indeed, Paul's choice of present participles (ἀπολλύμενοι, καταργούμενοι) to describe the fate of those who regard the gospel as 'foolishness' suggests that their destruction is not reserved for some eschatological future, but has already begun.[309] Those for whom the message about the cross is foolishness 'are already perishing' (1.18). The 'rulers of this age' who crucified the Lord of glory 'are already being brought to nothing' (2.6). And the rich and powerful in the church at Corinth are warned that, if they persist in a 'natural' or 'unspiritual' understanding which regards the cross as 'foolishness', they court their own destruction (2.14).

303. *Od.* 17.605–609.
304. Plato *Grg.* 486B.
305. So, already, Daly, *Aesop without Morals*, 20–21; Winkler, *Auctor and Actor*, 286–89.
306. *Vit. Aesop.* 87.
307. *Vit. Aesop.* 127–42. On Aesop as a φαρμακός ('one put to death for the purification of a city'), see esp. A. Wiechers, 'Aesop als Pharmakos' in *Aesop in Delphi*, Beiträge zur klassischen Philologie 2 (Meisenheim am Glan: Anton Hain, 1961) 31–42.
308. *Vit. Aesop.* 142.
309. See the discussion of the implications of Paul's choice of present participles in 1.18 and 2.6 in Heinrici, *Der erste Brief*, 67, 95.

2. *Assertion*

As the second moment in his analysis, Paul asserts that a reversal has occurred in the concepts of 'wisdom' and 'foolishness', so that what is regarded as 'foolishness' by the elite is actually 'wisdom', and vice versa.[310] Paul insists, in the strongest possible terms, that God is the agent of this reversal: God has destroyed the wisdom of the wise; God has nullified the discernment of the discerning (1.19). 'God has made foolish the wisdom of the world' (1.20b). The goal of God's decisive action is a reversal of the conventional polarities of knowledge and power: the low and despised experience divine favor, while the cultural elite are put to shame (1.26–28). God has brought about this transformation in secret, selectively revealing to the low and despised the 'wisdom' of the crucified Christ 'through the Spirit' (2.6–16). Despite appearances to the contrary, the transvaluation of 'wisdom' and 'foolishness' is now an accomplished fact: 'the wisdom of this world is foolishness with God' (3.19).

The extraordinary importance of this reversal of values in Paul's argument is indicated, first of all, by the amount of space he devotes to the subject. By far the greatest portion of the exposition in 1.18–3.23 is preoccupied with the motif of the divine overthrow of worldly wisdom.[311] Paul returns to the point again and again, repeatedly asserting its triumphant reality after every acknowledgement of the existence of a realm of elite wisdom (1.19–20,21b,24–25,30; 2.7,9–10,15–16), and even after his acceptance of the necessity of becoming a 'fool' (3.19–20)!

A second indication of the importance of this assertion is the fact that Paul appeals to the weightiest authorities in order to back it up: Scripture and the Spirit.[312] Immediately after announcing the reversal of values (1.18), Paul cites a passage from the scriptures, Isa. 29.14 (LXX), in confirmation (1.19). The formal manner in which Paul prefaces the quotation (γέγραπται γάρ)[313] demonstrates the authority that the Isaian oracle possessed for Paul.[314] Clearly, Paul felt that he had found a proof-

---

310.   So, already, Weiss, *Der erste Korintherbrief*, 25; Bertram, 'μωρός', 846; Wilckens, *Weisheit und Torheit*, 36.

311.   Wilckens, *Weisheit und Torheit*, 36–37.

312.   On Paul's citation of scripture as an 'argument from authority', see Collins, *First Corinthians*, 94.

313.   On the citation formula γέγραπται γάρ, see the comments of Heinrici, *Der erste Brief*, 68: 'Das γέγραπτα schliesst stets eine Berufung auf unantastbare Autorität des angezogenen Ausspruchs ein'; see also Collins, *First Corinthians*, 94; Lindemann, *Der erste Korintherbrief*, 44.

314.   The first part of the Isaian oracle (Isa. 29.13) already appears in the Jesus tradition in Mk. 7.6–7, indicating that the oracle belonged to early Christian apologetic; cf. A. Lindemann, 'Die Schrift als Tradition. Beobachtungen zu den biblischen Zitaten im Ersten Korintherbrief' in *Schrift und Tradition. Festschrift für Josef Ernst zum 70. Geburtstag*, eds. K. Backhaus and F. G. Untergassmair (Paderborn: Schöningh, 1996) 201–203.

text for his thesis about the divine reversal of wisdom and folly. This is particularly true of the version of the text that Paul cites from the Septuagint, for here God himself is presented as speaking: 'I will destroy the wisdom of the wise, and the discernment of the discerning I will nullify.'[315] Paul's choice of this text must have seemed especially effective to Corinthian opponents who were well-versed in the scriptures, such as the adherents of Apollos;[316] for in the larger context, Isaiah goes on to critique those who take pride in their wisdom, and to foretell the creation of a new order of things in which the deaf will hear and the blind will see.[317] Six times in the heart of his argument (1.18–3.23) Paul explicitly cites biblical material.[318] The important thing to notice is that in every case the appeal to Scripture serves the same purpose: to reinforce Paul's assertion about the reversal of wisdom and foolishness.

Not satisfied with an appeal to the Scripture, Paul also invokes the authority of the Spirit: 'and to us God has revealed these things through the Spirit' (2.10a).[319] Paul emphasizes the role of the Spirit in the reversal of values by making the Spirit the agent of the search for divine wisdom: 'for the Spirit searches (ἐραυνᾷ) everything, even the depths of God' (2.10b). Uniquely among his contemporaries, Paul reserves the activity of 'searching' (ἐραυνάω) to the Spirit, rather than human beings.[320] For Paul, it is not the wise man who seeks to know the truth, but the Spirit that

---

315. The Hebrew text of Isa. 29.14 is not formulated in the first person singular, and thus would not have been as well suited to Paul's purposes; see E. Ellis, *Paul's Use of the Old Testament* (Grand Rapids, MI: Eerdmans, 1957) 22–25; Stanley, *Paul and the Language of Scripture*, 185–86; Lindemann, *Der erste Korintherbrief*, 44.

316. So, already, Weiss, *Der erste Korintherbrief*, 27: 'Zunächst beruft sich Paulus auf die Schrift – um so angemessener, wenn er sich hier mit der Schrift-kundigen Apollos-Partei auseinandersetzt.' Similarly, Best, 'The Power and the Wisdom of God', 14, with reference to Paul's citation of the scriptures in 1.19, 31; 3.19–20.

317. Isa. 29.16, 18, 24; cf. F. Wilk, *Die Bedeutung des Jesajabuches für Paulus*, FRLANT 179 (Göttingen: Vandenhoeck & Ruprecht, 1998) 246; Collins, *First Corinthians*, 103.

318. The six explicit citations are: Isa. 29.14 in 1.19; Jer. 9.22–23 in 1.31; Isa. 64.3–4 in 2.9; Isa. 40.13 in 2.16; Job 5.12–13 in 3.19; and Ps. 93.11 in 3.20; see the analysis in Koch, *Die Schrift als Zeuge des Evangeliums*, 31, 36–37, 42, 71–72; Stanley, *Paul and the Language of Scripture*, 185–94; Collins, *First Corinthians*, 94–96; H. Drake Williams, *The Wisdom of the Wise: The Presence and Function of Scripture within 1 Cor. 1.18–3.23*, AGJU 49 (Leiden: Brill, 2001).

319. That the Spirit is invoked as an additional authority in 2.10–15 is indicated by the post-positive conjunction δέ in 2.10a, not translated in some versions (e.g., the NRSV), whose function is confirmatory and explicative; the variant γάρ ('for'), found in P46, B, several minuscles, and Clement of Alexandria, is an attempt at clarification. That the Spirit is the agent of revelation in 2.10a is clearly denoted by the preposition ὑπό with the genitive; see N. Turner, *A Grammar of New Testament, Greek*, vol. 3; *Syntax*, ed. J. H. Moulton (Edinburgh: T & T Clark, 1963) 267. On the function of 2.10–15 within Paul's argument, see Heinrici, *Der erste Brief*, 100: 'Begründung für die Sicherheit des Offenbarungsbesitzes aus dem Wesen des Geistes.'

320. In Philo (e.g., *De Fug.* 164–65; *Leg. All.* 384), the wise man seeks wisdom; in 4 Ezra 13.54–55; 14.37–41, Ezra himself searches for wisdom and understanding; in 1 Peter 1.10–12,

makes the divine mind accessible. Human beings 'receive' the Spirit, and with it 'the gifts bestowed by God' (2.12).[321] The means and source of authentic wisdom is nothing less than 'the Spirit of God' (2.11–13).[322]

A third indication of the importance of the reversal of wisdom and foolishness in Paul's argument is the elevated rhetoric of the passages in which the theme comes to expression. Whenever Paul asserts the divine reversal of values, there is a noticeable rise in the rhetorical tenor of the text. Examples span the spectrum from the smallest trope to the largest structural feature. In the six verses, 1.20–25, Paul employs the following rhetorical figures: *repetitio*,[323] *anaphora*,[324] *isocolon*,[325] *homoioteleuton*,[326] *paronomasia*,[327] *oxymoron*,[328] *chiasmus*,[329] *litotes*,[330] and *synkri-*

the prophets search for knowledge about salvation. Only Paul places the activity of 'seeking' (ἐραυνάω) exclusively with the Spirit. See A. R. Hunt, *The Inspired Body: Paul, the Corinthians, and Divine Inspiration* (Macon, GA: Mercer University Press, 1996) 39–56, 63–66.

321. See the discussion of τὰ χαρισθέντα in A. R. Brown, *The Cross and Human Transformation: Paul's Apocalyptic Word in 1 Corinthians* (Minneapolis: Fortress, 1995) 129–31.

322. On the Spirit as the source and means of divine wisdom in 2.10–16, see J. Reiling, 'Wisdom and the Spirit: An Exegesis of 1 Corinthians 2, 6–16' in *Text and Testimony: Essays in Honor of A. F. J. Klijn*, ed. T. Baarda, et al. (Kampen: Kok, 1988) 200–211; Brown, *The Cross and Human Transformation*, 103–104, 122–33.

323. The trio of rhetorical questions in 1.20a is an example of the rhetorical figure of *repetitio*; Weiss, *Der erste Korintherbrief*, 27; Collins, *First Corinthians*, 103. For other examples of a series of rhetorical questions expecting a negative answer, see Diodorus Siculus 14.67.1; Lucian *Dial. Deor.* 4.4; Josephus *Ant.* 10.156.

324. Each of the questions in 1.20a introduced by the interrogative adverb ποῦ ('where') is an instance of the rhetorical device of *anaphora*; Weiss, *Der erste Korintherbrief*, 27; Collins, *First Corinthians*, 103–104. For examples of the rhetorical use of ποῦ in several direct questions consecutively, see Epictetus *Diss.* 3.10.17; Libanius *Or.* 61, p. 337, 18F.

325. The two rhetorical questions in 1.20a and 1.20b are approximately the same length. The two questions would have exactly the same number of syllables, if the variant reading τούτου ('this'), attested by P11, a few majuscules (F, G, Ψ), and correctors of some of the most important manuscripts (א, C, D), were to be accepted; however, the reading without τούτου is better supported. Yet, as Weiss observes (*Der erste Korintherbrief*, 27 n.2), the second line is rhetorically nicer without the exact conformity.

326. E.g., the two clauses in 1.20; Weiss, *Der erste Korintherbrief*, 27.

327. E.g., Paul plays with two meaning of the term σοφία ('wisdom') in 1.21: on the one hand, σοφία is a divine attribute, activity, effluence; on the other hand, it is a human capacity, endeavor, attainment; Sir. 1.9–10; Wis. Sol. 7, 8. By using the term in both senses, in prepositional phrases in close proximity (ἐν τῇ σοφίᾳ τοῦ θεοῦ ... διὰ τῆς σοφίας), Paul shapes a playful contrast between the two types of 'wisdom'. Cf. Weiss, *Der erste Korintherbrief*, 29.

328. E.g., the stunning oxymoron 'the foolishness of preaching' in 1.21b; cf. Weiss, *Der erste Korintherbrief*, 29.

329. The antithetical comparisons μωρόν-σοφώτερον and ἀσθενές-ἰσχυρότερον in 1.25 form a *chiasmus* with δύναμις and σοφία in 1.24; Weiss, *Der erste Korintherbrief*, 34.

330. Paul's explanation of how God has overthrown worldly wisdom in 1.25 is a pointed example of the use of *litotes*, rhetorical understatement, so as to intensify; Collins, *First Corinthians*, 108.

sis.[331] Paul's use of parallelism and antithesis in the paragraph 1.26–31 is so skillful that it has aroused the admiration of students of ancient rhetoric: 'From any Greek orator the artistry of this passage would have called forth the utmost admiration.'[332] The three parts of the negatively formulated sentence in vs. 26 ('not many are wise according to human standards, not many are powerful, not many of noble birth') furnish the schema for the next three sentences, in which the paradoxical action of God is positively described (in 1.27–29).[333] 'The parallelism of these verses is carried out as precisely as the thought permits without sacrificing clarity to form.'[334] Even the greater length of the concluding clause (vs. 28–29), which exceeds the other two in the length and number of its members, corresponds to the requirements of the rhetoricians, who favored such pleonastic conclusions.[335]

Throughout the section that stretches from 1.18 to 2.16, the rhetoric is as high-flown and the construction is as skillful as in any passage of Paul.[336] At points, the elocution is so sonorous that it finds a parallel only in the most poetic and mystical portions of Romans:[337] 'What no eye has seen, nor ear heard, nor the human heart conceived, what God has prepared for

---

331.   The sentence 1.25 is an impressive instance of the technique of *synkrisis*, rhetorical comparison, in order to highlight the transcendence of divine wisdom and power. Each element in this carefully constructed sentence has its counterpart: 'God' contrasts with 'human beings'; 'foolishness' contrasts with 'wisdom'; 'weakness' contrasts with 'strength'. Cf. Collins, *First Corinthians*, 108.

332.   Blass-Debrunner-Funk, *A Greek Grammar of the New Testament*, } 490, p. 260.

333.   The construction of the passage is best viewed in the form which it is given by Weiss (*Der erste Korintherbrief*, 35–36), who reconstructs the probable wording of the original text, based upon variants in the manuscript tradition, as follows:

βλέπετε γάρ τὴν κλῆσιν ὑμῶν, ἀδελφοί,
ὅτι οὐ πολλοὶ σοφοί κατὰ σάρκα, // οὐ πολλοὶ δυνατοὶ // οὐ πολλοὶ εὐγενεῖς,
ἀλλὰ τὰ μωρὰ τοῦ κόσμου ἐξελέξατο ὁ θεὸς // ἵνα καταισχύνη τοὺς σοφούς,
καὶ τὰ ἀσθενῆ τοῦ κόσμου ἐξελέξατο ὁ θεὸς // ἵνα καταισχύνη τοὺς ἰσχυρούς,
καὶ τὰ ἀγενῆ καὶ τὰ ἐξουθενημένα // τὰ μὴ ὄντα // ἵνα τὰ ὄντα καταργήσῃ,
ὅπως μὴ καυχήσηται πᾶσα σάρξ ἐνώπιον τοῦ θεοῦ.

334.   Blass-Debrunner-Funk, *A Greek Grammar of the New Testament*, } 490, p. 260; cf. Collins, *First Corinthians*, 90.

335.   Blass-Debrunner-Funk, *A Greek Grammar of the New Testament*, } 490, p. 260, citing Cicero *De Orat*. 3.48.186; Demetrius *Eloc*. 18.

336.   Weiss, *Der erste Korintherbrief*, 25, 27, 30, 35; Collins, *First Corinthians*, 90–91.

337.   See esp. Rom. 8.27, where Paul again speaks of a divine 'searching' (ἐραυνάω) of hearts and of 'the mind of the Spirit'; in Rom. 8.28, Paul speaks of 'those who love God', as in 1 Cor. 2.9; later, in Rom. 11.25–36, there are more extensive parallels to the vocabulary of 1 Cor. 2.6–16 (μυστήριον, βάθος, σοφία, γνῶσις, ἀνεραυνάω, νοῦς), all in a strophic construction that lauds the inscrutability of the wisdom and knowledge of God. See Hunt, *The Inspired Body*, 64–65.

those who love him' (2.9).[338] The object of the extraordinary eloquence of this and other passages in 1.18–2.16 is always the same: the divine reversal of wisdom and folly. The same conviction animates the antithesis that emerges again and again, and provides the structural pattern of the discourse.[339] The opposition between 'the wisdom of the world' and 'the foolishness of our proclamation' (1.19–21), between 'the wise, powerful, nobly born' and 'the foolish, weak, low and despised' (1.26–28), between 'the rulers who crucified the Lord of glory' and 'those of us who love him' (2.6–9), between 'spiritual' and 'natural' persons (2.14–15) is created by God's decision to bring about a great reversal of values.

Despite obvious indications of the importance of the divine reversal of values, there is no consensus among scholars regarding the status or function of this aspect of Paul's argument.[340] The opinions of interpreters diverge widely in assessing the background and motivation of Paul's thought.[341] Some hold that Paul shares the world-view of apocalyptic, and for this reason opposes divine and human wisdom.[342] Others suggest that the antithetical structure of Paul's thought reflects a dualism rooted in a Gnostic conception of reality, in which God stands opposite the world.[343] In particular, Paul's discourse on 'wisdom among the perfect' in 2.6–16 has perplexed interpreters, and has given rise to an abundance of hypotheses.[344]

---

338.   The passage is rightly printed in strophic form by Nestle-Aland, *Novum Testamentum Graece*, 27th ed., 443. The origin of the saying that Paul quotes in 2.9 is uncertain. Origen (*PG* 13, 1769) asserts that the citation derives from an *Apocalypse of Elijah*. But the extant Greek and Coptic fragments of this apocalypse do not contain the saying. The wording of 2.9 has elements in common with Isa. 52.15 and 64.3 (LXX), but cannot be regarded as a citation of these passages. A similar saying is attributed to Jesus in the *Gospel of Thomas* 17. On the origin of Paul's citation, see Koch, *Die Schrift als Zeuge des Evangeliums*, 37–41; Lindemann, *Der erste Korintherbrief*, 66–67.

339.   On the prominence of antithesis in 1.18–2.16, see esp. S. Grindheim, 'Wisdom for the Perfect: Paul's Challenge to the Corinthian Church (1 Corinthians 2.6–16)', *JBL* 121/4 (2002) 705. The antithetical pattern of 1.18–2.16 is recognized by Brown, *The Cross and Human Transformation*, 76–77, but is explained as a function of Paul's apocalyptic frame of reference.

340.   On the lack of consensus among interpreters, see Hunt, *The Inspired Body*, 4–5.

341.   See the survey of scholarly opinion in Hunt, *The Inspired Body*, 4–10.

342.   R. Scroggs, 'Paul: Σοφός and πνευματικός', *NTS* 14 (1967–68) 33–55; J. Christiaan Beker, *Paul the Apostle: The Triumph of God in Life and Thought* (Philadelphia: Fortress Press, 1980); Brown, *The Cross and Human Transformation*.

343.   Wilckens, *Weisheit und Torheit*, esp. 52–213; Schmithals, *Gnosticism in Corinth*, *passim*.

344.   For the history of interpretation of this passage prior to 1973, see M. Winter, *Psychiker und Pneumatiker in Korinth: Zum religionsgeschichtlichen Hintergrund von 1. Kor. 2,6–3,4*, MThSt 12 (Marburg: Elwert, 1975) 3–55; for more recent theories, see Brown, *The Cross and Human Transformation*, 105–106; Hunt, *The Inspired Body*, 4–10; Grindheim, 'Wisdom for the Perfect', 692–701.

One cannot resist the impression that Paul's argument has not yet been understood, despite the arduous efforts of a number of researchers.[345]

The source of difficulty in understanding Paul's argument has long been recognized: it is the appearance of self-contradiction.[346] Having repeatedly denied that he preaches the gospel with 'eloquent wisdom' (1.17; 2.1,4), Paul now asserts, whether from pride or defensiveness, that he communicates hidden wisdom to the spiritually perfect: 'Yet among the perfect we do speak wisdom, ... divine wisdom hidden in a mystery' (2.6–7). It seems that Paul's insistence upon a reversal of values and the triumph of the divine purpose has led him to forget, momentarily, his former acknowledgement of the 'crucified Christ' as the sole content of his preaching (1.17,18,22; 2.2). In apparent contradiction of his previous statements, Paul now announces the possibility of communicating a 'wisdom for the perfect' (2.6). It is this appearance of self-contradiction that has perplexed and troubled interpreters.[347]

The interpretation that is offered here locates Paul's argumentative strategy in the comic-philosophic tradition. It will be suggested that Paul shared with his audience a set of assumptions regarding the 'wise fool', who asserts the existence of a wisdom more profound than that authorized by the educated elite. In the tradition that connects Socrates, Aesop and the mime, one encounters, as in Paul, an insistence on the overthrow of elite wisdom and a celebration of the triumph of a common sense that is the paradoxical possession of slaves and the poor. More than this general similarity of perspective, one also encounters in this tradition the three specific elements of Paul's argument which, taken together, provide its mode of operation: first, an emphasis on the divine initiative in the reversal of conventional notions of wisdom and foolishness; second, the recognition that the reversal of values is revealed to some, but hidden from others; and third, as a consequence of the foregoing, the acceptance of irony as the authentic mode of relationship to a world that remains ignorant of the divine reversal.

---

345.   For recognition of a fundamental gap in understanding, particularly of the enigmatic passage 2.6–16, see e.g., R. Bultmann, *Faith and Understanding* (New York: Harper & Row, 1969) 1.71–72; Conzelmann, *1 Corinthians*, 57; P. Stuhlmacher, 'The Hermeneutical Significance of 1 Corinthians 2.6–16' in *Tradition and Interpretation in the New Testament: Essays in Honor of E. Earle Ellis*, eds. G. F. Hawthorne and O. Betz (Grand Rapids, MI: Eerdmans, 1988) 328; Hunt, *The Inspired Body*, 5.

346.   So, already, Bultmann, *Faith and Understanding*, 1.71–72; clearly identified and emphasized by Conzelmann, *1 Corinthians*, 57.

347.   Bultmann, *Faith and Understanding*, 1.71–72; idem, *Theology of the New Testament*, 1.175 (New York: Charles Scribner's Sons, 1951), 181–82; E. Käsemann, *Exegetische Versuche und Besinnungen* (Göttingen: Vandenhoeck & Ruprecht, 1960) 1.267–76; Schmithals, *Gnosticism in Corinth*, 151; Wilckens, *Weisheit und Torheit*, 52–53, 60; Conzelmann, *1 Corinthians*, 57–61; Weder, *Das Kreuz Jesu bei Paulus*, 165–67.

All of the elements of Paul's argument for a reversal of values are established features of the Socratic tradition. As is well known, Socrates had a 'divine sign' (δαιμόνιον σημεῖον) that kept him from doing anything amiss.[348] Both Plato and Xenophon refer to this prophetic inner voice,[349] and it was a subject of fascination among Stoics and Middle Platonists.[350] Moreover, the wisdom of Socrates was attested by the highest religious authority, the Delphic oracle.[351] Plato's Socrates relates how his enthusiastic disciple Chaerephon went to Delphi and asked the god whether anyone was wiser than Socrates, and the priestess replied 'no one'.[352] Socrates was puzzled by the oracle's response, since he was not conscious of possessing any great wisdom.[353] So he set himself the task of interrogating the citizens of Athens to discover what the god could mean in asserting that he was the wisest of men.[354] Socrates' solution of the riddle embodies an insight into the relation between divine and human wisdom: 'The truth of the matter is pretty certainly this: that real wisdom is the property of God, and this oracle is his way of telling us that human wisdom has little or no value.'[355] Socrates concludes that the god simply took him as an example in order to say that the wisest man is the one who is aware of his lack of wisdom.[356] Thus, Socrates explains his philosophical investigations as 'obedience to the divine command', as an attempt 'to help the cause of god', as 'service to the god'.[357]

The greater wisdom of Socrates, as he carries out the mission given him by the deity, remains unrecognized by the majority. As observed above, politicians and orators accounted Socrates a 'complete fool' for occupying

348. On Socrates' 'divine sign', see the sensible discussion in Friedländer, *Plato*, 32–36; Guthrie, *Socrates*, 82–85.

349. Plato *Apol.* 31C-D, 40A-C; *Euthyphro* 3B; *Resp.* 496C; *Phdr.* 242B; Xenophon *Mem.* 1.1.2–4; 4.3.12; 4.8.1; *Apol.* 5, 12–13.

350. Cicero *Div.* 1.123; *SVF* III.37–38; Plutarch *De genio Socratis* esp. 9–12, 20–24; Apuleius *De deo Socratis* esp. 17–20; Maximus of Tyre *Diss.* 8, 9; see the discussion in Döring, *Exemplum Socratis*, 6–7, 10–11.

351. The reply that the Delphic oracle gave concerning Socrates in known from Plato *Apol.* 21A and Xenophon *Apol.* 14. For comparison of the two versions and discussion of the historicity and significance of the incident, see Edelstein, *Xenophontisches und platonisches Bild des Sokrates*, 34; Guthrie, *Socrates*, 85–89.

352. Plato *Apol.* 21A.

353. Plato *Apol.* 21B; see the analysis of Socrates' reaction to the oracle by Guthrie, *Socrates*, 86: 'Socrates himself chose to take the oracle very seriously, and regarded it as a turning point in his life.'

354. Plato *Apol.* 21B-22E.

355. Plato *Apol.* 23A; trans. H. Tredennick in *The Collected Dialogues of Plato*, ed. E. Hamilton and H. Cairns (Princeton: Princeton University Press, 1978) 9.

356. Plato *Apol.* 23A–B.

357. Plato *Apol.* 23B; cf. Guthrie, *Socrates*, 88–89.

himself with 'frivolity and nonsense'.[358] The guardians of Athenian culture construed Socrates' game of questions with no authorized answers as a malicious attack upon moral values and the gods.[359] Only a devoted group of disciples perceive that Socrates' ridiculous exterior conceals a serious core. As Alcibiades explains to his companions in the *Symposium*, 'Anyone listening to Socrates for the first time would find his arguments simply laughable... But if you open up his arguments, and really get into the skin of them, you'll find that they're the only arguments in the world that have any sense at all, and that nobody else's are so godlike.'[360]

Alcibiades perceives that Socrates' disavowal of knowledge is 'ironic': 'Take my word for it, there's not one of you that really knows him. But now I've started on him, I'll show him up. Notice, for instance,...how Socrates loves to appear utterly uninformed and ignorant... Don't you see that it's just his outer casing? He spends his whole life playing (παίζων) his little game of irony (εἰρωνευόμενος) and laughing up his sleeve at all the world.'[361] It is this same irony which makes Thrasymachus so angry in the *Republic*, where he complains of 'Socrates' usual affectation' (ἡ εἰωθυῖα εἰρωνεία Σωκράτους), his 'shamming ignorance', his 'old game of never giving a positive answer himself, but taking up everyone else's answer and refuting it'.[362] Plato is cautious in his account of Socratic 'irony', conscious of the negative meaning of the term: in the fourth century, the term εἴρων still described the worst type of 'dissembler', a man who would praise you to your face and attack you behind your back.[363] Thus, Plato takes care to place the accusation of εἰρωνεία against Socrates in the mouth of either a bitter opponent like Thrasymachus or an infamous politician like Alcibiades.[364] Yet there is something that one would call 'gentle irony'[365] in the dialogues where Socrates places himself on the same level with the

---

358. Plato *Grg.* 485D; Ps.-Plato *Hipp. Maj.* 304B.

359. For the indictment against Socrates – refusing to recognize the gods of the state and corrupting the youth – see Xenophon *Mem.* 1.1.1; Diogenes Laertius 2.40; paraphrases of the indictment are found in Plato *Apol.* 24B and *Euthyphro* 3B.

360. Plato *Symp.* 221E-222A; trans. M. Joyce in *The Collected Dialogues of Plato*, 572.

361. Plato *Symp* 216D-E. See the discussion of this passage and the questions it raises by M. Gourinat, 'Socrate était-il un ironiste?' *Revue de Metaphysique et de Morale* 91 (1986) 339–53; Vlastos, *Socrates, Ironist and Moral Philosopher*, 33–42.

362. Plato *Resp.* 337A; trans. Guthrie, *Socrates*, 126.

363. O. Ribbeck, 'Über den Begriff des εἴρων', 381–400; see esp. Aristophanes *Vesp.* 174; *Nubes* 449; Plato *Leg.* 908E; Aristotle *Eth. Nic.* 1124b30; Theophrastus *Char.* 1.

364. Guthrie, *Socrates*, 126; M. Gagarin, 'Socrates' *Hybris* and Alcibiades' Failure,' *Phoenix* 31 (1977) 22–37.

365. In the softened sense that the term begins to acquire in Aristotle *Eth. Nic.* 1127b22ff., where Socrates is adduced as an example of one who specializes in mock-modesty. See the analysis in P. W. Gooch, 'Socratic Irony and Aristotle's *Eirōn*: Some Puzzles', *Phoenix* 41 (1987) 95–104.

young men and says, 'Come now, let's look into this, you and I, for I don't know any more about it than you do.'[366]

Indeed, the Platonic Socrates includes himself within the ironic tension, making himself and his restless pursuit of wisdom the objects of parody.[367] Thus in the *Euthydemus*, Socrates portrays himself as a slave to the wisdom of two sophists, whom he asks to demonstrate how one should practice virtue.[368] Socrates first proposes to show them what his notion of philosophy is, and the sort of thing he should like to hear. Socrates pleads: 'If you think I am clumsy (ἰδιωτικῶς) and ridiculous (γελοίως) in doing this, don't laugh at me; I am only eager to listen to your wisdom, and so I will be daring enough to make a rough sketch before you.'[369] In the parody of dialectic that follows, Socrates plays the role of the anxious fool, confiding in his pupil Clinias, 'We have almost made ourselves ridiculous (γέλαστοι) before these strangers, you and I, son of Axiochus!'[370] Comedy turns into farce, when Socrates, having lost the knowledge he sought to catch, and becoming entangled in his own argument,[371] appeals to the sophists for help: 'When I was thrown into this difficulty, I cried out with all my voice, asking the strangers, as one calls upon the Dioscuri, to save us, the boy and myself, from these overwhelming waves of the *logos*.'[372]

Once again, the *Life of Aesop* provides suggestive parallels to Paul's argument, in respect to the overthrow of elite wisdom by what is deemed to be folly. Indeed, the thesis of the *Life of Aesop*, to the extent that a folk-book of this sort may be said to have a 'thesis', is that true wisdom resides outside the academy, and that even a deformed slave, who suffers every possible disadvantage, can manage to triumph over the guardians of Hellenic culture by exercise of his native wit and common sense.[373] The central section of the *Life* repeatedly stages this reversal of expectations through a running battle of wits between the slave Aesop and the philosopher Xanthus, in which the slave consistently out-thinks his master.[374] Xanthus is portrayed as the embodiment of the Hellenic standards of καλοκἀγαθία: he is handsome[375] and highly

---

366. E.g., Plato *Meno* 96D; *Alc. I* 124C; *Char.* 158D; *Laches* 201A-B. On Socratic irony in this broader sense, see Friedländer, *Plato*, ch. 7; Guthrie, *Socrates*, 126–28.

367. Friedländer, *Plato*, 145–47.

368. Plato *Euthyd.* 218D.

369. Plato *Euthyd.* 278D; trans. W. H. D. Rouse in *The Collected Dialogues of Plato*, 392.

370. Plato *Euthyd.* 279C.

371. Plato *Euthyd.* 291B-292E.

372. Plato *Euthyd.* 293A; trans. Friedländer, *Plato*, 146.

373. Daly, *Aesop without Morals*, 20–21; Winkler, *Auctor and Actor*, 282.

374. *Vit. Aesop.* 20–91.

375. The name of the philosopher is probably meant to suggest that he is handsome, since ξανθός = 'fair-haired'. The word is used in this sense with other synonyms of 'handsome' in *Vit. Aesop.* 32 to name the opposite of Aesop's physical appearance.

educated.[376] He enjoys a great repute and is followed by a group of admiring students.[377] Yet the proud philosopher is repeatedly fooled and made to appear a nincompoop by the meanest of his slaves. 'Aesop outwits the philosopher in simple matters in the privacy of the household, outshines him with common sense before his students, and answers questions that baffle Xanthus before the public assembly.'[378] The object of this overthrow is explicitly stated to be the elite wisdom sought by the Greeks. Indeed, the notion that the fruits of Hellenic culture deserve to be called 'wisdom' occasions an episode in which the slave is overheard 'laughing' behind the philosopher's back:

> Xanthus said, 'Aesop are you laughing with me or at me?'
> Aesop said, 'Oh, not at you.'
> Xanthus said, 'Well, then, at whom?'
> Aesop said, 'At the professor you studied under.'
> Xanthus said, 'You blackguard, this is blasphemy against the Hellenic world, for I studied at Athens under philosophers, rhetoricians, and philologists. And do you have the effrontery to set foot on the Muses' Helicon?'
> Aesop said, 'If you talk nonsense, you'll have to expect to be jeered at.'[379]

The pre-eminent role in the reversal of Aesop's fortunes is given to the goddess Isis and her daughters the Muses.[380] At the beginning of the tale, Aesop is mute, and hence the target of abuse by his fellow-slaves, who assume he is powerless to retaliate.[381] As a reward for Aesop's kindness to a priestess of Isis who has strayed from the highway and become lost, Aesop is granted the power of speech and the ability to conceive and elaborate tales.[382] The priestess petitions Isis: 'Oh, crown of the whole world, Isis of many names, have pity on this workman, who suffers and is pious, for the piety he has shown, not to me, oh mistress, but to your appearance. And if you are unwilling to repay this man with a livelihood of many talents for what the other gods have taken from him, at least grant him the power of speech, for you have the power to bring back to light those things which have fallen into darkness.'[383] The goddess subsequently appears to Aesop in a dream, and not only restores his voice, but asks that each of her daughters the nine Muses bestow on him

---

376. *Vit. Aesop.* 36.
377. *Vit. Aesop.* 20.
378. Daly, *Aesop without Morals*, 21.
379. *Vit. Aesop.* 36.
380. Daly, *Aesop without Morals*, 20–22; Winkler, *Auctor and Actor*, 286.
381. *Vit. Aesop.* 2.
382. *Vit. Aesop.* 4–7.
383. *Vit. Aesop.* 5.

something of her own talent too.[384] The passage in which the author describes the epiphany of Isis is the most poetic in the *Life*.[385] Even if elements of this rhetorical *ekphrasis* are borrowed from a classical source, the author has lavished effort on the description of the natural surroundings in which Aesop takes his siesta, and has produced a pastoral account of hypnotic beauty. To be sure, the account of Isis' miraculous intervention is only loosely attached to the rest of the *Life*, and is obviously the contribution of the author to the tradition that he inherited.[386] Nor do other episodes in the *Life* illustrate the piety in return for which Aesop is given the powers of speech and fabulation.[387] But the author's point in making Isis' miracle the inaugural event in the *Life* is less to emphasize the recompense for piety than to assert the necessity of divine intervention in order to alleviate Aesop's plight. On this basis, the priestess of Isis makes her appeal: only with the help of the goddess can a poor workman, who labors under every disability, hope to experience a reversal of fortune.

The gifts of the goddess, as great as they may be, remain unrecognized by the majority of those whom Aesop meets. Only a few are able to look beyond Aesop's grotesque appearance and grasp his astonishing cleverness. The motif of contrasting responses to Aesop is a constant feature in the *Life*, and must have belonged to the inherited tradition. On the way to the slave market in Ephesus, Aesop's fellow-slaves judge him to be the 'worst fool' they have ever seen, because he chooses to carry the heaviest load, a basket of bread. Only one of the slaves suspects the truth: 'He's no fool (οὐκ ἔστιν μωρός); he's starved and wants to get his hands on the bread so he can eat more than the rest.'[388] Similarly, in the lengthy section of the *Life* devoted to Aesop's service to Xanthus, the proud philosopher and most of his graduate students regard Aesop as 'a repulsive piece of human garbage'.[389] Speaking for the majority, one of the students advises the philosopher: 'Professor, if you pay attention to him, he'll soon drive you mad. Like body, like mind. This abusive and malicious slave isn't worth a penny.'[390] Only one of the scholars invited to Xanthus' banquet shows

384. *Vit. Aesop.* 6–7.
385. *Vit. Aesop.* 6–7; see the comments of Daly, *Aesop without Morals*, 22.
386. Perry, *Aesopica*, 5; Daly, *Aesop without Morals*, 22; Winkler, *Auctor and Actor*, 286. The association of Aesop with the Muses, on the other hand, probably belongs to the oldest core of the tradition; see Wiechers, *Aesop in Delphi*, 31–33.
387. What piety Aesop exhibits is in connection with the Muses, e.g., *Vit. Aesop.* 100: upon Aesop's return to Samos, his first act is to sacrifice to the Muses and to erect a shrine to them, with a statue of Mnemosyne.
388. *Vit. Aesop.* 18 (ms. G).
389. E.g., *Vit. Aesop.* 27, 31, 69.
390. *Vit. Aesop.* 55.

himself to be a true philosopher by answering the question that Aesop, serving as doorman, poses to each of the guests in a manner which demonstrates that he comprehends Aesop's coarse wit.[391] The selfish and corrupt citizens of Samos risk destruction by the Lydian king because they fail to perceive the wisdom Aesop offers: 'When the Samians saw Aesop, they burst out laughing and shouted, "How can this person solve our riddle? He has the look of a portentous monstrosity. Is he a frog, or a hedgehog, or a pot-bellied jar, or a drill sergeant for monkeys, or an imitation of a flagon, or a cook's gear, or a dog in a basket?" '[392] In the end, the Samians are only saved by Aesop's persistence and common sense: 'Men of Samos, why do you joke and gape at me? You shouldn't consider my appearance but examine my wits. It's ridiculous to find fault with a man's intelligence because of the way he looks. Many men of the worst appearance have a sound mind, etc.'[393]

Irony is the only successful resolution of the contrast between the transformation in Aesop wrought by the goddess and the perception that persists among the majority of those whom Aesop encounters. A cunning irony, generally masked as obtuseness, characterizes most of Aesop's relationships.[394] The irony seems particularly heavy-handed in the section of the *Life* devoted to Aesop's service to Xanthus. Looking for a pretext to give Aesop a beating, Xanthus sets Aesop a series of onerous tasks.[395] Aesop's repeated failure to fulfill the tasks as expected demonstrates, ironically, not the slave's incompetence, but rather the master's ignorance of how to give orders.[396] The irony in Aesop's relationship with Xanthus often takes the form of a reversal of the 'professor joke' known from the roughly contemporary *Philogelos*.[397] By taking Xanthus' words in a strictly literal sense, Aesop demonstrates that the philosopher does not know what he is saying: e.g., ordered to prepare 'lentil' for Xanthus' guests, Aesop bakes a single bean.[398] The repetition of this dull ruse is tedious for modern bourgeois readers. But one must reckon with the reality that such irony, disguised as obtuseness, provided the only

391.   *Vit. Aesop.* 77b (ms. W).

392.   *Vit. Aesop.* 87.

393.   *Vit. Aesop.* 88.

394.   E.g., the self-deprecating humor employed in Aesop's advice to the slave-dealer in *Vit. Aesop.* 15, and the laconic reply to the policeman in *Vit. Aesop.* 65.

395.   *Vit. Aesop.* 38–64.

396.   Stated explicitly as the goal of Aesop's actions in *Vit. Aesop.* 38.

397.   E.g., *Philogelos* 43. That some of the material in the *Philogelos* goes back at least as far as the first century, see Winkler, *Auctor and Actor*, 164. For analysis of the jokes featuring the learned fool called σχολαστικός, see Winkler, *Auctor and Actor*, 160–65.

398.   *Vit. Aesop.* 41; for similar humor, see 38–40, 42–43, 44–46.

defense, and occasional revenge, for those who routinely suffered mistreatment.

Nowhere does the cunning of slaves celebrate a more brilliant overthrow of traditional values than in the comedies of Plautus.[399] Here a new, inverted hierarchy is created, in which native wit, not wealth or birth, distinguishes the ruler from the ruled.[400] In the *Asinaria*, for example, the clever slaves Leonida and Libanus succeed in completely reversing the master-slave relationship, so that the low and despised are exalted, and the powerful and noble are brought to nothing.[401] The slaves begin by insisting that they be addressed as 'patrons' and receive supplication.[402] Not satisfied with these verbal enhancements of status, they demand tangible signs of subservience. The master is commanded to get down and rub the knees of his slave, and even to carry the slave upon his back![403] The reversal of status is epitomized by the jubilant cry of Libanus as he rides in triumph upon his master-as-horse: 'Hey, here is how the high and haughty ought to be humbled!'[404] As the climax of his ennoblement, the slave makes the ultimate demand: to be given divine honors – a statue, an altar, and a sacrifice to his godhead.[405]

The most characteristic and successful Plautine plots involve the outsmarting of a presumably smarter master by a slave.[406] In the *Bacchides*, the wily Chrysalus exults over the deception of the learned Nicobulus: 'How I fooled my old master, fully flimflammed him today, shrewdly

399. Needless to say, this reversal is already familiar from Greek comedy, e.g., the opening speech of Xanthias in Aristophanes' *Frogs*, and the relations between clever slaves and dull-witted masters in Menander. But, as Segal (*Roman Laughter*, 101) observes: 'Plautus is, in almost every sense, the most "saturnalian" comic playwright of them all; he turns *everything* topsy-turvy' (Segal's emphasis).

400. Segal, *Roman Laughter*, 103–104; W. S. Anderson, *Barbarian Play: Plautus' Roman Comedy* (Toronto: University of Toronto, 1993) 98–102.

401. For what follows, see the detailed and insightful analysis of Segal, *Roman Laughter*, 104–109, drawing upon E. Fraenkel, *Plautinisches im Plautus* (Berlin: Reimer, 1922) ch. 8 and P. Spranger, 'Historische Untersuchungen zu den Sklavenfiguren des Plautus und Terenz', no. 8, esp. 117–19.

402. Plautus *Asinaria* 650–54 for the demand to be called *patronos*; lines 662–699 for instances of supplication. See the observation of Segal, *Roman Laughter*, 106: 'Between line 662 and line 699, there are thirteen verbs of "beseeching", notably *orare* (five times), as well as *exorarier*, *obsecrare*, *petere*, and *supplicare*.'

403. Plautus *Asinaria* 670–71, 699–702. See further Segal, *Roman Laughter*, 108: 'This brace of erstwhile slaves has become the most finicky of masters. Leonida is not pleased with the way Argyrippus has rubbed his knees (line 678). Libanus indicates that his master is so bad a piece of horseflesh that he will send him off to work in the mills (lines 709–710), an ironic reminder of the plight of the stereotyped comic slave.'

404. Plautus *Asinaria* 702; trans. Segal, *Roman Laughter*, 116.

405. Plautus *Asinaria* 712–13, and 718, 731, where the demand for homage is satisfied.

406. Segal, *Roman Laughter*, 116–23, with numerous examples.

tricked a tricky oldster, rushed him, crushed him, now he swallows every
word I say!'[407] Near the end of the play, Nicobulus agonizes over the fact
that the wiles of a slave have made a wise man foolish (*dolis doctis
indoctum*):[408] 'Here's the one thing that pains me and makes my heart
crack. Here's the one thing that puts my whole soul on the rack: that a man
of my age should be made such a fool.'[409] Plautus typically deepens the
inversion by making the wise old man, who is the victim of comic
overthrow, a person of social or political rank, a senator.[410]

The irony inherent in the topsy-turvy situations created by Plautus cuts
both ways – against erstwhile slaves and erstwhile masters. Thus, in the
midst of scenes in which slaves celebrate their triumphs, they acknowledge
their lowly status in the everyday social order.[411] And even as the masters
comply with their slaves' outrageous demands, they hurl at them vulgar
epithets, such as *verbero* ('whipping-post') and *carnufex* ('gallows-bird'),
ironic reminders of normal circumstances, under which such behavior
would be harshly punished.[412] Conversely, Plautus gives the distinguished
victims of the servants' schemes expressive names that ironically recall
their former social status: e.g., Nicobulus, 'conquering in counsel', and
Periphanes, 'most notable'.[413] Plautus delights in scenes that capture the
inversion of a specific virtue, for which the wise and strong are
customarily respected. There is stunning irony in Periphanes' confession
that he and his colleague Apoecides, both renowned statesmen, have been
'thoroughly bamboozled both in person and in public' by an insignificant
slave.[414]

In assessing the effect of the reversal of status portrayed by Plautus, it is
important to take account of the 'saturnalian' atmosphere that pervades

---

407. Plautus *Bacchides* 642–44; trans. Segal, *Roman Laughter*, 118.
408. Plautus *Bacchides* 1095.
409. Plautus *Bacchides* 1099–1101; trans. Segal, *Roman Laughter*, 118. Cf. *Captivi* 781–87.
410. E.g., *Casina* 536 and *Epidicus* 189, where the elderly antagonists are termed *columen
senati*. See also *Asinaria* 871; *Mercator* 319.
411. E.g., Plautus *Asinaria* 650: Leonida: 'Now first of all, we don't deny we're both of us
your bondsmen.'
412. E.g., Plautus *Asinaria* 669, 696; cf. Segal, *Roman Laughter*, 107.
413. Duckworth, *The Nature of Roman Comedy*, 348; Segal, *Roman Laughter*, 121.
414. Plautus *Epidicus* 517, 521–24: Periphanes speaks first of his own public humiliation,
then of the greater disgrace of his prominent colleague Apoecides: 'What now for me, so often
spokesman for the senate? I've been bamboozled both in person and in public! But I'm not
half as fooled as he – who's famous as a framer of laws and legislation, founding father, and
always boasting of his shrewdness, too.' This speech is even more bitterly ironic in context, as
observed by Segal, *Roman Laughter*, 205–206 n. 139, since, in the preceding passages, these
two pillars of the state have engaged in much self-congratulation regarding their own
shrewdness.

the comedies.[415] Plautus' slave-heroes wildly exploit the liberty to misbehave temporarily enjoyed by slaves at the Roman Saturnalia.[416] Thus the 'revolutionary' actions of Plautine slaves stand under the protection of the god of the festival.[417] In a number of cases, Plautus attributes to his slaves a consciousness of the need for divine intervention, if their audacious schemes are to prove successful. As Epidicus spies the chance of victory, he exclaims: 'All the gods in heaven, not to mention twelve immortals more, now do battle by my side and aid me as my aides-de-camp!'[418] Even the impudent Tranio in the *Mostellaria* is obliged to seek divine refuge from his irate master: anticipating his master's attempt to slap handcuffs on him, Tranio leaps onto a nearby altar, and refuses to descend from his 'holy place', where he enjoys a heavenly immunity.[419]

Horace bases the lesson of one of his most biting satires on the saturnalian premise that the slave is wiser and freer than his master.[420] The satire is set during the Saturnalia, when slaves were treated with indulgence.[421] Horace's bondsman Davus takes advantage of the liberty of the season to lecture his master on his vices. Davus' tone at the opening of the dialogue is mock-humble and ironic: 'I've been listening some time, and wishing to say a word to you, but as a slave I dare not.'[422] In the sermon that follows, Davus relentlessly exposes his master's follies to ridicule, focusing on his inconsistency, lust, and voracity. Horace attempts to resist his slave's criticism, addressing him as *furcifer*, reminding him that he is stupid and lazy, and menacing him with dark looks and raised hands.[423] But the slave enjoys immunity according to the rules of the holiday. So he proceeds to demonstrate that the master is not the 'better man', but the 'greater fool'.[424] As the reversal of conventional roles – free

415. On the saturnalian quality of Plautus' comedies, see Spranger, 'Historische Untersuchungen zu den Sklaven-figuren des Plautus', 117; Segal, *Roman Laughter*, 32–33, 103.

416. On the temporary freedom and equality enjoyed by slaves during the Saturnalia, see Horace *Sat*. 2.3.5; 2.7.4; Martial 11.6.4.

417. On the incorporation of saturnalian customs into the *ludi Romani*, see W. Warde Fowler, *The Roman Festivals* (London: Macmillan, 1925) 177.

418. Plautus *Epidicus* 675–76; trans. Segal, *Roman Laughter*, 134.

419. Plautus *Mostellaria* 1064–1116.

420. *Sat*. 2.7. The satire addresses two questions: 'Who is the greater fool?' (2.7.42) and 'Who is free?' (2.7.83). The satire is thus an exploration of the Stoic paradox that 'only the wise man is free' (μόνος ὁ σοφὸς ἐλεύθερος); see Cicero *Paradoxa Stoicorum* 5. Horace treats a similar theme in *Sat*. 2.3, which also has the Saturnalia as its setting.

421. Horace *Sat*. 2.7.4; cf. *Sat*. 2.3.5.

422. Horace *Sat*. 2.7.1–2; trans. Fairclough, *Horace. Satires*, 225. Compare the ironic words of the slave Epidicus to the distinguished old men in Plautus *Epidicus* 257–58.

423. Horace *Sat*. 2.7.22, 39, 43–44.

424. Horace *Sat*. 2.7.41–42. See the commentary by Freudenburg, *The Walking Muse*, 225–26.

man/slave and wise man/fool – nears completion, Horace's anger is so aroused that he breaks the saturnalian spell and ends the lecture, by threatening to send Davus to hard labor on his Sabine farm.[425]

Judging from the extant fragments of the mime, the overthrow of conventional wisdom, and the embarrassment of authority-figures by tricky, irreverent slaves, were standard fare on the popular stage: for example, the fool in the *Charition* mime is the one who effects the heroine's rescue by making her captors drunk.[426] The fool also mocks the ecstatic dance of the king of the barbarians.[427] Here, too, there is an appeal for divine aid, so that the low may triumph: the fool prays to his obscene goddess, the 'lady Fartemis' (κυρία Πορδή), for protection and prosperity.[428] And there is irony of a broad and vulgar kind, e.g., the fool drinks to the king's 'bad health'.[429] Naturally, the level of irony in the mime depends upon the acuity of the mime-writer. A bitter cynicism characterizes the fool's response to the question of where justice is to be found in a London mime-papyrus: 'Among those who spit at each other!'[430]

It is clear how fully Paul participates in the comic-philosophic tradition whose outlines we have traced through the preceding pages. With others who adopt the 'grotesque perspective' in order to utter a subversive truth, Paul asserts that a divinely willed reversal has occurred in the conventional relations of knowledge and power. In the dichotomy that Paul erects between human and divine 'wisdom' (1.19–21), Paul seems closest to the Socratic insight into the meaning of the Delphic oracle: true wisdom belongs to God, human wisdom has no value.[431] But in his insistence that the foolish and weak in the world have been given a paradoxical wisdom that makes them superior to the educated and powerful (1.26–31), Paul reveals a bias in favor of the disadvantaged and

425. Horace *Sat.* 2.7.116–18. Compare the numerous threats of being sent *in pistrinum* directed at slaves in Plautine comedy, e.g., *Pseudolus* 494, 499, 500, 534, 1060.

426. *POxy* 413 ('Charition') 45–106, esp. 96.

427. *POxy* 413 ('Charition') 93–95; see the comments of Wiemken, *Der griechische Mimus*, 64–65; Page, *Select Papyri III*, 349.

428. *POxy* 413 ('Charition') 4–8.

429. *POxy* 413 ('Charition') 68.

430. *PLond* 1984, line 2; Page, *Select Papyri III*, 362–63.

431. Indeed, it does not seem impossible that Paul was consciously influenced by the Socratic tradition at this point, since the Chaerephon-oracle continued to be debated among various philosophical schools, e.g., Aristotle *apud* Diogenes Laertius 2.23 and Colotes of Lampsacus *apud* Plutarch *Adv. Col.* Q7, 1116E; 18, 1117D, among others; cf. H. W. Parke, 'Chaerephon's inquiry about Socrates', *CP* 56 (1961) 241–50. Dio Chrysostom made the Delphic oracle and Socrates' response the model for his own account of conversion to a philosophical life, esp. *Or.* 13; cf. *Or.* 12.14; see the discussion in Döring, *Exemplum Socratis*, 83–85, 88, 90, 98.

ignoble like that which comes to expression in the *Life of Aesop*.[432] With his argument for a divine overthrow of elite wisdom, Paul places himself in a tradition of popular thinking that would have been recognized by his reading public.

Accordingly, Paul insists, at the beginning of his argument, that God has taken the initiative in the overthrow of elite wisdom. He does this in the most effective way by citing a biblical oracle in which God himself is represented as speaking: 'I will destroy the wisdom of the wise, and the discernment of the discerning I will thwart' (1.19).[433] Paul's point is not merely that divine wisdom surpasses human understanding, but rather that the value of elite wisdom has been completely eliminated.[434] Paul sharpens this point by substituting ἀθετήσω ('I will nullify') for κρύψω ('I will hide') of the Septuagint.[435] In Paul's version of the biblical text, God has not merely 'hidden' understanding from the wise, but has 'brought it to nothing'.

The series of rhetorical questions that immediately follow the citation of Scripture represent the promise of the Isaian oracle as triumphantly fulfilled: 'Where is a wise man (σοφός)? Where is a learned one (γραμματεύς)? Where is a searcher (συζητητής) of this age?' (1.20a).[436] The sense of these questions is not simply that human wisdom fails when put to the test, because a truly wise person cannot be found, but rather that God has annihilated the basis of learned culture, so that one can no longer claim to be what the name of σοφός suggests.[437] Paul makes his point culturally specific by means of terms which refer to the educated elite among Jews and Greeks, respectively: the γραμματεύς is the Jewish scribe, not merely a skilled copyist, but an expert in Scripture and its wisdom;[438] the συζητητής is the philosophical researcher so highly esteemed in the Hellenic world, one who pursues wisdom by means of discussion,

432. Daly, *Aesop without Morals*, 20–21; Winkler, *Auctor and Actor*, 282.

433. On the force of the first person singular formulation of the Septuagint version of Isa. 29.14, see Lindemann, *Der erste Korintherbrief*, 44.

434. Heinrici, *Der erste Brief*, 68; Weiss, *Der erste Korintherbrief*, 27.

435. In this case, it seems clear that Paul has modified the language of the LXX in the interest of his argument, although the possibility cannot be excluded that he cites an alternate textual tradition; see the discussion in Heinrici, *Der erste Brief*, 68; Weiss, *Der erste Korintherbrief*, 27; Koch, *Die Schrift als Zeuge des Evangeliums*, 31, 36–37; Collins, *First Corinthians*, 103.

436. Heinrici, *Der erste Brief*, 69.

437. Weiss, *Der erste Korintherbrief*, 27.

438. The term γραμματεύς is not found elsewhere in Paul, but is frequent in the gospels as a designation for a scholar versed in the law of Moses. On the wisdom of the scribe, see esp. Sir. 38.24–39.11. Cf. Weiss, *Der erste Korintherbrief*, 28; Collins, *First Corinthians*, 104; Lindemann, *Der erste Korintherbrief*, 45.

debate, and dialectic.[439] Paul's questions mock the educated elite by means of
the very titles of their dignity: the wise men are not what they claim to be!

The high irony created by the three-fold anaphora in 1.20a rapidly
descends into farce through a final rhetorical question in the latter half of
the verse: 'Has not God made foolish the wisdom of the world?' The verb
μωραίνειν, pulled forward to the beginning of the sentence for emphasis,[440]
does not have the general sense 'to deprive of understanding or insight',[441]
but rather possesses all of the pejorative connotations associated with the
noun μωρός (weakness, imbecility): thus, God has 'made stupid' the
wisdom of the world.[442] Like 'Holy Trickery' to whom Plautine slaves give
thanks, God has 'bamboozled' the representatives of elite wisdom. Like the
Muses to whom Aesop offers sacrifice, God has made 'nincompoops' of
the philosophers and rhetoricians. And Paul has provocatively placed this
coarse, comic word at the beginning of a rhetorical question, demanding
that those who are enamored of 'learned eloquence' concede that they have
been 'made foolish' by God.

Not content merely to assert the reality of the divine overthrow of elite
wisdom, Paul proceeds in vs. 21 to explain why and how God has 'made
stupid' the wisdom of the world: 'For since, in the wisdom of God, the
world did not know God through wisdom, it pleased God, through the
foolishness of our proclamation, to save those who believe.'[443] In a single
sentence, Paul compresses the entire history of God's dealings with the
world, the first half recounting the fruitless outcome of the human search
for knowledge of the divine, and the second half announcing the saving
results of the revelation of God in Christ.[444] The sentence is thus a very
concise counterpart to the aetiological legends of the comic-philosophic

439.   The subject noun συζητής is not otherwise attested, but the verb συζητητεῖν and the
abstract noun συζήτησις are not uncommon; see Liddell-Scott-Jones, *Greek-English Lexicon*,
1670; Bauer, *Greek-English Lexicon*, 954. For the understanding of συζητητής as 'philosophical
researcher', see esp. M. Lautenschlager, 'Abschied von Disputierer. Zur Bedeutung von
συζητητής in 1 Kor 1,20', *ZNW* 83 (1992) 276–85; followed by Collins, *First Corinthians*, 104;
Lindemann, *Der erste Korintherbrief*, 45.

440.   Heinrici, *Der erste Brief*, 70.

441.   Rightly, Heinrici, *Der erste Brief*, 70; Weiss, *Der erste Korintherbrief*, 27.

442.   Heinrici (*Der erste Brief*, 70) calls attention to Horace *Od.* 1.34.2, *insaniens sapientia*,
and Lucian *Alex.* 40, where the wise are described as μωρόσοφοι. See also Lindemann, *Der
erste Korintherbrief*, 45: 'Die in 20b folgende abschliessende Frage besagt, dass Gott die σοφία
τοῦ κόσμου tatsächlich "dumm gemacht" hat.'

443.   For ἐπειδὴ γάρ as causal and explanative, see Bauer, *Greek-English Lexicon*, 360; cf.
Heinrici, *Der erste Brief*, 71: 'Nähere Erklärung über dies ἐμώρανεν ο θεός'; Collins, *First
Corinthians*, 105.

444.   The point is grasped by Heinrici, *Der erste Brief*, 71, despite the fact that he refers to
Rom. 1.18–3.20 as a fuller exposition of the theme. In Rom. 1.18–32, the subject is the tragic
human fall into sinfulness; in 1 Cor. 1.21, by contrast, the focus is on the divine initiative in
human history.

tradition, viz. the Isis-miracle that inaugurates the paradoxical career of Aesop, and the Chaerephon-oracle that initiates the philosophical mission of Socrates. Yet Paul's language is so well chosen, and the sentence is so tightly constructed, that none of the drama of divine intervention is sacrificed by abbreviation. The actors in the drama are figures of transcendent proportion: God, God's *Sophia*, and the world (ὁ κόσμος) treated as a thinking subject = 'humankind'.[445] The inception of the action lies outside time, before the beginning of history. Paul makes this clear by placing the phrase 'in the wisdom of God' at the beginning of the sentence: all that subsequently unfolds happens within the timeless purpose of God.[446] The contrast between the futility of the human quest for knowledge and the saving power of the divine revelation is captured by a skillful play on two senses of the word σοφία: on the one hand, human 'shrewdness', a quality in which, Herodotus tells us, the Greeks always took pride;[447] on the other hand, divine 'wisdom', the transcendent purpose which, according to Proverbs (8.22–31) assisted in the creation.[448] The turning point in the drama is precisely indicated by Paul's careful placement of words in the sentence: 'God' (τὸν θεόν) as the object of the failed human noetic quest is placed at the very end of the clause, and then, immediately, 'God' (ὁ θεός) is named at the beginning of the next clause, describing the divine initiative for salvation.[449] The verb that Paul uses to describe the divine initiative, εὐδοκέω, places the emphasis upon the divine 'choice', the divine 'pleasure', the divine 'delight',[450] and makes clear that God's intervention in human history is in no sense a 'reaction'.[451] Just at the moment when the account is most absorbing and gripping, Paul explodes with an oxymoron, 'the buffoonery of (our) proclamation', so preposterous that it trumps the irreverence of Plautus' slaves and the fools in the mime.[452]

Having asserted the divine overthrow of elite wisdom, and having related why and how this occurred, Paul now affirms the contrary: 'we, however, proclaim Christ crucified, ... divine power and divine wisdom' (1.23–24).[453] The boldness of Paul's formulation may now be appreciated,

445. Weiss, *Der erste Korintherbrief*, 29.

446. Heinrici, *Der erste Brief*, 71–72; Wilckens, *Weisheit und Torheit*, 33–34; Lindemann, *Der erste Korintherbrief*, 45.

447. Herodotus 1.60; cf. Weiss, *Der erste Korintherbrief*, 29.

448. Heinrici, *Der erste Brief*, 71.

449. Weiss, *Der erste Korintherbrief*, 29.

450. Heinrici, *Der erste Brief*, 72; Bauer, *Greek-English Lexicon*, 404.

451. Lindemann, *Der erste Korintherbrief*, 45.

452. Weiss, *Der erste Korintherbrief*, 29–30: 'Hier tritt die Paradoxie des paulinischen Gedankens packend hervor. Fast klingt es lästerlich, dass Gott, um die Menschen zu retten, Torheit angewandt habe.'

453. On the contrast between subjects and the shift in focus introduced by the expression ἡμεῖς δέ, see Collins, *First Corinthians*, 107; Lindemann, *Der erste Korintherbrief*, 46.

in light of our thesis that his argument participates in a tradition which celebrates the cleverness of slaves and the poor; for Paul's statement surpasses the limit of paradox in both directions. On the one hand, the object of Paul's proclamation is not merely a deformed slave or a barefoot philosopher, but the 'crucified', one who has experienced the extremity of human misery, and has touched bottom. Paul intensifies the wretchedness of his subject by the use of the perfect participle, ἐσταυρωμένος, as we have observed: Christ was not only crucified at a certain moment in the past, but *remains*, as the subject of Christian preaching, 'the one crucified'.[454] On the other hand, Paul insists that the founder of the Christian way of life is not merely the wisest of men, but is actually the 'power of God and wisdom of God'.[455] Again, this is the most ridiculous statement imaginable – that a gallows-bird should be the embodiment of divine attributes. And again, Paul intensifies the contrast by repeating the genitive attribute θεοῦ ('of God'), and by placing it emphatically before the noun it modifies.[456] Indeed, Paul embellishes the dramatic effect of the account of his proclamation (I would say 'hams it up', if the subject were not so serious) by his choice of the verb κηρύσσειν: earlier Paul had described his preaching as 'evangelizing' (1.17), now he characterizes his work as 'announcing a message as a herald'.[457] The image that is created is that of Paul appearing on the streets of Corinth as a 'divine messenger', like Mercury/Sosia in Plautus' *Amphitryon*, and breathlessly announcing that a 'gallows-bird' is the 'wisdom of God'.

In substantiation of the paradox,[458] Paul formulates an ironic maxim: 'For the foolishness of God is wiser than men and the weakness of God is stronger than men' (1.25). The content of Paul's statement is, again, as extreme as possible: in order to express the totality of the contrast between the divine and the human, Paul employs oxymora that sound positively blasphemous – 'God's folly,... God's weakness'.[459] The style of the

454. Lindemann, *Der erste Korintherbrief*, 47; Heckel, 'Der Gekreuzigte bei Paulus', 196–200.

455. Lindemann, *Der erste Korintherbrief*, 47.

456. Weiss, *Der erste Korintherbrief*, 33; Vos, 'Die Argumentation des Paulus in 1 Kor 1,10–3,4', 101.

457. Weiss, *Der erste Korintherbrief*, 32 n.1: 'An unserer Stelle mag κηρύσσειν einen feierlichen Ton haben: "als Herolde verkündigen".' Cf. Epictetus *Diss.* 3.22.69, who describes the true Cynic as ἄγγελος καὶ κατάσκοπος καὶ κῆρυξ τῶν θεῶν.

458. That 1.25 is meant as confirmation of the paradox articulated in 1.24 is indicated by the explanatory conjunction ὅτι and by the chiastic structure that unites vss. 24 and 25; Heinrici, *Der erste Brief*, 76–77; Weiss, *Der erste Korintherbrief*, 34; Lindemann, *Der erste Korintherbrief*, 47–48.

459. Weiss, *Der erste Korintherbrief*, 34.

sentence is that of an epigram, as commentators have observed.[460] Paul's maxim is reminiscent of the *sententiae* of the mime writer Publilius Syrus, whose 'sagacious verses' were so highly admired that a collection of his epigrams was published in the first century A.D. for the instruction of schoolboys.[461] Indeed, the balance and rhythm of Paul's formulation gives his sentence a lilting quality like the songs of the clever slaves in Plautus' comedies. With these oxymoronic verses, Paul brings his argument for a divine reversal of wisdom and foolishness to a triumphant (provisional) conclusion.[462]

In comparison with other witnesses to the comic-philosophic tradition, Paul's argument seems extreme and hyperbolic. The moral triumph over elite culture, which the *Life of Aesop* credits to a mentally well-endowed slave, is predicated by Paul of all those who, however lowborn or stupid, are 'called' by the 'word of the cross' (1.26–28). The insight into the true relation between divine and human wisdom, which occurred to an ironic philosopher at a certain moment in Athenian history, is now asserted by Paul to be the permanent possession of all those who believe his proclamation (1.21,24). The absoluteness of Paul's assertion is undeniable, and it is important to identify the causes of this totalizing tendency. Two factors are clearly discernable: first, an *apocalyptic* perspective, that repeatedly comes to expression in Paul's use of the term 'this age' (ὁ αἰὼν οὗτος),[463] that is, the present world period, in contrast to the coming messianic age;[464] and second, the conviction that God has taken *historic* action in the death of Christ, reflected in Paul's choice of aorist verbs (e.g., ἐμώρανεν, 1.20b).[465] These two aspects of Paul's faith give universal scope and concrete reality to Paul's account of the overthrow of elite wisdom that is missing from the other sources we have examined. Our suggestion is that these features would have been perceived by Paul's Corinthian

460. Heinrici, *Der erste Brief*, 76; esp. Conzelmann, *1 Corinthians*, 48: 'The sentence must be read in the first instance as a maxim on its own.... It expresses in epigrammatic form a timeless rule of the relation between divine and human power.'

461. Seneca *Ep. Mor.* 8.8 praises the epigrams of Publilius Syrus for their sagacity. For the vast collection of epigrams attributed to Syrus, many doubtless genuine, see Friedrich, *Publilii Syri Mimi Sententiae*.

462. C. Senft (*La Première Épitre de Saint-Paul aux Corinthiens*, 41) designates vs. 25 'la conclusion triumphale'.

463. 1 Cor. 1.20; 2.6, 8; 3.18; see the excursus in Weiss, *Der erste Korintherbrief*, 28; see the comments of Collins, *First Corinthians*, 104; Lindemann, *Der erste Korintherbrief*, 45. The expression ὁ αἰὼν οὗτος ('this age') means the same for Paul as ὁ κόσμος οὗτος ('this world'), or simply ὁ κόσμος ('the world'); cf. 1 Cor. 1.27; 3.19.

464. See, e.g., 4 Ezra 4.11; 7.50; Eth. En. 71.15; m.Abot. 2.7; see the discussion of these and other apocalyptic traditions in Brown, *The Cross and Human Transformation*, esp. 36–59.

465. Lindemann, *Der erste Korintherbrief*, 45: 'Der Aor. Verweist auf ein einmaliges, geschichtliches Handeln Gottes, also auf Jesu Kreuzestod.'

audience as specifically Christian (ultimately Jewish) augmentations of a popular tradition of cultural criticism which Paul shared with mime writers, satirists, and others.

In the serio-comic tradition we may hope to find an explanation of the most puzzling aspect of Paul's argument on behalf of a divine reversal of values, namely, the appearance of self-contradiction. As observed above, Paul claims in 2.6–16. that he communicates a 'wisdom for the perfect', after repeatedly disavowing the use of 'eloquent wisdom' in his proclamation of the gospel (1.17; 2.1,4). Paul's discourse of wisdom among the perfect in 2.6–16 seems to many interpreters an open contradiction of his former acknowledgement of the crucified Christ as the sole content of his preaching (1.17,18,22; 2.2).[466] Before seeking a new understanding of Paul's discourse in 2.6–16, it is important to grasp, in some detail, the reasons why this passage has perplexed and troubled interpreters.

The impression that Paul contradicts himself in the course of his argument is augmented by the highly unusual vocabulary employed in 2.6–16.[467] Words and phrases such as 'the perfect' (οἱ τέλειοι), 'mystery' (μυστήριον), 'hidden' (ἀποκεκρυμμένη), 'reveal' (ἀποκαλύπτειν), 'search' (ἐραυνᾶν), 'the deep things of God' (τὰ βάθη τοῦ θεοῦ), and 'receive the Spirit' (λαμβάνειν τὸ πνεῦμα), are rarely attested in Paul's extant correspondence.[468] Also remarkable is the concentration of forms and cognates of the verbs 'to know' (γινώσκειν) and 'to discern' (κρίνειν).[469] This represents a decided shift in the language used by Paul in the first part of the argument (1.18–2.5).[470] Even the term 'wisdom' (σοφία) seems to undergo a change in meaning: no longer a designation for 'learned eloquence', as in the first part of the letter (1.17; 2.1,4), the term now seems to describe a mysterious discourse.[471]

466. Bultmann, *Faith and Understanding*, 1.71–72; idem, *Theology of the New Testament* 1.175, 181–82; Käsemann, *Exegetische Versuche und Besinnungen* 1.267–76; Schmithals, *Gnosticism in Corinth*, 151; Wilckens, *Weisheit und Torheit*, 52–53, 60; Conzelmann, *1 Corinthians*, 57–61; Weder, *Das Kreuz Jesu bei Paulus*, 165–67.

467. So, already, W. Bousset, *Der erste Brief an die Korinther. Die Schriften des Neuen Testaments*, Vol. 2, ed. W. Bousset and H. Heitmüller (Göttingen: Vandenhoeck & Ruprecht, 1917) 84; Reitzenstein, *Hellenistic Mystery-Religions*, 426–36; Bultmann, *Faith and Understanding*, 1.71–73; Lührmann, *Das Offenbarungsverständnis bei Paulus*, 113–17.

468. Hunt, *The Inspired Body*, 4–5; Collins, *First Corinthians*, 124.

469. Note the verb γινώσκειν in 2.8 (twice),11,14,16, and compounds of κρίνειν in 2.13, 14,15 (twice); cf. Schmithals, *Gnosticism in Corinth*, 151; Hunt, *The Inspired Body*, 4.

470. Emphasized by Conzelmann, *1 Corinthians*, 60; Collins, *First Corinthians*, 124.

471. Wilckens, *Weisheit und Torheit*, 60, 80, 99, 206; Schmithals, *Gnosticism in Corinth*, 138–41, 151–55; Lührmann, *Das Offenbarungsverständnis bei Paulus*, 113–14; G. Theissen, *Psychological Aspects of Pauline Theology* (Philadelphia: Fortress Press, 1987) 345–52.

In addition to the strangeness of the language, there is the impression, shared by a number of scholars, that the discourse on 'wisdom among the perfect' in 2.6–16 fits rather awkwardly in its present context.[472] Attention is drawn to the abrupt beginning of the discourse,[473] and to the sudden shift to the first person plural.[474] Throughout the lengthy paragraph, Paul employs the first person plural, both in pronominal form,[475] and as the subject of verbs.[476] The distinctive 'we' style of this passage contrasts with the first person singular found in 2.1–5 and 3.1–4.16. The emphatic κἀγώ in 3.1 resumes the account of Paul's ministry among the Corinthians begun in 2.1, by returning to the first person singular.[477] Thus, a number of scholars express the opinion that the composition of the text would have been smoother, if 3.1 had followed directly on 2.5, without the intervening paragraph.[478] Contributing to the impression of 2.6–16 as a self-contained unit is the complex, yet elegant disposition of the paragraph, and the lofty, rhythmical tone that pervades the passage.[479]

On account of the strangeness of the vocabulary and the incongruity of the text, the discussion of 'wisdom among the perfect' in 2.6–16 is widely regarded as a 'digression' in Paul's argument.[480] The incongruity is felt to be so great that an origin of the discourse outside the present context has repeatedly been hypothesized. One interpreter thinks that the exposition reflects the kind of 'esoteric teaching' that Paul offered to advanced disciples at his school in Ephesus.[481] Noting the citations of Scripture in 2.9 and 2.16, another scholar conjectures that Paul has taken over a previously formulated 'midrash' on the subject of wisdom.[482] A third researcher suggests that 2.6–16 is 'the literary deposit of a form of oral communica-

---

472. So, already, Weiss, *Der erste Korintherbrief*, 52; H. Conzelmann, 'Paulus und die Weisheit', *NTS* 12 (1965–66) 238; cf. Lindemann, *Der erste Korintherbrief*, 59–60.

473. Conzelmann, 'Paulus und die Weisheit', 238.

474. Weiss, *Der erste Korintherbrief*, 52; Collins, *First Corinthians*, 122–23; Lindemann, *Der erste Korintherbrief*, 59.

475. The first person plural pronoun is found in 2.7,10,12 (twice), and 16. In three cases, the pronoun is drawn forward to the beginning of the sentence for emphasis. Note esp. 2.16, where Paul's exposition concludes with an emphatic 'we': 'But *we* have the mind of Christ!'

476. Note the first person plural verb forms in 2.6,7,12 (twice),13,16.

477. Weiss, *Der erste Korintherbrief*, 52; Collins, *First Corinthians*, 123; Lindemann, *Der erste Korintherbrief*, 59.

478. E.g., Weiss, *Der erste Korintherbrief*, 52; Widmann, '1 Kor 2,6–16: Ein Einspruch gegen Paulus'; Lindemann, *Der erste Korintherbrief*, 59.

479. J. Weiss, 'Beiträge zur paulinischen Rhetorik', 207–10; idem, *Der erste Korintherbrief*, 52.

480. Weiss, *Der erste Korintherbrief*, 52; Bultmann, *Faith and Understanding*, 1.71–73; Conzelmann, *1 Corinthians*, 57.

481. Conzelmann, 'Paulus und die Weisheit', 184–86.

482. E. Earle Ellis, *Prophecy and Hermeneutic in Early Christianity: New Testament Essays*, WUNT 18 (Tübingen: Mohr-Siebeck, 1978) 25–26, 59–60, 156–57, 213–16.

tion' that Paul offered to mature Christians, in order to lead them to 'a higher stage of consciousness' regarding the meaning of the cross of Christ.[483] Indeed, the anomalies in the pericope have led one interpreter to question whether the passage derives from Paul, and to propose that the paragraph is an interpolation, a pneumatic 'wisdom discourse', composed by one of Paul's Corinthian opponents, and taken up into the text of canonical 1 Corinthians in the process of redaction.[484]

Even those interpreters who raise no questions about the Pauline authorship of the section 2.6–16 nevertheless find it necessary to posit the influence of the theology of Paul's Corinthian opponents upon the formulation of the passage, in order to account for the unusual vocabulary.[485] Thus, several interpreters explain that Paul takes up the language and concepts of the Corinthian elite in order to correct them, but becomes so entangled in the theology of his opponents, that he ultimately falls prey to a primitive form of Gnosticism.[486] Other scholars maintain that Paul appropriates the terminology of his Corinthian opponents, but reinterprets their theology in an apocalyptic fashion, so as to put forward his own concept of 'wisdom'.[487]

Against these conjectures, it must be objected that the incongruity of the section 2.6–16 is not so drastic as has been asserted.[488] The vocabulary of the passage, while unusual, is not unique.[489] The key terms – 'perfect' (τέλειοι), 'mystery' (μυστήριον), 'hidden' (ἀποκερυμμένη), 'reveal' (ἀποκαλύπτειν), 'search' (ἐραυνᾶν), etc. – are found in other Pauline letters.[490] Even the concentration of such terms is not unexampled: much of this vocabulary reappears at the climactic moment of the argument of

483. Theissen, *Psychological Aspects of Pauline Theology*, 345–93, esp. 347–52.

484. Widmann, '1 Kor 2,6–16: Ein Einspruch gegen Paulus'. According to Widmann, the discourse was originally conceived as a reply by one of Paul's Corinthian opponents to Paul's charge that their faith was grounded upon human wisdom (p. 50).

485. E.g., Weder, *Das Kreuz Jesu bei Paulus*, 165–73, esp. 166: 'deutliche Anlehnung an korinthische Sprache'.

486. Bultmann, *Faith and Understanding*, 1.70–72; E. Käsemann, '1 Korinther 2,6–16' in idem, *Exegetische Versuche und Besinnungen* (Göttingen: Vandenhoeck & Ruprecht, 1960) 1.267–76; Wilckens, *Weisheit und Torheit*, 52–89; Schmithals, *Gnosticism in Corinth*, 138–41, 151–55.

487. D. Lührmann, *Das Offenbarungsverständnis bei Paulus* (Neukirchen-Vluyn: Neukirchener Verlag, 1965), 113–17; Pearson, *The Pneumatikos-Psychikos Terminology in 1 Corinthians* esp. ch. 4.

488. F. Lang, *Die Briefe an die Korinther*, NTD 7 (Göttingen: Vandenhoeck & Ruprecht, 1986) 41; Lindemann, *Der erste Korintherbrief*, 60.

489. Hunt, *The Inspired Body*, 64–65.

490. For the plural τέλειοι, see 1 Cor. 14.20 and Phil. 3.15; μυστήριον is found in 1 Cor. 15.51 and Rom. 11.25; 16.25; ἀποκαλύπτειν in 1 Cor. 3.13; 14.30; Gal. 1.16; 3.23; Phil. 3.15; Rom. 1.17,18; 8.18; ἐραυνᾶν in Rom. 8.27; βάθος in 2 Cor. 8.2; Rom. 8.39; 11.33.

Romans.[491] What is unique, precisely, is the concentration of such language in a passage whose focus is epistemic, rather than eschatological.[492] Moreover, there are significant elements of verbal continuity between 2.6–16 and the other sections of Paul's argument.[493] The key terms 'wisdom', 'mystery', 'crucify (cross)', 'Spirit', 'foolishness', and 'know' are already present in 1.18–2.5.[494] It has been argued, plausibly, that even the term 'wisdom' (σοφία) is used in the same sense in 2.6–16 as in the previous section of the argument (1.18–2.5): the 'wisdom' which is spoken 'in a mystery' (2.7) is nothing other than the message of the 'crucified Christ' (1.23; 2.1–2), 'who has become for us wisdom from God' (1.30).[495] The appearance of a shift in the meaning of the term 'wisdom' is merely the result of the antithetical structure of Paul's argument.[496]

Moreover, there are conspicuous structural parallels between 1.18–25 and 2.6–16.[497] The section on the preaching of the cross as foolishness in 1.18–25 finds its counterpart in a section on the preaching of the crucified

---

491. Where Paul envisions the future salvation of Israel (11.25–36), he speaks of the 'mystery' (μυστήριον) that he wants his readers to understand (11.25), and then breaks forth in praise of God in a hymnic form (11.33–36) that includes much of the vocabulary of 1 Cor. 2.6–16, such as βάθος, σοφία, γνῶσις, ἀνεραυνάω, and νοῦς. See Hunt, *The Inspired Body*, 64–65.

492. On 1 Cor. 2.6–16 as part of a 'critique of the epistemic vices' of the Corinthians, see Stowers, 'Paul on the Use and Abuse of Reason', 261.

493. Lang, *Die Briefe an die Korinther*, 41; Stuhlmacher, 'The Hermeneutical Significance of 1 Cor. 2.6–16', 333.

494. Especially significant as an element of verbal (and conceptual) continuity is the term μυστήριον ('mystery'), which already occurs in 2.1, and recurs in 4.1 (in the plural). To be sure, there is a widely attested variant in 2.1, μαρτύριον ('witness'), supported by the second corrector of Sinaiticus, B, D, F, G, C, and the Majority text. But the reading μυστήριον is also strongly attested: P46, the first hand of Sinaiticus, A, C, and a great many church fathers. The text-critical judgment is difficult: μαρτύριον could be an assimilation to 1.6; but μυστήριον could be an intrusion from 2.7. Internal evidence speaks in favor of μυστήριον, since μαρτύριον is seldom found in Paul's epistles (otherwise only in 2 Cor. 1.12, but in a different sense). The reading μυστήριον is chosen by the 27th edition of Nestle-Aland. Cf. Metzger, *A Textual Commentary on the Greek New Testament*, 545. An argument in favor of μαρτύριον as the original reading in 1 Cor. 2.1 is advanced by G. Fee, '1 Corinthians 1.2, 2.1, and 2.10' in *Scribes and Scripture: New Testament Essays in Honor of J. Harold Greenlee*, ed. D. A. Black (Winona Lake, IN: Eisenbrauns, 1992) 6–7; idem, *The First Epistle to the Corinthians*, 88, 91.

495. So, already, Wilckens, 'Zu 1. Kor 2,1–16', 501–37, esp. 513: the mysterious wisdom which Paul and his co-workers proclaim among the perfect (2.6–7) is 'a more penetrating interpretation of the word of the cross'; followed by G. Sellin, 'Das "Geheimnis" der Weisheit und das Rätsel der 'Christuspartei'', 81; Lang, *Die Briefe an die Korinther*, 41; Wolter, 'Verborgene Weisheit und Heil für die Heiden', 304; Schrage, *Der erste Brief an die Korinther*, 240; H. Merklein, *Der erste Brief an die Korinther: Kapitel 1–4*, ÖTK (Gütersloh: Gerd Mohn, 1992) 224; Grindheim, 'Wisdom for the Perfect', 694–97.

496. Wilckens, 'Zu 1. Kor 2,1–16', 513; Grindheim, 'Wisdom for the Perfect', 692–97.

497. Theissen, *Psychological Aspects of Pauline Theology*, 345; Stuhlmacher, 'The Hermeneutical Significance of 1 Cor. 2.6–16', 333.

Lord as wisdom in 2.6–16. The parallelism may be illustrated by juxtaposition:

The preaching as foolishness, 1.18–25	The preaching as wisdom, 2.6–16
(a) the word of the cross as foolishness to the wise of this world, vss. 18–20	(a) the wisdom of God as unrecognizable by the rulers of this age, vss. 6–9
(b) the decisive action of God through foolishness, vss. 20–21	(b) the agency of the Spirit which searches for wisdom, vss. 10–13
(c) the preaching as scandal and foolishness to Jews and Gentiles, power and wisdom for believers, vss. 22–25	(c) the preaching as foolishness to unspiritual people, but wisdom for the spiritual, vss. 14–16

In both sections, Paul has given his thought a chiastic structure (αβα).[498] The point of the studied parallelism is to highlight the contrast in values and to dramatize the divine reversal.

Thus, there is no reason to doubt the Pauline authorship of the passage 2.6–16. Nor are there compelling grounds for seeking to interpret the text primarily from the perspective of the addressees, or in terms of the theology of Paul's opponents.[499] The decisive factor in regard to the latter is the observation that the discourse in 2.6–16 is not polemically conceived.[500] Paul's account of his 'discourse of wisdom among the perfect' is not formulated in opposition to the theology of his rivals, but rather expounds a previously hidden dimension of his own preaching of the cross.[501]

And yet, the appearance of incongruity remains.[502] Even those interpreters who are most sympathetic to Paul's argument, and least inclined to pass judgment upon the consistency of Paul's thought,[503] must

---

498. Rightly, Weiss, *Der erste Korintherbrief*, 52.

499. Lindemann, *Der erste Korintherbrief*, 60.

500. Rightly, Conzelmann, *1 Corinthians*, 58–59.

501. Wilckens, 'Zu 1. Kor 2,1–16', 513; Sellin, 'Das "Geheimnis" der Weisheit', 81; Lindemann, *Der erste Korintherbrief*, 60.

502. Well expressed by G. Bornkamm, *Paul* (New York: Harper & Row, 1971) 163–64, who acknowledges that in 2.6–16 'at first glance, by trimming his gospel to suit the Corinthian "gnostics" Paul is apparently untrue to himself', but ultimately concludes that 'Paul comes back to where he started, and makes plain that he knows of no higher or deeper mysteries transcending the gospel than that comprised in the "word of the cross".'

503. E.g., Stuhlmacher, 'The Hermeneutical Significance of 1 Cor. 2.6–16', 331, who rejects 'Sachkritik' as practiced by Bultmann, and seeks to defend Paul against the charge of having deviated from his insight into the paradoxical character of the word of the cross (1.18–25) by accommodating himself to Gnostic theology in 2.6–16.

exert considerable effort to make 2.6–16 comprehensible in context,[504] and acknowledge that only detailed exegesis can demonstrate whether the wisdom discourse in 2.6–16 is congruent with Paul's theology of the cross.[505] Thus, it is important to identify as precisely as possible the factors in the text or context that contribute to the appearance of incongruity in regard to 2.6–16.

First, there is an undeniably antithetical moment at the beginning of the paragraph.[506] The contrast is signalled by the conjunction δέ in 2.6, which, even if it is copulative,[507] is also adversative.[508] If δέ should not be translated 'but' in this case, it must at least be rendered 'yet'.[509] The object of the contrast is sought most naturally in the preceding paragraph (2.1–5), where Paul denies that his proclamation was in 'words of wisdom'.[510] After Paul has just said that 'wisdom' is none of his concern, the statement, 'Yet we do speak wisdom among the perfect' (σοφίαν δὲ λαλοῦμεν ἐν τοῖς τελείοις), produces the effect of a sharp antithesis.[511]

Second, the vocabulary employed in 2.6–16 is certainly unusual, even if it is not unique; unusual in nature, in concentration, and in application to the possibility of knowledge.[512] The source of the uncommon vocabulary of 2.6–16 has long been recognized: Paul derives the characteristic vocabulary

504. Wilckens, 'Zu 1. Kor 2,1–16', 501–504; Sellin, 'Das "Geheimnis" der Weisheit', 72–73; Lang, *Die Briefe an die Korinther*, 27–59; Stuhlmacher, 'The Hermeneutical Significance of 1 Cor. 2.6–16', 332–34.

505. E.g., Lindemann, *Der erste Korintherbrief*, 61: 'Die Auslegung muss zeigen, inwiefern der Text im einzelnen im Kontext der paulinischen Theologie verständlich gemacht werden kann.'

506. Conzelmann, *1 Corinthians*, 60: 'σοφίαν δὲ λαλοῦμεν κτλ., "Yet we do speak wisdom, etc.," sounds like an emphatic antithesis.'

507. Heinrici, *Der erste Brief*, 92: 'fortführend'; Lindemann, *Der erste Korintherbrief*, 61: 'reihend'.

508. C. Holsten, *Das Evangelium des Paulus*. Vol. 1. *Der Brief an die Gemeinden Galatiens und der erste Brief an die Gemeinde in Korinth* (Berlin: Reimer, 1880) ad loc.: 'gegensätzlich'; Weiss, *Der erste Korintherbrief*, 52–53; Conzelmann, *1 Corinthians*, 60. For δέ as adversative and copulative, see Smyth, *Greek Grammar*, 644. The contrast denoted by δέ in 2.6 is augmented by the strongly adversative conjunction ἀλλά at the beginning of 2.7.

509. With the NRSV and most commentaries, e.g., Conzelmann, *1 Corinthians*, 56, 60; Lindemann, *Der erste Korintherbrief*, 57: 'aber'. The mixed force of δέ, both adversative and copulative, is well captured by the KJV: 'howbeit'.

510. Conzelmann, *1 Corinthians*, 60.

511. Rightly, Weiss, *Der erste Korintherbrief*, 52. The qualifications that follow, in 2;6b and 2.7 (δὲ οὐ..., οὐδέ..., ἀλλά), distinguish the σοφία θεοῦ from the σοφία λόγου that earlier formed the basis of the antithesis (1.17).

512. Even those interpreters who understand 2.6–16 as the logical continuation of the argument begun in 1.18–2.5 acknowledge that the vocabulary of the former passage is uncommon (so Collins, *First Corinthians*, 124), and that there is 'a certain tension between the theological content and the linguistic means of expression' (so Lang, *Die Briefe an die Korinther*, 41).

of the passage from the sphere of the mystery religions.[513] The term τέλειος, used with emphasis at the beginning of the paragraph,[514] is a *terminus technicus* of the mystery religions, designating one who has been initiated into the mystic rites.[515] The term μυστήριον (2.7) is likewise a technical term of Greco-Roman religion applied mostly to the mysteries with their secret rites and secret teachings.[516] Other terms used by Paul in this passage may have been connected with the mystery religions – such as 'mind' (νοῦς), 'knowledge' (γνῶσις), and 'spirit' (πνεῦμα).[517] But the injunction to secrecy regarding the mysteries, and the resulting incompleteness of our knowledge, make it impossible to be sure. Philosophers and Hellenistic Jewish writers, such as Philo, also appropriated the language of the mysteries in order to describe the human search for the divine mind.[518] But there is no reason to conclude that Paul has drawn the terminology of 2.6–16 from these intermediate sources, rather than the mysteries themselves, with which he elsewhere reveals an acquaintance.[519] Indeed, the solemn, elevated

513. Bousset, *Der erste Brief an die Korinther*, 84; Reitzenstein, *Hellenistic Mystery-Religions*, 426–36; Bultmann, *Faith and Understanding*, 1.71–73; Wilckens, *Weisheit und Torheit*, 54–60; Conzelmann, *1 Corinthians*, 59–61.

514. Weiss, *Der erste Korintherbrief*, 52.

515. Bauer, *Greek-English Lexicon*, 995–96, s.v. τέλειος 3, citing *Corp. Herm.* 4.4; Philodemus Περὶ θεῶν 1.24.12 (ed. H. Diels in *Abhandlungen der Königlichen Akademie der Wissenschaften zu Berlin*, Philosophisch-historische Klasse [1915] p. 41; 93); Iamblichus *Myst.* 3.7 (p. 114 Parthey); Philo *Somn.* 2.234. Cf. Apuleius *Met.* 11.26, 29. For this understanding of the term τέλειος in 1 Cor. 2.6, see Heinrici, *Das erste Sendschreiben*, 40–41; Reitzenstein, *Hellenistic Mystery-Religions*, 432–34; Wilckens, *Weisheit und Torheit*, 53–60; Conzelmann, *1 Corinthians*, 60–61.

516. Herodotus 2.51.2; Diodorus Siculus 1.29.3; 3.63.2; Socratic Ep. 27.3; Cornutus 28, p. 56.22; 57.4; Alciphron 3.26.1; *OGIS* 331.54; 528.13; 721.2; numerous references in Dittenberger, *SIG*, see index; cf. G. Bornkamm, 'μυστήριον', *TDNT* 4 (1967) 803–808; Bauer, *Greek-English Lexicon*, 661–62.

517. R. Reitzenstein and H. Schäder (*Studien zum antiken Synkretismus aus Iran und Griechenland* [Leipzig: Teubner, 1926] 161–70), followed by Wilckens (*Weisheit und Torheit*, 54–58), call attention to *Corp. Herm.* 4.4, where the terms 'mind' (νοῦς) and 'knowledge' (γνῶσις) are used to characterize the 'perfect' (τέλειοι), and to the so-called 'Naasene Sermon' in Hippolytus *Ref.* 5.8.21, 26, where the 'perfect man' (τέλειος ἄνθρωπος) is said to comprehend 'the ineffable mysteries of the Spirit' (τὰ τοῦ πνεύματος ἄρρητα μυστήρια), arguing for the influence of the language of the mysteries on both texts.

518. For philosophers who take up this usage, see esp. Plato *Phdr.* 249A-250C; *Symp.* 210A-212C; cf. Bornkamm, 'μυστήριον', 808–809; for the Stoics and Plutarch, see the texts assembled and discussed by Weiss, *Der erste Korintherbrief*, 74; G. Delling, 'τέλειος', *TDNT* 8 (1972) 70; Hunt, *The Inspired Body*, 23–30. Especially important is the appropriation of the language of the mysteries by Philo *Somn.* 2.230–34; *Leg. All.* 3.100, 134, 159, 219; *Cher.* 42, 48–49; see the discussion in E. Bréhier, *Les idées philosophiques et religieuses de Philon d' Alexandrie* (Paris: Vrin, 1950) 242–49; Bornkamm, 'μυστήριον', 809; Delling, 'τέλειος', 70–72; Hunt, *The Inspired Body*, 39–50; Lindemann, *Der erste Korintherbrief*, 62.

519. E.g., 2 Cor. 3.18; see Reitzenstein, *Hellenistic Mystery-Religions*, 454–55; Windisch, *Der zweite Korintherbrief*, 129.

tone of the passage, combined with the esoteric vocabulary, suggest that Paul wished to create the impression that he is presenting a mystery teaching designed only for initiates.[520]

Lastly, the paragraph 2.6–16 is characterized by the use of the verb λαλεῖν ('to speak') in 2.6, 2.7, and 2.13 (retrospectively in 3.1).[521] This verb, which is not otherwise found in 1 Cor. 1–4, is used exclusively in 2.6–16 to describe the act of communication of divine wisdom. This observation has consequences for the form, content, and tone of the passage in question. As to form, the consistent use of λαλεῖν indicates that the 'hidden wisdom' is an oral discourse.[522] That is to say, in 2.6–16 Paul is giving an account of a speech of some kind, an oral performance. As to content, it is important to observe that the majority of the uses of λαλεῖν in Paul are in reference to a higher, pneumatic speech, whose content is variously described as 'revelation', 'knowledge', 'prophecy', 'teaching', and 'mysteries' (1 Cor. 12–14).[523] As to tone, an ambiguity attaches to the verb λαλεῖν that does not characterize the other terms used by Paul in 1 Cor. 1–4 to designate the act of communication (εὐαγγελίζεσθαι, κηρύσσειν, and καταγγέλλειν). Although λαλεῖν has a broad usage in later Greek, and is often merely synonymous with λέγειν, a negative connotation survives from older Greek, where the verb denotes 'informal communication ranging from engagement in small talk to chattering and babbling'.[524] Occasionally, this negative connotation is audible in Paul – as when he contemplates the possibility of speaking on merely human authority (1 Cor. 9.8), or when he recollects how he once spoke as a child (1 Cor. 13.11). The ambiguity of the verb λαλεῖν introduces the possibility that the tone of the presentation in 2.6–16 is ironic.[525]

The history of research into the difficult passage 2.6–16 indicates where progress is to be made in understanding Paul's argument, and which avenues of inquiry are no longer productive. The attempt to determine the specific provenance of the concepts found in 2.6–16, and from this to reconstruct the theology of Paul's Corinthian opponents, must be regarded

---

520. Bornkamm, 'μυστήριον', 819.

521. Theissen, *Psychological Aspects of Pauline Theology*, 347; Lindemann, *Der erste Korintherbrief*, 58.

522. Theissen (*Psychological Aspects of Pauline Theology*, 347–49) suggests that the formal category is either 'wisdom discourse' or 'knowledge discourse', making reference to 1 Cor. 12.8 and 14.6.

523. Of the total of 47 uses of λαλεῖν in Paul, 25 are in 1 Cor. 12–14, mostly in reference to pneumatic speech and glossolalia.

524. Bauer, *Greek-English Lexicon*, 582 s.v. λαλέω. See esp. *POxy* 413 ('Charition') 67.

525. On the possibility of irony in 2.6–16, see R. Funk, 'Word and Word in 1 Corinthians 2.6–16' in idem, *Language, Hermeneutic, and the Kingdom of God: The Problem of Language in the New Testament and Contemporary Theology* (New York: Harper & Row, 1966) 280, esp. 285 n. 42: 'The choice of λαλοῦμεν heightens the irony.'

as failed, because its outcome is inconclusive. The language Paul uses to describe his discourse of wisdom in 2.6–16 was widely distributed in antiquity and was not limited to a particular intellectual tradition.[526] Representatives of Jewish wisdom, apocalyptic writers, Philo, Plutarch, and others employ similar language to describe the human search for knowledge of the divine.[527] Not surprisingly, this language later appealed to Christian Gnostics.[528] The wide distribution of the language of 'mystery', and the amenability of this vocabulary to the purposes of different thinkers, frustrates every attempt to identify precisely the tradition from which Paul has derived the concepts in 2.6–16.[529]

Nor is the background of Paul's thought in 2.6–16 the point at issue, in the final analysis, but rather the function of this passage in his broader argument. Elements of continuity in the wording, content, and structure of 1.18–2.16 make it clear that 2.6–16 was not conceived as a 'digression' in any sense, but as the continuation of the previous line of argument under an antithetical aspect. Thus, attention must focus on the function of the difficult passage 2.6–16 in the context of Paul's argument for the divine reversal of wisdom and folly. Is there a way of understanding Paul's 'discourse of wisdom among the perfect' that resolves the appearance of contradiction with his previous statements about the folly of the word of the cross?

The hypothesis that is offered here focuses on the function of the wisdom discourse 2.6–16 in the context of Paul's assertion about a reversal of values, by locating Paul's argumentative strategy in the comic-philosophic tradition. It will be suggested that the missing link in understanding is to be found in an assumption that Paul shares with his audience regarding the appearance of the grotesque outsider, who claims to possess a wisdom more profound than that authorized by the elite. To the rich and the powerful, such a figure invariably appeared to be a charlatan, a quack.[530] In 2.6–16, Paul is presenting a parody of himself and his apostolic colleagues as mystagogues propounding hidden wisdom to

---

526. Rightly, Hunt, *The Inspired Body*, 10, 60–61.

527. Arguing for a derivation of Paul's vocabulary from Jewish wisdom traditions, Wilckens, 'Zu 1 Kor. 2,1–16,' 501–37; Theissen, *Psychological Aspects of Pauline Theology*, 353–67; emphasizing the apocalyptic background, Brown, *The Cross and Human Transformation*, 45–64; calling attention to Philo's usage, Pearson, *The Pneumatikos-Psychikos Terminology in 1 Corinthians*; Horsley, 'Pneumatikos vs. Psychikos', 269–88; pointing to similar vocabulary in Plutarch, Hunt, *The Inspired Body*, 23–30.

528. Illustrated in detail by Wilckens, *Weisheit und Torheit*, 53–145.

529. Interpreters concede the 'complexity' of the background of Paul's thought in 1 Cor. 2.6–16, positing a combination of Jewish wisdom traditions with Gnosticism (so Theissen, *Psychological Aspects of Pauline Theology*, 353–54), or a merger of Jewish-Hellenistic wisdom traditions with apocalyptic traditions (thus Lang, *Die Briefe an die Korinther*, 40–41).

530. On the figure of the charlatan, see Ribbeck, *Alazon*, esp. 10–18 on the various types of 'learned impostors', including those who pretend to proficiency in prophecy and philosophy.

initiates. The fact that Paul is engaged in self-parody in 2.6–16, a fact seldom recognized by interpreters,[531] does not negate the seriousness of the 'wisdom' that he speaks about the crucified Christ, a wisdom communicated here in 'jesting-earnest'.

Let us attempt to trace the course of this development in Paul's argument. Having asserted in the strongest possible terms that God has nullified the wisdom sought by the elite (1.18–25), Paul then expounds the consequences of the divine intervention for both the noble and the commoner: the wise and the strong have been put to shame, while the low and despised have been empowered with a paradoxical wisdom that comes from God – the message about Jesus Christ (1.26–31).[532] After such an implausibly radical assertion, one could well expect that there would be realistic objections: 'But little of this was apparent, when you came preaching among us!' This anticipated rejoinder is the basis for Paul's concession that, when he came to Corinth, he did not preach in 'lofty words of wisdom', but 'in weakness and in fear and in much trembling' (2.1–3). As we have argued above,[533] Paul adopts the persona of the 'befuddled orator' from the mime, in order to make clear that he does not reject, but rather accepts, the comparison with a comic type which his detractors have suggested. Yet, Paul wished to establish that, despite all of his stammering weakness, the message that he preached was actually the saving wisdom of God (1.30; 2.4–5). But how was Paul to make this clear, without compromising his understanding of the word of the cross, and without capitulating to the value system of the elite, by claiming to be a wise man who makes use of 'eloquent wisdom'? The course that Paul chooses is that of self-parody: Paul presents a caricature of himself as a mystagogue imparting secret wisdom to initiates.

The brilliance of this strategy is manifold. First, by mocking himself and his proclamation, Paul undermines the impression that he makes any claim to be a 'wise man', at least as a wise man is defined by the elite. Second, by relying on the principle that a parody always preserves the parodied,[534] Paul asserts the existence of a mysterious wisdom that is capable of transforming the lives of those who receive it, despite the ineptitude of the communicators. Third, by his consistent use of the first person plural pronoun in this passage,[535] Paul includes all of the apostles and

---

531.　The exception in the history of research is Georgi, *Theocracy in Paul's Praxis and Theology*, 54–56, who recognizes parodistic elements in 1.18–2.16 and refers to the mime.

532.　On the function of 1.26–31 in Paul's argument, see Weiss, *Der erste Korintherbrief*, 34.

533.　See above, ch. 4 on 2.1–5.

534.　B. A. Babcock, *The Reversible World: Symbolic Inversion in Art and Society* (Ithaca: Cornell University Press, 1978) 99.

535.　1 Cor. 2.7,10,12,16; cf. Weiss, *Der erste Korintherbrief*, 52; Lindemann, *Der erste Korintherbrief*, 59

missionaries of Christ, even the eloquent and learned Apollos, in the satire
that he directs at himself, so that their earnest pretensions to sapiential
authority are simultaneously burlesqued. Finally, the force of Paul's self-
parody rests upon the familiarity of the comic type of the 'false prophet' or
'vagabond philosopher', who was constantly ridiculed in the popular
theater.[536] Indeed, with his appropriation of this persona, Paul joins a
serio-comic tradition that includes Socrates, Menippus of Gadara, and
others,[537] and thus would have been well known to Paul's audience,
especially those who participated in learned culture.

The figure of the charlatan (ἀλαζών) was a constant subject of parody on
the comic stage.[538] Aristophanes provides a colorful list of characters
whom he reckons among the swarm of 'learned impostors' (ἀλαζόνες)
worthy of ridicule: 'sophists, prophets, practisers of medicine, lazy long-
haired fops with rings and natty nails, dithyrambic and choric twisters of
songs, astronomical speculators'.[539] Among the surviving titles and fragments of comedy and mime devoted to these types, caricatures of prophets,
philosophers, and quack-doctors predominate.[540] Aristotle explains why
this should be so: 'prophecy, philosophy, and medicine are the commonest
fields of pretence and imposture, because these arts have two qualities: they
are useful to people and can be counterfeited without detection'.[541]

Wandering prophets (μάντεις), soothsayers (χρησμολόγοι), sorcerers
(γόητες), and mendicant priests (ἀγύρται) were all regarded as charlatans.[542]
The early comic poet Aristoxenus asks: 'Who among men furnishes the
maximum imposture (ἀλαζονία)?' and answers, 'the prophets'
(οἱ μάντεις).[543] Aristophanes heaps scorn upon the type: 'Here's a fellow
coming this way, with laurel round his head. Who can he be? He looks an
arrant humbug (ἀλαζών). Some seer (μάντις), I think.'[544] A fragment of the

536. Ribbeck, _Alazon_, 10–11; W. Süss, _De personarum anitquae comoediae atticae usu atque origine_ (Ph.D. diss., University of Bonn, 1905) 28.
537. Ribbeck, _Alazon_, 11–12; Helm, _Lucian und Menipp_, 81–84.
538. The foundational study is that of Ribbeck, _Alazon_, esp. 10–18; see also Süss, _De personarum antiquae comoediae_, 10–28; F. Cornford, _The Origin of Attic Comedy_ (Gloucester, MA: Peter Smith, 1968), 136–40.
539. Aristophanes _Nubes_ 331–33: πλείστους αὗται βόσκουσι σοοστάς, θουριομάντεις, ἰατροτέχνας, σφραγιδονυχαργοκομήτας, κυκλίων τε χορῶν ᾀσματοκάμπτας, ἄνδρας μετεωροφένακας.
540. Ribbeck, _Alazon_, 10.
541. The citation in context: Aristotle _Eth. Nic._ 4.7.13: οἱ μὲν οὖν δόξης χάριν ἀλαζονευόμενοι τὰ τοιαῦτα προσποιοῦνται ἐφ' οἷς ἔπαινος ἢ εὐδαιμονισμός, οἱ δὲ κέρδους ὧν καὶ ἀπόλαυσίς ἐστι τοῖς πέλας καὶ διαλαθεῖν ἔστι μὴ ὄντα, οἷον μάντιν σοφὸν ἰατρόν. διὰ τοῦτο οἱ πλεῖστοι προσποιοῦνται τὰ τοιαῦτα καὶ ἀλαζονεύονται· ἔστι γὰρ ἐν αὐτοῖς τὰ εἰρημένα.
542. Ribbeck, _Alazon_, 14; W. Burkert, 'ΓΟΗΣ. Zum griechischen "Schamanismus",' _Rheinisches Museum_ 102 (1962) esp. 38, 50–54.
543. Aristoxenus of Selinus _Hephaistion_ 8; citation in Ribbeck, _Alazon_, 14.
544. Aristophanes _Pax_ 1043–45; see also _Pax_ 1069, 1120–23; _Aves_ 983–85.

Ψεύδομαντις ('False-Prophet') by the comic poet Anaxandrides portrays the protagonist proudly defending his character: 'That I am an impostor (ἀλαζών), you find fault with this. But why? For this art conquers all the others completely, after flattery. Hence it is distinguished.'[545] Authors of Middle and New Comedy made the 'false prophet' an object of ridicule, as indicated by the titles of their plays: thus, the Μάντεις of Alexis, the ᾽Αγύρτης of Philemon, and the ῾Ιέρεια and the Μηναγύρτης of Menander.[546] In a surviving fragment of Menander's Θεοφορουμένη ('The Demoniac Girl'), two gentlemen propose to test whether a girl is really possessed by a god, or is only 'pretending' to be so.[547] Burlesque of soothsayers and diviners was popular fare on the Roman stage, as well: to Afranius, Pomponius, and Laberius are each attributed plays with the title *Augur*.[548] In a fragment of the *Augur* of Afranius (whose plays were performed even in imperial times), we hear of the prophetic 'trance' (*rabies*) of the soothsayer.[549]

Philosophers were also suspected of being charlatans, and were frequently presented in this guise in comedy and mime.[550] A quack-philosopher already appears in one of the mimes of Epicharmus,[551] 'using subtleties of argument to justify himself in playing tricks on his neighbors'.[552] Aristophanes portrays Socrates in the *Clouds* as a quack who engages in meteorological speculation and dispenses mysterious doctrines.[553] Pheidippides defines the characteristics of philosophers by reference to Socrates and his disciples: 'Faugh! These rogues, I know them. Those rank impostors (ἀλαζόνες), those palefaced, barefoot vagabonds you

---

545. Cited from Ribbeck, *Alazon*, 15: ὅτι εἴμ᾽ ἀλαζών, τοῦτ᾽ ἐπιτιμᾷς· ἀλλὰ τί; νικᾷ γὰρ αὕτη τὰς τέχνας πάσας πολὺ μετὰ τὴν κολακείαν. ἥδε μὲν γὰρ διαφέρει.

546. Ribbeck, *Alazon*, 15.

547. Menander Θεοφορουμένη 22–25; text cited according to the new edition of W. G. Arnott, *Menander*, Vol. 2, LCL (Cambridge, MA: Harvard University Press, 1996) 62–63. In what is probably a reference to the demoniac girl at line 12, the text reads ἀλαζονεύεται ('she's a humbug'), according to Arnott, pp. 60–61.

548. For the titles and fragments, see O. Ribbeck, *Comicorum Romanorum Fragmenta*, 164, 225; Bonaria, *Mimorum Romanorum Fragmenta*, 18–19.

549. Afranius fr. 1 in Ribbeck, *Comicorum Romanorum Fragmenta*, 164.

550. Ribbeck, *Alazon*, 10–13.

551. The fragment is best consulted in H. Diels, *Die Fragmente der Vorsokratiker*, 113–14.

552. Pickard-Cambridge, *Dithyramb, Tragedy and Comedy*, 376.

553. See the account of the components that make up Aristophanes' portrait of Socrates by Gigon, *Sokrates*, 19: 'des abstruss gelehrten Meteorologen, des unverschämten Hungerleiders und der zynischen Aufklärers in seiner Sokratesfigur zu einer widerspruchsvoll lebendigen Einheit verschmolzen...' On Socrates in the *Clouds* as the embodiment of the type of the ἀλαζών, see Reich, *Der Mimus*, 42, 66, 354–56. Cf. Betz, *Der Apostel Paulus und die sokratische Tradition*, 34.

mean: that Socrates, poor wretch, and Chaerephon.'[554] Xenophon felt it
necessary to defend Socrates against the charge of ἀλαζονεία, especially
because Socrates claimed to possess a 'divine sign', and relied upon it for
the advice he gave his disciples. Yet in the course of his defense, Xenophon
reflects the infamy which men of his class associated with the figure of the
ἀλαζών: 'Who would not admit that he wished to appear neither a fool
(ἠλίθιος) nor an impostor (ἀλαζών) to his companions? But he [Socrates]
would have been thought both, had he proved to be mistaken when he
alleged that his counsel was in accordance with divine revelation.'[555]

The surviving titles of Greek comedy of all periods reveal the popularity
of the quack-philosopher as a subject of caricature. Both Cratinus and
Eubulus composed plays with the title Πανόπται ('The All-Seeing Ones')
ridiculing philosophers.[556] The Σοφισταί of Plato Comicus probably
lampooned philosophical innovators.[557] Alexis' Πυθαγορίζουσα made light
of the followers of Pythagoras;[558] (the plays of Alexis remained popular
down to Roman times, and were adapted by Roman comedians).[559] The
Φιλόσοφοι of Philemon was doubtless also a parody.[560] Eupolis' Κόλακες
('Flatterers') ridiculed Callias, son of Hipponicus, for seeking out the
company of sophists.[561] In a fragment of this work, a sturdy steward
complains of Protagoras' behavior as a guest: 'The rogue pretends to know
(ἀλαζονεύεται) all about things in the heavens, but whatever is dished up
from the earth, he eats!'[562] Roman writers also delighted in the ridicule of
philosophers. Several fragments of the mimes of Laberius take the
philosophers as a subject for satire: one fragment mentions Democritus,
while others make scoffing reference to the Cynics and Pythagoreans.[563]

---

554. Aristophanes *Nubes* 102–103. The scholiast adds the explanation: 'Charlatans
(ἀλαζόνας): properly they are called liars; but he reasonably calls the philosophers impostors
since they profess to speak about what they do not understand'; cited in Ribbeck, *Alazon*, 11
n.1. See also the scholion on *Nubes* 363, where the chorus ironically praises Socrates, 'for you
hold your head high, haughtily, and cast your eyes sideways as you go', the scholiast observes:
'It is characteristic of the boastful impostors (ἀλαζόνες) not to have their gaze fixed on the
same object, but to move their eyes up and down, and to shift their gaze now hither, now
thither'; cited in Ribbeck, *Alazon*, 12 n.3.
555. Xenophon *Mem.* 1.1.5; see the analysis of this passage in O. Gigon, *Kommentar zum
ersten Buch von Xenophons Memorabilien* (Basel: F. Reinhardt, 1953) 6–9.
556. *Comicorum Atticorum Fragmenta*, ed. T. Kock (Berlin: Teubner, 1888) 1.11; 2.164; cf.
Ribbeck, *Alazon*, 11.
557. Kock, *Comicorum Atticorum Fragmenta*, 1.601f.
558. Kock, *Comicorum Atticorum Fragmenta*, 2.297f.; cf. Ribbeck, *Alazon*, 11.
559. Aulus Gellius *Noct. Att.* 2.23.1.
560. Kock, *Comicorum Atticorum Fragmenta*, 2.478ff.; Ribbeck, *Alazon*, 11.
561. Kock, *Comicorum Atticorum Fragmenta*, 2.258.
562. Frag. 146b in Kock, *Comicorum Atticorum Fragmenta*, 1.258; cf. Ribbeck, *Alazon*, 11.
563. Frags. 89, 48, 27 in Bonaria, *Mimorum Romanorum Fragmenta*, 62, 35, 23; cf. Beare,
The Roman Stage, 156–57.

A composite portrait of the philosopher as charlatan may be derived from the pages of Lucian, who repeatedly holds the philosophers up to ridicule.[564] The learned impostor is characterized by a gloomy seriousness, pallid countenence, long beard, and raised eyebrows.[565] His bearing is as haughty and self-important as if he had swallowed a spear.[566] His gaze is constantly roving from the heavens to the earth.[567] He claims to know the mysteries of the cosmos – the boundaries of heaven, the circumference of the sun, the distance from the sun to the moon, and the depth of the sea.[568] Lucian is determined to show these philosophers up as impostors: behind the appearance of the sage hides ignorance, delusion, and quarrelsomeness.[569]

Within the tradition that lampoons the prophets and philosophers, the turn to self-parody seems to have occurred in the person of the ironic Socrates.[570] As we have seen, Socrates repeatedly makes his own pursuit of wisdom the object of parody, acknowledging that his aporetic arguments make him appear to be a fool and an impostor.[571] In Plato's *Symposium*, Socrates seeks to initiate his companions into the worship of the god of love.[572] But telling the truth about Love in the Socratic manner evidently involves self-parody: not only does Socrates acknowledge that he may appear to be a 'fool' (καταγέλαστος) in his discourse on this lofty subject,[573] he casts himself in the role of the tardy student of a woman![574] In a highly creative adaptation of the conventional parody of the prophetic type, Plato portrays Socrates as an 'initiate' seeking revelation of the mysteries of Love from a Mantinean prophetess named

564. Ribbeck, *Alazon*, 12; Branham, *Unruly Eloquence*, 25.

565. Lucian *Dial. mort.* 10; *Pisc.* 44; *Somn.* 4; *Dial. Meretr.* 10; *Fug.* 7.

566. Lucian *Dial. mort.* 1, 2; cf. Epictetus *Diss.* 1.21.

567. Lucian *Somn.* 4. See the scholion on Aristophanes *Nubes* 363.

568. Lucian *Icaromen.* 6.

569. Lucian *Icaromen.* 6; *Bis acc.* 11; *Herm.* 12. On Lucian's disparaging of hypocritical philosophers, see M.-O. Goulet-Cazé, 'Le cynisme à l'époque impériale', *ANRW* 2.36.4 (1990) 2763–68.

570. On Socrates as the model for the self-parodic satirists of the later period (Menippus, Varro, Horace), see W. S. Anderson *Essays on Roman Satire* (Princeton: Princeton University Press, 1982) 29; Relihan, *Ancient Menippean Satire*, 43, 103, 180; Freudenburg, *The Walking Muse*, 9, 12, 21, 27.

571. E.g., Plato *Euthyd.* 278D, 279C, 291B-292E, 293A; *Gorgias* 490C-494E; *Symp.* 177D. Cf. Edelstein, *Xenophontisches und platonisches Bild des Sokrates*, 138–50; T. C. Brickhouse and N. D. Smith, 'The Paradox of Socrates' Ignorance' in *Plato's Socrates* (Oxford: Oxford University Press, 1994) 30–38.

572. See esp. the summation of the purpose of Socrates' speech in *Symp.* 212B, with the observations of K. Dover, *Plato. Symposium* (Cambridge: Cambridge University Press, 1980), 159.

573. Plato *Symp.* 198D, 199B.

574. See the discussion of this aspect by Nightingale, *Genres in Dialogue*, 128.

Diotima.[575] Throughout the passage, Plato employs the language of the
mystery-cults (μύειν, τέλεα, ἐποπτικά, κτλ.).[576] Diotima adopts the author-
itative tone of the mystagogue, giving assurances that the ineffable vision is
attainable, and raising the hopes of the candidate for initiation.[577] Socrates
struggles fervently to comprehend, and repeatedly expresses his amaze-
ment.[578] The self-parody is excruciating:[579] the Mantinean woman interrogates Socrates as he usually interrogates others,[580] condescending to him
and playing with him ironically.[581] At one point, Diotima insists that the
answer to Socrates' question 'would be clear even to a schoolboy'.[582] Socrates
is repeatedly forced to admit his ignorance and need of instruction.[583] She
chafes at his lack of understanding.[584] Faced with such a formidable mentor,
Socrates 'marvels'.[585] Worst of all, Diotima expresses doubt in Socrates'
ability to attain the vision of the higher mysteries.[586] By means of self-parody
and role-reversal, Socrates affirms the existence of a divine wisdom, at the
same time that he undermines the claims of the philosophers to possess it.

The most influential portrait of a prophetic charlatan in antiquity
was that of the Cynic satirist Menippus of Gadara (third century
B.C.)[587] In the *Necyia*, Menippus presented himself as a man who

---

575. At *Symp.* 201D Diotima is described as 'a woman who was deeply versed in many
fields of knowledge. It was she who brought about a ten years' postponement of the great
plague of Athens on the occasion of a certain sacrifice, and it was she who taught me the
philosophy of Love.' See the observations of Dover, *Plato. Symposium*, 137: 'If Plato invented
Diotima, he may have made her Mantinean because of the resemblance of the place-name to
μάντις "seer" and its cognates; "Diotima" could be analysed as "honoured by Zeus" or as
"honouring Zeus". Female religious experts were not unknown; Aeschines' mother (according
to Demosthenes 18.259f., a hilarious caricature) offered initiation into a minor mystery-cult.
It may be that cults of this kind were numerous, and normally in the hands of women.'

576. Esp. in *Symp.* 209E-210A: 'Well now, my dear Socrates, I have no doubt that even
you might be initiated (μυηθείης) into these, the more elementary mysteries of Love. But I
don't know whether you could apprehend the final revelation (τὰ τέλεα καὶ ἐποπτικά)'; see also
Symp. 210E. Cf. the comments of Dover, *Plato. Symposium*, 155: 'μύειν is "initiate", ἐπόπται
are those admitted to the final secrets of a mystery-cult (e.g. the Eleusinian mysteries).' Cf. C.
Riedweg, *Mysterienterminologie bei Platon* (Berlin: de Gruyter, 1987) 2–21.

577. *Symp.* 208C, 209E-212A. Cf. Dover, *Plato. Symposium*, 159.

578. *Symp.* 206B, 206C, 207C.

579. Lowenstam, 'Paradoxes in Plato's *Symposium*', 85–104, esp. 96–97.

580. *Symp.* 201E.

581. *Symp.* 202B.

582. *Symp.* 204B.

583. *Symp.* 206B, 207C.

584. *Symp.* 207C.

585. *Symp.* 208B.

586. *Symp.* 209E-210A.

587. Little is known of the historical Menippus. Diogenes Laertius' *Life of Menippus*
(6.99–101) is hostile and anecdotal. The report that Menippus was a slave at Sinope may
reflect assimilation to the life of Diogenes the Cynic. His works include *Necyia, Testaments,*

visited the underworld and came back as the prophet of a paradoxical truth – that 'the life of the common sort is best'.[588] In keeping with the Socratic precedent,[589] Menippus' self-portrayal was clearly self-parodic.[590] An important testimonium in the *Suda* describes Menippus' appearance:

> Menippus the Cynic went so far in his hocus-pocus that he took on the appearance of a Fury and said that he had come from Hades as an observer of sins and would go back down again to report to the divinities there. This was his attire: a gray, ankle-length cloak with a purple belt around it; an Arcadian cap with the twelve signs of the Zodiac woven into it on his head; tragic boots; an immense beard; and an ashen staff in his hand.[591]

Whatever the value of this report may be for knowledge of the historical Menippus, it is clear that the tradition identified the character portrayed in the *Necyia* as the embodiment of the prophetic charlatan.[592] In Menippus' *Necyia*, the answer to the most urgent question – 'What is the best kind of

---

Letters imagined to be from the gods' presence, the *Sale of Diogenes*, and a *Symposium*, among others. For discussion of the external evidence regarding Menippus, see Helm, *Lucian und Menipp*; J. Hall, *Lucian's Satire* (New York: Harper, 1981) 74–79. Lucian's description of Menippus' physical appearance and deportment in *Dial. Mort.* 1.2 recalls the fool in the mime: 'An old man, bald, with a decrepit cloak full of windows and open to every wind, a motley of flapping rags, always laughing and generally mocking those hypocritical philosophers' (Γέρων, φαλακρός, τριβώνιον ἔχων πολύθυρον, ἅπαντι ἀνέμῳ ἀναπεπταμένον καὶ ταῖς ἐπιπτυχαῖς τῶν ῥακίων ποικίλον, γελᾷ δ' ἀεὶ καὶ τὰ πολλὰ τοὺς ἀλαζόνας τούτους φιλοσόφους ἐπισκώπτει). For discussion of this passage, see J. Relihan, 'Old Comedy, Menippean Satire, and Philosophy's Tattered Robes', *Illinois Classical Studies* 15 (1990) 188.

588.   For reconstruction of Menippus' *Necyia*, see Relihan, *Ancient Menippean Satire*, 45–47. The quotation forms the climax of Lucian's *Menippus, or Necyomantia* 21, based upon Menippus' influential work.

589.   On the Platonic Socrates as a model for Menippus' literary personality, see Relihan, *Ancient Menippean Satire*, 43, 103, 109, 180. The subtexts of Menippus' *Necyia* are diverse, and include the *Odyssey*, bks. 9–12, Old Comedy (esp. Aristophanes), Platonic myth (esp. the myth of Er in the *Republic*), and the mime; see Reich, *Der Mimus*, 388–91; Branham, *Unruly Eloquence*, 17, 46–57; Relihan, *Ancient Menippean Satire*, 30–36.

590.   On the self-parodic quality of Menippean satire generally, and of the *Necyia* in particular, see Relihan, *Ancient Menippean Satire*, 18–20, 23, 41–42, 45–48.

591.   *Suda* s.v. φαιός; cited and discussed in Relihan, *Ancient Menippean Satire*, 45. Diogenes Laertius (6.102) attributes this costume to Menedemus, in the life that immediately follows that of Menippus. For analysis of this attribution, see J. Relihan, 'Vainglorious Menippus in Lucian's *Dialogues of the Dead*', *Illinois Classical Studies* 12 (1987) 194–95.

592.   For this picture of Menippus in the tradition, see Varro's Ταφὴ Μενίππου (F 539), which speaks of Menippus as 'an underworld lurker-in-the-shadows, an evil spirit, and let him keep people anxious, for they have worse fear of him than the fuller does of the owl'; cited in Relihan, *Ancient Menippean Satire*, 45–46, 233 n.40. A similar portrait of Menippus is found in Lucian's *Nec.* and *Dial. Mort.*; see the discussion in Branham, *Unruly Eloquence*, 15–17, 20–

life for human beings?' – is invested in a character who invites disbelief and cannot be taken seriously.

Unfortunately, Menippus' *Necyia* is lost.[593] But the influence of the work is so great that it is not difficult to form an impression of Menippus' character.[594] Moreover, it is generally acknowledged that Lucian's *Necyomantia* is based upon the lost work of Menippus.[595] Without entering into the debate over the extent to which Lucian has revised the *Necyia* for his own purposes,[596] we may assume that Lucian's Menippus is a recasting of the persona established by Menippus himself.[597] Indeed, the title of Lucian's work in its full form – Μένιππος ἢ Νεκυομαντεία ('Menippus, or Divination of the Dead') – suggests both dependence upon the Cynic satirist and fascination with the figure of the prophet as impostor.[598]

At the beginning of Lucian's *Necyomantia*, Menippus has just returned from the underworld in outlandish garb and spouting poetry: he wears

25; J. Relihan, 'Menippus in Antiquity' in *The Cynics: The Cynic Movement in Antiquity and Its Legacy*, ed. R. Bracht Branham and M.-O. Goulet-Cazé (Berkeley: University of California Press, 1996) 275.

593.   Indeed, all of the writings of Menippus are lost. A few fragments are preserved as quotations in later writers: Diogenes Laertius (6.29) cites Menippus' *Sale of Diogenes*; Athenaeus *Deip.* 629e, 664e, 32e quotes from Menippus' *Symposium* and *Arcesilaus*, and a hexameter line of an unassigned fragment. See the analysis in Relihan, *Ancient Menippean Satire*, 40.

594.   Not only Varro's Ταφὴ Μενίππου, mentioned above (n. 592), but also Seneca's *Apocolocyntosis* and Petronius' *Satyricon* are influenced by Menippus' *Necyia*. See K. Mras, 'Varros menippeische Satiren und die Philosophie', *Neues Jahrbuch für Philologie* 33 (1914) 390–420; E. Woytek, 'Varro' in *Die römische Satire*, ed. J. Adamietz (Darmstadt: Wissenschaftliche Buchgesellschaft, 1986) 311–55; M. D. Reeve, 'Apotheosis... per saturam', *CP* 79 (1984) 305–307; H. K. Riikonen, *Menippean Satire as a Literary Genre with Special Reference to Seneca's* Apocolocyntosis (Helsinki: Societas Scientiarum Fennica, 1987); J. Adamietz, 'Zum literarischen Charakter von Petrons *Satyrica*', *Rheinisches Museum* 130 (1987) 329–46; Relihan, *Ancient Menippean Satire*, 49–99. See also the fragment of Laberius' mime *Nekyomantia* in Ribbeck, *Comicorum Romanorum Fragmenta*, frag. 17.

595.   On this point in general, with bibliographic orientation, see W. H. Tackaberry, *Lucian's Relation to Plato and the Post-Aristotelian Philosophers* (Toronto: University of Toronto, 1930) 8–40; G. Anderson, *Lucian, Theme and Variation in the Second Sophistic* (Leiden: Brill, 1976) 139–40; Branham, *Unruly Eloquence*, 14–16; Relihan, *Ancient Menippean Satire*, 104–14, esp. the judgment, 104: 'The *Necyomantia* is commonly regarded as bearing the closest relation of any of Lucian's works to a work of Menippus.'

596.   The most detailed attempt to reconstruct Menippus out of Lucian is that of Helm, *Lucian und Menipp*, esp. 15–18; but see the critique of McCarthy, 'Lucian and Menippus', 3–55. For a survey of the debate on the debt owed to Menippus by Lucian and others, see Hall, *Lucian's Satire*, 64–150.

597.   This is the 'middle way' between extreme views of the relation between Lucian and Menippus proposed by Relihan, *Ancient Menippean Satire*, 39, 104, 228 n. 2.

598.   Relihan, *Ancient Menippean Satire*, 104. Νεκυομαντεία is also the title of the eleventh book of the *Odyssey*.

Odysseus' hat and Heracles' lion skin, carries Orpheus' lyre,[599] and speaks
in tags of Euripidean verse.[600] Menippus explains that his strange dress is a
disguise intended to make him look like others who have passed alive
through Hades, and that he speaks in verse as a consequence of having
recently associated with the shades of Homer and Euripides.[601] But
Menippus' costume and speech also serve to establish his persona on a
number of levels. The absurd attire recalls the dress attributed to
Menippus (by the *Suda*),[602] while the bits of poetry refer to the mixture
of verse and prose that define the style of Menippean satire.[603] At the same
time, Menippus' ludicrous appearance carries on the motif of self-parody
from the *Necyia*: Lucian mocks the mocker, suggesting that this comical
critic is not to be taken seriously.[604] Finally, Menippus' flamboyant
entrance evokes the theatrical context.[605] Lucian repeatedly emphasizes this
aspect: the interlocutor enjoins Menippus 'stop your play-acting';[606]
Menippus explains that his costume allowed him to pass through Hades
unimpeded 'as they do in the plays',[607] a reference to the many comedies
and mimes with this motif.[608] In this way, Lucian connects his dialogue
with the stage-world, where the false prophet was a fixture.

Lucian presents the account of what Menippus saw and heard in Hades
as an initiation into the mysteries. Lucian achieves this effect by the way in
which the account is introduced, and by the vocabulary employed in the
dialogical passages. Thus, Menippus is cast in the role of initiator, while
his interlocutor plays the part of initiate. Learning of Menippus' journey to
the underworld, a friend demands to know whether he heard anything that
would affect his life in the world above. Menippus replies: 'Yes, by Zeus, a
great deal; but it is not right to divulge these things to everyone nor make
known the secrets (τὰ ἀπόρρητα). Someone might indict me for impiety in
the court of Rhadamanthus.'[609] The interlocutor begs to hear the account,
appealing to friendship and his own initiation into the mysteries: 'In
Heaven's name, don't withhold your words from a friend! You will be

---

599.   Lucian *Nec.* 1: τὸ ἀλλόκοτον τοῦ σχήματος, πῖλος καὶ λύρα καὶ λεοντῆ.

600.   Euripides *Hecules Furens* 523–24; *Hecuba* 1; and two citations from lost plays of
Euripides, perhaps the *Peirithous* and the *Andromeda*. Cf. Branham, *Unruly Eloquence*, 20–21.

601.   Lucian *Nec.* 1, 8.

602.   Relihan, *Ancient Menippean Satire*, 105.

603.   On the mixture of prose and verse in Menippean satire, see Quintilian 10.1.95. For
discussion of the issue, see J. Wright Duff, *Roman Satire* (Berkeley: University of California
Press, 1937) ch. 5; Relihan, *Ancient Menippean Satire*, 12–13, 17–21.

604.   Relihan, *Ancient Menippean Satire*, 105.

605.   Branham, *Unruly Eloquence*, 20–21.

606.   Lucian *Nec.* 1.

607.   Lucian *Nec.* 8.

608.   E.g., Aristophanes *Ranae*, and Laberius *Necyomantia*.

609.   Lucian *Nec.* 2.

telling a man who knows to keep silent, and who, moreover, has been initiated into the mysteries (πρὸς μεμυημένον).'[610] In the dialogue that follows, Lucian prolongs the conceit of mystagogic instruction by means of the vocabulary employed in question and answer. For example, when the friend requests an explanation of a puzzling feature of the narrative, Menippus responds: 'Why, that, at any rate, is obvious and not at all shrouded in mystery (ἀπόρρητον).'[611]

In the first part of his discourse, Menippus relates the reason for his journey to Hades.[612] Menippus explains that his adolescent mind was troubled by the contradictions in Greek culture: the poets praised the gods for behavior which was forbidden by the laws.[613] So Menippus decided to go to the philosophers and ask them to show him the right path in life. But the philosophers' disagreements and inconsistencies soon convinced him that the ordinary person's way of life is best – indeed as good as gold.[614] This conclusion, however, was disappointing, for Menippus still felt 'foolish' (ἀνόητος). It was little consolation that in his ignorance he had the company of 'many wise men (σοφοί), widely renowned for intelligence'.[615] In his perplexity, Menippus resolved to go to Babylon and find a Zoroastrian mage who knew the incantations and rites for guiding one safely to the underworld.[616] There he planned to consult with Teiresias, the 'prophet and sage' (μάντις καὶ σοφός), about 'what is the best life'.[617]

The ritual preparations for the descent to the underworld are described by Menippus in great detail.[618] Ablutions, incantations, midnight consecrations with torches, blood sacrifices – all reflect the practice of ancient magic.[619] According to Plutarch, magical incantations formed part of the rites of initiation.[620] The burlesque of magical ceremonies was a popular subject in the mime. A fragment of a mime of Sophron portrays a

610.   Lucian *Nec.* 2.
611.   Lucian *Nec.* 8.
612.   At *Nec.* 2, Lucian divides Menippus' discourse into two parts: first, the purpose of the journey and the guide; then, what he saw and heard there. This division corresponds to the two stages of the mystagogic speech: the elementary mysteries and the final revelation; cf. Plato *Symp.* 209E-210A.
613.   Lucian *Nec.* 3.
614.   Lucian *Nec.* 4: ὥστε μοι τάχιστα χρυσσοῦν ἀπέδειξαν οὗτοι τὸν τῶν ἰδιωτῶν τοῦτον βίον.
615.   Lucian *Nec.* 6.
616.   Lucian *Nec.* 6.
617.   Lucian *Nec.* 6: τίς ἐστιν ὁ ἄριστος βίος.
618.   Lucian *Nec.* 7–10.
619.   For discussion of the magic ritual in *Nec.* 7–10, see esp. Helm, *Lucian und Menipp*, 15–19.
620.   Plutarch *De Superst.* 12.

sorceress and her assistant performing an occult ceremony.[621] This mime, or one with a similar theme, is depicted on a stucco relief from the Underground Basilica of the Porta Maggiore in Rome (Fig. 18).[622] The fresco, dated to the first half of the first century A.D.,[623] shows a woman in the center uttering incantations over a three-legged table on which repose several objects, among them a cup and a wand.[624] The sorceress is flanked by two figures wearing pointed hats and loin cloths, evidently mimic fools.[625] Thus, the magic rituals in Lucian's *Necyomantia* serve to remind his readers of familiar caricatures in the theater. At the same time, the elaborate preparations for the journey contribute to the parody of the quest for knowledge.[626] Of special interest is the emphasis Lucian places upon the speech of the magus, which is repeatedly characterized as 'murmuring', 'indistinct', and 'meaningless'. After the morning ablutions, Menippus reports, the σοφός 'would make a long address which I could not follow very well, for like an incompetent announcer at the games, he spoke rapidly and indistinctly'.[627] At the midnight consecrations, he 'murmured the incantation in an undertone'.[628] During the invocation of the spirits, 'he intermingled a number of foreign-sounding, meaningless words of many syllables'.[629]

What Menippus sees in the underworld is the ultimate reversal of status and values which, as we have seen, is consistently preached by the comic-philosophic tradition.[630] Before the throne of Minos, people of wealth and power are arraigned for their evil deeds, prosecuted by the most implacable of witnesses – their own shadows![631] The worst malefactors are found to be 'those puffed up with wealth and power' (οἱ ἐπὶ πλούτοις τε καὶ ἀρχαῖς τετυφωμένοι). Minos feels a special resentment toward their 'ephemeral imposture (ὀλιγοχρόνιος ἀλαζονεία) and arrogance, their failure to

---

621. Text and translation in Page, *Select Papyri* III, 328–31. Theocritus adapted Sophron's mime in his second idyll, 'The Spell', according to the scholiast on *Idyll* 2.69.

622. On the basilica and its frescos in general, see E. S. Strong, *Art in Ancient Rome* (London: Heinemann, 1929) 167–71. Fig. 18 is reproduced from Goldman, 'Two Terracotta Figurines from Tarsus', 31.

623. For the date, see E. S. Strong, 'Stuccoes of the Underground Basilica near the Porta Maggiore', *JHS* 44 (1924) 65–68.

624. Strong, 'Stuccoes of the Underground Basilica', 85.

625. Goldman, 'Two Terracotta Figurines from Tarsus', 30, 32.

626. Branham, *Unruly Eloquence*, 22.

627. Lucian *Nec.* 7: ῥῆσίν τινα μακρὰν ἐπιλέγων ἧς οὐ σφόδρα κατήκουον· ὥσπερ γὰρ οἱ φαῦλοι τῶν ἐν τοῖς ἀγῶσιν κηρύκων ἐπιτροχόν τι καὶ ἀσαφὲς ἐφθέγγετο.

628. Lucian *Nec.* 7: ἅμα καὶ τὴν ἐπῳδὴν ἐκείνην ὑποτονθορύσας.

629. Lucian *Nec.* 9: παραμιγνὺς ἅμα βαρβαρικά τινα καὶ ἄσημα ὀνόματα καὶ πολυσύλλαβα.

630. Branham, *Unruly Eloquence*, 23: 'First, he finds that justice in the underworld pursues a comic logic of role reversal and ego deflation.'

631. Lucian *Nec.* 11.

remember that they were mortal'.[632] 'So they were stripped of their short-lived splendor – I mean their wealth, birth, and power (πλούτους λέγω καὶ γένη καὶ δυναστείας) – and stood there naked, with hanging heads, reviewing, point by point, their happy life among us as if it had been a dream.'[633]

Lucian's critique of human vain-glory climaxes in a theatrical simile.[634] The stage metaphor, one of Lucian's favorite devices,[635] seems particularly well-suited to the *Necyomantia*, considering Menippus' penchant for self-dramatization, and the theatrical associations of many motifs.[636] The theatrical metaphor furnishes the most poignant moment in the work, because it successfully implicates the audience in the pageant of human folly.[637]

> When I saw these things, it seemed to me that human life is like a great pageant, choreographed and directed by Chance, who has distributed to the performers various and many-colored costumes. Taking one person, by chance, she attires him royally, placing a tiara upon his head, bodyguards by his side, and encircling his brow with the diadem; but upon another she puts the costume of a slave. One she makes up beautiful, but renders another ugly and laughable. I suppose the show (θέα) must have variety... For a brief span she lets each use his costume, but when the time of the pageant is over, each player gives back his props and lays aside his costume along with his body, becoming what he was before his birth, no different from his neighbor.[638]

Some of the actors in the play, through ignorance of their true condition, become angry and indignant when Chance demands the return of her trappings, erroneously believing that they are being robbed of their own property, instead of giving back what they had only borrowed for a time.[639] Thus the fundamental delusion is revealed to be the belief that wealth, birth and power constitute identity. The costumes and properties seduce the mortal players into believing in the reality of their roles; 'but Chance, like a cosmic ironist, sooner or later unmasks time's fools, leaving them like actors out of work, "sans everything".'[640] Menippus reflects: 'I suppose you have often seen these stage-folk who act in tragedies, and according to the demands of the plays become at one moment Creons, and again Priams

632. Lucian *Nec.* 12.
633. Lucian *Nec.* 12.
634. Lucian *Nec.* 16.
635. Kokolakis, *The Dramatic Simile of Life*, 44.
636. Relihan, *Ancient Menippean Satire*, 109–10.
637. Branham, *Unruly Eloquence*, 23–24.
638. Lucian *Nec.* 16; the translation adapts Harmon, *Lucian* IV, 99.
639. Lucian *Nec.* 16.
640. Branham, *Unruly Eloquence*, 24.

Figure 18.   Stucco relief from the Underground Basilica of Porta Maggiore, Rome. First century A.D.

and Agamemnons...And when at length the play comes to an end, each of them strips off his gold-bespangled robe, lays aside his mask, steps out of his buskins, and goes about in poverty and humility...That is what human affairs are like, or so it seemed to me as I looked.'[641]

Menippus' account of what he saw in the underworld is interrupted by the interlocutor, who reminds him of his promise to report the decree of the council of Hades.[642] Menippus relates that an assembly of the dead was convoked, and a motion was passed to punish the rich who in life had plundered, oppressed, and humiliated the poor: after their deaths, the bodies of the rich are to be tortured like other malefactors, but their souls are to be sent back to live in donkeys for 250,000 years, in which form they will be subject to the poor.[643] The fantastically long period of punishment, and the comical nature of the penalty inflicted, reveal a specific animus against the elite, that is also present in the *Life of Aesop*, and that characterizes products of the 'grotesque perspective' in general.[644]

The *Necyomantia* concludes with Menippus' account of his consultation with Teiresias, the goal of his journey. The Theban prophet is at first unwilling to divulge the secret of a happy life, but eventually yields; taking Menippus aside where they cannot be heard, Teiresias whispers in his ear: 'The life of the common sort is best.'[645] Teiresias advises Menippus to avoid the philosophers and to regard their speculations and syllogisms as 'nonsense' (λῆρος). The prophet urges Menippus to go on his way through life, 'laughing a great deal and taking nothing seriously' (γελῶν τὰ πολλὰ καὶ

641.   Lucian *Nec.* 16; trans. Harmon, *Lucian* IV, 101.
642.   Lucian *Nec.* 19.
643.   Lucian *Nec.* 20.
644.   Relihan, *Ancient Menippean Satire*, 110, 255 n. 23.
645.   Lucian *Nec.* 21: ὁ τῶν ἰδιωτῶν ἄριστος βίος. Cf. Plato *Phdr.* 236D where Socrates characterizes himself as an ἰδιώτης as opposed to the experts.

περὶ μηδὲν ἐσπουδακώς).[646] Menippus is now eager to return to life, and is shown a shortcut out of the underworld. Menippus re-emerges into the light through the oracular cave of the false prophet Trophonius.[647]

The parody of the quest for wisdom reaches an ironic climax. The wisdom that Menippus gains by such great effort is that which he knew before he began his journey: the simple life is best.[648] The concluding reference to the false prophet Trophonius is a reminder that the enthusiastic Menippus is not to be taken too seriously.[649] And yet, the irreducible truth of the superiority of the simple life survives all parody. Indeed, this truth is paradoxically reaffirmed by Menippus' fantastic journey with its inconsequential results.[650] Nor is Teiresias' concluding advice to be dismissed as a counsel of detachment; for, in fact, Teiresias echoes the traditional counsel of the archaic poet Simonides (sixth century B.C.): 'Above all, pursue only how to put the present in its proper place, and run on, laughing at most things and worried about nothing.'[651] The good sense of the common man triumphs. 'Liberated from the contradictions of those who presume to know what is to be taken seriously, Menippus returns eager to inform the powers that be of the reversals that await them.'[652]

For readers familiar with the tradition of parody of prophetic charlatans, Paul's adaptation of this parody in 1 Cor. 2.6–16 would have seemed clear, adroit, and daring. The object of our analysis must be to demonstrate that each of these characteristics is accurate: first, that Paul signals the parody of himself as a mystagogue by making use of language, style and motifs well known to his audience from the popular stage and Cynic satire; second, that Paul skilfully translates the parody into his theological debate with the Corinthians, while keeping the features of the genre intact; and third, that Paul boldly insists on the validity of the very sort of revelation which the parody contains – namely, the epiphany of the

---

646. Lucian *Nec.* 21. See R. Bracht Branham, 'The Wisdom of Lucian's Tiresias', *Journal of Hellenic Studies* 109 (1989) 159–60.

647. Lucian *Nec.* 22. Lucian also mocks the oracle of Trophonius in *Dial. Mort.* 10.

648. Branham, *Unruly Eloquence*, 22; Relihan, *Ancient Menippean Satire*, 22.

649. For this ironic interpretation of the reference to Trophonius at the end of the *Necyomantia*, see already J. Geffcken, 'Studien zur griechischen Satire,' *Neue Jahrbücher für das klassische Altertum* 27 (1911) 474; followed by Relihan, *Ancient Menippean Satire*, 22. On Trophonius and the mystery cults, see P. Bonnechere, 'Trophonius of Lebadea: Mystery aspects of an oracular cult in Boeotia' in *Greek Mysteries*, ed. M. Cosmopoulos (London: Routledge, 2003) 169–92.

650. Branham, *Unruly Eloquence*, 22, 25.

651. Simonides fr. 141; text and trans. in Relihan, *Ancient Menippean Satire*, 111, 255 n. 24.

652. Branham, *Unruly Eloquence*, 25.

crucified Christ as divine wisdom and power, though unrecognized by the rulers of this age (2.8) and dismissed as 'foolishness' (2.14).

The means by which Paul notifies his readers that he is presenting a parody of himself as a mystagogue in 2.6–16 are multifarious, consisting especially in the peculiarity of his word-choice, the solemnity of his style, and the character of his motifs and devices. We shall discover that the paragraph 2.6–16 as a whole, and the scene that it portrays, including its most oblique details, makes sense only by reference to the parodies of charlatans known to Paul's readers from the stage and satire. We may begin with those features of the text that mark a development in Paul's argument.

The turn in Paul's argument is indicated by contrast and ambiguity at the beginning of the paragraph (2.6).[653] The contrast is embodied not only in the conjunction δέ, which, as has been suggested, is weakly adversative ('yet', 'howbeit'),[654] but also, and primarily, in the term σοφία ('wisdom'), which is drawn forward to the very beginning of the sentence for emphasis,[655] and is used in a manner different from its previous uses in the epistle.[656] The difference consists in a deliberate ambiguity, created by the omission of the article, and by the absence of any qualifying phrases.[657] Only in the latter part of the verse, where the term is repeated (in a form of *epanalepsis*), is the nature of 'wisdom' indicated, and then only in a negative sense: 'not of this age nor of the rulers of this age who are perishing' (2.6b). Previously, whenever Paul has used the term σοφία, he has taken care to make clear precisely in what sense the term is being used, and this even when playing with different senses of the term in the tradition (1.21). The mechanism of precision is usually a qualifying genitive: thus 'wisdom' is either σοφία λόγου ('eloquent wisdom') or σοφία κόσμου ('worldly wisdom'), by which Paul denotes the 'learning' which is the prized object of the elite (1.17,19,20,21,22); or 'wisdom' is σοφία θεοῦ, the divine purpose and initiative, which has the paradoxical character of μωρία in the present age (1.21,24,30). But now, in 2.6, the term 'wisdom' is used in an unqualified and indefinite sense, destabilizing the previous categories, and forcing the reader to become more involved in the issue. In what sense does Paul, having rejected 'eloquent wisdom' (1.17; 2.1,4), now claim to communicate 'wisdom' among the initiates? In the verses that follow, Paul will qualify his 'wisdom' as 'of God' (2.7), and will intimate that the 'wisdom' that he communicates is nothing other than the paradoxical

653. Heinrici, *Der erste Brief*, 90: 'Die Auffassung des Ganzen ist entgegengesetzt.'
654. Weiss, *Der erste Korintherbrief*, 52–53; Conzelmann, *1 Corinthians*, 60.
655. Weiss, *Der erste Korintherbrief*, 52.
656. Weiss, *Der erste Korintherbrief*, 53.
657. Weiss, *Der erste Korintherbrief*, 53.

message of the crucified Christ (2.8).[658] But in the space that is momentarily opened up by contrast and ambiguity in 2.6, Paul introduces his self-parody.

A second indicator of a new direction in Paul's argument is the emergence of an anomalous vocabulary in 2.6, which evokes a different context than that of the preceding paragraphs, and begins to shape a new persona. The phrase, ἐν τοῖς τελείοις, upon which the major emphasis falls in the first sentence of the paragraph,[659] employs a *terminus technicus* of the mystery cults: the τέλειος is the one who has been fully initiated into the mysteries,[660] who has heard 'sacred words' and seen 'holy visions', and has thus become 'perfect'.[661] That Paul intends the term τέλειος to be understood in a technical sense with reference to the mysteries, and not in the moral-philosophical sense of 'mature' or 'fully developed',[662] is indicated by the words with which τέλειος is grouped in the verses that follow – μυστήριον, ἀποκεκρυμμένη κτλ.[663] For μυστήριον is likewise a technical term of Greco-Roman religion,[664] describing an 'initiation ceremony' in which a ritual is performed upon a participant, enabling him to attain 'a new state of mind through experience of

---

658. Grindheim, 'Wisdom for the Perfect', 694–97.

659. Weiss, *Der erste Korintherbrief*, 52: 'Der Satz hat einen Doppelton, den schwächeren auf σοφίαν, den stärkeren auf ἐν τοῖς τελείοις'; similarly, Conzelmann, *1 Corinthians*, 60.

660. Bauer, *Greek-English Lexicon*, 995–96, s.v. τέλειος 3, referring to *Corp. Herm.* 4.4; Philodemus Περὶ θεῶν 1.24.12 (ed. H. Diels in *Abhandlungen der Königlichen Akademie der Wissenschaften zu Berlin*, Philosophisch-historische Klasse [1915] p. 41; 93); Iamblichus *Myst.* 3.7 (p. 114, Parthey); Philo *Somn.* 2.234; etc. For this understanding of τέλειος in 1 Cor. 2.6, see Heinrici, *Das erste Sendschreiben*, 40–41; J. H. Kennedy, *St. Paul and the Mystery Religions* (London: Hodder & Stoughton, 1913), 130–34; Reitzenstein, *Hellenistic Mystery-Religions*, 432–34; Wilckens, *Weisheit und Torheit*, 53–60; Conzelmann, *1 Corinthians*, 60–61. More usual as a designation for 'initiate' is the cognate τελούμενος, e.g., Plato *Phdr.* 249C; Aristotle *fr.* 15 = Synesius *Dio* 10, p. 48a. On the word family τελειόω, τελετή, τελεστής, τελεστήριον, and so forth, see C. Zijerveld, Τελετή, *Bijdrage tot de kennis der religieuze terminologie in het Grieksch* (diss. Utrecht, 1934).

661. The reference is to Plutarch *fr.* 178 (ed. F. H. Sandbach, *Plutarch's Moralia* XV, LCL [Cambridge, MA: Harvard University Press, 1987] 316–19). Plutarch uses the term παντελής for 'perfect,' rather than τέλειος, and places this term in apposition to μεμυημένος ('initiated'). But the passage is a description of what it is like 'to be initiated' (τελεῖσθαι), and is therefore relevant to Paul's use of τέλειος. On the importance of this text for reconstructing the experience of initiation into the mysteries, see W. Burkert, *Ancient Mystery Cults* (Cambridge, MA: Harvard University Press, 1987) 91–92.

662. So, Weiss, *Der erste Korintherbrief*, 73–74; G. Delling, 'τέλειος', 75–76; Lindemann, *Der erste Korintherbrief*, 62, appealing to Wis. Sol. 9.6; Philo *Leg. All.* 1.92–94; 3.134, 159; Stobaeus *Ecl.* 2.7.198.

663. Rightly, Heinrici, *Das erste Sendschreiben*, 40–41; Conzelmann, *1 Corinthians*, 60–61.

664. On μυστήριον in this technical sense, see esp. G. Bornkamm, 'μυστήριον', 803–808; Bauer, *Greek-English Lexicon*, 661–62, citing, among other texts, Herodotus 2.51.2; Diodorus Siculus 1.29.3; 3.63.2; Socratic Ep. 27.3; Cornutus 28, p.56.22; 57.4; Alciphron 3.26.1; *OGIS* 331.54; 528.13; 721.2; and numerous texts in Dittenberger, *SIG*.

the sacred.'[665] The word family of μυστήριον largely overlaps with that of τέλειος in accounts of the mysteries,[666] so that Paul's association of the terms is decisive for his meaning. Both τέλειος and μυστήριον are made more specific by the addition of language which stipulates secrecy.[667] The customary adjectives are ἄρρητος ('not to be spoken') and ἀπόρρητος ('secret'),[668] for which Paul substitutes a synonym, ἀποκεκρυμμένη ('hidden').[669] Paul's appropriation of terminology which was in constant use to characterize the mysteries is intended to evoke a scene in which Paul presents a mystery teaching to initiates.[670]

A third indicator of the turn to self-parody in 2.6–16 is Paul's use of the verb λαλεῖν to designate his discourse. This verb, which is used repeatedly and exclusively in 2.6–16 to describe the communication of wisdom,[671] but is found nowhere else in 1 Cor. 1–4, gives the specific character to the paragraph.[672] And that character, as we have suggested, is ironic and self-mocking; for Paul's other uses of λαλεῖν in 1 Corinthians have something consistently ambivalent about them: λαλεῖν is the babbling talk of children who have not yet mastered adult language (13.11); λαλεῖν is the daemonic speech of one who says 'Let Jesus be cursed!' (12.3); and λαλεῖν is, above all, the unintelligible speech of 'tongues': 'the one who speaks (ὁ λαλῶν) in a tongue… speaks mysteries in a spirit (πνεύματι δὲ λαλεῖ μυστήρια), and no one understands him' (14.2).[673] A clear indication of the negative

665. The definition is that of Burkert, *Ancient Mystery Cults*, 7–8. Burkert calls attention to the importance of the Latin translation of μυστήρια, μύειν as *initia, initiare* in Varro *De ling. Lat.* 5.58; Cicero *De Leg.* 2.36; *De nat. deor.* 1.119; *Tusc. Disp.* 1.29; Livy 31.14.7; 39.9.4; and the bilingual inscription from Samothrace (late Hellenistic period) in *SEG* 29.799, which has *initiatei* corresponding to μύσται.

666. Burkert, *Ancient Mystery Cults*, 9, 137 n. 44, adducing Athenaeus' definition of τελεταί as festivals 'with some mystical tradition' (μετά τινος μυστικῆς παραδόσεως). See further, Bornkamm, 'μυστήριον', 804.

667. Burkert, *Ancient Mystery Cults*, 9. See esp. Dittenberger, *SIG*³ 873, 9–10: τὰ τε ἀπόρρητα τῆς κατὰ τὰ μυστήρια τελετῆς. See also Diodorus 1.23.2, τῆς τελετῆς καὶ τὸν μυστήριον, and 3.63.2, μυστήρια καὶ τελετάς.

668. *IG*³ 1.953; Euripides *fr.* 63; *Helen* 1307; *Bacch.* 470–72; *Rhesus* 943; Aristophanes *Nubes* 302; *Eccl.* 442; Plutarch *Pompey* 24.7; *SIG*³ 873, 9–10; Burkert, *Ancient Mystery Cults*, 9, 137 n. 44.

669. Plato *Phdr.* 273C, ἀποκεκρυμμένη τέχνη; Ps. Demetrius 155, κατηγορίαι ἀποκεκρυμμέναι. Cf. Vettius Valens 7.30, ἀποκρύφων. See Bauer, *Greek-English Lexicon*, 114 s.v. ἀποκρύπτω 2. See also the 'Naasene Hymn' quoted in Hippolytus *Ref.* 5.10.2: μυστήρια πάντα δ᾽ ἀνοίξω,…τὰ κεκρυμμένα τῆς ἁγίας ὁδοῦ ('All mysteries I shall disclose,… the hidden things of the holy way').

670. So already Bornkamm, 'μυστήριον', 819.

671. 1 Cor. 2.6,7,13; 3.1 (retrospectively summarizing).

672. Lindemann, *Der erste Korintherbrief*, 58: 'Der Abschnitt ist bestimmt duch das Stichwort λαλοῦμεν.'

673. The verb λαλεῖν is found 22 times in 1 Cor. 14 (excluding vss. 33b-35) in reference to glossolalia.

connotations of the term are the instances in which Paul contrasts λαλεῖν with unambiguous modes of discourse: thus, Paul distinguishes the tentative voice of human authority from the trustworthy pronouncement of the law, using λαλεῖν for the former and λέγειν for the latter (9.8); similarly, Paul insists that the one who 'speaks' (λαλῶν) in a tongue merely edifies himself, but the one who 'prophesies' (προφητεύων) edifies the church (14.4). Additional instances of contrast might be adduced.[674] The basis of the pejorative judgment upon the speech designated by λαλεῖν is its unintelligibility.[675] In most instances in which the verb λαλεῖν is employed, a restrictive 'only' or 'merely' is implicit: thus, Paul asks, 'Do I say (λαλῶ) this on (merely) human authority?' (9.8); and observes, 'the one who speaks (λαλῶν) in a tongue (only) builds himself up' (14.4).[676] The fact that Paul does not qualify his use of λαλεῖν in 2.6–16, as elsewhere, suggests that he is speaking tongue-in-cheek. Insight into the attitude that underlies Paul's usage is supplied by a passage from the *Life of Aesop*. When the goddess resolves to restore Aesop's speech, she removes from his tongue the impediment which prevents him from 'speaking' (λαλεῖν).[677] Awakening and finding that he is able to name the things which he sees, Aesop exclaims: 'I speak (λαλῶ)! By the Muses! Where have I gotten the power of speech (τὸ λαλεῖν)?'[678] The verb λαλεῖν expresses the awkward self-consciousness of one who seeks to utilize a discursive ability for which he is not prepared by education, class, or breeding.[679] The term is therefore most appropriate to Paul's parody of himself as a charlatan.

Speech plays an important role in initiation into the mysteries. The mystagogue not only performs rituals on the initiand, but also communicates a 'sacred tale' (ἱερὸς λόγος) about the fate of the god.[680] In a well-

674. E.g., 1 Cor. 12.3, λαλῶν Ἀνάθεμα Ἰησοῦς, εἰπεῖν Κύριος Ἰησοῦς. See also 14.2–3; 14.5, μείζων δὲ ὁ προφητεύων ἢ ὁ λαλῶν γλώσσαις.

675. 1 Cor. 14.2, 'no one understands'; 14.9, 'so with yourselves; if in a tongue you utter speech that is not intelligible (μὴ εὔσημον), how will anyone know what is being said (τὸ λαλούμενον)? For you will be speaking into the air'; 14.11, one who speaks in a tongue is like a 'foreigner' (βάρβαρος) whose sounds have no meaning; 14.23, 'If the whole church comes together and all speak in tongues (λαλῶσιν γλώσσαις), and ordinary people or unbelievers enter, will they not say that you are out of your mind (μαίνεσθε)?'

676. On this point, see already Vos, 'Die Argumentation des Paulus in 1 Kor 1,10–3,4,' 107.

677. *Vit. Aesop.* 7 (ms. G).

678. *Vit. Aesop.* 8 (ms. G).

679. For the use of λαλεῖν in reference to barbaric speech, see *POxy* 413 ('Charition') 67. The term has the connotation of the opposite of articulate discourse because of its association with the sounds of animals, birds, insects, etc.; see Liddell-Scott-Jones, *Greek-English Lexicon*, 1026–27 s.v. λαλέω II. 'chatter', 'chirp'. See Paul's own analogy of speech in tongues (λαλεῖν ἐν γλώσσαις) with the indistinct sounds produced by lifeless musical instruments in 1 Cor. 14.7–8.

680. On the ἱερὸς λόγος, see Herodotus 2.51; 2.62; 2.81; Diodorus 1.98.2; Ps.-Plato *Ep.* 7, 335A; Plutarch *De Isis.* 353D; Pausanias 2.13; 8.15.4. Cf. the Hellenistic inscription from the

known passage of the *Republic*, Plato provides a glimpse of the way in which charlatans utilized such mystagogic discourses in private initiations.[681] Plato allows that 'the strangest of all speeches' (οἱ λόγοι θαυμασιώτατοι) are those which 'begging priests' (ἀγύρται) and 'soothsayers' (μάντεις) present at rich men's doors to make them believe that they can expiate misdeeds by means of incantations and sacrifices.[682] In such speeches, the poets are routinely cited, along with passages from the books of Musaeus and Orpheus.[683] Mystical speeches and sacred hymns figure prominently in Demosthenes' caricature of Aeschines as an acolyte for his mother in the initiation which she offered into a minor mystery cult.[684] Aeschines 'read from the books', while his mother performed the ritual, and he led the initiands in the hymn: 'Here I leave my sins behind, Here the better way I find.'[685] Demosthenes ridicules the powerful tones with which the youthful Aeschines sounded forth the 'holy ululation'.[686] We have already noted the emphasis that Lucian places upon the lengthy speeches of the magus who consecrates Menippus for his journey to the underworld.[687] Paul's repeated and emphatic use of λαλεῖν is meant to evoke the murmuring, indistinct speeches of such mystagogues.

The scripture citation in 2.9 ('What no eye has seen, nor ear heard, etc.') contributes rhetorically to the parody Paul is creating, when its function in the discourse is understood. The attention of researchers has focused on the source of the quotation, but has produced no certain result,[688] because the quotation has not been found, either in the Old Testament,[689] or in

sanctuary of Dionysus at Halicarnassus in *SEG* 28.841, which invites the reader to join the rites 'in order that you may know the whole λόγος'. According to Chrysippus *fr.* 42, *SVF* II.17, the transmission of a λόγος about the gods is the essence of τελεταί. See the discussion of the role of speech in the mysteries by Burkert, *Ancient Mystery Cults*, 69–75.

681. Plato *Resp.* 364B-E. See the discussion of this important passage in Burkert, *Ancient Mystery Cults*, 71.

682. Plato *Resp.* 364B-C.

683. Plato *Resp.* 364C-E. The prophetic ἀλαζών with his book is already ridiculed in Aristophanes *Aves* 974–89. On the use of books in the mysteries, see Burkert, *Ancient Mystery Cults*, 70–71.

684. Demosthenes 18.259-60. The passage is of great importance as the most detailed description of a mystery cult in the classical period. Cf. H. Wankel, *Demosthenes, Rede für Ktesiphon über den Kranz* (Heidelberg: Winter, 1976) 132–149.

685. Demosthenes 18.259.

686. Demosthenes 18.259-60.

687. Lucian *Nec.* 7, 9.

688. The observation of Weiss (*Der erste Korintherbrief*, 58) is still valid: 'Über die Herkunft des Zitats ist noch keine Gewissheit erzielt.' See esp. the excursus on 'Das "Schriftwort" in 1 Kor 2,9' in Lindemann, *Der erste Korintherbrief*, 66–67, for a summary of recent research.

689. Hieronymus (*Vall.* IV.70) already suggests that Paul paraphrases Isa. 64.3 (LXX): ἀπὸ τοῦ αἰῶνος οὐκ ἠκούσαμεν οὐδὲ οἱ ὀφθαλμοὶ ἡμῶν εἶδον θεὸν πλὴν σοῦ, καὶ τὰ ἔργα σου ἃ ποιήσεις

apocryphal Jewish writings.[690] To be sure, there are many similar sayings in Jewish and Christian texts,[691] and even in Hellenistic literature.[692] But the frequency and distribution of the sentiment is a reflection of the importance of the concepts of hiddenness and revelation in ancient religion,[693] and does not simplify, but rather complicates the search for the source of the saying which Paul quotes. Almost overlooked in the quest for origins is the *form* of the citation,[694] which is the key to understanding its function in 2.6–16. For the citation is poetical,[695] a fact which recalls the role played by poetry in the speeches of the mystagogues. Plato asserts that 'for all their sayings' the begging priests and soothsayers 'cite the poets as witnesses' (τούτοις δὲ πᾶσι τοῖς λόγοις μάρτυρας ποιητὰς ἐπάγονται),[696] and adduces frequently cited passages from Hesiod and Homer, as examples.[697] Demosthenes' caricature of Aeschines' performance in the mysteries emphasizes the acolyte's 'holy ululation', and quotes two verses of the

---

τοῖς ὑπομένουσιν ἔλεον. For an attempt to reconstruct the history of the tradition leading from Isa. 64.3 to 1 Cor. 2.9, see H. Ponsot, 'D'Isaie LXIV,3 à I Corinthiens II,9,' *RB* 90 (1983) 229–42. But Paul's citation has little in common with Isa. 64.3, beyond the mention of 'hearing' and 'seeing'; thus, rightly, Heinrici, *Der erste Brief*, 98. A decisive argument against the derivation of 1 Cor. 2.9 from Isa. 64.3 is the observation of Weiss, *Der erste Korintherbrief*, 59: 'Sehr wenig glaublich ist vollends, dass Paulus von sich aus das τοῖς ὑπομένουσιν ἔλεον, das zu seinem Gedankengängen gut passen würde, durch das ihm so ungeläufige τοῖς ἀγαπῶσιν αὐτόν ersetzt hätte.'

690.   Origen (*Comm. In Matt.*, on Matt. 27.9) ascribes the quotation to the Apocryphon of Elijah. See Weiss, *Der erste Korintherbrief*, 59; P. Prigent, 'Ce que l'oeil n'a pas vu', *TZ* 14 (1968) 416–29. But the extant fragments of what is known as the Apocalypse of Elijah do not contain the saying quoted in 1 Cor. 2.9; see W. Schrage in *JSHRZ* V/3, 195–96. For an attempt to derive the saying from the Coptic Testament of Jacob, see E. von Nordheim, 'Das Zitat des Paulus in 1 Kor 2,9 und seine Beziehung zum koptischen Testament Jakobs', *ZNW* 65 (1974) 112–20; but O. Hofius ('Das Zitat 1 Kor 2,9 und das koptische Testament des Jakob', *ZNW* 66 [1975] 140–42) argues that the Test. Jac. is a late Christian work; supplemented and confirmed by H. F. D. Sparks, '1 Cor 2,9 A Quotation from the Coptic Testament of Jacob', *ZNW* 67 (1976) 269–76.

691.   See esp. Ps.-Philo *Lib. Ant. Bib.* 26.13; *b. Sanh.* 99a; *Ev. Thom.* 17; *Asc. Is.* 11.34. See the discussion in M. Philonenko, 'Quod occulus non vidit, I Cor. 2,9', *ThZ* 15 (1959) 51–53; Strack-Billerbeck, *Kommentar* (Munich: Beck), III.327–29; Koester, 'Gnostic Writings as Witnesses for the Development of the Sayings Tradition' 248–49. For the history of the saying in post-Pauline Christianity, see A. Lindemann, *Paulus im ältesten Christentum* (Tübingen: Mohr, 1979), 187–88, 265–69, 294–98, 324–25.

692.   Conzelmann, *1 Corinthians*, 63 n. 71 adduces Plutarch *Aud. poet.* 17E as a parallel.

693.   Rightly, Conzelmann, *1 Corinthians*, 63. On the hiddenness of the central revelation as a source of the attractiveness of the mystery cults, see Burkert, *Ancient Mystery Cults*, 45–48.

694.   The exception in the history of scholarship is Weiss, *Der erste Korintherbrief*, 58.

695.   The citation is rightly printed in strophic form in Nestle-Aland, 27th ed. See the analysis of Weiss, *Der erste Korintherbrief*, 58: 'Das Zitat ist symmetrisch gebaut: 3 Zeilen zu 13, 13, 15 Silben; der Ausdruck hat rhetorische Fülle.'

696.   Plato *Resp.* 364C.

697.   Plato *Resp.* 364D-E, citing Hesiod *Op.* 287–89 and Homer *Il.* 9.497–500.

hymn in which he led the initiands.[698] Plutarch mentions the 'solemn, sacred words' which welcome the initiate into the sacred rites.[699] Paul's citation of a poetical passage at the climax of the first section of his discourse mimics the citations of poetry and hymns by initiators into the mysteries, and thus contributes powerfully to the parody. The fact that Paul introduces the verses as sacred scripture, signalled by the citation formula καθὼς γέγραπται ('as it is written'),[700] also belongs to the parody of a mystagogic scene; for the citation of holy books was an established feature of the mysteries.[701] One recalls that the charlatans described by Plato performed private mysteries with 'many books of Musaeus and Orpheus' in hand;[702] and Aeschines assisted his mother in her initiations, by 'reading from the books while she performed the ritual'.[703]

The scriptural citation in 1 Cor. 2.9 is not the only portion of Paul's discourse characterized by rhythmical cadence and rhetorical fullness. Throughout the paragraph, Paul sustains a lofty, ceremonious tone and a fluidity of expression.[704] The repetition of key words and phrases in elegant, interlocking clauses (*anaphora*) gives the passage a hypnotic effect. Thus the style of the passage contributes to the impression of a mystagogue propounding a ἱερὸς λόγος.[705]

Among the stylistic features of 2.6–16, the one which contributes most to the parody of mystagogic speech is the studied indefiniteness of expression. We have already noted how the unqualified use of the noun σοφία creates ambiguity about the subject of Paul's discourse.[706] The same ambiguity attaches to the relative pronoun ἅ, which introduces the scripture citation in 2.9.[707] For ἅ ('things which') is both object and subject.[708] The dual role played by the relative pronoun creates confusion

---

698. Demosthenes 18.259.

699. Plutarch *fr.* 178.

700. Lindemann, *Der erste Korintherbrief*, 65: 'Paulus führt, wie καθὼς γέγραπται anzeigt, das Zitat als Wort der Heiligen Schrift an'; 67: 'Aber entscheidend ist, dass Paulus meint, er zitiere definitiv ein *Schriftwort*, d.h. in der ihm zur Verfügung stehenden Tradition hat das Logion offensichtlich diese Qualität gehabt.'

701. Burkert, *Ancient Mystery Cults*, 70–71.

702. Plato *Resp.* 364E.

703. Demosthenes 18.259.

704. Weiss, 'Beiträge zur paulinischen Rhetorik', 42–45.

705. Compare the style of the mystagogic speech of Diotima in Plato *Symp.* 201D-212C. See also Plato *Meno* 81A and *Papyrus Derveni*.

706. Cf. Weiss, *Der erste Korintherbrief*, 53.

707. ἅ is repeated for rhetorical effect in the third line of the citation. The variant ὅσα is not strongly attested.

708. That is to say, a demonstrative pronoun is concealed within the relative pronoun; on this usage, see Bauer, *Greek-English Lexicon*, 725 s.v. ὅς b. Cf. Conzelmann, *1 Corinthians*, 56 n. 4: 'ἅ, "things that", is both object and subject'; similarly, Lindemann, *Der erste Korintherbrief*, 66.

about the construction of the sentence.[709] Moreover, the content of the pronoun remains unspecified: *what* it is which eye has not seen nor ear heard, we are not told.[710] Because the reference of the pronoun is unknown, it is impossible to determine the original meaning of the saying.[711] The resulting ambiguity frustrates historians, but contributes powerfully to the air of mystery surrounding the discourse. The relationship of the phrase ἐν μυστηρίῳ (in 2.7) is likewise ambiguous.[712] ἐν μυστηρίῳ may be taken either with σοφία ('wisdom') or with λαλεῖν ('to speak').[713] In the first case, the phrase describes the inscrutable nature of the divine purpose: θεοῦ σοφίαν ἐν μυστηρίῳ = 'God's mysterious wisdom'.[714] In the second case, the phrase designates the manner in which wisdom is communicated: λαλοῦμεν θεοῦ σοφίαν ἐν μυστηρίῳ = 'we speak divine wisdom in the form of a mystery'.[715] A decision between these

709.   Rightly, Conzelmann, *1 Corinthians*, 56 n. 4. Older commentators (Grotius, Godet, *et al.*) suggested that a verb must be supplied (γέγονε, ἐστί, or ἐγνώκαμεν); see Heinrici, *Der erste Brief*, 98 for literature. Hofmann (*Der erste Brief*, 31) takes the citation in vs. 9 as an introduction to vs. 10, so that ἅ is the object of ἀπεκάλυψεν. But against this speaks the conjunction δέ in vs. 10, and Paul's practice of concluding an argument with a citation of scripture. Schrage (*Der erste Brief an die Korinther*, 1.247, 256) sees ἅ as dependent upon λαλοῦμεν.
710.   Rightly, Lindemann, *Der erste Korintherbrief*, 66: 'Was dieses Objekt inhaltlich ist, wird nicht gesagt.'
711.   Lindemann, *Der erste Korintherbrief*, 66.
712.   Rightly, Weiss, *Der erste Korintherbrief*, 54: 'Fraglich ist die Beziehung von ἐν μυστηρίῳ.'
713.   Weiss, *Der erste Korintherbrief*, 54–55; Conzelmann, *1 Corinthians*, 56 n. 1, 62. An older generation of interpreters even construed ἐν μυστηρίῳ with τὴν ἀποκεκρυμμένην (Theodoret, Grotius); see Heinrici, *Der erste Brief*, 96 for references.
714.   Thus the majority of interpreters, e.g., Heinrici, *Der erste Brief*, 96; Lietzmann, *An die Korinther*, 16; Lindemann, *Der erste Korintherbrief*, 63–64. Those who embrace this construction excuse the absence of an article before ἐν μυστηρίῳ by appealing to Rom. 5.15, δωρεὰ ἐν χάριτι. An unexpressed participle, οὖσαν or γενομένην, must be supplied in order to complete the thought. ἐν must be taken in a modal sense. Against this interpretation is the resulting redundancy with τὴν ἀποκεκρυμμένην, which expresses essentially the same thought as ἐν μυστηρίῳ, taken as a qualifier of σοφία.
715.   So, Weiss, *Der erste Korintherbrief*, 55: 'so würde es doch zweifellos möglich sein, zu sagen: λαλεῖν ἐν μυστηρίῳ, d.h. in der Form eines Geheimnisses; das geht leicht über in die Nuance: "als ein Geheimnis".' Similarly, Bauer, *Greek-English Lexicon*, 662 s.v. μυστήριον 1 b: 'λαλοῦμεν θεοῦ σοφίαν ἐν μυστηρίῳ, *we impart the wisdom of God in the form of a mystery* (ἐν μυστηρίῳ = in a mysterious manner [Laud. Therap. 11] or = secretly, so that no unauthorized person would learn of it [cp. Cyr. of Scyth. P. 90,14 ἐν μυστηρίῳ λέγει].' In favor of this interpretation is the naturalness of the connection of the prepositional phrase with a verb in close proximity. As a parallel construction, one may point to 1 Cor. 14.6, ἐὰν μὴ ὑμῖν λαλήσω ἢ ἐν ἀποκαλύψει ἢ ἐν γνώσει ἢ ἐν προφητεία ἢ ἐν διδαχῇ. G. Dautzenberg ('Botschaft und Bedeutung der urchristlichen Prophetie nach dem Ersten Korintherbrief (2.6–16; 12–14)'

constructions is impossible.[716] The expression οἱ ἄρχοντες τοῦ αἰῶνος τούτου ('the rulers of this age') is also ambiguous, and for this reason has occasioned much debate among interpreters.[717] Although the immediate reference is to political authorities,[718] as argued above, the mystical context also suggests the demonic powers,[719] who control the earthly rulers responsible for the death of Jesus.[720] Where so many elements are genuinely ambiguous, it is impossible to resist the impression that the ambiguity is deliberate. The indefiniteness of Paul's expression is in keeping with 'the obligation of secrecy, deemed essential for all true mysteries'.[721] Ambiguity preserves the boundary between what is not to be spoken and what must be intimated, in order to attract initiates.[722]

The topics and motifs of Paul's discourse are drawn from the mystery cults and bear direct reference to the conventions of initiation rituals. First, there is the sharp distinction between those who are 'in' and those who are 'out'. This dichotomy, so essential to the identity and function of a mystery

---

in idem, *Studien zur paulinischen Theologie* [Göttingen: Vandenhoeck & Ruprecht, 1999] 40–42) regards λαλοῦμεν ἐν μυστηρίῳ (2.7) as analogous to λαλεῖ μυστήρια in 14.2, and on this basis describes 2.6–16 as 'prophetische Rede'.

716.   Conzelmann, *1 Corinthians*, 56 n. 1.

717.   The debate is already underway in the early church; see the summary of arguments by Theodore of Mopsuestia in K. Staab, *Paulus-kommentare aus der griechischen Kirche aus Katenenhandschriften* (Münster: Aschendorff, 1933) 174. Chrysostom and Theodoret support the political interpretation, while Origen and Theodore advocate the demonological; cf. Heinrici, *Der erste Brief*, 95; Weiss, *Der erste Korintherbrief*, 53 n. 2. For a summary of the debate among modern scholars, see Clarke, *Secular and Christian Leadership in Corinth*, 116–18.

718.   As decisively argued by Schniewind, 'Die Archonten dieses Äons, 1 Kor. 2,6–8', 104–109; followed by Miller, 'ἀρχόντων τοῦ αἰῶνος τούτου', 522–28; Carr, 'The Rulers of this Age', 20–35; Fee, *The First Epistle*, 104; Wolff, *Der erste Brief*, 17; among others.

719.   So, Dibelius, *Die Geisterwelt im Glauben des Paulus*, 24; Weiss, *Der erste Korintherbrief*, 53–54; Lietzmann, *An die Korinther*, 12; Wilckens, *Weisheit und Torheit*, 61–63; Conzelmann, *1 Corinthians*, 61; Schrage, *Der erste Brief*, 1.250, 253–54; among others.

720.   Also arguing in favor of a double reference to political and demonic powers is A. Feuillet, *Le Christ Sagesse de Dieu d'après les Épître pauliniennes* (Paris: Gabalda, 1966) 25–36.

721.   Burkert, *Ancient Mystery Cults*, 45.

722.   Compare the famous account of initiation into the mysteries of Isis in Apuleius *Met.* 11.23.6–8: 'Studious reader, you may terribly wish to know what was said and done there. I would tell you if it were allowed, you would know if it were permitted to hear; but both your ears and my tongue should incur the pain of rash curiosity. But I shall not keep you in suspense with religious desire nor shall I torture you with prolonged anguish; listen, therefore, and believe it to be true. I approached the frontier of death, I set foot on the threshold of Persephone, I journeyed through all the elements and came back, I saw at midnight the sun, sparkling in white light, I came close to the gods of the upper and nether world and adored them from near at hand. Behold, now I have told you, and what you have heard, you must now forget; therefore I have only told that which may be divulged without offence for the understanding of the profane.'

cult,[723] is asserted and maintained throughout the paragraph 2.6–16. Thus, 'the initiates' (οἱ τέλειοι) of 2.6 imply the uninitiated. Those who have received 'the spirit of God' are set opposite those who have received 'the spirit of the world' (2.12). The 'spiritual' (πνευματικός) person is contrasted with the 'natural' (ψυκικός) person (2.14). The composition of these groups matters less to Paul than to modern interpreters,[724] for Paul leaves their identities unspecified.[725] What matters to Paul is simply the distinction between the spiritual and the unspiritual, a concern wholly in keeping with the organization of the mysteries. The boundary between the initiated and the uninitiated was carefully guarded in the mysteries, as we can see from one of Dio Chrysostom's analogies: the uninitiated, who stand outside, at the gates, may hear a mystic word cried out, or glimpse fire above the walls, but remain ignorant of the secret reserved for the *mystai*.[726]

A second motif drawn from the mystery cults is the myth of the god's redemptive suffering, alluded to, and, indeed, briefly summarized, in 2.7–8 ('But we speak God's hidden wisdom in a mystery, which God decreed before the ages for our glory, which none of the rulers of this age understood; for if they had understood, they would not have crucified the Lord of glory'). The term 'myth' is used here, not in a pejorative sense, but with the meaning that it has in the mysteries, where it designates a traditional account of the fate of the god communicated to initiates.[727]

723. Burkert, *Ancient Mystery Cults*, 45–46.

724. Much energy has been expended in the attempt to identify these groups. Some hold that the τέλειοι are all Christians: thus, Bornkamm, 'μυστήριον', 819; Du Plessis, ΤΕΛΕΙΟΣ 184; Winter, *Pneumatiker und Psychiker in Korinth*, 214; Fee, *First Epistle*, 100–103; Schrage, *Der erste Brief*, 1.249; Merklein, *Der erste Brief an die Korinther: Kapitel 1–4*, 225, 234; Wolff, *Der erste Brief*, 54; Collins, *First Corinthians*, 129; Thistelton, *First Epistle*, 233, 267–68; Lindemann, *Der erste Korintherbrief*, 61–63. Others argue that the τέλειοι are a higher class of believers: so, Allo, *Première Épître aux Corinthiens*, 40; Wilckens, *Weisheit und Torheit*, 53; R. Schnackenburg, 'Christian Adulthood according to the Apostle Paul', *CBQ* 25 (1963) 357–58; M. E. Thrall, *The First and Second Letters of Paul to the Corinthians* (Cambridge: Cambridge University Press, 1965) 24; Scroggs, 'Paul: Σοφός and πευνματικός', 44–48; Pearson, *The Pneumatikos-Psychikos Terminology in 1 Corinthians*, 34–35; Barrett, *First Epistle*, 69; Conzelmann, *1 Corinthians*, 60; Stuhlmacher, 'The Hermeneutical Significance of 1 Cor. 2.6–16', 334; Theissen, *Psychological Aspects of Pauline Theology*, 352; M. Bockmuehl, *Revelation and Mystery in Ancient Judaism and Pauline Christianity* (Grand Rapids MI: Eerdmans, 1997) 164–65; A. Standhartinger, 'Weisheit in *Joseph und Aseneth* und den paulinischen Briefen', *NTS* 47 (2001) 496.

725. Grindheim, 'Wisdom for the Perfect', 708: 'There seems to be an intentional ambiguity on Paul's part [with respect to the identity of the τέλειοι].

726. Dio Chrysostom *Or*. 36.33–34. Indeed, the boundary between the initiated and the uninitiated was so firm that one might be required to undergo a second initiation when one moved from group to group within the same cult, as Lucius-Apuleius discovered when he went from Corinth to Rome and sought the company of the worshipers of Isis in *Met*. 11.27.2, 29.5.

727. Burkert, *Ancient Mystery Cults*, 73–75.

Interpreters recognize that vs. 8b is, in effect, a Pauline summary of the passion narrative.[728] Preceded by a reference to what God decreed before the ages began, vss. 7–8 constitute a brief 'redemptive history', culminating in the crucifixion of Jesus.[729] Precisely such a mythological narrative structured as a sequence of actions performed by a god is the 'sacred tale' (ἱερὸς λόγος) communicated to initiates in the mysteries.[730] Indeed, some historians of religion hold that the account of the 'sufferings' (πάθη) of the god is 'the proper content of *mysteria*'.[731] Mystery *logoi* of the 'suffering god' are attested for Dionysus, Attis, and Osiris.[732] Referring to this central aspect of the mysteries, Paul presents the crucifixion of Jesus as the content of the hidden wisdom which he teaches to initiates. Indeed, the application of the lofty title 'Lord of glory', a divine predicate,[733] to *the crucified one*, a usage unparalleled in Paul,[734] may reflect the language of the mysteries, where the suffering, anthropomorphic actant, paradigmatically Dionysus, is described as the 'god' or 'lord' of the mystery.[735]

---

728.   E.g., Heinrici, *Der erste Brief*, 95, 97; Lindemann, *Der erste Korintherbrief*, 64.

729.   A number of scholars find a reference to redemptive history in 2.7–8, i.e., A. Robertson and A. Plummer, *A Critical and Exegetical Commentary on the First Epistle of St. Paul to the Corinthians*, ICC (Edinburgh: T. & T. Clark, 1914) 43; Bultmann, *Theology of the New Testament*, 1.106; N. A. Dahl, 'Formgeschichtliche Beobachtungen zur Christusverkündigung in der Gemeindepredigt' in *Neutestamentliche Studien für Rudolf Bultmann* (Berlin: Töpelmann, 1954) 4; Barrett, *First Epistle*, 71; Fee, *First Epistle*, 105.

730.   On the role of the μῦθος of Demeter and Persephone in the Eleusinian mysteries, see M. Nilsson, *Geschichte der griechischen Religion* (Munich: Beck, 1961) 1.469; N. Richardson, *The Homeric Hymn to Demeter* (Oxford: Oxford University Press, 1974). The myth of Dionysus is explicitly connected with the mysteries in Diodorus 3.62.8; see the discussion of this and other texts in M. L. West, *The Orphic Poems* (Oxford: Oxford University Press, 1983) 140–75; Burkert, *Ancient Mystery Cults*, 73, 155 n.38. For the Greek texts on Isis-Osiris, see Diodorus 1.21–22 and Plutarch *De Iside*; J. Gwyn Griffiths, *The Origins of Osiris* (Berlin: Hessling, 1966). For the ἱερὸς λόγος of Attis, see Pausanias 7.17.10–12; Arnobius 5.5–7; H. Hepding, *Attis, seine Mythen und sein Kult* (Berlin: Topelmann, 1967) 37–41.

731.   Burkert, *Ancient Mystery Cults*, 75, citing Herodotus 2.171; Diodorus 1.97.4; see also Bornkamm, 'μυστήριον', 805.

732.   Dionysius of Halicarnassus *Ant. Rom.* 2.19; Pausanias 7.17.10–12; Plutarch *De Iside* 25, 360D; *De E* 389A; *Def. Or.* 415A.

733.   Ps. 28.3 (LXX), ὁ θεὸς τῆς δόξης, echoed in Acts 7.2; cf. Eph. 1.17, ὁ θεὸς . . . ὁ πατὴρ τῆς δόξης. The epithet 'Lord of glory' is frequent in *Eth. En.*, e.g., 22.14; 25.3,7; 27.3,5, etc., esp. 63.2, 'the Lord of glory and the Lord of wisdom'. Cf. Ps. 24.7, ὁ βασιλεὺς τῆς δόξης.

734.   Commentators note the anomalous character of the description of the crucified as the 'Lord of glory', observing that this usage corresponds more to Johannine christology (John 1.14; 2.11). Elsewhere, Paul reserves the epithet 'glory' to the resurrected and exalted Christ, e.g., Phil. 3.21. To speak of the crucified Christ as the 'Lord of glory' seems to contradict Paul's *kenosis* doctrine, according to which the incarnate Christ emptied himself of his 'glory' (Phil. 2.7). See esp. Weiss, *Der erste Korintherbrief*, 56; Conzelmann, *1 Corinthians*, 63.

735.   E.g., Plato *Phdr.* 265B, where Dionysus is lord (θεός) of the τελεστικὴ μανία. Cf. Diodorus 1.23.2; 3.63.2; Burkert, *Ancient Mystery Cults*, 9, 73–75, 137 n.47.

As in the mysteries, Paul suggests that the fate of the initiate corresponds to that of the god represented in myth and ritual. Paul makes this connection in elegant fashion by using the same word, δόξα ('glory'), to designate the destiny of the Christians that he employs as a qualitative genitive to characterize the Lord Jesus: 'for our glory... the Lord of glory' (2.7–8).[736] This is the principle of *sympatheia* described by ancient commentators on the mysteries: 'They cause sympathy of the souls with the ritual..., so that the initiands assimilate themselves to the holy symbols, leave their own identity, become at home with the gods, and experience divine possession.'[737] Thus, a number of scholars regard the identification of the initiate with the fate of the god as the distinguishing characteristic of the ancient mysteries.[738] By the structure and formulation of his sentence in 2.7–8, Paul evokes the moment when the glorious being of the Christians is unveiled through assimilation to the fate of their glorious Lord.[739]

The motif of the 'searching' of a divine figure ('the Spirit') in 2.10 also derives from the mystery religions. To be sure, the concept of the search for divine knowledge, and the term ἐραυνᾶν (classical ἐρευνᾶν) used by Paul, was broadly current in Hellenism: thus, the poet acknowledges that the human mind is unable to 'search out' divine counsels;[740] Plato's Socrates 'searches' for true wisdom.[741] But it is in the mystery cults that the search of a divine figure (Demeter, Isis) is connected with salvation and results in revelation for the initiates, as in Paul. In the Homeric *Hymn to Demeter*, which contains the foundation myth of the Eleusinian Mysteries, the goddess roams the earth with burning torches in her hands, searching in grief for her lost daughter Persephone.[742] The stages of Demeter's

---

736. The connection between εἰς δόξαν ἡμῶν and ὁ κύριος τῆς δόξης is detected by Weiss, *Der erste Korintherbrief*, 57; Conzelmann, *1 Corinthians*, 63 n.63.

737. Proclus *In Remp.* II. 108,17–30 (Kroll); text and translation cited in Burkert, *Ancient Mystery Cults*, 114, 171 n.161.

738. Bornkamm, 'μυστήριον', 805; W. D. Berner, 'Initiationsriten in Mysterienreligionen, im Gnosticismus und im antiken Judentum' (diss. Göttingen, 1972) 266–67; E. Lohse, *Umwelt des Neuen Testaments* (Göttingen: Vandenhoeck & Ruprecht, 1974) 171–79; Burkert, *Ancient Mystery Cults*, 74–75.

739. Paul's evocation of the principle of *sympatheia* renders moot the question of whether εἰς δόξαν ἡμῶν refers to the future glorification of believers (so the majority of interpreters, e.g., Heinrici, *Der erste Brief*, 96; Schrage, *Der erste Brief*, I.251–52; Collins, *First Corinthians*, 130) or the present glory bestowed by Christ (Conzelmann, *1 Corinthians*, 62; Lindemann, *Der erste Korintherbrief*, 64).

740. Pindar *fr.* 61; see also uses of ἐρευνᾶν in connection with the seer's craft in Sophocles *OT* 562–68, 725; Euripides *Med.* 669; cf. Hunt, *The Inspired Body*, 15–17.

741. Plato *Ap.* 23B, 41B; *Tht.* 174B; *Leg.* 821A; see also Philo *Leg. All.* 3.84; *Fug.* 165; Judith 8.14; cf. Conzelmann, *1 Corinthians*, 66 n.94; Hunt, *The Inspired Body*, 18–19, 40–43, 56.

742. *Hymn. Hom. Cer.* 47–53; see the commentary on this passage by Richardson, *The Homeric Hymn to Demeter*.

mournful search (her wandering with torches, her fasting and abstention from washing, etc.) serve as the model for the ritual actions of the initiand.[743] Similarly, the devotees of Isis imitate the search of their goddess for Osiris, beating their breasts and wailing, then loudly rejoicing when the god is found.[744] Two aspects of Paul's account of the Spirit's search, in particular, suggest that it is meant to recall the mystery cults. First, there is the verb ἐραυνᾶν (ἐρευνᾶν), which is weakened when it is translated, as is customary, 'to search'; for the image which the verb evokes, when one surveys its uses, is more sensual than mental: a scouring, a combing, a search that penetrates the farthest recesses, and fathoms the depths.[745] The verb recalls Demeter's anxious, nine-day search for her daughter, and is even more reminiscent of the initiand's search at the beginning of the mysteries, as recounted by Plutarch: 'there is straying and wandering, the weariness of running this way and that', and then, finally, 'a marvellous light, open country and meadow lands, sacred music and holy visions'.[746] Second, there is the expression τὰ βάθη τοῦ θεοῦ ('the depths of God'), for which there is no precise parallel, either in the Septuagint or in the New Testament.[747] Yet the substance is present in Socrates' account of the 'depth' (βάθος) of the 'reverend and awful' philosopher Parmenides,[748] and in Paul's own encomium of the 'depth' (βάθος) of the wisdom and knowledge of God in Rom. 11.33, passages which employ the language of the mysteries. Paul's reference to the 'depths' through which the Spirit searches evokes the subterranean chambers associated with the mysteries, like the grotto of Pluto at Eleusis.[749] In his account of the ritual journey of an initiate, Plutarch speaks of 'frightening paths in darkness that lead nowhere'.[750] One recalls that Lucian's Menippus descends into the depths in the parody of an initiation ritual in the *Necyomantia*.[751]

Probing more deeply the foundational assumptions of the mysteries, Paul explains that the Christian's capacity to comprehend the things of

---

743. Richardson, *The Homeric Hymn to Demeter*, 211–217; Burkert, *Ancient Mystery Cults*, 77; M. L. West, *Homeric Hymns*, LCL (Cambridge, MA: Harvard University Press, 2003) 8.

744. Firmicus *Err.* 2.9; cf. Seneca *Apoc.* 13; Vitruvius 8 *praef.*; Juvenal 6.527; Lactantius *Inst. Epit.* 18 (23); Augustine *Civ. Dei* 6.10; Burkert, *Ancient Mystery Cults*, 75, 77.

745. See Liddell-Scott-Jones, *Greek-English Lexicon*, 686, s.v. ἐρευνάω and ἐραυνάω, with the insightful discussion in Weiss, *Der erste Korintherbrief*, 60–61.

746. Plutarch *fr.* 178; trans. F. H. Sandbach, *Plutarch's Moralia*, 319; cf. Burkert, *Ancient Mystery Cults*, 91–92.

747. Rightly, Lindemann, *Der erste Korintherbrief*, 68. The closest is Judith 8.14 (βάθος καρδίας ἀνθρώπου); see also *Test. Job* 37.6, τὰ βάθη τοῦ κυρίου.

748. Plato *Tht.* 183E; see already Heinrici, *Der erste Brief*, 100.

749. Burkert, *Ancient Mystery Cults*, 95.

750. Plutarch *fr.* 178; Burkert, *Ancient Mystery Cults*, 162 n.11.

751. Lucian *Nec.* 10, 22.

God derives from the Spirit of God which he has received: 'For what human being knows what is truly human except the human spirit that is within him? So also no one comprehends what is truly God's except the Spirit of God. Now we have received not the spirit of the world, but the Spirit that is from God, so that we may understand the gifts bestowed on us by God' (2.11–12). Paul's explanation is more than an application of the general philosophical principle of 'like by like'.[752] Rather, Paul makes reference to the concept of genealogy in the mysteries, through which the identity and privilege of the initiate is established.[753] According to the texts of the Orphic gold *lamellae*, the initiate is to respond to the guardians of Hades with the declaration: 'I am a son of Earth and of star-filled Heaven.'[754] This statement presupposes that the initiate has come to know his origins in the mysteries.[755] As a result of this self-knowledge, 'kinship' is established between the initiate and the god.[756] Alluding to this aspect of initiation, Paul asserts that the Christian's privileged access to the secrets of God derives from his reception of the Spirit.

Paul's insistence that he restricts the disclosure of 'spiritual things to those who are spiritual' (πνευματικοῖς πνευματικὰ συγκρίνοντες)[757] in 2.13 likewise draws upon a basic concept of the mysteries: the commensurability of

752. Thus, Conzelmann, *1 Corinthians*, 66, tracing the principle through the history of ancient philosophy: Democritus 68B.164 in Diels, *Fragmente*, 2.176; Plato *Prot.* 337C–338A; *Resp.* 508A–511E; *Tim.* 45C; Poseidonius; Manilius *Astronomica* 2.115–16; Sextus Empiricus *Math.* 7.92–93; Cicero *Nat. deor.* 2.32.81–38.97; 2.61.153–67; *Tusc. Disp.* 1.20.46; Philo *Mut. Nom.* 6; *Gig.* 9; see C. W. Müller, *Gleiches zu Gleichem: Ein Prinzip frühgriechischen Denkens* (Wiesbaden: Harrassowitz, 1965) 2–7.

753. On the principle of 'genealogy' in the mysteries, see Burkert, *Ancient Mystery Cults*, 76.

754. M. L. West, 'Three Papyri of Hesiod Corrigenda', *Zeitschrift für Papyrologie und Epigraphik* 18 (1975) 229–36; J. Breslin, *A Greek Prayer* (Malibu, CA: J. Paul Getty Museum, 1985).

755. Burkert, *Ancient Mystery Cults*, 76.

756. In the pseudo-Platonic *Axiochus* (371D), a dying man is termed 'kinsman of the gods' in a context which refers to the Eleusinian mysteries; see also Ps.-Plato *Ep.* 7, 334B, which speaks of the 'kinship' of initiates among themselves and with the gods; see further Apuleius *Met.* 11.24.5; cf. Burkert, *Ancient Mystery Cults*, 76–77, 99–100.

757. There is much debate among commentators over the interpretation of the phrase πνευματικοῖς πνευματικὰ συγκρίνοντες. Debate arises from uncertainty about the gender of πνευματικοῖς and the ambiguity of συγκρίνοντες. When πνευματικοῖς is taken as neuter, the phrase may be translated 'interpreting spiritual things in spiritual terms' – thus Conzelmann, *1 Corinthians*, 56, 67; Fee, *The First Epistle*, 115, among others. But when πνευματικοῖς is construed as masculine, then 'interpreting spiritual things to spiritual persons'; so, Weiss, *Der erste Korintherbrief*, 65; Lindemann, *Der erste Korintherbrief*, 71. In favor of the second interpretation is the continuation of Paul's argument in vss. 14–15, in which the ψυχικὸς ἄνθρωπος is set opposite the πνευματικός.

knowledge.[758] In the mysteries, access to sacred knowledge is granted only to those who have become fit to receive it – a principle which imposes conditions upon candidates for initiation.[759] Philo reflects this principle, when he explains how he guides readers into the deeper meaning of Scripture: 'We are teaching divine mysteries to initiates who are worthy to receive the holiest secrets' (τελετὰς γὰρ ἀναδιδάσκομεν θείας τοὺς τελετῶν ἀξίους τῶν ἱερωτάτων μύστας).[760] Commenting on Aristotle's pronouncement about the mysteries, Synesius explains that the pure vision is granted to the τελούμενοι, but only 'after they have become fit for the purpose'.[761] The principle of the commensurability of knowledge not only establishes the basic distinction between the initiate and the uninitiated,[762] but also creates grades of status among those who are undergoing initiation: thus, the μύστης who has received 'preliminary initiation' is distinguished from the ἐπόπτης who has 'seen' the blessed vision.[763] Paul alludes to this principle and the distinctions it introduces in his explanation of why he speaks wisdom only among 'the

758. On this concept in general, see Bornkamm, 'μυστήριον', 804; Burkert, *Ancient Mystery Cults*, 69, 80, 90–92.

759. Bornkamm, 'μυστήριον', 804: 'Receiving the mysteries is linked to certain conditions which are more or less difficult to attain; by entrance qualification and dedication, the candidate is separated from the host of the uninitiated and enters into the fellowship of initiates who know each other by confessional formulae or symbolical signs.' Plato already alludes to this principle in an influential passage of the *Phaedrus* (249C), which clearly refers to the Eleusinian mysteries: 'he who ever approaches to the full vision of the perfect mysteries (τελέους ἀεὶ τελετὰς τελούμενος), he alone becomes perfect (τέλεος ὄντως μόνος γίγνεται)'.

760. Philo *Cher*. 42. The whole passage (*Cher*. 42–48) is modeled on a mystery λόγος. See the commentary in Riedweg, *Mysterienterminologie bei Platon, Philon*, 71–92.

761. Synesius *Dio* 10, p. 48a (commenting on Aristotle *fr*. 15). See Riedweg, *Mysterienterminologie bei Platon, Philon*, 127–30.

762. See the inscription from the sanctuary of Dionysus at Halicarnassus in *SEG* 28.841; see also Dio Chrysostom *Or*. 36.33–34. See the discussion in Bornkamm, 'μυστήριον', 804; Burkert, *Ancient Mystery Cults*, 69, 90, 153 n.14. It is noteworthy that the only occurrence of the term μυστήριον in the gospels (Mark 4.11 and parallels) reflects the distinction between insiders and outsiders in respect to knowledge: 'To you has been given the mystery of the kingdom of God, but to those outside, everything is in parables.'

763. The distinction between the μύστα who undergo 'preliminary initiation' and the ἐπόπται who experience the 'perfect mysteries' is already presupposed in Plato *Symp*. 209E-F; see Riedweg, *Mysterienterminologie bei Platon, Philon*, 5–6. See also Apuleius *Met*. 11.28.5; 11.30.4, where Lucius first becomes a *cultor*, then, after several initiations, becomes a member of the *pastophori* in Rome; see Burkert, *Ancient Mystery Cults*, 40, 90–91; K. Clinton, 'Stages of Initiation in the Eleusinian and Samothracian Mysteries' in *Greek Mysteries: The Archaeology and Ritual of Ancient Greek Secret Cults*, ed. M. B. Cosmopoulos (London: Routledge, 2003) 50–78.

initiates':[764] 'And we communicate these things, not in speeches (λόγοι) taught by human wisdom, but (in speeches) taught by the Spirit, interpreting spiritual things (πνευματικά) to those who are spiritual. The psychical person, however, does not receive the things of God's Spirit, for they are foolishness to him and he is not able to understand them, because they are spiritually discerned. But the spiritual person discerns all things...' (2.13–15). Paul's use of the term λόγοι ('speeches') in this context to designate the form of what is taught is significant, since λόγοι played an important role in initiation into the mysteries: a λόγος about the gods was transmitted to the μύσται, but withheld from the uninitiated.[765] The πνευματικά (neut. pl.) which Paul interprets to 'spiritual persons' may be meant to recall the 'sacred objects' shown to initiates in the mysteries, to which cryptic reference is made in the 'password' (σύνθημα) given to initiates.[766] The verb συγκρίνειν is a felicitous choice for a parody of mystagogic instruction, since συγκρίνειν means both 'to compare'[767] and 'to interpret'.[768] Paul exploits the ambiguity to emphasize both the compatibility of knowledge and the need for interpretation. Common to both meanings is the principle of commensurability.[769] The interpretation of dreams plays an important role in initiation into the mysteries.[770]

Paul concludes his parody of mystagogic instruction with the high-spirited exclamation: 'But we have the mind of Christ!' (2.16b).[771] Here,

764. The identity of the πνευματικοί of vs. 13 with the τέλειοι of vs. 6 is generally recognized: see already Heinrici, *Das erste Sendschreiben*, 40–41; Weiss, *Der erste Korintherbrief*, 52, 65, 73–74; Conzelmann, *1 Corinthians*, 67; Grindheim, 'Wisdom for the Perfect,' 702–709.

765. See the discussion of the 'knowledge' that was acquired by initiates through transmission of a ἱερὸς λόγος in Burkert, *Ancient Mystery Cults*, 69–70, 81, citing Chrysippus *fr.* 42, *SVF* II.17, among other texts.

766. On the 'password' and the 'sacred objects,' see Clement of Alexandria *Protrepticus* 21.2; Arnobius 5.26; see the insights of A. Delatte, *Le cycéon, breuvage rituel des mystères d'Eleusis* (Paris: Du Cerf, 1955) 5–8; Burkert, *Ancient Mystery Cults*, 94–95.

767. Bauer, *Greek-English Lexicon*, 953 *s.v.* συγκρίνω 2; in favor of this meaning, see Reitzenstein, *Hellenistic Mystery-Religions*, 429–30: 'by comparing spiritual gifts and revelations (which we already possess) with spiritual gifts and revelations (which we receive)'; followed by Lietzmann, *An die Korinther I*, 14; Schrage, *Der erste Brief* 1, 262.

768. Bauer, *Greek-English Lexicon*, 953 *s.v.* συγκρίνω 3. Note esp. the use of συγκρίνω in the LXX for the interpretation of dreams: Gen. 40.8, 16, 22; 41.12–13, 15; Dan. 5.7, 12 (Theod.); see also *Joseph and Asenath* 4.14. In favor of this meaning, see Weiss, *Der erste Korintherbrief*, 64–65; Lindemann, *Der erste Korintherbrief*, 71.

769. Reflected in the primary meaning, 'to bring things together, combine'; see Bauer, *Greek-English Lexicon*, 953 *s.v.* συγκρίνω 1. See esp. Maximus of Tyre *Dial.* 16.4c: συνετὰ συνετοῖς λέγων ('speaking wise things to the wise').

770. See Apuleius *Met.* 11.17, where the date of the initiation of Lucius is determined by a dream; Artemidorus *Oner.* 2.39, where the Eleusinian divinities appear in a dream.

771. On the hyperbolic quality of the concluding assertion in 2.16b, see Weiss, *Der erste Korintherbrief*, 67.

too, Paul makes allusion to the mysteries, in which saving knowledge is achieved by union with the deity.[772] In a text such as the *Poimandres*, which makes use of the language of the mysteries,[773] 'mind' (νοῦς) is bestowed as a heavenly gift upon the one who seeks knowledge of God.[774] The person thus favored receives divine 'mind' (ἔννοια) and becomes the teacher of his brothers.[775] Appropriating this language, Paul portrays himself as an inspired teacher of the Christian mystery.[776] Paul emphasizes the one with whom he has achieved unity by replacing κυρίου of the Septuagint with Χριστοῦ, in his quotation of Isa. 40.13.[777] Paul is the mystagogue of 'Christ crucified'.[778]

Beyond the motifs and topics, the structure and composition of 2.6–16 mark the paragraph off from its literary context as a unit, a kind of 'interlude'.[779] The disposition of the passage is extraordinarily elegant, divided into three parts, according to an αβα schema:[780] a) vss. 6–9, the hidden wisdom which is not of this age; b) vss. 10–12, the Spirit which searches the depths of God; c) vss. 13–16, the spiritual persons who are able to receive divine wisdom.[781] Each of the sub-sections is further divided and constructed on the same αβα pattern (e.g., vs. 6 = α, vs. 7 = β, vs. 8 = α), the first sub-section expanded by a citation of scripture (vs. 9), and the last climaxed by a rhetorical question and its ironic reply (vs. 16).[782] Paul has

---

772. Reitzenstein, *Hellenistic Mystery-Religions*, 431–32; Weiss, *Der erste Korintherbrief*, 68; Collins, *First Corinthians*, 137–38.

773. The *Poimandres* has a Hellenistic Jewish background, as demonstrated by B. A. Pearson, 'Jewish Elements in *Corpus Hermeticum* 1 (*Poimandres*)' in R. van den Broek and M. J. Vermaseren, *Studies in Gnosticism and Hellenistic Religions Presented to G. Quispel* (Leiden: Brill, 1981) 336–48.

774. *Herm. Wr.* 1.2ff.; Reitzenstein, *Hellenistic Mystery-Religions*, 432; R. Behm, 'νοῦς,' *TDNT* 4.958–59.

775. *Corp. Herm.* 1.1ff.; 32; Reitzenstein, *Hellenistic Mystery-Religions*, 432.

776. Weiss, *Der erste Korintherbrief*, 68; Conzelmann, *1 Corinthians*, 65, 69; Jewett, *Paul's Anthropological Terms*, 377.

777. The change of κυρίου to Χριστοῦ is deliberate, as can be seen from Rom. 11.34, where Paul quotes Isa. 40.13 without alteration; so, already, Weiss, *Der erste Korintherbrief*, 68–69; W. Willis, 'The "Mind of Christ" in 1 Corinthians 2,16', *Biblica* 70 (1989) 117.

778. Cf. 1 Cor. 1.17, 23; 2.2; Willis, 'The "Mind of Christ" in 1 Corinthians 2,16', 118.

779. Weiss, *Der erste Korintherbrief*, 52 describes 2.6–16 as an 'Einlage'.

780. The αβα schema is created by the resumption of σοφίαν λαλοῦμεν (vs. 6) in the phrase ἃ καὶ λαλοῦμεν (in vs. 13); on this point, see Weiss, *Der erste Korintherbrief*, 52; Lindemann, *Der erste Korintherbrief*, 59.

781. For the tripartite division of 2.6–16, see Weiss, *Der erste Korintherbrief*, 52; Lindemann, *Der erste Korintherbrief*, 59.

782. On the expansion of the first sub-section (a) through the scripture citation in vs. 9, see Weiss, *Der erste Korintherbrief*, 52. On the climactic rhetorical question and thetic reply in vs. 16, see Lindemann, *Der erste Korintherbrief*, 59.

exerted all of his rhetorical ability to create the impression of a complex, yet elegant, oral performance.[783]

As one looks back over this remarkable paragraph, it is evident how fully the device of self-parody has served Paul's purposes. Within his larger argument, Paul wished to assert that the message of the crucified Christ is 'the wisdom of God', without gainsaying his former acknowledgment that the word of the cross is 'foolishness' to the elite. In Paul's parody, authority is simultaneously asserted and undermined: the mysterious power of the word of the cross is fully maintained, while the seriousness of the messenger is mocked and destabilized. To the wise, powerful and well-born in Corinth, Paul says: 'I know that you view me as a charlatan who goes from door to door offering private initiations through the strangest of all discourses. So I appear, and so do all who preach the message of the crucified Lord. And yet, the wisdom and power of the message survives all ridicule. Indeed, those from whom this wisdom is hidden are shown to be pretentious fools, who do not know how to live, and who are doomed to die.' The combination of truth and jest in Paul's discourse is wholly in keeping with the paradoxical style of the serio-comic (σπουδογέλοιον) which connects Paul with the tradition of Socrates and Menippus, who prefigure Paul's literary strategy.[784]

In conclusion, our reading of Paul's discourse of 'wisdom for the initiates' in 2.6–16 attributes to Paul a greater complexity of perception and motivation than is generally recognized by interpreters. Accordingly, Paul's response to the claims of certain teachers to communicate 'wisdom' is neither simple affirmation nor simple rejection, but a profound appreciation of the ambiguity of the undertaking. In Paul's discourse of 'wisdom for the initiates,' one simultaneously hears two voices (the product of Paul's ironic consciousness): on the one hand, the voice of the mystagogic preacher communicating hidden wisdom to initiates; on the other hand, the voice of the apostolic author mocking the competence of his own efforts. Paradoxically, Paul's decision to parody himself, and his

783. Weiss, 'Beiträge zur paulinischen Rhetorik,' 42–45; Theissen, *Psychological Aspects of Pauline Theology*, 347–49.

784. On the σπουδογέλοιον ('jesting-earnest') as a generic niche in Hellenistic literary tradition whose purpose was to convey truth under cover of jest, see G. C. Fiske, *Lucilius and Horace. A Study in the Classical Theory of Imitation* (Madison: University of Wisconsin, 1920) 18–19, 47–49, 88–92, 96–97, 100–101, 143–47, 168–75; Grant, *Ancient Rhetorical Theories of the Laughable*, 20, 50–51, 55–61; Branham, *Unruly Eloquence*, 26–28. Hermogenes describes the Socratic dialogue as a πλοκὴ σπουδαῖα καὶ γελοῖα (Spengel, *Rhetores Graeci*, 2.445). Menippus is expressly called σπουδογέλοιος by Strabo (16.2.29). The well-known line of Horace (*Sat.* 1.23–24), *ridentem dicere verum quid vetat*, appears to be a conscious paraphrase of the Greek σπουδογέλοιον. For the mimes of Sophron as σπουδαιογέλοια, see the scholiast on Demosthenes *Olyn.* 2.19.

capacity to do so, enhances his own moral authority, and undermines that of his apostolic rivals, with their earnest pretensions to eloquent wisdom.

3. *Affirmation*

As the final moment in his analysis, Paul affirms that, despite the divine reversal of values, the message about the cross remains 'foolishness' in this present age. Although the overthrow of the wisdom of the world is accomplished in the purpose of God (1.21) through the cross of Christ (1.17, 23), the event remains unrecognized by the rulers of this age (2.6–8). The violence of the rulers against Jesus is perpetuated against his followers as ridicule, shame, and derision (1.26–28). The apostles of Christ are 'reviled,... persecuted,... slandered... to this very day' (4.12–13). Therefore, Paul concludes, 'No one should deceive himself. If anyone among you thinks that he is wise in this age,[785] let him become a fool (μωρὸς γενέσθω), that he may become wise' (3.18).

The small amount of space devoted to the final step in Paul's analysis belies the importance of the affirmation for his argument as a whole. For although the resolution that the Christian must 'become a fool' is explicitly articulated only here, at the climax of the theological analysis,[786] the attitude is presupposed throughout, and controls the development of Paul's thought.[787]

It is clear that 3.18–19a, and the paragraph which these verses introduce (3.18–23), is the summation of the argument developed since 1.10. The wording of the conditional sentence in 1.18 ('If someone among you thinks that he is wise in this age, let him become a fool, etc.') recalls Paul's decision with respect to his own preaching in 2.2: δοκεῖ is the counterpart

---

785. There is considerable debate among commentators over the construal of the phrase ἐν τῷ αἰῶνι τούτῳ ('in this age'), whether, that is, it belongs to the protasis as a qualification of σοφός... ἐν ὑμῖν, or to the apodosis modifying μωρός. Weiss (*Der erste Korintherbrief*, 87) argues that when ἐν τῷ αἰῶνι τούτῳ is taken with the protasis, the result is a stylistically inelegant doublet of ἐν ὑμῖν. Thus, ἐν τῷ αἰῶνι τούτῳ should be regarded as the energetic beginning of the apodosis: 'in this age, let him become a fool...' However, Paul does not elsewhere begin statements with prepositional phrases refering to 'this age'; thus Robertson and Plummer, *A Critical and Exegetical Commentary on the First Epistle of St. Paul to the Corinthians*, 70. For further discussion, see Lindemann, *Der erste Korintherbrief*, 91. In terms of the content and meaning of the verse, the phrase 'in this age' describes the horizon of both wisdom and foolishness. Consequently, one should entertain the possibility that the ambiguous placement of the phrase ἐν τῷ αἰῶνι τούτῳ is deliberate, whatever the resulting stylistic inelegance.

786. Several commentators refer to 3.18–23 as the 'peroration' of the rhetorical argument begun in 1.18 (or 1.10): thus, Schrage, *Der erste Brief*, I.311; Merklein, *Der erste Brief an die Korinther. Kapitel 1–4*, 280; Collins, *First Corinthians*, 162–63.

787. Wilckens, *Weisheit und Torheit*, 9.

of ἔκρινα, while ἐν ὑμῖν is repeated to establish the context of judgment.[788] What is required of the Corinthians is a resolve like that which Paul made when he came to Corinth preaching the crucified Christ.[789] Similarly, the justification for the resolution, supplied in 3.19a ('For the wisdom of this world is foolishness with God'), echoes the paradoxical formulation in 1.20.[790] The pair of scriptural texts cited in 3.19b-20 recall Paul's quotation of Isa. 24.14 in 1.19.[791] The paraenetic inference that Paul draws with respect to human boasting in 3.21a is reminiscent of the admonitions of 1.29, 31.[792] Finally, Paul's reference to himself, Apollos, and Cephas in 3.22 recalls the party slogans of 1.12.[793] Paul thus forms a rhetorical *inclusio* around the development of his argument since the beginning of the letter.[794] The point of this 'ring-composition'[795] is to bring the reader to embrace the decision to 'become a fool'.

The significance of Paul's affirmation of foolishness and the implications of his resolution become apparent only when Paul's decision is placed in the cultural tradition that connects Socrates, satire, and the mime. For in this tradition, the necessity of becoming a fool is consistently recognized and affirmed. Moreover, one discovers that the decision to become a fool serves pedagogical purposes, by constructing a scenario that enables critical self-insight and liberation from the tyranny of conventional wisdom.

We may begin with Socrates, who is depicted in the writings of his followers as a teacher who avowed ignorance in order to bring his contemporaries to self-knowledge.[796] As we have seen, Socrates did not attempt to correct the impression that he was a foolish, comic figure.[797] On the contrary, he spoke of his own wisdom as 'a sorry thing, and questionable, like a dream'.[798] His characteristic utterance took the form of a disavowal of knowledge: 'What I do not know, I do not think that I know.'[799] Socrates' detractors construed his appropriation of the role of the

788. Weiss, *Der erste Korintherbrief*, 86.
789. Weiss, *Der erste Korintherbrief*, 87.
790. Lindemann, *Der erste Korintherbrief*, 91.
791. Collins, *First Corinthians*, 162.
792. Lindemann, *Der erste Korintherbrief*, 91.
793. Collins, *First Corinthians*, 162–63; Lindemann, *Der erste Korintherbrief*, 91.
794. Collins, *First Corinthians*, 87, 162.
795. Lindemann, *Der erste Korintherbrief*, 91.
796. On Socrates' avowal of ignorance and his educational intent, see W. Jaeger, 'Socrates als Erzieher' in *Paideia. Die Formung des griechischen Menschen*, Vol. 2 (Berlin, 1954) 74–82; Friedländer, *Plato. An Introduction*, 137–53; Vlastos, *Socrates, Ironist and Moral Philosopher*, ch. 1; Stokes, 'Socrates' Mission', 26–81.
797. Plato *Apol.* 21A-24A. See the other texts assembled and discussed by Reich, *Der Mimus*, 354–60.
798. Plato *Symp.* 175E.
799. Plato *Apol.* 21D; see Guthrie, *Socrates*, 85–89, 122–25.

fool as an ironic game, the act of a dissembler, accusing him of malicious irony, and even of hubris.[800] But Plato insists that Socrates' profession of ignorance is genuine.[801] Socrates claims that he knows nothing but how much he desires knowledge.[802] Socrates always includes himself in the admission of ignorance to which the exercise of dialectic drives his interlocutors at the conclusion of the aporetic dialogues: 'I too am ignorant'.[803] To be sure, the Platonic Socrates knows that his consciousness of his own ignorance makes him 'wiser to some small extent' than other men.[804] But this knowledge does not result in hubris, nor is his irony a disguise for contempt. Ignorance is the necessary attitude of the lover of wisdom, who is all too aware of what he lacks.[805] If there is dissimulation in Socrates' approach, when he places himself on the same level as the young men,[806] it is an expression of a sincere, pedagogical intent to bring others with him as companions on the ascent to knowledge of the beautiful and the good.[807]

The stories in the *Life of Aesop* are also imbued with the recognition that the wise man must become a fool. The wisdom of Aesop, like that of Socrates, is aporetic and sceptical.[808] Asked by his philosopher-master what he knows, Aesop answers, 'Nothing at all' (ὅλως οὐδέν). The point of Aesop's avowal of ignorance is to expose the ambitions of the professional intellectuals as baseless. The philosopher's students grasp the point, and are momentarily liberated from their pretensions: 'Hey! He's wonderful.... No man alive knows everything. That's why he said he knew nothing. That's why he laughed.'[809] In the running battle of wits between master and slave that makes up the central section of the *Life*, Aesop teases and provokes Xanthus by interpreting his commands in a stupidly literal sense.[810] In these exchanges, Aesop's liberated simplicity is repeatedly contrasted with the philosopher's bondage to conventional wisdom.

800. Plato *Symp.* 219C; see the discussion in M. Gagarin, 'Socrates' *Hybris* and Alcibiades' Failure,' *Phoenix* 31 (1977) 22–37. According to Diogenes Laertius (2.19), Timon of Phlius lampooned Socrates as a 'dissembler'.

801. Friedländer, *Plato. An Introduction*, 140–44; Brickhouse and Smith, 'The Paradox of Socrates' Ignorance', 30–38.

802. Plato *Symp.* 177D; see the discussion in Lowenstam, 'Paradoxes in Plato's *Symposium*', 85–104.

803. Friedländer, *Plato. An Introduction*, 141–42.

804. Plato *Apol.* 21D; cf. Guthrie, *Socrates*, 85–89; C. D. C. Reeve, *Socrates in the Apology* (Indianapolis: University of Indiana, 1989) 15–18.

805. Plato *Resp.* 336E; cf. Friedländer, *Plato. An Introduction*, 143.

806. Plato *Alc I* 124C; *Char.* 158D; *Meno* 96D; *Laches* 201A.

807. Plato *Symp.* 212B; cf. Friedländer, *Plato. An Introduction*, 141–42.

808. Daly, *Aesop without Morals*, 21; Winkler, *Auctor and Actor*, 283.

809. *Vit. Aesop.* 25; trans. Daly, *Aesop without Morals*, 42–43.

810. *Vit. Aesop.* 20–91.

Because the philosopher assumes that he must answer every question, he becomes ashamed and suicidal, while Aesop, who admits that his knowledge is minimal, saves the lives of the Samians.[811] The purpose of Aesop's foolishness is pedagogical. In a fable that Aesop relates to king Croesus, the grotesque little man compares himself to a harmless insect whose drone is a solace to wayfarers: 'Poor as my body is, I utter words of commonsense and thereby benefit the life of mortals.'[812]

The slaves in Plautine comedy persist in foolery, despite the lashes, gashes and crosses with which they are threatened, exclaiming, with impudent resolve, *non curo*! ('I don't care!').[813] Paradoxically, the foolishness in which Plautine slaves inure themselves is shown to be true shrewdness, the path to a higher freedom.[814] Similarly, the fool in the *Charition* mime readily embraces the suggestion that he suborn the barbarian king with undiluted wine.[815] Thereby, he descends to a deeper level of foolishness, joining in the drunken dance of the barbarians, but in the process, he effects the escape of his mistress.[816]

A convincing case has recently been made that Horace chooses to portray himself as a buffoon in the *Satires*, in the service of his moralistic intent.[817] Rejecting the conventional role of *sapiens*, Horace carefully crafts a persona of foolishness: he is hot-tempered and ill-suited to polite society, his toga hangs askew, his haircut is lopsided, he wears a floppy shoe.[818] The satirist describes his behavior at dinner as that of a graceless boor: he gets drunk and pisses on the dinner couch, breaks an antique goblet, grabs a piece of pullet from the wrong side of the plate, and so on.[819] Horace's description of himself in these passages reveals the strong influence of comedy and mime.[820] Horace clearly places himself in the class of the *stulti* (fools).[821] The issue is not whether the historical Horace ever dressed in such a way or misbehaved at Maecenas' table. Rather, the

---

811.   *Vit. Aesop.* 84–85.

812.   *Vit. Aesop.* 99; trans. Daly, *Aesop without Morals*, 78.

813.   Plautus *Persa* 264; *Bacchides* 268–71; *Pseudolus* 1325; *Asinaria* 319, 545–51. See the discussion in Segal, *Roman Laughter*, 143–58.

814.   E.g., Plautus *Epidicus* 728–33; *Mostellaria* 1178–81. Cf. Segal, *Roman Laughter*, 158–65.

815.   *POxy* 413 ('Charition') lines 50–55.

816.   *POxy* 413 ('Charition') 60–107; see the comments of Wiemken, *Der griechische Mimus*, 64–66.

817.   Freudenburg, *The Walking Muse*, 21–33.

818.   Horace *Sat.* 1.3.29–34, with the analysis of Freudenburg, *The Walking Muse*, 27–29. Cf. Horace *Ep.* 1.1.94–97.

819.   Horace *Sat.* 1.3.90–94, with the commentary of Armstrong, *Horace*, 37–41.

820.   See, e.g., Plautus *Miles gloriosus* 648–56; Freudenburg, *The Walking Muse*, 27, 29.

821.   See esp. Horace *Sat.* 1.3.76–79; see the note on this passage in Fairclough, *Horace. Satires*, 38.

satirist has chosen to render himself as a bumpkin or buffoon, in accordance with a well-known comic type,[822] in order to teach those who trust in the stability of conventional beliefs and institutions that they do not know how to live; they crucify slaves for the slightest offence and refuse to forgive friends their trespasses.[823] In a comic inversion of the Stoic paradox, Horace insists that 'only the fool is truly wise'.[824]

In a letter of advice to his young friend Lucilius, Seneca explains that one who seeks the Supreme Good in life will find himself in opposition to the common conception of what is true and good, and must even be willing to be considered a fool.[825] Summoning the example of Socrates, Seneca summarizes his teaching as follows: 'Follow these rules of conduct, if my words carry weight with you, in order that you may be happy. And let some men think you even a fool (*stultus*). Allow any man who so desires to insult you and work you wrong; but if only virtue dwell with you, you will suffer nothing. If you wish to be happy, if you would be in good faith a good man, let one person or another despise you.'[826]

Readers familiar with the tradition of cultural criticism that connects Socrates and Cynic satire with comedy and mime would have recognized three implications of Paul's admonition to 'become a fool'. First, Paul's affirmation of the necessity of foolishness is a recognition of the tyranny of conventional wisdom. The power of worldly wisdom is so great that it results in self-deception, as Paul points out: 'Let no one deceive himself' (μηδεὶς ἑαυτὸν ἐξαπατάτω). Hence, the critique of conventional wisdom must employ indirection, a dialectical movement of self-denial. In his attempt to educate the politician Alcibiades, Socrates assumes the ridiculous guise of a Silenus.[827] But the spell of elite culture is so strong that Alcibiades is unable to understand the strange, truly loving Socrates; ultimately, Alcibiades abandons the philosophical life, 'overcome by the honor conferred by the crowd'.[828] The *Life of Aesop* embodies the same insight into the tyranny of conventional wisdom in the story of the death of Aesop

822. Corbett, *The Scurra*, 64; Freudenburg, *The Walking Muse*, 32–33.
823. Horace *Sat.* 1.3.76–98.
824. For the Stoic saying 'Everyone save the wise man is a fool' or 'mad', see, e.g., *SVF* III.165,26; III.166,28; III.167,31.
825. Seneca *Ep.* 71.1–7; this passage is quoted in connection with 1 Cor. 4.8–13 by Stowers, 'Paul on the Use and Abuse of Reason', 260.
826. Seneca *Ep.* 71.7; trans. R. M. Gummere, *Seneca. Epistles 66–92*, LCL (Cambridge, MA: Harvard University Press, 1994) 77.
827. Plato *Symp.* 215A-B, 217A, 221D-222A; see the commentary of Dover, *Plato. Symposium*, 164–65; Bury, *The Symposium of Plato*, 143.
828. Plato *Symp.* 216B; see Gagarin, 'Socrates' *Hybris* and Alcibiades' Failure', 22–37.

at the hands of the Delphians.[829] When Aesop comes to Delphi, he gives an exhibition of his commonsense, fabulistic wisdom, as elsewhere. But the pale, greybearded men of Delphi remain unresponsive and give Aesop nothing.[830] Aesop attempts to illustrate the 'bondage' of the Delphians to conventional wisdom by telling the story of the ancestral origin of the Delphians as slaves sent to the shrine of Apollo as spoils of war.[831] But the Delphians remain trapped in convention, anxious over their 'reputation'; so they devise a plot to kill Aesop by a trick.[832] In keeping with this tradition, Paul recognizes the tyranny of conventional wisdom.

Second, Paul's decision to 'become a fool' is a reflection of the paradoxical nature of wisdom in the present age. Paul's formulation of the paradox is absolute: anyone who wishes to be wise in this age must become a fool. In his embrace of paradox, Paul places himself in the Socratic tradition. In the writings of his followers, Socrates is depicted as a philosopher who embraced paradox as the proper mode of beauty and truth. Socrates is paradoxical in appearance, behavior, and argument. One need only recall the comical scene in Xenophon's *Symposium* in which Socrates challenges the handsome Critobulus to a contest of beauty.[833] Socrates praises his bulging eyes which see the world from all sides, his flaring nostrils which catch scents from all about, and his wide mouth which can bite off the biggest portion.[834] Similarly, in the *Memorabilia*, Socrates offers his services as a procurer to the beautiful courtesan Theodote, making fun of his own habit of attracting rich gentlemen.[835] Socrates' λόγοι are likewise paradoxical: his arguments have a ridiculous exterior that conceals a serious core.[836] Alcibiades explains that 'Socrates wraps his arguments up in just the kind of expressions you'd expect of an insufferable satyr. He talks about pack asses and blacksmiths and shoemakers and tanners,... But if you open up his arguments and get into the skin of them, you'll find that they're the only arguments in the world

---

829.   *Vit. Aesop.* 124–42. On the antiquity and complex history of this piece of the Aesop saga, see Wiechers, *Aesop in Delphi*, 31–33; G. Nagy, *The Best of the Achaeans* (Baltimore: Johns Hopkins University Press, 1979) 280–90.

830.   *Vit. Aesop.* 124.

831.   *Vit. Aesop.* 126.

832.   *Vit. Aesop.* 127–42.

833.   Xenophon *Symp.* 4.20; 5.1–9; see Reich, *Der Mimus*, 358.

834.   Xenophon *Symp.* 5.5,6,7.

835.   Xenophon *Mem.* 3.11,16–17; Reich, *Der Mimus*, 358.

836.   It is doubtless because of the serio-comic character of Socratic discourse that Aristotle (*Poet.* 1447b8–10) mentions the Σωκρατικοὶ λόγοι and the mimes of Sophron in the same breath.

that have any sense at all.'[837] Plautus' comedies repeatedly enact the implicit paradox that only the foolish slaves are shrewd and truly free.[838] Horace bases a saturnalian dialogue on the same paradoxical premise: the slave Davus demonstrates that he is wiser and freer than his master.[839] To make sure that his Corinthian readers grasp his point, Paul formulates his insight concerning the paradoxical nature of wisdom in a statement that recalls, and comically reverses, one of the *paradoxa Stoicorum* ('everyone save the wise man is a fool').[840]

Third, Paul's decision to 'become a fool' implies a pedagogical purpose. This intent is embodied not only in the purpose clause in 3.18b, ἵνα γένηται σοφός ('in order that he may be wise'), but must be assumed to be present throughout, even in ironic and caustic passages (such as 3.1–4 and 4.8). This is the conclusion to which one is led by the constancy of this motif in the comic-philosophic tradition. Socrates is the prime example: 'he assumed the role of an ignorant man' in order to disabuse others of their pretensions to knowledge.[841] Socrates' foolishness was a guise that enabled him to play his pedagogical game of question and answer.[842] Aesop is presented in the *Life* as the educator of philosophers and kings; his deformity is a grotesque façade behind which he dismantles conventional assumptions about wisdom and power.[843] Horace ingeniously embodies the motif of the educative purpose of assumed folly in his presentation of the diatribe of the slave Davus as some scraps of lectures picked up by the door-keeper of the Stoic philosopher Crispinus.[844] To the degree that Paul's Corinthian readers were able to apprehend the pedagogical purpose behind his foolishness, they may have been able to tolerate, and perhaps even to appreciate, passages such as 3.1–4, 4.8, and 4.14–21, which strike modern readers as condescending, sarcastic, and threatening.

837. Plato *Symp.* 221E-222A. See C. L. Griswold, 'Irony and Aesthetic Language in Plato's Dialogues' in *Philosophy and Literature*, ed. D. Bollig (New York: Scribners, 1987) 71–99, esp. 76–82.
838. Segal, *Roman Laughter*, 158.
839. Horace *Sat.* 2.7, esp. line 42.
840. *SVF* III.165,26; III.166,28; III.167,31; Cicero *Paradoxa Stoicorum* 5. On allusion to Stoic paradoxes in 1 Cor. 4.9–13, see Stowers, 'Paul on the Use and Abuse of Reason,' 260–61.
841. Quintilian *Inst. Orat.* 9.2.46.
842. Jaeger, 'Socrates als Erzieher', 74–76; Friedländer, *Plato. An Introduction*, 141–42.
843. E.g., *Vit. Aesop.* 87–88; see Winkler, *Auctor and Actor*, 287–91.
844. Horace *Sat.* 2.7.44–45.

4. *Consequences*

Paul's theological analysis has consequences for all who are addressed by the 'foolishness' of 'the word of the cross': the Corinthians, Paul's missionary rivals, and Paul himself and his colleagues. Discussion of these consequences is concentrated in the section 3.1–4.21, but is not limited to these chapters. Already in the *narratio* of the letter (1.11–17), and later, when Paul makes the Corinthians (1.26–31) and himself (2.1–5) examples of his argument, he reveals his understanding of the way in which various responses to 'the word of the cross' determine one's fate in the divine economy. As Paul portrays these consequences, he draws freely upon characters from farce and mime, in keeping with the theatrical metaphor he has developed throughout these chapters.

First, we examine Paul's elucidation of the consequences for the Corinthian Christians. As 'the word of the cross' evokes two, diametrically opposed responses from hearers (1.18), so is it twofold in its effect.[845] On the one hand, the judgment of 'foolishness' rebounds upon the ones who render it, so that their lives become paradoxically moronic and shameful (1.27–28), despite their participation in elite culture. On the other hand, those who are called and who respond in faith (1.21b, 26) find themselves suddenly empowered, endowed with wisdom, justice, and liberty (1.30). These consequences are the result of the divine reversal that the event of the crucified Christ manifests.[846]

In the *narratio* of the letter (1.11–17), where Paul briefly recounts the incidence of faction among the Corinthians, he portrays the quarrelsome Corinthians as the partisans of various theater actors, whose rivalry threatens to destroy civic concord.[847] Paul achieves this effect by formulating his impression of the divisiveness of the Corinthians in a series of slogans which mimic the cheers of fans of star actors in the theater: 'What I mean is this – that each of you says, "I am [a partisan] of Paul!" or "I am [a partisan] of Apollos!" or "I am [a partisan] of Cephas!" etc.' (1.12). The closest formal parallel to the slogans in 1.12 is found in Quintilian's account of a choice between leaders of rival schools of rhetoric: 'Asked whether he was an adherent of Theodorus or Apollodorus, a certain teacher of rhetoric replied: "I am [a partisan] of the Thracian!" (*Ego parmularius sum*).'[848] Like Paul, Quintilian ironizes the

---

845. Heinrici, *Der erste Brief*, 67; Weiss, *Der erste Korintherbrief*, 25; Wilckens, *Weisheit und Torheit*, 21; Collins, *First Corinthians*, 102.

846. See the thoughts of A. Badiou, *Saint Paul: The Foundation of Universalism* (Stanford, CA: Stanford University Press, 2003) 46–47, 55.

847. For this understanding of 1.11–17, see already Welborn, *Politics and Rhetoric in the Corinthian Epistles*, 14–15.

848. Quintilian *Inst. Orat.* 2.11.1–2.

tendency to partisanship by appropriating a cry from the amphitheater, where partisans of star gladiators identified themselves and expressed their enthusiams by shouting their allegiance to various champions.[849] In 14–15 A.D., riots caused by the partisans of actors in Rome were of such magnitude that they are mentioned by six different historians.[850] Tiberius and the senate took harsh measures to quell the riots and restore the peace: the actors (*histriones*) and the 'heads of the factions' were banished from Italy.[851] Paul's caricature of the adherents of Apollos, Cephas, and others is as ominous as it is comical: in their admiration for these virtuosi apostles, the Corinthians make themselves quarrelsome partisans of actors, rowdy members of theater claques; moreover, the strife which their partisanship foments risks punitive intervention by the One to whom all things are placed in subjection, who will not tolerate divisions in the body of Christ.

At two points in the epistle, Paul insists that those Corinthians who pronounce the judgment of 'foolishness' upon the 'word of the cross' have shown themselves to be 'children' in matters of the spirit. In the first instance, Paul explains that since the Corinthians are still 'like infants in Christ' (ὡς νηπίοις ἐν Χριστῷ),' he is obliged to nourish them with 'milk' (γάλα) rather than with 'solid food' (3.1–2). The point of the metaphor[852] is obviously the spiritual immaturity of the Corinthians.[853] In the second instance, Paul highlights the misbehavior of the Corinthian 'children' (τέκνα) by means of a well-developed allusion to 'The Guardian' mime in 4.14–21, as argued above.[854] These childhood metaphors gain vividness and

---

849. Groups came to the amphitheater organized as guilds, sat in compact armies under acknowledged leaders, called *capita factionem* or *duces* (Suetonius *Tib.* 37; *Nero* 20.3), and engaged in unison cheering. See L. Robert, *Les Gladiateurs dans l'Orient grec*. Bibliothèque de l'Ecole des hautes études 278 (Paris: Hakkert, 1940) 41; R. MacMullen, *Enemies of the Roman Order* (Cambridge, MA: Harvard University Press, 1966) 168–70.

850. Tacitus *Ann.* 1.77; Dio Cassius 57.14.10; Velleius Paterculus 2.126.2; Suetonius *Tib.* 37; Zosimus 1.6.1; and, arguably, Valerius Maximus 2.4.1. See the discussion of this famous episode by E. J. Jory, 'The Early Pantomime Riots' in *Maistor: Classical, Byzantine and Renaissance Studies for Robert Browning* (Canberra: Australian Association for Byzantine Studies, 1984) 57–66; W. J. Slater, 'Pantomime Riots,' *Classical Antiquity* 13 (1994) 120–44. On Roman theater riots in general, see H. Bollinger, *Theatralis Licentia* (Basel: Winterthur, 1969).

851. Tacitus *Ann.* 4.14.4; cf. Velleius Paterculus 2.126.2. The actors who caused the riots are often described as 'pantomimes' in literature on the episode. But Tacitus' use of the less precise term *histriones*, and his reference to 'the old Oscan farce,' suggest that those who caused the riots were mime actors. On partisanship caused by actors, see in general, Leppin, *Histrionen*; C. Rouché, *Performers and Partisans at Aphrodisias in the Roman and Late Roman Periods* (London: Society for the Promotion of Roman Studies, 1993).

852. For other transferred uses of νήπιος in Paul, see 1 Thess. 2.7; Gal. 4.3; Rom. 2.20.

853. See the discussion in W. Grundmann, 'Die NHΠIOI in der urchristlichen Paränese', *NTS* 5 (1958/59) 188–205.

854. See above, ch. 4.

resonance from the theatrical context which Paul's language evokes. Unruly, mischievous children populate the mime. A fragmentary mime-papyrus in the British museum refers to a young girl (παρθένος κόρη), her cruel brother (σύγγονε βάρβαρε), a sister (φιλάδελφε), a nurse (τροφέ), and an indulgent father (γενέτης ἀγρώτατος).[855] The plot of the mime (to the degree to which it can be reconstructed) concerns the girl's attempt to keep her misbehavior a secret.[856]

As an additional consequence of the judgment of 'foolishness' upon the 'word of the cross', Paul portrays leading figures in the Corinthian church as arrogant and abusive patrons. In 4.8, Paul addresses those who are 'filled', and 'rich', and who 'reign like kings'. The first two appellatives are straightforward indicators of social status: 'satiety' is a characteristic of the rich, and is constantly connected with 'wealth' in ancient literature.[857] More revealing as an indicator of the relationship between Paul and certain persons at Corinth is the third expression, 'you reign like kings' (ἐβασιλεύσατε). By the first century, 'king' (*rex*) was the client's term for a rich patron.[858] Horace calls his patron Maecenas 'king and father' (*rex paterque*).[859] Juvenal's hapless clients refer to the rich patrons whose largesse they pursue as 'kings'.[860] By styling certain persons at Corinth as 'kings', Paul ridicules their pretension to patronal position over himself and his colleagues. Juvenal satirizes kingly patrons who invite their clients to the table, but give them nothing to eat.[861] The queenly matron in the adultery mime crucifies her slaves and exploits her clients.[862] Like the arrogant patrons in satire and mime, certain Corinthians are guilty of neglect and abuse of social inferiors. They feast luxuriously and celebrate their status, while the poor, dishonored apostles are hungry, thirsty, naked, beaten, and homeless (4.8–13). Paul ironically reminds these patrons of what they have forgotten: that everything they 'have' they have 'received' as a gift; thus they have earned no 'distinctions' and have nothing of which to 'boast' (4.7).

---

855. Milne, *Catalogue of the Literary Papyri in the British Museum* (1927) no. 52, p. 39; text and translation in *Popular Mime*, ed. I. C. Cunningham, LCL (Cambridge, MA: Harvard University Press, 2002) 412–15.

856. See the reconstruction of the plot by Page, *Select Papyri III*, 368.

857. For 'satiety' (κόρος) as a characteristic of the rich, see, e.g., Philo *In Flacc.* 77; Dio Chrysostom *Or.* 7.17; Lucian *De Merc. Cond.* 8. For the connection of 'satiety' with 'wealth,' see esp. Luke 6.24–25; Dio Chrysostom *Or.* 1.67; 30.19. For other texts in this regard, see Marshall, *Enmity in Corinth*, 183–84, 188–89; Fitzgerald, *Cracks in an Earthen Vessel*, 133–35.

858. G. Highet, '*Libertino Patre Natus*', *American Journal of Philology* 94 (1973) 279; cited in connection with 1 Cor. 4.8 by Martin, *Slavery as Salvation*, 210 n. 13.

859. Horace *Ep.* 1.7.37–38.

860. Juvenal 5.14, 130, 137, 161; 7.45; 10.161.

861. Juvenal 5.156–73.

862. *POxy* 413 ('Adulteress') 123–24, 166–70.

Wholly opposite is the consequence for those who find themselves 'called' by the 'word of the cross' and who respond in 'faith' (1.21b, 24, 30): paradoxically, they experience empowerment with divine wisdom (θεοῦ σοφία), so that their lives gain the qualities that define ideal citizens – 'a sense of justice' (δικαιοσύνη), 'sanctity' (ἁγιασμός), and 'freedom' (ἀπολύτρω-σις).[863] Paul makes it clear for whom the cross-gospel has this unexpected consequence: for the most part, they are members of the lower class, those who lack education, wealth, and birth (1.26).[864] It is at this point that failure to understand Paul's thought is most significant. A diligent researcher of the folly of the message of the cross opines that, because the cross was such a horror to slaves and the poor, the message of the crucifixion of the Son of God 'was hardly an attraction to the lower classes of Roman and Greek society'.[865] Nothing could be further from an adequate understanding of the psycho-social dynamic of Paul's gospel. Consideration of the tradition that Paul appropriates may help us avoid this misunderstanding.

In literature written from 'the grotesque perspective,' the fate of slaves and the poor is the source of a 'laughter of liberation'.[866] Plautine slaves defy whippings, tortures and crucifixion, giving thanks to 'Holy Trickery'.[867] In the process, Plautus' slaves show themselves to be shrewder and freer than their masters.[868] One may assume that Plautus' audience, especially slaves and the poor, delighted in the sight of a rascally slave such as Tranio perched majestically on an altar,[869] and that they participated in his temporary 'divinity', especially since they knew that tomorrow, both they and he would again be subject to the unquestioned power of the masters.[870] With all the references to whippings, tortures and crucifixion, 'Plautine comedy must have given rise to a laughter of liberation.'[871] Similarly, Aesop is mocked and beaten, and finally driven to his death by the citizens of Delphi. Yet, the *Life of Aesop* is the story of the triumph of a deformed slave over the guardians of Hellenic culture.[872] The story-tellers

---

863. On δικαιοσύνη as a civic virtue, see H. J. Krämer, *Arete bei Platon und Aristoteles* (Heidelberg: Winter, 1959) 93; A. W. H. Adkins, *Merit and Responsibility* (Oxford: Oxford University Press, 1960) 287–91; J. M. Rist, *Human Value* (Leiden: Brill, 1982) 17–18.

864. Theissen, *The Social Setting of Pauline Christianity*, 71–73.

865. Hengel, *Crucifixion in the Ancient World*, 61–62. Hengel argues that it was mainly for the 'ancient bourgeoisie of the self-made man who had made their way up from the mass of the people' that the message about a crucified redeemer was attractive.

866. The phrase is derived from Segal, *Roman Laughter*, 9.

867. E.g., Libanius in Plautus *Asinaria* 545–51.

868. Segal, *Roman Laughter*, 163–64.

869. Plautus *Mostellaria* 1064–1116.

870. Plautus *Mostellaria* 1178–79.

871. Segal, *Roman Laughter*, 9.

872. Daly, *Aesop without Morals*, 19–23.

who contributed to the *Life*, and those for whom the stories were told, must have delighted in the subversion of the claims of the cultured elite to a monopoly on knowledge.[873] The fool in the mime is ugly, deformed and beaten; he appears upon the stage bearing the instrument of his own torture (ῥάβδος).[874] Yet the fool is the hero of that genre of entertainment which, by the middle of the first century, 'practically monopolized the stage'.[875] For the common people who delighted in the mime, the fool was a locus of value and meaning. This psycho-social dynamic explains the extraordinary popularity of the *Laureolus* mime, in which a runaway slave was crucified on the stage.

Paul's gospel of a 'crucified Christ' builds upon this dynamic and supercedes it. In the message that the annointed one of God had died the contemptible death of a slave, slaves and the poor heard that they had been 'chosen' by God. 'Consider your calling, brothers and sisters, that not many of you were wise in a human sense, not many powerful, not many well-born; but God chose the foolish of the world, . . . and God chose the weak of the world, . . . and God chose the low-born of the world and the despised, mere nothings . . . ' (1.26–28). Or, to put it the other way around, the message that a piece of human garbage, one of those whom life had demolished, and who had touched bottom, has been vindicated by God and is now 'the Lord of glory' – this message is a power capable of rescuing those who trust in it from despair over the nothingness of their lives (1.18b, 21b, 24). So that, even if they live in the shadow of the cross and die a bit every day, and even if the cross should be their tomb, as it was of their fathers and grandfathers, even there life would have value and meaning, because the one who died in this contemptible way was the annointed one of God.

Second, Paul spells out the consequences of 'the message about the cross' for his apostolic rivals, Apollos and Cephas (3.5–4.5). Paul includes himself in this company, to the degree to which he has been made, unwittingly, the object of partisan rivalry among the Corinthians.[876] Paul makes it clear that he and his apostolic rivals are merely 'servants' (διάκονοι),[877] not the sophists and scholars they are taken to be by the

---

873. Winkler, *Auctor and Actor*, 279–86.

874. Wüst, 'Mimos', 1748.

875. W. Beare, 'Mimus', *OCD* (1970) 688.

876. As Paul turns to consider the consequences for Apollos and himself in 3.5, the conjunction οὖν makes clear that the evaluation of status which follows is a function of the situation of partisanship in the community. More precisely, οὖν draws a conclusion from an unexpressed affirmative answer to the question of the preceding verse: 'For when someone says, "I am a partisan of Paul!" and another says, "I am a partisan of Apollos!" are you not all-too-human?' See Lindemann, *Der erste Korintherbrief*, 79–80.

877. The Cynic concept of the philosopher as διάκονος or 'servant' of God does not lie in the background of Paul's thought at this point; cf. Conzelmann, *1 Corinthians*, 73 n. 37.

Corinthians (3.5). In a series of well-constructed metaphors, Paul portrays himself, Apollos and Cephas as farm workers (3.6–9), construction laborers (3.9–15), and household stewards (4.1–5).[878] Paul's intention in evoking these humble occupations is to diminish the importance attributed to the apostles. This is clear, first of all, from the logic of the metaphor: neither Apollos nor Paul may be regarded as a maestro, because each has been assigned the position of servant by Christ (καὶ ἑκάστῳ ὡς ὁ κύριος ἔδωκεν, 3.5b).[879] Paul further denigrates the apostles by the way in which he poses the question of their status, using the neuter τί ἐστιν, rather than the masculine τίς;[880] thus, not '*Who* is Apollos?' but '*What* is Apollos?' (3.5).[881] It is difficult to resist the impression that the priority given to Apollos in this passage, where he is named first, reflects the overestimation of the eloquent man of culture (ἀνὴρ λόγιος) by certain Corinthians.[882]

Paul combats the tendency to see the apostles as star performers, by casting them in subordinate roles. The farmer, the builder, and the steward are all roles played by fools in comedy, farce, and mime. Paul first compares himself and Apollos to farm workers (γεωργοί):[883] 'I planted, Apollos watered, but God caused the growth' (3.6). Paul insists that the one who plants and the one who waters are part of the same farming operation ('they are one', ἕν εἰσιν), but observes (3.8), rather surprisingly, that 'each will receive his own wage (μισθός) in accordance with his own labor (κόπος)'. Paul completes the image (3.9) by characterizing the apostles as 'co-laborers' (συνεργοί) employed by God,[884] and by telling the Corinthians, 'you are God's field (γεώργιον)'.

The farmer (γεωργός/ἄγροικος, *rusticus*) was a fixture of the comic stage, ridiculed for the boorishness of his conduct, in comparison with the

---

878. On the metaphoric field in general, see R. Bach, 'Bauen und Pflanzen' in *Studien zur Theologie der alttestamentlichen Überlieferungen*, ed. R. Rendtorff (Tübingen: Siebeck-Mohr, 1961) 7–32; J. Shanor, 'Paul as Master Builder. Construction Terms in First Corinthians', *NTS* 34 (1988) 461–71; P. von Gemünden, *Vegetationsmetaphorik im Neuen Testament und seiner Umwelt. Ein Bildfelduntersuchung*, NTOA 18 (Göttingen: Vandenhoeck & Ruprecht, 1993) 272–75.

879. Lindemann, *Der erste Korintherbrief*, 80.

880. Part of the manuscript tradition has τίς rather than τί in 3.5 (P46 vid, $\aleph^2$, C, D, F, G Ψ); but this reading rests upon a misunderstanding of Paul's purposes.

881. Lindemann, *Der erste Korintherbrief*, 80; Collins, *First Corinthians*, 145.

882. With Weiss, *Der erste Korintherbrief*, 75. Lindemann (*Der erste Korintherbrief*, 80), however, sees only a stylistic reason why Apollos is named first, noting the chiasmus in 3.4–5.

883. That Paul has the term γεωργοί in mind, when he describes himself as having 'planted' and Apollos as having 'watered' in 3.6, is clear from the designation of the Corinthian church as a γεώργιον in 3.9.

884. The genitive θεοῦ in 3.9 does not suggest that Paul and Apollos are collaborators with God, but rather underscores the fact that the workers belong to God, are in God's employ; see Collins, *First Corinthians*, 146; Lindemann, *Der erste Korintherbrief*, 82.

sophistication of the city-dweller.[885] The figure already makes his appearance in the 'Αγρωστῖνος (*Rustic*) of the mime-writer Epicharmus.[886] That the farmer was also a character in the mimes of Sophron is indicated by the titles 'Αγρωστῖνος (*Rustic*) and 'Ωλιεὺς τὸν ἀγροιώταν (*The Fisherman to the Farmer*).[887] Aristophanes provides several examples of the type: Dikaiopolis and Trygaios in *Acharnians* and *Peace*,[888] and the country fellows caricatured in the *Ecclesiazusae*, clad in rough tunics, shod in clodhoppers, bearded, leaning on their staffs, and singing some old man's song.[889] Antiphanes' "Αγροικος portrayed a farmer named Boutalion,[890] whom the scholiast describes as a μωρός.[891] Menander, whom Paul elsewhere quotes,[892] composed a *Farmer* (Γεωργός); in the surviving fragments, we meet an old bachelor farmer living austerely in a country deme where he works like a day-laborer, wielding his heavy, two-pronged mattock.[893] Quintilian attests that this comedy remained popular in the first century.[894] The farmer was a favorite subject of Atellan farce:[895] he bore the name of Bucco,[896] and was fat-cheeked, greedy, and

---

885. See O. Ribbeck, 'Agroikos, eine ethologische Studie', *Abhandlungen der königlichen sächsischen Gesellschaft der Wissenschaften* 23 (1888) 1–45.

886. Text and fragment in Kaibel, *Comicorum graecorum fragmenta*; cf. Nicoll, *Masks, Mimes and Miracles*, 38.

887. Ribbeck, 'Agroikos', 6; text and translation of the sparse fragments of the latter mime in *Sophron. Mimes*, ed. I. C. Cunningham, LCL (Cambridge, MA: Harvard University Press, 2002) 320–21.

888. Aristophanes *Achar.* 180–81, 254, 371; *Pax* 190–91, 350–51; see Ribbeck, 'Agroikos', 7–9.

889. Aristophanes *Ec.* 268–79.

890. Athenaios *Deip.* 7.313b, 8.358d.

891. Schol. On Aristophanes *Ran.* 990, cited in Ribbeck, 'Agroikos', 10 n.1.

892. 1 Cor. 15.33: 'Bad company corrupts good morals', a citation of Menander *Thais* fr. 218 (Koch). The sentence is also attributed to Euripides (fr. 1013, Nauck), by whom Menander was heavily influenced. See the discussion in Weiss, *Der erste Korintherbrief*, 367; Koch, *Die Schrift als Zeuge des Evangeliums*, 42–45; Collins, *First Corinthians*, 560–61; Lindemann, *Der erste Korintherbrief*, 353.

893. Text, translation and introduction in *Menander. The Principal Fragments*, ed. F. G. Allinson, LCL (Cambridge, MA: Harvard University Press, 1964) 324–39. A second Menandrean portrait of the farmer is found in the Δύσκολος. See the discussion in Ribbeck, 'Agroikos', 11–15.

894. Quintilian *Inst. Orat.* 11.3.91.

895. Pomponius composed a *Rusticus* and Novius an *Agricola*; titles in Ribbeck, *Comicorum Romanorum Fragmenta*, 225, 254. See Ribbeck, 'Agroikos', 27; Nicoll, *Masks, Mimes and Miracles*, 72, 77.

896. Among the farces of Pomponius is a 'Bucco on Bail' (*Bucco auctoratus*), a 'Bucco Adopted' (*Bucco adoptatus*), and a 'Bucco the Gladiator'. See Beare, *The Roman Stage*, 133–35.

stupid.[897] The crudest portrait of the farmer is that found in the mime, where he was played as a country Priapus.[898]

A clear image of the farmer is conveyed by Theophrastus, who devotes one of his character studies to ἀγροικία ('like a farmer' or 'boorishness').[899] Theophrastus' portrait is influenced by comedy, and is subtle and rather sympathetic.[900] One may confirm and supplement this portrait by references in Horace, Athenaios, and others.[901] The farmer is immediately recognizable by his appearance and demeanor: he is shod in big, floppy clodhoppers;[902] his tunic hangs askew;[903] his beard is long and unkempt, or badly trimmed;[904] his haircut is lopsided;[905] his fingernails are grimy and unclipped;[906] his whole person is dirty[907] and odiferous;[908] his gait and demeanor are clumsy.[909] Indeed, 'gracelessness' (ἀσχημοσύνη) is the hallmark of the farmer's behavior:[910] the farmer is the sort who talks in a loud, 'barnyard' voice;[911] he is quick with swear words;[912] he sings at the baths;[913] he drinks a pungent liquor, and then goes to the assembly, careless of how strongly his breath smells;[914] 'he sits down with his cloak hitched up above his knee, revealing his nakedness.'[915] The farmer is more comfortable with his servants than with family members or friends: 'he asks advice from his servants on the most important matters, and describes to hired laborers in the field all the proceedings of the city assembly';[916] he seduces his cook, and then joins her in grinding up the daily ration of meal and handing it

---

897.　See esp. Plautus *Bacchides* 1088: 'fools, idiots, dotards,...Buccos' (*stulti, stolidi, fatui,...buccones*). For the visual appearance of the character, see Dieterich, *Pulcinella*, 92; Nicoll, *Masks, Mimes and Miracles*, 69–70; Beare, *The Roman Stage*, 129.

898.　Ribbeck, 'Agroikos', 27, citing an anonymous mime fragment. Cf. Tibullus 1.4.7.

899.　Theophrastus *Char.* 4; text and trans. in *Theophrastus. Characters*, ed. J. Rusten, LCL (Cambridge, MA: Harvard University Press, 2002) 60–63.

900.　Rusten, *Theophrastus. Characters*, 147.

901.　The references are assembled by Ribbeck, 'Agroikos,' 33–45.

902.　Theophrastus *Char.* 4.4; Horace *Sat.* 1.3.31; Athenaios *Deip.* 13.565e.

903.　Horace *Sat.* 1.3.32; Ovid *Ars* 1.514; Athanaios *Deip.* 1.21b.

904.　Aristophanes *Ec.* 272–73; Varro fr. 1.

905.　Horace *Sat.* 1.3.31; *Ep.* 1.1.94; Ovid *Ars* 1.517.

906.　Horace *Ep.* 1.1.104; Ovid *Ars* 1.519.

907.　Horace *Ep.* 1.7.83.

908.　Plautus *Mostellaria* 39; Horace *Sat.* 1.1.27; Ovid *Ars* 1.521.

909.　Alexis fr. 263, cited in Ribbeck, 'Agroikos', 35.

910.　Ribbeck, 'Agroikos,' 35–39.

911.　Theophrastus *Char.* 4.5.

912.　Horace *Ep.* 2.1.146.

913.　Theophrastus *Char.* 4.15; Seneca *Ep.* 56.1–2.

914.　Theophrastus *Char.* 4.2–3.

915.　Theophrastus *Char.* 4.7.

916.　Theophrastus *Char.* 4.9.

out to the household.[917] He is most familiar of all with the barnyard
animals: he omits a polite greeting for those whom he passes in the street,[918]
but stands and gawks at the sight of a cow, an ass, or a goat;[919] he eats his
breakfast right from the storeroom, as he is feeding his plough-animals;[920]
he goes with the dog to answer the door and, grabbing the dog
affectionately by the snout, says 'This fellow looks out for our property
and household!'[921]

The humor in Paul's analogy in 3.6–9 is mostly implicit, consisting in
the contrast between the 'farmer' (γεωργός, *rusticus*) and the 'urbanite'
(ἀστεῖος, *urbanus*) – contrasting stereotypes ingrained in the ancient
audience.[922] Apollos (insofar as we know him) appears to be the epitome
of the ἀστεῖος: city-bred, learned, eloquent – perhaps also witty and
charming. To portray Apollos as a farmer is in itself funny, without
evoking the details of the comic type. At one point only does Paul allude
to a specific feature of the farmer-type, namely, in reference to the 'wage'
which each farm-worker receives in accordance with his 'labor' (3.8b).
This parenthetical remark is rather unexpected,[923] given Paul's insistence,
in the phrases that precede and follow (3.8a, 3.9a), on the unity of
purpose and the equality of status of the apostolic co-laborers. But the
farmer was notoriously concerned about his money (φιλάργυρος).[924]
Theophrastus captures this trait: 'He rejects a silver coin that he gets
from someone because it looks too much like lead, and trades for
another.'[925]

Paul next compares himself and the other apostles with construction
workers laboring upon a building (3.9c,10–17). The image is elaborated in
greater detail than that of the agricultural workers, permitting Paul to
make points about his relationship to his rivals, and to raise questions
about the quality of their workmanship.[926] The Corinthian church is
immediately declared to be 'God's building' (θεοῦ οἰκοδομή), later identified

---

917. Theophrastus *Char*. 4.10.
918. Terence *Ad*. 80, 432, 720.
919. Theophrastus *Char*. 4.8.
920. Theophrastus *Char*. 4.9, 11.
921. Theophrastus *Char*. 4.12.
922. Ribbeck, 'Agroikos', 46.
923. Lindemann, *Der erste Korintherbrief*, 81: 'Überraschend ist nun allerdings die
Nachbemerkung in 8b.'
924. Aristophanes *Nu*. 133; *Ran*. 718ff.; Plautus *Casina* 9; Ribbeck, 'Agroikos', 8.
925. Theophrastus *Char*. 4.13; trans. J. Rusten, *Theophrastus. Characters*, 63.
926. The context makes clear that the same apostles and missionaries are meant as in 3.5–
6 and 3.22, although neither Apollos nor Cephas is mentioned by name in 3.10–17; so, rightly,
H. W. Hollander, 'The Testing by Fire of the Builders' Work: 1 Corinthians 3.10–15', *NTS* 40
(1994) 92. Cf. I. Kitzberger, *Bau der Gemeinde. Das paulinische Wortfeld* οἰκοδομή/(ἐπ)οικοδομεῖν,
fzb 53 (Wurzburg: Echter Verlag, 1986) 70.

specifically as a 'temple' (ναός) (3.16). Paul describes himself as a 'skilled master-builder' (σοφὸς ἀρχιτέκτων), who has 'laid a foundation' (θεμέλιον ἔθηκα). Paul observes that 'another is now building upon it (ἐποικοδομεῖ)', and that 'each should take care how he builds (ἐποικοδομεῖ)'. Paul extends the metaphor by listing various building materials – permanent and impermanent, flammable and non-flammable: 'gold, silver, precious stones, wood, hay, straw' (3.12). The metaphor takes a dramatic turn, with Paul's declaration that 'the work' (τὸ ἔργον) of each builder will be 'tested' by fire: 'If the work that someone has built on the foundation survives, he will receive a wage (μισθός). If someone's work is burned up, he will be penalized (ζημιωθήσεται).'

The terminology of Paul's extended metaphor is drawn directly from the everyday usage of construction work.[927] The ἀρχιτέκτων, or 'master builder', was a familiar figure at the construction site, the director of the work of others.[928] The θεμέλιος is the 'foundation stone' of a house;[929] even the expression κείμενος θεμέλιος ('laid foundation') is a technical term of the building industry, as attested by an inscription from the third century B.C.[930] The use of 'hay' (χόρτος) and 'straw' (καλάμη) as cheap building materials in the houses of the poor, and the dangerous flammability of such products, is noted by historians.[931] Paul's repeated reference to the 'work' (ἔργον) of each builder (3.13, 14, 15) finds a parallel in an Arcadian inscription which lists the specific tasks performed by sub-contractors employed in the building of a temple.[932] The same inscription mentions penalties imposed upon builders who fail to finish their work on time, or who harm other workers, or damage property.[933]

Paul ingeniously exploits the logic of the construction metaphor to denigrate his rivals. In this effort, the nuances of the technical vocabulary play an important role. The ἀρχιτέκτων, for example, is not a 'manual laborer' (ἐργάτικος), but the 'head of the workers' (ἐργατῶν ἄρχων), according to Plato;[934] his price is a thousand times above the ordinary

927. See esp. the Arcadian inscription of the fourth century B.C. in C. D. Buck, *Greek Dialects* (Chicago: University of Chicago Press, 1955) 201–203. See also A. Fridrichsen, 'Exegetisches zu den Paulusbriefen' (1930) and '*Themelios*, 1. Kor. 3,11' (1946) in idem, *Exegetical Writings. A Selection*, ed. C. Caragounis and T. Fornberg, WUNT 76 (Tübingen: Mohr-Siebeck, 1994) 203–10, 228–30; Shanor, 'Paul as Master Builder', 461–71.

928. Plato *Pol.* 259E. Cf. Euripides *Alc.* 348; Maximus of Tyre *Diss.* 6.4.

929. On θεμέλιος λίθος as the 'foundation' of a house, see Aristophanes *Aves* 1137; Lk. 6.48–49; Acts 16.26.

930. Cited in Fridrichsen, '*Themelios*, 1. Kor. 3,11', 228–30.

931. Diodorus Siculus 5.21.5; 20.65.1.

932. Buck, *Greek Dialects*, 201–203; Collins, *First Corinthians*, 149. For ἔργον with special reference to a building, see Aristophanes *Aves* 1125; Polybius 5.3.6; Diodorus Siculus 1.31.9.

933. Buck, *Greek Dialects*, 203; Collins, *First Corinthians*, 149.

934. Plato *Pol.* 259E.

construction worker.⁹³⁵ Aristotle observes that the 'master-craftsmen' (ἀρχιτέκτονες) relate to their 'underlings' (ὑπηρέται) as 'masters' (δεσπόται) relate to their 'slaves' (δοῦλοι).⁹³⁶ By designating himself the ἀρχιτέκτων, Paul is not merely reminding the Corinthians of the foundational role of his preaching, he is distinguishing himself from other missionaries and apostles, whose work is subordinate. They are 'hirelings' who work for a 'wage' (μισθός), while Paul's foundation-laying is a 'gift' (χάρις) of the divine benefactor (3.10). It falls within the logic of the construction metaphor that Paul lists the various building materials used by the sub-contractors and contemplates the perishability of each product; for the ἀρχιτέκτων is responsible for the design of the whole building and the execution of the project.⁹³⁷ It is a rhetorical master-stroke that Paul applies to himself as ἀρχιτέκτων the additional attribute σοφός, used in the clever, idiomatic sense of 'skilled': against those who regard themselves as 'wise' because of their lofty eloquence (1.17,20; 2.1), Paul insists that the foundational role given to him in the construction of God's house corresponds to the higher level of his 'skill,' and thus proves that he is truly 'wise'.⁹³⁸

The construction metaphor is sufficiently broad and complex to permit Paul to insert observations of a nearly allegorical precision. Thus he glosses his account of the 'foundation' that has been laid with the explanation – 'which is Jesus Christ' (3.11b). And he makes clear that the fire which will test the work of the builders is the conflagration of 'the day' (ἡ ἡμέρα) of the Lord (3.13), the eschatological day of judgment, whose essential characteristic is fire.⁹³⁹ Yet, the image of construction remains fully self-consistent and is not compromised by these allegorical references. It belongs to the logic of the construction metaphor that no one who continues to work on a building can alter the existing foundation (θεμέλιον γὰρ ἄλλον οὐδεὶς δύναται θεῖναι παρὰ τὸν κείμενον),⁹⁴⁰ without creating a different structure altogether.⁹⁴¹ The reference to the fire of the last day does not negate the fact that 'dread of fire was a daily obsession' among

935. Plato *Amat.* 135B: τέκτονα μὲν ἂν πρίαιο πέντε ἢ ἓξ μνῶν, ἄκρον ἀρχιτέκτονα δ' οὐδ' ἂν μυρίων δραχμῶν ('you might be able to buy a builder for 5 or 6 minas, but you'd need more than 10,000 drachmas for a master-builder'). See also Aristotle *Met.* 1, 981a30.

936. Aristotle *Pol.* 1.2.5, 1254a1.

937. Lindemann, *Der erste Korintherbrief*, 84.

938. Collins, *First Corinthians*, 149, 155, who senses the cleverness and the irony of Paul's idiomatic use of σοφός.

939. D. W. Kuck, *Judgment and Community Conflict. Paul's Use of Apocalyptic Judgment Language in 1 Corinthians 3.5–4.5* (Leiden: Brill, 1992) 93–95, 148–49, esp. 179–80.

940. 3.10; note the logical connection of the conjunction γάρ.

941. Lindemann, *Der erste Korintherbrief*, 84.

the inhabitants of the large cities of the Roman Empire.[942] With his metaphor of the construction workers, Paul has created a scene of realism and unity worthy of a one-act play.

Clearly, the intention of Paul's construction metaphor is to diminish the importance attributed to the apostles. The emissaries and messengers of the Christ are not sophists and scholars, as some in Corinth suppose, but are rightly compared with craftsmen and artisans, even common laborers. One senses a Socratic precedent behind Paul's analogy. Socrates, one recalls, found material for his arguments in the work of 'blacksmiths and shoemakers and tanners'.[943] In his search for wisdom, Socrates turned to artisans and handworkers, and found that they had command of a field of technical skill, and in this respect were wiser than the politicians and poets, who had no understanding at all, despite their reputation for wisdom.[944] Indeed, Socrates himself was regarded as a βάναυσος: his father is said to have been a stonemason (λιθουργός), and Socrates himself was brought up in this craft.[945] One also senses the influence of farce and mime upon Paul's construction metaphor. The titles of farces and mimes reveal how many were devoted to the trades and occupations: e.g., Pomponius' *Piscatores* ('The Fishermen') and *Medicus* ('The Doctor'), Novius' *Fullones* ('The Fullers').[946] A number of Laberius' mimes indicate subjects taken from ordinary professions, e.g., *Fullo* ('The Fuller'), *Piscator* ('The Fisherman'), *Salinator* ('The Salt-Miner'), *Restio* ('The Rope-Dealer').[947] A mimic fool depicted as a ὑπηρέτης, perhaps a rower, survives in a terracotta statuette from Tarsus, dated to the first century A.D.[948]

Paul's construction metaphor is rich in possibilities for slapstick humor. It is not difficult to imagine the clownish workers scrambling over the construction site, competing for materials, colliding with one another. Someone shouts 'fire!,' the workers flee, and the curtain falls. Paul encourages such a comical reading by a phrase at the end of the paragraph: αὐτὸς δὲ σωθήσεται, οὕτως δὲ ὡς διὰ πυρός, 'he (that is, the builder) himself will be saved, but only, as the saying goes, "through fire"' (3.15b). This

---

942. Carcopino, *Daily Life in Ancient Rome*, 33, citing Juvenal 3.197–98: 'No, no, I must live where there is no fire and the night is free from alarms!'; 3.199–207, where the poor man is startled from his sleep by flames in his attic; 14.305–308, the rich man fears that his mansion will burn, destroying his bronzes, pillars of marble, etc..

943. Plato *Symp.* 221E.

944. Plato *Apol.* 22D.

945. Aristoxenus fr. 51 (Wehrli); Lucian *Somn.* 9–12; see the discussion in Zeller, *Die Philosophie der Griechen*, 2.1, 52; Guthrie, *Socrates*, 58–59.

946. E. Wölfflin, 'Atellanen und Mimentitel,' *Rheinisches Museum* 43 (1888) 308–309; Nicoll, *Masks, Mimes and Miracles*, 68–69.

947. Bonaria, *Mimorum Romanorum Fragmenta I*, 9–103.

948. Goldman, 'Two Terracotta Figurines from Tarsus', 22–34; see Fig. 11 above.

statement, and especially its final phrase, ὡς διὰ πυρός, has occasioned much consternation among interpreters,[949] with some imagining that Paul refers to the fires of purgatory![950] But the comparative and qualifying expression οὕτως δὲ ὡς ('in this way, as follows, as it were') makes it clear that the salvation of which Paul speaks is meant to be understood in a metaphorical sense, as part of the construction image he has been developing since the beginning of the paragraph.[951] In fact, the phrase διὰ πυρός is a common idiom describing a narrow escape from danger:[952] 'so, διὰ πυρὸς ἰέναι (as we say) "to go through fire and water," dash through any danger'.[953] The preposition διά is to be taken in a local rather than an instrumental sense.[954] The picture that Paul presents is that of the 'unexpected and narrow escape of those whose works will not stand up to the fiery test'.[955] As the fire ignites, the workers escape from the 'penalty' about to be imposed upon their sloppy construction, by running through the walls of the burning building!

Third, Paul compares himself, Apollos, and Cephas with household stewards (4.1–5). Paul admonishes his Corinthian readers, 'Let a person consider us in this way, as servants (ὑπηρέται) of Christ and stewards (οἰκονόμοι) of the mysteries of God' (4.1). Paul then states the criterion for evaluating stewards, the essential qualification of the steward's job description: 'that he be found trustworthy' (4.2). Projecting himself entirely into the metaphor, and speaking in the first person, as one of the stewards whose accounts are about to be audited, Paul declares: 'To me it is a matter of complete indifference whether I am judged by you or by any human court' (4.3). Paul avows, defensively, that he has a clean 'conscience' (σύνοιδα), but insists that judgment be postponed until the Lord comes, who, like the master of the house, is alone worthy to judge

---

949. For a survey of conflicting interpretations of Paul's statement in 1 Cor. 3.15b, see Lindemann, *Der erste Korintherbrief*, 87–88.

950. This interpretation goes back to Origen; see E. Koch, 'Fegfeuer', *TRE* 11, 70–71. See J. Gnilka, *Ist 1. Kor. 3,10–15 ein Schriftzeugnis für das Fegfeuer?* (Düsseldorf: Triltsch, 1955); J. Michl, 'Gerichtsfeuer und Purgatorium zu 1 Kor. 3,12–15' in *Studiorum Paulinorum Congressus* (Rome: Pontifico Instituto Biblico, 1963) 395–401.

951. On οὕτως δὲ ὡς as a marker of what follows as metaphorical, see Blass-Debrunner-Funk, *A Greek Grammar of the New Testament*, 897.1; Bauer, *A Greek-English Lexicon*, 742 *s.v.* οὕτως 2; Collins, *First Corinthians*, 160.

952. E.g., Aristophanes *Lys.* 133; Xenophon *Symp.* 4.16; *Oec.* 21.7: καὶ διὰ πυρὸς καὶ διὰ παντὸς κινδύνου. See also Crates *Ep.* 6. Rightly recognized by Conzelmann, *1 Corinthians*, 77: 'Paul is obviously borrowing from a common phrase'; Lindemann, *Der erste Korintherbrief*, 87: 'die Terminologie dabei ist durchgängig der Alltagssprache entnommen'.

953. Liddell-Scott-Jones, *Greek-English Lexicon*, 1555 *s.v.* πῦρ II.

954. Rightly, Kuck, *Judgment and Community Conflict*, 183–84.

955. Kuck, *Judgment and Community Conflict*, 183; see also Weiss, *Der erste Korintherbrief*, 83; Barrett, *First Corinthians*, 89; F. Lang, 'πῦρ', *TDNT* 6, 944.

his stewards: he will bring to light whatever may have been covered up; then, each steward will receive the 'praise' (ἔπαινος) that is his due (4.4–5).

The major-domo, or chief steward, was a stock character of comedy and mime.[956] Pollux describes the character as being ruddy complexioned, with reddish hair arranged in the form of a σπεῖρα ('coiled hair dressing'), and bushy, raised eyebrows.[957] The type is easily identified among the extant terracottas (e.g., Fig. 19).[958] Plautus has left an unforgettable portrait of the type in the *Pseudolus*, where the title character is described as 'a red-haired fellow, potbellied, with thick legs, swarthy complexioned, with a big head, sharp eyes, red mouth, and tremendous feet';[959] he stands, hand on hip, with an attitude of self-confident regality,[960] threatening to 'fillet' the other servants, 'the way a cook does a lamprey';[961] his speech is peppered with military metaphors.[962] A parable in Luke's Gospel (16.1–8), obviously influenced by comedy and mime,[963] presents the figure of the household manager with subtlety and realism: charged with squandering his master's property, a steward (οἰκονόμος) shrewdly cooks the books to ensure his future employment. The type of the steward was so well established that it might be evoked in literature for purposes of ridicule: i.e., the figure of the chief steward colors Seneca's portrait of Claudius as an officious fool in the *Apocolocyntosis*.[964]

Paul's vocabulary is exceedingly well chosen to support the image of the apostles as household managers. The comparative expression οὕτως ... ὡς is employed again at the beginning of the paragraph to mark what follows as another metaphor.[965] The οἰκονόμος was the chief household slave: he enjoyed a position of authority over other slaves and had responsibility for

956.   On this character type, see Nicoll, *Masks, Mimes and Miracles*, 28–30; Bieber, *History of the Greek and Roman Theatre*, 159–60; Beacham, *The Roman Theatre*, 35–38.

957.   Pollux *Onom.* 4.150; cf. Robert, *Die Masken der neueren attischen Komödie*, 108–109.

958.   Fig. 19 depicts a mime actor in the role of the chief household slave; terracotta figure now in the J. Paul Getty Museum; picture in Beacham, *Spectacle Entertainments of Early Imperial Rome*, 10, Fig. 3. For other examples, see Bieber, *Denkmäler zum Theaterwesen*, 135 no. 89, Tab. 73.1, 2, 4; 57 no. 30, Tab. 89; 162 no. 138, Tab. 94.1; 169 no. 168, Tab. 105.3; Nicoll, *Masks, Mimes and Miracles*, Fig. 13–15.

959.   Plautus *Pseudolus* 1218–19.

960.   *Ibid.*, 458–61.

961.   *Ibid.*, 38–61.

962.   E.g., *Ibid.*, 383.

963.   J. Albert Harrill, 'The Farce of the Dishonest Manager (Luke 16.1–8): Roman Slave Comedy and Early Christian Self-Definition', 2003 Annual Meeting of the Society of Biblical Literature.

964.   Seneca *Apoc.* 7.4–5; 8.3; 15.2.

965.   Bauer, *A Greek-English Lexicon*, 742, *s.v.* οὕτως 2; Weiss, *Der erste Korintherbrief*, 84; contra Conzelmann, *1 Corinthians*, 82 n. 1; Lindemann, *Der erste Korintherbrief*, 95, for whom οὕτως looks backward, summarizing what has preceded.

Figure 19.   Terracotta of a mime actor. J. Paul Getty Museum, Malibu, CA.

his master's possessions.[966] Despite the scope of his responsibility, he remained a slave, as indicated by the term with which Paul pairs οἰκονόμος in 4.1 – ὑπηρέτης, that is, an 'underling', a 'subordinate', an 'assistant'.[967] If he failed to discharge his duties prudently, he might be beaten, or might even be killed.[968]

Paul brilliantly captures the ambiguity of the steward's position, by means of a colloquial expression at the beginning of vs. 2, ὧδε λοιπόν, and the axiomatic statement which it introduces: ζητεῖται ἐν τοῖς οἰκονόμοις, ἵνα πιστός τις εὑρεθῇ. The little idiom, ὧδε λοιπόν, which has provoked much speculation among interpreters,[969] is evidently a verbal gesture of annoyance by one who is forced to concede that a general truth is applicable in the present case. So much is suggested by a lively passage of

966. Philo *De Jos.* 37; Epictetus *Diss.* 3.22.3; Luke 12.42–48; 16.1–8; cf. *EDNT* 2.568–75; Collins, *First Corinthians*, 168.

967. Philo *De Sac.* 44; *Post.* 50; cf. *EDNT* 3.398–402; Weiss, *Der erste Korintherbrief*, 93: 'bezeichnet ὑπηρέτης, das einer niederen Sphäre entnommen ist, wohl mehr ein untergeordnetes Hand-langer-Verhältnis'; similarly Collins, *First Corinthians*, 172.

968. See esp. Luke 12.42–48.

969. See the extensive discussion in Weiss, *Der erste Korintherbrief*, 94–95; A. Fridrichsen, 'Sprachliches und Stilistisches zum Neuen Testament', *Kungliga Humanistika Vetenskap – Samfundet i Uppsala, Arsbok 1943* (Uppsala: Almqvist & Wiksell, 1943) 25–26; M. Thrall, *Greek Particles in the New Testament. Linguistic and Exegetical Studies*, NTTS 3 (Grand Rapids, MI: Eerdmans, 1962) 26–27; Blass-Debrunner-Funk, *A Greek Grammar of the New Testament*, 451.6; Lindemann, *Der erste Korintherbrief*, 96.

dialogue in Socratic style in Epictetus.[970] A rich Roman of consular rank is interrogated by a philosopher regarding the care and keeping of his soul.[971] When the philosopher presses to know whether the rich man's care for his soul is genuine, Epictetus warns the philosopher of the growing annoyance of the citizen: 'In this case then, there comes the danger (ὧδε λοιπὸν ὁ κίνδυνος), that first he will say, "What is that to you, good sir? Are you my master?" and after that, if you persist in annoying him, that he will lift his fist and give you a blow.'[972] Paul uses the idiom in precisely this way. The expressions ζητεῖται ('it is required'), ἐν τοῖς οἰκονόμοις ('among stewards'), and τις ('one') all contribute to the general, almost proverbial, character of the utterance: 'it is required of stewards that each one be found trustworthy'.[973] Paul concedes the principle, but signals his annoyance at the application to his own case, by the verbal equivalent of a raised fist and a proffered blow – ὧδε λοιπόν. It is the kind of bellicose gesture that distinguished the chief household slave in comedy and mime.[974]

Paul's verbal gesture in 4.2 forms the transition to a concise and lively 'speech in character' in vss. 3–5. Paul fully inhabits the role he has assigned himself in the metaphor, and speaks in the first person singular as one of the stewards whose accounts are about to be audited. The phrase, ἐμοὶ δὲ εἰς ἐλάχιστόν ἐστιν,[975] a free formulation compounded of ἐλάχιστον ἐστιν and εἰς ἐλάχιστον γίνεται,[976] expresses the cavalier attitude of the steward toward the possibility of an audit: 'But to me it is a matter of complete indifference whether I am judged by you or by any human court!' (4.3). Entirely in character, Paul employs another common usage (σύνοιδα + the reflexive),[977] to disavow consciousness of anything against himself (4.4a). Employing a term with a broad judicial usage, ἀνακρίνειν,[978] Paul

---

970. The passage is often adduced as a parallel to 1 Cor. 4.2; so, e.g., Weiss, *Der erste Korintherbrief*, 95; Conzelmann, *1 Corinthians*, 82; Bauer, *A Greek-English Lexicon*, 1101 *s.v.* ὧδε 2; Lindemann, *Der erste Korintherbrief*, 96.

971. Epictetus *Diss.* 2.12.17–25. The discourse is devoted to the topic of how to keep a philosophical argument from ending with 'a scornful laugh or an insult' (2.12.1–4).

972. Epictetus *Diss.* 2.12.24; the translation modifies W. A. Oldfather, *Epictetus*, Vol. 1, LCL (Cambridge, MA: Harvard University Press, 1967) 297. Note also the use of the expression τὸ ὧδε to characterize an 'unpleasant' (δύσκολον) way of doing philosophy in Crates *Ep.* 6.

973. Weiss, *Der erste Korintherbrief*, 94–95; Collins, *First Corinthians*, 172.

974. The expression ὧδε occurs frequently in the mimes of Herodas, e.g., 2.98; 3.96; 4.42; 5.85; 7.113, 126.

975. The phrase is found nowhere else in Paul's letters; cf. Collins, *First Corinthians*, 172.

976. Bauer, *A Greek-English Lexicon*, 284, *s.v.* εἰμί 2cb.

977. Job 27.6; Epictetus *Diss.* 3.23.15; *POxy* 898,20; Horace *Ep.* 1.1.61: *nil conscire sibi, nulla pallescere culpa*; cf. H.-J. Eckstein, *Der Begriff Syneidesis bei Paulus. Eine neutestamentlich-exegetische Untersuchung zum Gewissensbegriff*, WUNT II/10 (Tübingen: Mohr-Siebeck, 1983) 205–213.

978. Liddell-Scott-Jones, *Greek-English Lexicon*, 109.

repeatedly insists that no one other than the Lord is competent to 'examine' him (4.3a, 4c). When the Lord comes, like the master of the household, 'he will shed light' (φωτίζειν) upon 'the things hidden in darkness' (τὰ κρυπτὰ τοῦ σκότους) and will expose 'the intentions of hearts' (αἱ βουλαὶ τῶν καρδιῶν) – expressions found nowhere else in Paul's extant correspondence, but entirely appropriate to the metaphor of an audit of a steward's accounts. Like the clever slaves in Plautine comedy,[979] Paul and his fellow stewards long to hear sweet words of 'praise' (ἔπαινος) from their Lord (4.5).

To make certain that the Corinthians have comprehended the purpose of his metaphors, Paul summarizes: 'I have applied (μετεσχημάτισα) these things to myself and Apollos for your benefit, brothers and sisters, so that you might learn through us the meaning of the principle, 'Not beyond the things which are written',[980] so that none of you may be puffed up in favor of the one [apostle] and against the other' (4.6). By means of the term μετασχηματίζω, Paul makes clear that throughout he has been teaching with the aid of figures of speech.[981] The figures warn against becoming 'puffed up' (φυσιοῦσθαι), as the unhappy result of partisanship.[982] Paul wishes the Corinthians to understand that, as the apostles of Jesus Christ, he and Apollos are not star performers worthy of adulation, but bit-players in the mime of life.

Finally, Paul expounds the consequences of 'the message about the cross' for himself and his missionary colleagues, that is, for those who have conformed their lives to the fate of 'the crucified Christ' (4.9–13). As demonstrated in detail above,[983] Paul portrays himself and his fellow apostles as 'buffoons' (μωροί) in a 'play' (θέατρον) 'staged' (ἀπέδειξεν) by God (4.9–10). Paul's vocabulary in this paragraph is explicitly theatrical: like the poor fools in the mime, Paul and his colleagues are 'weak,... hungry,... naked,... given the knuckle-sandwich, etc' (4.10–11). Yet, one senses that the suffering and mistreatment that Paul describes is more than metaphorical, that the line between theatrical image and social reality is

---

979. On the words of praise which the Plautine slave seeks to extract from his master, see Segal, *Roman Laughter*, 128–34.

980. On the meaning of this difficult phrase, see the suggestions of Fitzgerald, *Cracks in an Earthen Vessel*, 124–27; Welborn, *Politics and Rhetoric in the Corinthian Epistles*, 43–75.

981. See esp. Ps.-Demetrius *De Eloc.* 287, 292–94, where the simplex form, σχηματίζειν, means 'to say something with the aid of a figure of speech'. See Hooker, '"Beyond the things which are written"', 27–32; B. Fiore, 'Covert Allusion in 1 Cor. 1–4', *CBQ* 47 (1985) 85–102; J. S. Vos, 'Der ΜΕΤΑΣΧΗΜΑΤΙΣΜΟΣ in 1 Kor 4,6', 154–72, esp. 171; Bauer, *A Greek-English Lexicon*, 642, *s.v.* μετασχηματίζω 3.

982. For the connection of the verb φυσιόω (and its cognate φυσάω) with partisanship, see, e.g., Demosthenes 19.314; Xenophon *Mem.* 1.2.25; cf. Welborn, *Politics and Rhetoric in the Corinthian Epistles*, 55–56.

983. See ch. 4, on 1 Cor. 4.9–13.

precariously thin, that having put on the mask of the 'fool of Christ', Paul will not take it off. At one point, this intuition seems especially ominous and poignant, namely, at the climax of the paragraph, where Paul echoes the judgment of the rich and powerful upon the clownish apostles: 'We have become like the refuse (περικαθάρματα) of the world, the scum (περίψημα) of all things, to this very day' (4.13). As we have seen, the terms κάθαρμα and περίψημα had become vulgar epithets by the time of Paul, terms of abuse exchanged as insults by fools in the mime.[984] But in their ancient sense, the terms κάθαρμα and περίψημα applied to those unfortunate souls, paupers and the deformed, who were put to death for the purification of the city.[985] One recalls that Aesop, who is repeatedly referred to as περικάθαρμα and κάθαρμα in the *Life*,[986] was hounded to his death by the men of Delphi as a wretched 'scapegoat' (φαρμακός).[987] Thus one wonders whether the older sense of these terms still echoes in Paul, and whether, at this point, Paul has moved beyond metaphor, and has begun to accept 'the word of the cross' as the literal truth of his own life.

984.   See above ch. 4 n. 246.
985.   See above ch. 4 n. 242, 243.
986.   *Vit. Aesop.* 14, 30, 31.
987.   See esp. A. Wiechers, 'Aesop als Pharmakos', 31–44.

Chapter 7

ACCEPTANCE OF THE ROLE

We have discovered that Paul was not alone among intellectuals in the early Empire in his appropriation of the role of the fool.[1] Laberius, Horace, and Juvenal, among others, adopted the persona of the fool, because of the greater freedom of thinking and speaking which the role permitted.[2] Paul's acceptance of the role of the fool mirrors the dialectical strategy of mime-writers and satirists who exploited the socially shameful status of the fool for the utterance of a dangerous truth. Speaking as a fool, Paul is able to challenge the reliance upon wealth and knowledge by the leaders of the church at Corinth, and the sense of superiority which these things engendered.

Yet, comparing Paul with his contemporaries, one has the unmistakable sense that Paul's acceptance of the role of the fool is qualitatively different. Laberius takes the stage and acts the part of a runaway slave;[3] but when the performance is over, Caesar restores his gold ring, and Laberius resumes his place in the audience among the knights.[4] Horace portrays himself as a rustic buffoon,[5] and permits one of his slaves to describe him as a 'great fool'.[6] But at the end of the day, Horace recovers his dignity in the simple life on his Sabine farm: dipping his hands into a limpid, icy stream, Horace reflects, 'What do *I* pray for? For what I now have, or even less; that I live out the rest of my days in my own sweet way, if the gods mean me to survive a while longer; for a good supply of books and food, enough for the year. Beyond that, simply not to waver.'[7]

---

1. See ch. 5 above.
2. Macrobius *Sat.* 2.7.2–7; Horace *Sat.* 2.7; Juvenal *Sat.* 9.
3. Macrobius *Sat.* 2.7.4. For the conclusion that Laberius played the part of a 'fool' (*actor secundarum partium*), see R. Till, 'Laberius und Caesar', 278 n. 78.
4. Macrobius *Sat.* 2.3.10, 7.3.8; Seneca *Contr.* 7.3.9.
5. Horace *Sat.* 1.3.29–34, 90–94; cf. Armstrong, *Horace*, 37–41; Freudenburg, *The Walking Muse*, 21–33.
6. Horace *Sat.* 2.7, esp. 2.7.39–115; cf. Freudenburg, *The Walking Muse*, 225–26.
7. Horace *Ep.* 1.18.107–12; trans S. P. Bovie, *Satires and Epistles of Horace* (Chicago: University of Chicago Press, 1966) 219. This portrait of dignity restored comes at the end of

These provisional appropriations of the fool's persona by the poets only throw into sharper relief the grim account of Paul's sufferings as the fool of Christ in 4.9–13: 'For I suppose that God has put us apostles on show last of all, as people condemned to death, because we have become a theater-act to the world, both to angels and to human beings. We are fools on account of Christ, . . . we are weak, . . . we are dishonored; . . . we are hungry and thirsty, we are naked, we are beaten, we are homeless, and we toil, laboring with our own hands; [we are] reviled, . . . harrassed, . . . slandered . . . ; we have become like the refuse of the world, the scum of all things, to this very day.' Even Juvenal's bitterness over the penury of his existence[8] pales to nothing beside Paul's pathos-laden account of the infamy of his life on account of Christ. Thus, we may conclude with a few observations on the source of Paul's acceptance of the role of the fool, the implications of Paul's choice for his rhetoric, and the limits of Paul's identification with the crucified Christ.

We may begin by dismissing the notion that the difference between Paul and his contemporaries in respect to the fool's role is merely the reflection of a difference in social class. To be sure, Paul is an artisan, a stage carpenter,[9] if the author of Acts is to be believed,[10] not a minor bureaucrat, like Horace. One might assume that Paul would identify more readily with a role that lay closer to his own social experience. But as Horace and Juvenal painfully attest, the freedom that an author enjoyed as the client of a wealthy patron was 'the freedom of the fool'.[11] According to Juvenal, the free meals, the forced flattery, the begging for petty favors took away the self-respect from a client's life.[12] In a world controlled by rich patrons, the life of an intellectual must have seemed as contingent and capricious as

---

an epistle in which Horace offers counsel to a young friend who is so eager to become the client of a wealthy patron that he resembles 'a mime-player acting the second part' (*Ep.* 1.18.14).

8.   E.g., Juvenal *Sat.* 3.124–25, 147–51; 5.19–23; 7.66–67.

9.   Bauer, *A Greek-English Lexicon*, 928–29, *s.v.* σκηνοποιός.

10.   Acts 18.3. On the historical reliability of the report that Paul was a σκηνοποιός, see Lüdemann, *Early Christianity according to the Traditions in Acts*, 202.

11.   The phrase is that of W. R. Johnson (*Horace and the Dialectic of Freedom*, 23), describing Horace's gradual self-understanding in his relationship with his patron Maecenas. See also P. L. Bowditch, *Horace and the Gift Economy of Patronage* (Berkeley: University of California Press, 2001). On patronage in general, see R. Saller, *Personal Patronage under the Early Empire* (Cambridge: Cambridge University Press, 1982); A. F. Wallace-Hadrill, ed., *Patronage in Ancient Society* (London: Routledge, 1989).

12.   See the eloquent account of the evolution of literary patronage from Horace to Juvenal in Highet, *Juvenal the Satirist*, 6–8, esp. 7, describing the increase in servility among intellectuals toward the end of the first century A.D.: 'The life of a "client" was horrible: without self-respect, without hope of independence unless after long servitude, without any real leisure, and without any real work—a lifetime of standing in waiting-rooms and loitering

that of a fool in the mime. Indeed, the Corinthian correspondence reveals that Paul himself was drawn into patron-client relationships.[13] Unable to support himself by the work of his hands, Paul accepted a gift from Stephanas.[14] Our final glimpse of Paul in Corinth shows him as the guest of Gaius, the wealthiest of the Corinthian Christians, and the 'host' of the whole church.[15]

No, the source of the difference between Paul and Horace with respect to the fool's role does not reside solely in social circumstance. If Paul himself is to be believed, it is also a matter of theology, of 'faith' (1.21b). Horace's gods provided for the peace and prosperity of those who are capable.[16] But because of the event of the crucified Christ, Paul has come to believe that God has chosen the nothings and nobodies. As a contemporary philosopher has observed, 'the most radical statement'[17] in the text on which we have been commenting is the following: 'But God has chosen the foolish of the world in order to shame the wise; and God has chosen the weak of the world in order to shame the strong; and God has chosen the low-born of the world and the despised, things that are not, in order to bring to nothing those that are' (1.27–28).[18] Because Paul believes that, in the cross of Christ, God has affirmed nothings and nobodies, he is able to embrace the role of the fool as the authentic mode of his own existence. Paul's appropriation of the role of the fool is a profound, but not unexpected, maneuver, given the way in which Jesus was executed and the socially shameful experience of Jesus' early followers.

On the basis of this belief, and the social experience in which it is grounded, Paul creates a discourse that is consistent with the event of the crucified Christ. On the one hand, this means that the discourse of 'eloquent wisdom' (σοφία λόγου) is abolished (1.19–20; 2.1,4), because God has chosen the foolish things.[19] On the other hand, and more importantly,

in corridors and bowing to blind eyes and begging for petty favours, the friend of a man who was neither your equal nor your companion, the dependant of a man who treated you as a useless ornament, the flatterer of a man whom you hated and who usually knew it.'

13.   Chow, *Patronage and Power*.

14.   1 Cor. 16.15–18, inferring a gift from the term ὑστέρημα in 16.17. For ὑστέρημα in this sense, see Phil. 2.30.

15.   Rom. 16.23. On the possibility that Erastus, the Corinthian οἰκονόμος, was also the client of Gaius, see de Vos, *Church and Community Conflicts*, 201–202: 'Rom. 16.23 reads as if Erastus has visited Gaius' house just as the letter was being written … If that was the case, it could imply that Gaius was somewhat socially superior: Erastus' visit may have been as an *amicus* (*cliens*) to his "patron" who was promoting his career.'

16.   Horace *Carm. Saec.*

17.   Badiou, *Saint Paul*, 47.

18.   See the comments on this passage by Georgi, *Theocracy in Paul's Praxis and Theology*, 54–55.

19.   Badiou, *Saint Paul*, 46–47.

it signals the emergence of a discourse in which folly, weakness, and baseness are articulated almost without euphemism. We have discovered that the law of the euphemism governed discourse about the μωρός in the Greco-Roman world: as a euphemism consists in the substitution of a pleasing expression for something that one does not want to hear mentioned, so the poor devil on the street, hungry and half-naked, might become the subject of discourse only in the language of jest. The rare authors who describe the poor whom they happen to meet—Philo, Seneca, Apuleius, scrupulous and sympathetic spirits all—invariably use language which likens these poor creatures to fools in the mime.[20] But because Paul has come to believe that *God has chosen* the weak and the low-born, he deconstructs the euphemisms, employing a language which involves less mimicry and no ambiguity. Paul describes the lives of the foolish, weak, dishonored apostles with a literalism of expression that bears comparison with Rilke's account of vagrants in the streets of Paris,[21] or Orwell's account of tramps on the roads of London.[22] To the rich and powerful in Corinth, Paul says: these fools at whom you laugh in the mime of life, whose weakness and poverty is a welcome reminder of what it is like to belong to the upper class, whose grotesque suffering is a source of amusement—these dishonored fools are the apostles of Christ!

Of particular importance as a moment in Paul's invention of a new, more literal Christian discourse is the emergence within Paul's vocabulary of the language of the 'cross' (σταυρός). As Cicero and Varro attest, it was this cruel and disgusting term which the cultured elite of the Roman world least wanted to hear.[23] The 'cross' was an ominous lacuna at the center of public discourse.[24] When the cross was mentioned at all, it was generally as the subject of jest.[25] But Paul seizes on this unspeakable word and pronounces it with a vengeance. Indeed, Paul summarizes the whole content of the gospel in a single phrase, ὁ λόγος τοῦ σταυροῦ ('the word of the cross'), a reduction of astonishing harshness. Paul's choice of the perfect participle, ἐσταυρωμένος, to describe more precisely the Christ whom he proclaims (1.23; 2.2) can only be viewed as provocative: Paul insists that the continuing and present significance of Christ, even after his

20. Philo *In Flacc.* 6.36–38; Seneca *Epist. Mor.* 12.3; Apuleius *Met.* 1.6–7.

21. Rainer Maria Rilke, *The Notebooks of Malte Laurids Brigge*, trans. S. Mitchell (New York: Random House, 1983) esp. 38–41.

22. George Orwell, *Down and Out in Paris and London* (New York: Harcourt, 2002). I owe this reference to my colleague and friend, Mark Harding.

23. Cicero *Pro Rabirio* 5.16; Varro *De Lingua Latina*; see above ch. 1.

24. See the discussion in ch. 6 above, esp. the silence of Caesar, Lucretius, Virgil, and the younger Pliny.

25. See Meggitt, 'Laughing and Dreaming at the Foot of the Cross', 9–14, and ch. 6 above.

resurrection, consists in nothing other than the fact that he *is* 'the crucified'.[26] It is not difficult to imagine how vulgar and shocking this language must have sounded to the Corinthian elite.

From what is known of Paul's letters, it would seem that the language of the 'cross' entered into Paul's discourse at this moment in his correspondence with Corinth. The pre-Pauline kerygmatic formulae do not contain the word at all.[27] The formula preserved in 1 Cor. 15.3b speaks of the death of Christ (Χριστὸς ἀπέθανεν), but not of the *manner* of his death.[28] Evidently, the manner of Jesus' death was not of great interest to the pre-Pauline tradition.[29] In Paul's earliest epistle, 1 Thessalonians, both the noun and the verb are lacking.[30] If 1 Thess. 1.9b-10 reflects the outline of Paul's preaching in the early years of his mission,[31] then the manner of Jesus' death was not emphasized. All of this changes dramatically in the Corinthian correspondence, specifically in the text which has been the object of our study, where the noun and the verb are concentrated (1.13, 17,18,23; 2.2,8).[32] Of special importance is the programmatic statement in 2.2: 'For I decided (ἔκρινα) not to know anything among you except Jesus Christ and him crucified (ἐσταυρωμένον).' If the aorist tense of κρίνειν is to be taken seriously, Paul recollects a moment in the history of his relationship with the Christian community at Corinth when he 'decided' to proclaim Christ as 'the crucified'.[33] From this point on, Paul does not look back, but rather interprets the whole of Christian existence according to a 'theology of the cross'.[34] It is well-founded speculation that the shame involved in being labelled a 'fool' by his Corinthian detractors led Paul to interrogate the ground of the truthfulness of this perception, and to

---

26. So, already, Kuhn, 'Kreuz', 720; Heckel, 'Der Gekreuzigte bei Paulus', 196–200.

27. So, rightly, Heckel, 'Der Gekreuzigte bei Paulus,' 194. The expression θανάτου δὲ σταυροῦ ('death of the cross') in the pre-Pauline hymn in Phil. 2.6–10 is an addition to the hymn by Paul himself; see U. B. Müller, *Der Brief des Paulus an die Philipper*, ThHK 11/1 (Leipzig: Evangelische Verlagsanstalt, 1993) 105.

28. Heckel, 'Der Gekreuzigte bei Paulus', 194–95.

29. The word σταυρός is found only once in the mouth of Jesus in the gospels, namely, in the saying about bearing one's cross in Mark 8.34//Matt. 16.24; Luke 9.23 and Q, Luke 14.27; Matt. 10.38; cf. J. Schröter, *Erinnerung an Jesu Worte*, WMANT 76 (Neukirchen-Vluyn: Neukirchener Verlag, 1997) 379–417.

30. W. Schrage, 'Der gekreuzigte und auferweckte Herr', *ZThK* 94 (1997) 25–38, esp. 25–26; Heckel, 'Der Gekreuzigte bei Paulus', 195.

31. G. Lüdemann, *Paul, Apostle to the Gentiles* (Philadelphia: Fortress Press, 1984) 107.

32. Outside of 1 Cor. 1–4, the verb is found only once in the Corinthian correspondence, 2 Cor. 13.4.

33. In favor of seeing 1 Cor. 2.2 as a reference to a development in Paul's thought, see U. Schnelle, *Wandlungen im paulinischen Denken*, SBS 137 (Stuttgart: Katholisches Bibelwerk, 1989) 49–54.

34. Gal. 2.19; 3.1; 5.11, 24; 6.12, 14; Phil. 2.8; 3.18; Rom. 6.6; cf. Bultmann, *Theology of the New Testament*, § 33.1, I, 292–94.

comprehend more fully the importance of the shameful manner of Jesus' death.

Yet, there is a limit to Paul's ability to identify himself with the fate of the crucified. The language in which Paul describes himself as a ʽμωρός on account of Christ' is not, finally, as intensely literal as that employed by Jesus in his parable of the beggar Lazarus (Luke 16.20–21). In Paul, there is still an aesthetic distance, a need for mimicry, a sense of shame. It is noteworthy how long Paul delays and how much he equivocates before finally employing a personal form of the concept 'foolishness' in 3.18.[35] Paul accepts the role of the fool of Christ, but only after a thorough theological analysis, in the course of which he redefines the terms 'wisdom' and 'foolishness' in a paradoxical sense. It should not be surprizing that Paul offered such resistance to the ignomy of being regarded as a μωρός. The educational level reflected in Paul's epistles is relatively high, providing evidence of social origins far from the bottom of Greco-Roman society.[36] In accepting the role of the μωρός, Paul had a considerable distance to fall. But we should be grateful for this distance and this resistance, for without it we would not possess one of the most interesting chapters in the history of Christian thought.

---

35. So, already, W. Caspari, 'Über den biblischen Begriff der Torheit', 692.

36. See the balanced and insightful discussion by A. Malherbe, 'Social Level and Literary Culture' in idem, *Social Aspects of Early Christianity* (Philadelphia: Fortress Press, 1983) 29–59.

BIBLIOGRAPHY

Reference Works

Balz, H., and G. Schneider, eds. *Exegetisches Wörterbuch zum Neuen Testament*. 3 vols. Stuttgart: Kohlhammer, 1980–1983.

Bauer, W. *A Greek-English Lexicon of the New Testament and Other Early Christian Literature*. Trans. and rev. W. F. Arndt, F. W. Gingrich, and F. W. Danker, 3rd ed. Chicago: University of Chicago Press, 2000.

Blass, F., and and A. Debrunner. *A Greek Grammar of the New Testament and Other Early Christian Literature*. Trans. and rev. R. W. Funk, Chicago: University of Chicago Press, 1961.

Denniston, J. D. *The Greek Particles*. Oxford: Clarendon Press, 1987.

Galling, K. von, ed. *Die Religion in Geschichte und Gegenwart*. 6 vols. Tübingen: Mohr-Siebeck, 1957–1962.

Glare, P. G. W. *Oxford Latin Dictionary*. Oxford: Clarendon Press, 1982.

Hammond, N. G. L., and H. H. Scullard. *The Oxford Classical Dictionary*. Oxford: Clarendon Press, 1970.

Kittel, G., and G. Friedrich, eds. *Theological Dictionary of the New Testament*. 10 vols. Trans. and ed. G. W. Bromiley. Grand Rapids, MI: Eerdmans, 1964–1976.

Klauser, T., and E. Dassman, eds. *Reallexikon für Antike und Christentum*. 14 vols. Stuttgart: Hiersemann, 1950–.

Lampe, G. W. H. *A Patristic Greek Lexicon*. Oxford: Clarendon Press, 1961.

Liddell, H. G., and R. Scott. *Greek-English Lexicon, With a Revised Supplement*. Rev. H. S. Jones and R. McKenzie. Oxford: Clarendon Press, 1996.

Lindsay, W. M. *Glossaria Latina*. 3 vols. Paris: Societe Belles Lettres, 1926.

Moulton, J. H., and G. Milligan. *The Vocabulary of the Greek Testament Illustrated from the Papyri and Other Non-Literary Sources*. London: Hodder & Stoughton, 1930; repr. Grand Rapids, MI: Eerdmans, 1976.

Robertson, A. T. *A Grammar of the Greek New Testament in Light of Historical Research*. New York and London: Hodder & Stoughton, 1914; repr. Nashville: Broadman Press, 1931.

Smyth, H. W. *Greek Grammar*. Cambridge, MA: Harvard University Press, 1956.

Turner, N. *A Grammar of the New Testament Greek*, Vol. 3: *Syntax*. Ed. J. H. Moulton. Edinburgh: T. & T. Clark, 1963.

Wissowa, G., W. Kroll, et al., eds. *Paulys Realencyclopädie der classischen Altertumswissenschaft*. Stuttgart: Metzler; München: Druckenmüller, 1894–1978.

Texts, Editions, Translations

Editions and translations of Greek and Latin authors are from the Loeb
Classical Library unless otherwise indicated.

Acta Apostolorum Apocrypha. Ed. by R. A. Lipsius and M. Bonnet. Darmstadt:
Wissenschaftliche Buchgesellschaft, 1959.
Acta Sanctorum. Ed. by T. Ruinart. Paris: Societé d' Edition "Les Belles Lettres,"
1689–1701.
Aesopica. Ed. by B. E. Perry. New York: Arno Press, 1980.
Aesop without Morals. Trans. L. W. Daly. New York: Thomas Yoseloff, 1961.
The Apocrypha and Pseudepigrapha of the Old Testament. 2 vols. Ed. by R. H.
Charles. Oxford: Clarendon Press, 1964
Artemidori Daldiani Onirocriticon Libri V. Ed. by R. A. Pack. Leipzig: Teubner,
1963.
Artemidorus. *The Interpretation of Dreams (Oneirocritica)*. Trans. by R. J. White.
Park Ridge, NJ: Noyes Press, 1975.
Athenaeus. The Deipnosophists. Vol. 7 Ed. C. Gulick. Cambridge, MA: Harvard
University Press, 1993.
Choricii Gazaei Opera. Ed. by R. Foerster. Leipzig: Teubner, 1929.
Comicorum Atticorum Fragmenta. Ed. T. Kock. Berlin: Teubner, 1888.
Comicorum Graecorum Fragmenta. Ed. by G. Kaibel. Berlin: Weidmann, 1958.
Comicorum Romanorum Fragmenta. Ed. O. Ribbeck. Leipzig: Teubner, 1897.
Commentarii ad Homeri Iliadem et Odysseam. Ed. by G. Stallbaum. Leipzig:
Teubner, 1825–1830.
Corpus Medicorum Graecorum. 5.4.2. Ed. by G. Helmreich. Leipzig: Teubner, 1923.
*Corpusculum Poesis Epicae Graecae Ludibundae I: Parodum Epicum Graecorum et
Archestrati Reliquiae*. Ed. by P. Brandt. Leipzig: Teubner, 1888.
The Cynic Epistles. Ed. by A. J. Malherbe. SBLSBS 12. Missoula, MT: Scholars
Press, 1977.
Demetrius. On Style. Ed. W. Rhys Roberts. Cambridge, MA: Harvard University
Press, 1973.
Epictetus. 2 vols. Ed. W. A. Oldfather. Cambridge, MA: Harvard University Press,
1967.
Excerpta de comoedia. Ed. P. Wessner. Leipzig: Teubner, 1902.
Die Fragmente der griechischen Historiker. 3 vols. Ed. by F. Jacoby. Berlin:
Weidmann, 1923–1950.
Die Fragmente der Vorsokratiker. Ed. H. Diels. Berlin: Weidmann, 1934.
The Greek Anthology. Vol. 3. Ed. W. R. Paton. Cambridge, MA: Harvard
University Press, 1993.
Hermes Trismegiste. Corpus Hermeticum. 4 vols. Ed. by A. D. Nock and A. J.
Festugiere. Paris: Societé d'Edition "Les Belles Lettres," 1980.
Herodas. Mimes. Ed. I. C. Cunningham. Cambridge, MA: Harvard University
Press, 1993.
Homer. *The Odyssey*. Trans. by R. Fitzgerald. New York: Farrar, Strauss and
Giroux, 2000.

The Homeric Hymn to Demeter. Ed. and trans. by N. Richardson. Oxford: Oxford University Press, 1974.

Homeric Hymns. Ed. M. L. West. Cambridge, MA: Harvard University Press, 2003.

Horace. Satires, Epistles, and Ars poetica. Ed. H. Fairclough. Cambridge, MA: Harvard University Press, 1991.

Inscriptiones Graecae. Ed. F. Hiller von Gaertringen. 2 vols. Berlin: Reimer, 1895.

Josephus III. The Jewish War, Books IV-VII. Ed. H. Thackeray. Cambridge, MA: Harvard University Press, 1979.

Justinus' des Philosophen und Märtyrers Apologien. Ed. by J. Pfättisch. Münster: Aschendorff, 1933.

Juvenal. Ed. G. G. Ramsey. Cambridge, MA: Harvard University Press, 1979.

Lucian. Vol. 2. Ed. A. H. Harmon. Cambridge, MA: Harvard University Press, 1968.

Lyrica Graeca Selecta. Ed. by D. L. Page. Oxford: Oxford University Press, 1968.

The Third and Fourth Books of Maccabees. Ed. and trans. by M. Hadas. New York: KTAV Press, 1976.

Macrobius. *The Saturnalia*. Trans. by P. V. Davies. New York: Columbia University Press, 1969.

Menander. Vol. 2. Ed. W. G. Arnott. Cambridge, MA: Harvard University Press, 1996.

Menander. The Principal Fragments. Ed. F. G. Allinson. Cambridge, MA: Harvard University Press, 1964.

Mimorum Romanorum Fragmenta. Ed. M. Bonaria. Geneva: Instituto di Filologia Classica, 1955.

Minor Latin Poets. Ed. J. W. Duff. Cambridge, MA: Harvard University Press, 1934.

New Testament Apocrypha. 2 vols. Ed. by E. Hennecke and W. Schneemelcher. Trans. by R. McL. Wilson. Philadelphia: Fortress Press, 1963.

Nonii Marcelli De Compendiosa Doctrina Libros. Ed. W. M. Lindsay. Leipzig: Teubner, 1903.

Novum Testamentum Graece. 27th edition. Ed. by E. Nestle and K. Aland. Stuttgart: Deutsche Bibelgesellschaft, 1993.

Novum Testamentum Graecum. 2 vols. Ed. by J. J. Wettstein. Graz, Oesterreich: Akademische Druck -und Verlagsanstalt, 1962.

Orientis Graeci Inscriptiones Selectae. 2 vols. Ed. by W. Dittenberger. Leipzig: Hirzel, 1903–1905.

The Oxyrhynchus Pappyri. Ed. by B. P. Grenfell and A. S. Hunt. London: Egypt Exploration Fund, 1903.

Papyri Graecae Magicae: Die Griechischen Zauberpapyri. Ed. K. Preisendanz. Stuttgart: Teubner, 1973.

Philonis Alexandrini in Flaccum. Ed. by H. Box. London: Oxford University Press, 1939.

Philogelos der Lachfreund, von Hierokles und Philagrios. Ed. by A. Thierfelder. München: Heimeran, 1968.

The Philogelos or Laughter-Lover. Trans. B. Baldwin. Amsterdam: Gieben, 1983.

Plato. *The Collected Dialogues of Plato.* Ed. and trans. by E. Hamilton and H. Cairns. Princeton: Princeton University Press, 1978.
Plato. Gorgias. Ed. by E. R. Dodds. Oxford; Oxford University Press, 1959.
Plato. Symposium. Ed. K. Dover. Cambridge: Cambridge University Press, 1980.
Platonis Opera: Platonis Phaedon. Ed. D. Wyttenbach. Lugduni-Batavorum: H. W. Hazenberg, 1830.
T. Macci Plauti Miles Gloriosus. Ed. M. Hammond. Cambridge, MA: Harvard University Press, 1997.
Pliny. Letters. Vol. 2. Ed. B. Radice. Cambridge, MA: Harvard University Press, 1976.
Popular Mime. Ed. I. C. Cunningham. Cambridge, MA: Harvard University Press, 2002.
Publilii Syri Mimi Sententiae. Ed. by O. Friedrich. Leipzig: Tuebner, 1880.
Scaenicae Romanorum Poesis Fragmenta II, Comicorum Romanorum Fragmenta. Ed. by O. Ribbeck. Hildesheim: Olms, 1962.
Select Papyri III. Ed. D. L. Page. Cambridge, MA: Harvard University Press, 1988.
Seneca. *Apocolocyntosis.* Ed. P. T. Eden. Cambridge: Cambridge University Press, 1984.
Seneca IV. Ad Lucilium Epistulae Morales. Ed. R. Gummere. Cambridge, MA: Harvard University Press, 1994.
Seneca. Moral Essays II. Ed. J. Basore. Cambridge, MA: Harvard University Press, 1994.
Septuaginta. Ed. by A. Rahlfs. Stuttgart: Deutsche Bibelgesellschaft, 1935.
Stoicorum Veterum Fragmenta. 4 vols. Ed. J. von Arnim. Leipzig: Teubner, 1905–1924.
Suetonius. 2 vols. Ed. J. C. Rolfe. Cambridge, MA: Harvard University Press, 1979.
Sylloge Inscriptionum Graecarum. 4 vols. Ed. by W. Dittenberger. Leipzig: Teubner, 1915–1924.
Tacitus V. The Annals, Books XIII-XIV. Ed. J. Jackson. Cambridge, MA: Harvard University Press, 1981.
M. Terenti Varronis de Lingua Latina quae supersunt. Ed. by G. Goetz and F. Schoell. Leipzig: Teubner, 1910.
Tertulliani Opera I. Ed. E. Dekkers (Turnholti: Typographi Brepols, 1954).
Theophrastus. Characters. Ed. J. Rusten. Cambridge, MA: Harvard University Press, 2002.

Literature

Abbott, F. 'The Theater as a Factor in Roman Politics under the Republic.' *Transactions of the American Philological Association* 38 (1907): 49–56.
Adamietz, J. 'Zum literarischen Charakter von Petrons Satyrica.' *Rheinisches Museum* 130 (1987): 329–346.
Adkins, A. W. H. *Merit and Responsibility.* Oxford: Oxford University Press, 1960.
Agamben, G. *Remnants of Auschwitz: The Witness and the Archive.* New York: Zone Books, 2002.

Aletti, J. N. 'Sagesse et mystère chez Paul. Reflexion sur le rapprochement de deux champs lexicographiques.' In *La Sagesse biblique de l'Ancien au Nouveau Testament*, ed. by J. Trublet, 357–384. Paris: Du Cerf, 1995.

Alföldy, G. *The Social History of Rome*. Baltimore: Johns Hopkins University Press, 1991.

Allo, E. B. *Saint Paul. Première Épître aux Corinthiens*. Paris: Gabalda, 1934.

Altizer, T. J. J. *Toward a New Christianity*. New York: Harcourt Brace, 1967.

Anderson, G. *Lucian, Theme and Variation in the Second Sophistic*. Leiden: Brill, 1976.

Anderson, R. D. *Ancient Rhetorical Theory and Paul*. Kampen: Kok Pharos, 1996.

Anderson, W. S., ed. *Essays on Roman Satire*. Princeton: Princeton University Press, 1982.

— *Barbarian Play: Plautus' Roman Comedy*. Toronto: University of Toronto, 1993.

André, J. M. 'Die Zuschauerschaft als sozialpolitischer Mikrocosmos zur Zeit des Hochprinzipats.' In *Theater und Gesellschaft im Imperium Romanum*, ed. J. Blänsdorf, 165–173. Tübingen: Francke, 1990.

Appel, H. *Der Hebräerbrief: Ein Schreiben des Apollos an Judenchristen der Korinthischen Gemeinde*. Leipzig: Deichert, 1918.

Armstrong, D. *Horace*. New Haven: Yale University Press, 1989.

Arndt, E. *De ridiculi doctrina rhetorica*. Kirchain: M. Schmersow, 1904.

Arnott, P. *Public and Performance in the Greek Theatre*. London: Routledge, 1989.

Asting, R. *Die Verkündigung des Wortes im Urchristentum, dargestellt an den Begriffen 'Wort Gottes,' 'Evangelium' und 'Zeugnis.'* Stuttgart: Kohlhammer, 1939.

Attridge, H. *The Epistle to the Hebrews*. Philadelphia: Fortress Press, 1989.

Auguet, R. *Cruelty and Civilization: The Roman Games*. London: Routledge, 1994.

Aune, D. E. *Revelation*. 3 vols. Nashville: Thomas Nelson, 1998.

Babcock, B. A. *The Reversible World: Symbolic Inversion in Art and Society*. Ithaca: Cornell University Press, 1978.

Bach, R. 'Bauen und Pflanzen.' In *Studien zur Theologie der alttestamentlichen Überlieferung*, ed. R. Rendtorff, 7–32. Tübingen: Mohr-Siebeck, 1961.

Badiou, A. *Saint Paul: The Foundation of Universalism*. Stanford, CA: Stanford University Press, 2003.

Baird, W. 'One Against the Other: Intra-Church Conflict in 1 Corinthians.' In *The Conversation Continues: Studies in Paul and John*, ed. R. T. Fortna and B. R. Gaventa, 116–136. Nashville: Abingdon, 1990.

Bakhtin, M. *Rabelais and His World* (Cambridge, MA: MIT Press, 1968).

Baldwin, B. 'The Philogelos: An Ancient Joke Book.' In *Roman and Byzantine Papers*. Amsterdam: Gieben, 1989: 624–637.

Barclay, J. M. G. 'Thessalonica and Corinth: Social Contrasts in Pauline Christianity.' *Journal for the Study of the New Testament* 47 (1992): 49–74.

Barnes, T. D. 'Christians and the Theater.' In *Roman Theater and Society. E. Togo Salmon Papers I*, ed. W. J. Slater, 161–180. Ann Arbor: University of Michigan Press, 1996.

Barrett, C. K. 'Christianity at Corinth.' In *Essays on Paul*, 1–27. Philadelphia: Westminster, 1982.

— *A Commentary on the First Epistle to the Corinthians.* New York: Harper and Row, 1968.

Barth, K. *The Resurrection of the Dead.* New York: Revell, 1933.

Barton, C. *The Sorrows of the Ancient Romans: The Gladiator and the Monster.* Princeton: Princeton University Press, 1993.

Bartsch, S. *Actors in the Audience: Theatricality and Doublespeak from Nero to Julian.* Cambridge, MA: Harvard University Press, 1994.

Baumann, R. *Mitte und Norm des Christlichen. Eine Auslegung von 1 Korinther 1,1– 3,4.* Münster: Aschendorff, 1968.

Beacham, R. *The Roman Theatre and its Audience.* Cambridge, MA: Harvard University Press, 1992.

— *Spectacle Entertainments of Early Imperial Rome.* New Haven: Yale University Press, 1999.

Beare, F. 'Zeus in the Hellenistic Age.' In *The Seed of Wisdom*, ed. W. McCullough, 47–57. Toronto: University of Toronto Press, 1964.

Beare, W. 'Mimus.' *The Oxford Classical Dictionary*, ed. N. G. L. Hammond and H. H. Scullard. 2nd ed. Oxford: Clarendon Press, 1970: 688.

— *The Roman Stage.* London: Methuen, 1977.

— 'Mime. Greek.' *The Oxford Classical Dictionary*, ed. S. Hornblower and A. Spawforth. 3rd ed. revised. Oxford: Oxford University Press 2003: 982.

Becatti, G. *The Art of Ancient Greece and Rome.* Englewood Cliffs, NJ: Prentice, 1975.

Behm, R. 'νοῦς.' *Theological Dictionary of the New Testament* 4 (1967): 951–960.

Beker, J. C. *Paul the Apostle: The Triumph of God in Life and Thought.* Philadelphia: Fortress Press, 1980.

Bellemore, J. 'Gaius the Pantomime.' *Antichthon* 28 (1994): 64–79.

Bengel, J. A. *Gnomon of the New Testament.* 3 vols. Edinburgh: T. & T. Clark, 1877.

Bergmann, B., ed. *The Art of Ancient Spectacle.* New Haven: Yale University Press, 1999.

Berner, W. D. 'Initiationsriten in Mysterienreligionen, im Gnosticismus und im antiken Judentum.' Diss. Göttingen, 1972.

Bertram, G. 'μωρός.' *Theological Dictionary of the New Testament* 4 (1967): 832– 847.

Best, E. 'The Power and the Wisdom of God: 1 Corinthians 1.18-25.' In *Paolo a una Chiesa Divisa (1 Cor. 1-4)*, ed. L. de Lorenzi, 21–30. Rome: Abbazi di S. Paolo, 1980.

Betz, H. D. *Der Apostel Paulus und die sokratische Tradition.* Tübingen: Mohr-Siebeck, 1972.

— *Galatians. A Commentary on Paul's Letter to the Churches in Galatia.* Philadelphia: Fortress Press, 1979.

— *2 Corinthians 8 and 9. A Commentary on Two Administrative Letters of the Apostle Paul.* Philadelphia: Fortress Press, 1985.

— *Lukian von Samosata und das Neue Testament.* TU 76. Berlin: Akademie-Verlag, 1961.

— 'The Problem of Rhetoric and Theology according to the Apostle Paul.' In *L'Apôtre Paul: Personalité, Style et Conception du Ministére*, ed. A. Vanhoye, Leuven: Leuven University Press, 1986.

— *Sermon on the Mount*. Minneapolis: Fortress Press, 1995.

Bieber, M. *Die Denkmäler zum Theaterwesen im Altertum*. Berlin: Vereinigung Wissenschaftlicher Verleger, 1920.

— *The History of the Greek and Roman Theater*. Princeton: Princeton University Press, 1961.

Bjerkelund, C. J. *Parakalo: Form, Funktion und Sinn der Parakalo-Sätze in den paulinischen Briefen*. Oslo: Universitetsforlaget, 1967.

Black, D. A. *Paul, Apostle of Weakness: Astheneia and its Cognates in the Pauline Literature*. New York: Peter Lang, 1984.

Blänsdorf, J., ed. *Theater und Gesellschaft im Imperium Romanum*. Tübingen: Francke, 1990.

Bockmuehl, M. *Revelation and Mystery in Ancient Judaism and Pauline Christianity*. Grand Rapids, MI: Eerdmans, 1997.

Bohatec, J. 'Inhalt und Reihenfolge der "Schlagwörte der Erlösungsreligion," 1 Kor. 1.26-31.' *Theologische Zeitung* 4 (1948): 252–271.

Bollinger, H. *Theatralis Licentia*. Basel: Winterthur, 1969.

Bompaire, J. *Lucian écrivain: Imitation et création*. Paris: Boccard, 1958.

Bonaria, M. *Romani Mimi*. Rome: In aedibus Athenaei, 1965.

Bonnechare, P. 'Trophonius of Lebadea: Mystery Aspects of an Oracular Cult in Boetia.' In *Greek Mysteries: The Archaeology and Ritual of Ancient Greek Secret Cults*, ed. M. B. Cosmopoulos, 169–192. London: Routledge, 2003.

Borghi, E. 'Il tema sophia in 1 Cor 1-4.' *Rivista Biblica* 40 (1992): 421–458.

Bornkamm, G. *Die Vorgeschichte des sogenannten Zweiten Korintherbrief*, SHAW.PH 1961, 2. Abhandlung. Heidelberg: Winter, 1961.

— 'μυστήριον.' *Theological Dictionary of the New Testament* 4 (1967): 803–819.

— *Paul*. New York: Harper and Row, 1971.

Bousset, W. *Der erste Brief an die Korinther*. Göttingen: Vandenhoeck & Ruprecht, 1917.

Bovie, S. P. *Satires and Epistles of Horace*. Chicago: University of Chicago Press, 1966.

Bowditch, P. L. *Horace and the Gift Economy of Patronage*. Berkeley: University of California Press, 2001.

Bradley, K. *Slavery and Society at Rome*. Cambridge: Cambridge University Press, 1994.

— *Slaves and Masters in the Roman Empire: A Study in Social Control*. New York and Oxford: Oxford University Press, 1987.

Branham, R. Bracht. *Unruly Eloquence: Lucian and the Comedy of Traditions*. Cambridge, MA: Harvard University Press, 1989.

— 'The Wisdom of Lucian's Tiresias.' *Journal of Hellenic Studies* 109 (1989): 154–168.

Braun, H. *Gesammelte Studien zum Neuen Testament und seiner Umwelt*. Tübingen: Mohr-Siebeck, 1962.

Braund, S. M. *The Roman Satirist and Their Masks*. London: Bristol Classical Press, 1996.

Bréhier, E. *Les idées philosophiques et religieuses de Philon d'Alexandrie*. Paris: Vrin, 1950.

Breslin, J. *A Greek Prayer*. Mailbu, CA: J. Paul Getty Museum, 1985.

Brickhouse, T. C. and N. D. Smith. 'The Paradox of Socrates' Ignorance.' In *Plato's Socrates*, 30–38. Oxford: Oxford University Press, 1995.

Broneer, O. 'Corinth, Center of St. Paul's Missionary Work in Greece.' *Biblical Archaeologist* 14 (1951): 90–98.

Brown, A. P. *The Cross and Human Transformation: Paul's Apocalyptic Word in 1 Corinthians*. Minneapolis: Fortress Press, 1995.

Brown, R. E. *The Death of the Messiah: From Gethsemane to the Grave: A Commentary on the Passion Narratives in the Four Gospels*, Vol. 1. New York: Doubleday, 1994.

Buck, C. D. *Greek Dialects*. Chicago: University of Chicago Press, 1955.

Bultmann, R. *Faith and Understanding*. New York: Harper and Row, 1969.

— *Theology of the New Testament*. Vol. 1. New York: Charles Scribner's Sons, 1951.

Bünker, M. *Briefformular und rhetorische Disposition im 1. Korintherbrief*. Göttingen: Vandenhoeck & Ruprecht, 1983.

Burge, E. L. 'The Irony of Socrates.' *Antichthon* 3 (1969): 5–17.

Burke, T. 'Paul's Role as "Father" to His Corinthian "Children" in Socio-Historical Context (1 Corinthians 4.14-21).' In *Paul and the Corinthians. Studies on a Community in Conflict. Essays in Honour of Margaret Thrall*, ed. T. Burke and J. Elliott, 95–114. Leiden: Brill, 2003.

Burkert, W. ΓΟΗΣ. Zum griechischen "Schamanismus".' *Rheinisches Museum* 102 (1962): 38–54.

— *Ancient Mystery Cults*. Cambridge, MA: Harvard University Press, 1987.

Calvin, J. *Commentarius in epistolam priorem ad Corinthios*. Brunsvigae, 1892.

Cameron, A. *Circus Factions: Blues and Greens at Rome and Byzantium*. Oxford: Oxford University Press, 1976.

Carpocino, J. *Daily Life in Ancient Rome*. New Haven: Yale University Press, 1977.

Carr, A. W. 'The Rulers of this Age—1 Corinthians ii.6-8.' *New Testament Studies* 23 (1976/1977): 20–35.

Carter, T. L. ' "Big Men" in Corinth.' *Journal for the Study of the New Testament* 64 (1997): 45–71.

Caspari, W. 'Über den biblischen Begriff der Torheit.' *Neue kirchliche Zeitschrift* 39 (1928): 668–695.

Castellani, V. 'Plautus versus *Komoidia*: Popular Farce at Rome.' In *Themes in Drama: Farce*, ed. J. Redmond, 53–82. Cambridge: Cambridge University Press, 1988.

Castelli, E. *Imitating Paul: A Discourse of Power*. Louisville, KY: Westminster/ John Knox, 1991.

Caster, M. *Lucien et la pensée religieuse de son temps*. Paris: Les Belles Lettres, 1938.

Chalmers, W. R. 'Plautus and His Audience.' In *Roman Drama*, eds. T. A. Dorley and D. R. Dudley, 21–50. London: Routledge, 1965.

Chow, J. K. *Patronage and Power: A Study of Social Networks in Corinth*. Sheffield: Sheffield Academic Press, 1992.

Chroust, A.-H. *Socrates, Man and Myth*. London: Routledge, 1957.

Cicu, L. *Problemi e strutture del mimo a Roma*. Venezia: Edizioni Gallizzi, 1988.

Clarke, A. D. *Secular and Christian Leadership in Corinth: A Socio-Historical and Exegetical Study of 1 Corinthians 1-6*. Leiden: Brill, 1993.

Clemen, C. *Die Einheitlichkeit der paulinischen Briefe an der Hand der bisher mit Bezug auf sie aufgestellten Interpolations-und Compilationshypothesen*. Göttingen: Vandenhoeck & Ruprecht, 1894.

Clinton, K. 'Stages of Initiation in the Eleusinian and Samothracian Mysteries.' In *Greek Mysteries: The Archaeology and Ritual of Ancient Greek Secret Cults*, ed. M. B. Cosmopoulos, 50–78. London: Routledge, 2003.

Coenen, J. *Lukian Zeus tragodos: Überlieferungsgeschichte, Text und Kommentar*. Meisenheim am Glan: Hain, 1977.

Collins, R. F. *First Corinthians*. Collegeville, MN: Michael Glazier, 1999.

Conzelmann, H. 'Paulus und die Weisheit.' *New Testament Studies* 12 (1965–1966): 231–244.

— *An Outline of the Theology of the New Testament*. London: SCM Press, 1969.

— *1 Corinthians*. Philadelphia: Fortress Press, 1975.

Corbeill, A. *Controlling Laughter: Political Humor in the Late Roman Republic*. Princeton: Princeton University Press, 1996.

Corbett, P. B. *The Scurra*. Edinburgh: Scottish Academic Press, 1986.

Cornford, F. *The Origin of Attic Comedy*. Gloucester, MA: Peter Smith, 1968.

Cox, H. *The Feast of Fools*. Cambridge, MA: Harvard University Press, 1969.

Crusius, O. *Untersuchungen zu den Mimiamben des Herondas*. Leipzig: Teubner, 1892.

Cullmann, O. *Vorträge und Aufsätze*, ed. K. Fröhlich. Tübingen: Mohr-Siebeck, 1966.

Dahl, N. 'Formgeschichtliche Beobachtungen zur Christusverkündigung in der Gemeindepredigt.' In *Neutestamentliche Studien für Rudolf Bultmann*, 3–9. Berlin: Töpelmann, 1954.

— 'Paul and the Church at Corinth according to 1 Corinthians 1.10-4.21.' In *Christian History and Interpretation: Studies Presented to John Knox*, ed. W. R. Farmer and C. F. D. Moule, 313–335. Cambridge: Cambridge University Press, 1967.

Dautzenberg, G. 'Botschaft und Bedeutung der urchristlichen Prophetie nach dem Ersten Korintherbrief (2.6-16; 12-14).' In *Studien zur paulinischen Theologie*, 31–57. Göttingen: Vandenhoeck & Ruprecht, 1999.

Davis, J. A. *Wisdom and Spirit: An Investigation of 1 Corinthians 1.18-3.20 against the Background of Jewish Sapiential Traditions in the Greco-Roman Period*. Lanham, MD: University Press of America, 1984.

Deissmann, A. *Paulus*. Tübingen: Mohr-Siebeck, 1925.

— *Light from the Ancient East*. Grand Rapids: Baker Book House, 1927.

Delatte, A. *Le cycéon, breuvage rituel des mystères d'Eleusis*. Paris: Du Cerf, 1955.

Delling, G. 'τέλειος.' *Theological Dictionary of the New Testament* 8 (1972): 67–87.

De Lorenzi, A. '*Madeia Perimadeia* in Petronio e un mimo perduto di P. Siro.' *Rivista Indo-Greca-Italica di Filologia* 13 (1929): 2–14.

Denniston, J. D. *Greek Prose Style*. Oxford: Clarendon Press, 1952.

Dessen, C. S. *The Satires of Persius. Iunctura Callidus Acri*. London: Bristol Classical Press, 1996.

Dibelius, M. *Die Geisterwelt im Glauben des Paulus*. Göttingen: Vandenhoeck & Ruprecht, 1909.

Dickison, S. K. 'Claudius: Saturnalicius Princeps'. *Latomus* 36 (1977): 634–47.

Dieterich, A. *Pulcinella. Pompejanische Wandbilder und römische Satyrspiele*. Leipzig: Teubner, 1897.

Dietrich, W. 'Kreuzesverkündigung, Kreuzeswort und Kreuzesepigraph. Randbemerkungen zum "Kreuz Christi" bei Paulus.' In *Theokratia. Festgabe für Karl Heinrich Rengstorf*, 214–221. Leiden: Brill, 1973.

Dinkler, E. *Signum Crusis. Aufsätze zum Neuen Testament und zur Christlichen Archäologie*. Tübingen: Mohr-Siebeck, 1967.

Dobschütz, E. von. 'Religionsgeschichtliche Parallelen zum Neuen Testament.' *Zeitschrift für die neutestamentliche Wissenschaft* 21 (1922): 69–72.

Döring, K. *Exemplum Socratis. Studien zur Socratesnachwirkung in der Kynisch-stoischen Popularphilosophie der frühen Kaiserzeit und im frühen Christentum*. Wiesbaden: Franz Steiner, 1979.

Drerup, E. *Demosthenes im Urteile des Altertums*. Würzburg: Becker, 1923.

Duckworth, G. E. *The Nature of Roman Comedy*. Princeton: Princeton University Press, 1952.

Ducos, M. 'La condition des acteurs à Rome. Données juridiques et sociales.' In *Theater und Gesellschaft im Imperium Romanum*, ed. J. Blänsdorf, 19–33. Tübingen: Francke, 1990.

Duff, A. M. *Freedmen in the Early Roman Empire*. Cambridge: Cambridge University Press, 1958.

Duff, J. Wright. *Roman Satire*. Berkeley: University of California Press, 1937.

Du Plessis, P. J. ΤΕΛΕΙΟΣ. *The Idea of Perfection in the New Testament*. Kampen: Kok, 1959.

Dupont, F. *Acteur-Roi ou le théâtre dans la Rome antique*. Paris: Du Cerf, 1985.

Ebner, M. *Leidenslisten und Apostelbrief. Untersuchungen zu Form, Motivik und Funktion der Peristasenkataloge bei Paulus*. Würzburg: Echter, 1991.

Eckstein, H.-J. *Der Begriff Syneidesis bei Paulus. Ein neutestamentlich-exegetische Untersuchung zum Gewissensbegriff*. Tübingen: Mohr-Siebeck, 1983.

Edelstein E. *Xenophontisches und platonisches Bild des Sokrates*. Berlin: Ebering, 1935.

Edwards, C. 'Beware of Imitations: Theater and the Subversion of Imperial Identity.' In *Reflections of Nero: Culture, History and Representation*, ed. J. Elsner and J. Masters, 83–97. Chapel Hill, NC: University of North Carolina Press, 1994.

Eitrem, S. 'Sophron.' *Symbolae Osloenses* 12 (1933): 10–13.

Ellis, E. Earle. *Paul's Use of the Old Testament*. Grand Rapids, MI: Eerdmans, 1957.

— *Prophecy and Hermeneutic in Early Christianity. New Testament Essays*, WUNT 18 (Tübingen: Mohr-Siebeck, 1978).

Engels, D. *Roman Corinth: An Alternative Model for the Classical City*. Chicago: University of Chicago Press, 1990.

Erasmus, D. *Moriae Encomium*. In *Opera Omnia*, ed. C. Miller. Amsterdam: North-Holland Publishing Company, 1979.

Fantham, R. E. 'Mime: The Missing Link in Roman Literary History.' *Classical World* 82.3 (1989): 153–163.

— 'Mime. Roman.' *The Oxford Classical Dictionary*, ed. S. Hornblower and A. Spawforth. 3rd ed. revised. Oxford: Oxford University Press, 2003: 982–83.

Farmer, K. 'Folly, Fool, Foolish, Simple.' In *The Westminster Theological Wordbook of the Bible*, ed. D. E. Gowan, 140–144. Louisville, KY: Westminster Press, 2003.

Fee, G. *The First Epistle to the Corinthians*. Grand Rapids, MI: Eerdmans, 1987.

— '1 Corinthians 1.2, 2.1, and 2.10.' In *Scribes and Scriptures: New Testament Essays in Honor of J. Harold Greenlee*, ed. D. A. Black, 1–12. Winona Lake, IN: Eisenbrauns, 1992.

Feuillet, A. *Le Christ Sagasse de Dieu d'après les Épître pauliniennes*. Paris: Gabalda, 1966.

Fiedler, P. 'μωρία.' In *Exegetical Dictionary of the New Testament*, Vol. 2, ed. H. Balz and G. Schneider, 449–450. Grand Rapids, MI: Eerdmans, 1981.

Field, F. *Notes on the Translation of the New Testament*. Oxford: Oxford University Press, 1899.

Fiore, B. 'Covert Allusion in 1 Cor. 1-4.' *Catholic Biblical Quarterly* 47 (1985): 85–102.

Fiske, G. C. *Lucilius and Horace. A Study in the Classical Theory of Imitation*. Madison: University of Wisconsin Press, 1920.

Fitzgerald, J. T. *Cracks in an Earthen Vessel: An Examination of the Catalogues of Hardships in the Corinthian Correspondence*. Atlanta: Scholars Press, 1988.

— 'Paul, the Ancient Epistolary Theorists, and 2 Corinthians 10-13' In *Greeks, Romans, and Christians: Essays in Honor of Abraham J. Malherbe*, eds. D. Balch, E. Ferguson, and W. A. Meeks, 190–200. Minneapolis: Augsburg Press, 1990.

Forbes, C. ' "Strength" and "Weakness" as Terminology of Status in St. Paul: The Historical and Literary Roots of a Metaphor, with Special Reference to 1 and 2 Corinthians.' B.A. thesis, Macquarie University, 1978.

— 'Early Christian Inspired Speech and Hellenistic Popular Religion.' *Novum Testamentum* 28 (1986): 257–270.

Fowler, W. Warde. *The Roman Festivals*. London: Macmillan, 1925.

Fraenkel, E. *Plautinisches im Plautus*. Berlin: Reimer, 1922.

Frank, T. 'The Status of Actors at Rome.' *Classical Philology* 26 (1931): 11–20.

Freud, S. *Jokes and Their Relation to the Unconscious*. Trans. J. Strachey. New York: Norton, 1963.

— 'Instincts and Their Vicissitudes.' In *General Psychological Theory*. Ed. P. Rieff. New York: Collier, 1963.

— *Introductory Lectures on Psychoanalysis*. Ed. J. Strachey. New York: Norton, 1966.

Freudenburg, K. *The Walking Muse: Horace on the Theory of Satire*. Princeton: Princeton University Press, 1993.

Fridrichsen, A. *Exegetical Writings. A Selection*, eds. C. Caragounis and T. Fornberg. Tübingen: Mohr-Siebeck, 1994.

— 'Sprachliches und Stilistisches zum Neuen Testament.' In *Kungliga Humanistika Vetenskap-Samfundet I Uppsala, Arsbok 1943.* Uppsala: Almqvist & Wiksell, 1943.

Friedländer, L. *Roman Life and Manners under the Early Empire.* 4 vols. Trans. L. Magnus and J. H. Freese, 7th edition. London: Routledge, 1908–1913.

Friedländer, P. *Plato. The Dialogues, First Period.* Princeton: Princeton University Press, 1965.

— *Plato. An Introduction.* Princeton: Princeton University Press, 1969.

Funk, R. *Language, Hermeneutic, and the Kingdom of God: The Problem of Language in the New Testament and Contemporary Theology.* New York: Harper and Row, 1966.

— 'The Apostolic Parousia: Form and Significance.' In *Christian History and Interpretation: Studies Presented to John Knox*, ed. W. R. Farmer and C. F. D. Moule, 249–269. Cambridge: Cambridge University Press, 1967.

Furneaux, H. *The Annals of Tacitus.* Oxford: Oxford University Press, 1907.

Furnish, V. P. *II Corinthians.* New York: Doubleday, 1984.

Gaca, K. 'Paul's Uncommon Declaration in Rom. 1.18-32 and Its Problematic Legacy for Pagan and Christian Relations.' *Harvard Theological Review* 92.2 (1999): 165–198.

Gagarin, M. 'Socrates' *Hybris* and Alcibiades' Failure.' *Phoenix* 31 (1977): 22–37.

Gagliardi, D. *Il Comico in Petronio.* Palermo: Palumbo, 1980.

Galinsky, K. *Augustan Culture.* Princeton: Princeton University Press, 1996.

Gardner, J. F. and T. Wiedemann, *The Roman Household: A Sourcebook.* London: Routledge, 1991.

Garland, R. *The Eye of the Beholder: Deformity and Disability in the Graeco-Roman World.* Ithaca: Cornell University Press, 1995.

Garnsey, P. *Social Status and Legal Privilege in the Roman Empire.* Oxford: Oxford University Press, 1970.

Garnsey, P. and R. Saller. *The Roman Empire: Economy, Society, and Culture.* London: Duckworth, 1987.

Garton, C. *Personal Aspects of the Roman Theatre.* Toronto: University of Toronto Press, 1972.

— 'A Register of Roman Actors.' In *Aufstieg und Niedergang der römischen Welt* 2.30.1 (1980): 580–609.

Gaventa, B. R. 'Mother's Milk and Ministry in 1 Corinthians 3.' In *Theology and Ethics in Paul and His Interpreters. Essays in Honor of Victor Paul Furnish*, Eds. E. Lovering and J. Sumney, 101–113. Nashville: Abingdon Press, 1996.

Gazza, V. 'I tre scritti affini di Luciano: Ζεὺς ἐλεγχόμενος, Ζεὺς τραγῳδός, θεῶν ἐκκλησία.' *Aevum* 27 (1953): 1–17.

Gebhard, E. R. 'The Theater and the City.' In *Roman Theater and Society*, ed. W. J. Slater, 113–128. Ann Arbor: University of Michigan Press, 1996.

Geffcken, J. 'Studien zur griechischen Satire.' *Neue Jahrbücher für das klassische Altertum* 27 (1911): 393–493.

Gelzer, T. 'Aristophanes und sein Sokrates.' *Museum Helveticum* 13 (1956): 65–93.

Gemünden, P. von. *Vegetationsmetaphorik im Neuen Testament und seiner Umwelt. Ein Bildfelduntersuchung.* Göttingen: Vandenhoeck & Ruprecht, 1993.

Genet, O. 'L'interpretation de la mort de Jésus en situation discursive. Un cas-type: L'articulation des figures de cette mort en 1-2 Corinthiens.' *New Testament Studies* 34 (1988): 506–535.

Gentili, B. *Theatrical Performances in the Ancient World: Hellenistic and Early Roman Theatre.* Amsterdam: J. C. Gieben, 1979.

Georgi, D. *The Opponents of Paul in Second Corinthians.* Philadelphia: Fortress Press, 1986.

— *Theocracy in Paul's Praxis and Theology.* Minneapolis: Fortress Press, 1991.

— 'Jüdischer Synkretismus' (unpublished essay).

Giancotti, F. *Mimo e Gnome: Studi su Decimo Laberio e Publilio Siro.* Firenze: G. D'anna, 1967.

Gibb, H. O. *'Torheit' und 'Rätsel' im Neuen Testament. Der antinomische Strukturcharakter der neutestamentlichen Botschaft.* Stuttgart: Kohlhammer, 1941.

Gigon, O. *Sokrates, sein Bild in Dichtung und Geschichte.* Bern: Francke, 1947.

— *Kommentar zum ersten Buch von Xenophons Memorabilien.* Basel: F. Reinhardt, 1953.

Gill, D. W. J. 'Erastus the Aedile.' *Tyndale Bulletin* 40 (1989): 293–301.

— 'In Search of the Social Elite in the Corinthian Church.' *Tyndale Bulletin* 44 (1993): 323–337.

Gilula, D. 'Greek Drama in Rome: Some Aspects of Cultural Transposition.' In *The Play Out of Context*, ed. H. Scolnicov and P. Holland. Cambridge: Cambridge University Press, 1989.

Gnilka, J. *Ist 1. Kor. 3.10-15 ein Schriftzeugnis für das Fegfeuer?* Düsseldorf: Triltsch, 1955.

Godet, F. *Commentary on St. Paul's First Epistle to the Corinthians.* Vol. 1. Edinburgh: T. & T. Clark, 1889.

Gold, B. K., ed. *Literary and Artistic Patronage in Augustan Rome.* Austin: University of Texas Press, 1982.

Goldberg, S. 'Terence and the Death of Comedy.' In *Drama and the Classical Heritage*, eds. C. Davidson, R. Johnson, and J. Stroupe, 52–64. New York: Scribner's Press, 1993.

Goldman, H. 'Two Terracotta Figurines from Tarsus.' *American Journal of Archaeology* 47 (1943): 22–34.

Golvin, J.-C. *L'amphithéatre romain.* Paris: Du Cerf, 1988.

Gooch, P. W. *Partial Knowledge: Philosophical Studies in Paul.* Notre Dame, IN: University of Notre Dame Press, 1987.

— 'Socratic Irony and Aristotle's *Eirōn*: Some Puzzles.' *Phoenix* 41 (1987): 95–104.

Goulder, M. D. 'Sophia in 1 Corinthians.' *New Testament Studies* 37 (1991): 516–534.

— *Paul and the Competing Mission in Corinth.* Peabody, MA: Hendrickson, 2001.

Goulet-Cazé, M.-O. 'Le cynisme à l'époque impériale.' *Aufstieg und Niedergang der römischen Welt* 2.36.4 (1990): 2763–2768.

Gourinat, M. 'Socrate était-il un ironiste?' *Revue de Metaphysique et de Morale* 91 (1986): 339–53.

Grant, M. *The Ancient Rhetorical Theories of the Laughable.* Madison: University of Wisconsin Press, 1924.

Grant M. and A. Mulas. *Eros in Pompeii: The Erotic Art Collection of the Museum of Naples*. New York: Stewart, Tabori & Chang, 1975.

Grant, R. M. 'The Wisdom of the Corinthians.' In *The Joy of Study. Papers on New Testament and Related Subjects Presented to Honor Frederick Clifton Grant*, ed. S. E. Johnson, 51–55. New York: Macmillan, 1951.

— 'The Description of Paul in the *Acts of Paul and Thecla*.' *Vigiliae Christianae* 36 (1982): 1–4.

Greenidge, A. H. J. *Infamia: Its Place in Roman Public and Private Law*. Oxford: Oxford University Press, 1894.

Griffin, M. *Seneca, a Philosopher in Politics*. Oxford: Oxford University Press, 1976.

Griffith, J. G. 'Juvenal and the Stage-Struck Patricians.' *Mnemosyne* 15 (1962): 256–261.

Griffiths, J. Gwyn. *The Origins of Osiris*. Berlin: Hessling, 1966.

Grindheim, S. 'Wisdom for the Perfect: Paul's Challenge to the Corinthian Church (1 Corinthians 2.6-16).' *Journal of Biblical Literature* 121/4 (2002): 689–709.

Griswold, C. L. 'Irony and Aesthetic Language in Plato's Dialogues.' In *Philosophy and Literature*, ed. D. Bollig, 71–99. New York: Scribner's, 1987.

Grosheide, F. W. *Commentary on the First Epistle to the Corinthians*. Grand Rapids, MI: Eerdmans, 1953.

Grube, G. M. A. *A Greek Critic: Demetrius on Style*. Toronto: University of Toronto Press, 1961.

Grundmann, W. 'δύναμαι', *Theological Dictionary of the New Testament* 2 (1963): 284–371.

— 'Die NHΠIOI in der urchristlichen Paränese.' *New Testament Studies* 5 (1958/1959): 188–205.

Grysar, C. J. *Der römische Mimus*. Vienna: Akademie der Wissenschaften, 1854.

Guthrie, W. C. K. *Socrates*. Cambridge: Cambridge University Press, 1971.

Haas, C. *Alexandria in Late Antiquity: Topography and Social Conflict*. Baltimore: Johns Hopkins University Press, 1997.

Haenchen, E. *The Acts of the Apostles*. Philadelphia: Westminster Press, 1971.

Hall, J. *Lucian's Satire*. New York: Harper, 1981.

Hanson, J. A. *Roman Theater-Temples*. Princeton: Princeton University Press, 1959.

Hardie, A. *Statius and the Silvae*. Liverpool: S. Cairns, 1983.

Harding, M. ' "Killed All the Day Long": The Powerful and Their Victims in the New Testament Era.' Paper presented to the Annual Meeting of the Society of Biblical Literature, 2001.

Harrill, J. Albert. 'The Farce of the Dishonest Manager (Luke 16.1-8): Roman Slave Comedy and Early Christian Self-Definition.' Paper presented to the Annual Meeting of the Society of Biblical Literature, 2003.

Harris, R. 'Who Sent Apollos to Corinth?' *Expositor* 11 (1916): 175–183.

Hartman, L. 'Some Remarks on 1 Cor. 2.1-5.' *Svensk Exegetisk Arsbok* 39 (1974): 109–120.

Hausrath, A. von. *Der Vier-Kapitel-Brief des Paulus an die Korinther*. Heidelberg: Bassermann, 1870.

Hays, R. *First Corinthians*. Louisville, KY: John Knox Press, 1997.

Heckel, T. 'Der Gekreuzigte bei Paulus und im Markusevangelium.' *Biblische Zeitschrift* 46 (2002): 190–210.

Heckel, U. *Kraft in Schwachheit. Untersuchungen zu 2. Kor. 10-13*. Tübingen: Mohr-Siebeck, 1993.

Heinrici, C. F. G. *Das erste Sendschreiben des Apostel Paulus an die Korinther*. Berlin: Hertz, 1880.

— *Der erste Brief an die Korinther*. Göttingen: Vandenhoeck & Ruprecht, 1896.

Helm, R. *Lucian und Menipp*. Leipzig: Teubner, 1906.

Hemer, C. J. *The Book of Acts in the Setting of Hellenistic History*. Tübingen: Mohr-Siebeck, 1989.

Hengel, M. *Crucifixion in the Ancient World and the Folly of the Message of the Cross*. Philadelphia: Fortress Press, 1977.

— *Juden, Griechen und Barbaren*. Stuttgart: Katholisches Bibelwerk, 1976.

— '*Mors turpissima crucis*: Die Keuzigung in der antiken Welt und die "Torheit" Des "Wortes vom Kreuz",' In *Rechtfertigung. Festschrift für Ernst Käsemann Zum 70. Geburtstag*. Ed. J. Friedrich, W. Pöhlmann and P. Stuhlmacher. Tübingen: Mohr-Siebeck, 1976.

Hengel, M. and U. Heckel. *Paulus und das antike Judentum*. Tübingen: Mohr-Siebeck, 1994.

Hepding, H. *Attis, seine Mythen und sein Kult*. Berlin: Topelmann, 1967.

Héring, J. *The First Epistle of St. Paul to the Corinthians*. London: Epworth, 1962.

Hermann, L. 'Laureolus.' In *Hommages à Henry Bardon*, eds. M. Renard and P. Laurens, 225–234. Bruxelles: Latomus, 1985.

Hicks, E. L. 'St Paul and Hellenism.' *Studia Biblica et Ecclesiastica* 4 (1896): 1–14.

Highet, G. *Juvenal the Satirist. A Study*. Oxford: Clarendon Press, 1954.

— '*Libertino Patre Natus*.' *American Journal of Philology* 94 (1973): 268–281.

— 'Petronius the Moralist.' In *The Classical Papers of Gilbert Highet*, ed. R. J. Ball, 191–209. New York: Columbia University Press, 1983.

Hirschfeld, O. 'Augustus und sein Mimus Vitae.' *Wiener Studien* 5 (1883): 116–119.

Hock, R. *The Social Context of Paul's Ministry: Tentmaking and Apostleship*. Philadelphia: Fortress Press, 1980.

Hodgson, R. 'Paul the Apostle and the First Century Tribulation Lists.' *Zeitschrift für die neutestamentliche Wissenschaft* 74 (1983): 59–80.

Hofius, O. 'Das Zitat 1 Kor 2,9 und das koptische Testament des Jakob.' *Zeitschrift für die neutestamentliche Wissenschaft* 66 (1975): 140–142.

Hollander, H. W. 'The Testing by Fire of the Builders' Work: 1 Corinthians 3.10-15.' *New Testament Studies* 40 (1994): 89–104.

Holsten, C. *Das Evangelium des Paulus. Vol. 1. Der Brief an die Gemeindan Galatiens und der erste Brief an die Gemeinde in Korinth*. Berlin: Reimer, 1880.

Hooker, M. D. '"Beyond the things which are written"? An Examination of 1 Corinthians 4,6.' *New Testament Studies* 10 (1963): 127–132.

Hopding, H. *Attis, seine Mythen und sein Kult*. Berlin: Töpelmann, 1967.

Hopkins, K. *Conquerors and Slaves: Sociological Studies in Roman History*. Cambridge: Cambridge University Press, 1978.

— *Death and Renewal*. Cambridge: Cambridge University Press, 1983.

Horsfall, N. 'Epic Burlesque in Ovid *Met*. Viii 260ff..' *Classical Journal* 74 (1979): 19–32.

Horsley, R. 'Pneumatikos vs. Psychikos: Distinctions of Spiritual Status Among the Corinthians.' *Harvard Theological Review* 69 (1976): 274–284.

— 'Wisdom of Word and Words of Wisdom in Corinth.' *Catholic Biblical Quarterly* 39 (1977): 224–239.

Hotze, G. *Paradoxien bei Paulus. Untersuchungen zu einer elementaren Denkform in seiner Theologie*. Göttingen: Vandenhoeck & Ruprecht, 1997.

Hubbard, M. *Propertius*. London: Duckworth, 1974.

Huber, G. *Das Motiv der 'Witwe von Ephesus' im lateinischen Texten der Antike und des Mittelalters*. Tübingen: Mohr-Siebeck, 1990.

Hülsemann, M. *Theater, Kult und bürgerlicher Widerstand im antiken Rom*. Frankfurt: Peter Lang, 1987.

Humphries, R. A. 'Paul's Rhetoric of Argumentation in 1 Corinthians 1-4.' Ph.D. diss., GTU, 1979.

Hunt, A. R. *The Inspired Body: Paul, the Corinthians, and Divine Inspiration*. Macon, GA: Mercer University Press, 1996.

Hunter, R. L. *The New Comedy of Greece and Rome*. Cambridge: Cambridge University Press, 1985.

Hyldahl, N. 'The Corinthian "Parties" and the Corinthian Crisis.' *Studia Theologica* 45 (1991): 19–32.

Jaeger, W. *Paideia: The Ideals of Greek Culture*. 3 vols. New York: Oxford University Press, 1939–1944.

— 'Socrates als Erzieher.' In *Paideia. Die Formung des griechischen Menschen*. Vol. 2. Berlin: Walter de Gruyter, 1954.

Jewett, R. *Paul's Anthropological Terms: A Study of Their Use in Conflict Settings*. Leiden: Brill, 1971.

Johnson, W. R. *Horace and the Dialectic of Freedom: Readings in Epistles I*. Ithaca: Cornell University Press, 1993.

Jonas, H. *Gnosis und spätantiker Geist*. Göttingen: Vandenhoeck & Ruprecht, 1966.

Jones, M. R. *'Voluptatis Artifices*: The Social Position of Roman Theatrical Performers During the Republic and the Principate of Augustus.' Ph.D. diss., Yale University, 1995.

Jory, E. J. 'Associations of Actors in Rome.' *Hermes* 98 (1970): 223–253.

— 'The Early Pantomime Riots.' In *Maistor: Classical, Byzantine and Renaissance Studies for Robert Browning*, ed. A. Moffatt, 57–66. Canberra: Australian Association for Byzantine Studies, 1984.

— 'Publilius Syrus and the Element of Competition in the Theatre of the Republic.' In *Vir Bonus Discendi Peritus. Studies in Celebration of Otto Skutsch's Eightieth Birthday*, ed. N. Horsfall, 73–81. London: University of London Institute of Classical Studies, 1988.

Judge, E. A. *The Social Pattern of the Christian Groups in the First Century*. London: Tyndale Press, 1960.

— 'The Early Christians as a Scholastic Community.' *Journal of Religious History* 1 (1960): 129–141.

— 'Paul's Boasting in Relation to Contemporary Professional Practice.' *Australian Biblical Review* 16 (1968): 37–50.

— 'St. Paul and Socrates.' *Interchange* 13 (1973): 106–16.

— 'The Reaction against Classical Education in the New Testament.' *Journal of Christian Education* 77 (1983): 7–14.

Jürgens, H. *Pompa diaboli. Die lateinischen Kirchenväter und das antiken Theater.* Stuttgart: Kohlhammer, 1972.

Jüthner, J. *Hellenen und Barbaren.* Leipzig: Dieterich, 1923.

Kalinka, W. 'Das Nichtwissen des Sokrates.' *Wiener Studien* 50 (1932): 36–46.

Kammler, H.-Ch. *Kreuz und Weisheit. Eine exegetische Untersuchung zu 1 Kor 1,10-3,4.* Tübingen: Mohr-Siebeck, 2003.

Käsemann, E. *Exegetische Versuche und Besinnungen.* Göttingen: Vandenhoeck & Ruprecht, 1960.

— *Perspectives on Paul.* Philadelphia: Fortress Press, 1971.

Kasher, A. *The Jews in Hellenistic and Roman Egypt: The Struggle for Equal Rights.* Tübingen: Mohr-Siebeck, 1985.

Kastner, K. 'Christi Dornenkrönung und Verspottung durch die römische Soldateska.' *Biblische Zeitschrift* 6 (1908): 378–392.

Kauffman, C. 'Enactment as Argument in the *Gorgias*.' *Philosophy and Rhetoric* 12 (1979): 114–129.

Kennedy, J. H. *The Second and Third Epistles of St. Paul to the Corinthians.* London: Methuen, 1900.

— *St. Paul and the Mystery Religions.* London: Hodder & Stoughton, 1913.

Kent, J. H. *Corinth*, Vol. 8, Pt. 3: *The Inscriptions, 1926–1950.* Princeton: American School of Classical Studies, 1966.

Ker, D. P. 'Paul and Apollos—Colleagues or Rivals?' *Journal for the Study of the New Testament* 77 (2000): 75–97.

Kessissoglu, A. I. 'Mimus Vitae.' *Mnemosyne* 41 (1988): 385–388.

Kierkegaard, S. *The Present Age*, trans. A. Dru. New York: Harper and Row, 1962.

Kindermann, H. *Das Theaterpublikum der Antike.* Salzburg: Otto Müller, 1979.

Kindstrand, J. F. *Bion of Borysthenes: A Collection of the Fragments with Introduction and Commentary.* Uppsala and Stockholm: Almquist and Wiksell, 1976.

Kitzberger, I. *Bau der Gemeinde. Das paulinische Wortfeld* οἰκοδομή/(ἐπ)οικοδομεῖν. Wurzburg: Echter Verlag, 1986.

Klauck, H.-J. *Hausgemeinde aund Hauskirche im frühen Christentum.* Stuttgart: Katholisches Bibelwerk, 1981.

Klostermann, E. *Das Matthäusevangelium.* Tübingen: Mohr-Siebeck, 1971.

Knox, J. *Philemon Among the Letters of Paul.* New York: Harper, 1959.

Koch, D. A. *Die Schrift als Zeuge des Evangeliums. Untersuchungen zur Verwendung und zum Verständnis der Schrift bei Paulus.* Tübingen: Mohr-Siebeck, 1986.

Koch, E. 'Fegfeuer.' *Theologische Realenzyklopädie* 11. 70–71.

Koester, H. 'Gnostic Writings as Witnesses for the Development of the Sayings Tradition.' In *The Rediscovery of Gnosticism*, Vol. 1, ed. B. Layton, 238–261. Leiden: Brill, 1980.

Köhler, L. 'Salz, das dumm wird.' *Zeitschrift des deutschen Palästina-Vereins* 59 (1926): 131–140.

Kokolakis, M. *The Dramatic Simile of Life*. Athens, 1960.

Konradt, M. 'Die korinthische Weisheit und das Wort vom Kreuz: Erwägungen zur korinthischen Problemkonstellation und paulinischen Intention in 1 Kor 1-4.' *Zeitschrift für die neutestamentliche Wissenschaft* 94 (2003): 181–214.

Körte, A. 'Bruchstück eines Mimus.' *Archiv für Papyrusforschung* 6 (1913) 1–8.

— Review of Reich, *Der Mimus*. In *Neue Jahrbücher für das klassische Altertum* 11 (1903): 537–549.

— 'Sophron.' RE 3 (1950): 1100–1103.

Kotansky, R. 'The Cohn Beaker: The Inscription.' *J. Paul Getty Museum Journal* 9 (1981): 87–92.

Krämer, H.-J. *Arete bei Platon und Aristoteles*. Heidelberg: Winter, 1959.

Kraus, W. 'Hegemon.' *Der Kleine Pauly. Lexicon der Antike* 2 (1979): 967.

Krentz, E. 'Paul, Games, and the Military.' In *Paul in the Greco-Roman World. A Handbook*, ed. P. Sampley, 344–383. Harrisburg, PA: Trinity Press International, 2003.

Kroll, W. 'Stupidus.' RE 4 (1931): 422–423.

Krueger, D. *Symeon the Holy Fool: Leontius's 'Life' and the Late Antique City*. Berkeley, CA: University of California Press, 1991.

— 'Tales of Holy Fools.' In *Religions of Late Antiquity in Practice*, ed. R. Valantasis, 177–186. Princeton: Princeton University Press, 2000.

Kuck, D. W. *Judgment and Community Conflict. Paul's Use of Apocalyptic Judgment Language in 1 Corinthians 3.5-4.5*. Leiden: Brill, 1992.

Kuhn, H.-W. 'Jesus als Gekreuzigter in der frühchristlichen Verkündigung bis zur Mitte des 2. Jahrhunderts'. *Zeitschrift für Theologie und Kirche* 72 (1975): 1–46.

— 'Die Kreuzesstrafe während der frühen Kaiserzeit. Ihre Wirklichkeit und Wertung in der Umwelt des Urchristentums.' *Aufstieg und Niedergang der römischen Welt* 2.25.1 (1982): 648–693.

— 'Kreuz.' *Theologische Realenzykklopädie* 19 (1990): 713–725.

Lampe, P. 'Paulus als Zeltmacher.' *Biblische Zeitschrift* 31 (1987): 256–261.

— 'Theological Wisdom and the "Word about the Cross": The Rhetorical Scheme of 1 Corinthians 1-4.' *Interpretation* 44 (1990): 117–131.

— 'Acta 19 im Spiegel der ephesinischen Inschriften.' *Biblische Zeitschrift* 36 (1992): 59–76.

Lanciani, R. *Ancient Rome in the Light of Recent Discoveries*. London: Macmillan, 1888.

Landvogt, P. *Epigraphische Untersuchung über den Oikonomos: Ein Beitrag zum hellenistischen Beamtenwesen*. Strasbourg: M. Dumont Schauberg, 1908.

Lang, F. 'πῦρ.' *Theological Dictionary of the New Testament* 6 (1968) 928–52.

— *Die Briefe an die Korinther*. Göttingen: Vandenhoeck & Ruprecht, 1986.

Laqueur, R. *Hellenismus*. Giessen: Universität Giessen, 1925.

Lassen, E. M. 'The Use of the Father Image in Imperial Propaganda and 1 Corinthians 4.14-21.' *Tyndale Bulletin* 42 (1991): 127–136.

Laubscher, H. P. *Fischer und Landleute. Studien zur hellenistischen Genreplastik*. Mainz: von Zabern, 1982.

Lautenschlager, M. 'Abschied vom Disputierer. Zur Bedeutung von συζητητής in 1 Kor 1,20.' *Zeitschrift für die neutestamentliche Wissenschaft* 83 (1991): 276–285.

Lees-Causey, C. 'The Cohn Beaker: Figured Scene.' *The J. Paul Getty Museum Journal* 9 (1981): 83–86.

Lefèvre, E. 'Politics and Society in Plautus *Trinummus*.' In *Theater and Society in the Classical World*, ed. R. Scodel, 177–190. Ann Arbor: University of Michigan Press, 1993.

Legrand, P. *The New Greek Comedy*. London: W. Heinemann, 1917.

— 'Théocrite.' *Revue des écrites anciennes* 36 (1934): 21–30.

Leo, F. 'Inschriftliches Citat aus Laberius' Hermes 48 (1913) 147.

Leppin, H. *Histrionen: Untersuchungen zur sozialen Stellung von Bühnenkünstlern im Westen des Römischen Reiches zur Zeit des Republik und des Principats*. Bonn: Habelt, 1992.

Lesky, A. *Geschichte der griechischen Literatur*. Bern-München: Francke, 1963.

Levick, B. 'The Senatus Consultum from Larinum.' *Journal of Roman Studies* 73 (1983): 97–115.

— *Claudius*. New Haven: Yale University Press, 1990.

— *Tiberius the Politician*. London: Routledge, 1999.

Lietzmann, H. *An die Korinther I/II*. Tübingen: Mohr-Siebeck, 1949.

Liftin, D. *St. Paul's Theology of Proclamation: 1 Corinthians 1-4 and Greco-Roman Rhetoric*. Cambridge: Cambridge University Press, 1994.

Lightfoot, J. B. *Notes on the Epistles of St. Paul*. London: Macmillan, 1904.

— *St. Paul's Epistles to the Colossians and to Philemon*. Repr. of 1879 ed. Grand Rapids, MI: Eerdmans, 1976.

Lim, T. 'Not in Persuasive Words of Wisdom, but in the Demonstration of the Spirit and Power.' *Novum Testamentum* 29 (1987): 137–149.

Lindemann, A. 'Die Schrift als Tradition. Beobachtungen zu den biblischen Zitaten im Ersten Korintherbrief.' In *Schrift und Tradition. Festschrift für Josef Ernst zum 70. Geburtstag*, eds. K. Backhaus and F. G. Untergessmair, 199–211. Paderborn: Schöningh, 1996.

— *Der erste Korintherbrief*. HNT 9/1. Tübingen: Mohr-Siebeck, 2000.

— *Paulus im ältesten Christentum*. Tübingen: Mohr, 1979.

Lindsay, W. M. *Nonii Marcelli De Compendiosa Doctrina Libros* (Leipzig: Tuebner, 1903).

— *Der erste Korintherbrief*. Tübingen: Mohr-Siebeck, 2000.

Lintott, A. *Violence in Republican Rome*. Oxford: Clarendon Press, 1968.

— *Imperium Romanum: Politics and Administration*. London: Routledge, 1993.

Little, A. M. G. 'Plautus and Popular Drama.' *Harvard Studies in Classical Philology* 49 (1938): 205–228.

Löschke, G. 'Korinthische Vasen mit der Rückführung des Hephaistos'. *Mittheilungen Des kaiserlichen deutschen archäologischen Instituts, Athenische Abteilung* 19 (1894): 517–524.

Lohse, E. *Umwelt des Neuen Testaments*. Göttingen: Vandenhoeck & Ruprecht, 1974.

Lowenstam, S. 'Paradoxes in Plato's *Symposium*.' *Ramus* 14 (1985): 85–104.

Lüdemann, G. *Early Christianity according to the Traditions in Acts*. Minneapolis: Fortress Press, 1989.

— *Paul, Apostle to the Gentiles*. Philadelphia: Fortress Press, 1984.

— *Paul: The Founder of Christianity* (Amherst, NY: Prometheus Books, 2002).

Lührmann, D. *Das Offenbarungsverständnis bei Paulus*. Neukirchen-Vluyn: Neukirchener Verlag, 1965.

Lütgert, W. *Freiheitspredigt und Schwarmgeister in Korinth*. Gütersloh: Bertelsmann, 1908.

Lyngby, H. 'De dramatiska problememi Oxrhynchus-mimen Μοιχεύτρια.' *Eranos* 26 (1928): 23–55.

MacMullen, R. *Enemies of the Roman Order*. Cambridge, MA: Harvard University Press, 1966.

— *Roman Social Relations 50 B.C. to A.D. 284*. New Haven: Yale University Press, 1974.

Magalhäes-Vilhena, V. de. *Le problème de Socrate*. Paris: Presses Universitaires de France, 1952.

Malherbe, A. *Social Aspects of Pauline Christianity*. Philadelphia: Fortress, 1983.

— 'A Physical Description of Paul.' *Harvard Theological Review* 74 (1986): 170–175.

Maly, K. *Untersuchungen zur pastoralen Führung des Apostels Paulus im 1. Korintherbrief*. Stuttgart: Katholisches Bibelwerk, 1967.

Manson, T. W. 'The Problem of the Epistle to the Hebrews.' *Bulletin of the John Rylands Library* 32 (1949): 1–17.

Manteuffel, G. von. *De opusculis Graecis Aegypti e papyris ostracis lapidibusque Collectis*. Warsaw: Société des sciences et des letters de Varsovie, 1930.

— 'Zwei Bemerkungen zu den griechischen Mimen aus Ägypten.' *Hermes* 65 (1930): 125–128.

— 'Über einige Papyri der Warschauer Sammlung.' *Münchener Beiträge zur Papyrus-Forschung* 19 (1934): 434–439.

— *Papyri Varsovienses*. Warsaw: Univ. Varsovie facult. Litt., 1935.

Marshall, P. *Enmity in Corinth: Social Conventions in Paul's Relations with the Corinthians*. Tübingen: Mohr-Siebeck, 1987.

Martin, D. *Slavery as Salvation: The Metaphor of Slavery in Pauline Christianity*. New Haven: Yale University Press, 1990.

— *The Corinthian Body*. New Haven: Yale University Press, 1995.

Mason, H. J. 'Lucius at Corinth.' *Phoenix* 25 (1971): 155–65.

— 'Fabula Graecanica: Apuleius and His Greek Sources.' In *Aspects of Apuleius' Golden Ass*, ed. B. L. Hijmans. Groningen: Bouma's, 1978.

Maxey, M. *Occupations of the Lower Classes in the Roman Society*. Chicago: University of Chicago Press, 1938.

Mayor, J. E. B. *Juvenal*. Cambridge: Macmillan, 1853.

McCarthy, B. P. 'Lucian and Menippus.' *Yale Classical Studies* 4 (1934): 3–58.

McCarthy, K. *Slaves, Masters, and the Art of Authority in Plautine Comedy*. Princeton: Princeton University Press, 2002.

McKeown, J. C. 'Augustan Elegy and Mime.' *Proceedings of the Cambridge Philological Society* 25 (1979): 71–84.

Meggitt, J. 'Laughing and Dreaming at the Foot of the Cross: Context and Reception of a Religious Symbol.' *Journal for the Study of Religion, Ethics, and Society* 1 (1996): 9–14.

— *Paul, Poverty and Survival*. Edinburgh: T. & T. Clark, 1998.

Merklein, H. *Der erste Brief an die Korinther I*. Gütersloh: Gerd Mohn, 1992.

Metzger, B. M. *A Textual Commentary on the Greek New Testament.* London and New York: United Bible Societies, 1971.

Meyer, E. *Der Papyrusfund von Elephantine.* Leipzig: Teubner, 1912.

Meyer, H. A. W. *Der erste Brief an die Korinther.* Göttingen: Vandenhoeck & Ruprecht, 1839.

Michl, J. 'Gerichtsfeuer und Purgatorium zu 1 Kor. 3,12-15.' In *Studium Paulinorum Congressus,* ed. 395–401. Rome: Pontifico Instituto Biblico, 1963.

Millar, F. 'The World of the *Golden Ass.' Journal of Roman Studies* 71 (1981): 63–75.

Miller, G. 'ἀρχόντων τοῦ αἰῶνος–A New Look at 1 Corinthians 2.6-8.' *Journal of Biblical Literature* 91 (1972): 522–528.

Mitchell, M. M. *Paul and the Rhetoric of Reconciliation: An Exegetical Investigation of the Language and Composition of 1 Corinthians.* Tübingen: Mohr-Siebeck, 1991.

Mitchell, S. 'Festivals, Games, and Civic Life in Roman Asia Minor.' *Journal of Roman Studies* 80 (1990): 183–190.

Modrzejewski, J. *The Jews of Egypt: From Ramses II to Emperor Hadrian.* Princeton: Princeton University Press, 1995.

Moeller, W. O. 'The Riot of 59 A.D. at Pompeii.' *Historia* 19 (1970): 84–95.

Moffat, J. *The First Epistle of Paul to the Corinthians.* London: Hodder & Stoughton, 1938.

Moltmann, J. *Theology of Play.* New York: Harper and Row, 1972.

Mommsen, Th. *The History of Rome.* London: Macmillan, 1880.

Moore, T. J. *The Theater of Plautus: Playing to the Audience.* Austin: University of Texas Press, 1998.

Mras, K. 'Varros menippeische Satiren und die Philosophie.' *Neues Jahrbuch für Philologie* 33 (1914): 390–420.

Müller, C. W. *Gleiches zu Gleichem. Ein Prinzip frühgriechischen Denkens.* Wiesnbaden: Harmsowitz, 1965.

Müller, U. B. *Der Brief des Paulus an die Philipper.* Leipzig: Evangelische Verlagsanstalt, 1993.

Munck, J. 'The Church without Factions. Studies in 1 Corinthians 1-4.' In *Paul and the Salvation of Mankind.* Richmond: John Knox Press, 1959.

Nagy, G. *The Best of the Achaeans.* Baltimore: Johns Hopkins University Press, 1979.

Nesselrath, H. G. *Lukians Parasitendialog. Untersuchungen und Kommentar.* Berlin: De Gruyter, 1985.

Nicoll, A. *Masks, Mimes and Miracles: Studies in the Popular Theatre.* New York: Harcourt, Brace, 1931.

Nigg, W. *Der christliche Narr.* Zürich: Artemis, 1956.

Nightingale, A. W. *Genres in Dialogue: Plato and the Construct of Philosophy.* Cambridge: Cambridge University Press, 1995.

Nilsson, M. *Geschichte der griechischen Religion.* München: Beck, 1961.

— *A History of Greek Religion.* New York: Norton & Co., 1968.

Nordheim, E. von. 'Das Zitat des Paulus in 1 Kor 2,9 und seine Beziehung zum koptischen Testament Jakobs.' *Zeitschrift für die neutestamentliche Wissenschaft* 65 (1974): 112–120.

O'Day, G. R. 'Jeremiah 9.22-23 and 1 Corinthians 1.26-31: A Study in Intertextuality.' *Journal of Biblical Literature* 109 (1990): 259–267.

Oepke, A. 'ἀπόλλυμι.' *Theological Dictionary of the New Testament* 1 (1964): 394–397.

Opelt, I. 'Esel,' *Reallexikon für Antike und Christentum* 6, 592–595.

Orth, E. *Logios.* Leipzig: Norske, 1926.

Orwell, G. *Down and Out in Paris and London.* New York: Harcourt, 2002.

Panayotakis, C. *Theatrum Arbitri: Theatrical Elements in the* Satyrica *of Petronius.* Leiden: Brill, 1995.

Parke, H. W. 'Chaerephon's inquiry about Socrates.' *Classical Philology* 56 (1961): 241–250.

Parker, H. N. 'The Observed of All Observers: Spectacle, Applause, and Cultural Poetics in the Roman Theater Audience.' In *The Art of Ancient Spectacle*, eds. B. Bergmann and C. Kondoleon, 163–180. New Haven: Yale University Press, 1999.

Payne, S. 'Imagery of Paul the Stagehand.' (Unpublished paper).

Pearson, B. *The Pneumatikos-Psychikos Terminology in 1 Corinthians: A Study in the Theology of the Corinthian Opponents of Paul and Its Relation to Gnosticism.* Missoula, MT: Scholars Press, 1973.

— 'Jewish Elements in *Corpus Hermeticum* 1 (*Poimandres*).' In *Studies in Gnosticism and Hellenistic Religions Presented to G. Quispel*, eds. R. van den Broek and M. J. Vermaseren, 336–348. Leiden: Brill, 1981.

Penna, R. *Wisdom and Folly of the Cross,* Vol. 2 of *Paul the Apostle: A Theological and Exegetical Study.* Collegeville, MN: Liturgical Press, 1996.

Perrochat, P. *Pétrone. Le Festin de Trimalcion.* Paris: Presses Universitaires de France, 1952.

Perry, B. E. *Studies in the Text History of the Life and Fables of Aesop.* Haverford, PA: American Philological Association, 1936.

Philonenko, M. 'Quod occulus non vidit, I Cor. 2,9.' *Theologische Zeitschift* 15 (1959): 48–60.

Pickard-Cambridge, A. W. *Dithyramb, Tragedy and Comedy.* Oxford: Clarendon Press, 1927.

Pickett, R. *The Cross in Corinth: The Social Significance of the Death of Jesus.* Sheffield Academic Press, 1997.

Plank, K. *Paul and the Irony of Affliction.* Atlanta: Scholars Press, 1987.

Pogoloff, S. *Logos and Sophia: The Rhetorical Situation of 1 Corinthians.* Atlanta: Scholars Press, 1992.

Ponsot, H. 'D'Isaie LXIV,3 à I Corinthiens II,9.' *Revue Biblique* 90 (1983): 229–42.

Popkes, W. '1 Kor 2,2 und die Anfänge der Christologie.' *Zeitschrift für die neutestamentliche Wissenschaft* 95 (2004): 64–83.

Potter, D. 'Performance, Power, and Justice in the High Empire.' In *Roman Theatre and Society*, ed. W. J. Slater, 129–160. Ann Arbor: University of Michigan Press, 1996.

Préaux, J.-G. 'Deus Christianorum Onocoetes.' In *Hommages à L. Hermann*, 639–654. Bruxelles: Latomus, 1960.

Preston, K. 'Some Sources of Comic Effect in Petronius.' *Classical Philology* 10 (1915): 28–39.

Prigent, P. 'Ce que l'oeil n'a pas vu.' *Theologische Zeitschrift* 14 (1968): 416–429.

Prümm, K. 'Dynamis in griechisch-hellenistischer Religion und Philosophie als Vergleichsbild zu göttlicher Dynamis im Offenbarungsraum.' *Zeitschrift für Theologie und Kirche* 83 (1961): 393–430.

Purcell, N. 'Does Caesar Mime?' In *The Art of Ancient Spectacle*, eds. B. Bergmann and C. Kondoleon, 187–194. New Haven: Yale University Press. 1999.

Radice, B. *Erasmus. Praise of Folly*. London: Penguin Books, 1993.

Ramsaran, R. A. 'Resisting Imperial Domination and Influence: Paul's Apocalyptic Rhetoric in 1 Corinthians.' In *Paul and the Roman Imperial Order*, ed. R. Horsley, 89–102. Harrisburg, PA: Trinity Press International, 2004.

Rapp, A. 'A Greek "Joe Miller"'. *Classical Journal* 46 (1951): 286–318.

Rawson, E. 'Theatrical Life in Republican Rome and Italy.' *Proceedings of the British School at Rome* 53 (1985): 97–113.

— '*Discrimina Ordinum*: The Lex Julia Theatralis.' *Proceedings of the British School at Rome* 55 (1987): 83–114.

— *Roman Culture and Society: The Collected Papers of Elizabeth Rawson*, ed. F. Millar. Oxford: Oxford University Press, 1991.

— 'The Vulgarity of the Roman Mime.' *Tria lustra. Liverpool Classical Monthly* 150 (1993): 255–260.

Reardon, B. P. *Collected Ancient Greek Novels*. Berkeley: University of California Press, 1989.

Reese, J. M. 'Paul Proclaims the Wisdon of the Cross: Scandal and Foolishness.' *Biblical Theology Bulletin* 9 (1979): 147–153.

Reeve, C. D. C. *Socrates in the Apology*. Indianapolis: University of Indiana, 1989.

Reeve, M. D. 'Apotheosis...per saturam.' *Classical Philology* 79 (1984): 305–307.

Reich, H. *Der Mimus. Ein litterar-entwickelungsgeschichtlicher Versuch*. Berlin: Weidmann, 1903.

— 'Der Mann mit dem Eselkopf, ein Mimodrama, von klassischen Altertum verfolgt bis auf Shakespeares Sommernachtstraum.' *Jahrbuch der deutschen Shakespeare-Gesellschaft* 40 (1904): 15–29.

— *Der König mit der Dornenkrone*. Leipzig: Teubner, 1905.

Reiling, J. 'Wisdom and the Spirit: An Exegesis of 1 Corinthians 2,6-16.' In *Text and Testimony: Essays in Honor of A. F. J. Klijn*, ed. T. Baarda et. al., 200–211. Kampen: Kok, 1988.

Reinmuth, E. 'Narratio und argumentatio—Zur Auslegung der Jesus-Christus-Geschichte im Ersten Korintherbrief. Ein Beitrag zur mimetischen Kompetenz des Paulus.' *Zeitschrift für Theologie und Kirche* 92 (1995): 13–27.

Reitzenstein, R. and H. Schäder. *Studien zum antiken Synkretismus aus Iran und Griechenland*. Leipzig: Teubner, 1926.

— *Hellenistic Mystery-Religions: Their Basic Ideas and Significance*. Pittsburgh: Pickwick Press, 1978.

Relihan, J. 'Vainglorious Menippus in Lucian's *Dialogues of the Dead*.' *Illinois Classical Studies* 12 (1987): 185–206.

— 'Old Comedy, Menippean Satire, and Philosophy's Tattered Robes.' *Illinois Classical Studies* 15 (1990): 180–196.

— *Ancient Menippean Satire*. Baltimore: Johns Hopkins University Press, 1993.

— 'Menippus in Antiquity.' In *The Cynics: The Cynic Movement in Antiquity and Its Legacy*, ed. B. Bracht Branham and M.-O. Goulet-Cazé, 265–293. Berkeley: University of California Press, 1996.

Reynolds, R. W. 'The Adultery Mime.' *Classical Quarterly* 40 (1946): 77–84.

Ribbeck, O. 'Über den Begriff des εἴρων.' *Rheinisches Museum* 31 (1876): 381–400.

— *Alazon. Ein Beitrag zur antiken Ethologie*. Leipzig: Teubner, 1882.

— 'Agroikos, eine ethologische Studie.' *Abhandlungen der königlichen sächsischen Gesellschaft der Wissenschaften* 23 (1888): 1–45.

Richardson, N. J. *The Homeric Hymn to Demeter*. Oxford: Oxford University Press, 1974.

Richardson, P. 'The Thunderbolt in Q and the Wise Man in Corinth.' In *From Jesus to Paul: Studies in Honor of Francis Beare Wright*, eds. P. Richardson and J. C. Hurd, 90–102. Waterloo: Laurier, 1984.

Richlin, A. *The Garden of Priapus: Sexuality and Aggression in Roman Humor*. New Haven: Yale University Press, 1983.

Richter, G. M. A. 'Grotesques and the Mime.' *American Journal of Archaeology* 17 (1913): 148–156.

Riedweg, C. *Mysterienterminologie bei Platon*. Berlin: de Gruyter, 1987.

Rieks, R. 'Mimus und Atellanae.' In *Das römische Drama*, ed. E. Lefèvre, 348–377. Darmstadt: Wissenschaftliche Buchgesellschaft, 1978.

Riikonen, H. K. *Menippean Satire as a Literary Genre with Special Reference to Seneca's Apocolocyntosis*. Helsinki: Societas Scientiarum Fennica, 1987.

Rilke, R. M. *The Notebooks of Malte Laurids Brigge*. Trans. by S. Mitchell. New York: Random House, 1983.

Rist, J. M. *Human Value*. Leiden: Brill, 1982.

Robert, C. *Die Masken der neueren attischen Komödie*. Halle: Niemeyer, 1911.

Robert, L. *Les Gladiateurs dans l'Orient grec*. Paris: Hakkert, 1940.

Robertson, A. and A. Plummer. *A Critical and Exegetical Commentary on the First Epistle of St. Paul to the Corinthians*. Edinburgh: T. & T. Clark, 1914.

Robinson, O. F. 'Slaves and the Criminal Law.' *Zeitschrift der Savigny-Stiftung für Rechtsgeschichte* 98 (1981): 223–227.

Rohde, E. *Psyche*. New York: Harcourt, Brace, 1925.

Rosenblüth, M. *Beiträge zur Quellenkunde von Petrons Satiren*. Berlin: Weidmann, 1909.

Rostrup, E. 'Oxyrhynchus Papyrus 413.' In *Oversigt over het Kgl. Danske Videnskabernes Selskabs Forhandlinger*, 63–91. Copenhagen, 1915.

Roueché, C. *Performers and Partisans at Aphrodisias in the Roman and Late Roman Periods*. London: Society for the Promotion of Roman Studies, 1993.

Russo, C. F. *L. Annaei Senecae Divi Claudii ΑΠΟΚΟΛΟΣΥΝΤΩΣΙΣ*. Firenze: Nuova Italia, 1985.

Saller, R. *Personal Patronage under the Early Empire*. Cambridge: Cambridge University Press, 1982.

Sallmann, K. 'Christen vor dem Theater.' In *Theater und Gesellschaft im Imperium Romanum*, ed. J. Blänsdorf, 243–260. Tübingen: Francke, 1990.

Sandbach, F. H. *The Comic Theatre of Greece and Rome*. London: Routledge, 1985.

Sanders, B. 'Imitating Paul: 1 Cor. 4.6.' *Harvard Theological Review* 74 (1981): 253–263.

Sandy, G. 'Scaenica Petroniana.' *Transactions of the American Philological Association* 104 (1973): 329–346.

Sänger, D. 'Die δυνατοί in 1 Kor. 1,26.' *Zeitschrift für die neutestamentliche Wissenschaft* 76 (1985): 285–291.

Scheibler, I. 'Zum ältesten Bildnis des Sokrates.' *Münchner Jahrbuch der bildenden Kunst* 40 (1989): 25–33.

Schenk, W. 'Der 1. Korintherbrief als Briefsammlung.' *Zeitschrift für neutestamentliche Wissenschaft* 60 (1969): 219–43.

— 'Korintherbriefe.' *Theologische Realenzyklopädie* 19 (1990): 620–640.

— ' "Kreuzestheologie" bei Paulus? Zu den "cultural codes" σταυρός, σκόλοψ, ξύλον.' In *Ja und Nein. Festschrift für Wolfgang Schrage*, 93–109. Neukirchen: Neukirchener Verlag, 1998.

Schlier, H. 'Kerygma und Sophia. Zur neutestamentlichen Grundlegung des Dogmas.' In *Die Zeit der Kirche. Exegetische Aufsätze und Vorträge*, 206–232. Freiburg: Herder, 1956.

Schmidt, K. L. 'Ἰησοῦς Χριστὸς κολαφιζόμενος und die "colaphisation" der Juden.' In *Aux sources de la tradition chrétienne, Mélanges M. Goguel*, 218–227. Neuchâtel: Delachaux & Niestle, 1950.

— 'ἔθνος in the New Testament.' *Theological Dictionary of the New Testament* 2 (1964): 369–372.

— 'κολαφίζω'. *Theological Dictionary of the New Testament* 3 (1965): 818–821.

Schmidt, P. L. 'Nero und das Theater.' In *Theater und Gesellschaft im Imperium Romanum*, ed. J. Blänsdorf, 149–164. Tübingen: Francke, 1990.

Schmiedel, P. *Die Briefe an die Thessalonicher und an die Korinther*. Freiburg: Mohr, 1893.

Schmithals, W. *Die Gnosis in Korinth. Eine Untersuchung zu den Korintherbriefen*. Göttingen: Vandenhoeck & Ruprecht, 1965.

— *Gnosticism in Corinth*. Trans. by J. Steely. Nashville: Abingdon, 1971.

Schnackenburg, R. 'Christian Adulthood according to the Apostle Paul.' *Catholic Biblical Quarterly* 25 (1963): 350–61.

Schneider, J. 'σταυρός.' *Theological Dictionary of the New Testament* 7 (1971): 572–584.

Schnelle, U. *Wandlungen im paulinischen Denken*. Stuttgart: Katholisches Bibelwerk, 1989.

Schniewind, J. 'Die Archonten dieses Äons, 1 Kor. 2,6-8.' In *Nachgelassene Reden und Aufsätze*, ed. Ed. Kähler, 104–109. Berlin: Töpelmann, 1952..

Schottroff, L. *Der Glaubende und die feindliche Welt. Beobachtungen zum gnostischen Dualismus und seiner Bedeutung für Paulus*. Tübingen: Mohr-Siebeck, 1970.

Schrage, W. *Der erste Brief an die Korinther, Vol. 1*. Neukirchen-Vluyn: Neukirchener Verlag, 1991.

— 'Der gekreuzigte und auferweckte Herr.' *Zeitschrift für Theologie und Kirche* 94 (1997): 25–38.

Schröter, J. *Erinnerung an Jesu Worte*. Neukirchen-Vluyn: Neukirchener Verlag, 1997.

Schürer, E. *The History of the Jewish People in the Age of Jesus Christ,* Vol. II, ed. G. Vermes. Edinburgh: T. & T. Clark, 1979.

Schwarz, E. 'Wo's Weisheit ist, ein Tor zu sein.' *Wort und Dienst* 20 (1989): 219–235.

Scobie, A. 'Slums, Sanitation and Mortality in the Roman World.' *Klio* 68 (1986): 397–409.

Scroggs, R. 'Paul: Σοφός and πνευματικός.' *New Testament Studies* 14 (1967/68): 33–55.

Segal, E. *Roman Laughter: The Comedy of Plautus.* Cambridge, MA: Harvard University Press, 1952.

— *The Death of Comedy.* Cambridge, MA: Harvard University Press, 2001.

Sellin, G. 'Das "Geheimnis" der Weisheit und das Rätsel der "Christuspartei" (zu 1 Kor 1-4).' *Zeitschrift für die neutestamentliche Wissenschaft* 73 (1982): 69–96.

— 'Hauptprobleme des Ersten Korintherbriefes.' *Aufstieg und Niedergang der römischen Welt* 2.25.4 (1987): 2940–3044.

Senft, C. *La première Épître de Saint Paul aux Corinthiens.* Neuchatel-Delachaux, 1979.

Shanor, J. 'Paul as Master Builder. Construction Terms in First Corinthians.' *New Testament Studies* 34 (1988): 461–471.

Shaw, G. *The Cost of Authority. Manipulation and Freedom in the New Testament.* Philadelphia: Fortress Press, 1982.

Shipley, G. *The Greek World after Alexander 323–30 B.C.* London: Routledge, 2000.

Siegert, F. *Argumentation bei Paulus.* Tübingen: Mohr-Siebeck, 1985.

Skutsch, O. 'Publilius Syrus.' *Real-Encyclopädie der classischen Altertumswissenschaft* 23 (1959): 1920–1923.

Slater, N. W. *Reading Petronius.* Baltimore: Johns Hopkins University Press, 1990.

Slater, W. J. 'Actors and Their Status in the Roman Theatre in the West.' *Journal of Roman Archaeology* 7 (1994): 364–368.

— 'Pantomime Riots.' *Classical Antiquity* 13 (1994): 120–144.

— *Roman Theater and Society. E. togo Salmon Papers I.* Ann Arbor: University of Michigan Press, 1996.

Smit, J. F. M. 'What is Apollos? What is Paul? In Search for the Coherence of First Corinthians 1.10-4.21.' *Novum Testamentum* 44 (2002): 231–251.

Smith, R. and K. Erim. *Aphrodisias Papers 2: The Theatre.* Ann Arbor: University of Michigan Press, 1991.

Söding, T. '"Was schwach ist in der Welt, hat Gott erwählt" (1 Kor 1,27). Kreuzestheologie und Gemeinde-Praxis nach dem Ersten Korintherbrief,' 260–271. In *Das Wort vom Kreuz. Studien zur paulinischen Theologie.* Tübingen: Mohr-Siebeck, 1997.

Sparks, H. F. D. '1 Cor 2,9: A Quotation from the Coptic Testament of Jacob.' *Zeitschrift für die neutestamentliche Wissenschaft* 67 (1976): 269–276.

Spranger, P. *Historsche Untersuchungen zu den Sklavenfiguren des Plautus und Terenz.* Wiesbaden: Steiner, 1961.

Srebrny, S. 'De mimi Graeci fragmento Londinensi.' *Eos* 30 (1927): 401–412.

Staab, K. *Paulus-kommentare aus der griechischen Kirche aus Katenenhandschriften.* Münster: Aschendorff, 1933.

Staerman, M. *Die Blütezeit der Sklavenwirtschaft in der römischen Republik.* Wiesbaden: Steiner, 1969.

Stählin, G. *Skandalon. Unteruschungen zur Geschichte eines biblischen Begriffs.* Gütersloh: Mohn, 1930.

— 'περίψημα.' *Theological Dictionary of the New Testament* 6 (1968): 84–93.

Standhartinger, A. 'Weisheit in *Joseph und Asenath* und den paulinischen Briefen.' *New Testament Studies* 47 (2001): 482–501.

Stanley, C. *Paul and the Language of Scripture. Citation Technique in the Pauline Epistles.* Cambridge: Cambridge University Press, 1992.

Stansbury, H. A. 'Corinthian Honor, Corinthian Conflict: A Social History of Early Roman Corinth and Its Pauline Community.' Ph.D. diss., University of California at Irvine, 1990.

Ste Croix, G. E. M. de. *The Class Struggle in the Ancient Greek World.* Ithaca: Cornell University Press, 1981.

Sterling, G. 'Wisdom Among the Perfect: Creation Traditions in Alexandrian Judaism and Corinthian Christianity.' *Novum Testamentum* 37 (1995): 355–384.

Stillwell, R. *Corinth II: The Theatre.* Princeton: The American School of Classical Studies at Athens, 1952.

Stokes, M. 'Socrates' Mission.' In *Socratic Questions. New Essays on the Philosophy of Socrates and its Significance*, ed. B. S. Grower, 260–272. London: Routledge, 1992.

Stowers, S. K. 'Paul on the Use and Abuse of Reason.' In *Greeks, Romans, and Christians: Essays in Honor of Abraham J. Malherbe*, ed. D. Balch, E. Ferguson and W. Meeks, 253–286. Minneapolis: Fortress Press, 1990.

Strack, H. and P. Billerbeck. *Kommentar zum Neuen Testament aus Talmud und Midrasch.* 7 vols. Munich: Beck, 1922–61.

Strecker, C. *Die liminale Theologie des Paulus.* Göttingen: Vandenhoeck & Ruprecht, 1999.

Strong, E. S. 'Stuccoes of the Underground Basilica near the Porta Maggiore.' *Journal of Hellenic Studies* 44 (1924): 62–70.

— *Art in Ancient Rome.* London: Heinemann, 1929.

Stuhlmacher, P. 'The Hermeneutical Significance of 1 Corinthians 2.6-16.' In *Tradition and Interpretation in the New Testament: Essays in Honor of E. Earle Ellis*, eds. G. F. Hawthorne and O. Betz, 328–347. Grand Rapids, MI: Eerdmans, 1988.

Sudhaus, S. 'Der Mimus von Oxyrhynchus.' *Hermes* 41 (1906): 247–277.

Süss, W. *De personarum antiquae comoediae atticae usu atque origine.* Ph.D. diss., University of Bonn, 1905.

Swiderek, A. 'Le Mime Grec en Egypte.' *Eos* 47 (1954): 63–74.

Tackaberry, W. H. *Lucian's Relation to Plato and the Post-Aristotelian Philosophers.* Toronto: University of Toronto Press, 1930.

Taylor, L. R. 'Republican and Augustan Writers Enrolled in the Equestrian Centuries.' *Transactions of the American Philological Association* 99 (1968): 469–472.

Tengström, E. 'Theater und Politik im Kaiserlichen Rom.' *Eranos* 75 (1977): 43–56.

Theis, J. *Paulus als Weisheitslehrer. Der Gekreuzigte und die Weisheit Gottes in 1 Kor 1-4*. Regensburg: F. Tustet, 1991.

Theissen, G. 'Legitimation und Lebensunterhalt: Ein Beitrag zu Soziologie urchristlicher Missionare.' *New Testament Studies* 21 (1975): 192–221.

— *The Social Setting of Pauline Christianity. Essays on Corinth*. Philadelphia: Fortress Press, 1982.

— *Psychological Aspects of Pauline Theology*. Philadelphia: Fortress Press, 1987.

Thiel, H. van. *Der Eselsroman*. 2 vols. München: Beck, 1971–1972.

Thiele, G. 'Die Anfänge griechischen Komödie.' *Neue Jahrbücher für das klassische Altertum* 5 (1902): 413–416.

Thrall, M. *Greek Particles in the New Testament. Linguistic and Exegetical Studies*. Grand Rapids, MI: Eerdmans, 1962.

— *The First and Second Letters of Paul to the Corinthians*. Cambridge: Cambridge University Press, 1965.

Till, R. 'Laberius und Caesar.' *Historia* 24 (1975): 260–286.

Treggiari, S. 'Urban Labour in Rome: *Merecenarii* and *Tabernarii*.' In *Non-Slave Labour in the Greco-Roman World*, ed. P. Garnsey, 48–64. Cambridge: Cambridge Philological Society, 1980.

Tuckett, C. 'Paul and the Jesus Tradition: The Evidence of 1 Corinthians 2.9 and the Gospel of Thomas 17.' In *Paul and the Corinthians. Studies on a Community in Conflict. Essays in Honor of Margaret Thrall*, eds. T. Burke and J. Elliott, 55–73. Leiden: Brill, 2003.

Turk, E. *Macrobius. Die Quellen seiner Saturnalien*. Ph.D. diss., Freiburg, 1961.

Usener, H. *Kleine Schriften IV*. Leipzig: Teubner, 1912.

Veyne, P. 'Apulée à Cenchrées.' *Revue Philologique* 39 (1965): 240–250.

— *Le pain et le cirque: Sociologie historique d'un pluralisme politique*. Paris: Seuil, 1976.

— *A History of Private Life I: From Pagan Rome to Byzantium*. Cambridge, MA: Harvard University Press, 1992.

Vlastos, G. *Socrates, Ironist and Moral Philosopher*. Ithaca: Cornell University Press, 1991.

— 'The Socratic Elenchus.' *Oxford Studies in Ancient Philosophy* 1 (1983): 71–91.

Vogt, J. *Ancient Slavery and the Ideal of Man*. Cambridge, MA: Harvard University Press, 1975.

Vollenweider, S. 'Weisheit am Kreuzweg. Zum theologischen Programm von 1 Kor 1 und 2.' In *Kreuzestheologie im Neuen Testament*, eds. A. Dettwiler and J. Zumstein, 43–58. Tübingen: Mohr-Siebeck, 2002.

Volz, P. *Die Eschatologie der jüdischen Gemeinde im neutestamentlichen Zeitalter*. Tübingen: Mohr-Siebeck, 1934.

Vos, C. S. de. *Church and Community Conflicts: The Relationship of the Thessalonian, Corinthian, and Philippian Churches with Their Wider Civic Communities*. Atlanta: Scholars Press, 1999.

Vos, J. S. 'Der ΜΕΤΑΣΧΗΜΑΤΙΣΜΟΣ in 1 Kor 4,6.' *Zeitschrift für die neutestamentliche Wissenschaft* 86 (1995): 154–72.

— 'Die Argumentation des Paulus in 1 Kor 1,10-3,4.' In *The Corinthian Correspondence*, ed. R. Bieringer, 87–119. Leuven: Leuven University Press, 1996.

Voss, F. *Das Wort vom Kreuz und die menschliche Vernunft. Eine Untersuchung zur Soteriologie des 1. Korintherbriefes.* Göttingen: Vandenhoeck & Ruprecht, 2002.

Voutiras, E. 'Τέλος ἔχει τὸ παίγνιον: Der Tod eines Mimus.' *Epigraphica Anatolica* 24 (1995): 61–72.

Vretska, K. 'Sophron.' *Der Kleine Pauly. Lexicon der Antike* 5 (1975): 281.

Wachsmuth, C. 'Senecas *Apocolocyntosis.*' *Rheinisches Museum* 18 (1863): 370–376.

Waddell, W. G. 'Hegemon.' *Oxford Classical Dictionary* (1978): 492.

Walbank, M. E. H. 'The Foundation and Planning of Early Roman Corinth.' *Journal of Roman Archaeology* 10 (1997): 95–130.

Walker, W. O. '1 Corinthians 2.6-16: A Non-Pauline Interpolation?' *Journal for the Study of the New Testament* 47 (1992): 75–94.

Wallace-Hadrill, A. F. *Patronage in Ancient Society.* London: Routledge, 1989.

Wanamaker, C. 'The Rhetoric of Power: Ideology in 1 Corinthians 1-4.' In *Paul and the Corinthians. Studies on a Community in Conflict. Essays in Honour of Margaret Thrall*, eds. T. Burke and J. Elliott, 115–138. Leiden: Brill, 2003.

Wankel, H. *Demosthenes, Rede für Ktesiphon über den Kranz.* Heidelberg: Winter, 1976.

Watzinger, C. 'Mimologen.' *Mittheilungen des deutschen archäologischen Instituts, Athenische Abteilung* 26 (1909): 1–8.

Weder, H. *Das Kreuz Jesu bei Paulus. Ein Versuch über den Geschichtsbezug des Christlichen Glaubens nachzudenken.* Göttingen: Vandenhoeck & Ruprecht, 1981.

Weiher, A. 'Philosophen und Philosophenspott in der attischen Komödie.' Ph.D. diss., München, 1913.

Weinreich, O. *Senecas* Apocolocyntosis. *Die Satire auf Tod/Himmel-und Höllenfahrt des Kaisers Claudius.* Berlin: Weidmann, 1923.

— *Studien zu Martial: Literarhistorische und Religionsgeschichtliche Untersuchungen.* Stuttgart: Teubner, 1928.

— *Epigramm und Pantomimus.* Heidelberg: Winter, 1948.

Weiss, J. 'Beiträge zur paulinischen Rhetorik.' In *Theologische Studien, Bernhard Weiss zu seinem 70. Geburtstag dargebracht*, 165–247. Göttingen: Vandenhoeck & Ruprecht, 1897.

— *Der erste Korintherbrief.* Göttingen: Vandenhoeck & Ruprecht, 1910.

— *Das Urchristentum*, ed. R. Knopf. Göttingen: Vandenhoeck & Ruprecht, 1917.

Welborn, L. L. 'On the Discord in Corinth: 1 Corinthians 1–4 and Ancient Politics.' *Journal of Biblical Literature* 106 (1987): 85–111.

— 'A Conciliatory Principle in 1 Cor. 4.6.' *Novum Testamentum* 29 (1987): 320–346.

— 'The Identification of 2 Corinthians 10-13 with the Letter of Tears.' *Novum Testamentum* 37 (1995): 138–153.

— *Politics and Rhetoric in the Corinthian Epistles.* Macon, GA: Mercer University Press, 1997.

— 'The Runaway Paul: A Character in the Fool's Speech.' *Harvard Theological Review* 92 (1999): 115–163.

— 'Μωρὸς γενέσθω: Paul's Appropriation of the Role of the Fool in 1 Corinthians 1-4.' *Biblical Interpretation* 10 (2002): 420–435.

Welch, K. 'Negociating Roman Spectacle Architecture in the Greek World: Athens and Corinth.' In *The Art of Ancient Spectacle*, eds. B. Bergmann and C. Kondoleon, 125–145. New Haven: Yale University Press, 1999.

West, A. B. *Corinth*, Vol. 8, Pt. 2: *Latin Inscriptions, 1896–1926*. Cambridge, MA: Harvard University Press, 1931.

West, M. L. *The Orphic Poems*. Oxford: Oxford University Press, 1983.

— 'Three Papyri of Hesiod Corrigenda.' *Zeitschrift für Papyrologie und Epigraphik* 18 (1975): 229–36.

Westermann, W. L. 'Sklaverei.' *Real-Encyclopädie der classischen Altertumswissenschaft* Suppl. VI, 980–981.

White, P. 'Positions for Poets in Early Imperial Rome.' In *Literary and Artistic Patronage in Ancient Rome*, ed. B. Gold, 50–66. Austin: University of Texas Press, 1982.

Widmann, M. '1 Kor. 2,6-16: Ein Einspruch gegen Paulus.' *Zeitschrift für die Neutestamentliche Wissenschaft* 70 (1979): 44–53.

Wiechers, A. *Aesop in Delphi*. Meisenheim am Glan: Hain, 1961.

Wiedemann, T. *Emperors and Gladiators*. London: Routledge, 1992.

Wiemken, H. *Der griechische Mimus. Dokumente zur Geschichte des antiken Volkstheaters*. Bremen: Schünemann, 1972.

Wilamowitz-Moellendorf, U. von. *Die Textgeschichte der griechischen Bukoliker*. Berlin: Weidmann, 1906.

Wilcken, U. 'Hellenen und Barbaren.' *Neue Jahrbücher des klassischen Altertums* 17 (1906): 457–471.

Wilckens, U. *Weisheit und Torheit: Eine exegetisch-religionsgeschichtliche Untersuchung zu I. Kor. 1 und 2*. Tübingen: Mohr-Siebeck, 1959.

— 'σοφία.' *Theological Dictionary of the New Testament* 7 (1972): 465–526.

— 'Zu 1 Kor 2,1-16.' In *Theologia Crucis—Signum Crucis*, ed. C. Andresen and G. Klein, 501–537. Tübingen: Mohr-Siebeck, 1979.

Wiles, D. *The Masks of Menander. Sign and Meaning in Greek and Roman Performance*. Cambridge: Cambridge University Press, 1991.

Wilk, F. *Die Bedeutung des Jesajabuches für Paulus*. Göttingen: Vandenhoeck & Ruprecht, 1998.

Williams, D. J. *Paul's Metaphors—Their Context and Character*. Peabody, MA: Hendrickson, 1999.

Williams, D. K. *The Terminology of the Cross and the Rhetoric of Paul*. Atlanta: Scholars Press, 1998.

Williams, G. 'Phases in Political Patronage of Literature in Rome.' In *Literary and Artistic Patronage in Ancient Rome*, ed. B. Gold, 3–27. Austin: University of Texas Press, 1982.

Williams, H. Drake. *The Wisdom of the Wise: The Presence and Function of Scripture within 1 Cor 1.18–3.23*. Leiden: Brill, 2001.

Willis, W. 'The "Mind of Christ" in 1 Corinthians 2,16.' *Biblica* 70 (1989): 110–122.

Windisch, H. '"Ελλην.' *Theological Dictionary of the New Testament* 2 (1964): 504–516.

— *Der zweite Korintherbrief*. Göttingen: Vandenhoeck & Ruprecht, 1924.

Winkler, J. J. *Auctor and Actor. A Narratological Reading of Apuleius's* Golden Ass. Berkeley: University of California Press, 1991.

Winter, B. W. *Philo and Paul among the Sophists*. Cambridge: Cambridge University Press, 1997.

Winter, F. *Die Typen der figürlichen Terrakotten II*. Berlin: Spemann, 1903.

Winter, M. *De mimis Oxyrhynchiis*. Ph.D. diss., Leipzig Universität, 1906.

— *Psychiker und Pneumatiker in Korinth: Zum religionsgeschichtlichen Hintergrund von 1. Kor. 2,6–3,4*. Marburg: Elwert, 1975.

Wiseman, J. 'Corinth and Rome I: 228 B.C.–A.D. 267.' *Aufstieg und Niedergang der römischen Welt* 2.7.1 (1981): 438–548.

Wiseman, T. P. '*Pete nobiles amicos*: Poets and Patrons in Late Republican Rome.' In *Literary and Artistic Patronage in Ancient Rome*, ed. B. Gold, 28–29. Austin: University of Texas Press, 1982.

— *Catullus and His World. A Reappraisal*. Cambridge: Cambridge University Press, 1985.

— 'The Games of Flora.' In *The Art of Ancient Spectacle*, eds. B. Bergmann and C. Kondoleon, 195–204. New Haven: Yale University Press, 1999.

Wistrand, M. *Entertainment and Violence in Ancient Rome: The Attitudes of Roman Writers of the First Century A.D*. Gotheborg: Universitatis Gothoburgensis, 1993.

Witherington, B. *Conflict and Community in Corinth: A Socio-Rhetorical Commentary on 1 and 2 Corinthians*. Grand Rapids, MI: Eerdmans, 1995.

Wolff, Ch. *Der erste Brief des Paulus an die Korinther*. Berlin: Evangelische Verlagsanstalt, 1982.

Wölfflin, E. 'Atellanen und Mimentitel.' *Rheinisches Museum* 43 (1888): 308–309.

Wolter, M. 'Apollos und die ephesinischen Johannesjünger (Act 18,24-19,7).' *Zeitschrift für die neutestamentliche Wissenschaft* 78 (1987): 49–73.

— Verborgene Weisheit und Heil für die Heiden.' *Zeitschrift für Theologie und Kirche* 84 (1987): 297–319.

— 'Dumm und skandalös: Die paulinische Kreuzestheologie und das Wirklichkeitsverständnis des christlichen Glaubens.' In *Das Kreuz Jesu. Gewalt—Opfer—Sühne*, ed. R. Weth, 44–63. Nuekirchen: Neukirchener Verlag, 2001.

Woytek, E. 'Varro.' In *Die römische Satire*, ed. J. Adamietz, 311–355. Darmstadt: Wissenschaftliche Buchgesellschaft, 1986.

Wrede, W. *Paulus*. Tübingen: Mohr-Siebeck, 1907.

— 'Über Aufgabe und Methode der sogenannten neutestamentlichen Theologie'. In *Das Problem der Theologie des Neuen Testaments*, ed. G. Strecker. Darmstadt: Wissenschaftliche Buchgesellschaft, 1975.

Wuellner, W. 'Haggadic Homily Genre in 1 Corinthians 1-3.' *Journal of Biblical Literature* 89 (1970): 199–204.

Wüst, E. 'Mimos.' *Real-Encyclopädie der classischen Altertumswissenschaft* 15.2 (1932): 1727–1764.

Yavetz, Z. 'Plebs sordida.' *Athenaeum* 43 (1965): 295–311.

— *Plebs and Princeps*. Oxford: Oxford University Press, 1988.

Yilmaz, H. and S. Sahin. 'Ein Kahlkopf aus Patara.' *Epigraphica Anatolica* 21 (1993): 77–91.

Young, N. H. '*Paidagogos*: The Social Setting of a Pauline Metaphor.' *Novum Testamentum* 29 (1987): 150–176.

Zahn, T. *Das Evangelium des Matthäus*. Leipzig: Hinrichs, 1903.

Zanker, P. *The Mask of Socrates: The Image of the Intellectual in Antiquity.* Berkeley: University of California Press, 1995.

Zaurich, K.-Th. 'Demotische Fragmente zum Ahikar-Roman.' *Folia Rara W. Voigt LXV. d.n. celebrati ... dedicata,* ed. H. Franke, 180–185. Wiesbaden: Frank Steiner, 1976.

Zeitz, H. 'Der Aesoproman und seine Geschichte: eine Untersuchung im Anschluss an die neugefundenen Papyri.' *Aegyptus* 16 (1936): 225–256.

Zeller, E. *Die Philosophie der Griechen,* 2.1: *Socrates und die Sokratiker.* Leipzig: Teubner, 1922.

Zijerveld, C. Τελετή. *Bijdrage tot de kennis der religieuze terminologie in het Grieksch.* Ph.D. diss., Utrecht, 1934.

Zumstein, J. 'Das Wort vom Kreuz als Mitte der paulinischen Theologie.' In *Kreuzestheologie im Neuen Testament,* eds. A. Dettwiler and J. Zumstein, 27–41. Tübingen: Mohr-Siebeck, 2002.

Zuntz, G. *The Text of the Epistles: A Disquitition upon the Corpus Paulinum.* London: Oxford University Press, 1953.

INDEX OF ANCIENT REFERENCES

Firmicus	
Math.	
4.14.3	66n.129,
	72n.177
Fronto	
61.155	113n.94
Gellius	
NA	
1.11.12	38n.23
2.23.1	194n.559
10.3.5	67n.142
16.7	5n.25,
	113n.92
16.7.1	44n.63
16.7.4	58n.67
19.13.3	58n.67
Herodas	
Mime	
2.18–20	94n.359
2.22–23	95n.362
2.25–27	94n.356
2.28–30	95n.363
2.42–45	94n.359
2.48	94n.358
2.60–61	94n.357
2.60–63	94n.355
2.60–65	94n.360
2.74–78	94n.360
2.95–98	94n.358
2.98	245n.974
3.5–6	88n.312
3.5–8	87n.303
3.10	88n.309
3.14	88n.309
3.18–19	88n.312
3.19–21	87n.303
3.19–26	88n.311
3.22–36	87n.302
3.26–29	89n.317
3.31–32	89n.318
3.32	88n.309
3.36–49	88n.312
3.58–88	87n.305
3.58–90	90n.319,
	109n.59
3.88–92	87n.305
3.93–97	87n.306
3.96	245n.974
4.42	245n.974

5	138n.148
5.85	245n.974
6	138n.148
7.113	245n.974
7.126	245n.974
Herodotus	
1.60	179n.447
2.51	208n.680
2.51.2	188n.516,
	206n.664
2.62	208n.680
2.81	208n.680
2.134–35	154n.260
3.132.2	130n.87
3.159.1	130n.87
2.171	215n.731
3.80.3	128n.72
3.125.3	130n.87
4.43.2	130n.87
4.77.1	30n.45
4.146	128n.72
6.30.1	130n.87
6.67.3	51n.10
7.194.1–2	130n.87
Hesiod	
Op.	
287–89	210n.697
Hipponax	
fr.	
108	94n.352
Historia Augusta, Duo Maxim.	
9.3–5	113n.90
Historia Augusta, M. Antonin.	
29	113n.90
Historia Augusta, Tyr.	
30.33	48.93
Homer	
Il.	
1.92	93n.350
2.212–65	35n.6
9.497–500	210n.697

Od.	
3.222	93n.350
4.240–64	149n.225
9–12	197n.589
11	198n.598
13.500–507	158n.291
17.202–203	149n.222
17.281	158n.291
17.298–99	158n.292
17.604–605	158n.292
17.605–609	160n.303
19.33–34	93n.350
Horace	
Ars poet.	
212–13	8n.53
Epist.	
1.1.61	245n.977
1.1.94–97	226n.818
1.1.104	237n.906
1.7.37–38	128n.71
1.7.83	237n.907
1.16.46–48	133n.106
1.18.10–14	46n.81,
	58n.68,
	64n.118,
	86n.291
1.18.14	37n.20,
	38n.21,
	64n.117,
	249n.7
1.18.107–12	248n.7
1.19.15	64n.121,
	95n.364
2.1.146	237n.912
Od.	
1.34.2	178n.442
Sat.	
1.2.55	58n.67,
	58n.69,
	61n.101
1.2.57	6n.35,
	58n.67,
	58n.69,
	61n.101
1.3.76–77	137n.138
1.3.82–83	137n.139
1.3.80–83	133n.106
1.5	5n.30

INDEX OF NAMES